INTRODUCTION TO
CLINICAL PSYCHOLO

INTRODUCTION TO CLINICAL PSYCHOLOGY:

Science and Practice

Bruce E. Compas

University of Vermont

Ian H. Gotlib

Stanford University

Boston   Burr Ridge, IL   Dubuque, IA   Madison, WI   New York   San Francisco   St. Louis
Bangkok   Bogotá   Caracas   Kuala Lumpur   Lisbon   London   Madrid   Mexico City
Milan   Montreal   New Delhi   Santiago   Seoul   Singapore   Sydney   Taipei   Toronto

McGraw-Hill Higher Education ✌

*A Division of The **McGraw-Hill** Companies*

INTRODUCTION TO CLINICAL PSYCHOLOGY: SCIENCE AND PRACTICE

Published by McGraw-Hill, a business unit of The McGraw-Hill Companies, Inc., 1221 Avenue of the Americas, New York, NY 10020. Copyright © 2002 by The McGraw-Hill Companies, Inc.

Some ancillaries, including electronic and print components, may not be available to customers outside the United States.

This book is printed on acid-free paper.

5 6 7 8 9 0 QPF/QPF 0 9 8 7 6

ISBN   978-0-07-012491-2
MHID 0-07-012491-4

Vice president and editor-in-chief: *Thalia Dorwick*
Publisher: *Stephen D. Rutter*
Senior sponsoring editor: *Melissa Mashburn*
Editorial coordinator*: Cheri Dellelo*
Senior marketing manager: *Chris Hall*
Lead project manager: *Peggy J. Selle*
Senior production supervisor: *Laura Fuller*
Coordinator of freelance design: *Michelle D. Whitaker*
Cover designer: *So Yon Kim*
Cover image: *"Qu'est-ce que c'est le point" By Jean-Claude Gaugy Copyright 1999; Collection of Museum of Art, St. Louis University*
Senior photo research coordinator: *Lori Hancock*
Photo research: *Billie Porter*
Supplement producer: *Sandra M. Schnee*
Media technology senior producer: *Sean Crowley*
Compositor: *GAC/Indianapolis*
Typeface: *10.5/12 Times Roman*
Printer: *Quebecor World Fairfield, PA*

The credits section for this book begins on page 511 and is considered an extension of the copyright page.

Library of Congress Cataloging-in-Publication Data

Compas, Bruce E.
    Introduction to clinical psychology / Bruce E. Compas, Ian H. Gotlib. — 1st ed.
        p.   ;   cm.
    Includes bibliographical references and index.
    ISBN 0–07–012491–4 (alk. paper)
    1. Clinical psychology.   I. Gotlib, Ian H.   II. Title.
    [DNLM: 1. Psychology, Clinical. WM 105 C7369i 2002]

RC467 .C596   2002
616.89—dc21

2001042796
CIP

www.mhhe.com

BRIEF CONTENTS

CONTENTS

PREFACE

Our primary goal in writing *Introduction to Clincial Psychology: Science and Practice* is to provide advanced undergraduate psychology students and beginning graduate students with an engaging, contemporary vision of the field of clinical psychology. We are both clinical scientists and practicing clinical psychologists, and we have both served as directors of APA-approved graduate training programs in clinical psychology. In writing this book, we draw on our experience in all these roles to provide students with an up-to-date, science-based, and forward-looking perspective on our field. Indeed, because of our active involvement in clinical research, we emphasize in this book the scientific basis for the practice of clinical psychology. Because of this science-based focus, we place considerable importance on linking science with the practice of clinical psychology.

We have assumed that students using this book will have had some exposure both to clinical psychology through an introductory-level course in abnormal psychology and to basic methods in psychological research design and statistics. With this foundation, we believe that students are well prepared to understand and appreciate the more advanced issues that we present in this text.

TEXT ORGANIZATION

There are three major sections in the text. In section I, we survey the field of clinical psychology. We describe the unique and defining features of the field, its history, and its development. Because of our emphasis on the scientific foundation of the practice of clinical psychology, we also provide an overview of the types of methods that are used in research in clinical psychology. We review the major theories that form the basis for both research and practice in clinical psychology, and we describe current research and thinking about psychopathology. In this section, we also introduce the reader to four cases that we use throughout the text to illustrate important facets of clinical psychology. These four cases represent a range of psychopathology and include a case of attention deficit/hyperactivity disorder in a child, bulimia nervosa in an adolescent, social phobia in an adult, and depression in an elderly woman.

In section II, we focus on assessment in clinical psychology. We describe how clinical psychologists measure and learn about psychological aspects of people and their problems. We discuss the general process of assessment and then describe specific types of assessment procedures, including interviewing strategies and formats for both children and adults, intellectual and neuropsychological assessment, personality assessment using objective and projective personality tests, and behavioral assessment. Throughout these chapters we continue to focus on our four cases, describing how each of the different approaches to assessment might be used with these individuals.

In section III, we address intervention in clinical psychology. We begin this section with an overview of intervention, including the promotion of health and positive behaviors, the prevention of psychopathology and physical illness, and the psychological treatment of psychopathology and illness. We then describe in detail three broad approaches to the treatment of psychopathology: (a) psychoanalytic, psychodynamic, and interpersonal approaches; (b) humanistic, existential, and experiential approaches; and (c) behavioral and cognitive approaches. For all these perspectives, we discuss relevant theory and research, describe the application of each therapy to specific psychological disorders, and once again illustrate how the therapies would be applied to our four cases. Consistent with our emphasis on clinical science, we devote an entire chapter to a description of similarities and differences across these different treatment approaches; to a discussion of how clinical psychologists conduct research and evaluate the effectiveness of psychotherapy; and to a presentation of which approaches to psychotherapy have been found in clinical research to be most effective in the treatment of specific disorders.

Finally, in the closing chapter of this book, we provide a synthesis of the advances that have been made in the field, the challenges that currently face clinical psychology, and the opportunities that we think are open to students in the future.

KEY FEATURES OF THE TEXT

A number of features of the text are particularly noteworthy. First, we emphasize a scientific approach to the field of clinical psychology. We both earned our PhDs from scientist-practitioner clinical psychology graduate programs that are based on the Boulder model of training. Because of our scientific training, we believe strongly in the reciprocal and mutually interactive nature of research and practice. As you will see throughout the text, however, we recognize that maintaining that link between research and practice is an important challenge for this field. We believe that research and practice should inform one another—that one cannot have or develop valid assessment or treatment procedures without strong clinical science—and that clinical practice is crucial in identifying the areas in greatest need of study. Therefore, throughout the text, we draw extensively on the latest research findings that guide the practice of clinical psychology in assessment and intervention.

Second, we have used four case studies to make more concrete the application of research to understanding and helping individuals in distress. We introduce these case studies in the opening chapter of the book and follow them through the process of diagnosis, assessment, and treatment. We chose these cases to reflect a range of different types of psychopathology. We also chose theses cases to cover the life span and to raise important issues related to gender and ethnic diversity. These four cases, along with many other clinical examples that we include throughout the book, help bring to life the differences among various theoretical approaches to the conceptualization, assessment, and treatment of psychopathology. For example, we describe in some detail the school shootings that occurred in Littleton, Colorado, on April 20, 1999, in order to raise questions about how different conceptualizations of human behavior would explain this act and about how humanistic approaches to psychotherapy, in particular, would contribute to understanding this situation.

Third, other texts treat important areas of clinical psychology such as clinical child psychology, clinical health psychology, prevention and health promotion, and neuropsychology as ancillary topics in separate chapters. Because we believe that these areas are integral parts of the field, we have woven them throughout this text, both through the use of the cases and through integrating these topics where appropriate with other chapter content.

Fourth, we have included material throughout to encourage students to engage in active critical thinking. For example, in our presentation of psychological theories that guide and shape assessment and intervention in clinical psychology (chapter 4), we guide students through the process of evaluating the strengths and weaknesses of these theories. Similarly, in our discussion of research on the effectiveness of psychotherapy (chapter 15), we provide students with the features of sound research methods to enable them to judge the quality of the research that has been conducted to date.

Finally, we have taken several steps in this book to enhance students' learning experience. For example, we have boldfaced key terms and names and listed them at the end of each chapter. For each chapter we also list useful resources, including books and professional journals. The CD-ROM packaged with the book as well as the accompanying website, <www.mhhe.com/compas>, includes focus questions for each chapter, additional chapter material to keep the content as up-to-date as possible, and key links to relevant resources on the Internet.

Also, a computerized text bank is available to instructors.

ACKNOWLEDGMENTS

First and foremost, we wish to express our deepest appreciation to our families for their love, patience, and encouragement throughout the process of writing this book. Our heartfelt thanks go to Carly, Colin, and Pam (BEC), and to Laura (IHG). This book would not have been possible without their support.

We are also grateful to a number of individuals who have helped bring this project to fruition. First, at McGraw-Hill we would like to thank Jane Karpacz and Melissa Mashburn for their help in overseeing the project and Cheri Dellelo for her encouragement, guidance, and technical assistance. Second, we appreciate the assistance of several students at the University of Vermont and Stanford University over the course of this project, some of whom have already gone on to start their careers in clinical psychology: Laurie Raezer, Sandra Baker, Jonathan Rottenberg, Pamela Schraedley, Saskia Traill, and Ryan Bogdan.

Finally, we wish to thank the following individuals who provided informative reviews that helped us sharpen our thinking and our writing: Charles R. Carlson, University of Kentucky; Ephrem Fernandez, Southern Methodist University; David Gard, San Francisco State University; William M. Grove, University of Minnesota; Nancy Hebben, Harvard University Extension School; Cooper B. Holmes, Emporia State University; Randolph M. Lee, Trinity College; Raymond P. Lorion, University of Pennsylvania; Janet R. Matthews, Loyola University; Richard M. McFall, Indiana University; Suzanne Meeks, University of Louisville; Jodi Mindell, St. Joseph's University; G. H. Morton, University of Massachusetts, Amherst; Larry L. Mullins, Oklahoma State University; Michael Murtagh, Bridgewater State College; Peggy W.

Nash, Broward Community College; Charles Neuringer, University of Kansas; Kenneth Olson, Fort Hays State University; Patricia Paul, Aurora University; Vicky J. Perkins, University of Oklahoma; Paul R. Rasmussen, Furman University; Carol Terry, University of Oklahoma; Amy W. Wagner, University of Wyoming; Patricia A. Wisocki, University of Massachusetts, Amherst; and Doris J. Wright, Kansas State University.

ABOUT THE AUTHORS

DR. BRUCE E. COMPAS received his PhD in Clinical Psychology from the University of California, Los Angeles. He is currently Professor of Psychology, Medicine, and Pediatrics at the University of Vermont, where he also serves as the Director of the Clinical Psychology Training Program. Dr. Compas's research is focused on psychological, interpersonal, and physiological processes of self-regulation and coping in response to stress and adversity. This work includes studies of adults and families coping with cancer; children and adolescents coping with chronic pain; and children and adolescents coping with parental depression; and also includes the development of interventions to enhance coping and self-regulation in children, adolescents, and adults. Dr. Compas's research has been supported by grants from the National Institute of Mental Health, the National Cancer Institute, and several private foundations, and he has published more than 100 scientific articles. He has served on the editorial boards of numerous journals, including the *Journal of Consulting and Clinical Psychology,* the *Journal of Clinical Child Psychology, Health Psychology, Psychological Bulletin, Developmental Psychology,* and the *Journal of Personality and Social Psychology.* Dr. Compas is a Fellow of the American Psychological Association and the American Psychological Society.

DR. IAN H. GOTLIB received his PhD in Clinical Psychology from the University of Waterloo. He is currently a Professor of Psychology at Stanford University and Director of the Stanford Mood and Anxiety Disorders Laboratory. Dr. Gotlib is very active in clinical research. In his research Dr. Gotlib examines information-processing styles of depressed children, adolescents, and adults, patterns of brain activation of depressed patients in response to different emotional stimuli, and the emotional, cognitive, behavioral, and biological functioning of children of depressed mothers. Dr. Gotlib's research has been supported by grants from the National Institute of Mental Health and the Medical Research Council of Canada. Dr. Gotlib has published more than 150 scientific articles and has written or coauthored several books in the areas of depression and stress. In addition, he has been Associate Editor of *Cognition and Emotion, Cognitive Therapy and Research,* and the *Journal of Social and Personal Relationships*, and has served on the editorial boards of the *British Journal of Clinical Psychology*, the *Journal of Abnormal Psychology*, and *Psychological Assessment*. Dr. Gotlib is a Fellow of the American Psychological Association, the American Psychological Society, and the American Psychopathological Association.

INTRODUCTION TO THE FIELD

Clinical psychology is an exciting and growing field that encompasses both research and practice related to psychopathology and to mental and physical health. In chapters 1 through 5, we introduce you to this field. We describe the unique and defining features of clinical psychology, its history, and its foundations (chapters 1 and 2). Our emphasis throughout this book is on the scientific basis of clinical psychology practice, and we provide an overview of the types of methods that are used in clinical psychological research (chapter 3). We offer a review of the major theories that form the basis for research and practice in clinical psychology (chapter 4), and we describe current research and thinking about psychopathology (chapter 5). We describe four cases that we will use to illustrate important facets of clinical psychology throughout this text, and we introduce you to these cases in chapter 1.

AN OVERVIEW OF CLINICAL PSYCHOLOGY

INTRODUCTION

The opportunities and challenges facing the field of clinical psychology at the outset of the twenty-first century are enormous. A recent national study of psychiatric disorders in America, the National Comorbidity Survey, found that approximately 30 percent of adults, or over 70 million people, were diagnosed with at least one psychiatric disorder during the previous 12 months (Kessler et al., 1994). As you read these words, more than 10 million Americans are suffering from mood disorders, including major depression, bipolar disorder, and dysthymia (Kessler et al., 1997). Over 15 million individuals are battling anxiety disorders such as generalized anxiety, phobias, obsessive compulsive disorder, and post-traumatic stress disorder (Kessler et al., 1999). More than 1 million Americans suffer from major mental illness in the form of schizophrenic disorders. Eating disorders affect the lives of over 500,000 individuals, mostly young adult women. Mental health problems affecting children and adolescents are pervasive and on the increase, including disruptive behavior disorders, attention deficit disorder, depression, and anxiety disorders that affect millions of children and adolescents (Achenbach & Howell, 1993).

Mental health problems have pervasive effects on the ability of millions of individuals to function effectively in daily living. Impairment attributable to mental health problems includes poor school achievement and job performance, disrupted interpersonal relationships, and decreased quality of life (e.g., Kessler et al., 1999; Kessler, Walters, & Forthofer, 1998). For example, individuals who suffer from agoraphobia or from severe depression may be unable to leave their homes. Children who are diagnosed with attention deficit disorder often are unable to perform adequately in school. Alcohol and substance abuse are associated with significant impairment in work and in disrupted marital relationships. And mental health problems can result in legal problems and criminality, such as that associated with juvenile delinquency, antisocial behavior, and substance abuse.

Mental health problems can also have profound effects on physical health and illness. Cardiac patients who experience depressive symptoms after a heart attack are at substantially increased risk for a second heart attack (e.g., Frasure-Smith et al., 1999). The most pervasive type of substance abuse, cigarette smoking, is the number one cause of lung cancer, one of the least treatable and most deadly forms of cancer (American Cancer Society, 2000). Eating disorders, including bulimia and anorexia nervosa, lead to a number of short- and long-term health problems related to poor nutrition. Ineffective management of life stress is a contributor to a host of health problems, including hypertension and decreases in the body's immune system (Adler et al., 1999).

Understanding, treating, and preventing mental health problems and their associated effects is the business of clinical psychology. Clinical psychologists play a central role in the assessment, diagnosis, treatment, and prevention of these problems. Through the use of psychological tests, interviews, and observation of behavior, clinical psychologists help identify and diagnose mental health problems. Through the practice of various forms of psychological treatments (e.g., cognitive behavior therapy, interpersonal psychotherapy, marital and family therapy), clinical psychologists are on the front line in the treatment of mental health problems. Clinical psychologists are increasingly involved in the treatment of behavioral and psychological factors that are related to physical disease, including cancer, heart disease, diabetes, asthma, and chronic pain, to mention only a few. Clinical psychologists are also involved in the delivery of programs to prevent mental health problems and to promote positive mental and physical health. Moreover, clinical psychologists are involved in research to better understand the nature and causes of mental health and physical health problems, to improve methods of assessment and diagnosis, and to develop and evaluate the effectiveness of new methods of treatment and prevention. As a result, clinical psychologists engage in work in which the stakes are high and the opportunities are great to contribute to meaningful changes in the lives of others. At the same time, the work undertaken by clinical psychologists is difficult and challenging, because these problems are complex and the level of understanding of many mental health problems (and physical diseases) is still at an early stage.

In this book we introduce you to the exciting and challenging field of clinical psychology. Throughout this text we draw on research in clinical psychology and other areas of psychology to provide you with an understanding of the scientific basis for clinical psychology practice. In addition to this emphasis on research, an important way to gain an understanding of the clinical psychology field is through the careful consideration of individual cases. To help you gain this perspective, you will follow the cases of four individuals (Jason, Allison, Phillip, and Maria) who are introduced in the case example box at the end of this chapter (see box 1.3). We will follow these four individuals throughout this book to help you understand and apply the knowledge and methods of the field of clinical psychology.

THE FIELD
OF CLINICAL PSYCHOLOGY

Concern for, and fascination with, human psychological problems began long before the origins of clinical psychology. Thus, as we will point out in chapter 2, the field of clinical psychology is embedded in a rich historical context. Before a consideration of this field's evolution, however, it is helpful to define the nature, scope, and purpose of clinical psychology.

Table 1.1 presents four definitions of clinical psychology that span a period of almost 80 years. The definition offered by Lightner Witmer, the founder of the first psychological clinic in the United States in 1896, is viewed by many psychologists as the original definition of the field. Witmer defined clinical psychology as a discipline concerned with the study of individuals, by observation or experimentation, with the goal of facilitating change in those individuals. In part because he worked with school-age children who were experiencing problems in learning, Witmer saw psychological treatment as educational in nature. A similar definition was offered by the clinical section of the American Psychological Association (APA) in 1935 that emphasized the application of psychological methods of observation and measurement for the purpose of facilitating the adjustment of individuals. The APA in 1981, and more recently the **Society of Clinical Psychology of the APA** in 2000, offered definitions of the field that echo the themes represented in the earlier definitions. These recent definitions continue to identify the primary goals of clinical psychology as the application of knowledge to better understand and alleviate a wide range of problems experienced by individuals in their lives. The definition presented by the Society of Clinical Psychology makes the most explicit link between psychological science and clinical practice, a theme that is emphasized throughout this book.

Although there are common elements in these definitions, they also reflect changes over the past 80 years in how clinical psychologists have

TABLE 1.1
Definitions of Clinical Psychology: 1912–2000

- Lightner Witmer in 1912: "For the methods of clinical psychology are necessarily involved whenever the status of an individual mind is determined by observation and experiment, and pedagogical treatment applied to affect change, i.e., the development of such a mind." (1907, Psychological Clinic, v.1, p.1).
- American Psychological Association (APA) in 1935: "Clinical psychology is a form of applied psychology which aims to define the behavior capacities and behavior characteristics of an individual through methods of measurement, analysis, and observation; and which, on the basis of an integration of these findings with the data received from physical examinations and social histories, gives suggestions and recommendations for the proper adjustment of the individual." (Brown, 1935, Psychological Clinic, 23, p. 5).
- APA in 1981: "a clinical psychologist is a professional who applies principles and procedures to understand, predict, and alleviate intellectual, emotional, psychological, and behavioral problems" (Specialty Guidelines for the Delivery of Services by Clinical Psychologists, Washington, DC: APA).
- Society of Clinical Psychology of APA in 2000: "The field of clinical psychology integrates science, theory and practice to understand, predict, and alleviate maladjustment, disability, and discomfort as well as to promote human adaptation, adjustment, and personal development. Clinical psychology focuses on the intellectual, emotional, biological, psychological, social, and behavioral aspects of human functioning across the life span, in varying cultures, and at all socioeconomic levels."

thought about their field. First, there has been a gradual expansion of the range, or scope, of clinical psychology. Witmer (1907) first defined the field as focused on problems of intellectual functioning and learning, or in his terminology, problems of the mind. This definition contrasts with the most recent definition offered by the APA Society of Clinical Psychology (2000) that includes problems at multiple levels of human functioning—intellectual, emotional, biological, psychological, social, and behavioral. Thus, these definitions suggest that an increasingly wider range of problems has been included in the purview of clinical psychology. Whereas clinical psychology originally was concerned with problems that fall within the domain of learning and education, it now is most strongly concerned with psychopathology (see chapter 5), and physical illness and health (e.g., Compas et al., 1998). Second, the degree of emphasis on *observing* and *understanding* human functioning, as contrasted with efforts to *change* human behavior, has shifted across these definitions. As we will present in more detail in chapter 2, this change is reflected in the increased involvement of clinical psychology in psychological intervention (psychotherapy and other methods of behavior change) as compared with psychological assessment.

In our view, however, these definitions fail to emphasize the most important characteristic that sets clinical psychology apart from other mental health professions. Clinical psychology involves not only the generation of scientific knowledge about human functioning and psychological problems but also the application of the science of psychology to the goals of understanding and improving the well-being of individuals. It is this close link between the science of psychology and efforts to understand and alleviate psychological problems in the lives of individuals that is the cornerstone of clinical psychology. Clinical psychologist **Richard McFall** (1991) has offered one of the strongest presentations of this view of the field in his **"Manifesto for a Science of Clinical Psychology"** (see box 1.1). The cardinal principle of this manifesto is, "Scientific clinical psychology is the only legitimate and acceptable form of clinical psychology" (p. 76). McFall argues that the alternative to this form of clinical psychology, *unscientific* clinical psychology, is untenable in its reliance on intuition and subjective judgment. Psychological science provides the most objective basis for the practice of clinical psychology, because it offers a knowledge base that is accumulated across numerous

Richard McFall, Ph.D., a clinical psychologist at Indiana University, has been a strong advocate for a scientific approach to the practice of clinical psychology. Dr. McFall is an active researcher in the area of social competence, and throughout his career has been concerned with the nature of the relationship between clinical research and practice. Dr. McFall served as the president of the Academy of Psychological Clinical Science from 1995 to 1998. (Photo courtesy of Richard McFall.)

studies that have been held to standards of scientific rigor and that offer clear evidence for the practice of clinical psychology.

For the purposes of this text, **clinical psychology** is defined as the branch of psychology devoted to the generation of psychological knowledge and the application of knowledge from the science of psychology for the purpose of understanding and improving the mental and physical well-being and functioning of an individual or group of individuals. This definition reflects not only what clinical psychology is, but also what it should be; that is, emphasis is given to the application of existing scientific knowledge and the generation of new information. Clinical psychology will contribute to the broader fields of psychology and behavioral science and will serve the needs of the public only if it is committed to a scientific basis for all its endeavors.

Although few clinical psychologists take on the roles of scientist and practitioner equally, clinical psychology as a field both contributes to and benefits from the knowledge base of psychology. Through the generation and application of psychological science, clinical psychologists aim to improve the psychological functioning and well-being of individuals. Clinical psychologists are concerned with individuals who are experiencing significant emotional distress, whose behavior is distressing or disturbing to others, or whose problems are manifested in an identifiable psychological disorder (Strupp & Hadley, 1977).

CLINICAL PSYCHOLOGY AND OTHER AREAS OF PSYCHOLOGY

Links Between Clinical Psychology and Other Areas of Psychology

At the most fundamental level, clinical psychology shares a common knowledge base with all of psychology—a knowledge base drawn from over 100 years of research on human behavior, emotion, cognition, and biology. Clinical psychology involves the application of this knowledge base of psychological science, and consequently, there is a bond between clinical psychology and basic research in psychology (e.g., Kihlstrom, 1995; Onken & Blaine, 1997). Basic psychological science provides the foundation for clinical psychology in the same way that that basic research in biochemistry, anatomy, physiology, microbiology, and genetics forms the basis for medicine and other health professions (Kihlstrom). A wide range of basic psychological science is relevant to clinical psychology, including research on emotion and motivation; perception, attention, learning, and memory; neuropsychology; thought and communication; social influence and social cognition; family processes and social networks; and sociocultural and environmental

processes (National Advisory Mental Health Council Behavior Science Task Force, 1995).

Some of the most important models for understanding clinical problems have been developed from research and theory in other areas of psychology. For example, theories of depression that emphasize the role of causal attributions or explanatory style have their roots in observations of animals' responses to inescapable shock (e.g., Overmier & Seligman, 1967; Seligman & Maier, 1967) and in social psychological research on the ways that people interpret the causes of events in their daily lives (e.g., Kelley, 1967, 1973). Martin Seligman (1975) and his colleagues integrated findings from these two areas to generate a theory of "learned helplessness" that has been applied to depression in humans. The theory has subsequently undergone several revisions (e.g., Abramson, Metalsky, & Alloy, 1989; Abramson, Seligman, & Teasdale, 1978; Alloy, Abramson, & Francis, 1999) that have integrated more complex explanations of cognitive processes that may be involved in helplessness and depression (the model is now referred to as the hopelessness model of depression). These revisions were strongly influenced by research in basic experimental psychology (e.g., Alloy & Abramson, 1979).

Basic research in cognitive psychology and cognitive science has also contributed significantly to recent advances in clinical psychology. For example, research on biases in the ways that people attend to emotional information in the environment has helped researchers to understand some of the cognitive processes that may underlie depression and anxiety (e.g., Gotlib, Kurtzman, & Blehar, 1997). Researchers in cognitive psychology have shown that emotions such as depressed or anxious mood, as well as clinical depression and anxiety are related to the ways that people attend to and process information in the world (Mathews & MacLeod, 1994). Using carefully controlled laboratory tasks, researchers have found that anxious individuals selectively attend to threatening as opposed to nonthreatening information at both conscious

BOX 1.1

A MANIFESTO FOR A SCIENCE OF CLINICAL PSYCHOLOGY

In 1991 Professor Richard McFall of Indiana University served as president of Section III (the Society for the Science of Clinical Psychology) of the Division of Clinical Psychology (now the Society of Clinical Psychology) of the American Psychological Association. In his presidential address (and in a subsequent article published in *The Clinical Psychologist*), Professor McFall offered a challenge to clinical psychology—that the only legitimate form of clinical psychology is that which is based in scientific research. Although 10 years have passed since McFall made this declaration, his points still apply today. The following excerpts provide a sample of the challenge that McFall laid out for the field.

Cardinal Principle: Scientific Clinical Psychology is the Only Legitimate and Acceptable Form of Clinical Psychology

This first principle seems clear and straightforward to me—at least as an ideal to be pursued without compromise. After all, what is the alternative? Unscientific clinical psychology? Would anyone openly argue that unscientific clinical psychology is a desirable goal that should be considered seriously as an alternative to scientific clinical psychology?

Probably the closest thing to a counter argument to this proposed Cardinal Principle is the commonly offered rationalization that science doesn't have all the answers yet, and until it does, we must do the best we can to muddle along, relying on our clinical experience, judgment, creativity, and intuition (cf. Matarazzo, 1990). Of course, this argument reflects the mistaken notion that science is a set of answers, rather than a set of processes or methods by which to arrive at answers. Where there are lots of unknowns—and clinical psychology certainly has more than its share—it is all the more imperative to adhere as strictly as possible to the scientific approach. Does anyone seriously believe that a reliance on intuition and other unscientific methods is going to hasten advances in knowledge? The systematic procedures of science represent the best methods yet devised for exploring the unknown.

So the alternative to scientific clinical psychology probably is not unscientific clinical psychology. Are there any other alternatives or contrasts? The most frequently mentioned is Clinical Practice. The dichotomy between science and practice is the classic one—the one codified in the Boulder Model of clinical training with its hyphenated characterization of clinical psychologists as "scientist-practitioners." The implication commonly attributed to the hyphenated Boulder Model is that there are two legitimate types of clinical psychology: clinical science and clinical practice.

and nonconscious levels (MacLeod & Rutherford, 1998). Similarly, depressed people have been found to attend more strongly to negative than to positive stimuli (Gotlib & Cane, 1987) and to have better memory for negative than for positive information (Mathews & MacLeod).

Another important example of the relation between clinical psychology and other areas of psychology can be found in the development of one of the most widely used and well-documented forms of psychological treatment—behavior therapy. The roots of behavior therapy can be found in basic research on operant and classical conditioning of behavior, research that has a long history involving both animals and humans (O'Donohue, 1998). Conditioning theory has been used to explain how certain types of psychological problems develop or are learned and how they might be treated or unlearned. For example, models of classical conditioning have

BOX 1.1. (continued)

This is the dichotomy one hears, for example, from undergraduates who are applying to graduate training programs in clinical psychology and are struggling with making what they perceive to be the difficult, but necessary, career choice between science and practice. When I counsel these undergraduates, I try to persuade them that they are not framing the issue correctly—that there really is no choice between science and practice. I tell them that all clinical psychologists must be scientists first, regardless of the particular jobs they fill after they earn their degrees; that becoming a clinical scientist does not mean that they are committed to working in a laboratory or university; and that choosing not to receive the best scientific training possible, by purposely opting for a training program that does not emphasize scientific training, means that they will not be prepared to do any form of psychological activity as well. What I am saying to them, of course, is that all forms of legitimate activity in clinical psychology must be grounded in science, that all competent clinical psychologists must be scientists first and foremost, and that clinicians must ensure that their practice is scientifically valid.

First Corollary: Psychological services should not be administered to the public (except under strict experimental control) until they have satisfied these four minimal criteria:

1. The exact nature of the service must be described clearly.

2. The claimed benefits of the service must be stated explicitly.

3. These claimed benefits must be validated scientifically.

4. Possible negative side effects that might outweigh any benefits must be ruled out empirically.

This Corollary may look familiar. It is adapted from recommendations made by Julian B. Rotter in the Spring 1971 issue of *The Clinical Psychologist* . . . Rotter offered this analogy:

Most clinical psychologists I know would be outraged to discover that the Food and Drug Administration allowed a new drug on the market without sufficient testing, not only of its efficacy to cure or relieve symptoms, but also of its short term side effects and the long term effects of continued use. Many of these same psychologists, however, do not see anything unethical about offering services to the public—whether billed as a growth experience or as a therapeutic one—which could not conceivably meet these same criteria. (p. 1)

Second Corollary: The primary and overriding objective of doctoral training programs in clinical psychology must be to produce the most competent clinical scientists possible (McFall, 1991).

---

been applied to the acquisition and development of fears and anxieties (e.g., Bouton, 1998; Bouton, Mineka, & Barlow, 2001). These models of conditioning have then been used to develop treatments that involve the extinction of fearful behavior and the acquisition of new, more competent behavior in its place (Barlow, Esler, & Vitali, 1998).

The rapidly growing field of clinical health psychology has also benefited from the work of clinical psychologists, social psychologists, physiological psychologists, and pediatric psychologists as well as physicians and immunologists (e.g., Andersen, Kiecolt-Glaser, & Glaser, 1994; Compas et al., 1998; Taylor, Repetti, & Seeman, 1997). Collaborative research efforts have led to a clearer understanding of the ways that psychological factors contribute to disease, the relationship between psychological and biological processes in health and disease,

Lyn Abramson, Ph.D., a Professor at the University of Wisconsin, and Lauren Alloy, Ph.D., a Professor at Temple University, are clinical psychologists who proposed an influential hopelessness theory of depression. Abramson and Alloy's work examining cognitive aspects of depression has contributed greatly to our understanding of this debilitating disorder. (Photos courtesy of Lyn Abramson, left; and Lauren Alloy, right.)

how individuals cope with disease and aversive aspects of medical treatment, and how to increase the adherence and compliance of patients who are required to follow long-term treatment regimens.

Despite the clear link between basic psychological science and the applied aspects of clinical psychology, this alliance has been an uneasy one. One of the most significant problems for the field is how to maintain a connection between clinical psychology and the rest of psychological science (Barlow, 1981; Davison & Lazarus, 1994). Many practicing clinical psychologists report that they do not find basic research in psychology to be relevant to the kinds of activities in which they engage during their day-to-day work in assessing and treating people with psychological problems. Practitioners often view psychological research as favoring the internal validity of an experiment

(careful control over the variables that are manipulated in the laboratory) over the external validity of the findings of the research (the applicability of the research to people in the real world). On the other hand, this separation between science and practice may also be the result of the decreased emphasis on scientific training in many professional psychology programs. As we discuss in chapter 2, the tension between basic areas in psychology and clinical psychology poses one of the major challenges in the present and future development of the field.

Unique Features of Clinical Psychology

Although clinical psychology is tied to the rest of psychology through scientific research, clinical psychology is, at the same time, different from developmental, social, physiological, learning, and other areas of psychology. Clinical psychology is unique specifically in its commitment to the use of psychological research to enhance the well-being of individuals. Korchin (1976) defined this approach as the **clinical attitude:** "Whether we are concerned with understanding, control (i.e., clinical intervention), or prediction, we need knowledge of the peculiar structure of a particular person which, in turn, requires clinical investigation of how such factors are ordered for him [*sic*]. But this process is not independent of general or differential knowledge; indeed, it is guided by it. Understanding of the ways in which relevant factors relate in general provides a framework for visualizing their relations in the specific case" (p. 30). Thus, clinical psychologists use psychological knowledge about people in general to understand and help specific individuals.

Clinical psychology is not the only arm of the broader field of psychology that is concerned with the application of psychological knowledge to help people. Other applied areas of psychology include counseling psychology, school psychology, community psychology, industrial/organizational psychology, and applied developmental psychology. Clinical psychology shares many common features with these other areas of psychology, yet is distinct from even these areas in its emphasis on psychological assessment, treatment, and prevention of psychopathology.

Perhaps the cloudiest distinction lies between clinical psychology and **counseling psychology.** Students in both clinical and counseling psychology doctoral programs are trained in methods of psychological assessment and treatment of various types of psychological problems and disorders. Historically, counseling psychology has been concerned more with problems of everyday living and with enhancing the adjustment of well-functioning individuals, whereas clinical psychology focused on more severe forms of psychopathology. Furthermore, counseling psychology programs have traditionally been based

in schools or departments of education, whereas clinical psychology programs have been based in departments of psychology. These distinctions have become less clear over the years, to the point where clinical and counseling psychologists are now often difficult to distinguish. Training programs in the two fields remain separate at most universities and colleges, however, and most counseling psychology programs are still based in departments or schools of education rather than in departments of psychology.

CLINICAL PSYCHOLOGY AND OTHER MENTAL HEALTH PROFESSIONS

Just as clinical psychology is not separate from the rest of psychology, it also is connected with the other branches of the mental health professions. Professionals in the field of mental health come from psychiatry, clinical social work, counseling, psychiatric nursing, and other types of applied psychology. Although each of these fields is involved in the delivery of services to individuals suffering from psychological problems and although some are involved in clinical research, each differs from clinical psychology in important ways.

Psychiatrists are physicians, doctors of medicine, and therefore receive education and training that is quite different from that received by clinical psychologists. Training as a psychiatrist begins with four years of medical school and a medical internship that is required of all physicians. Specific training in psychiatry begins only after a physician receives her or his M.D. and typically takes the form of 4-year residency training in psychiatry, with further specialized training (e.g., child psychiatry) following the completion of residency. The training of all physicians, including psychiatrists, is grounded in the basic physical and biological sciences. This training, however, does not necessarily include training in research in the behavioral sciences, an important difference from the training of clinical psychologists. Psychiatrists in practice are typically involved in prescribing psychotropic medication for the treatment of psychopathology and to a lesser extent in conducting psychotherapy and managing the medical care of psychiatric patients. Thus, psychiatrists and clinical psychologists are alike in that both may be involved in conducting psychotherapy, but they differ in that psychiatrists are trained to prescribe medication, whereas clinical psychologists are trained in methods of psychological assessment and in behavioral science research. If the current movement within a large portion of psychology to achieve limited medication prescription privileges for clinical psychologists is successful, this change would have a significant effect on the relationship between clinical psychology and psychiatry (DeLeon, 1996).

Although these two fields have very different intellectual traditions and draw from somewhat different bases of knowledge about human behavior, there are instances of collaboration in research and practice between psychiatry and psychology. Psychiatrists and psychologists have collaborated on a wide range of research, including epidemiologic studies (Kessler et al., 1994), investigations of the causes of psychopathology (Gotlib et al., 1991), and most extensively in the area of treatment research (e.g., Hollon & Beck, 1996). Psychologists and psychiatrists often collaborate in clinical practice, with psychiatrists monitoring the evaluation and use of psychotropic medication, and psychologists providing expertise in assessment and psychotherapy.

As we will point out in chapters 12 through 15, some of the most significant advances in psychotherapy research and methods have come from the field of psychiatry. For example, Joseph Wolpe, one of the founders of behavior therapy through his work on systematic desensitization for the treatment of anxiety, and Aaron Beck, the founder of cognitive therapy for depression,

were trained in psychiatry. It is noteworthy, however, that Wolpe, Beck, and others have worked in close collaboration with clinical psychologists in the development and evaluation of their approaches to psychotherapy.

Clinical social workers receive a master of social work (MSW) after typically two years of graduate training. Social work training includes course work in the theory and practice of social work, but the emphasis of this training is on two years of supervised fieldwork in community agencies or mental health settings. Clinical or psychiatric social workers typically conduct psychotherapy on an individual or group basis and are involved in the coordination of a wide range of social and psychological services for the people they serve. In contrast to the training for clinical psychologists, training for clinical social workers does not involve preparation for psychological assessment or research; in contrast to psychiatrists, clinical social workers are not trained in the administration of psychoactive medication. On the other hand, social work training retains a strong emphasis on working with people in the community and in coordinating services that are designed to meet all their needs and problems beyond those that can be met through psychotherapy or medication alone. Activities include social casework (e.g., investigating potential child abuse, facilitating reentry to the community from hospitals); group, marital, and personal counseling; and social welfare planning. Clinical social workers can be licensed as independent practitioners of psychotherapy at the master level.

Psychiatric nurses receive their basic training in nursing as part of a two-year program to become a registered nurse. Psychiatric nursing is an area of specialization within nursing that involves concentrated training in working with individuals with psychiatric disorders. Most often, psychiatric nurses work in hospital settings with inpatient populations. Activities carried out by psychiatric nurses include individual and group counseling, hospital administration, and mental health education. Psychiatric nurses work closely with other medical professionals, especially psychiatrists, and are often involved in managing the treatment of psychological problems through psychoactive medication.

WHAT CLINICAL PSYCHOLOGISTS DO, AND WHERE THEY DO IT

Although clinical psychology is a distinct area within the field of psychology, clinical psychologists are remarkably heterogeneous in the day-to-day work that they do and in the settings in which they work. Examples of the types of work conducted by clinical psychologists are included in table 1.2.

Tasks of Clinical Psychologists

One of the most exciting aspects of clinical psychology is the variety of activities that clinical psychologists can become involved in as part of

their work. These activities include research, teaching, assessment and diagnosis, prevention, treatment, consultation, and administration. Although most clinical psychologists are involved in some combination of these activities, very few are involved in all these endeavors at any one point in their careers or even over the course of their careers.

Research   Most research in clinical psychology is carried out or supervised by faculty members in universities and colleges, although some research is conducted by clinical psychologists working in applied settings, such as hospitals and clinics. Research in clinical psychology is a widely varied enterprise, ranging from investigations of problems that can be observed and studied in animals in laboratory settings to studies of the effectiveness of a certain type of psychotherapy for a specific clinical problem with patients in community clinics or hospitals. For example, important research on the nature and

TABLE 1.2
A Sampling of Settings in Which Clinical Psychologists Work

Setting	Primary role	Primary duties
College or university	Professor	• **Teaching** • **Research** • **Supervision of clinical training**
Mental health center	Clinical psychologist	• **Assessment** • **Diagnosis** • **Treatment (psychotherapy)** • **Administration**
Medical hospital	Clinical Psychologist, medical psychologist, rehabilitation psychologist	• **Assessment** • **Diagnosis** • **Treatment (psychotherapy)** • **Consultation/liaison to medical professionals**
Psychiatric hospital	Clinical psychologist	• **Assessment** • **Diagnosis** • **Treatment (psychotherapy)**
Independent practice	Clinical psychologist	• **Assessment** • **Diagnosis** • **Treatment (psychotherapy)**

development of anxiety disorders has been carried out using a variety of methods. In a classic series of studies of anxiety responses in rhesus monkeys, **Dr. Susan Mineka,** currently at Northwestern University, and her colleagues demonstrated that fears and anxiety can be acquired through processes of classical conditioning and observational learning (e.g., Cook & Mineka, 1990; Mineka & Cook, 1986). We will describe this research in more detail in chapter 2. Professor **David Barlow** and his associates (e.g., Barlow, Esler, & Vitali, 1998; Barlow et al., 2000), currently at Boston University, are conducting exciting research on the treatment of adults suffering from anxiety disorders. These researchers have shown that anxiety disorders can be treated effectively through psychological interventions that change the ways that patients think and by teaching such skills as the ability to relax. Mineka's and Barlow's approaches to studying anxiety are linked by psychological theory and research (Bouton, Mineka, & Barlow, 2001).

Teaching   Clinical psychologists who work in colleges and universities are also involved in teaching, both with undergraduates who are majoring in psychology (and students from other majors who take psychology courses) and graduate students who are pursuing their master's or doctorate in clinical psychology. Clinical psychology faculty typically teach undergraduate courses such as abnormal psychology, personality, introduction to clinical psychology, and child clinical psychology. The majority of teaching is carried out though classroom instruction or individual instruction in research. In addition, however, a large amount of teaching by clinical psychologists involves clinical teaching and supervision of graduate students who are learning skills in psychological research, assessment, and intervention. Graduate students are trained in psychological assessment and psychotherapy in clinic settings under the direct supervision of clinical psychologists. Typically, the student sees the patient or client and meets weekly with the

supervisor to formulate an understanding of the case, to read and discuss the psychological research that is relevant to the case and the type of assessment or treatment that is being pursued, and to evaluate and plan weekly sessions with the client. Often, the supervisor will directly observe the student working with a patient (through a one-way mirror) or listen to audiotapes of sessions with the student to review the process of the sessions.

Assessment   One of the unique skills of clinical psychologists involves the ability and training to carry out detailed psychological **assessments.** As described in detail in chapters 6 through 10, assessment includes the administration and interpretation of standardized psychological tests, the use of structured clinical interviews, systematic observation of a client's behavior, and an examination of the settings or environments in which the individual functions day to day.

Psychologists who work in clinical practice, whether in a clinic setting or in their own independent office, devote varying amounts of their time to assessment. For example, one psychologist may devote a great deal of his or her time to conducting evaluations of the psychological functioning of individuals who have filed for workers' compensation for psychological disabilities related to work stress. Another might conduct frequent evaluations of children's psychological status as it pertains to decisions regarding custody after a divorce, and still another might conduct evaluations of individuals who have been incarcerated for committing sexual offenses. In contrast, other psychologists may be involved in assessment of only those clients to whom they provide psychotherapy.

Treatment   Perhaps the most common image of a clinical psychologist is that of someone who conducts individual, group, or family psychotherapy. This image is reasonably accurate, because practicing psychologists devote a great proportion of their time to the delivery of psychological treatment using any of the dozens of approaches to psychotherapy. **Treatment** may be conducted with individual children, adolescents, or adults or with couples, families, or groups of individuals with similar types of problems. A typical individual psychotherapy session lasts 50 minutes (rather than an hour, to allow the psychologist time to write notes and prepare for subsequent appointments) and may follow a relatively prescribed format depending on the orientation of the psychologist. Clinical psychology is placing an increasing emphasis on the use of treatments that have been validated in empirical research (i.e., they have been shown to work in carefully controlled studies) and standardized through detailed manuals describing the treatment methods (Chambless & Hollon, 1998; Woody & Sanderson, 1998).

Prevention   Although the **prevention** of psychopathology is a high priority for all types of mental health practitioners, significantly less time and effort is devoted to the prevention than to the treatment of mental health problems. The reasons for this lack of attention to prevention are complex and are the subject of further discussion in chapter 11. Prevention programs include teaching social skills to school-age children, teaching adults ways to cope with work-related stress and its consequences, helping families cope with the possible effects of divorce, and teaching patients with physical illness how to cope with their disease and the adverse side effects of treatment. Psychologists engage in prevention-related activities as part of their duties in mental health centers and in consultation with organizations such as businesses and schools. Clinical psychologists are likely to become increasingly more involved in prevention efforts, in part as a result of pressure from health maintenance organizations and insurance companies to reduce the cost of health care. Preventing the onset of psychological and medical disorders can be, in the long run, much more cost effective than treating disorders once they arise.

Consultation   Clinical psychologists also offer their services through advice and **consultation** to other professionals. For example, a clinical psychologist might serve as a consultant in a school, providing information and guidance to teachers and counselors who themselves work directly with children. Another psychologist might provide advice and consultation to a business that is struggling with a high rate of alcohol abuse among its employees. The base of operations for consultation services performed by psychologists may be independent practice or a large consulting firm that specializes in this type of work.

Administration   Although clinical psychologists are not specifically trained to be administrators, clinical psychologists may assume administrative positions in the various settings in which they serve. Such positions include serving as the director of the clinical psychology training program within a university psychology department, chairperson of a psychology department, director of a mental health center, or director of psychological services in a hospital or health maintenance organization.

Settings in Which Clinical Psychologists Work

Given the wide range of tasks in which clinical psychologists are involved, it is not surprising that clinical psychologists work in a remarkably wide array of settings. These settings include community mental health centers, independent practice, psychiatric hospitals, general medical hospitals, residential treatment centers for children and adolescents, universities and colleges, school systems, prisons, courts and police departments, government, and industry. The specific roles that clinical psychologists serve vary both across and within these settings, with research, assessment, and treatment being the most commonly represented activities in these various contexts.

The settings that most people associate with the work of clinical psychologists include mental health clinics, psychiatric hospitals, and independent practice. In these and other settings, clinical psychologists are involved in psychological assessment (including psychological testing and the systematic observation of behavior) and in psychological treatment (typically individual, group, or family psychotherapy based on any of several theoretical models). These same functions, however, are actually carried out by clinical psychologists in a much wider range of settings. Psychologists are engaged in these activities in medical hospitals, in separate medical psychology units within hospitals, or as members of interdisciplinary teams in cancer centers, burn units, pediatric wards, and rehabilitation units.

Norcross, Krag, and Prochaska (1997) conducted a survey and found that in 1995, 15 percent of clinical psychologists were employed in academic settings (colleges and universities), 30 percent in hospitals or clinics (including psychiatric hospitals, general hospitals, outpatient mental health clinics, medical schools, and mental health centers), and 40 percent in private or independent practice. Interestingly, the proportion of clinical psychologists employed in independent practice rose steadily from the 1970s through the 1990s: Twenty-three percent were employed in private practice in 1973, 31 percent in 1981, 35 percent in 1986, and 40 percent in 1995. We will consider this trend in terms of its implications for the future development of clinical psychology in chapter 2.

The APA periodically surveys its members and provides information on the employment of psychologists. Results were released recently indicating that the settings in which psychologists work have changed from 1973 to 1995. In 1973, approximately 58 percent of all doctoral-level psychologists worked in academic settings (colleges, universities, and medical schools), and 12 percent worked in business settings (including private practice and other clinical settings). By 1995 these numbers had changed dramatically:

The proportion of psychologists in academic settings had declined to 35 percent while the percentage in applied, health-care-related settings had grown to 39 percent. Specifically, 10 percent were employed in private nonprofit settings, 22 percent in private for-profit settings (includes businesses and incorporated private practices), and 17 percent were self-employed (i.e., individual independent practice). These figures reflect the large increase in the proportion of psychologists receiving degrees in clinical psychology and pursuing careers in applied settings. Examples of the work of clinical psychologists are presented in box 1.2.

MODELS OF TRAINING IN CLINICAL PSYCHOLOGY

In most of the United States and Canada, clinical psychologists are defined by successful completion of doctoral-level training in clinical psychology from an accredited institution, including the successful completion of an accredited year-long internship in an applied setting and successful completion of a national examination for licensure as a psychologist (although some states allow individuals to practice as psychologists with a master's degree). Within the United States, two distinct models of training have developed, one leading to a doctor of philosophy (**PhD**) degree in psychology and the other to a doctor of psychology (**PsyD**) degree. The fundamental difference between the two models of graduate training lies in their relative emphasis on the importance of psychological research in the training of doctoral-level clinical psychologists.

The APA provides periodic (every 5 to 7 years) review of clinical psychology doctoral programs that apply for accreditation. The APA applies criteria for accreditation that address the quality of the faculty, the course curriculum, characteristics of clinical training, research training, admissions criteria, quality of students in the program, the outcomes (careers) of students who graduate from the program, and the standards

BOX 1.2

A SAMPLING OF CLINICAL PSYCHOLOGISTS IN PRACTICE

Gerard Banez, Ph.D., is a Pediatric Clinical Psychologist in the Cleveland Clinic. Dr. Banez works in collaboration with pediatricians in treating children who have problems such as chronic headache and abdominal pain, children who have been hospitalized and have to undergo painful medical procedures (e.g., children with cancer who need to have their bone marrow treated), and children who experience behavioral problems such as attention deficit disorder and anxiety disorders. Dr. Banez conducts psychological evaluations of children, conducts behavior therapy to treat problems, and consults with pediatricians to help determine the role of psychological treatment in a child's overall medical care.

David Baker, Ph.D., is a clinical psychologist in a university-based psychology clinic that serves the community. Dr. Baker conducts individual psychotherapy with adults who are experiencing a wide range of problems, including depression, anxiety disorders, personality disorders, and sexual dysfunction. He bases much of his work on cognitive-behavioral treatments that have been evaluated and are presented in systematic manuals to guide treatment. He sees approximately five to six clients each day in 50-minute sessions. In addition to meeting with clients, he writes case summaries of each session and conducts psychological testing as needed for the formulation and evaluation of his cases.

Karen Fondacaro, Ph.D., is a clinical psychologist who works in forensic clinical psychology. She practices in a psychology clinic that specializes in work with sexual offenders and victims of sexual abuse. She conducts groups for juvenile offenders who have been convicted of sexual abuse, counsels parents whose children have been abused, provides individual and group psychotherapy for children who have been abused, and conducts work in state prisons with incarcerated men and women who have been convicted of crimes related to sexual abuse. As part of her work she also conducts evaluations of children who have experienced sexual abuse in order to determine the nature and the extent of the psychological effects of abuse.

Rose Colletti, Ph.D., is a clinical psychologist who spends a portion of her time working in a comprehensive breast care center that treats women with breast cancer. Dr. Colletti works as part of a multidisciplinary team of surgeons, medical oncologists, radiation oncologists, and nurses to offer comprehensive care to breast cancer patients and their families. She meets with each patient when the patient receives her diagnosis, conducts a brief evaluation of the patient's psychological status and identifies possible individual, group, and family services that may be needed. She helps patients cope with the stress of breast cancer, using techniques that have been shown to be effective in managing anxiety, depression, and stress. Dr. Colletti is also involved in research as part of a randomized clinical trial comparing the efficacy of two different psychological interventions for women with breast cancer.

Janice Peyser, Ph.D., is a clinical neuropsychologist who works in a large medical center, providing and supervising neuropsychological evaluations and consultation to a wide range of departments and clinics within the medical center. Dr. Peyser conducts neuropsychological testing for patients with head injuries that result from accidents, for patients suffering from Alzheimer's disease or dementia, and for patients suffering from severe mental illness (e.g., schizophrenia). As part of her work, she supervises the neuropsychological testing of other psychologists and coordinates the training of psychology doctoral students who are receiving practicum or internship training in the medical center. Dr. Peyser is also involved in research, including a study of the effects of chemotherapy on the neuropsychological functioning (memory, sustained attention, fine motor coordination) of cancer patients.

and procedures that the program employs in the training of students. In the fall of 2000 the APA listed 200 accredited doctoral programs in clinical psychology, of which 159 were PhD programs and 41 were PsyD programs (see the APA website (www.apa.org) for a complete list of APA-accredited clinical psychology programs).

PhD Training Model

The scientist-practitioner model of training is represented in PhD clinical psychology programs. This model of training was first formally articulated in a report commissioned by the APA and chaired by David Shakow in 1947 (Shakow, 1948) and subsequently at a conference in Boulder, Colorado (Raimy, 1950). It is typically referred to as the **Boulder Model** of training in clinical psychology (Baker & Benjamin, 2000). Students are required to develop skills both as psychological researchers and as practicing psychologists. Although the balance of these two types of training activities is rarely exactly 50-50 in any single program, all Boulder Model programs share a commitment to a relative balance of training in the science and the application of clinical psychology (Belar, 2000).

These programs are housed mostly in university-based departments of psychology that are also committed to educating undergraduates in psychology and to the graduate training of students in other areas of psychology (e.g., learning, developmental, cognitive, social). Students complete course work in basic areas of psychology and also participate in specialized seminars on topics in clinical psychology. Students are required to carry out at least two pieces of original research: a master's thesis or its equivalent and a second research project that constitutes their doctoral dissertation. This research is usually on a topic relevant to clinical psychology and often involves applied research on the nature, measurement, etiology, prevention, or treatment of some form of psychopathology or health-related problem. In addition, students must complete a specified number of hours of training in clinical practice (typically psychological assessment and psychotherapy) during their years in graduate school, followed by a full-year, 40-hours-per-week internship in an applied setting under the supervision of licensed clinical psychologists. Programs that have achieved accreditation by the APA must comply with a set of guidelines regarding the types of courses and research and clinical training experiences that are required of students for completion of the degree. A typical Boulder Model program requires four years of work at a university (course work, research, clinical practica) followed by an internship in the fifth year.

The rationale for the balance of training in research and practice is that, regardless of the specific career they pursue, clinical psychologists will need to draw on both sets of skills. For clinical psychologists who are actively involved in research, it is essential to be able to draw on experience working with people who have clinically significant problems. This experience keeps researchers in touch with the issues and problems that are faced by such people. Without this contact with people who are suffering from psychological problems, it is too easy for researchers to select research questions and problems because they are the ones that are most easily answered, are the most fashionable in the field, or are best suited for the methodologies that are available. Similarly, it is essential for clinical psychologists who are primarily involved in clinical practice to have a solid foundation in psychological research. Without training in research methods, practicing clinicians will be unable to stay informed of the latest developments in research concerned with psychopathology, assessment, or treatment. Clinicians need to be trained in research so that they can be educated consumers of the research advances that will emerge during the course of their career.

PsyD Training Model

Programs that grant a PsyD degree in clinical psychology to their graduates differ from PhD programs in the balance of training devoted to research and clinical practice. Although some PsyD training programs are based in universities, most exist in separate freestanding professional schools devoted solely to the training of professional psychologists. In these programs, relatively little emphasis is given to clinical research and relatively more training is devoted to skills in psychological assessment and intervention. Although students in these programs may conduct original clinical research for their dissertation, PsyD programs allow students an alternative to complete this requirement through other means, such as a review of the literature on a topic relevant to clinical psychology or a detailed case study.

The rationale behind practitioner-oriented models of training is twofold (Korman, 1974). First, there is a large body of knowledge and skills that a student needs to learn to become a competent clinician, and competence in the skills needed for clinical practice requires more time than can be devoted to them in a program that emphasizes both research and practice. Second, because most clinical psychologists do not go on to conduct research, they need relatively less training in research. Proponents of this model contend that it is no longer possible to acquire the necessary foundation of both clinical and research skills in the span of four to five years of doctoral training.

The Essential Role of Research in Clinical Psychology Training

A struggle over the identity of clinical psychology has developed between those advocates of the scientist-practitioner model (or more recently, a clinical science model) and advocates of the professional model of training. Some clinical psychologists have argued that the scientist-practitioner model has outlived its usefulness, if it was even a viable model in the first place. In spite of the people who have argued for the move toward greater professionalization of clinical psychology, however, the scientist-practitioner model remains strong in university-based training programs (Belar & Perry, 1992; Benjamin & Baker, 2000).

As the knowledge base of psychology in general, and clinical psychology in particular, continues to expand at an ever-increasing pace, the importance of sound scientific training for clinical psychologists will become even more important in the future. The continued importance of research training for clinical psychologists does not imply that all or even the majority of clinical psychologists are expected to go on to pursue research as part of their career. On the contrary, it is recognized that the majority of those students who receive their PhD in clinical psychology will spend their careers delivering psychological services to those in need of such assistance. Nevertheless, it is essential that practitioners of a scientifically based clinical psychology are capable of consuming and utilizing the vast knowledge base generated by psychological research.

Recognition of the central role of psychological science in the training and functioning of the clinical psychologist does not imply that science is a purely objective or infallible approach to knowledge. In fact, science is heavily influenced by the personal values and biases of researchers in the types of questions that they try to answer in their work and in the choice of the methods they use to answer these questions. Furthermore, the interpretation of scientific data is often open to debate with regard to the meaning and significance of the findings (cf. Mahoney, 1976). Despite these limitations, however, psychological science will continue to offer the basis for the practice of clinical psychology as long as psychologists accept the limits of science.

HOW A CLINICAL PSYCHOLOGIST THINKS

Although the science and the practice of clinical psychology may sound different, they are linked by a common way of thinking about people and the problems they experience. A series of four tasks are central to how clinical psychologists think about people and problems, whether in generating research and knowledge for the field as a whole or for gaining a better understanding of a given individual. These tasks are **description, explanation, prediction,** and **change** of human functioning.

Description

Accurate understanding of any individual or any psychological problem begins with a careful description of the person and the contexts in which she or he lives. In individual cases this description includes attention to the nature of the person's current functioning as well as a careful documentation of his or her prior development. In the broader field of clinical psychology, this description includes the development of systems for classification or categorization (taxonomies) of problems that are considered the subject matter of the field, the development of sound tools for the measurement of these problems, and documentation of the prevalence of these problems.

Imagine that you are working as a clinical psychologist, and an adolescent is referred to you for help. Brian is 16 years old. Approximately one year ago his parents went through a very difficult divorce. Following his parents' divorce, Brian, his mother, and younger sister moved to a new town in order for his mother to begin a new job and for the family to try to "start over." Because Brian's father did not provide regular financial support, the family was faced with significant economic difficulties as they tried to get by on his mother's salary. Brian did not adjust well either to his parents' divorce or to the move to a new school and town. He had diffi-

culty making new friends at school and became progressively more withdrawn and lonely. Three months before coming to see you, Brian became severely depressed and made a serious, but uncompleted, suicide attempt. You are faced with a number of important questions in your initial meetings with him. Is there a specific pattern of behaviors, thoughts, or feelings that characterize the difficulties that Brian is experiencing? Are these problems unique to him, or are they similar to difficulties experienced by other people? After some initial information has been obtained about a person, clinical psychologists must formulate a series of questions to systematically gain more information.

The initial questions that you ask about Brian should be guided by a sound theory of human behavior and by research that pertains to the problems of the individual client. With regard to this case, it is important that you draw on research examining the prevalence, causes, and correlates of adolescent suicide attempts. Research suggests that adolescent suicide attempts are related to depression, stressful life events, and difficulties or conflict within the family (e.g., Lewinsohn, Rhode, & Seeley, 1996; McKeown et al., 1998; Wagner, 1997). Furthermore, research suggests that the degree to which adolescents' parents, particularly mothers, are involved in and willing to cooperate with treatment predict how well suicidal adolescents will recover (King et al., 1997). In addition, you may want to know about Brian's strengths and competencies. In what areas of life has he been successful? What aspects of life are satisfying to him? And it will be essential for you to evaluate Brian's current suicidal thoughts and plans in order to assess the likelihood that he may make another attempt to take his life. Answers to these questions are part of the task of developing a careful, detailed *description* of the scope and nature of Brian's problems, his strengths and capabilities, and the environment or context in which he lives.

When clinical psychologists function as researchers they are faced with the same initial need for careful description. Clinical science is concerned first with identification of patterns of problematic behaviors, emotions, and thoughts that can be carefully and reliably documented in more than one individual at more than one point in time (e.g., Kessler et al., 1994). Accurate description is dependent on tools for reliably measuring the behaviors, thoughts, and feelings of individuals. The most important observations and descriptions are those that discern patterns of behavior across individuals or within the behavior of a single individual over time. For example, is there a consistent pattern of behaviors and emotions that is characterized by withdrawal from interactions with others, sadness, and suicidal intention or attempt? Is Brian representative of a larger group of individuals who display a similar pattern of behaviors?

As we will explain in more detail in chapter 5, Brian is suffering from Major Depressive Disorder as defined by the *Diagnostic and Statistical Manual, 4ᵗʰ Edition* (DSM-IV) of the American Psychiatric Association (1994). Although the DSM-IV is a *psychiatric* diagnostic classification system, clinical psychologists have made significant contributions to its development (e.g., Barlow, 1991; L. A. Clark, Watson, & Reynolds, 1995; Davidson & Foa, 1991; Widiger et al., 1991), as well as to epidemiological research on the incidence, prevalence, and course of disorders. For example, Peter Lewinsohn and his colleagues at the Oregon Research Institute have collected extensive data on the prevalence of major depressive disorder in over 1,700 adolescents in Oregon. These studies have shown that approximately 20% of adolescents have experienced at least one episode or Major Depressive Disorder by the time they are 18 years old (e.g., Lewinsohn et al., 1993). Furthermore, depressive symptoms and a diagnosis of depression in adolescence are associated with a number of other problems, including risk for suicide, poor academic performance, and impaired social relationships (Gotlib, Lewinsohn, & Seeley, 1995). Such data place Brian's problems into a broader context of the nature of depression during adolescence.

Explanation

Description of an individual or a psychological problem is not adequate for complete understanding of that person or problem. It is imperative that clinical psychologists develop careful models to explain how or why the problem developed, either in an individual or in people in general. This task includes the development and testing of models of etiology or cause, including but not limited to the use of experimental methods to test causality. The explanation enterprise of psychological science and of psychological practice involves the generation of hypotheses about an individual or a problem, hypotheses that can then be carefully and rigorously tested.

Why did Brian attempt to take his life? *Why* has he sunk into a behavioral pattern in which he is overwhelmed by daily responsibilities and feels that he has lost control over his own life? Certainly a provocative hypothesis would center on his parents' divorce. But what is the basis for this hypothesis? What do you know about the psychological consequences of the parental divorce and the losses and stresses that are associated with divorce? And what is the correspondence between such a loss and later depression, suicidal ideation, or suicide attempts?

The answers to these questions lie beyond information that you can obtain by examining a single case such as Brian's. Here you must turn to the broader science of psychology for an explanation of the problems that Brian is experiencing. Research concerned with the consequences of parental divorce and other types of separation and loss should provide guidance in understanding Brian's experience (Sandler et al., 2000). It will be important to determine if the short-term consequences during the first weeks and months following parental divorce are the same as, or different from, the long-term consequences over a period of years. It will also be important to determine whether it makes a difference if the divorce is associated with high levels of conflict between the parents, as compared with divorces that are worked out more amicably.

Explaining the nature and cause of a problem requires that clinical psychologists avoid the temptation to latch onto easy explanations. In spite of the salience of his parents' divorce and its timing in relation to Brian's suicide attempt, you must consider other competing explanations. Brian's current difficulties could be due in large part to aspects of his experience, such as characteristics of his family, or to biological factors, such as dysregulation in his central nervous system or an inherited risk for developing depression. Moreover, his parents' divorce may be only one element, perhaps the final trigger, in a much more complex set of factors that led to Brian's current problems.

The types of explanations that have been developed by psychologists for psychological problems will be presented in more detail in chapter 4. These explanations are rooted in both broad models of human beings and their behavior and in more circumscribed models of specific behaviors or problems. A number of different theories have been proposed to explain the causes of Major Depressive Disorder. These various theories emphasize the role of biological factors (e.g., Howland & Thase, 1999), cognitive schemas and networks (e.g., Beck, 1976; D. Clark, Beck, & Alford, 1999), conditioning and learning processes (e.g., Lewinsohn & Gotlib, 1995), interpersonal relationships (e.g., Klerman & Weissman, 1993), and an integration of one or more of these factors (e.g., Goodman & Gotlib, 1999). For example, one theoretical perspective on depression has focused on the ways in which individuals interpret and attribute the causes of events in their lives and generate expectations about future events (e.g., Gotlib & Abramson, 1999). This model hypothesizes that individuals are prone to develop depression to the extent that they have a characteristic negative

way of interpreting and attributing the causes of stressful events in their lives. An episode of depression may be triggered when an individual with a depressive cognitive style encounters a stressful event that activates the negative way of thinking (e.g., Metalsky & Joiner, 1992). This perspective has been supported by considerable empirical evidence and may provide an explanation for why Brian became depressed in response to his parents' divorce and the subsequent changes in his life.

Prediction

The most stringent and necessary test of any explanation is to see if it leads to predictions that are supported by empirical research. The importance of prediction, like description and explanation, is evident in the work of clinical psychologists helping individuals as well as in the work of clinical researchers trying to understand a problem in the general population. Prediction is possible only through repeated observations in which conditions are either controlled or well understood.

As you treat Brian's depression, you must try to predict the course of his symptoms in the initial weeks and months of his treatment. He has made an attempt to take his own life, and you must make a judgment about the likelihood that he will make another suicide attempt. What factors would be useful in trying to predict subsequent suicidal thinking or attempts? Even if he does not make another attempt on his life, you must make a prediction about the likely course of his current problems. Are these problems likely to continue, will they remit on their own, or is psychological treatment or medication necessary? Are there certain psychological treatments that are likely to be effective in treating his depression?

In research, prediction is tested in two ways: (a) longitudinal studies of the course of problems as they occur in real life; and (b) experimental studies testing specific predictions or hypotheses under controlled circumstances. For example, following the first of these methods, clinical psychologists have studied the course of depressive symptoms and Major Depressive Disorder during adolescence (e.g., Compas et al., 1997; Gotlib, Lewinsohn, & Seeley, 1995; Hankin et al., 1998). The results of these studies indicate that both symptoms of depression and episodes of Major Depressive Disorder increase over the course of adolescence, with more girls than boys experiencing depression during the adolescent decade.

Although the findings of longitudinal research are valuable, studies of this type are inherently limited in the inferences that can be drawn about the role of events, such as the loss of a loved one or parental divorce, in causing depression. This limitation is because these studies typically fail to take into account the functioning of individuals *before* they experienced such events. On the other hand, studies using experimental methods to examine the effects of loss (and many other important clinical problems) are unethical in research involving people—investigators cannot expose research participants to highly stressful or traumatic experiences. However, strong experimental evidence on the effects of separation and loss has been obtained in experiments with animals. The classic research of psychologist Harry Harlow and his colleagues, continued in the work of Stephen Suomi and his associates, are important examples of this work (e.g., Suomi, 1998). The findings from both human and animal research in this area point to important individual differences in response to loss. In both methods, the goal of the clinical researcher is to try to identify cause-and-effect relationships regarding important clinical problems.

Change

Because clinical psychology involves the application of psychological knowledge to alleviate human problems, it is not enough for clinical psychologists to describe, explain, or predict human functioning. Clinical psychologists must also be concerned with producing change in people's lives. Specifically, clinical psychologists develop and carry out planned and controlled interventions for the treatment and prevention of psychopathology, for coping with and prevention of some forms of physical illness, and for the promotion of psychological and physical health. Facilitating change is a goal of researchers and practicing clinicians alike.

Efforts to change people's lives must be based on research evidence that allows the clinician to make reasonable predictions about the effects of specific interventions. For example, what should you expect if you encourage Brian to discuss his feelings, including both his sense of sadness and his feelings of anger, about his parents' divorce? Is this discussion likely to lead to meaningful and lasting changes in his behavior, thoughts, and emotions? Alternatively, what is likely to happen if you systematically encourage and reward Brian for increasing his involvement in pleasant and constructive activities involving school, sports, and friends? Will making changes in his behavior be sufficient to alleviate his deep feelings of loss related to his parents' divorce? And from a different perspective, it may be important to change how Brian thinks about his parents, about himself, and about the reasons for his parents' divorce. If Brian learns to think about his parents' divorce in a different way, will this new way of thinking lead to meaningful changes in his emotions and behaviors?

Clinical psychologists are concerned with developing much more than a set of techniques for helping people change (e.g., Kanfer & Goldstein, 1991). They are committed to developing a broad set of principles to understand how and why people change (Borkovec, 1997). Clinical psychologists are more than technicians who can follow a set of procedures designed to help a person deal with a problem or change some aspect of his or her behavior. Clinical psychologists need to understand whether certain techniques work with some people or some problems and not others, and they need to understand the reasons that these techniques work. Without this type of comprehensive understanding of the mechanisms of how people change, psychologists cannot continue to systematically improve the ways that they can help people, and they may be unaware of ways to generalize their current methods to different people or problems.

One of the most active areas of research in clinical psychology focuses on the efficacy and effectiveness of psychotherapy (e.g., Hollon, 1996; Seligman, 1996). The psychological treatment of depression has been a particularly important and active area of psychotherapy research, with research being guided by several different theoretical models of depression. For example, based on the groundbreaking work of psychiatrist Aaron Beck (1976; Beck et al., 1979), clinical psychologists have contributed to the development and evaluation of research on cognitive therapy for depression. This research has demonstrated that cognitive therapy is one of several effective treatments for Major Depressive Disorder (e.g., Hollon & Beck, 1996). Clinical psychologists have also conducted research to determine how and why cognitive therapy produces beneficial effects in the treatment of depression (e.g., DeRubeis et al., 1996).

SUMMARY AND CONCLUSIONS

In this chapter we have reviewed the definition and characteristics of the field of clinical psychology. Clinical psychology involves the application of knowledge from the science of psychology to understand and aid individuals who are experiencing mental health problems. We have emphasized the relationship between psychological science and clinical application. Clinical psychology is both tied to and distinct from other areas of psychology. The common bond with other areas of psychology lies in the shared commitment to psychological research, while the unique features of clinical psychology involve the application of research to the understanding, treatment, and prevention of psychopathology. Clinical psychology is also distinct from other mental health fields, including psychiatry, clinical social work, and psychiatric nursing.

Clinical psychologists work in a variety of settings including universities, medical hospitals, psychiatric hospitals, psychological clinics, and independent practice. They are involved in activities that include research, teaching, and administration as well as the assessment, diagnosis, treatment, and prevention of psychopathology. Although clinical psychologists function both as scientists and as practitioners, their work in these two realms is unified by a systematic way of thinking about people and problems. Thus, a psychologist—whether trying to help an individual cope with a traumatic event in his or her life or trying to arrive at a broader understanding of how people in general cope with trauma—must engage in careful description, explanation, prediction, and change of the person or problem.

KEY TERMS AND NAMES

Assessment
David Barlow
Boulder Model
Clinical attitude
Clinical psychology
Clinical social work
Consultation
Counseling psychology
Description, explanation, prediction, change
"Manifesto for a Science of Clinical
   Psychology"

Richard McFall
Susan Mineka
PhD training in clinical psychology
Prevention
Psychiatry
PsyD training in clinical psychology
Society of Clinical Psychology of the American
   Psychological Association
Treatment

RESOURCES

Books
American Psychological Association. (2000).
   Graduate study in psychology. Washington, DC:
   Author.
Sternberg, R. J. (1997). *Career paths in psychology:
   Where your degree can take you*. Washington, DC:
   American Psychological Association.
American Psychological Association. (1993). *Getting
   in: A step-by-step plan for gaining admission to
   graduate school in psychology*. Washington, DC:
   Author.

Sayette, M. A., Mayne, T. J., & Norcross, J. C.
   (1998). *Insider's guide to graduate programs in
   clinical and counseling psychology*. New York:
   Guilford Press.
Journals
American Psychologist
Clinical Psychology: Science and Practice
Clinical Psychology Review

BOX 1.3

CASE EXAMPLES

In each of the following instances, imagine that you are a clinical psychologist working in a community mental health center, and these individuals have come to the clinic for help.

Jason, age 8

Jason's mother, Mrs. Newman, is seated in the clinic waiting area with a sullen look on her face. As you greet her, Jason enters the front door of the clinic carrying a can of soda. He is a tall, slender, 8-year-old African American boy with closely cut black hair. When you ask them to follow you to your office, Mrs. Newman has to prod Jason to accompany her, and he does so with a scowl. During your initial interview with Jason and his mother, Jason is quiet and offers very little information, even when you ask him questions directly. He squirms uncomfortably in his chair and slurps loudly from his soda can. Mrs. Newman begins by complaining that her son had noticed the soda machine on the way into the clinic. She reports that she told him she did not want him to buy a drink right now, but he insisted, began to make a scene, and she gave him a dollar to avoid a fuss. As his mother is talking, Jason is leaning back in his chair, and almost falls over backwards several times. His mother reports the following information: She was asked by Jason's teacher to take him to a psychologist because of his behavior. Currently in the third grade, Jason has been experiencing difficulties in school since he was in first grade. His teachers describe Jason as a very challenging student who has trouble paying attention and following basic classroom rules. He is out of his seat much of the time, disrupting other students as they try to work. Jason has difficulty completing his assignments in school and rarely completes his homework. His teachers note that the little work that Jason does complete is often sloppily written and disorganized. This past year, Jason's teachers have noted that he has become increasingly angry, surly, and disrespectful in class. He talks back to teachers when they try to reprimand him, often refuses to follow their instructions, and

appears to be unconcerned about the consequences of his misbehavior. Despite his problems in school, Mrs. Newman reports that Jason is a very bright boy and that his teachers share this view of him.

You ask Jason if he agrees with what his mom has reported. As you talk with Jason, you offer him paper and colored markers to draw while he talks. At different points during your interview with him, as a way of helping him to feel more comfortable, you ask if he can draw a picture of what he is talking about. He acknowledges that he gets into trouble at school, but he reports that this trouble is because of problems caused by other children. Jason feels that other children at school, particularly a group of boys in his class, purposefully try to make him angry and provoke a fight. For example, he reports that he dropped a notebook filled with his school papers in the hallway, and another boy stepped on the papers with a very muddy shoe. Jason says that he knew that the other boy had stepped on his papers on purpose, and he lashed out at the boy, pushing him into the wall and wrestling him to the floor. With great anger in his voice, Jason reports that he was punished by his teacher for this incident while the other boy was let off without any consequences.

Throughout the interview, Jason squirms in his chair, gazes around the room, and taps his feet on the floor. He appears impatient and eager to leave, asking his mother on several occasions if they could go. As you are speaking with him, he gets up out of his chair several times and looks at the books and professional journals you have on your shelves, taking the books down and glancing through the pages. His mother asks him not to touch things in the office but he ignores her requests. You ask him if he finds the books interesting and if he has any questions about the books or any of the other materials in your office. He does not respond to your question, puts the books down, and sullenly returns to his chair for the remainder of the interview.

You will learn more about Jason again in chapters on psychopathology (chapter 5), assessment

BOX 1.3 (continued)

(chapter 6), behavioral assessment (chapter 10), intelligence testing (chapter 8), and cognitive-behavioral therapy (chapter 14).

Allison, age 17

Allison is seated in the waiting room alone reading a magazine, and she quickly rises when you greet her and follows when you ask her to join you. Upon entering your office, Allison immediately states that her mother had called to make an appointment for her and had pressured her to come to the clinic. When you ask Allison to explain why she thinks her mother wanted her to come to the clinic, she quickly launches into a description of her current concerns in an anxious and wavering voice. Allison reports that she has always been a good student in school but that it is becoming increasingly more difficult to achieve perfect grades. She received all As throughout grade school and middle school, but since entering high school she reports that she has received "several Bs." She says that her mother and father worry a great deal about her grades and that they have been very concerned about the drop in her school performance. When you ask her how she feels about school, she becomes tearful and reports that she constantly feels anxious about school. She is always anxious before exams, even when she knows she has studied the material carefully. When you ask her what type of grades she would like to get, she states that "nothing less than perfect will do. I have to be perfect."

After Allison describes her worries about her schoolwork, you ask if there are other things about which she is concerned. She reports that when she entered high school, she became preoccupied with her weight and other aspects of her physical appearance. She insisted that her parents buy a scale for her, and she weighs herself in the morning before school, upon coming home from school, before and after dinner, and again before going to bed. Her eating has become increasingly more independent of the rest of her family; she often eats in her room while watching television or doing her homework. Her parents are unaware that she is using money she earns from her job after school to purchase large

quantities of junk food (e.g., cookies, chips). Her mother recently went into Allison's room to clean it and found empty cookie and potato chip bags under the bed and stuffed in the corner of her closet. She confronted Allison when she returned from school, and it was at this time that her mother insisted that she would make an appointment for Allison at the clinic. After a long silence, Allison discloses that she binges on these foods alone in her room and then slips into the bathroom and purges herself of the food by placing her finger down her throat and forcing herself to vomit. She is tearful as she describes this behavior and implores you not to tell her parents that she is making herself vomit after eating.

As you continue the interview, Allison shares with you how important it is to her to be thin and attractive. Although Allison is physically slim, she reports that she feels fat and bloated. She describes in detail that she feels that her thighs are too fat, her waist is too large, her breasts are large and flabby, and her cheeks are chubby. She says that she knows that she shouldn't be bingeing and forcing herself to vomit, but that she is terrified of becoming fat.

You will learn more about Allison in chapters on psychopathology (chapter 5), personality assessment (chapter 9), behavioral assessment (chapter 10), and psychodynamic therapy (chapter 12).

Phillip, age 43

Phillip is seated with his wife in the waiting area when you meet him. They follow you to your office and sit together on your sofa. You ask Phillip to tell you a bit about himself and why he and his wife came to see you. He states that he has been married to Elaine for 15 years, and that they have three children: a daughter, age 12, and two sons, ages 7 and 9. Until recently, Phillip worked for a large and established computer company, where he had been employed for more than 10 years. Just over a year ago Phillip left that job to join a small new computer software company. In his new job Phillip leads a group that is responsible for developing new programs for corporate financial analysis. Unlike his former job, this job requires him to make frequent

BOX 1.3 (continued)

presentations to the upper level managers at the company about new software programs that his work group has developed. These presentations have become an essential part of his job, and in large part, they determine the success or failure of the ideas developed by his group.

The decision to change jobs was a difficult one for Phillip and his family. Although there were exciting opportunities and more potential for growth at the new company, Phillip had to give up the security of working for an established corporation. The decision process caused significant distress for Phillip and his family. His relationship with Elaine became strained, and although the move did not affect their children directly, they nevertheless seemed to be reacting negatively to the stress experienced by their parents. They were often uncharacteristically oppositional and also sometimes seemed withdrawn and isolated from their friends and family.

Three weeks ago, Phillip was scheduled to make a presentation to a group of managers in a Friday morning meeting. Although he felt that he knew the material very well, he found it difficult to think about the presentation and avoided doing so until the night before. Then he lay awake most of the night worrying about the presentation. He thrashed in bed, sweating, his heart pounding. Phillip went to work the next day, only to leave before his presentation. He reported to his manager that he was coming down with the flu and could not deliver his talk. Although he felt an immediate sense of relief, he also felt guilty and worried over the consequences of his failure. A week later he was talking on the telephone at work when he suddenly felt short of breath; his heart was racing, and he became light-headed. He experienced a pain in his chest and he felt certain

that he was having a heart attack. Phillip hung up the phone and sat stooped over at his desk for several minutes until he finally caught his breath.

Because of these experiences, Phillip made an appointment with his physician for a checkup. His physical examination revealed no abnormalities in Phillip's blood pressure or heart rate or in the results of his electrocardiogram. After Phillip described his symptoms to his physician, the doctor told Phillip that he did not appear to have a heart problem but, rather, might have a problem with anxiety. Phillip talked with his wife about the physician's diagnosis, and they decided that it might be helpful for Phillip to see a psychologist. His wife agreed to accompany him, and he arranged for an appointment with you.

As you spend more time talking with Philip, he reports that he has felt anxious and fearful all his life. He describes himself as having been very shy as a child and somewhat of a loner in school. Phillip focuses on the immediate problem of the presentations at work and recalls having trouble making oral presentations as early as elementary school. In fact, he states, he planned and schemed ways to avoid making speeches and presentations throughout high school and college. During college, for example, if he attended the first day of class and found that the course required an oral presentation, he would immediately drop the course and find an alternative that did not require a presentation. Phillip's previous job did not require him to make presentations, and he had forgotten about this source of anxiety until it came flooding back to him earlier this month.

Because of these physical symptoms, Phillip has become preoccupied with his health. The stress around Phillip's change of job as well as his recent physical difficulties has affected his relationship

BOX 1.3 (concluded)

with his wife and children, and he has come to you for help.

You will learn more about Phillip in the chapters on theory (chapter 4), psychopathology (chapter 5), interviewing (chapter 7), humanistic therapy (chapter 13), and cognitive-behavioral therapy (chapter 14).

Maria, age 73

Maria is seated beside her son in your waiting room, staring at the floor. She does not look up when you enter the room, but does when you call her name. She accompanies you, with her son, slowly to your office. When you ask her to tell you about herself, she replies that she lives alone in the house that she shared with her husband of 48 years, until his death two years ago. Maria, a 73-year-old Latina, reports that since her husband's death she has become increasingly isolated and despondent, leaving her house only to shop for the small amount of groceries she needs each week and to attend church on Sundays. She tells you that her three children were so concerned that she was spending all her time at home that her eldest son phoned to make this appointment for her. Her son, who lives an hour's drive from Maria (the nearest of the three siblings to their mother), brought her to this appointment. Maria appears sad and is relatively unresponsive at the beginning of the interview. She moves slowly when she walks, and she is very slow to respond to your questions, often pausing for several seconds before offering a labored reply. Although there is little emotion in her voice, Maria's replies to your questions are detailed and thoughtful.

During the course of the first interview, you find out that Maria spends most of her time alone at home, either watching television or in bed. She reports that she has great difficulty sleeping, and even when she is able to sleep she typically wakes very early in the morning. Most days Maria does not bother to bathe or dress in the morning, spending much or all of the day in her nightgown and housecoat. Maria and her son both report that these feelings and behaviors are a dramatic change from how she was before her husband passed away. She and her husband used to love to socialize. They had a large group of friends and always had dinner parties. Now, however, Maria states that the thought of being with friends without her husband continues to make her feel very sad.

In this initial interview, Maria talks about her husband constantly and with a great deal of affection. She reports that it feels as if he died very recently rather than two years ago. Maria states that instead of going out she stays at home and does crossword puzzles. She reports that she used to love to watch the news, but finds it hard to do that now because the news makes her feel sad and discouraged about the world. Maria says that she thinks about her husband all the time and wonders, sometimes, whether she should "join him." When she says this, her son looks at you with concern. You ask Maria if she plans to take her life, and she replies that she has no plans to do so. Her son tells you that he and his siblings are worried about the lack of improvement in their mother's mood and behavior over the past year, and they are hoping that you will be able to help her.

You will learn more about Maria in the chapters on psychopathology (chapter 5), assessment (chapter 6), interviewing (chapter 7), intelligence testing (chapter 8), psychodynamic therapy (chapter 12), and humanistic therapy (chapter 13).

CLINICAL PSYCHOLOGY: PAST AND PRESENT

INTRODUCTION

The history of clinical psychology, like that of many fields, is typically presented as a collection of names and dates. It is important to understand the individuals who have shaped the field of clinical psychology and to know when landmark events in the field occurred (examples of important events in the history are presented in the timeline in table 2.1). Tracing the progression of the development of the field and the individuals who have influenced it provides an important perspective on the roots of clinical psychology as

it exists today. However, the primary significance of clinical psychology's relatively short history does not lie in names and dates. Rather, its historical importance comes from an understanding of the factors that have shaped the field into its current form and the forces that are likely to influence its development in the future. Three things are striking about the history of clinical psychology. First, many of the significant events and forces that have influenced its development have come from *outside* rather than from within psychology. Second, there have been significant advances in the *science* of clinical psychology, in some instances represented by breakthrough pieces of research, but most often through the slow and gradual accumulation of knowledge across many studies. And third, clinical psychology has emerged as a *profession* only recently and is still working to define its identity.

TABLE 2.1

Timeline: Events in Research, Assessment, Treatment, and the Profession of Clinical Psychology

Date	Area of impact	Event
1879	Research	Wundt establishes the first psychology laboratory for research at the University of Leipzig, Germany.
1892	Profession	Hall and others establish the American Psychological Association.
1895	Treatment	Freud and Breuer publish *Studies on Hysteria,* presenting their model of intrapsychic processes and the basis for neuroses (anxiety disorders).
1896	Treatment	Witmer opens first psychological clinic at the University of Pennsylvania.
1900	Treatment	Freud publishes The *Interpretation of Dreams,* providing the basis for psychoanalytic psychotherapy.
1905	Assessment	Binet and Simon in France develop the first intelligence test to evaluate the intellectual abilities of French schoolchildren.
1907	Profession	Witmer publishes first issue of *The Psychological Clinic,* the first professional journal devoted to clinical psychology.
1910	Profession and treatment	Freud lectures at Clark University, introducing psychoanalytic thought to American psychology.
1910	Profession	Flexner Report calls for introduction of scientific education and training in medical education.
1917	Assessment	United States enters World War I; at the request of the army, psychologists develop the Army Alpha (verbal) and Army Beta (nonverbal) intelligence tests for selection of inductees into the army.
1919	Profession	The Section on Clinical Psychology is established within the American Psychological Association.
1921	Assessment	Rorschach publishes *Psychodiagnostik,* describing the use of his set of inkblots in diagnosis of psychiatric patients.
1935	Assessment	Murray and Morgan publish the Thematic Apperception Test (TAT) for use in projective assessment of personality.
1939	Assessment	Wechsler publishes the Wechsler-Bellevue Intelligence Test, the first intelligence test for adults and the precursor of the current Wechsler Adult Intelligence Test–3rd Edition.
1941	Treatment	United States enters World War II; army trains psychologists to provide psychological treatment for soldiers with "shell shock" (PTSD).
1942	Treatment	Rogers publishes *Counseling and Psychotherapy,* one of the first major works on the psychological treatment of mental disorders that offered an alternative to Freudian psychoanalysis.
1943	Assessment	Hathaway publishes the Minnesota Multiphasic Personality Inventory (MMPI), the first "objective" personality test.

TABLE 2.1 (concluded)

Date	Area of impact	Event
1945	Profession	Connecticut establishes the first law for the certification of professional psychologists, providing the precursor to current licensing laws.
1946	Profession	U.S. Veterans' Administration provides funds to universities for the training of clinical psychologists to help with the treatment of the psychological casualties of World War II.
1949	Profession	Conference on Graduate Education in Clinical Psychology held at the University of Colorado, Boulder (the Boulder Conference).
1952	Treatment and research	Eysenck publishes paper that reviews research on the effectiveness of psychotherapy and concludes that psychotherapy is no more effective than no treatment.
1952	Assessment	The American Psychiatric Association publishes the first edition of the *Diagnostic and Statistical Manual of Mental Disorders* (the DSM).
1958	Treatment and research	Wolpe publishes the first paper describing the use of "reciprocal inhibition" in the treatment of anxiety.
1959	Research	Bandura and Walters describe a social learning theory of aggression, introducing the concept of vicarious learning through observation.
1968	Research and assessment	Mischel publishes *Personality and Assessment,* challenging some of the assumptions of traditional personality testing and promoting a behavioral approach to assessment.
1969	Assessment	Bijou et al. publish paper describing one of the first uses of systematic observation of behavior as a means of assessment of children.
1973	Profession	Conference on doctoral education held in Vail, Colorado; professional school (PsyD) model of training in clinical psychology is endorsed.
1974	Treatment	Smith and Glass publish the first meta-analysis of the effects of psychotherapy, providing a new way of synthesizing and quantifying the effectiveness of psychological treatment.
1974	Treatment	Mahoney publishes *Cognition and Behavior Modification,* an important step in the development of cognitive models of psychotherapy.
1979	Treatment	Beck and colleagues publish *Cognitive Therapy of Depression,* solidifying the development of cognitive therapy.
1980	Assessment	The American Psychiatric Association publishes the third edition of the DSM (DSM-III), providing a more research-based approach to the classification of psychiatric disorders.
1988	Profession	The American Psychological Society is created, in part a result of the split between scientists and practitioners within the American Psychological Association.
1994	Assessment and research	The American Psychiatric Association publishes the fourth edition of the DSM (DSM-IV).
1995	Treatment and research	The Task Force of the Division of Clinical Psychology of the American Psychological Association offers criteria to evaluate empirically supported treatments for specific psychiatric disorders.

More fundamental than the questions of how and when clinical psychology developed is the question of *why* the science and profession of clinical psychology developed so rapidly during the second half of the twentieth century. The field came into being for two reasons. First, throughout history there has been a need to provide care and services for individuals who are experiencing psychological problems, and clinical psychology emerged in part to help meet this need. The needs of individuals with psychological problems had been addressed in very different ways over the course of history before clinical psychology stepped in to help fill this role. Second, some of the founders of scientific psychology in the late 1800s and early 1900s felt that one objective of their new science should be to contribute to the welfare of others. William James, G. Stanley Hall, and other founders of American psychology shared a belief that one of the responsibilities of the new field of psychology was to benefit human welfare in a broad sense. Thus, a societal need existed, and some members of the psychological community felt a responsibility to fill this need. As we will point out, however, the greatest growth of clinical psychology occurred during the second half of the twentieth century, spurred by events that began during the First and Second World Wars.

Early Approaches to Mental Health Care

The commitment to helping individuals in psychological distress certainly did not begin with the field of clinical psychology. The major functions that are served by clinical psychologists today (understanding and aiding individuals who are suffering from psychological disorders or are experiencing significant psychological distress) were met by other individuals and institutions in societies for centuries before the emergence of psychology as a profession. In various societies and at different points in history, who has been responsible for meeting the psychological needs of individuals has depended on how mental health and mental disorder have been viewed. Professions that have taken responsibility for the care and welfare of individuals who suffer from psychological or psychiatric disorders have included the clergy or other religious groups, physicians, and individuals committed to social welfare. It is important to recognize that psychologists have only recently joined these other groups in the field of mental health (see Alloy, Jacobson, & Acocella, 1999; Nolen-Hoeksema, 1998).

For much of recorded history, treatment of psychological problems was carried out by religious institutions. The treatment of mental health problems by religious methods is based in *demonology,* the view that these problems are the result of forces of evil. Writings from the Old Testament and the Talmud refer to madness that is the result of punishment by God, and throughout the Middle Ages in Europe, the church was responsible for explaining the causes of psychological disturbance and providing treatment for it (most often in the form of punishment). For example, disturbed and disordered behavior that today is considered evidence of psychosis (e.g., hallucinations, delusions) used to be interpreted as evidence of possession by the devil and was treated through exorcisms, torture, or death by burning at the stake.

An alternative to demonology emerged in the form of medical explanations of psychological problems—the *somatogenic* perspective. The earliest medical or biological explanation of emotional and behavioral disorders can be found in the writings of Hippocrates in the fourth century B.C. Hippocrates believed that psychological problems, like physical illnesses, were caused by imbalances in the four bodily fluids (black bile, yellow bile, blood, and phlegm). As biological explanations for psychological problems emerged, medical professionals became involved in the identification and treatment of such disorders. Unfortunately, from the 1500s through the 1800s, medical treatment of psychological problems primarily took the form of placement of individuals in psychiatric hospitals and asylums that offered little if anything in the way of treatment. Patients were held as prisoners in horrible conditions, little care or treatment was available, and even humane treatment was often lacking. In contrast to these early approaches, more recent developments in biological explanations of psychopathology have led to major advances in diagnosis and treatment.

Advances in Mental Health Care

Only recently, and only in some cultures around the world, have psychological problems come to be viewed at least partly as the result of disturbances and problems in behavior (the *psychogenic* hypothesis) and, as a result, have come within the purview of psychology. One major change in thinking about and treatment of psychological problems occurred with the advent of moral treatment in the 1800s. Led by physicians and others concerned with social reform in the United States and Europe (e.g., Philippe Pinel in France and Benjamin Rush in the United States), the moral treatment movement was based on the conviction that individuals with psychological problems deserved humane care and treatment. As part of the moral treatment movement, efforts were made to improve the inhumane conditions and methods that characterized asylums and mental hospitals at that time. One of the most dramatic changes in the conceptualization and treatment of psychological problems occurred late in the nineteenth century with the emergence of truly psychological explanations of these problems. French physicians Jean Charcot, Hippolyte Bernheim, and Pierre Janet began to experiment with the use of hypnosis in the treatment of some psychological problems and introduced the notion that psychological methods of treatment could be an alternative to medical and religious approaches. Their theories led to the pioneering work of Sigmund Freud, an Austrian neurologist, who is perhaps the best-known

proponent of psychological explanations for disorders of behavior and emotion. We will discuss these people in greater detail in chapter 4.

Conceptualizations of psychopathology continue to develop. Much current research and theory in clinical psychology reflects a *biopsychosocial* model in which biological, psychological, and social factors are all considered important in understanding mental health problems (e.g., Keefe & France, 1999; Plomin & Rutter, 1998). Biological factors include the role of genetics that may contribute to vulnerability to some forms of psychopathology, neurological damage in the brain and central nervous systems, and dysregulation of neurotransmitters in the brain and central nervous system. Psychological factors include cognitive processes of attention; self-perception; causal attributions; and processes of the experience, expression, and regulation of emotions. Social factors include stressful life events, conditions of chronic stress, interpersonal relationships, and the broad social and cultural contexts in which disorders may develop. Complex conceptualizations of psychopathology that combine these many elements have now replaced more simplistic explanations that focus on only one factor.

THE EMERGENCE OF CLINICAL PSYCHOLOGY WITHIN THE FIELD OF PSYCHOLOGY

As reflected in this brief history of the conceptualization and treatment of psychological problems, the origins of clinical psychology cannot be tied to a single person or event. Instead, a number of individuals responding to a variety of forces were involved in the emergence of the field in the United States and Europe in the late nineteenth and early twentieth centuries. Because clinical psychology involves the application of knowledge from the scientific study of human behavior, it is noteworthy that *the science of psychology preceded the profession of psychology.*

This order is in contrast to many other professions in which professional practice began before the science of the field. Training in the practice of law, for example, was carried out through apprenticeship to a practicing attorney long before formal training programs in law were established in universities (Routh, 1994). Similarly, medicine was practiced for centuries before the scientific basis of the field was fully developed. The nature of medical education and training, and indeed the entire field of medicine, was reshaped in 1910 by an influential report by Abraham Flexner (Regan-Smith, 1998). The **Flexner Report** called for the introduction of training in basic science as a component in all medical training and education—prior to 1910, medical practitioners were not required to be trained in science. Clinical psychology followed the opposite path—the science of psychology was established before the application of psychology began, a precedent that has led to considerable conflict within the field.

Most historians mark the origins of psychology with the development of Wilhelm Wundt's laboratory for the study of perception and behavior in Germany in the mid-1800s. Wundt was trained as a philosopher, and research conducted in his laboratory was novel in its attempt to study observable processes of human sensation and perception under relatively controlled and experimental conditions. Wundt had a major effect on American psychology through the relatively large number of Americans who received their doctoral training in his laboratory at the University of Leipzig.

The field of psychology that began to emerge in the United States in the latter part of the nineteenth century was an academic discipline committed to the scientific study of human behavior. The focus of much of the early research in psychology (e.g., examination of the characteristics of color vision) had little to do with the types of psychological problems that are the focus of clinical psychology today. Nevertheless, many pioneers of American psychology recognized that one of the important values of psychology would include its application to the effort to solve human problems.

One of the doctoral students who worked with Wundt was a young American named **Lightner Witmer.** Formal training in psychology did not exist in the United States in the late nineteenth century, and as a result, Witmer and others who were interested in the scientific study of human behavior had no choice but to leave the United States and seek their education in Europe. After receiving his doctoral degree with Wundt, Witmer returned to the United States to accept a position in the psychology department at the University of Pennsylvania, where he could

Lightner Witmer opened the first Psychological Clinic in 1896 at the University of Pennsylvania, designed to treat children with learning difficulties. Witmer founded a new branch of psychology dedicated to helping people, and called this new field "clinical psychology." (Photo courtesy Archives of the History of American Psychology-The University of Akron.)

continue to conduct his research on processes of perception.

The course of Witmer's work took a different turn in the spring of 1896, however, when a schoolteacher asked for Witmer's assistance in working with an otherwise bright 14-year-old boy who was having severe difficulty with spelling and recognizing written words (McReynolds, 1987, 1997). Witmer conducted a careful evaluation of the boy's problems and developed an intensive treatment program to try to improve his reading and spelling skills. This case spurred Witmer to open the first Psychological Clinic in 1896 at the University of Pennsylvania, designed specifically to treat children with learning difficulties. He called for the founding of a new branch of psychology dedicated to the goal of helping people and coined the term *clinical psychology* to describe this new field.

That same year, 1896, Witmer presented his ideas about the applications of psychology to the treatment of human problems to the members of the newly formed American Psychological Association, and he received a cool reception at best (McReynolds, 1997; Riesman, 1976). The APA members' negative response was due to several factors. Although there was some support for the application of psychological knowledge to solving human problems, the majority of psychologists considered themselves to be scientists and did not regard the role described by Witmer as appropriate for them. They did not wish to endanger their identification as scientists, which was tenuous enough in those early years, by moving their profession into what they felt were premature applications. Even if they had considered his suggestions to be laudable, few if any psychologists were trained or experienced to perform the functions Witmer proposed. The chilly response from members of the APA is somewhat surprising given that Witmer emphasized that clinical psychology should involve the careful application of the science of psychology. Witmer used the term *clinical psychology* to refer to a method of teaching and research and not merely

as an extension of the word *clinic,* a place where persons are examined (Reisman).

Witmer persuaded the University of Pennsylvania administration to offer formal training in clinical psychology, and its 1904–05 catalog announced that students in clinical psychology could take courses for credit in psychology and in the medical school (Riesman, 1976). By 1907, Witmer had been able to raise sufficient funds to establish a hospital school for the training of mentally retarded children as an adjunct to his clinic, and to found and serve as the first editor of a professional journal, *The Psychological Clinic* (see box 2.1). For his efforts, Witmer is now widely considered to be the founder of clinical psychology.

In understanding the origins of clinical psychology, it is important to consider that the first psychological clinic was dedicated to helping children with learning problems, which was a clear and logical application of the research on human learning and memory that was being conducted by psychologists at the time (e.g., Witmer, 1907/1996). Thus, the field of clinical psychology originated in an attempt to apply what was being learned in the basic science of psychology at the time. As Witmer himself stated,

> here was a simple developmental defect of memory; and memory is a mental process of which the science of psychology is supposed to furnish the only authoritative knowledge. It appeared to me that if psychology was worth anything to me or to others it should be able to assist in a retarded [*sic*] case of this kind.

The evolution of the field of clinical psychology after Lightner Witmer can be best understood through an examination of how clinical psychologists came to be involved in each of four different activities: research, assessment, treatment, and prevention. Clinical psychologists became involved in these endeavors at different points during the twentieth century and for very different reasons. You as students must comprehend the role of clinical psychologists in these

BOX 2.1

Vol. I, No. 1   March 15, 1907

THE PSYCHOLOGICAL CLINIC

A Journal for the Study and Treatment
of Mental Retardation and Deviation

Editor:
LIGHTNER WITMER, Ph.D.,
University of Pennsylvania.

Associate Editor:
HERBERT STOTESBURY, Ph.D.,
The Temple College,
Philadelphia.

Associate Editor:
JOSEPH COLLINS M.D.,
Post Graduate Medical College,
New York.

CONTENTS

THE PSYCHOLOGICAL CLINIC PRESS
West Philadelphia Station, Philadelphia, PA.

Lightner Witmer established the first professional journal devoted to clinical psychology in 1907.

BOX 2.1 (concluded)

December 2000   Volume 68, Number 6

Journal of
Consulting and Clinical Psychology

Copyright © 2000 by the American Psychological Association, Inc.

Regular Articles

(Contents continue)

The Journal of Consulting and Clinical Psychology, published by the American Psychological Association, is a prominent research journal in clinical psychology. (Table of contents from the December 2000 issue of *Journal of Consulting and Clinical Psychology.* Copyright © 2000 by the American Psychological Association. Reprinted with permission.)

four activities both to understand forces in this field's past and to anticipate changes in its future.

During the early years, clinical psychology was a science and profession dominated by males (Snyder, McDermott, Leibowitz, & Cheavens, 2000). For example, in 1917, only 13 percent of APA members were women. Although women made progress in the fields of developmental and school psychology, from 1920 through 1974 women comprised only 24 percent of graduates with doctoral degrees in clinical psychology (Snyder et al.). By 1994, however, 68.7 percent of students admitted to doctoral programs in clinical psychology were women. Thus, the composition of clinical psychology has changed from being overwhelmingly male to being overwhelmingly female. It is important to possess an understanding not only of the events that shaped clinical psychology, but also of the broader social context in which the field has developed.

How Clinical Psychologists Became Involved in Research

Witmer and the other founders of clinical psychology were researchers who were interested in the application of their research to the benefit of others. Clinical researchers try to add to these bodies of knowledge both to increase their understanding of psychopathology, illness, and health and to improve their methods for its treatment and prevention. Because of their broad training in basic behavioral science, clinical psychologists are able to draw on and contribute to research in a variety of different areas and to collaborate with professionals from other disciplines.

Clinical psychological research has steadily grown in its scope since the early 1900s. This subfield now includes research on the basic characteristics and prevalence of psychopathology (epidemiology), the causes of psychopathology (etiology), the measurement of behavior and psychological characteristics of individuals (assessment), the role of the brain and central nervous system (clinical neuropsychology), the treatment of psychopathology (psychotherapy), the prevention of psychopathology and the promotion of psychological health, and the links between psychological factors and physical health and illness (health psychology/behavioral medicine). There has been landmark research in each of these areas during the past 70 years, the results of which led to substantial changes in knowledge about a particular problem or issue. Some of the leading journals for the publication of research in clinical psychology are described in table 2.2, and examples of seminal research in clinical psychology are presented in table 2.3.

Clinical psychology has been shaped not only by findings from research studies by also by important reviews of research evidence and by the development of new methods for clinical practice. Two examples are particularly prominent in this regard. In the early 1950s, the field of psychotherapy was in its early stages of development, and much of the practice of psychotherapy was based on the psychoanalytic model developed by Freud. Research on the effectiveness of this approach to psychotherapy was very limited, however—most practitioners simply assumed that the methods they were using were effective in treating their patients. Given this widespread acceptance of the belief that psychotherapy was effective, a paper published in 1952 by British psychologist **Hans Eysenck** created enormous controversy. Eysenck argued that there was little or no evidence that psychotherapy was any more effective than no treatment at all. He reached this conclusion by comparing two sources of data: the results of 24 studies that had been conducted on the outcomes of psychotherapy, and information on rates of recovery from emotional distress in the absence of treatment, or what is referred to as spontaneous remission.

Eysenck reported that treated individuals actually did *worse* than did people who received no psychotherapy: Whereas 72 percent of the individuals who did not receive treatment recovered from their problems, only 44 percent of those

TABLE 2.2
Sampling of Research and Professional Journals Related to Clinical Psychology

Journal of Consulting and Clinical Psychology
　　This journal, published bimonthly by the APA, is the premier journal in clinical psychology for the publication of research related to psychological treatment.

Journal of Abnormal Psychology
　　This journal, a quarterly publication of the APA, is the preeminent psychological journal about research on the nature, course, and causes of psychopathology.

Psychological Assessment
　　Also issued quarterly by the APA, this journal publishes research concerned with methods for the assessment and diagnosis of psychopathology and other psychological factors related to mental health.

Clinical Psychology: Science and Practice
　　Published quarterly by the Society of Clinical Psychology of the APA, this journal provides reviews and critical discussions of research and professional issues in the field.

Professional Psychology: Research and Practice
　　Published bimonthly by the APA, this journal presents articles on the application of psychology, including the scientific basis of the profession of psychology, and articles that present assessment, treatment, and practice implications.

Behavior Therapy
　　Published by the Association for the Advancement of Behavior Therapy, this journal publishes articles on the effectiveness of various methods of behavior therapy and cognitive-behavior therapy as well as research articles on psychopathology.

receiving psychoanalysis and 64 percent of those receiving "eclectic" psychotherapy (unspecified forms of talk psychotherapy) recovered. Although the rates of improvement presented by Eysenck are much lower than those found in many studies that have been published since the appearance of his paper, his report had a significant impact on the field. Eysenck challenged clinical psychologists and other mental health professionals to provide better evidence for the effectiveness of their treatment methods. Initiated by Eysenck's paper, more and better research on the effects of psychotherapy has been conducted, leading to more effective methods of treatment and a better understanding of how and why psychotherapy works. The current evidence on the effects of psychotherapy is much more positive than the perspective offered by Eysenck 50 years ago (see chapter 15).

A second example of research that changed the field is a short but important book, *Statistical Versus Clinical Prediction* published by psychologist **Paul Meehl** in 1954, that had a significant impact on psychological testing and assessment. Before Meehl published his book, psychologists relied heavily on their subjective judgments and intuitions in interpreting the results of psychological tests. This approach, referred to as clinical judgment or clinical prediction, was based on the assumption that clinical psychologists learn a unique set of skills that allows them to make accurate judgments about people and to predict such things as patients' ability to benefit from psychotherapy, people's potential for success in a job, or the likely course of individuals' psychological problems. Meehl challenged these assumptions by demonstrating that judgments based on statistical data representing patterns of behavior in large samples of people provide a more accurate basis for making judgments and predictions about specific individuals than do the subjective judgments of single clinicians. The findings reported by Meehl in 1954 still hold true today (Dawes, Faust, & Meehl, 1989; Meehl, 1997)—statistically based predictions are still more accurate than clinical judgment.

TABLE 2.3.

Sampling of Research That Has Shaped the Field of Clinical Psychology

1952   Eysenck, Hans J. (1952). The effects of psychotherapy: An evaluation. *Journal of Consulting Psychology, 16,* 319–324. This provocative review of research on the efficacy of psychotherapy concluded that therapy was no more effective in treating "neuroses" than no treatment at all. This article spurred the field to become more active in generating careful research to examine the efficacy of psychotherapy.

1954   Meehl, Paul E. (1954). *Statistical versus clinical prediction: A theoretical analysis and a review of the evidence.* Minneapolis: University of Minnesota Press. This relatively brief book provided a critical analysis of the use of subjective, or "clinical," judgment in the process of psychological testing and evaluation. Meehl showed that the use of statistical data is more effective in making important judgments and evaluations of human behavior.

1954   Rogers, Carl R. (1954). *Psychotherapy and personality change.* Chicago: University of Chicago Press. This book provided the basis for the development of a new approach to psychotherapy that was in direct contrast to traditional Freudian psychoanalysis and to behavior therapy that was emerging at that time. Equally important, this book spurred careful research on the process and outcome of psychotherapy.

1958   Wolpe, J. (1958). *Psychotherapy by reciprocal inhibition.* Stanford, CA: Stanford University Press. This book reported on the first use of the behavioral technique known as systematic desensitization in the treatment of anxiety disorders. The treatment involved one of the first applications of behavioral principles to the treatment of a psychological problem.

1969   Bandura, A. (1969). *Principles of behavior modification.* New York: Holt, Rinehart, & Winston. This book provided an integration of research on the use of behavioral methods in the treatment of psychological and behavioral disorders. In addition, it marked a break from many of the principles of traditional (or radical) behaviorism. Most importantly, Bandura outlined his research on modeling and vicarious learning—the fact that learning could take place by observing others rather than only through direct reinforcement of one's own behavior. This research opened the door for new methods of treatment that involved modeling and social learning procedures.

1979   Smith, Mary L., & Glass, Gene V. (1979). Meta-analysis of psychotherapy outcome studies. *American Psychologist, 32,* 752–760. This important article reported the first use of a statistical technique called *meta-analysis* to integrate the results of many different studies of the effectiveness of psychotherapy. The authors' conclusion of their analyses indicated that psychotherapy was significantly and meaningfully more effective than no treatment. The comparison of different types of psychotherapy was not as conclusive, and many readers interpreted these findings as an indication that all therapies are about equally effective in treating psychological problems. Subsequent research has challenged this perspective.

1985   Elkin, Irene, Parloff, Morris B., Hadley, Suzanne W., & Autry, Joseph H. (1985). NIMH Treatment of Depression Collaborative Research Program: Background and research plan. *Archives of General Psychiatry, 42,* 305–316. [Also Elkin et al. (1989). National Institute of Mental Health Treatment of Depression Collaborative Research Program: General effectiveness of treatments. *Archives of General Psychiatry, 46,* 971–982]. This landmark study involved the comparison of two methods of psychotherapy (cognitive therapy and interpersonal psychotherapy) and medication in the treatment of major depressive disorder. The findings of the study are complicated and have been interpreted in a number of different ways. However, the major findings suggested that the three forms of treatment were all somewhat superior to placebo treatment and that they were roughly equivalent to one another.

Although single groundbreaking studies and commentaries have clearly important effects on the field of clinical psychology, they are relatively rare and do not represent how most of the growth and development in the field occurs. Rather, the greatest contribution of research in clinical psychology is the slow and gradual accumulation of knowledge that comes from the results of dozens of studies on a particular topic. For example, procedures for the treatment of anxiety disorders have been developed through the efforts of a large number of different researchers who have conducted many series of carefully designed studies using a wide variety of research methods (Barlow, 1998). These procedures include the treatment of generalized anxiety disorder (Barlow et al., 1998), panic disorder (Clark et al., 1999), post-traumatic stress disorder (e.g., Foa, Keane, & Friedman, 2000), and specific phobias (Clark et al.).

One of the most striking features of research in clinical psychology today is the breadth of topics that are included within the field. Throughout much of the first century of clinical psychology, three topic areas have been focal points of research: the nature and etiology of psychopathology; the reliability and validity of methods of psychological assessment, especially psychological tests; and psychotherapy efficacy (whether or not psychotherapy can work) and effectiveness (whether psychotherapy actually does work in practice). Today, however, research in clinical psychology extends well beyond these core topics of research. Clinical psychologists now investigate the role of psychological factors in the development of physical disease (e.g., cancer, heart disease), the relative effectiveness of psychotherapy as compared with medication in the treatment of psychopathology, the prevention of violent behavior, the long-term consequences of sexual assault and rape, and many, many other topics.

How Clinical Psychologists Became Involved in Assessment

Since its inception, psychology has been uniquely concerned with the measurement of differences between individuals on important cognitive and personality characteristics. The study of differences between individuals on psychological tests and measurements began with the work of Sir Francis Galton in England in the late 1800s. Galton was fascinated by the work of his cousin Charles Darwin on differences in characteristics both between and within species, and in the process of natural selection that is influenced

by these differences. Galton focused on the concept of individual differences between people, especially in various aspects of perception and mental abilities. Early interest in individual difference testing in the United States is marked by the work of James McKeen Catell at the University of Pennsylvania. Trained in Wundt's laboratory in Germany and influenced by a meeting with Galton in England, Catell constructed tests to measure various facets of sensorimotor functioning. As a result of these early influences, one strong thread through the history of clinical psychology is the development of tests and other procedures to assess and measure characteristics of individuals.

Around the time that Witmer was developing an application of psychology to help children who were experiencing difficulties learning in school, events in Europe were also leading to the development of methods to measure children's potential for learning. In 1904, the Minister of Public Instruction in Paris wanted to ensure that children with limited intellectual skills were still provided with an education. **Alfred Binet** and Theodore Simon were commissioned by the French government to develop a tool to aid in decisions about the appropriate educational programs for French schoolchildren. Binet was a French researcher trained in both law and medicine. In order to study individual differences, he felt it was necessary to sample a wide range of complex intellectual processes so that the spread of scores obtained by different individuals would be broad (Reisman, 1976). This work resulted in the first formal test of intelligence, the 1905 Binet-Simon scale, consisting of 30 items of increasing difficulty. By 1908 this original simple test had been expanded into an instrument composed of 59 tests grouped at age levels from three to thirteen years according to the percentage of children of a particular age who passed a given item (Reisman).

Interest in Binet's work grew over the next few years, and versions of the Binet-Simon scale were imported to the United States. The version that eventually became the accepted U.S. translation and standardization of the Binet-Simon scale (the Stanford-Binet Intelligence Test) was developed by psychologist Louis Terman of Stanford University. Terman was one of several American psychologists who were interested in developing ways to measure and quantify human intelligence. Through their work, Terman and others provided psychologists with another application of their field. This early application was rooted in an aspect of the science of psychology at the time, the psychometric study of individual differences (see box 2.2).

If the development of clinical psychology had followed the path set by Witmer, Terman, and others in the early 1900s, it would have slowly emerged as a field that was based on the careful application of the young science of psychology. This is not what happened, however. Indeed, much of the rest of the history of the field is marked by decisions made by psychologists to move into new areas and new applications even though the scientific knowledge in these areas may not have been sufficient to warrant such an application. There were often powerful social forces pressing psychologists to step forward to address an important issue or assume an important role. The results of these decisions have been far-reaching, because the field of clinical psychology has expanded at a rate that has at times challenged its scientific knowledge base and expertise. We will now consider the first of these powerful external events that shaped clinical psychology: World War I.

World War I: A Test for Clinical Psychology
As the United States prepared to enter the war that was raging in Europe in 1917, the American military was faced with an unprecedented task—the conscription and creation of a massive army and navy. There was an enormous need to evaluate quickly and accurately the qualifications of over 1 million young men as potential members of the armed forces (Driskell & Olmstead, 1989). Physicians were enlisted in the task of conducting physical evaluations of these draftees to determine whether they were physically fit to serve during the war. But the military recognized the need to also evaluate the mental and intellectual qualifications of these potential soldiers. Physicians could not fill this role, because the evaluation of mental functioning was not within their realm of expertise. Based on their knowledge of human learning and memory and the measurement of individual differences in human intelligence, psychologists were called on to fill this role.

In 1917, a group of psychologists, headed by APA president Robert Yerkes, undertook the task of developing tools to measure the mental abilities of future soldiers (Driskell & Olmstead, 1989). The psychological tests that were available and in use at the time (e.g., the test developed by Binet and Simon) required individual administration. Consequently, these tests were impractical for use with the large number of recruits involved in the military. Therefore, Yerkes and his colleagues set about the task of developing a quick and efficient test of intelligence that could be administered to large groups of individuals simultaneously. This effort yielded two tests, the **Army Alpha** (a test of verbal skills) and the **Army Beta** (a test of nonverbal skills). The enduring consequence of this work is that it established psychologists as experts in the measurement of individual characteristics in ways that were practical and useful. It is unlikely that this first large-scale application of scientific psychological knowledge and methods would have occurred without strong pressure from external sources, in this case the U.S. military.

Advances in Psychological Testing and Assessment   In addition to the powerful social forces that led clinical psychology to become involved in psychological assessment and testing, significant advances in research have also played an important role. For example, the publication of the **Minnesota Multiphasic Personality Inventory (MMPI)** by psychologist **Starke Hathaway**

BOX 2.2

CONSIDERING THE POLITICAL CONTEXT OF THE HISTORY OF PSYCHOLOGY

The advances made by the pioneers of intelligence testing at the beginning of the twentieth century continue to the latest versions of these tests today. Intelligence tests now, just as in Binet's time, can and should be used to ensure that individuals who need special services receive the help and assistance that they deserve. On the other hand, it is equally important to recognize that not all these pioneers were driven by goals involving equal access to opportunities and optimal development for all people.

Throughout its history, intelligence testing has been associated with theories of the nature of individual differences in intellectual abilities. These theories have included ones that posit that differences among individuals are greatly influenced by their genetic endowment. Unfortunately, genetic differences in intellectual ability have often been equated with lines that divide individuals by their social status. Carried to the extreme, genetic theories of individual differences in intelligence have been used as the basis for advocating selective breeding of human beings in order to advance the "quality of the race." In fact, the eugenics movement in the United States advocated just such an approach during the early part of the twentieth century.

It is startling and disconcerting that the pioneers of intelligence testing were eugenicists. Influenced by the writing of English biologist Sir Francis Galton, Louis Terman and other American psychologists were active in the eugenics movement in the United States in the early 1900s. Galton was interested in measuring the mental and physical characteristics of the average Englishman with the goal of improving the "British race." Galton developed numerous tests of sensory discrimination and collected a mass of assorted data on all the aristocrats, professional men, and university personnel he could convince to serve as subjects. Galton set up an "Anthropometric Laboratory" at the International Health Exposition of 1884 where, for a threepence fee, visitors could have their physical characteristics measured and could take tests of vision, hearing, muscular strength, reaction time, and breathing power.

Galton believed that bright parents tend to have bright children and that parents with good physiques pass on good physiques to their offspring. Therefore, he suggested, a better race of human beings could be developed by carefully selecting for mating those who are most fit to receive an education and to become parents. As Schultz and Schultz (1987) state, "Galton's ultimate aim was to encourage the birth of the more eminent or fit individuals and to discourage the birth of the unfit. To help achieve this end, he founded the science of *eugenics* and argued that the human strain, not unlike livestock, could be improved by artificial selection. . . . He proposed that intelligence tests be developed for use in choosing the brightest men and women for selective breeding . . . those who achieved the highest scores be introduced to one another and offered financial inducements for marrying and having a large number of children" (p. 117). Thus, Galton began to develop intelligence tests with the goal of identifying individuals who should be mated. These ideas were influential in shaping the thinking of Terman and other American psychologists.

Galton's contributions to psychology, and to science in general, were far-reaching. Among his accomplishments are composite photography, systems for describing weather, the rudimentary form of the correlation coefficient, the ticker tape, the questionnaire method, the discovery of eidetic imagery (photographic memory), the development of percentile values, and perhaps his greatest contribution, the use of statistical methods in scientific investigation (Reisman, 1976). Despite these accomplishments, however, it is painfully clear that the scientific contributions of Galton and others can be, and have been, used in ways that do not equitably promote the welfare of all people.

in 1943 represented a major change in the way that psychologists measured personality and psychopathology. As we will discuss in greater detail in chapter 7, the MMPI relies on statistical comparisons of the test responses of an individual to those of a large sample of other people who have already been tested. These comparisons are used to determine the degree to which the individual is similar to a group of people with known personality characteristics, or people with a specific type of psychopathology. Thus, the MMPI represented an important shift away from the more clinical, subjective approach to assessment and toward a more statistical, empirically based method of assessment.

Another important advance in assessment occurred during the 1960s with the recognition that direct observations of people's behavior might represent an important source of information, perhaps more valid, in fact, than relying on their responses to psychological tests. The first applications of behavioral observation as a means of assessment were conducted in schools and psychiatric hospitals, settings in which it was rather easy for a psychologist to observe an individual's behavior and in which the environment was relatively contained and controlled. For example, Bijou, Peterson, Harris, Allen, and Johnston (1969) described a method for the experimental study of young children in natural settings, including their home, school, and other institutions, as well as the behavior of parents, peers, and professional workers (see chapter 8). In general, research has shown that behavioral observations can be conducted in a manner that is reliable (different raters independently generate similar ratings of the same individual) and that these observations can be useful in formulating and evaluating the effects of treatment.

How Clinical Psychologists Became Involved in Treatment

In the late 1800s and early 1900s, the treatment of psychopathology was dominated by the field of psychiatry, largely because of the influence of Freud and the development of psychoanalysis as the primary method for treating psychopathology. With his training as a neurologist, it would have been natural for Freud to assume that the treatment of psychopathology was an extension of the treatment of other disorders of the nervous system and, therefore, a task best left to trained physicians. Surprisingly, it was not Freud but his followers who argued that the practice of psychotherapy should be limited to those with medical training.

One of the earliest ways in which psychologists became involved in the treatment of psychological problems was through the child guidance movement in the early 1900s. In 1909 William Healy established a child guidance clinic in Chicago to provide services for children with psychological problems. The clinic was staffed by psychiatrists, social workers, and psychologists who treated children and adolescents, primarily for problems that are now labeled Conduct Disorder and Oppositional Defiant Disorder in the DSM-IV. Based mostly on Freud's psychoanalytic theory, psychologists conducted therapy in which children were encouraged to engage in play and the therapist would offer psychoanalytic interpretations of their play.

With the exception of the early work of clinical psychologists in child guidance clinics, the involvement of clinical psychologists in the treatment of psychopathology has been primarily fueled by forces from outside psychology. In much the same way that the First World War was critical in increasing the role of psychologists in assessment, the Second World War played an integral role in the emergence of clinical psychologists as providers of treatment for psychopathology.

World War II: Clinical Psychology and the Treatment of Psychopathology　The Second World War renewed the need for psychologists to evaluate the competencies of thousands of men and women who were being enlisted in the armed services. Psychologists were once again asked to administer psychological tests to

draftees. World War II and the period that followed it are most noteworthy, however, for the
emergence of a new set of skills for psychologists. Clinical observations of soldiers who had
experienced the stress of combat led to the identification of a syndrome of symptoms of psychological trauma that were displayed by many
soldiers. This syndrome was labeled "shell
shock" or "battle fatigue" at the time, but is
now known as Post-Traumatic Stress Disorder
(PTSD). The primary symptoms of PTSD are
high levels of anxious arousal, recurrent and persistent intrusive thoughts and emotions pertain-
ing to the trauma, and persistent efforts to avoid
all reminders and thoughts about the traumatic
event. Physicians and others involved in providing medical assistance to combat soldiers noted
that the symptoms could be managed most effectively if the victims were treated as quickly as
possible and in the context of battle. Those soldiers for whom treatment was delayed and
administered in a hospital removed from the bat-
tlefield were more likely to suffer extended and
more severe reactions than those who received
immediate psychological attention.

The dilemma faced by the armed services in
addressing the needs of these thousands of "psychological casualties" was the insufficient number of trained individuals available to provide
treatment. Medical personnel, including those
physicians trained in the relatively young field of
psychiatry, were needed to treat physical casualties. Psychologists were called on once again to
fill a need because they were perceived as having
the most representative set of skills needed for
the task (Strickland, 1986).

During this time the majority of people who
pursued college and graduate degrees were male,
and as a result, most clinical psychologists were
men. However, women in psychology emerged
as an important force during the Second World
War (Strickland, 1988). Experimental, social, applied, and clinical psychologists all developed
new respect for each other as they worked together and brought their own special skills to the
military and to national defense. Interestingly,
women psychologists were excluded from APA's
war mobilization effort. Women within psychology founded the National Council of Women
Psychologists and worked to help with community problems, such as reducing the stress of war
on civilians and giving advice about child care to
women who worked outside their homes during
the war, many for the first time. This organization was just one example of the struggles of
women to achieve equal status with men in clinical psychology.

The end of World War II brought rapid and
dramatic changes in the field of clinical psychology. At the conclusion of the war, the armed services and the Veterans' Administration (VA)
were faced with the task of providing care for
more than 40,000 psychologically wounded
veterans who had returned home. Too few psychiatrists were available to manage this task;
consequently, the VA chose to draw on psychology as a new source of professionally trained
mental health personnel. At this time, the membership of APA, including psychologists in all
specializations, was barely 4,000. The VA system
estimated that 4,700 *clinical* psychologists were
needed to provide treatment for psychological
casualties from World War II. To meet this need,
the VA invested enormous amounts of money
to pay for the training of doctoral-level clinical
psychologists. Consequently, whereas in 1946
there were no formal university programs to train
clinical psychologists, by 1950 half of all PhDs
in psychology were being awarded in clinical
psychology.

Alternative Approaches to Psychotherapy
The role of psychologists in conducting psychotherapy was expanded by more than just the military and VA hospitals. **Carl Rogers,** one of the
founders of humanistic psychology, was also influential in involving psychologists in psychotherapy during this period. Rogers provided a
strong impetus to move psychotherapy out of
the exclusive realm of medicine, psychiatry,
and psychoanalysis. While he was director of
the Rochester Child Guidance Center, Rogers

spearheaded an effort to loosen the hold of psychiatrists on the practice of psychotherapy, arguing that trained and qualified clinical psychologists could perform as well as medically trained analysts. With the publication in 1942 of his book *Counseling and Psychotherapy,* Rogers not only identified psychotherapy as a legitimate activity for clinical psychologists but also offered the first model of psychotherapy that was not based on psychoanalytic theory.

Finally, the role of psychologists in providing treatment for psychological disorders was also fueled by advances in theory and research on learning and conditioning processes that led to behaviorally oriented treatments. As models of classical conditioning and operant conditioning of behavior emerged over the course of the early and mid 1900s, psychologists began to see the potential value of these models for explaining and treating maladaptive behavior. For example, the early work of Watson, Raynor, and Jones showed the role that conditioning and learning play in the development of fears (e.g., Jones, 1924a, 1924b). Among the first to apply behavioral models to treatment was psychiatrist Joseph Wolpe (1958), who suggested that "neurotic" behaviors (anxiety disorders) were learned through a process of conditioning and could be unlearned by a similar process, which he called "reciprocal inhibition" (see chapter 14).

Psychotherapy research has been one of the most active areas of empirical investigation for clinical psychologists (see chapter 15). We have already noted several important events in psychotherapy research, including Rogers's (1942) early research on client-centered therapy, Eysenck's (1952) critical evaluation of the effectiveness of psychotherapy, and Wolpe's (1958) work on the use of behavioral methods to treat anxiety. Other landmark studies in psychotherapy research include the first evidence of the efficacy of cognitive therapy in the treatment of depression (Rush, Beck, Kovacs, & Hollon, 1977), the first use of the statistical technique of meta-analysis to integrate and evaluate large

numbers of different studies of the effects of psychotherapy (Smith & Glass, 1977), the first evidence that behavioral methods could be used to treat sexual dysfunction (Lobitz & LoPiccolo, 1972), and comparisons of the efficacy of various forms of psychotherapy and pharmacotherapy in the treatment of depression (e.g., Rush, Beck, Kovacs, & Hollon, 1977) and anxiety disorders (Power, Simpson, Swanson, & Wallace, 1990).

How Clinical Psychologists Became Involved in Prevention of Psychopathology

The treatment of psychopathology, like the treatment of any problem or disorder, can reduce the prevalence or number of existing cases of disorder. Treatment cannot, however, reduce the incidence of new cases of a disorder. That is, no matter how effective psychologists become in treating problems related to anxiety, depression, eating disorders, or substance abuse, to name but a few, the treatment of existing problems will not reduce the number of new individuals who develop these problems. Recognition of this simple fact provided the impetus for the development of prevention efforts in public health in general and for the prevention of psychopathology in particular.

Prevention of psychological problems was not an integral part of the goals of clinical psychology as the science and profession developed during the first half of the twentieth century. Beginning in the 1950s, however, a number of factors increased psychologists' awareness of the importance of prevention in dealing with mental health concerns in American society. The report of the United States Joint Commission on Mental Illness and Health in the late 1950s, President Kennedy's initiative for new programs to combat mental retardation and psychological disorders in 1963, and the development of comprehensive community mental health centers in the 1960s were all landmark events in moving prevention into mental health programs and policies in the United States (Albee & Gullotta, 1997). All these initiatives highlighted the need to reduce the incidence of new cases of psychopathology. In addition, they emphasized the unequal access of Americans to mental health treatment. Individuals of lower socioeconomic status (as reflected in levels of education and occupation) have less access to mental health professionals and are less able to pay for such services because of lack of income and lack of health insurance to cover the costs of such services. Prevention programs that can eliminate some of the social factors that contribute to the development of psychological problems may be able to eliminate some of these inequities.

Clinical psychologists have played a central role in the development of prevention programs to reduce the incidence of new cases of a wide range of psychological problems and disorders. Prevention programs focus primarily on children as psychologists attempt to prevent the onset of disorders early in children's lives. Prevention includes programs to prevent aggressive behavior and conduct disorder (e.g., Dodge, 2000), depression (e.g., Clarke et al., 1995), and substance use and abuse (e.g., Botvin, 1999).

The Development of
Clinical Psychology as a Profession

As clinical psychologists have acquired new skills and roles, particularly in the areas of assessment and treatment, psychology has needed to organize itself as a profession to monitor and regulate the activities of those who present themselves to the public as clinical psychologists. What does it mean to say that you are a clinical psychologist? What skills, competencies, and credentials must you have in order to use this label for yourself? What are the ethical and professional standards that govern psychologists' interactions with their clients? What assurances are provided to the public that the methods used

by clinical psychologists have been proven to be effective? These issues have all had to be addressed as clinical psychology has worked to define and regulate itself as a profession. The APA has played a leading role in the development and regulation of the profession of psychology, including establishing ethical principles for the practice of psychology, accrediting training programs in clinical psychology, and working with state legislatures and the U.S. Congress to support legislation to monitor and regulate the practice of psychology.

Academic research–oriented psychologists and applied psychologists have often found it difficult to integrate scientific psychology and professional psychology (Strickland, 1986). During the early part of the twentieth century, clinical and other applied psychologists complained that their interests were not being met within the APA. As a result, in 1917 fifteen of the 375 members of APA broke off to form the American Association of Clinical Psychology. With the threat of losing more members, APA reluctantly agreed to consider certifying some members as "consulting psychologists" and two years later established a special Clinical Section to handle professional issues. In the early 1930s, the New York State Psychological Association, in an attempt to deal with issues of ethics, licensing, and standardization of training, became the Association of Counseling Psychologists (ACP). In 1937, the clinical section of the APA disbanded, left the APA again, and joined ACP, which was renamed the American Association for Applied Psychology (AAAP). This move represented a significant split between the scientific and applied aspects of psychology. In a reflection of this split, in 1939 Carl Rogers discussed the possibility of awarding professional psychologists a doctor of psychology degree (similar to the current PsyD degree) rather than a PhD. In 1939 AAAP published a model certification act for state affiliates who could use such a document in their state legislative efforts within states to gain certification or registration for psychologists.

This model certification was a major factor leading to the establishment of state boards for the licensing of psychologists.

The split between scientific and applied psychology was addressed in the 1940s when APA changed its membership standards. The APA previously had required that its members must have at least two research publications beyond the dissertation. In 1945 APA was restructured in ways that were particularly supportive of practitioners, including an elimination of the requirement of publications for membership. The impetus for this change came from the need to unify psychologists for the purpose of responding to the country's wartime needs. The APA bylaws were expanded to include the advancement of psychology not only as a science but also as a profession and as a means of promoting human welfare. An arm of the APA, the Practice Directorate, is devoted specifically to issues that pertain to psychology as a profession. The Practice Directorate supports legislation that is important to psychology, conducts public education campaigns, and engages in efforts to support practicing psychologists.

The tension between research and applied interests of psychology arose again in the 1980s when academic psychologists raised concerns that APA had become too involved with the practice of psychology and was ignoring psychological research. These concerns led to the formation of a new organization, the American Psychological Society (APS), in 1988. The APS is strongly committed to the promotion of scientific research in basic and applied psychology and provides an alternative for psychologists who worry that APA has become more of a guild to protect the practice of psychology in ways that are not tied to the scientific basis of the field. The two groups function independently of one another with separate governing bodies, separate annual conventions, and separate scientific journals. However, many psychologists, and many scientifically oriented clinical psychologists in particular, are members of both organizations.

The Development of Models of Training in Clinical Psychology

As we noted in chapter 1, there are two models of training in clinical psychology. One emphasizes a balance of training in both research and practice, and the second places more emphasis on clinical/professional training.

The Boulder Conference   As doctoral training in clinical psychology expanded during and following the Second World War, there was a need to regulate and monitor the type of training that students received in such programs. The APA took the lead in this area, establishing accreditation criteria that included course curricula, research training, qualifying examinations, and clinical training (APA Committee on Training in Clinical Psychology, 1947). Carl Rogers, the president of APA, appointed **David Shakow** to formulate a model for training in clinical psychology. Shakow recommended that training in clinical psychology should produce professionals who are well equipped to conduct research, assessment, and psychotherapy. This training should be accomplished in four years of study at the doctoral (PhD) level, including course work in psychology, psychological research, and supervised clinical practicum experiences in assessment and psychotherapy. The curriculum should include courses in research methods, core areas of psychology (e.g., learning, social psychology, developmental psychology), disciplines related to psychology (e.g., biology, sociology), the psychodynamics of behavior, diagnostic (assessment) methods, and methods of psychotherapy. Shakow proposed that the third year of training should consist of a year-long, full-time internship in a clinical setting followed by a final year of training that is devoted to doctoral dissertation research. The report also recommended that master's-level training in clinical psychology should be discontinued and that the professional field should be identified only at the doctoral level.

David Shakow, Ph.D., was appointed by Carl Rogers in 1947 to help formulate a model for training in clinical psychology. Shakow's emphasis on the integration of science and practice formed the foundation for the Boulder model of training in clinical psychology. (Photo courtesy Archives of the History of American Psychology-The University of Akron.)

Spurred by Shakow's report, a landmark event in the development of clinical psychology as a profession occurred with the conference on training in clinical psychology in Boulder, Colorado in 1949 (Benjamin & Baker, 2000; Raimy, 1950). The outcome of this meeting, often called the **Boulder Conference,** was the formulation of a "scientist-practitioner" model of training for clinical psychologists. The recommendation of this meeting was that students in clinical psychology should be trained as psychologists first and practitioners second. That is, clinical psychologists were defined as individuals who are trained and skilled in both the science of psychology and the application of psychological knowledge. This two-pronged approach, still referred to as the Boulder model, has set the stan-

dards for training in clinical psychology for over 50 years.

The Vail Conference   The wisdom of trying to train clinical psychologists to be both competent scientists and practitioners was questioned vigorously in the years following the Boulder Conference (e.g., Albee & Loeffler, 1971). In a series of conferences and papers, some clinical psychologists argued for the need for an alternative approach to training, one that placed greater emphasis on clinical training and less emphasis on scientific training (e.g., APA, 1967; Hoch, Ross, & Winder, 1966). An alternative approach emerged in 1968 when Donald Peterson presented the model for the first professionally oriented clinical psychology training program at the University of Illinois (Peterson, 1968). His efforts culminated in another training conference, this time held in Vail, Colorado, in 1973. At this meeting there was, as expected, a reaffirmation of support for the Boulder model as one approach to the training of clinical psychologists. But a second approach, a professional model of training, also emerged from the **Vail Conference** with significant support. The professional model validated the importance of knowledge of psychological research but deemphasized the importance of training in research skills for clinical psychologists. Training programs could now receive accreditation from the APA by following either the scientist-practitioner model or the new professional training model. During this time period the number of programs offering the PsyD (doctor of psychology) degree grew rapidly, and most of the programs that offered this degree developed in freestanding professional schools of psychology, schools that were independent of universities. The development of separate schools of professional psychology that were not a part of university psychology departments contributed further to the widening gap between practicing clinical psychologists and psychologists involved in basic research. Professional schools were not designed to train students in research in basic areas of psychology, and their faculties did not include researchers in these core areas. The number of clinical psychology training programs has grown rapidly in recent years, due primarily to the increase in the number of PsyD programs (see figure 2.1).

Licensure and Regulation of the Profession

Licensure. In addition to the certification of graduate programs that is carried out by APA, the practice of clinical psychology is also regulated in the United States by procedures of licensure and certification (Drum & Hall, 1993). Many different professions are regulated at the state level, including lawyers and physicians, as well as clinical psychologists. In addition, many of these professions are regulated by national organizations that oversee the certification of their competency to practice the profession. The primary goal of these regulatory mechanisms and laws is to provide the public with some assurance that they will receive a certain standard of care or service from workers who represent themselves as professionals from a specific discipline.

Figure 2.1

APA Accredited Doctoral Programs in Clinical Psychology: 1948–1996.

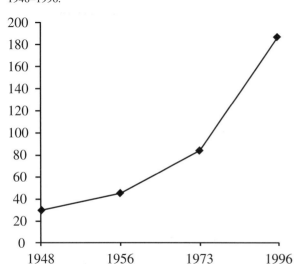

The first law requiring certification to practice psychology was instituted in Connecticut in 1945. Certification and licensing laws specify the type of training required to represent oneself to the public as a psychologist. For example, **psychology licensing laws** in most states stipulate that a psychologist must have received a doctoral degree, that is, either a **PhD** or a **PsyD in clinical psychology** from an accredited university or professional school. These laws spell out the types of courses that must be taken during graduate school and the type and amount of supervised clinical training that a psychologist must receive. Furthermore, all states require successful completion of the national licensing exam (the Examination for Professional Practice in Psychology) in psychology in order to become licensed as a psychologist. This exam is a comprehensive multiple-choice exam covering all areas of psychology; in addition, some states also require an oral exam that focuses on the practice of clinical psychology. State licensing laws are typically written by state legislators and are overseen by licensing boards comprised of both psychologists and nonpsychologists. Licensing laws have become a central means of public and professional regulation of clinical psychology.

The standards that are covered by licensing laws include requirements not only for graduate education in clinical psychology but also for the types of continuing education programs and activities in which psychologists must participate to have their license renewed on a regular basis (typically every two years). The continuing education requirements are intended to ensure that licensed psychologists are staying abreast of the latest developments in the field, especially changes in research that have occurred in the time since they completed their degree. In reality, however, continuing education programs on psychopathology, assessment, and treatment are not required to present material that has been supported by scientific evidence (Dawes, 1994). As a result, most continuing education requirements actually do little to assure the public that a licensed psychologist will be up to date on the latest findings in the field.

Ethical guidelines for psychology An important step in the regulation of the practice of psychology came with the development of the standards for ethical conduct of the APA. The first set of ethical guidelines was published in 1953, and the most recent revision appeared in 1992 (APA, 1992). These standards cover a wide range of activities in which psychologists are engaged, including teaching, research, and general conduct. A significant portion of the guidelines is concerned with standards of conduct for the professional practice of psychology, including standards

for psychological testing and psychotherapy (see table 2.4 for examples of the Ethical Principles of Psychologists). The Ethical Principles address such issues as client confidentiality, privacy, protection from harm, informed consent, and the nature of the relationship between psychologists and their clients.

The Ethical Principles outlined by APA reflect, to some degree, the integration of science and practice. For example, standards for psychological assessment and testing include reference to the need for establishing the reliability and validity of the tests and procedures that are used. Proper reliability and validity ensure that the information generated by tests and other methods

TABLE 2.4

A Sampling from the American Psychological Association Ethical Principles of Psychologists

2. Evaluation, Assessment, or Intervention
    2.02 Competence and Appropriate Use of Assessments and Interventions
        (a) Psychologists who develop, administer, score, interpret, or use psychological assessment techniques, interviews, tests, or instruments do so in a manner and for purposes that are appropriate in light of the research on and evidence of the usefulness and proper application of the techniques.
    2.08 Test Scoring and Interpretation Services
        (a) Psychologists who offer assessment of scoring procedures to other professionals accurately describe the purpose, norms, validity, reliability, and applications of the procedures and any special qualifications applicable to their use.
        (b) Psychologists select scoring and interpretation services (including automated services) on the basis of evidence of the validity of the program and procedures as well as on other appropriate considerations.
        (c) Psychologists retain appropriate responsibility for the appropriate application, interpretation, and use of assessment instruments, whether they score and interpret such tests themselves or use automated or other services.
4. Therapy
    4.02 Informed Consent for Therapy
        (a) Psychologists obtain appropriate informed consent to therapy or other related procedures, using language that is reasonably understandable to participants. The content of informed consent will vary depending on many circumstances; however, informed consent generally implies that the person (1) has the capacity to consent, (2) has been informed of significant information concerning the procedure, (3) has freely and without undue influence expressed consent, and (4) consent has been appropriately documented.
5. Privacy and Confidentiality
    5.03 Minimizing Intrusions of Privacy
        (a) In order to minimize intrusions on privacy, psychologists include in written and oral reports, consultations, and the like, only information germane to the purpose for which the communication is made.
        (b) Psychologists discuss confidential information obtained in clinical or consulting relationships, or evaluative data concerning patients, individual organizational clients, students, research participants, supervisees, and employees, only for appropriate scientific or professional purposes and only with persons clearly concerned with such matters.

of assessment can be trusted when it is used to make important decisions in people's lives. At this point, however, it is noteworthy that the ethical principles are silent with regard to whether *treatments* should be shown to be effective before they are offered to the public. Concern with empirically validating the efficacy and effectiveness of treatments emerged as an important issue for clinical psychology in the 1990s (Chambless & Hollon, 1998), and we will return to this issue in greater detail in chapter 15.

CLINICAL PSYCHOLOGY TODAY AND IN THE YEAR 2010

Clinical psychology enters the twenty-first century as a strong and growing field. Clinical psychologists are well established as researchers in the areas of psychopathology, psychotherapy, and behavioral medicine. As practitioners, clinical psychologists operate both independently and in cooperation with professionals in a variety of other disciplines. Despite these strengths, the field is faced with a number of challenges in the coming years, challenges that you will confront should you choose clinical psychology as a career. We now briefly consider five critical issues that clinical psychology must address. These five are by no means the only issues or problems on the horizon; they do represent, however, the types of challenges that present and future clinical psychologists will face in research, training, and clinical practice. As you consider these issues and their possible effects on the future of clinical psychology, it is instructive to take some guidance from the lessons to be learned from the first 100 years of the history of the field.

Challenge 1: The Link Between Science and Practice

Despite the goal to train psychologists who are well versed in research and practice, the communication between researchers and practitioners is poor (e.g., Beutler, Williams, Wakefield, &

Entwistle, 1995; Edelson, 1994; Havens, 1994). Researchers are dismayed by reports that most practicing psychologists do not stay informed of the latest developments in psychological research. Practitioners bemoan the nature of psychological research, noting that it often has little relevance for the day-to-day activities that they carry out in the real world. The result has been a breakdown in the link between clinical research and clinical practice (Kanfer & Goldstein, 1991).

The challenge is how to make research more relevant to, and representative of, the issues faced by practitioners in the real world. Furthermore, there must be improved communication of the many exciting findings from psychological research to those who are involved in the practice of psychology, and communication of the observations and experiences of practitioners to those who are conducting research. The field needs researchers who are not afraid to tackle the important questions that need to be asked about the nature, measurement, treatment, and prevention of psychopathology. The field needs individuals who can translate these facts into information that can be put into practice by professional psychologists (Kanfer & Goldstein, 1991). Practicing psychologists can return to Witmer's original model of a research-based clinical psychology in which each case is treated as an opportunity to gather important data about human problems and solutions to these problems. Based on the history of clinical psychology, however, we can anticipate that the tension between scientific and nonscientific camps will continue (see box 2.3).

Challenge 2: Prescribing Rights for Clinical Psychologists

In this society the prescription of medication for any disorder, whether the problem is primarily physical or psychological in nature, typically has been the exclusive purview of physicians. The medical profession has argued that physicians are uniquely trained in the basic biological sciences and in the knowledge base of medical

BOX 2.3

WHAT IF CLINICAL PSYCHOLOGY WASN'T BASED IN SCIENCE? A LOOK TO THE PAST FOR AN ANSWER

The debate about the role of psychological research in the practice of clinical psychology is likely to continue in the future. An interesting perspective on this issue comes from the past. The 1920s and 1930s were a period in which ideas were presented to the public in the name of psychology, but these ideas had little or no basis in psychological research (Benjamin, 1986). This spread of "pop" psychology resulted in an intense public backlash against the field. Grace Adams, a writer during this period, became one of the sternest critics of the overselling of psychology. Benjamin wrote of Adams, "Her 1928 article in the *American Mercury,* entitled 'The Decline of Psychology in America,' was a vociferous attack on applied psychology: She argued that psychology had forsaken its scientific roots so that individual psychologists might achieve popularity and prosperity." In an article for the *Atlantic Monthly,* Adams (1934) chided psychologists for masquerading as scientists when their discipline was only groping for a philosophy of hope. She wrote, "for all its theories, [psychology] has performed no miracles. It has renamed our emotions 'complexes' and our habits 'conditioned reflexes,' but it has neither changed our habits nor rid of us our emotions" (p. 92).

These early criticisms came about because psychology was promising more than it could deliver. If psychologists overstate what they are capable of providing to the public, both the field of clinical psychology and individual practitioners will be held accountable for their claims. However, clinical psychology has no need to oversell itself. Clinical psychologists have made enormous advances in their understanding of the nature, causes, and course of different forms of psychopathology. Procedures have been developed to reliably and validly measure a wide range of human behaviors and characteristics. Psychotherapy has been shown, through decades of careful research, to be an effective way to treat a host of psychological disorders. Perhaps the real challenge for clinical psychologists is to be as clear about what they do not yet understand as they are about what they already know. If clinical psychologists are not able to concede the limits of their knowledge, they may once again be held up to uncomfortably close public scrutiny and accountability.

practice to utilize medication as a tool to treat disease. Recently, however, the right to prescribe specific types of medication has been established by nonphysicians, including optometrists, dentists, and nurse practitioners.

There has been a growing movement by some psychologists to challenge the exclusive control by psychiatry of **prescription privileges** for psychoactive medication. Specifically, psychologists have argued that the needs of the nation's mentally ill cannot be adequately met if psychiatrists alone are allowed to prescribe medication for the treatment of problems such as schizophrenia, depression, anxiety disorders, and eating disorders (DeLeon & Wiggins, 1996). Some psychologists have argued that, with appropriate training, clinical psychologists can take on the task and responsibility of limited prescription privileges for psychoactive medication in the treatment of psychopathology.

Few issues in clinical psychology have produced more heated debate than the arguments surrounding prescription privileges. Physicians have argued that psychologists lack adequate training necessary to prescribe medications in a careful, ethical, and effective manner. Proponents of psychologists acquiring prescription rights, including the leadership of the APA, argue that psychologists can be trained to effectively prescribe medication for psychological disorders (DeLeon & Wiggins, 1996). Further, proponents have argued that it is in the best interest of underserved populations who are in need of psychoactive medication and other psychological services to increase the numbers and types of professionals who are trained to prescribe medication. The level of conflict is especially high *within* the field of clinical psychology (e.g., Barkley, 1991; DeLeon, Fox, & Graham, 1991; DeNelsky, 1991).

In considering the impact of extending prescription rights to psychologists, it is important to understand the effects that such a change would have on the nature of clinical psychology and on the ways in which psychologists think about people and their problems (Hayes & Heiby, 1996). The addition of course work and practical training necessary to build the competencies to prescribe psychoactive medication would mean either extending the length of time required for training or replacing aspects of training that are already in place (Riley, Elliott, & Thomas, 1992). A concern raised by many psychologists is that research training would be decreased in order to accommodate the time and effort needed for training in psychopharmacology, thus further eroding the scientific training of clinical psychologists. Similarly, clinical psychologists may devote less time to keeping up with new developments in psychotherapy (Hayes & Heiby). Finally, introducing prescription privileges for clinical psychology may have a pervasive effect on the ways that psychologists think about human problems and solutions to those problems. Access to prescription rights may lead psychologists away from the continued development of nonmedical explanations and treatments of psychopathology.

Challenge 3: A Diverse Society

The composition of the U.S. population is changing at a remarkable rate. The degree of diversity in ethnic and cultural groups who live in this country is expanding rapidly. The fabric of American society is enriched by the interweaving of individuals from Asian, African, Hispanic, and European cultures and heritages. It is projected that by the year 2010 there will be no majority culture group in the United States; Americans will be fully composed of groups of different "minorities." Furthermore, American society continues to become an older society, with an increasingly older average age and a larger portion of the population over the age of 65. The proportion of the population age 85 and over is projected to double to 7 million from 1994 to 2020, and to double again by 2040 (U.S. Bureau of the Census, 1996).

How is clinical psychology preparing itself to meet the needs of a diverse, pluralistic society? Even more fundamentally, how well does psychology understand the needs of an ethnically and culturally diverse society? Two steps are needed with respect to this issue. First, clinical psychologists need a better knowledge base of the types of mental health problems and concerns that are faced by individuals in different ethnic groups. Clinicians have precious little information concerning the prevalence and manifestation of various forms of psychopathology across cultural and ethnic groups. This information is critical if psychologists are going to provide valid and effective assessment and treatment to different populations. Second, clinicians need a better understanding of how different segments of society conceptualize solutions to, and help for, their problems. For example, it is not at all clear that psychotherapy, as it is currently practiced, is an applicable solution to the problems faced by inner-city African American youth or by families that have recently immigrated from Southeast Asia. A broader understanding of the similarities and the differences among various cultural groups is a pressing need for the future development of clinical psychology.

Challenge 4: Employment Needs

Many of you who are reading this text will go on to become clinical psychologists. But how many clinical psychologists will this society need in the future? Arguments have been made that the schools are currently training too many clinical psychologists, essentially flooding the market with individuals who have this professional training (e.g., Albee, 2000). Counterarguments have been offered that it is difficult or impossible to accurately estimate the number of psychologists who are needed, especially in light of the ever-expanding roles that psychologists can fill.

Clinical psychology has seen rapid and substantial growth since its inception early in the twentieth century. Based on statistics compiled by the National Science Foundation and the APA, as of 1998 (the most recent year for which comprehensive data are available) there were approximately 87,000 doctoral-level psychologists (psychologists who had earned a PhD or PsyD degree). Approximately half, or over 40,000, of these psychologists had earned their degree in clinical psychology. The U.S. Department of Labor projects that employment of psychologists will grow about as fast as the average for all occupations through the year 2008. Employment in health care settings (including mental health and physical health care), the primary settings in which clinical psychologists work, is projected to grow the fastest. Based on data available for 1998 from the APA, less than 1 percent of doctoral-level psychologists were unemployed and seeking jobs—a very strong statement about the employment market for doctoral-level psychologists.

Clinical psychology has come to comprise an increasingly larger segment of the field of psychology. As shown in figure 2.2, clinical psychologists increased from 35 percent of all PhD level psychologists in 1975 to 50 percent of PhD psychologists in 1995. Of the new doctoral degrees awarded in 1997 (the most recent year with complete data), 36 percent of all new PhDs in psychology were awarded in clinical psychology. When statistics include PsyDs, new doctorates in clinical psychology comprise 47 percent of all new doctorates awarded in psychology in 1997. Graduates with a PsyD degree comprised 21 per-

cent of all doctoral degrees awarded in psychology in 1997, a figure that is likely to continue to grow in the future.

Steady growth is also reflected in the number of new students enrolled in graduate programs in psychology and the number of doctorates awarded in clinical psychology over the past 25 to 30 years. In 1974, 1,036 new (first-year) students enrolled in clinical psychology. This number had grown to 2,219 by 1996, an increase of 114 percent in 22 years. The most dramatic rise came in the period from 1979 to 1987 (an increase of 74.8 percent), a direct result of the rapid growth in the number of new professional schools of psychology during this period. By comparison to this enormous growth in clinical psychology, new enrollments in all the basic areas of psychology combined (e.g., cognitive, developmental, experimental, social) grew from 4,191 to 4,828 from 1974 to 1996, an increase of only 15 percent.

When considering the composition of clinical psychology and other mental health professions, it is important to go beyond the total numbers of professionals and consider the distribution of each group in terms of the representation of women and ethnic minorities. In clinical psychology, the proportion of women has risen steadily since the origin of the field as a male-dominated profession in the early part of the twentieth century (Snyder et al., 2000). Recent statistics indicate that 57 percent of clinical psychologists in 1983 were women, rising to 60 percent by 1991.

The figures reflecting representation of ethnic minorities are quite different, however. In 1983, only 8.6 percent of clinical psychologists were African Americans, and only 1.1 percent were Hispanic Americans. By 1991, the percentage of clinical psychologists who were African Americans had declined to 7.8 percent and the percentage of Hispanic Americans had risen only slightly, to 3.8 percent. In contrast, in 1983 18.2 percent of social workers were African American and 6.3 percent were Hispanic American. These

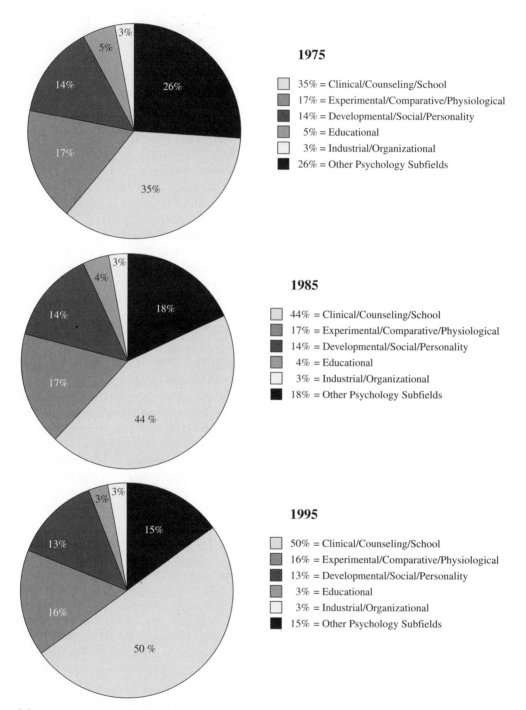

1975

35% = Clinical/Counseling/School
17% = Experimental/Comparative/Physiological
14% = Developmental/Social/Personality
5% = Educational
3% = Industrial/Organizational
26% = Other Psychology Subfields

1985

44% = Clinical/Counseling/School
17% = Experimental/Comparative/Physiological
14% = Developmental/Social/Personality
4% = Educational
3% = Industrial/Organizational
18% = Other Psychology Subfields

1995

50% = Clinical/Counseling/School
16% = Experimental/Comparative/Physiological
13% = Developmental/Social/Personality
3% = Educational
3% = Industrial/Organizational
15% = Other Psychology Subfields

Figure 2.2
Percentages of Psychologists in Clinical and Other Areas of Psychology.

figures rose to 21.9 percent and 7.2 percent, respectively, by 1991. Thus, although clinical psychology has shown excellent progress in fairly representing women within the field, progress in the representation of ethnic minorities has lagged far behind both the proportion of minorities in the U.S. population as a whole and the proportion in other mental professions. Clearly, an important task for the field of clinical psychology is to increase the diversity of those who make up members of the profession in order to better represent an increasingly diverse society in the United States.

Challenge 5:
Managed Care and the Health Care Industry

The character of health care in America has changed dramatically in the past decade with the emergence of **managed health care** playing a major role. Under managed health care systems, decisions about an individual's health care are managed, or regulated, either by the company that provides the health care services or by the insurance company that supports the cost of services. The growth of managed care has had a major impact on the way that psychological services are provided to individuals. Prior to the develop-

ment of managed care systems, many individuals carried health insurance policies that included mental health services, including psychological testing and psychotherapy provided by a clinical psychologist. The individual was able to choose a psychologist, and the cost of the psychologist's services would be reimbursed by the insurance company. For the most part, there were no stipulations about the types of problems for which an individual could seek help, nor were there limits placed on the number of sessions that would be reimbursed. Furthermore, an individual was allowed to select a licensed psychologist of her or his choice, and insurance companies would cover most or all of the cost of these services.

The provision of mental health care has changed dramatically under managed care. Most current systems require that approval be obtained from a managed care worker before services from a psychologist can be sought. The psychologist is typically required to specify a diagnosis that is being treated, and a limited number of sessions are approved for reimbursement. Additional sessions are added only upon review by the managed care worker. And patients are allowed to choose a psychologist only from a preapproved list from the managed care company.

SUMMARY AND CONCLUSIONS

The history of clinical psychology is rooted in the ways that societies have viewed mental health and psychopathology for centuries. Early approaches (referred to as demonology) were based in religious beliefs and emphasized the role of evil spirits and the devil as the source of abnormal behavior. The belief that psychopathology is caused by physical processes (the somatogenic perspective) dates to the time of the ancient Greeks and is a dominant viewpoint today. The notion that psychological factors are the cause of psychopathology (the psychogenic perspective) can be found in the early work of Freud and is a

dominant view in modern clinical psychology. Current perspectives have integrated biological, psychological, and social factors in the understanding of psychopathology, as represented in emerging biopsychosocial theories.

Lightner Witmer is viewed as the founder of clinical psychology in the United States through his work in establishing the first psychological clinic in 1896. The development of the field was strongly influenced by the need for psychologists to provide important services during the First and Second World Wars. Psychologists were called to develop tests of mental abilities for prospective soldiers during World War I and to provide treatment for shell shock (Post-Traumatic Stress Disorder) during World War II.

Following World War II, clinical psychology grew rapidly as the VA provided support for the training of clinical psychologists to work with psychological casualties of the war. The scientist-practitioner model of training was developed at the Boulder Conference in 1949, and the professional school model of training (as exemplified in PsyD programs) was outlined at the Vail Conference in 1973. Both models of training are represented in clinical psychology today.

The history of clinical psychology can be traced through advances and landmark events in research, assessment, treatment, and prevention and through the development of the profession of clinical psychology (see table 2.1 for a Timeline of some of these events). The field is now faced with a number of interesting and challenging issues that will shape the nature of clinical psychology in the twenty-first century (e.g., prescription privileges; diversity in society; managed health care). We have outlined some of these issues here, and we return to them at the close of this book (chapter 16).

KEY TERMS AND NAMES

Army Alpha and Army Beta tests
Alfred Binet
Boulder Conference
Hans Eysenck
Flexner Report
Starke Hathaway
Managed health care
Paul Meehl
Minnesota Multiphasic Personality Inventory
  (MMPI)

PhD in clinical psychology
Prescription privileges for psychologists
Psychology licensing laws
PsyD in clinical psychology
Carl Rogers
David Shakow
Vail Conference
Lightner Witmer

RESOURCES

Books

McReynolds, P. (1997). *Lightner Witmer: His life and times.* Washington, DC: American Psychological Association.

Routh, D. K. (1994). *Clinical psychology since 1917: Science, practice, and organization.* New York: Plenum Press.

Routh, D. K., & DeRubeis, R. J. (Eds.). (1998). *The science of clinical psychology: Accomplishments and future directions.* Washington, DC: American Psychological Association.

Walker, C. E. (Ed.). (1998). *Comprehensive clinical psychology: Vol. 1. Foundations.* Oxford, England: American Book.

Journals

Professional Psychology: Research and Practice
History of Psychology
Professional Practice of Psychology

RESEARCH METHODS IN CLINICAL PSYCHOLOGY

INTRODUCTION

Janis lay on the examining table in the emergency room (ER) of the university hospital for the fourth time in the past two months. Her senior year of college was almost half over but she felt that school, and her life in general, was spinning out of control. She had high hopes of completing her degree in English and then applying for a job in a large publishing firm in New York City. Now she feared that she would be unable to complete the fall semester, much less her degree or the start of her career. The problem that brought her yet again to the ER made school and work seem insignificant—she had an overwhelming sense that she was going to die of a heart attack.

She told the doctor on call that this episode had been typical of the others that had happened earlier this fall. Two of her closest friends had rented a movie to watch with her in her apartment. The film was a romantic comedy, not frightening in any way. About 30 minutes into the movie, however, Janis's heart began to race uncontrollably, feeling as if it was about to explode in her chest. Her body began shaking and she started to sweat profusely. As the agonizing moments passed, she began to have difficulty catching her breath, and she felt that she was about to suffocate. She felt a dull pain in her chest, and she was terrified that she was having a heart attack. Janis began to sob, terrified that she was about to die. Although she was having difficulty talking, she insisted that her friends either call an ambulance or drive her to the hospital. Too frightened that something could go wrong if they drove her, her friends called 911 and waited with her for the ambulance to arrive.

By the time she arrived at the hospital, Janis's symptoms had subsided, and the doctor provided Janis with medication to further help to calm her. When the doctor interviewed Janis about her recent and past history of health problems, several things were noteworthy. First, there was no evidence that Janis had experienced a heart attack on this or any of her previous hospital visits. Furthermore, her medical records indicated that she was in good health, including her blood pressure and resting heart rate. Second, Janis had a history of problems related to anxiety, beginning when she was 10 years old. For example, she had experienced difficulties with public speaking, starting with class presentations in junior high school. She recalled that her mother had also experienced anxiety problems. Janis's mother had been ill a great deal when Janis was young and was often preoccupied with her own health. Her mother also worried constantly about Janis's health and the possibility that Janis would be injured in an automobile crash or some other type of accident. The third noteworthy piece of information in her history was that Janis had been smoking cigarettes since she was 17 years old, and she currently smoked between 8 and 10 cigarettes a day. She had tried numerous times to quit, because she knew all the health risks associated with smoking. However, she reported that smoking was one of the few things that seemed to calm her when she felt tense or nervous.

Janis reported that she had become increasingly withdrawn and anxious in the past month. She now avoided places where the previous episodes had occurred; for example, one incident took place in a movie theater and even though Janis loved movies, she would no longer go to the theater out of fear that another episode would occur. In fact, her fear of having other incidents was becoming so pervasive she often found it hard to think of anything else.

Janis's problem presents an interesting puzzle, one that has been a focus for researchers and clinicians in clinical psychology and psychiatry for decades. As we will explain in this chapter, Janis is suffering from Panic Disorder and is at risk for developing an accompanying problem of Agoraphobia. What is known about Panic Disorder? What causes it? Can it be treated? In chapters 1 and 2 we have made the case that the field of clinical psychology is based on the broad science of psychology and that the methods used in the practice of clinical psychology must be evaluated using rigorous scientific methods. Therefore, we now consider the basic characteristics of research in clinical psychology. To provide an example of clinical psychological research, we will draw on findings from studies of the prevalence, causes, course, and treatment of Panic Disorder.

THE ROLE OF RESEARCH IN CLINICAL PSYCHOLOGY

Research lays a foundation of knowledge for understanding the phenomena of interest to clinical psychologists, including psychopathology, mental health, and the relationship between psychological factors and physical disease. Research also provides a body of evidence to guide clinical practice, including empirically validated methods to assess people and their problems and empirically supported methods of prevention and treatment. Psychological tests and other assessment methods used in clinical practice should be based on research that has established their reliability and validity (e.g., Hunsley & Bailey, 1999). Research findings should also identify those interventions that have been shown to be more effective than no treatment or alternative forms of treatment (e.g., Chambless & Hollon, 1998; Weisz, Hawley, Pilkonis, Woody, & Follette, 2000). Just as research informs clinical practice, clinical experiences provide a source of ideas and hypotheses for research. Research also provides ideas for new directions and applications for the field of clinical psychology, including links between clinical psychology and research in other behavioral, biological, and social sciences.

Because of the wide range of questions that confront researchers in clinical psychology, a variety of methods are used in research in this field (Hayes, Barlow, & Gray-Nelson, 1999; Kazdin, 1998). Research designs used by clinical psychologists range from single-case designs that study one individual at a time to large-scale, multisite studies involving hundreds or even thousands of participants. Clinical psychologists conduct research in many different settings, including experimentally controlled laboratories as well as naturalistic settings such as hospitals, clinics, schools, and the community. Clinical researchers utilize various methods of data analysis, ranging from complex multivariate statistics used with large samples to nonstatistical methods in single-case studies. The methods that are chosen by researchers shape the types of questions that are asked, reflect the hypotheses that are being tested, and influence the interpretation of findings.

THE RESEARCH PROCESS

The process of research in clinical psychology, like research in other areas of psychology and in other sciences, involves the unfolding of a story. The story begins with a question that, when framed properly, can be answered with an acceptable degree of certainty. Pursuing the answers to questions involves six broad steps: generation of hypotheses, selection of measures of key variables, selection of a research design, selection of a sample, hypothesis testing, and interpretation and dissemination of results. Throughout this process, it is imperative that researchers follow clear guidelines and standards

for ethical treatment of participants (human or animal) in research.

Generating Hypotheses

Any piece of research begins with a question that needs to be answered. Why do more women than men experience clinical depression (Nolen-Hoeksema, Larson, & Grayson, 1999)? What is the role of human genetics in the development of infantile autism (Rutter, Silberg, O'Connor, & Siminoff, 1999)? How stable are certain personality characteristics, such as extroversion or sociability, across the life span (McRae & Costa, 1997)? What role does poverty play in the development of psychopathology (McLoyd, 1998)? Is psychotherapy effective in the treatment of eating disorders such as Bulimia Nervosa and Anorexia Nervosa (Wilson, 1999)? These questions are among the thousands that have been posed and examined through research by clinical psychologists.

In order to serve as the focus of scientific research, a question needs to be refined into a **hypothesis.** A hypothesis goes further than a question in that it reflects the researcher's best educated idea about the expected answer to a question. Furthermore, a hypothesis can be tested to determine if the **null hypothesis** (i.e., that there is no difference or no relationship between the variables being studied) can be rejected with some degree of certainty or statistical probability. Some types of descriptive research (e.g., epidemiological research to determine the prevalence of different forms of psychopathology) may not be framed in terms of hypotheses. Instead, descriptive research attempts to provide information that defines the extent or parameters of a particular behavior, personality characteristic, or psychological disorder (e.g., Kessler et al., 1994). Research that is aimed to predict, explain, or change human behavior, however, is best represented as a specific hypothesis that can be tested. The statistical methods employed by psychologists allow researchers to determine the probability that the null hypothesis is false and that a hypothesized relationship among different variables did not occur simply by chance (see the section titled, "Testing Hypothesis").

Research hypotheses can emerge from at least three sources—careful observations of a clinical case or cases, a theory concerned with human behavior or psychopathology, and the results of previous research. A skilled clinical researcher is first and foremost an astute observer of human behavior. One the richest and most relevant sources of observations is the interactions of clinical psychologists with their clients or patients (Davison & Lazarus, 1994). For example, a clinical psychologist who treats aggressive and noncompliant children may observe that these children frequently come from families in which there is a high degree of conflict and anger between the parents. This observation raises the possibility that conflict and discord in marital relationships can contribute to childhood aggression and noncompliance (e.g., Cummings, 1998; Emery & Forehand, 1996). Equally plausible, however, is the hypothesis that aggressive and disobedient behavior by a child can contribute to tension and arguments between parents. In this way, observations of individual cases raise questions whose answers require other methods and additional information.

A theory can serve as an important source of hypotheses about a variety of clinical problems. A theory serves as a road map for a clinical psychologist, providing a sense of what to expect and why it should be expected. Nevertheless, the central propositions of any theory cannot be left as mere abstractions. A strong theory must lend itself to empirical evaluation and testing. For example, operant behavior theory predicts that any behavior that is followed by positive consequences should increase in frequency (O'Donohue, 1998). The theory further predicts that the frequency and intensity of a behavior will be greatest when positive consequences are administered contingent on only a portion of the occur-

rences of the behavior, in a variable pattern, that is, a pattern in which the proportion (ratio) of responses that are followed by positive consequences varies over the course of time. Thus, a researcher can do more than ask a question about the effects of positive consequences on behavior. The researcher can hypothesize that a variable ratio pattern of reinforcement will increase behavior more rapidly than no reinforcement or more than reinforcement that is administered contingent on every occurrence of the behavior. This hypothesis could then be tested in relation to clinically relevant behaviors, such as the development and maintenance of a child's disruptive or noncompliant behavior.

Hypotheses can also emerge directly from the findings of previous research. This includes studies carried out by other researchers as well as an investigator's own previous work. Knowledge of prior research is important to avoid pursuing the answers to questions that have already been resolved, to learn from the tribulations and mistakes of others, and to draw on the findings of previous studies as an important source of future hypotheses. Keeping abreast of research in psychology has become a daunting task, however, as the field has grown to include thousands of active researchers publishing their findings in hundreds of journals around the world. Computerized literature search programs such as *PsychLit, PsychInfo,* and *MedLine* have been enormously helpful in expediting the process of bringing oneself up to date on current research on a topic. But these methods are not a substitute for reading broadly in many areas of psychology to develop hypotheses that reflect basic as well as applied research. Some of the most interesting research hypotheses emerge from unexpected and serendipitous sources, which often are the result of reading outside one's own area of interest (see box 3.1 for an example of basic research on emotion).

The strongest examples of psychological research involve sequential studies in which the findings of one investigation serve as the starting

BOX 3.1

FINDINGS FROM RESEARCH ON EMOTION AND THE BRAIN

Recent advances in understanding human emotions, including processes in the brain that are related to emotion, have opened new avenues for research in clinical psychology. A pioneer in this area of research is Richard Davidson, Professor of Psychology at the University of Wisconsin–Madison. Davidson's research has provided fascinating new insights into the areas of the brain that are involved in the experience and regulation of different types of emotions. Davidson recently received the 2000 Distinguished Scientific Contribution Award from the American Psychological Association (Davidson, 2000a). Davidson's research has provided a foundation of knowledge about the underlying biological structures that relate to important clinical problems, including anxiety disorders and depression. Specifically, his work has provided groundbreaking information on the role of several areas of the brain (e.g., the prefrontal cortex, amygdala, hippocampus) in the experience and regulation of emotions. Davidson

uses a variety of technologies, including positron-emission tomography and functional magnetic resonance imaging, to measure functioning in different brain regions after exposure to emotionally arousing stimuli.

The clinical implications of this research are far-reaching. For example, researchers and clinicians have long recognized that there are substantial differences among individuals in the ways that they respond to and are affected by emotionally threatening and stressful events and stimuli. Davidson has established that one source of these individual differences lies in the ways that people's brains respond to emotions (Davidson, 2000b). One source of such differences is in the relative activity in the left and right portions of the prefrontal cortex, because the left hemisphere plays a larger role in positive emotions and the right hemisphere in negative emotions (e.g., Davidson, Marshall, Tomarken, & Henriques, 2000).

point for the next study in the series. Thus, the best research is comprised not of isolated experiments or studies but rather of systematic, cohesive, and programmatic efforts by researchers to tackle a complex set of questions in a series of investigations. In some instances, a series of studies can be planned in advance, because the researcher knows a sequence of questions that he or she wishes to answer. In other cases, however, one study will yield unexpected or serendipitous findings that lead in new and unexpected directions. In either case, researchers need to be prepared to learn from the findings of one investigation to guide their hypotheses in the next step in the process. Some of the best examples of programmatic research in clinical psychology involve the use of basic research on a clinical disorder to form the foundation for interventions to treat or prevent the problem. For example, research on the factors that place children at risk

for the development of aggressive and violent behavior problems has led to the development of interventions in childhood to prevent the onset of these problems (e.g., Coie et al., 1999; Greenberg et al., 1999).

Measuring Key Variables

Selection of Measures   Once a set of hypotheses has been developed, the next challenge for the researcher is to determine how to measure the key variables, or constructs, that are the focus of the study. Measurement involves assessment of characteristics of people's thoughts, emotions, behavior, and physiology and the environments in which they function. A number of difficult decisions must be made with regard to the measurement of people and environments. First, the aspects of the person or the environment that are most central to the research goals and hypotheses must be determined. A researcher cannot, however, measure everything that might be relevant to the question at hand. Measurement of a large number of variables is impractical, because participants in research often cannot or will not invest the amount of time that a researcher desires. More importantly, including too many measures is not scientifically sound, because the inclusion of more and more measures increases the chances of finding effects that are spurious. That is, the more measures that are taken, the more likely it is that some of them will achieve statistically significant effects merely by chance, a phenomenon referred to as **Type I error** (Kazdin, 1998). In general, researchers should measure only those factors that are most important to their hypotheses.

Second, specific methods must be selected to measure the variables of interest in the study. Assessment methods used in clinical research include direct observations (e.g., observations of parents and children interacting with each other; Reuter & Conger, 1998); self-reports by participants in the research (e.g., self-reports of symptoms of depression and anxiety; Steer, Clark, Beck, & Ranieri, 1999); measures of physiological reactivity and recovery (e.g., heart rate variability, skin conductance; Cacioppo, Berntson, & Crites, 1996); and performance on structured experimental tasks (e.g., continuous performance tasks; Nigg, Hinshaw, & Halperin, 1996). Each of the methods of measurement has its inherent strengths and weaknesses. For example, self-reports from participants are necessary to assess certain aspects of thoughts and emotions because there are aspects of private experience that are not accessible any other way (Stone et al., 2000). On the other hand, self-reports are subject to certain types of problems, including biases in the ways that individuals may want to present themselves to others, the inability to accurately report on certain aspects of one's own thoughts and emotions, and unwillingness to disclose certain types of information (Nisbett & Wilson, 1977; Stone et al.). Observational methods are strong in terms of their objectivity and ability to measure

behavior as it occurs in response to specific events or conditions in the environment. Observations cannot be used, however, to measure private thoughts and internal emotional states. One solution to the problems inherent in each form of measurement is to use different types of measures in the same study to determine the degree to which the findings converge across different types of measurement as opposed to findings that are unique to one type of measure (Campbell & Fiske, 1959; Kazdin, 1998).

Third, the researcher must determine if tried-and-true measures of these constructs have been developed and used in previous research, or if new measures need to be constructed to pursue the goals of this study. Whenever possible, researchers use measures that have established levels of *reliability* and *validity* and (when appropriate) that have normative data available on populations that are similar to the participants in the study. These factors provide a degree of assurance that the measure can be trusted—that the results are to some degree consistent and accurate. In some instances, a researcher will want to measure a variable for which an adequate instrument is not available. In these cases, the researcher is faced with the task of developing and validating a new measure in order to carry out the study. It is not acceptable, however, to simply employ a new measure or technique for the purposes of the study without paying careful attention to establishing its reliability and validity (see the discussion on measurement development in this section). Some of the different types of reliability and validity that are important in research in clinical psychology are presented in table 3.1.

An example of these difficult decisions can be found in research on the nature of anxiety disorders. Anxiety can be measured at a number of different levels, including the experience and emotions of the individual (e.g., "I feel tense and anxious"), observations made by others of overt manifestations of anxiety (e.g., "I could see his hands were shaking and I could hear a trembling in his voice"), and measures of physiological arousal (e.g., elevated heart rate, blood pressure,

TABLE 3.1
Types of Reliability and Validity in Clinical Psychology Research

Reliability	Definition
Inter-rater	Degree of agreement in the ratings provided by two observers of the same behavior
Internal consistency	Degree to which responses (e.g., items on a test) are correlated with one another
Test-retest	Stability of responses or ratings on the same measure at two points in time

Validity	
Construct	Degree to which the measure reflects the concept that it is intended to measure; often tested with factor analysis
Concurrent	Association between the measure and a criterion (a related construct) at the same point in time
Predictive	Association between the measure and a criterion (a related construct) at a future point in time
Convergent	Degree of association between two measures that are presumed to measure the same construct
Discriminant	Lack of association between two measures that are presumed to measure different constructs

skin conductance). None of these approaches to measurement represents the "right" way to assess anxiety, and the issue is clouded by the fact that the three approaches often yield different results (e.g., Cuthbert, Levin, Miller, & Kozak, 1983; Greenwald, Cook, & Lang, 1989; Lang, Levin, Miller, & Kozak, 1983). For example, some individuals may experience high physiological arousal but do not report subjective experiences of fear or anxiety, and conversely, some individuals with very low levels of arousal feel very anxious. The failure of different types of measures to converge (i.e., to provide the same information on the variable that is being measured) does not in and of itself imply that any one of the measures is invalid. However, it presents the researcher with a challenge in the interpretation of the different sources of information.

Investigators must pay close attention to the distribution, or differences, in the scores of individuals on different measures. Distribution is reflected in indices of the central tendencies of scores (mean and median) and the variability of these scores (standard deviation and variance). By comparing the responses of a single individual to those of others who are similar in age and other demographic characteristics, the researcher is often able to determine the degree to which the individual deviates from typical functioning on this measure. In order to make comparisons with the responses of others, the researcher must have access to good *normative* data on the measure on a representative sample of individuals.

A great deal hinges on the quality of the measures selected for use in research. If these tools fail to produce information that is at least minimally reliable (consistent) and valid (truthful), any findings of the research will be suspect. Inadequate measures will undermine the likelihood that the same or similar results could be replicated in the future. Measures must also be consistent with one's theoretical perspective on the problem. If a researcher is interested in investigating a psychoanalytic explanation of the causes of anxiety, she or he will need to use measures that can assess the unconscious processes that, according to psychoanalytic theory, are thought to underlie overt anxiety. In contrast, a behaviorally oriented researcher will want to measure the antecedent and consequent conditions in the environment that are hypothesized to elicit and maintain anxiety according to this theory. The use of similar measures in both research and clinical practice will increase the likelihood that research findings will be applicable to practitioners and that clinical practice can generate data that will stimulate research.

Measurement Development   As we noted in chapter 2, the roots of clinical psychology lie in the development and use of psychological tests, most notably intelligence tests. Since these initial efforts in the early 1900s to measure intellectual functioning, clinical psychologists have played a leading role in the development of tests of personality, psychopathology, life events and experiences, and neuropsychological functioning as well as the development of methods for the systematic observation of behavior. The development of these various techniques of measurement has provided a foundation for research and the practice of clinical assessment.

The development of any psychological test begins with a clear definition of the construct to be measured. The constructs that are of greatest interest to psychologists are hypothetical—they do not exist in some tangible form that can be touched but are represented only as a set of ideas. Intelligence and personality are examples of hypothetical constructs, important concepts that cannot be directly (physically) measured. Therefore, the first task for researchers is to develop a way to sample behaviors or responses that represent the construct, which is often reflected in the selection of items to include on a test. Once a set of items has been selected, researchers must obtain information on the ways that samples of people respond to those items. The most useful items will be those that distinguish between individuals. That is, a test item that elicits the same response from everyone tells you something about the strength of that item as a stimulus but responses to the item tell you little or nothing about differences among people who take the test. Furthermore, researchers are interested in identifying items that can distinguish among people in predictable and meaningful ways. Responses to test items need to be related to other criteria that can be used to understand the meaning of test responses. For example, a measure of symptoms of depression should distinguish between patients who have a diagnosis and those who do not.

A psychological test is of little use if it simply consists of a group of undifferentiated items. Most of the aspects of human functioning that psychologists measure have different facets to them. For example, most theories of intelligence

hypothesize that intellectual functioning is comprised of different elements; similarly, theories of personality propose that there are different dimensions of personality. Therefore, researchers are interested in identifying patterns of relationships among responses to test items or questions. To identify these patterns, researchers often use the statistical procedure called *factor analysis* to either explore the associations among responses to test items or to confirm a hypothetical model of how responses to test items are interrelated. Factor analysis examines the patterns of correlations among items on a test in order to determine if there are relatively distinct sets of items that are correlated with one another more than they are correlated with other items. These sets of correlated items are referred to as factors and can be used to form separate scales that comprise the items in a measure.

Many clinical psychologists are more interested in the ways that people actually perform on specific tasks or behave in the environments in which they live than in the ways that people respond to questions on a psychological test. Behaviorally oriented psychologists have carried out extensive research to develop reliable and valid ways to assess behavior (e.g., S. J. Beck, 2000). The development of a sound method for observation of behavior is contingent on a clear operationalization of what the behavior is and on agreement among observers as to the presence and absence of the target behavior.

Selecting a Research Design

Armed with a clear set of hypotheses and appropriate measures to assess the important constructs under investigation, a clinical psychologist is prepared to design a study. There are four basic types of research designs (but many variations within each) from which to choose—single-case designs, descriptive designs, correlational designs, and experimental designs. Moreover, all these designs can be cross-sectional (one point in time) or longitudinal (over the course of time). The choice of which design to use depends on the nature of the question being asked and on ethical and practical limitations that may constrain the research. No one type of research design is inherently superior to others—each is simply better suited to answer some questions than others.

Single-case designs are a set of methods developed in behavioral psychology to study individual cases in a controlled manner. Unlike purely descriptive "case studies," single-case experimental designs involve the systematic introduction and, in some instances, the withdrawal of experimental conditions accompanied by ongoing measurement of the relevant variables (e.g., Barlow & Hersen, 1984; Kazdin, 1998). An individual serves as his or her own "control" in the sense that the person is observed under normal or nonexperimental conditions as well as under conditions specifically created by the experimenter. First, data are collected to establish a "baseline" for the behavior—the rate or frequency of the behavior under the initial conditions (A). Then the experimental condition is introduced, and the behavior continues to be observed to determine if the rate or frequency of the behavior changes with the introduction of the experimental condition (B). In an A-B-A single-case design, the experimental condition is then withdrawn (return to A) and the behavior continues to be observed to determine whether the rate or frequency returns to the level observed during the initial baseline period. The behavior of the person is examined as a function of the introduction and withdrawal of the experimental condition. For example, the effects of a particular type of reinforcer (e.g., a parent's praise and attention) on behavior can be observed by an experimenter who systematically introduces and withdraws the reinforcer and observes the changes in behavior that may accompany the presence or absence of the reinforcement. An alternative approach is a **multiple baseline design** in which more than one behavior is studied in sequence. A baseline period is established for each behavior, and the experimental condition is implemented to change each of the behaviors one at a time.

Although single-case designs were originally used typically to study a small number of very discrete behaviors, they are now used to study increasingly complex patterns of behavior. For example, Lucyshyn, Albin, and Nixon (1997) used a single-case design to evaluate the effects of family-based behavioral treatment for a child with severe disabilities and severe behavior problems. This study focused on a program to change self-injurious, aggressive, and destructive behaviors in a 14-year-old girl. The researchers used a multiple baseline approach in which they implemented several different interventions through the parents' behavior (e.g., changing the ways that the parents responded to the child's self-injuries) with their daughter in different settings (e.g., dinner at home, in restaurants, in the grocery store). The frequency of the girl's problem behaviors was assessed during the baseline condition, during the training period in which the parents were taught to respond differently to her behavior, and during follow-up. The rates of the girl's problem behaviors decreased in each of the different settings following the program to change the ways that her parents responded to these behaviors.

Descriptive research designs are used in clinical psychology to report on the prevalence or incidence of a human characteristic or problem in the population. The goal of this type of research is to describe a particular phenomenon without trying to predict or explain when or why it occurs. A descriptive approach is used most frequently in *epidemiological* studies in which researchers try to identify the prevalence of different forms of psychopathology. Descriptive studies are often an important first step in research on a particular problem or disorder, because they allow the researchers to define the scope of a problem in the population. Researchers involved in descriptive research are primarily concerned with accurate measurement of the problem and with the representativeness of the sample that they include in their study. If participation in a study is biased toward a particular segment of the population, the results of the study could misrepresent the prevalence of a problem as higher or lower than it actually is in the population as a whole. This type of research does not attempt to predict or understand the causes of a problem, however, because other variables that might be hypothesized to be causes or correlates of the problem typically are not measured.

Epidemiological research is designed to establish the number, or *prevalence,* of disorders in a population at a particular point in time as well as the onset, or *incidence,* of new cases during a specified period of time (e.g., the past year). Epidemiology has a long history in the field of public health, where studies have been conducted to understand the prevalence and incidence of physical disease (e.g., Klienbaum et al., 1982; Lilienfield & Lilienfield, 1980). Epidemiological methods have been used more recently to estimate the extent of psychiatric disorders within populations or countries.

The National Institute of Mental Health supported a major epidemiological study of psychopathology in adults, the National Comorbidity Survey (NCS), in the early 1990s (Kessler, 1994; Kessler et al., 1994). This study included a large sample of adults in the community (more than 8,000 participants) who were interviewed using a standardized diagnostic interview. A specific goal of this large project was to determine the degree to which individuals have more than one type of psychopathology (the co-occurrence of two or more disorders in the same individual is referred to as comorbidity). In a summary of the initial findings it was reported that nearly 50 percent of respondents reported at least one lifetime disorder, and close to 30 percent reported at least one 12-month disorder. The most common disorders were Major Depressive Disorder, Alcohol Dependence, Social Phobia, and Simple Phobia (Kessler et al.).

One important use of epidemiological data is to determine the different probabilities of an individual developing a psychiatric disorder as a function of various demographic factors. This information is examined through the use of odds ratios—determining the odds (or probability) that individuals will meet the criteria for a specific disorder if they possess one demographic characteristic (e.g., being female) as opposed to another (e.g., being male). For example, in the NCS data, 21.3 percent of women met criteria for an affective disorder in their lifetime compared with 12.7 percent of men (Kessler et al., 1994). These figures show an odds ratio of 1.76 for affective disorder for women compared to men; that is, women were 1.76 times more likely (slightly less than twice as likely) to have developed an affective disorder in their lifetime than were men (Kessler et al.).

Correlational research designs are used to determine the degree to which there is an *association between two or more variables.* A simple (or bivariate) **correlation** represents the relationship that is observed between two variables in a sample of individuals. The same two variables are assessed for each person in the sample and a *correlation coefficient* is calculated to provide a numerical representation of the magnitude and direction of this association. This coefficient can range from positive 1.00 (one variable increases in value at exactly the same rate as the other variable increases in value), to zero (no association between the variables), to negative 1.00 (one variable decreases in value at exactly the same rate as the other variable increases in value).

Figure 3.1 illustrates examples of two sets of correlational data between two variables. In these hypothetical data, cancer patients were asked to report on the degree to which they blamed themselves for the cause of their cancer (e.g., "It is my fault that I developed cancer," "I did something to deserve to get cancer"), on their current symptoms of depression, and on their sense of optimism and hope for the future (see Glinder & Compas, 1999, for an example of research on self-blame and cancer). Figure 3.1a represents a positive correlation between self-blame attributions (the vertical axis) and symptoms of depression (the horizontal axis). As reflected in the figure, patients who are higher in self-blame are also higher in depressive symptoms—a significant positive correlation between self-blame and depressive symptoms. In contrast, figure 3.1b shows that patients who blame

FIGURE 3.1A

Positive correlation between self-blame attributions and symptoms of depression in cancer patients.

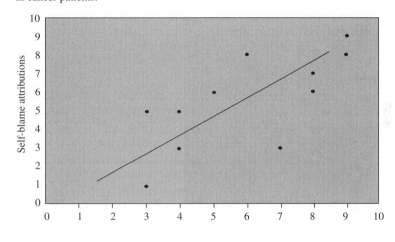

Depressive symptoms

FIGURE 3.1B

Negative correlation between self-blame attributions and optimistic beliefs in cancer patients.

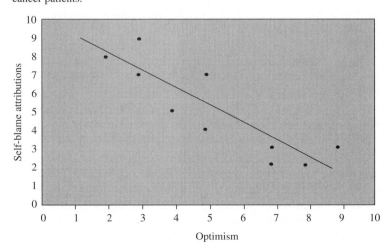

Optimism

themselves for their cancer are lower in their sense of optimism about the future—a significant negative correlation between self-blame and optimism.

Correlations can be calculated either at a single point in time (cross-sectional research) or over the course of time (prospective or longitudinal research). Cross-sectional correlations allow researchers to determine the degree to which two variables are associated at the same point in time or coincide with the occurrence of a particular event. For example, Nolen-Hoeksema (2000) examined the correlation between cognitive rumination (thinking repetitively and passively about one's negative emotions and focusing on one's symptoms of distress) and symptoms of depression. In a sample of over 1,300 adults, some of whom met diagnostic criteria for Major Depression and most who were not clinically depressed, she found a significant positive correlation ($r = .48$) between rumination at the beginning of the study (Time 1) and depressive symptoms measured at the same point in time. She also examined the relationship between rumination at the beginning of the study and depressive symptoms 1 year later (Time 2). Initial cognitive rumination at Time 1 was also correlated with depressive symptoms at Time 2 ($r = .40$). Thus, adults' tendency to ruminate about their feelings was related to more depressive symptoms a year later.

Most researchers who use correlational designs in their research recognize that more than two variables may be important in understanding the problem that they are investigating. When researchers are interested in determining the associations among more than two variables at a time, they will use **multiple correlation** or **multiple regression designs** in their research. These designs are more complex than simple correlational designs but are much more representative of the complicated associations among multiple factors as they occur in the world. Nolen-Hoeksema (2000) in her study of rumination and depressive symptoms, wanted to determine if the relationship between Time 1 rumination and Time 2 depressive symptoms would still be significant after taking into account how depressed the participants were at Time 1. That is, perhaps the association between initial rumination and later depressive symptoms was due to the degree of depressive symptoms that participants reported at the first assessment. In fact, depressive symptoms at Time 1 were strongly correlated with depressive symptoms at Time 2 ($r = .61$). To address this possibility, Nolen-Hoeksema conducted a multiple regression analysis in which Time 1 depressive symptoms and Time 1 rumination were both tested as predictors of Time 2 depressive symptoms. Time 1 rumination was still a significant predictor of Time 2 depressive symptoms, even when Time 1 depressive symptoms were taken into account. Thus, there is something unique about cognitive rumination at Time 1 that helps to explain depressive symptoms at Time 2.

A more powerful method to assess the associations among variables in a correlational design is the use of structural equation modeling (SEM) techniques to analyze data. These methods provide more stringent tests than multiple regression analyses in several ways. SEM analyses include statistical methods to account or control for error in the measures that are used; in other words, no measure is perfectly reliable, and the error in the measure can be accounted for in SEM. Furthermore, SEM analyses allow researchers to test complex models that include many different relationships among multiple variables as complete models, rather than testing each of these relationships separately.

In spite of the important information that can be obtained from correlational designs, correlations cannot be used to infer causation. Knowing that two or more variables are correlated does not inform researchers about the direction of the relationships among the variables. Studies in which variables are assessed at more than one point in time (prospective or longitudinal designs) are an improvement over cross-sectional research designs. Prospective designs allow researchers to determine the temporal (over time) relationships between variables and the temporal precedence (the degree to which one variable came first) of one variable over another. Although longitudinal correlational designs can be used to determine if one variable occurred before another, it is still impossible to infer causality from this approach. The longitudinal association between two variables may be bidirectional (i.e., each variable may exert a causal effect on the other rather than only one being a cause and the other an effect). More importantly, like cross-sectional correlational designs, longitudinal designs still fail to control for other variables that may have caused both of the variables that were measured. For example, maternal depression is related to a wide range of behavior problems in children whose mothers are depressed (Gotlib & Goodman, 1999). However, depressive symptoms in a mother and behavior problems in her children may both be affected by other factors, including high levels of marital conflict within the family or economic hardship (Goodman & Gotlib, 1999). Only experimental designs can be used to determine causal relations among variables.

Experimental research designs involve the control or manipulation of one or more variables (the independent variables) to determine their effect on a second variable or set of variables (the dependent variables). Because the independent variable is under the control of the researcher, it is possible to determine if changes in this factor *cause* changes to occur in the dependent variable. In addition to being able to control the independent variable, the researcher must be able to randomly expose individuals to different levels of the independent variable in order to control for any unanticipated differences in participants who are exposed to different conditions within the experiment. In laboratory experiments, different stimuli or conditions (the independent variables) are controlled or manipulated by the researcher. These studies often include different

types of participants (another independent variable), such as patients who are diagnosed with a specific type of psychopathology and a comparison group of participants who do not suffer from psychopathology. The dependent variables involve the aspects of behavior, cognition, emotion, or physiology that are of interest to the investigator.

Experimental designs are used in two primary ways in clinical psychology research. First, researchers conduct controlled experiments to study the possible causal relationship between two (or more) variables. Experimental studies of psychopathology are important to an understanding of the possible causes of psychological disorders. However, ethical concerns obviously mitigate against any research that actually causes a psychological disorder. Rather, experimental studies are conducted on analogues (representations) of psychopathology, or they are conducted with patients already suffering from a type of psychopathology to learn about factors that are relevant to an understanding of the disorder. Experimental research conducted with animals can have important implications for an understanding of psychopathology in humans, because research ethics allow for somewhat different procedures to be used with animals. For example, researchers have studied the startle probe reflex (a reflexive eye blink response to a sudden noise or physical stimulus) in animals to better understand the role of this response in vulnerability to anxiety (e.g., Falls, 1998; Hamm, Greenwald, Bradley, & Lang, 1993). Studies of the startle probe reflex in humans have produced similar findings (e.g., Lang, 1995; Larson, Sutton, & Davidson, 1998).

The second major area in which experimental designs are used in clinical psychology is in studies that are designed to evaluate the effectiveness of an intervention to prevent or treat a problem and in which participants are *randomly assigned* to a group that receives the intervention or to an alternative condition (a control group). Random assignment to groups in treatment studies makes it more likely that the groups are equivalent on all the important variables that relate to the possible effects of treatment. If the groups are identical except for their exposure or lack of exposure to the treatment, any differences between the groups after the completion of the treatment are inferred to have been caused directly by the treatment.

An example of an experimental design can be found in a study on the effectiveness of two different treatments for childhood Social Phobia (Beidel, Turner, & Morris, 2000). Children (ages 8 to 12) with Social Phobia were randomly assigned to either a behavioral treatment program that taught social skills and exposure to situations that elicit social anxiety or to a placebo treatment that did not include methods to specifically reduce Social Phobia and anxiety. Measures of anxiety, other symptoms of psychopathology, and social skills were taken before and after treatment. Figure 3.2 presents the mean scores for the children in the treatment and placebo intervention conditions on a measure of Social Phobia and anxiety before and after treatment. The researchers found a significant interaction between the type of group (the behavioral treatment versus the control group) and time (before and after treatment). The Social Phobia symptoms in the group that received the behavioral treatment decreased from pretreatment to posttreatment, while the symptoms in the placebo group did not change. Because the participants were randomly assigned to one group or the other, the changes from pretreatment to posttreatment can be attributed to the effects of the treatment; that is, in this true experiment, the effects that are observed can be attributed to the presence versus absence of the treatment.

The research literature on the effects of psychotherapy is enormous, with a long and rich history, and we present a more detailed review of the findings in chapter 15. Hundreds of studies over the past 50 years have compared many different forms of psychotherapy to no treatment, to various forms of placebo treatments that often involve attention from a counselor or therapist

Deborah C. Beidel, Ph.D., is a Professor in the Clinical Psychology program at the University of Maryland and co-director of the Maryland Center for Anxiety Disorders. Dr. Beidel's research focuses on the etiology and treatment of anxiety disorders in children and adults. Dr. Beidel also plays an active role in the American Psychological Association's accreditation of internships in clinical psychology. (Photo courtesy of Deborah Beidel.)

but do not include the aspects of treatment that are hypothesized to contribute to change, and to psychoactive medications for the treatment of many disorders (e.g., depression, anxiety, eating disorders). Through the efforts of the scores of researchers that have engaged in this challenging and important area of research, the beneficial effects of psychotherapy are now well established (e.g., DeRubeis & Crits-Christoph, 1998; Kazdin & Weisz, 1998). Continued work is needed, however, to answer more complex questions about

FIGURE 3.2

Mean anxiety scores for behavioral treatment group and control group before and after treatment (from Biedel, Turner, & Morris, 2000).

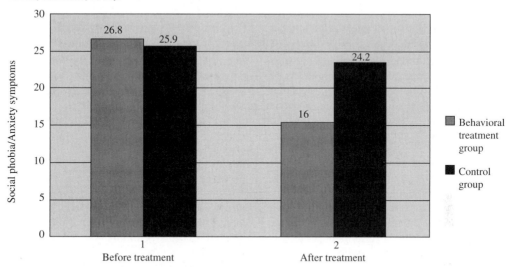

how various therapies help and why some individuals respond more favorably to treatment than other individuals do. Important questions to be addressed include: What components of a treatment are necessary and sufficient to produce change? Which treatment is more or most effective for a particular population? What processes occur during treatment that may contribute to treatment outcome? We return to these issues in Chapter 15.

Which design is best? There is sentiment among some researchers that experimental research designs are superior to descriptive or correlational approaches because only experimental designs can be used to determine true causal relationships. This view is a misrepresentation of the broad scope of the research process, however, because each type of research design is useful for addressing some questions and hypotheses and not others. Clinical psychologists are often interested in observing things as they occur in the natural environment, and descriptive and correlational designs are best suited for this purpose. In other instances, clinical psychologists are interested in determining cause-

and-effect relations among variables or in determining the effects of a specific form of treatment, goals that are addressed only with experimental designs. Furthermore, ethical constraints often limit the types of research designs that can be used. Researchers cannot ethically cause significant distress or psychopathology to occur in participants in human research. The first priority of any researcher is the welfare of the individuals who participate in the research, and any risks that are involved must be within reasonable limits and must be justified by the potential benefits of the research (see box 3.2). As a result, much of the research on the causes and course of psychopathology must rely on descriptive and correlational designs combined with analogue or animal research that uses experimental designs to test similar hypotheses.

Selecting a Sample

Who should participate in a study once it has been designed? Selection and recruitment of a sample is important to the ultimate generalizability (external validity) of the research findings. If

BOX 3.2

RESEARCH ETHICS

All research, whether with humans or animals, is guided by principles that protect the welfare of the participants. Three principles are paramount in research with human participants. First, all participants must be fully informed about the nature of the research in advance, and they must be capable of freely providing their consent to participate. Second, to the extent that there are any risks involved in the research, the potential benefits of the study must outweigh the possible risks to the participants. Third, the privacy and confidentiality of the participants must be protected.

Informed consent is the first step in all human research. Researchers achieve informed consent by providing potential participants with a written description of the study that describes the goals of the study, the procedures that will be used, any potential risks, possible benefits, and their rights as participants in research. Investigators are required to provide all participants a summary of these aspects of the research in nontechnical (lay) language and the opportunity to ask any questions that they may have about the study. Participants then provide written agreement to enroll in the research by signing the consent form. Participants under the age of 18 years old are presumed to be unable to provide true informed consent, because they may not be able to understand the nature of the research or the conditions of consent. Consent from a parent or guardian is required along with assent by the young person.

Researchers must carefully consider the possible risks that a subject may encounter in the study. One risk in clinical psychological research is the mild degree of emotional distress that may be experienced by participants when they respond to questions in an interview or on a questionnaire that are related to troubling experiences in their lives or to troubling aspects of themselves or their relationships. Researchers must ensure that participants are aware of any such risks in advance, that they are free to withdraw from the study if they feel too distressed, and that some form of follow-up support or counseling is provided should it be necessary. In many instances, participants do not directly benefit from their involvement in the study; however, their participation may lead to benefits for others based on the findings of the study.

All participants in research have the right to have their identity protected. All information obtained in the context of research must be protected. Therefore, all research records are typically kept without any information that could be used to identify the participants, and all materials are kept safely locked and secure at the research site.

Research protocol and ethics are overseen at universities and colleges by institutional review boards (IRBs) whose job it is to review all research protocols before they are enacted to ensure that all of the criteria mentioned here have been met. Investigators are required to submit annual reports to their IRB regarding the progress on a study until it is terminated, and researchers are required to report any ethical problems encountered in their research to the IRB for review.

the sample is not a **representative sample** of the larger population from which it is drawn, the results of the study may be biased or influenced by the characteristics of the sample. For example, a sample may differ from the general population in terms of demographic characteristics, such as sex, age, education level, income, and ethnic or racial background. These characteristics may influence the findings of the study, because the results may differ as a function of one or more of these characteristics. Although the results are certainly reflective of other groups who are similar to the sample in the study, it would be incorrect to generalize the findings to the population as a whole. In research with clinical samples, it is additionally important to determine the extent to which the sample is representative of the clinical population to which the results are to be generalized. This representativeness includes the diagnosis or problem, whether the sample is intended to represent individuals receiving hospital versus outpatient care, and the severity and duration of the problem.

Selecting a representative sample is important in many types of research, including epidemiological research and treatment studies. For example, if the rate of alcohol abuse is influenced by factors such as age, income, and education level, then estimates of the frequency of this problem in the population could be dramatically affected if a sample was biased on one or more of these factors (McCrady & Epstein, 1999). Similarly, if the effectiveness of a particular treatment is evaluated with a sample that is biased with regard to age or sex or socioeconomic status, the effects that are observed for the sample may not hold true for subgroups with the broader population.

One egregious error in psychological research has been the consistent underrepresentation of large segments of the population, most notably ethnic minorities and the poor. Much or most research in clinical psychology has been limited to participation by Caucasian, primarily middle and upper social class individuals (Belar, 1998; Sue, Kuraski, & Srinivasan, 1999). This error has been due to a variety of factors but has made it difficult to extend the findings of much psychological research to those populations who are in greatest need. Efforts to include more ethnic minorities and more poor individuals in clinical psychological research are a high priority.

The generalizability of research findings is affected by the context in which the research is conducted as much as by the sample that participates in the research. For example, if a researcher is interested in the effectiveness of a particular form of psychotherapy, the initial studies of its effects are likely to be conducted in a university-based clinic and the therapy is most likely carried out by doctoral students or practicing psychologists who have received special training in conducting this particular form of therapy. This type

of study is essential in a determination as to whether the therapy can work. The investigator is certainly interested, however, in generalizing the findings of this research, conducted in the laboratory, to the use of this form of psychotherapy in community settings and as practiced by psychologists or trained therapists who are not directly affiliated with the university where the technique is being developed and tested. Even though the populations who receive treatment in the two settings may be similar in some respects, the differences in these two types of settings have been found to affect the outcome of the therapy. For example, John Weisz of the University of California, Los Angeles has shown that therapies for children and adolescents produce statistically significant and large effects in university-based studies but only small or nonsignificant effects when they are studied in community settings (e.g., Weisz et al., 1993).

Testing Hypotheses

Once a study has been completed and the data are in hand, psychologists rely on the use of *inferential statistics* to evaluate the degree to which the null hypothesis has been rejected. The specific type of statistical procedure that is used depends on the research design that was employed. Correlation or multiple regression analyses are used to test hypotheses in correlational research. Correlation and regression coefficients reflect the degree and direction of association between variables. In contrast, analysis of variance (ANOVA) and related statistics are typically used to test hypotheses in experimental research. The results of an ANOVA (reflected in the F statistic) indicate the reliability and magnitude of the difference between groups or within a group either across time or under different conditions.

A first step in evaluating the findings of a study is to determine how likely it is that these results could have occurred by chance. This test is referred to as the **statistical significance** of the findings—the probability that the pattern of data that was observed did not occur by chance. Psychology as a field has established a specific criterion of acceptable certainty that findings are not a chance occurrence. Psychologists will accept findings that are likely to have occurred by chance no more than 5 out of 100 times. This statistic is represented by the notation "$p < .05$," indicating that the probability that the observed finding occurred by chance is less than 5 in 100. The statistical significance of a finding represents its reliability or trustworthiness. It gives investigators an indication of the likelihood that the same outcome would be found again if the study were replicated.

A statistically significant finding is "significant" only in that it is not due to chance—an important piece of information to be sure, but not the only thing researchers need to know. Statistical significance establishes that a finding is reliable but does not indicate whether the finding is meaningful (J. Cohen, 1994). Statistical significance is influenced by two factors: the magnitude or size of the finding and the size of the sample. For example, a correlation of $r = .40$ will be statistically significant at the .05 level with a sample larger than 50, but it will not reach significance with a smaller sample. Conversely, a correlation of greater magnitude ($r = .75$) will achieve statistical significance with a sample of less than 50. As the size of the sample increases, the size of the coefficient (in correlation analyses) or the size of the difference between groups (in an analysis of variance) that is required to reach statistical significance becomes smaller (J. Cohen, 1992).

The meaning of the finding can be better expressed by the magnitude or size of the effect—the **effect size.** The effect size is an index of the degree of association between two variables or the magnitude of the difference between groups, given that the effect has achieved the traditional criterion for statistical significance. Rules of thumb have been developed to distinguish effects that are small, medium, and large for psychological research (J. Cohen, 1988). For example,

correlation coefficients that achieve statistical significance and range from $r = .10$ to .25 are considered small effects; $r = .25$ to .37 are considered medium effects; and correlations that are greater than $r = .37$ are considered large effects.

A third important step in examining a hypothesis is to determine if the findings of a study are clinically meaningful. The **clinical significance** of a finding depends on more than the statistical significance or reliability of the finding—it also depends on the size or magnitude of the effect in relation to criteria that are used to establish what constitutes psychopathology (Jacobson & Truax, 1991). Is the effect sufficiently large that it reflects a meaningful difference in the well-being or functioning of the individuals involved? Let's look, for example, at a study in which a researcher recruited 200 clinically depressed individuals and randomly assigned them to receive a form of psychotherapy or to be placed on a waiting list for a specified period of time. As one of the measures of symptoms of depression, the researcher used the Beck Depression Inventory (BDI; A. T. Beck, Steer, & Gorbin, 1988), a self-report questionnaire that is widely used to measure depressive symptoms. Previous research has found that nondepressed samples receive an average score of 5 on the BDI and that clinically depressed individuals typically score greater than 20. The mean scores for the treatment and control groups in this study were 28 and 29 before treatment was administered and 21 and 29 after treatment. This finding indicates that the treatment group's score on the BDI went down 7 points as a result of psychotherapy while the control group's score did not change. The researcher analyzes these data and finds that this result is a statistically significant difference—the groups did not differ on the BDI before treatment, but after treatment the treated group (mean score = 21) scored significantly lower than did the control group (mean score = 29). Closer scrutiny of these findings indicates, however, that the mean for the treated group is still above the score that reflects high depressive symptoms.

Even though the decline in the participants' depression was *statistically* significant, it does not reflect a *clinically* meaningful change, because the majority of the treated group is still highly depressed after receiving psychotherapy. This example illustrates the need to look beyond the statistical significance of the findings to understand the statistics' meaning for the people and problems that are the focus of clinical research.

Interpreting and Disseminating Findings

The final step in the research process is to place the meaning or implications of a study in a broader context. What are the ramifications of the findings for understanding the nature, causes, and course of psychological problems? What are the implications for the prevention or treatment of psychopathology? What do the results mean for establishing public policy related to mental health?

A first step in the process of sharing the results of research is to submit them to review for publication in peer-reviewed professional journals. Articles that are published in peer-reviewed scientific journals have been evaluated by other researchers and experts in the field prior to publication. The review process ensures that the work that is published meets certain accepted criteria for scientific quality. Of course, research journals differ dramatically in the degree of rigor that is required for a paper to be accepted for publication. The most rigorous journals in clinical psychology (e.g., *Journal of Consulting and Clinical Psychology, Journal of Abnormal Psychology, Behavior Therapy*) accept 20 percent or fewer of the papers that are submitted and reviewed. Other journals apply less rigorous standards and accept larger proportions of the papers that are reviewed. Therefore, although the review process as a whole provides some assurance that a published paper has been subjected to certain criteria, some journals are much more stringent than others in applying these criteria. Peer-reviewed journals are important in that they

shape and influence the scientific basis of clinical psychology.

The findings of clinical research are not designed solely for advancing the science of clinical psychology, however. Clinical research is also designed to improve the conditions of people with psychological problems. Therefore, researchers have an obligation to translate their findings into information that can be used for the general good. Research results should be communicated to the public, to practicing psychologists, and to officials who formulate mental health policies and allocate money for mental health programs. The final resting place for research results should not be in a scientific journal—publication should be only one of several outlets for communicating the findings of research in clinical psychology. It is imperative that clinical psychologists take great care in how the findings of their research are shared with the public. Practicing psychologists and their clients as well as policy makers are hungry for information that will help them understand the nature, causes, and treatment of psychological problems. Eagerness to find solutions for these problems often leads some audiences to be less critical of the results of research. Furthermore, many of the interested audiences are not trained in research methods and statistics, which leaves them at the mercy of researchers in interpreting the meaning and significance of their work. Therefore, researchers have an obligation to be highly self-critical and to stringently test their hypotheses to ensure the public that they have been confirmed beyond reasonable doubt.

An important task for any field is the integration and synthesis of the results of many separate studies on a common topic. The challenge of such an integration is to identify the consistencies that have emerged in the findings. One approach has been to review and describe or count the findings and the degree to which they converge. For example, a researcher might review studies of psychotherapy for the treatment of a specific disorder and count how many studies have reported beneficial effects and how many have not. However, this approach does not take into account several important factors, including the quality of the studies, the size of the samples, and the size of the effects that were found. A quantitative approach to reviewing findings, called **meta-analysis,** allows researchers to derive a numerical index, the overall **effect size,** that synthesizes the findings of multiple studies. An effect size is a quantitative index of a particular type of statistical test that reflects the aggregation of findings across multiple studies. Meta-analyses of research on the effects of psychotherapy have played an important role in helping the field evaluate the degree to which psychotherapy is effective in treating psychopathology (e.g., Smith & Glass, 1977; Weisz, Weiss, Han, & Granger, 1995) and the degree to which certain treatments are effective for specific disorders (e.g., Abramowitz, 1997; Thase et al., 1997).

Obtaining Support for Research

Conducting research is expensive. Before undertaking a study, researchers often need to obtain financial support for costs that are incurred in carrying out their work. Costs that are associated with any research study include the salaries for the research staff, equipment and materials needed to carry out the study, and compensation for participants. Large-scale studies can cost millions of dollars to conduct. Therefore, researchers are faced with the task of seeking and obtaining funding for their work. The two primary sources for research support are government agencies (e.g., the National Institutes of Health [NIH]; the National Science Foundation [NSF]), and private foundations that are devoted to providing funds for research (e.g., the John D. and Catherine T. MacArthur Foundation; the William T. Grant Foundation). One of the major sources of funding for research in clinical psychology is the National Institute of Mental Health (NIMH), a branch of the NIH. NIMH

funds research on basic behavioral, emotional, cognitive, and biological processes related to psychopathology; epidemiological research; prevention research; and studies examining the effects of psychological and pharmacological treatments of psychopathology. Clinical psychological research is also supported by other NIH agencies to the extent that their research is related to the populations that are served by these agencies (e.g., National Institute of Drug Abuse; National Cancer Institute; National Institute of Child Health and Human Development).

Given the high cost of most research, it is not surprising that competition for research funding is intense. Only a modest proportion of grants submitted to NIH are awarded funding. The exact percentage of submitted proposals that are approved to receive funding varies from year to year, but is most often less than 20 percent. Applications for funding are reviewed by committees composed of other researchers who are experts in their field, who rank the applications for eligibility for funding.

PANIC DISORDER: AN EXAMPLE OF RESEARCH IN CLINICAL PSYCHOLOGY

We now return to Janis, our case example of Panic Disorder (PD) that we introduced in the opening pages of this chapter. As you will recall, she presented at the ER complaining of chest pain, an extremely rapid heart rate, shaking, sweating, and shortness of breath to the point that she felt she was going to suffocate. Janis had experienced a Panic Attack, as defined in the DSM-IV. Furthermore, because she had experienced four episodes of this type during the previous two months, she meets the DSM-IV criteria for PD (the symptoms of a Panic Attack are presented in table 3.2). A Panic Attack is a terrifying experience, so frightening it can lead to overwhelming fear and anxiety of experiencing another attack. Janis has now developed significant anxiety that she will have another attack and

TABLE 3.2
DSM-IV Criteria
for Panic Attack and Panic Disorder

Panic Disorder is marked by recurrent, spontaneous Panic Attacks. During the attack, a person may experience the following symptoms:

Noticeably quick or pounding heart rate
Pain or other discomfort in the chest
Sweating
Shaking
Difficulty breathing, shortness of breath
Dizziness
Tingling sensations
Fear of going crazy or losing control
Fear of dying
Derealization or depersonalization
Choking sensation
Nausea
Cold or hot flashes

To be diagnosed as a Panic Attack, four or more symptoms should be present. Those who experience Panic Attacks usually describe them as occurring "out of the blue." One Panic Attack does not result in a diagnosis of Panic Disorder. To become Panic Disorder, the initial Panic Attack will be followed by one month (or more) of one (or more) of the following:

Constant worry about having another Panic Attack
Constant worry about the cause of the attack (i.e., heart attack)
Major behavioral change related to the Panic Attack

Epidemiological Research on Panic Disorder

PD was one of the diagnoses that was included in the National Comorbidity Study (NCS) that we discussed in chapter 1 (Kessler et al., 1998). Recall that the NCS involved psychiatric diagnostic interviews administered to over 8,000 adults in the United States (aged 15 to 54 years old) to establish the current and lifetime prevalence of DSM disorders (at the time of the study, the DSM-III-R was used). The lifetime rate for PD was found to be 3.4 percent, and approximately 15 percent of the respondents had experienced a Panic Attack in their life. Approximately 3 percent of the sample had experienced a Panic Attack in the prior month, and approximately 1 percent met criteria for PD in the previous month. About half of the individuals with a lifetime history of Panic Attack and PD also met lifetime criteria for a history of major depression. Women were more than twice as likely as men to experience Panic Attacks and PD. Such epidemological data have helped to establish estimates of the prevalence of psychopathology and helped determine the types of services that need to be available for the treatment of problems. The findings from the NCS suggest that PD has a relatively high prevalence and that the high proportion of women relative to men indicates that Janis's case may be relatively typical.

has begun to restrict her activities in response to this fear.

What is known about PD? How prevalent is it? What are possible causes of PD? Can it be treated? Fortunately for Janis, there is now extensive psychological research that has addressed all these issues. In this way, research on PD provides excellent examples of each of the types of research reviewed in this chapter. Furthermore, this research exemplifies systematic, programmatic research on a topic that helps clinicians understand its nature, causes, course, and treatment.

Correlational Research on Panic Disorder

Many studies have examined the correlates of PD, and a number of findings are relevant to understanding Janis's problems. First, the likelihood of developing PD is significantly greater if other members of the family have a history of anxiety disorders, especially if family members specifically have PD. Several studies have found that, compared with individuals who do not have a psychiatric disorder, individuals who suffer from PD have a greater likelihood of having first-degree relatives (parents, siblings) who suffer from anxiety disorders (Goldstein et al., 1994; Goldstein, Wickramaratne, Horwath, & Weissman, 1997). Thus, Janis's recollection of her mother's problems with anxiety suggests that she may have a positive family history for anxiety disorder.

Second, several studies have shown that "anxiety sensitivity" is a risk factor for the development of PD. Anxiety sensitivity refers to the tendency to believe that emotional and physical arousal signify something potentially harmful. One specific type of anxiety sensitivity involves fears of some physical sensations, including the fear that rapid heartbeat and shortness of breath are indications that something is physically wrong. Two large longitudinal studies, one with adolescents (Hayward, Killen, Kraemer, & Taylor, 2000) and one with young adults (Schmidt, Lerew, & Jackson, 1999), found that high levels of anxiety sensitivity predicted later Panic Attacks and the development of PD. These findings may be relevant to understanding Janis's case, because she appears to become extremely frightened when she experiences an increased heart rate and shortness of breath.

A third line of important correlational research has found that cigarette smoking is also a risk factor for later onset of PD. For example, Breslau and Klein (1999) examined the association between smoking and later PD in two large epidemiological samples of over 4,000 individuals. The researchers found that smoking predicted an increased risk for PD and that the risk was even higher for those who were currently smoking as compared with those who had quit smoking. In contrast, a diagnosis of PD did not predict later smoking, suggesting that smoking increases the risk for PD, but PD does not lead to increased smoking. A similar recent study of adolescents by P. Cohen et al. (2000) provides further evidence on the association between cigarette smoking and anxiety disorders in adolescence and young adulthood. Janis's cigarette smoking may have contributed to her increased risk for panic attacks and the development of PD.

Experimental Research on Panic Disorder

As we noted in this chapter, experimental research on psychopathology is difficult to conduct because it is, of course, unethical to experimentally create a psychological disorder. However, if proper safeguards are taken, researchers can create analogues, or imitations, of experiences that are related to psychopathology. One line of research related to PD is exemplary in this regard. It is hypothesized that individuals who suffer from PD are extremely sensitive to what are called interoceptive cues—internal sensations, especially physical sensations. Given the heightened level of anxiety sensitivity in people with PD, these individuals may be especially prone to misinterpret even small increases in heart rate and minor difficulties in breathing as indications of a physical problem. To investigate this possibility, researchers have devised a method in which participants use a mask to breathe air that has about a 5 percent level of carbon dioxide (CO_2), slightly higher than normal. The presentation of CO_2-enriched air mimics the feelings of shortness of breath and suffocation that are a central symptom of panic attacks.

In a series of studies, patients with PD have been found to be hypersensitive to breathing the CO_2-enriched air and react to it with significantly higher levels of anxiety than do individuals without PD. Klein (1993) has labeled this heightened sensitivity an increased suffocation alarm. That is, all human beings become somewhat distressed by the feeling of being suffocated, but individuals who are prone to PD have an extraordinarily heightened level of this alarm. J. G. Beck, Ohtake, and Shipherd (1999) found that PD patients responded with heightened levels of anxiety and a more rapid rate of breathing when they were presented with air that was either higher than normal in CO_2, or lower than normal in oxygen. In an interesting extension of this research, van Beek and Griez (2000) found that first-degree relatives of PD patients also were more reactive to a CO_2 challenge than were control subjects (see also Zvolensky, Eifert, Lejuez, & McNiel, 1999). These studies provide carefully controlled evidence that individuals with PD respond with more anxiety than do non-PD individuals to identical physical sensations. This finding is consistent with the hypothesis that Panic Attacks are caused by the misinterpretation of interoceptive cues. Janis appears to display this heightened sensitivity to her heart rate and her respiration.

Treatment of Panic Disorder

It is fortunate for Janis that in addition to excellent research on the nature and correlates of PD, there has been outstanding research in methods for the treatment of PD. In fact, studies on the treatment of PD provide some of the best evidence available on psychological methods for the treatment of psychopathology. Two treatments are well established as effective in the treatment of PD: cognitive therapy as developed by psychologist David Clark and his colleagues at Oxford University, and panic control therapy (a more behavioral treatment) developed by psychologist David Barlow of Boston University. When we say that the effectiveness of these treatments is well established, we mean that the treatments have been shown to be more effective than control comparisons in randomized controlled studies. Furthermore, the beneficial effects of both these treatments have been replicated in more than one study conducted by independent investigators in different research settings. Thus, these studies have shown statistically significant differences in PD as a result of treatment by either cognitive or behavioral therapy (see Barlow, Esler, & Vatali, 1998, for a review on studies of the treatment of PD). Researchers have not stopped at demonstrating that these treatments can produce statistically significant effects, however. Research has also shown that these results are clinically significant, because typically more than 75 percent of those people who are treated are free of symptoms of PD after

the completion of treatment, and they remain symptom free at follow-up assessments months later (Barlow et al.).

Further research has shown that the effects of cognitive and behavioral treatments are not limited to the special conditions under which some research studies are carried out. Similar to most research on the effects of psychotherapy, the majority of the original studies on the treatment of PD were carried out by researchers at universities and medical schools by specially trained therapists under carefully controlled conditions. More recently, comparable effects have been obtained under conditions in which the treatments are delivered in community clinics by practicing psychologists. For example, Stuart, Treat, and Wade (2000) found that 89 percent of patients treated with cognitive-behavioral therapy in a community health center were free of panic symptoms at follow-up.

A more complete understanding of any psychological treatment can be obtained by examining which aspects of the treatment are responsible for producing beneficial effects, and which elements, if any, appear to be unnecessary. Research of this type has been conducted on treatments for PD. For example, Schmidt et al. (2000) examined the importance of a specific treatment component, breathing retraining, as a component of behavior therapy for PD. By randomly assigning PD patients to behavior therapy with and without breathing retraining, they found that it was not a necessary element of treatment. The researchers note that this finding is important because although breathing retraining appears to be an attractive component of treatment, these results suggest it should not be included as part of behavior therapy. Conversely, Schmidt and Woolaway-Bickel (2000) found significance in the quality of home-based practice in cognitive-behavioral therapy for PD. Homework involved the practicing of skills and exposure methods (e.g., patients with cardiac fears were assigned to complete aerobic exercises; patients with hypersensitivity to dyspnea cues were assigned to repeatedly hyperventilate). Therapists' ratings of patient compliance with homework assignments significantly predicted positive changes on most outcome measures. Thus, patients should be encouraged to complete home-based practice, an important element of effective treatment.

Finally, researchers need to establish that a treatment is as or more effective than alternative forms of treatment. In the treatment of PD, several medications have been found to be effective forms of treatment (e.g., imipramine, alprazolam). Therefore, the comparison of psychological and pharmacological treatments is important. Several studies have shown that cognitive and behavioral treatments are at least as effective as medication in the treatment of PD, and some research has suggested that other benefits may favor the use of psychological treatments over medication. Barlow, Gorman, Shear, and Woods (2000), in a paper published in the prestigious *Journal of the American Medical Association,* compared cognitive-behavioral therapy, imipramine, and the combination of the two treatments in a randomized, place-controlled trial. Both treatments were superior to a placebo treatment, and the findings suggest that cognitive-behavioral therapy was more durable and was better tolerated by the patients.

These findings provide strong evidence that there are highly effective treatments to help Janis overcome her PD. Through either cognitive therapy or panic-control therapy, it is likely that Janis can be free of panic attacks in several months and that she is likely to remain symptom free long after the completion of treatment. In this way, careful psychological research has provided clear evidence to guide the understanding and treatment of a person in significant need of help.

SUMMARY AND CONCLUSIONS

The foundation of clinical psychology lies in the research that has been generated on the nature and causes of psychopathology, the development of measures of personality and behavior, and the evaluation of the effects of psychotherapy and other forms of intervention to relieve or prevent psychological distress. The research process follows a series of steps that include the generation of hypotheses, the choice of measures, the selection of a research design, the identification of a sample, the testing of the hypothesis, and the interpretation and dissemination of findings. Clinical psychologists use several different types of research designs, including single-case designs, descriptive methods, correlational designs, and experimental methods. Using both correlational and experimental methods to conduct studies in the laboratory and in the natural environment, clinical psychologists have made significant contributions to the scientific study of human behavior.

KEY TERMS AND NAMES

Clinical significance
Concurrent validity
Construct validity
Convergent validity
Correlation
Correlational research designs
Descriptive research designs
Discriminate validity
Effect size
Experimental research designs
Hypothesis
Internal consistency reliability

Inter-rater reliability
Meta-analysis
Multiple baseline design
Multiple correlation
Multiple regression
Null hypothesis
Predictive validity
Representative sample
Single-case design
Statistical significance
Test-retest reliability
Type I error

RESOURCES

Books

Barlow, D. H., & Hersen, M. (1984). *Single-case experimental designs: Strategies for studying behavior change* (2nd ed.). Elmsford, NY: Pergamon.

Hayes, S. C., Barlow, D. H., & Nelson-Gray, R. O. (1999). *The scientist-practitioner: Research and accountability in the age of managed care* (2nd ed.). Boston: Allyn & Bacon.

Holmbeck, G. N., Kendall, P. C., & Butcher, J. N. (Eds.). (1999). *Handbook of research methods in clinical psychology* (2nd ed.). New York: John Wiley.

Kazdin, A. E. (1998). *Research design in clinical psychology* (3rd ed.). Boston: Allyn & Bacon.

Journals

Journal of Consulting and Clinical Psychology
Journal of Abnormal Psychology
Archives of General Psychiatry
Journal of Clinical Child Psychology

CHAPTER FOUR

MODELS OF DEVELOPMENT, BEHAVIOR, AND PERSONALITY

INTRODUCTION

On the morning of April 20, 1999, two students walked into Columbine High School in Littleton, Colorado. By noon, in the deadliest high school shooting in U.S. history, Eric Harris, age 18, and Dylan Klebold, age 17, had killed 12 students and one teacher, wounded 23 others, and then took their own lives. They were armed with two sawed-off shotguns, a 9 mm semiautomatic rifle,

a semiautomatic handgun, and dozens of home-made bombs. Five days later, over 70,000 people attended a memorial service for the victims of the shooting. Parents of one of the slain children filed a $250-million, wrongful-death lawsuit against Eric Harris's and Dylan Klebold's parents. Harris's and Klebold's parents wrote and sent letters of remorse to the victims' families and said that they had no idea their sons were capable of killing.

In the year following the shooting, the Columbine teacher who had made a frantic 911 call from the school library on April 20 took a leave of absence; another 17-year-old Columbine student was arrested on suspicion of threatening to "finish the job" started by Eric Harris and Dylan Klebold; a Florida teenager used the Internet to threaten a Columbine student and was quickly arrested; the mother of a student who was paralyzed in the shooting entered a pawnshop, asked to look at a handgun, and used the gun to kill herself; and in the first of many copycat threats and school shootings, six students were injured in a mass shooting in a high school in Atlanta.

How are we to understand these particular events and the development and causes of violent, antisocial behavior more generally? Rates of violence among children, teens, and adults continue to rise alarmingly both in the United States and worldwide (Chappell & DiMartino, 2000). Understanding the causes of violence is essential to the development of interventions to prevent and treat such problems, and clinical psychologists play a central role in both these tasks. There are many possible explanations for violent, aggressive behavior. One perspective maintains that aggression is an inherent part of human nature, a part of all of our personalities, that needs to be controlled through socialization (e.g., Altemeyer, 1996). Another view holds that extreme aggression reflects an underlying biological deficit or disorder that is present in the genetic endowment or neurological structure of only a small number of individuals who are qualitatively distinct from other people (e.g., DiLalla & Gottesman, 1991). Yet another perspective contends that violence and aggression are the result of learning and environmental conditions that shape our ability to regulate emotions and behavior (e.g., Bandura, 1997; Widom, 2000). It is important to realize that the way in which psychologists view the causes and development of violence and aggression will have profound im-

plications for the choices they will make in trying to prevent and treat such behavior.

In the specific case of aggression and violence, clinical psychologists must develop or adopt a theory or conceptual model to explain more broadly why and how various forms of psychopathology occur. The model that they use will determine how they assess and treat different forms of abnormal behavior as well as whom they may identify as being at high risk for developing psychopathology. There is no shortage of theories and models of human behavior to explain the causes of abnormal behavior. In fact, for new students of clinical psychology, one of the most challenging and perplexing aspects of this field is the frustratingly large number of theories from which to choose. Nevertheless, it is critical to know the major theories of behavior and psychopathology and to understand the strengths and weaknesses of each theory.

In this chapter we will describe the major theoretical models in clinical psychology and encourage you to think critically about them. Before we do that, though, we will discuss briefly why a theory is necessary to a clinical psychologist. We offer a number of criteria for selecting a conceptual model on which to base one's work and will then discuss three of the most widely used conceptual models in clinical psychology: the psychodynamic, behavioral/cognitive, and humanistic models. We will also discuss, albeit more briefly, recent biological models of psychopathology that are being integrated into current psychological theories. These models will help you understand the approaches to clinical assessment and therapy that we present in later chapters.

PURPOSE OF A THEORY

Whether considering the behavior or problems of a single individual or of groups of people more generally, clinical psychologists are confronted with a dizzying array of information. Should clinicians be more concerned with overt, observable behavior; or with thoughts or emotions that individuals experience internally and report verbally; or perhaps with physiological and other biological processes that are occurring within the person? Should clinical psychologists consider the situations and contexts in which the person is functioning? Because we all (including clinical psychologists) would be overwhelmed if we had to process *all* the information about people that is available to us at any given moment, we tend to focus selectively on certain types of information. The specific theory, or conceptual framework, held by a clinical psychologist determines what information she or he will attend to and what information will be ignored.

Thus, an essential role for theory in clinical psychology is to organize and structure the way psychologists think about people and their problems. A theory functions like a road map to assist psychologists in trying to plot their course for dealing with individuals and their psychological problems. Clinical psychologists will be more efficient in treating patients' emotional difficulties with the aid of a theory or conceptual model than would be the case if treatment were based on trial and error with every patient. And even if a treatment is effective, the absence of a theory increases the possibility that the treatment might not be replicated in the future with another patient who presents a similar problem. In fact, the application of theory has led to the development of "road maps" for clinical psychologists in the form of carefully detailed manuals for many forms of psychological treatment that are based on well-articulated theoretical models of specific psychological problems (e.g., Greenberger & Padesky, 1995; Lamm, Jones, Hayward, & Bright, 1999; Mufson, Moreau, Weissman, & Klerman, 1993; Wells, 1997).

CRITICAL THINKING ABOUT THEORY

An adequate theory for use in clinical psychology should meet six basic criteria: (a) It should offer the most *parsimonious* explanation of the problem in question; (b) its central principles should be *logical and internally consistent;*

(c) the theory should offer *clear, testable hypotheses;* (d) it should be *supported by empirical research;* (e) it should be capable of explaining *diverse problems* in people of *diverse backgrounds;* and (f) it should be capable of *changing and developing* in response to new input and information. The essential tasks for any theory are to account for the facts that are known and to predict new facts yet to be found.

Parsimony

The law of **parsimony** that guides all scientific theory states that the best explanation of any phenomenon is always the simplest explanation. That is, the best theory to explain any problem or set of observations will include only those elements and propositions that are both *necessary and sufficient* to account for what has been observed—any other elements in a theory are superfluous. The need for parsimony is balanced, of course, by the concern that the theory should not be too simple to adequately explain the phenomenon. Thus, a good theory must embody the critical features of the phenomenon while leaving out the trivial or unnecessary details (Judson, 1980). As we will point out in this chapter, searching for the optimal balance between parsimony (simple but complete) and reductionism (overly simplistic) is a challenge for theories of human behavior. For example, psychodynamically oriented clinical psychologists contend that behavioral theories of psychopathology are reductionistic—they are too simplistic and ignore important internal determinants of behavior. On the other hand, behaviorists argue that psychodynamic theories are not parsimonious—they are unnecessarily complex and contain speculations about unobservable aspects of human nature that are not relevant in understanding human behavior.

Logic and Internal Consistency

A sound theory must possess **internal consistency;** that is, it must be consistent within itself.

Furthermore, one proposition must lead to the next in a cumulative fashion, with each element building logically on those that came before it. It is critical, of course, that the elements of the theory do not contradict each other. At the core of all psychological theories are fundamental assumptions about human nature. For example, theories differ in their assumptions about what newborns bring with them into the world. Some theories posit that infants are "blank slates" upon which experience will write and create personality and character (see Berney, 1998; Ouellet, 1976). In contrast, other theories assume that people bring inherently positive or negative characteristics into the world, typically described in terms of needs or drives that hold the potential for good or evil (Freud, 1923; Maslow, 1971; Rogers, 1961). All other elements of a theory build on these basic assumptions. It should be apparent, therefore, that it is impossible to simply pick and choose elements from different psychological theories without generating a host of inconsistencies and contradictions. For example, one cannot theorize that all of human behavior is developed through experience with the environment, a basic principle in some behavioral theories, at the same time that one calls into play innate drives and needs as explanations for behavior, such as those postulated by Freud, Maslow, and Rogers.

Testability

A theory should generate hypotheses that can be subjected to testing. From the perspective of philosophy of science, a theory should generate a set of propositions that are falsifiable, that is, that are capable of being disproved. Testability of a theory is related to its logic and internal consistency—theories that are not internally consistent may not be easily tested, because the essential elements cannot be formulated in ways that allow them to be evaluated. To be testable, the central elements of a theory must be capable of being operationalized and measured. Testability is eas-

iest if the elements can be measured through direct observation by an external observer, rather than measured indirectly through an individual who provides information to which only he or she has access. An important task for clinical psychologists, therefore, is to develop ways of measuring internal psychological experiences that allow objective tests of specific theories. This challenge is not unique to psychology, of course, because other sciences, including physics and astronomy, must also deal with elements of theory that cannot easily be observed. Importantly, as you will see throughout this book, psychology is making great strides in being able to measure reliably aspects of human functioning that were previously inaccessible to objective measurement, and these gains are permitting empirical tests of theories that were not possible when the theories were originally formulated.

Support Through Empirical Research

A theory must be tested in empirical research. As elegant, elaborate, and fascinating as a theory may be, it will be of little use to clinical psychologists until it has been put to the test of accounting for the thoughts, emotions, and behaviors of real people, especially of people experiencing psychological problems. Ultimately, a theory is only as strong as the evidence that has been garnered in its support. Unfortunately, it is not always clear what constitutes acceptable data or evidence in support of a theory. For example, in the 1920s John Watson's challenge of the validity of introspection and self-report as acceptable evidence in the study of human behavior represented a turning point in the development of psychological theory. In the years following this challenge, behavioral theories were tested only with data that could be corroborated through direct observation (cf. Skinner, 1953). Another turning point, frequently referred to as the cognitive revolution, occurred when mental events and covert cognitive processes were once again regarded as acceptable data for the testing of cognitive theories (e.g., Dember, 1974; Mahoney, 1974), a perspective that gave rise to new and innovative research paradigms in cognitive psychology. As a general principle, theory should be supported by strong scientific investigation.

Application to Diverse Problems and Diverse People

Clinical psychologists deal with people of widely divergent backgrounds who present with a diverse range of problems. As this society continues to grow into a more diverse and pluralistic society, there will increasingly be large differences in the ages and cultural backgrounds of individuals who come for assessment and treatment. Thus, a theory that is useful to clinical psychologists cannot be limited in its scope to only some categories of people and their difficulties. A theory must be sensitive to these differences if it is to be helpful to clinical psychologists who work with diverse populations. The ability of a theory to account for diversity is a function both of the way in which the theory was constructed and of the types of research that are conducted to test it. Thus, a strong theory should not be bound by the constraints of the time and the culture in which it was developed. Similarly, diversity should also characterize the people who are included in research studies designed to test the theory. Most grand theories of psychology are concerned with the search for fundamental laws or truths about human nature; unfortunately, much of the research conducted to test these theories is sorely lacking in diversity, a point made salient in Robert Guthrie's (1998) book *Even the Rat Was White.*

Change and Growth Capability

The relation between theory and empirical data is a two-way street, each influencing the other. Judson (1980) reports a conversation with Joshua Lederberg, a geneticist who shared a Nobel Prize for discovering the fact that some bacteria mate, passing copies of their DNA to the other: "You go back and forth from observation to theory. You don't know what to look for without a theory; and you can't check the theory without looking at the fact; and the fact is only meaningful in the light of some theoretical construction" (p. 184). Empirical data are essential to corroborate the central ideas of a theory and to guide further elaboration of the theory. This means, of course, that the theory must be capable of change in response to challenges by data—the alternative is dogmatic adherence to a theory despite contrary evidence.

THEORIES OF BEHAVIOR, DEVELOPMENT, AND PSYCHOPATHOLOGY

Now that we have armed you with some knowledge for evaluating the qualities of the various theories used by clinical psychologists, we turn our attention to four of the most influential theories. We will return to each of these theories in more depth in the chapters on clinical research, assessment, and intervention. Keep in mind that you need to evaluate each theory in light of the criteria we have outlined.

Psychoanalytic and Psychodynamic Theories

Freud   The oldest and most widely debated theory of psychopathology begins with the work of **Sigmund Freud,** a brilliant Austrian neurologist who developed his thinking about personality and psychopathology during the late 1800s and early 1900s. Although Freud's original psychoanalytic theory has undergone many revisions to create other psychodynamic theories (e.g., Adler, 1959; Bowlby, 1969–1980; Jung, 1935/56), his theory remains the benchmark against which virtually all other theories in the field are compared. Because Freud's theory was the first example of modern thinking about psychopathology, most other theories are to some degree an extension of, or a reaction against, his thinking.

Freud formulated a comprehensive theory of development, personality, and psychopathology. A major part of this theory concerns the *structure* of personality. Freud assumed that we are born with a predetermined set of psychological needs, drives, or instincts, which comprise the *id*. These innate drives lead us to seek immediate gratification of sexual and aggressive needs. Simply put, Freud postulated that we are driven to experience pleasure and avoid pain. Freud described two other aspects of personality that are shaped primarily by experiences with the environment. The *superego* is the internalization of moral principles, or the conscience, and the rules that govern all organized societies. Finally, the *ego* is the individual's connection to the world. It involves an awareness of oneself and the ability to accurately perceive and interact with one's environment. The ego must try to balance the sexual and aggressive drives of the id and the moral constraints of the superego.

Not surprisingly, Freud theorized that in the course of normal development an individual's instinctual drives (represented by the id), the constraints of reality (represented by the ego), and societal rules (represented by the superego) will inevitably come into *conflict*. It is not possible to gratify all of one's needs and wants as they arise; consequently, this goal of the id will conflict with the constraints of the ego and the values of the superego. These internal conflicts would cause the individual a great deal of anxiety if she or he were aware of them. Freud postulated, however, that much of what is important in determining our behavior, including these clashes among the id, ego, and superego, is not within conscious awareness; rather, it is rooted at various depths within the *unconscious*. Freud believed that the unconscious is filled with unacceptable memories, feelings, impulses, and so on, material that would cause us to become anxious if we were aware of it. To keep from experiencing this emotional discomfort, we develop *defense mechanisms*. Defense mechanisms operate outside of our conscious awareness; that is, we do not realize

that we are using defense mechanisms, which allow us to continue to function without experiencing the distress that would certainly engulf us if we were aware of the unacceptable material lying under the cover of our defense mechanisms.

How did Freud come to postulate links between (a) unacceptable material that lies outside human awareness and (b) distress and anxiety? Freud developed his theory as he was treating patients, which had a strong influence on the development of his formulations. In fact, Freud's interest in psychopathology began in part with cases that were presented to him in his role as a neurologist. Freud was trained as a physician; consequently, he was guided in his thinking by a "medical model." That is, all illnesses were presumed to have an organic or physical cause and should be treated accordingly, with physically based therapies.

As a neurologist, Freud treated patients who were suffering from what were then conceptualized as neurological conditions and who were experiencing weak or damaged nerves. A turning point in Freud's thinking came with his observation that symptoms of a disorder that was diagnosed at the time as "conversion hysteria" did not respond to any available neurological treatment. Primary among these symptoms was physical paralysis or anesthesia with no known organic basis. Importantly, Freud noticed that the paralysis or anesthesia experienced by these patients occurred on their bodies in patterns that did not conform to existing knowledge about the central nervous system. For example, some patients exhibited what was called "glove anesthesia," in which they reported experiencing no feeling or sensation in one of their hands from the wrist down. Anatomically it is impossible to invoke a physical explanation for this disorder, because nerves that are responsible for the experience of sensation in the hands extend up along the arms and do not stop and start in a band around the wrist; if the nerves were damaged, the numbness would not be confined to the hand. Freud's observation that these symptoms could not have a physical cause posed a direct challenge to the thinking of his colleagues, who attributed hysterical paralysis to subtle, undetectable lesions in the central nervous system. Freud's thoughts on this issue are reflected in his first important psychological paper in 1893, "Some Points for a Comparative Study of Organic and Hysterical Motor Paralyses."

We should point out here that although Freud was clearly fighting an uphill battle against mainstream thinking in neurology, he was not alone in trying to develop a psychological explanation for illnesses that were presumed to be organic in nature. In fact, at the same time that Freud was beginning to develop his ideas in Austria, the French neurologists Hippolyte Bernheim and Jean Charcot were advocating hypnosis as a procedure to alleviate hysterical neurosis. Freud went to France to investigate Bernheim's and Charcot's claims and to study with them. Together, the researchers observed that when patients were induced into a hypnotic state, the symptoms of the hysteria were often relieved. Thus, patients with hysterical paralysis could move their limbs, and patients with hysterical blindness could see. Importantly, the symptoms returned once the patients were no longer under hypnosis. Freud reasoned that if the patients' primary physical symptoms could be reduced or changed through hypnosis, they could not be purely organic in origin. As Mitchell and Black (1995) stated, "The problem is not in the flesh—the hand, the eyes, the legs are intact. The problem is an idea, out of awareness—the idea that the patient cannot feel, cannot see, cannot walk. . . . It was ideas, not nerves, that were the source of trouble" (p. 3).

But how could ideas so powerfully affect physical functioning? Freud began to examine this question through his collaboration with Josef Breuer, an internist in Vienna. Breuer was treating a young woman named Bertha Pappenheim (later referred to as Anna O.), who, while caring for her sick father, developed a number of symptoms, including headaches, paralyses, distorted

vision, and speech dysfunctions. Breuer attempted to remove Pappenheim's symptoms through posthypnotic suggestions but was unsuccessful. He observed, however, that under hypnosis Pappenheim recalled painful and aversive emotional experiences of which she was unaware while she was conscious and not under hypnosis. More importantly, as she expressed these emotions while under hypnosis (a process she called "chimney sweeping," later referred to as *catharsis*), over time her symptoms disappeared. Freud and Breuer hypothesized that these symptoms were traumatic experiences and feelings that had been transformed, or "converted," into physical symptoms. This hypothesis marked the origin of psychoanalytic theory with the publication of *Studies on Hysteria* in 1895 by Freud and Breuer, in which they stated that "hysterics suffer mainly from reminiscences" (p. 7).

Interestingly, Freud and Breuer differed in their ideas about *how* certain experiences come to generate feelings that are ultimately split off from conscious awareness. Breuer believed that the dissociated experiences occurred during periods of altered consciousness, such as stress and fatigue. Freud took a different position and argued that the experiences that were kept out of awareness were determined not by an altered state of consciousness, but rather by the *content* of the particular experience. Thus, Freud believed that experiences that are disturbing or unacceptable to the person or that are otherwise inconsistent or incompatible with the rest of the person's conscious feelings or beliefs are actively blocked from awareness. And he believed further that what was necessary for removal of the symptoms caused by this dissociation was for the individual to become aware of the blocked material. As we will explain in chapter 12, this awareness is, in large part, the overarching goal of the form of psychotherapy developed by Freud: psychoanalysis.

Although it would appear that Freud and Breuer had begun a remarkable collaboration, they soon went their separate ways. Freud became interested in free association, or allowing the patient to say whatever came to mind in an uninterrupted flow of ideas, as an alternative technique to the use of hypnosis. Equally important, against the pervasive values of the time, Freud pursued the possible significance of sexuality in understanding personality development and the causes of psychopathology. Freud had become increasingly impressed by the regularity with which his patients' free associations led to "memories" of a sexual nature, dating from childhood. Often these remembered scenes involved sexual abuse at the hands of a parent or relative. Indeed, in 1896 Freud published papers and gave lectures describing a "seduction theory" of hysteria, arguing that childhood sexual abuse was a necessary precondition for the illness. The response, as you can imagine, was icy. Krafft-Ebing, an eminent Viennese psychiatrist, called Freud's theory "a scientific fairy tale." Freud himself soon began to have doubts about it, writing that the uncovering of these "memories" too often failed to produce the expected symptom relief. He still believed that sexual abuse did exist (Karon & Widener, 1995), but even in Freud's own family a sibling had developed hysterical symptoms and, if Freud's theory were correct, it would identify his father as a child abuser, something Freud could not accept.

Freud altered his seduction hypothesis to revise the traditional definition of sexuality. Instead of referring specifically to adult copulation and reproduction, Freud conceptualized sexuality as a general drive for sensual gratification of different kinds and hypothesized that it was present in all individuals from infancy onward. He framed this drive for sexual gratification within a broader *stage theory* of development. Freud believed that personality and psychopathology are outcomes of an invariant sequence of stages of psychosexual development. He postulated that during the first five years of life, individuals pass through the *oral* stage, then through the *anal* stage, and then through the *phallic* stage. The quality of the progression to a new stage depends on the extent to which the individual successfully negotiated the demands of the preceding stage. At each stage the basic needs must be gratified in a way that is consistent with that particular developmental level. For example, Freud hypothesized that during the first two years of life the infant must be able to gratify his or her oral needs through sucking and feeding. Similarly, in the second and third years of life, the child must gratify her or his anal needs through attempts to control bodily functions. Failure to have one's needs adequately gratified at a particular level of development will lead the individual to become *fixated at,* or focused on, that source of gratification. A person who is fixated at a specific psychosexual stage continually tries to receive the form of gratification that is characteristic at that stage (e.g., oral pleasure, anal control), even though the method of gratification is no longer developmentally appropriate.

As you can see, Freud essentially formulated a theory of normal personality development. Each of us progresses through the same sequence of psychosexual stages, and we must try to resolve the emotional issues relevant to each stage as best we can. Because unresolved conflicts and experiences at each stage would cause considerable anxiety, we develop and use defense mechanisms to keep such information from reaching awareness. But the conflicts, urges, memories, and feelings are present nonetheless, constantly pressing for expression and affecting behavior (see box 4.1 and figure 4.1). As our defenses weaken, the unacceptable material in our unconscious becomes more accessible, and we experience increased distress in the form of anxiety or depression. For Freud, the anxiety or depression is seen as a symptom of underlying, unconscious conflicts and material, most commonly involving sexual and aggressive instincts. Indeed, Freud would likely have little difficulty attributing the Columbine shootings to an explosive expression of innate aggressive instincts and a drive for self-destruction that was poorly regulated by the ego and superego.

BOX 4.1

DO UNCONSCIOUS PROCESSES AFFECT HUMAN BEHAVIOR?

Freud postulated that memories, attitudes, instincts, and feelings that are unacceptable to us, or that would cause us to experience anxiety are contained in the *id*. Our defense mechanisms work to prevent these memories and emotions from reaching our consciousness. Because these defense mechanisms are not perfectly efficient, some of this unconscious material does affect our behaviors, thoughts, and feelings even though we do not realize it. Although the id is certainly not a physical structure in our bodies, Freud's underlying premise is that thoughts and feelings *about which we are unaware* nevertheless affect our behavior. Because of the pervasiveness of the unconscious, Freud believed that we often do not have access to the reasons or motivation for much of our behavior.

Is there evidence that factors outside of our awareness can influence our behavior? In an influential article published in *Psychological Review* in 1977, Richard Nisbett from the University of Michigan and Timothy Wilson from the University of Virginia argued that we may have little or no direct access to our higher order mental processes, such as those involved in making judgments, solving problems, and initiating behavior (Nisbett & Wilson, 1977). Essentially, Nisbett and Wilson claim that we do not really know or are unaware of *why* we make certain judgments or engage in certain behaviors and, worse yet, we readily offer explanations for these choices that we fully believe but that are often wrong.

Nisbett and Wilson (1977) review a number of areas of research in which subjects engage in behaviors, are asked why they did so, and offer completely inaccurate explanations and justifications. There is a large literature, for instance, examining the effects of the presence of others on helping behavior. The

well-documented, consistent finding in this area of study is that the greater the number of people that are present in a situation, the less likely it is that any of them will help someone in need (e.g., Baumeister, 1996; Bickman, 1994). Interestingly, Latané and Darley (1968) reported that every subject in a number of studies they reviewed claimed that their behavior was not influenced by the other people who were present.

Nisbett and Wilson (1977) report a series of studies with even more dramatic results. In one study, for example, they asked subjects to learn specific word pairs in a list that were meant to increase the probability of the subject giving a particular response to a subsequent target question. For instance, subjects learned the word pair "ocean-moon" with the expectation that when they were later asked to name a detergent, they would be more likely to respond with "Tide" than would subjects who did not learn this word pair. In fact, that is exactly what happened: Subjects who learned specific word pairs were twice as likely to give the expected target response as were subjects who learned different word pairs. More importantly, when subjects were asked why they said "Tide," they almost never mentioned the word pair cue "ocean-moon" as a reason for their response.

Nisbett and Wilson (1977) describe a number of other similar studies, all of which demonstrate very effectively not only that we are not aware of why we engage in behaviors or make decisions, but also that we invariably offer an explanation or justification that we firmly believe. So, to return to the issue of the unconscious and defense mechanisms, Freud's assertion that our behavior is influenced, if not determined, by material in our unconscious is indeed supported by the results of empirical research.

Freud treated only a limited number of different psychological disorders, and as a result, he attempted to explain the causes of only a fraction of the various disorders with which

psychologists deal today. The basic principles of his theory, however, have been applied to the full spectrum of psychopathology. In each case, it is assumed that the symptoms of the disorder are

The Freudian Unconscious. The Freudian unconscious emphasizes motivational explanations for phenomena such as slips of the tongue. (Reprinted with permission from *Psychology Today* Magazine, Copyright © 1987 Sussex Publishers, Inc.)

only the surface manifestations of an underlying conflict. Symptoms are simply the form through which the person is able to express the internal conflicts that she or he is experiencing.

Freud and his contemporaries relied on a single method, the *case study,* to test their complex and fascinating hypotheses about the psychological roots of psychopathology. They made careful observations of individual patients who presented with specific problems. Early in the development of psychoanalytic theory, it was Freud's systematic observations of his patients' thoughts and emotions released under hypnosis that led him to theorize about the importance of unconscious processes as determinants of overt behavior. The use of case studies as a method of scientific inquiry, however, is extremely limited. Observations of individual cases are important in *generating hypotheses,* but case studies cannot

be used to *test and disprove* hypotheses. Indeed, overreliance on case observations represents a major shortcoming in the early development of psychoanalytic theory as a scientific approach to understanding psychopathology.

Ego Psychology and Object Relations   Psychoanalytic theory has been subjected to numerous changes and revisions since Freud's original work. As you will see, the changes that have occurred in psychoanalytic theory have both downplayed the roles of sexuality and aggression and paid greater attention to the role of the ego, that aspect of the personality that represents conscious and rational thought. Freud's focus on sex and aggression is understandable when one considers the social and cultural context in which he developed his theory. Freud's world was characterized by the rigid morality of the Victorian era, the rapid changes in technology and social order that occurred throughout the western world in the early twentieth century, and the horror and devastation of two world wars. Undoubtedly, Freud's exposure to a strict morality regarding sexuality, restrictive views about the role of women within society, and the worst aspects of human nature profoundly shaped his views of personality and psychopathology.

Nevertheless, several of Freud's followers felt that he focused too strongly and too narrowly on instinctual aggression and sexuality. Freud had argued strongly that human behavior is rooted in biological factors, in particular, by instincts housed in the id. He saw the ego simply as a servant to the id and its instinctual drives. In one major derivation of psychoanalytic theory, a group of theorists, referred to now as **ego psychologists,** disagreed with this formulation. This group, which included Erik Erikson (1956), Heinz Hartmann (1939), and Freud's daughter Anna (1946), contended that behavior is determined not only by the id but by the ego as well. In fact, Anna Freud greatly expanded her father's conceptualization of defense mechanisms, focusing on the role of the ego in implementing the defenses. As we will discuss in more detail in chapter 12, these psychologists shifted the focus of both psychoanalytic theory and treatment from the id to the ego. They argued that the ego is, in large part, independent of the id rather than subservient to it. They maintained that the ego has its own sources of gratification and motivation, such as love and creativity, as well as its own adaptive functions, such as thinking, perceiving, learning, remembering, and communicating with the environment. Contrary to Freud's view, these ego psychologists also believed that personality is not solidified by early childhood or puberty; rather, they argued that personality development continues into adulthood.

Perhaps the best known theory of ego psychology is that formulated by Erik Erikson (1950, 1959). Erikson developed a stage theory of psychological development that differed in significant ways from the model proposed by Freud. Whereas Freud focused on the critical role of the unconscious and its effect on our feelings and behaviors, Erikson was more concerned with how the conscious aspects of the ego developed through culture and social relationships. He formulated a theory of ego development in which the ego unfolds across a sequence of psychosocial stages, or crises, beginning with basic trust versus mistrust of others; including autonomy versus shame and self-doubt, personal initiative versus guilt and intimacy versus isolation; and ending with ego integrity versus despair. Erikson described these stages of ego development in terms of conflicts, or tensions, but the conflicts are not based in internal, libidinal drives. Rather, Erikson focused on important tasks in social development and on the development of a sense of self and identity. Importantly, Erikson believed that these tasks and stages of development extend well beyond early childhood and encompass the entire life cycle, from infancy to old age.

A second major derivation of psychoanalytic theory is **object relations** theory, a school of therapy associated primarily with British analysts such as Melanie Klein (1932, 1948), Donald Fairburn (1952), and John Bowlby (1969–1980) as well as with European-born analysts who moved to America, such as Margaret Mahler (Mahler, Pine, & Bergman, 1975), Otto Kernberg (1976, 1980), and Heinz Kohut (1971, 1977). In understanding the impetus for, and rise of, object relations theory, it is important to recognize that in many ways and like many of his contemporaries, Freud likened human beings to animals. Drawing on Darwin's revolutionary and captivating theory of evolution, Freud postulated that humans are "wired" like the animals from which they evolved, driven by instincts to pursue simple pleasures. Through socialization, they learn to channel their animal nature and base instincts into socially acceptable forms of civilized living.

In the 1940s, a group of theorists, spurred by the groundbreaking work of Melanie Klein, proposed the view that the human infant is not "animal-like and instinctual." Rather, these theorists espoused a more positive view of human nature, contending that the infant is born ready and wired for interpersonal interaction and positive social development. The motivating force of the libido of the infant is to bond with an interpersonal "object," or person, typically a parent. Object relations theorists argued that, just as ducklings become imprinted onto whatever caregiving object appears at the right time (Lorenz, 1966), infants become psychologically attached to their early caregivers and, more important, build their emotional lives in accord with the quality of the early caregiving received by that object. If the caregiver (object) encourages a secure attachment and relationship with the infant, the infant's natural positive interpersonal and intrapsychic growth will be allowed to develop. On the other hand, an abusive or neglectful early interpersonal object, resulting in inadequate parenting, will block this growth.

One of the strongest proponents of object relations theory was John Bowlby, a British psychiatrist. Like Freud, Bowlby was influenced by Darwin's theory of evolution, but whereas Freud focused on humankind's ascent from the lower species, Bowlby emphasized the evolution and natural selection survival value of *attachment,* the infant's instinctual motivation to bond to its mother. Thus, the mother is important to the infant initially because of her role as a need-gratifying object. The infant's subsequent personality development and emotional security is a function of the availability and quality of the infant's attachment figure, or object. Similarly, Bowlby believed that many forms of psychopathology stem from a basic anxiety related to fear of separation from the attachment object.

The term *object* in this context, therefore, refers to external representations of internal psychological processes, most importantly, significant people early in the patient's life. Thus, object relations theory clearly places a greater emphasis on interpersonal relationships than did original Freudian theory. Unlike psychoanalytic theory's strong focus on internal drives, object relations theory and therapy emphasizes the role that human (object) relationships play in the development of personality. As we will describe in greater detail in chapter 12, therapists working from this perspective seek to understand the patients' internal representations of significant others (sometimes referred to as "person schemas") and the way patients interact with important people in their lives.

Interpersonal Approaches Finally, several theorists have broadened the object relations perspective, emphasizing the importance of interpersonal relationships in determining behavior and psychopathology. For example, Alfred Adler, who was one of Freud's original students, Eric Fromm, Karen Horney, and Erik Erikson (whose work we described in the previous section) all developed theories that are based in part on psychodynamic principles but that have an important emphasis on interpersonal processes. It was psychiatrists Harry Stack Sullivan (1953, 1956) and Adolf Meyer (1957) who offered the first systematic interpersonal theories of psychopathology and psychotherapy. Both Sullivan and

Meyer believed that the most salient aspects of personality and psychopathology involved the person's relationship to his or her social environment. Indeed, Sullivan (1940) went so far as to define personality as "the relatively enduring pattern of recurrent interpersonal situations which characterize a human life" (p. xi). Although Sullivan believed that the roots of interpersonal relationships lie in early childhood experiences, he felt that the most important manifestations of these experiences, and ultimately their resolution, were in the person's current social relationships and interactions.

Two interpersonal approaches are currently dominant in clinical psychology: the interpersonal model of Gerald Klerman and Myrna Weissman (Klerman, Weissman, Rounsaville, & Chevron, 1984; Weissman & Markowitz, in press), and the various family systems models (e.g., Kerr & Bowen, 1988; Minuchin, 1974; see Goldenberg and Goldenberg, 2000, for a detailed description of these models). The interpersonal approach of Klerman and Weissman does not take a specific position on the etiology of psychopathology, but rather emphasizes the interpersonal context of psychological disorders once they have developed. Klerman and Weissman recognize that psychological problems affect the person's social relationships and argue that these relationships play an important role in maintaining problems once they develop. This observation has led to the development of an approach to psychotherapy that focuses on changing the nature of the current interpersonal relationships in the individual's life. We describe this approach to treatment, known as interpersonal psychotherapy, in greater detail in chapter 12.

Family systems theories focus on relationships within the family and assume that these relationships are strongly *interdependent.* Systems theories assume that families, like any natural system, possess certain characteristics that are directed at maintaining structure and homeostasis within the system (von Bertalanffy, 1973). The structure of the family is defined by the roles or functions that individual members play within the family and by the nature of the relationships among the members. The behavior and emotions of any member have direct ramifications for the behavior and emotions of other members. System theories define psychopathology in terms of dysfunction within the family rather than an individual. The symptoms experienced by a family member are seen as an expression of dysfunction within the family rather than pathology that is unique to the individual.

Behavioral and Cognitive Theories

During the late 1800s and early 1900s, as Freud's ideas were being presented first to an astonished medical community in Europe and then to the fledgling field of psychology in Europe and the United States, a different way of conceptualizing human behavior and psychopathology was emerging from research laboratories and academic departments of psychology. This perspective stood in stark contrast to Freudian theory. Rather than formulating hypotheses about processes and constructs—such as the id, defense mechanisms, and psychosexual stages—that are not observable this new perspective emphasized instead the development of a set of principles or laws that could be used to explain overt, observable, behavior. Labeled "behaviorism," this approach focused on principles of *learning,* which can be defined as "a relatively permanent change in the probability of exhibiting a specific behavior" (Mowrer & Klein, 1989, p. 3). Learning theories offer an explanation of the conditions that lead to the initiation, continuation, and termination of specific behaviors. Two traditions emerged early in the development of theories of learning: one from the reflex tradition in the work of the Russian physiologist Ivan Pavlov, called **Pavlovian,** or **classical, conditioning,** and the other from the work of B. F. Skinner and his colleagues, called **instrumental,** or **operant, conditioning.**

Classical, or Pavlovian, Conditioning The original observations of the Nobel Prize–winning Russian physiologist Ivan Pavlov are well known to any student who has had even a brief introduction to the field of psychology. In the early 1900s Pavlov was studying the digestive system of the dog. In conducting experiments with dogs, Pavlov noticed that some dogs salivated before the food reached their mouths. It seemed that the presence of meat alone made the dogs salivate. Pavlov observed further that the dogs in fact began to salivate when they heard the footsteps of the assistant who was bringing the food. He referred to this phenomenon initially as *psychic secretion,* but later used the term *conditioned reflex* instead. Pavlov reasoned that the dogs had learned to associate the sound of footsteps with the subsequent appearance of food, so that the footsteps (an initially neutral stimulus) eventually were sufficient alone to elicit salivation.

In America, **John Watson,** a Professor of Psychology at Johns Hopkins University, read Pavlov's writings and, by 1919, began to develop early behavioral principles based in large part on Pavlov's work. Watson called for a reliance on overt, observable data, which meant a focus on behavior (what people do) rather than on subjective reports (what people think and feel). It is important to recognize that Watson did not deny the existence of thoughts or introspection; rather, he believed that data based on observable behaviors required fewer inferences than did data based on self-reported thoughts or feelings and were, therefore, more scientifically valid.

Watson believed that humans are born with three basic emotions: fear, rage, and love. These three emotions, he thought, are elicited by specific but very limited stimuli. Moreover, these specific stimuli are hardwired, or biologically based, in human beings, eliciting the same emotions in virtually everyone. In attempting to account for the full range of human emotional expression and for differences in emotional behavior among individuals, Watson posited that we learn more elaborate emotional responses by association, or conditioning. In one famous experiment that he conducted with his graduate student Rosalie Rayner, Watson and Rayner (1920) used principles of classical conditioning (derived from Pavlov's work with dogs) to condition fear in an 11-month-old infant, who is now known to introductory psychology students simply as "Little Albert." Watson and Rayner presented a slightly positive stimulus (a white rat) to Albert and then proceeded to startle the infant by clanging heavy steel bars above his head (a procedure that almost certainly would not pass the standards of human subjects ethics review boards today). After only five pairings (or associations) of the aversive stimulus (noise from the clanging steel bars) with the previously positive stimulus (the white rat), Albert began to show overt signs of distress and soon withdrew in fright from the rat. This distress-and-avoidance response not only persisted as long as four months later, even after Watson and Rayner no longer clanged the steel bars when the rat was presented to Albert, but further, it generalized to other white furry objects, including a white rabbit and even a Santa Claus mask with a white fuzzy beard.

Despite the ethical problems of causing Little Albert's distress, Watson and Rayner's experiment was a landmark study. It represented the first empirical demonstration that supported Watson's hypothesis that emotions can be learned. Furthermore, it was the first laboratory demonstration of an "experimental neurosis" in a human—the acquisition of anxiety in response to stimulus that does not represent a realistic threat. Watson's focus was on relatively mechanistic, automatic processes in learning and conditioning. We have come a long way since Watson's work. Tolman (1932, 1952) introduced the concept of expectancy theory. He hypothesized that people are capable of understanding the structure of their environment and that they form expectations regarding the likelihood that certain behaviors will lead to desired goals. Thus, as early as the 1930s Tolman began to integrate cognitive concepts with behavioral theories to understand

human functioning. More recently, Rescorla (1988) articulated the limitations of the early mechanistic theories of conditioning: "Traditional descriptions of conditioning as the acquired ability of one stimulus to evoke the original response to another because of their pairing are shown to be inadequate. They fail to characterize adequately the circumstances producing learning, the content of that learning, or the manner in which that learning influences performance. Instead, conditioning is now described as the learning of relations among events so as to allow the organism to represent its environment" (p. 151).

It is clear now that conditioning is not the result of simply pairing one stimulus with another. Indeed, the co-occurrence of stimuli at the same time, or in the same location, does not necessarily result in learning (Bouton, 2000). In fact, classical conditioning theory underwent profound changes when psychologists observed that all stimuli and responses are not equivalent in producing conditioning. In a landmark study, Garcia and Koelling (1966) demonstrated that it was easier to associate internal pain (e.g., a stomachache) with a gustatory stimulus (e.g., smell) than with an auditory-visual stimulus, whereas it was easier to associate peripheral pain (e.g., a prick to the skin) with an auditory-visual stimulus than with a gustatory stimulus.

Current theories of classical conditioning recognize the importance of the context or setting in which specific stimuli occur and affect behavior. Individuals respond not only to a particular stimulus but also to the other features of the environment in which the stimulus is presented. The context influences both the acquisition of new behavior and the extinction or discontinuation of behavior as well (Bouton, 1993). Extinction is not simply the unlearning of a prior behavior or association, but rather, it seems to involve the learning of new associations with the environment. Because prior behaviors are not really unlearned, patterns of behavior that have been extinguished can recur when the individual is presented with the context in which the original learning took place. The role of context in the acquisition and extinction has important implications for behavioral methods in the treatment of psychopathology (e.g., Bouton, 2000; Bouton & Swartzentruber, 1991), an issue that we will discuss in detail in chapter 14.

Classical conditioning, or associative learning, is hypothesized to be involved in the etiology of a number of emotional disorders. For example, because it is clear that autonomic nervous system arousal can be conditioned, anxiety can be learned, as Watson demonstrated with Little Albert. An entire class of DSM disorders involves elevations in level of anxiety, including phobias, panic, and post-traumatic stress disorder (e.g., Bouton, Mineka, & Barlow, 2001). Consequently, classical conditioning explanations have been formulated for these anxiety disorders as well as for some of the sexual deviations, like fetishes. Interestingly, human beings and other organisms appear to be predisposed to associate anxiety with some stimuli but not with others. For example, phobic anxiety frequently occurs in response to spiders and snakes, animals that can be poisonous, but not to rabbits and turtles, animals that do not pose threats to humans. As we mentioned in chapter 2, psychologist Susan Mineka at Northwestern University has demonstrated in a series of experiments that although monkeys can be conditioned to be afraid of snakes, they cannot be conditioned to show fear to flowers (e.g., Mineka, 1992). The roots of this differential conditioning probability may be an evolutionary process in which species acquire the ability to become fearful primarily to conditions that are truly threatening (see box 4.2).

Operant, or Instrumental, Conditioning Before the publication of **B. Frederick Skinner's** book *Science and Human Behavior* in 1953, studies of learning and conditioning were influenced almost exclusively by Pavlovian principles, particularly classical conditioning. With his seminal book, Skinner underscored the impor-

Susan Mineka, Ph.D., is a Professor at Northwestern University. A clinical psychologist, Dr. Mineka conducted innovative research with monkeys demonstrating that fears are learned more readily to certain classes of stimuli, a finding that supports the concept of biological preparedness.

tance of instrumental, or operant, conditioning in understanding other ways of learning. Whereas classical conditioning theory focuses on the *antecedents* of behavior or the environmental conditions that *precede* behavior, operant theory emphasizes the *consequences* of behavior or the environmental conditions that *follow* behavior. Positive consequences (stimuli) that follow a behavior (response) will increase the likelihood of the behavior being exhibited again in the future (positive reinforcement), as will the removal of negative stimuli following the behavior (negative reinforcement). Similarly, negative consequences of a behavior should have the effect of reducing the probability that the behavior will be emitted in the future (punishment). These operant principles are based, in large part, on Thorndike's (1927) law of effect, which basically states that organisms will repeat behaviors for which they have been rewarded and will not

BOX 4.2

CAN WE LEARN TO FEAR ANYTHING?

The conditioning explanations of the acquisition of fears and phobias seem to fit with common sense and are also consistent with clinical experience. Many irrational fears and phobias develop following an intense aversive experience with a particular stimulus. Nevertheless, there are some facts that raise questions about the validity of learning theory explanations for the development of phobias. Seligman (1971), in particular, identified a number of problems with conditioning explanations for the etiology of fears and phobias. For example, whereas conditioned fear responses that are learned in a laboratory situation are usually easy to extinguish, actual phobias are extremely persistent and resistant to change. Furthermore, if the conditioning explanation is correct, that people "learn" fear in response to frightening objects, why are more people not phobic of guns, knives, cars, electrical sockets, or other potentially harmful objects? These are surprisingly uncommon fears. In fact, although people could develop phobic responses to a virtually unlimited number of objects, most phobias involve a very small number of stimuli, such as snakes, heights, dogs, closed-in spaces, and insects.

To explain this relatively restricted range of stimuli to which people and animals show fear responses, Seligman suggested that animals (including humans) are **biologically prepared,** on the basis of neural pathways, to learn fear to some stimuli and not to others. Seligman and other theorists postulate that this biological preparedness is a result of evolutionary natural selection over hundreds of thousands of years. That is, individuals within a species who easily learned fear responses to truly dangerous stimuli like heights, snakes, and insects and who avoided situations involving these stimuli were more likely to survive, reproduce, and pass on genes to their offspring that facilitate that pattern of learning.

Is there empirical support for this concept of biological preparedness? Indeed there is, both in animals and in humans. For example, in an elegant series of studies, psychologist Susan Mineka and her colleagues at Northwestern University (e.g., Mineka & Cook, 1993; Mineka, Davidson, Cook, & Keir, 1984) demonstrated that rhesus monkeys learn fear to dangerous stimuli far more easily than to benign objects. Mineka began by showing that young monkeys who are raised by parents who are afraid of snakes do not themselves exhibit this fear if they have no direct experience with snakes. Thus, simply being born to parents who fear snakes is not sufficient to produce a fear of snakes in the offspring. Mineka then had offspring of wild-reared parent monkeys observe their parents showing fear responses to snakes. After only eight minutes of observation, five of six young monkeys acquired an intense fear of snakes, a fear that did not diminish even after three months. Finally, when young monkeys watched a videotape of another monkey in the top of the frame showing a fear response to either a snake or a flower presented in the bottom frame, they subsequently showed a fear response only to a snake, even though they observed the identical modeled fear response to both a snake and a flower. Thus, it is clear that monkeys are "prepared" to show fear or become phobic to some stimuli but not to others.

And it is not just monkeys who show selective conditioning. Psychologist Arne Öhman in Sweden has demonstrated that although people can be conditioned to show fear to pictures of snakes, houses, and faces by pairing electric shock with the pictures, the conditioned fear to the houses and faces diminishes very quickly, while the fear learned to the snakes is much more resistant to extinction (Öhman, 1996). Considered together, the empirical evidence does indicate that we are biologically prepared to learn to be afraid of a small subset of objects in our environment.

repeat behaviors that have been ignored, or for which they have been punished.

Contrary to what many people may think, continuously reinforcing a behavior is not the most powerful way to increase and maintain its frequency. Research that examines the effects of different schedules of reinforcement has demonstrated that a behavior will be learned and maintained most strongly if it is reinforced only some of the time that it occurs. This intermittent conditioning is one of the main reasons gambling is such a difficult behavior to stop—bets have been reinforced some of the time, and there's a belief that the next bet will win, even though the last one did not. In fact, the belief that a good poker hand must be due to arrive after a string of bad hands is known as the "gambler's fallacy"—each hand is, of course, independent of the one before.

Social Learning Theory An important shift in behavioral theory occurred when Albert Bandura of Stanford University conducted a classic series of studies of learning through observation, or *modeling.* Bandura (1969, 1986) argued that operant and instrumental conditioning could not account for many behaviors and demonstrated that a behavior could be learned by observing other people model the behavior, even if the observer received no direct reinforcement. Bandura referred to this phenomenon as "vicarious" learning or conditioning, and it set the stage for extensive research that challenged some of the original principles of behaviorism. Indeed, it was Bandura's research that provided the foundation for studies that examined the impact on young children of watching violence on television and being exposed to violence in the media. It is not difficult to see how social learning theory would explain the shootings at Columbine: Eric Harris and Dylan Klebold learned their violent behavior by observing violence around them—in the media, in music, and on the Internet. They witnessed the attention that perpetrators receive and interpreted that attention as reinforcing, even glorifying. Together, Harris and Klebold engaged in the behaviors they had seen modeled by others. And, of course, the copycat school shootings that took place following the Columbine shootings can be explained using exactly the same

Albert Bandura, Ph.D., a clinical psychologist at Stanford University, has been a major figure in psychology for over 40 years. He played an integral role in formulating social learning theory, and pioneered the use of modeling to treat fears and phobias. Dr. Bandura also developed the theory of self-efficacy, and recently has extended this concept to the understanding of functioning at a societal level.

principles, but now Harris and Klebold are the models.

In general, classical and operant conditioning and social learning theories are concerned with explaining observable phenomena—behaviors that can be seen by others and that can be attributed to objectively defined antecedent or consequent conditions in the environment. Although in the original development of these behavioral theories, cognitive (and even unconscious) processes were viewed as intriguing, mental processes were not considered to be measurable phenomena and, therefore, were not the subject of scientific inquiry (e.g., Skinner, 1953). This strict adherence to observable behavior and events and the exclusion of any consideration of mental processes led learning theories to be characterized as reductionistic and mechanistic explanations of human functioning. The evolution of learning theory, however, has led to the development of current models of behavior that are anything but mechanistic. Indeed, modern learning theory focuses strongly on the associative processes through which organisms, including human beings, learn about the world around them and their relationship to that world (e.g., Bouton, 1993; Mower & Klein, 2001). These associative processes clearly involve a consideration of mental, or cognitive, activity. Thus, in much the same way that caricatures of Freudian theory overlooked the subtleties of subsequent developments of the theory, many descriptions of learning theories as "mechanistic" fail to capture the complexity of these more recent models.

Cognitive Theories   Cognitive theories of psychopathology are the most recent and rapidly growing entrant to the field of clinical psychology. The cornerstone of cognitive theories is that individuals are affected not only by the objective world around them but also by their subjective *perceptions and interpretations* of the world. People who perceive and interpret events more negatively are predicted to be more likely to develop depression or anxiety than are people with a more positive perspective on their environment. Many cognitive theorists believe that even though cognitions cannot be observed, they can be treated and changed in much the same way as overt behaviors. This "behavioral" view of cognitions has led to the development of the field of cognitive behavior therapy, which we describe in detail in chapter 14.

One of the most influential cognitive theorists in clinical psychology is **Aaron Beck** (1967, 1976), who originally developed what is now referred to as cognitive therapy out of his clinical experience with depressed patients. Beck observed that the dreams of depressed patients were replete with negative content—themes of

loss and failure, of abandonment and rejection. These observations led him to emphasize the importance of negative thoughts in depression, to posit that negative cognitions played a central role in the onset and maintenance of this disorder. At that time, this formulation was a significant departure from the prevalent views of depression as a disorder of mood. Beck was arguing that depression is not a disorder of emotion, but rather is first and foremost a disorder of thought. Of course, Beck was not the first person to emphasize the importance of cognition in influencing behavior; as Buddha is said to have stated many centuries ago, "All that we are arises with our thoughts. With our thoughts, we make our world."

Beck postulated that depressed people are characterized by what he called a "negative cognitive triad"; that is, they have a negative view of themselves, their world, and their future. Depressed people believe that they are unworthy of love or success, that their environment is unsupportive, and that their future is hopeless. Beck theorized that depressed people are also characterized by "negative schemas," cognitive structures that lead them to perceive and interpret their experiences in a negative manner. These schemas are essentially sets of negative expectancies about relationships, competencies and abilities, self-concept, and so on, that develop out of adverse early experiences. Beck argued that these negative schemas function as a vulnerability factor, or diathesis, for the development of depression. In a diathesis-stress model of psychopathology, the onset of a disorder is caused by the interaction of a diathesis, or predisposition to the disorder, and a stressor from the environment that "activates" the diathesis. With respect to depression, Beck hypothesized that when people who have schematic expectancies of loss or failure encounter a stressful life circumstance that is relevant to a particular schema, the schema will lead them to have negative thoughts of failure and loss. These cognitions, in turn, act to disrupt adaptive behavior, reduce motivation, and worsen mood, resulting ultimately in depression.

In short, therefore, Beck proposed that adverse early experiences involving loss, failure, or rejection lead individuals, as children and adolescents, to develop negative schemas around these themes. These schemas are latent, or unconscious, until they are activated by a relevant stressful life event. Once they are activated, they lead the individual to engage in persistent negative thinking, which leads, in turn to depression. As you can imagine, it was not a large step for Beck (1976) to extend this formulation to explain the development of anxiety in essentially the same way he had for depression. In his formulation of anxiety, Beck postulated that individuals who have early experiences that involve danger or threat develop strong schemas around these themes and, when they encounter situations in the environment that activate these danger or threat schemas, the resultant negative cognitions lead them to experience anxiety or panic.

Cognitive models of psychopathology have been the focus of extensive research (e.g., Abramson et al., in press; Gotlib & Neubauer, 2000; Haaga, Dyck, & Ernst, 1991). The results of this research indicate that a variety of different types of psychopathology are characterized by dysfunctional ways of thinking. The evidence is less clear, however, concerning the causal role of cognitions. That is, most research suggests that people with serious problems such as depression or anxiety are characterized by negative ways of thinking. Findings are less clear that these dysfunctional patterns of thinking actually precede the onset of these problems. The role of cognitive processes as a possible cause of psychopathology remains one of the most active areas of research within clinical psychology.

It is unlikely that we will ever really know why Eric Harris and Dylan Klebold shot their classmates, but theorists trying to understand the killings from a cognitive-behavioral perspective would likely focus on environmental factors that reinforced the boys' aggressive behaviors, like violent computer games or Internet-based peer or support groups. Behaviorists may also theorize that the two boys learned to associate guns and bombs with status and power. Finally, cognitive theorists would emphasize Harris's and Klebold's schemas, which filtered their perceptions and interpretations of events in their world and permitted them to justify their actions.

Humanistic Theories

A third force emerged during the 1950s in American psychology, partly in reaction to the dominance of psychoanalytic and behavioral theories of the time. This third perspective argued for a more positive view of human nature, in contrast to the negative view of human nature espoused by Freudian theory and the neutral stance proposed by behaviorists. A large and loosely associated group of **humanistic theories** were developed based on the shared assumption that people have an innate capacity for, and a tendency toward, positive growth and experience.

The roots of humanistic psychology can be found with William James and the origins of psychology in the United States. James received training in philosophy, physiology, and medicine during his struggle to develop a personal and professional identity (Reisman, 1976). Among the many influences on his career, James's thinking was affected by the writings of the French philosopher Charles Renouvier, who believed that the capacity for liberty or free will was one of the defining characteristics of human nature. James incorporated the concepts of *free will* and the *sense of self* as cornerstones for his emerging views on psychology. These themes have remained central in humanistic psychology throughout the twentieth century.

The most influential of the humanistic theories is the *person-centered* theory of **Carl Rogers** (1951, 1961). Rogers shared with Freud the assumption that human beings are born with innate drives and needs. He differed radically from Freud, however, concerning their nature. Whereas Freud saw the instincts as oriented toward the selfish satisfaction of personal gratification and having the potential for destructiveness, Rogers saw an innate drive toward actualization of all of one's competencies and potential. In Rogers's terms, human beings are born with an innate tendency toward self-actualization and positive growth. In contrast to Freud, Rogers also emphasized the role of conscious processes and the current environment over unconscious factors and past experience.

Three elements are central to Rogerian theory: the *experience* of the individual, the development of a *self-concept,* and the availability of *unconditional positive regard* from people in the individual's social environment. Rogers believed that each person has her or his own unique vantage point on the world and that each viewpoint is valid in its own right. The *phenomenological perspective* maintains that people react to their perceptions of the world and to their experience of the world and their inner emotions and thoughts rather than to an external objective reality. For Rogers's approach, in direct contrast to the behavioral approach, the most important psychological data were the subjective impressions and experiences of the individual.

The concept of the self emerged from Rogers's emphasis on the phenomenological experience of the individual. Rogers proposed that individuals possess a perception of their *real self* that is distinct from their *ideal self.* The real self is how the person actually perceives his or her own competencies and weaknesses, that is, one's current identity. In contrast, the ideal self is composed of personal aspirations, or the way one would like to be. According to Rogers, the greater the discrepancy between the real self and the ideal self, the greater the personal dissatisfaction and anxiety experienced by the individual. As a person proceeds along the path toward self-actualization and realization of his or her personal potential, the discrepancy between the real and ideal selves decreases, and the individ-

ual experiences a greater sense of personal congruence.

Rogers believed that, although people possess the potential for self-direction and control over their lives, the process of self-actualization is also influenced by the environment. As we will discuss in greater detail in chapter 13, a necessary environmental condition for personal growth is the experience of unconditional positive regard. Unconditional positive regard is the acceptance and valuing of an individual despite whatever personal shortcomings and problems he or she may possess. Unconditional regard frees the person to attend to her or his own personal values and wishes, to pursue personal goals and directions for development of the self. The absence of unconditional positive regard implies that a person is valued and loved only conditionally, that one's personal worth is contingent on meeting the expectations and values of others. Rogers believed that this type of conditional acceptance leads to greater discrepancy between the real and ideal selves, leads the individual to lose a sense of connection with his or her personal experience, and ultimately contributes to the development of psychopathology. It is this loss of connection with personal experience that humanistically oriented theorists would emphasize in trying to understand the reasons for the Columbine killings.

Biological Theories

Every thought, emotion, and behavior that human beings exhibit is associated with some aspect of biological functioning. Each time we think, feel, or act, there is activity in our central nervous system. It is essential, therefore, for clinical psychologists to consider the biological underpinnings of the actions that they observe or that their clients report. This statement does not mean, of course, that all thoughts, emotions, and actions are *caused* by biological factors. In many instances, biological processes within the central nervous system may reflect the result of thoughts or emotions, may act as a final common pathway for the expression of some action that has been caused at another level.

We will discuss biological models of behavior, development, and psychopathology at two general levels. First, the field of **behavioral genetics** is concerned with identifying the heritability of behavior. Researchers in this field have attempted to determine the degree to which specific aspects of personality and psychopathology are influenced by the genetic information that is passed from parents to their children. Second, researchers and theorists in the broad interdisciplinary field of **behavioral neuroscience** study the role of biological processes, especially neurotransmitters within the central nervous system, in determining thoughts, emotions, and actions. Although behavioral genetics and behavioral neuroscience are complementary aspects of biological theories about human functioning, they rely on very different research methods and utilize different levels of analysis.

Behavioral Genetics Behavioral geneticists are concerned with the degree to which information encoded in the DNA of genes can contribute to individual differences in behavior and development (e.g., Plomin & Rutter, 1998). Most pertinent to clinical psychology, behavioral geneticists have tried to understand the extent to which specific psychological disorders or symptoms of psychopathology are inherited. Research in this field involves comparing the behavior and psychological functioning of individuals who vary in the degree of genetic similarity and in the similarity of the environments in which they have been raised, with the goal of assessing the degree to which genes, environments, and their combination influence behavior, development, and psychopathology (Goodman & Gotlib, 1999).

The research designs that behavioral geneticists have used most frequently involve *adoption* studies, which compare adopted children with their biological and adopted parents or compare adopted and biological siblings, and *twin* studies, which compare monozygotic (identical) and dizygotic (fraternal) twins reared in either the same or different environments. We know that biological siblings and biological parents and their children share, on average, 50 percent of the same genes. In contrast, there is no shared genetic information between adoptive parents and adopted siblings. Thus, in adoption studies, comparisons of the degree of similarity between children and their biological parents (or siblings) and children with their adoptive parents (or siblings) offer a sort of natural experiment in which the degree of genetic similarity is controlled. In twin studies, comparisons of the degree of similarity that is observed within pairs of monozygotic twins (who share 100 percent of their genes) and within pairs of dizygotic twins (who share, on average, 50 percent of their genes) offer another opportunity to try to explain similarities in behaviors and personality. The uncontrolled factor in such studies could be the types of environments to which these individuals have been exposed, however, and steps need to be taken to control or account for the similarity and dissimilarity in the experiences of these individuals.

Research in behavioral genetics examining the heritability of psychopathology has yielded two important findings. First, genetics appear to play an important role in many forms of psychopathology, explaining 30 percent to 60 percent of the variance in different disorders (e.g., Goodman & Gotlib, 1999; Plomin, 1991). Second, and perhaps more important, it now appears unlikely that genes determine behavior directly. Rather, genes appear to exert their influence through complex interactions between individuals and their environments (cf. Goodman & Gotlib, 1999; Plomin, DeFries, McClearn, & Rutter, 1997). For example, Kendler et al. (1995) have demonstrated that people who are at genetic risk for depression are more likely to respond to stressful events by becoming depressed than are people without the genetic risk factors.

Behavioral Neuroscience Scientists examining the functions of the central nervous system have made remarkable strides over the past two decades, due in part to the development of complex technologies that permit a more comprehensive understanding of the ways in which information is transmitted from one neuron to the next. An understanding of the endocrine system, including hormonal processes, and its relation to behavior has increased dramatically as well. Indeed, it is now clear that there is an underlying physiological element to many forms of psychopathology.

Information that guides thoughts, emotions, and motor behavior is transmitted within the nervous system from one nerve cell, or neuron, to another. The transmission of information is in the form of an electrical impulse within a neuron that is transmitted across the space, or synapse, between two neurons by chemicals called *neurotransmitters*. The impulse that is carried by the first neuron triggers the release of neurotransmitters into the synapse to carry the message to the next neuron in the sequence. The information that is transmitted depends on the neurotransmitters that are emitted by the first neuron, on processes that operate in the synapse that either facilitate or impede the movement of the neurotransmitters across this space, and on the capacity of the second neuron to accept the neurotransmitters that have been sent. Three outcomes are possible for neurotransmitters that are released into the synapse: (a) These chemicals may reach the dendritic ending of the next neuron, successfully transmitting the message; (b) the neurotransmitters may return to the axonal ending of the original neuron in the sequence, either through a reuptake process or through binding to an autoreceptor site on the axon; or (c) neurotransmitters may be broken down by enzymes that are present in the synapse. Once the neurotransmitter is broken down, it can no longer successfully bind to the dendrite and therefore cannot transmit the message.

In general, biological theories of psychopathology focus on imbalances in levels of neurotransmitters in the synapse that lead to unsuccessful transmission of the neural message. These imbalances can be the result of (a) insufficient levels of certain neurotransmitters, (b) excessive levels of other neurotransmitters, or (c) levels of other biochemical substances (i.e., chemicals that are not neurotransmitters but affect the neurotransmitters) in the synapse that affect the transmission. The enzymes that act on neurotransmitters may destroy them before they are able to successfully carry their message to the next neuron in the sequence, or they may fail to metabolize the transmitters, allowing excessive levels to be taken back into the initial neuron through the reuptake process. Although there are dozens of different types of neurotransmitters, three in particular have been studied extensively because of their association with different forms of psychopathology: norepinephrine, dopamine, and serotonin. Norepinephrine has been implicated in our response to stressful and dangerous situations; dopamine has been found to play an important role in schizophrenia; and serotonin appears to be involved in the onset of emotional disorders such as depression and anxiety as well as in suicide attempts. See table 4.1 for a comparison of the theories.

APPLICATION OF THEORY: UNDERSTANDING MAJOR DEPRESSION

The usefulness of these four theories is best seen through their application to an understanding of the causes of an important human problem. We will now describe how these theories can be put into action to explain clinical depression. All four theories recognize the presence of severe depressive symptoms such as dysphoric mood, sleep difficulties, loss of appetite leading to a significant weight loss, inability to experience pleasure in previously rewarding activities, low sense of self-worth, and suicidal thoughts or attempts. They differ, however, in their explanations of the cause of these symptoms.

TABLE 4.1
How Well Does Each Theory Meet the Criteria for a Good Theory?

	Parsimony	Internal consistency	Testable hypotheses	Empirical support	Diversity	Changeability
Psychodynamic theories	Mixed—early model was poor, but more recent interpersonal theories are better	Good	Mixed—it is difficult to assess most constructs and test predictions, but recent work is better	Mixed—few studies examine theoretical constructs; recent work examining unconscious is better	Poor—they do not attempt to explain diversity	Poor—theory has changed little in response to empirical findings
Behavioral/ cognitive theories	Good—original behavioral theories may have been too reductionistic, but more recent integrations are broader	Good	Good—constructs are clearly operationalized and testable	Good—large literature supports principles of behavioral and cognitive theories	Good—diversity may be explained by different learning histories, environmental factors	Good—theories have evolved in response to data, particularly cognitive theories
Humanistic theories	Poor—several concepts appear to be unnecessary or redundant	Mixed	Poor—it is difficult to operationalize major constructs	Poor—there are few studies of humanistic constructs	Poor—they do not attempt to explain diversity	Poor—theories have changed little
Biological theories	Good—these theories rarely implicate unnecessary constructs; they are sometimes criticized for being reductionistic	Good	Good—constructs and variables are operationalized and testable	Good—there is a large literature on biological factors in psychopathology	Poor—little attention is given to individual differences	Good—theories have evolved in response to data

BOX 4.3

UNDERSTANDING PHILLIP FROM DIFFERENT THEORETICAL PERSPECTIVES

We have discussed four different theoretical approaches to understanding the development of psychopathology. To provide you with a better sense of some of the similarities and differences among these perspectives, we describe how a clinician would use each of these approaches to try to understand the same individual, in this case Phillip from chapter 1. Recall that Phillip is a 43-year-old married man with three children. He changed jobs about a year ago and recently has been experiencing symptoms of anxiety and panic. Phillip reports that he has been shy all his life and has avoided situations that would require him to speak in front of a group. Phillip's recent job move has added stress to his relationships with his wife and children, and his anxiety symptoms are causing him to become preoccupied with his health.

From a psychoanalytic perspective, most forms of anxiety are conceptualized as resulting from internal conflicts among the id, the ego, and the superego. More specifically, a psychoanalytic explanation for Phillip's anxiety would postulate that the standards he has internalized in his superego are restrictive and demanding. These standards determine what is acceptable behavior and what is unacceptable. Psychoanalysts might hypothesize further that Phillip is afraid of disappointing his "superego," which is really the internalization of his parents. Therefore, the discrepancy and conflict between Phillip's high standards and his likely not-as-high

behavior leads him to experience anxiety. Phillip's reports of being shy as a child are consistent with the psychoanalytic position that the origins of psychopathology are likely to be in early childhood, probably within the first five years of life. Phillip's particular problem with public speaking likely stems from a unconscious fear that he will start to verbalize unacceptable material that is housed in the id and that he will be powerless to prevent that from happening. The anxiety is being experienced as physical difficulties, something that psychoanalysts might suggest is the first step on the road to the development of a conversion hysteria disorder. More recent psychodynamic perspectives would emphasize the social nature of Phillip's anxiety and might implicate early problematic bonding experiences with his parents or current difficulties in his social environment as factors that are likely contributing to his anxiety.

A behavioral view of Phillip's difficulties would focus strongly on his learning history. Classical conditioning theorists would assume that at some earlier point, Phillip learned to associate fear with making oral presentations. Perhaps Phillip was ridiculed for a talk he gave, or perhaps he simply observed someone else being embarrassed while giving a speech. In either case, the association between public speaking and fear is now established, and Phillip becomes anxious when faced with the prospect of making a presentation. Compounding this situation, from an

Psychoanalytic / Interpersonal Perspective

Freud recognized the significance of loss as an immediate precipitant of depression. He hypothesized that adverse events early in childhood leave some individuals vulnerable to depression later in life. Specifically, Freud theorized that failure to receive appropriate gratification of one's needs in the oral stage results in excessive dependency on others and inadequate develop-

ment of the ego. Freud believed that this failure of gratification was often due to inadequate parenting. When an individual experiences a significant loss as an adult, feelings of rejection and abandonment are reactivated and, Freud suggested, the individual experiences anger toward the parent. Because we typically adopt, or internalize, characteristics of our caregiver, the anger toward this person is also experienced as anger toward ourself. Thus, for Freud, early loss leaves

BOX 4.3 (concluded)

operant conditioning perspective, Phillip is being reinforced each time he avoids giving a speech. When it appears that he will be unable to avoid making a presentation, Phillip's level of anxiety increases to the point where he experiences physical symptoms. Similarly, from a more cognitive perspective, Phillip's anxiety is seen as a product of negative schemas, learned early in his childhood, that lead him to interpret events in his world as threatening and dangerous. As a child, Phillip may not have been prepared for his presentations in school and thus performed poorly. Those experiences would have led him to have expectations for failure, which are activated automatically now as an adult each time Phillip must give a speech. In addition, Phillip is likely misinterpreting mild physical symptoms of anxiety and is becoming even more anxious about experiencing a heart attack.

Humanistic theorists hypothesize that anxiety develops when there is a discrepancy between an individual's "ideal self," or aspirations, and her or his "real self," or current level of functioning. In explaining Phillip's anxiety, therefore, humanists would suggest that he has set his standards too high, elevating his ideal self to a level that is not attainable by his actual performance. They might also hypothesize that Phillip is concerned about receiving positive regard from others in his environment, because he is basing his self-concept on his perception of how others view him. A lack of unconditional positive regard from others around him leads Phillip to place excessive importance on the regard he receives

from others for performing well. This pressure causes Phillip to experience symptoms of anxiety in situations in which he must obtain positive regard from others.

Finally, biological approaches to understanding Phillip's anxiety would focus on genetic and neurochemical factors that contribute to the development of anxiety disorders. It appears that both panic disorder and social phobia may have a moderate genetic component. Therefore, biological theorists might hypothesize that there is a history of anxiety disorder in Phillip's family of origin and that he has a genetic makeup that leaves him vulnerable to experiencing anxiety. Other theorists would suggest that Phillip has a hyperactive central noradrenergic system that increases his biological reactivity to stress, resulting in symptoms of anxiety. Finally, the results of recent studies using functional Magnetic Resonance Imaging (fMRI) procedures would lead clinical neuroscientists to hypothesize that Phillip has difficulties regulating his emotional functioning because of abnormal brain activations in the locus ceruleus and amygdala in response to stressful stimuli.

As you can see, some of these perspectives implicate early experience, whereas others focus on current functioning; some emphasize underlying processes (both psychological and biological), whereas others focus on observable behaviors. Ultimately, it is likely that some form of integration of these theories will be most useful in understanding people like Phillip.

us dependent and at risk for experiencing anger, self-hate, and depression if we encounter later loss events that activate these feelings.

From a more interpersonal and object-relations perspective, depression is viewed being caused and maintained by problematic interpersonal relationships and particularly by the loss of an important relationship (e.g., Gotlib & Beach, 1995; Weissman & Klerman, 1993). Depression may be triggered by disruptions in important interpersonal relationships, most notably the loss of an important relationship. The role of interper-

sonal relationships in causing depression is not limited to a loss, however. Symptoms of depression can be conceptualized in part as a maladaptive attempt to deal with a difficult social environment. Under stress, individuals who are vulnerable to depression because of poor interpersonal skills or problematic early relationships may become excessively dependent on, and seek reassurance from, others around them. And as they become more depressed, their relationships become further strained. The sadness, self-deprecation, and irritability that characterize depression can alienate people who are close to the depressed individual, eventually driving away the sources of support and attachment that the individual needs most and further exacerbating the depressive symptoms.

Behavioral / Cognitive Perspective

A behavioral perspective on depression also involves the concept of loss. In this view, however, the emphasis is on the tangible loss of reinforcement in one's environment (Lewinsohn, 1974; Lewinsohn, Hoberman, Teri, & Hautzinger, 1985). The loss of a significant relationship is likely to lead to a reduction in the sources of reinforcement in a person's life. From the perspective of operant theory, this loss of reinforcement will lead to a reduction in the behaviors being emitted by the individual. This phenomenon is seen in symptoms of social withdrawal and decreased activity that are characteristic of people with depression. The loss of reinforcement and subsequent decrease in behavior initiates a vicious cycle in which people's social withdrawal further decreases their opportunities to obtain reinforcement, further inhibiting their behavior. To make matters worse, depressed people often receive reinforcement, in the form of sympathy and concern, for the very behaviors they are trying to stop. In short, adaptive behaviors are extinguished and depressive behaviors are reinforced in a vicious downward cycle.

More cognitively, some individuals are hypothesized to develop a way of thinking about themselves, the world, and the future that predisposes them to be vulnerable to depression. This dysfunctional style of thinking alone, however, is not sufficient to cause depression; it must be *activated* by experience of a stressful life event. Once a stressor has triggered or activated a dysfunctional cognitive style, depression-prone individuals begin to selectively attend to and interpret information in their world in negative ways. They focus on negative experiences to the exclusion of positive events, and they distort

ambiguous or neutral experiences in a negative way. They blame themselves for negative events and never notice positive aspects of their environment. These negative ways of thinking are hypothesized to directly influence the individual's emotions and behaviors, leading to the core symptoms of depression.

Humanistic Perspective

From the humanistic perspective, depression is the result of the loss of unconditional positive regard, leading to an unmanageable disparity between the real and ideal selves. When positive regard is experienced as conditional on only certain behaviors, humanistic theory predicts that people will focus on external values and ideals to guide their behavior. This focus will lead people to be out of touch with their own inner experience and to lose sight of their personal goals and values as guides for behavior. Further, an external ideal may be established as the standard for the ideal self, a standard that is unrealistic or unattainable for an individual. The result is a wide disparity between the real and ideal selves, and this disparity is experienced as low self-worth, a hallmark of depression.

Biological Perspective

Biological theories have contributed two sources of information on the causes of the depression—behavioral genetic research on the heritability of depression, and research on the dysregulation of neurotransmitters in depression. Evidence for the heritability of depression is stronger for bipolar disorder (which used to be called manic-depression) than for unipolar depression (e.g., Wallace, Schneider, & McGuffin, in press). Interestingly, however, there is evidence that a vulnerability to unipolar depression may, at least in part, be inherited. For example, in a study of 1,033 pairs of women who were either fraternal or identical twins, Kendler, Neale, Kessler, Heath, and Eaves (1992) found that the concordance (agreement) rate for the occurrence of depression was higher for identical twins than for fraternal twins, even after accounting for environmental factors. Scientists have also demonstrated that neurotransmission processes in depressed individuals are different than those in nondepressed individuals. More specifically, depression is characterized by elevated levels of cortisol produced in the hypothalamic-pituitary-adrenal axis of the central nervous system and by decreased levels of serotonin or norepinephrine in the central nervous system. This dysregulation of neurotransmitters is hypothesized to contribute to the disruption of a number of biological processes involved in depression, including sleep, arousal, and response to stress (e.g., Shelton, Hollon, Purdon, & Loosen, 1991; Siever & Davis, 1985).

Integrating Theories: Toward a Biopsychosocial Perspective

Which of these theories offers the "correct" explanation for the cause of depression? How can psychologists determine which perspective represents the truth? Certainly, one step in this process is to examine the empirical evidence that has been gathered to test these theories. As you might have expected, there is some empirical support for each of these theories, and one of these perspectives has not been shown to be clearly superior to the others in explaining the cause of depression. Research in this area is still at an early stage, and more evidence is needed before clear conclusions can be drawn. Compounding this situation is the fact that depression is a complex phenomenon—it is likely that there are multiple forms of depression, each with a different etiology. Finally, it is likely that all these models are correct to some degree and that biological, psychological, and social processes all operate in the development of depression.

In fact, researchers and theorists have come to recognize some of the common elements in these theories and have offered more integrative models of depression (e.g, Akiskal & McKinney, 1975; Goodman & Gotlib, 1999; Gotlib & Hammen, 1992; Shelton et al., 1991). Integrative models acknowledge that depression (and other forms of psychopathology) have multiple causes. The etiology of a complex problem may have multiple pathways, and all or only some of these paths may be operating in a single case. This view suggests that there may be several different factors that are *sufficient* to cause depression, but that no single factor is a *necessary* cause.

The integration of biological, psychological, and social models represents an important next step in the development of theories of behavior and psychopathology. Integration of different theories must still be balanced, however, against the need to develop the most parsimonious explanation for a problem. A critical task for clinical researchers is to determine which factors are essential for specific psychological problems to occur and which are correlates or consequences of these problems (cf. Barnett & Gotlib, 1988). In the next chapter we turn our attention to the classification and diagnosis of psychological problems.

SUMMARY AND CONCLUSIONS

Theories are critical in clinical psychology. They help clinicians to organize the way they think about people and their situations, and they influence the approach clinicians take to assessment and treatment. Among meeting a number of other criteria, a good theory should offer clear, testable hypotheses and should be supported by empirical research. Several major theories of psychopathology are widely used in clinical psychology. Psychoanalytic and psychodynamic theories, first developed by Freud, postulate that psychopathology, and particularly anxiety, is caused by unconscious conflicts among the id, ego, and superego. These conflicts involve unacceptable feelings and memories that the person keeps from awareness through the use of various defense mechanisms. Behavioral and cognitive theories focus on the learning of maladaptive behaviors through classical or operant conditioning or on the operation of cognitive schemas, or filters, through which people interpret events in their world. Humanistic theories take a more positive view of human nature and conceptualize psychopathology as arising from blocked drives for self-actualization and self-fulfillment. Finally, biological theories emphasize the contribution of genetic or neurochemical functioning to the development of psychopathology.

These theories vary in the extent to which they meet the criteria set forth for evaluating the strength of a good theory. It is almost certain that no single theory will explain all forms of psychopathology. Clinical psychologists are beginning to integrate aspects of these theories into broader biopsychosocial theories of psychopathology. As promising as these more comprehensive theories are, however, they have been formulated too recently to have met all the criteria for a strong theory, and much work remains to be done in testing these theories.

KEY TERMS AND NAMES

Aaron Beck
Behavioral genetics
Behavioral neuroscience
Biological preparedness
Classical, or Pavlovian, conditioning
Cognitive theories
Ego psychology
Sigmund Freud

Humanistic theories
Internal consistency
Object relations
Operant, or instrumental, conditioning
Parsimony
Carl Rogers
B. Frederick Skinner
John Watson

RESOURCES

Books

Freud, S., & Breuer, J. (1895). *Studies on hysteria* (Vol. 2; J. Strachey, Ed.). London: Hogarth Press.

Bandura, A. (1986). *Social foundations of thought and action: A social cognitive theory.* Englewood Cliffs, NJ: Prentice-Hall.

Mahoney, M. J. (1976). *The scientist as subject.* Cambridge, MA: Ballinger.

Journals

Theory and Science
Journal of the American Psychoanalytic Association
Psychoanalytic Psychology
Journal of the Experimental Analysis of Behavior
Journal of Humanistic Psychology
Personal Relationships

CHAPTER FIVE

DIAGNOSIS AND CLASSIFICATION IN CLINICAL PSYCHOLOGY

INTRODUCTION

In chapter 1 we presented the case of Brian, a 16-year-old adolescent whose parents had recently divorced. Brian and his mother and sister moved to a new town after the divorce to try to make a fresh start. Within six months of this move, Brian's school performance and social functioning had deteriorated markedly. He had not made any new friends since the move and had also lost contact with his old schoolmates. He was finding it difficult to concentrate, and, consequently, his schoolwork was suffering. Brian was also losing weight and waking up in the middle of the night, often finding it difficult

to fall back to sleep. He was feeling increasingly lonely, and six months after he moved to the new town with his mother and sister, Brian made a serious suicide attempt.

As clinical psychologists, what are we to think when an individual cannot sleep, does not want to eat, and feels sad and despondent most of the time? How are we to understand these behaviors and feelings? What does it mean when these problems are accompanied by a serious decline in performance at school or work? How are problems of eating and sleeping related to Brian's social and academic difficulties? And how is a suicide attempt tied to these other problems? Finally, what should we make of these problems in a teenage boy or girl, compared with the same problems in a 40-year-old man or woman? These questions are central to the task of defining and classifying psychopathology.

The process of classifying psychological problems involves the descriptive phase in the thinking of clinical psychologists that we discussed in the first chapter. That is, when clinicians attempt to classify the types of psychological problems that people experience, they are trying to describe accurately and systematically the nature and scope of these problems. Several issues are central to an understanding of how clinical psychologists think about psychopathology, and these issues are the focus of this chapter. The first issue involves the general need for classification—should psychologists try to classify people or the problems that they experience, and if so, why? Second, what systems have been developed for the classification of psychopathology, and how well do these systems work in helping clinical psychologists understand the psychological problems that are experienced and exhibited by children, adolescents, and adults? And finally, what improvements can be made to the ways that psychologists think about, classify, and diagnose various forms of psychopathology?

THE IMPORTANCE OF CLASSIFICATION

Is Brian's reaction to the divorce of his parents unique? That is, are Brian's problems "one of a kind," or are they representative of those of a group of people who display a similar pattern of problematic thoughts, behaviors, and emotions? And are we in a better position to understand and help Brian if we have knowledge of people who seem to exhibit similar patterns of behaviors and feelings? These questions are at the core of the decision concerning whether we should try to classify psychological problems in a systematic manner. If we work within an assumption that each individual is unique with respect to the causes of, and the potentially useful treatments

for, his or her psychological difficulties, then there is no need to try to classify Brian's problems with those of other individuals. If, however, we believe that Brian's problems are not unique, that his difficulties may be similar to those experienced and displayed by other people, that they may share common causes and may be treated with a common therapeutic approach, then we may gain a better understanding of Brian by being able to compare his situation with that of a large group of individuals.

The concept of similarity among individuals, contrasted with the uniqueness of each person, lies at the heart of debates over the importance and usefulness of systems for classifying psychopathology. As we will explain in this chapter, Brian's problems are not unique. A constellation of sad affect, disrupted social functioning, sleep and appetite problems, poor work or school performance, and suicidal thoughts or attempts is often observed in adolescents and adults. A constellation, or collection, of symptoms is known as a **syndrome.** Much can be gained by recognizing that Brian's problems reflect a syndrome or disorder that has been labeled *Major Depressive Disorder* (American Psychiatric Association, 1994). We will use depression, and Brian's problems in particular, as an instructive example of the classification of psychopathology.

Classification as a Characteristic Activity of Humans

Classification of people and their problems has been a hotly contested issue throughout much of the history of clinical psychology and psychiatry. On the one hand, many professionals have argued that classification or diagnostic systems are necessary to facilitate our understanding of people and their problems, to provide a basis for an understanding of the etiology and course of different types of problems, and to provide adequate treatment to those in need of help (Clark, Watson, & Reynolds, 1995). On the other hand, critics have argued that classification systems for personality and psychopathology are inherently problematic because they can lead to the dehumanization of individuals and contribute to the development of stereotypes of individuals who are placed in certain diagnostic categories (Kutchins & Kirk, 1997). Critics also argue that stigmas and other negative attitudes are attached to the labels that emerge from classification systems (Tucker, 1998; see below).

This debate can be informed by a larger body of research that suggests that the tendency to classify and categorize information about the world, including information about people, is an inherent feature of the way that human beings process knowledge. Researchers in cognitive psychology, social psychology, and cognitive science have shown that people organize and group information on the basis of perceived similarity of the elements on a variety of different dimensions (Genero & Cantor, 1987; Medin & Heit, 1999). Searching for patterns and structures in the information that we take in is necessary if we are to manage the morass of stimuli and information that confront us at every moment. Although we may not be aware that we are doing so, without our constant efforts to organize incoming information we would be overwhelmed by stimuli from the environment and would be unable to make effective judgments and decisions. Clinical psychologists are faced with this same basic need for structure and organization when they try to identify similarities and differences among the people that they try to help.

Classification as a Characteristic of Science

In addition to helping us understand our world, classification is also a fundamental characteristic of science. All of nature, from the level of atomic and molecular structures to the organization of the solar system and galaxies, is characterized by pattern and structure. A major task of all fields of science is to identify the structures and patterns that exist in nature, including those that are reflected in the behaviors, thoughts, and emotions

of people. The development of a reliable and valid system of classification, called a **taxonomy,** is a necessary step in the advancement of any science, including the science of human behavior and psychopathology.

Virtually all biological and physical sciences utilize taxonomies as part of their efforts to understand the phenomena they study. For example, one of the most significant observations of pattern in the history of science was the development of the periodic table of the elements by Dmitry Mendeleyev in 1869. By identifying the rules that govern the most basic elements in chemistry, Mendeleyev developed a classification system that not only allowed him to organize known elements into families, but further, led him to predict the existence of elements that had not yet been discovered. Since the early 1800s, scientists had known that substances were made up of atoms. Through the middle 1800s they were trying to understand the natural organization of the elements out of which other forms of matter were built; they measured the elements' atomic weights relative to the weight of the lightest known element, hydrogen, and tried to characterize the chemical behavior of each element (Judson, 1980). Despite these efforts, however, no useful system for organizing and classifying elements had been developed. Mendeleyev realized that if he arranged the elements according to increasing atomic weight, similar chemical properties appeared cyclically, an observation that led him to propose the periodic law of the elements (Judson). Mendeleyev was able to identify the natural pattern and structure that characterized the basic elements, and the resulting system was invaluable to physicists and chemists in their understanding of the basic characteristics of the elements and their relationships to one another.

Clinical psychologists and other mental health professionals and researchers are faced with a similar task. They have struggled for many years to determine whether there is an inherent structure or organization to the types of behavioral, emotional, and cognitive problems for which people either seek or require professional help. A critical assumption underlying efforts to classify psychological problems is that human behavior, including dysfunctional behavior, is a natural phenomenon and is therefore governed by the same rules that dictate structure and order in all of nature. But even if that assumption is valid, how does one decide what elements are essential in classifying human behavior? And how are those elements related to each other? In developing a classification system, or taxonomy, of psychopathology, how many categories should there be? Should the categories be broad or narrow? As you might expect, having categories that are too narrow may lead psychologists mistakenly to treat similar disorders as different. By the same token, having categories that are too broad may lead us to treat different disorders as if they were the same. And perhaps overriding all these decisions, how do we decide that a behavior or condition is problematic or serious enough to warrant a diagnosis at all?

The Benefits and Costs of Classification

The decision to classify psychopathology has both benefits and costs. There are two major benefits of classification in clinical psychology. First, organized information about the characteristics of people whom we try to help can be useful when clinicians make treatment decisions. Thus, if a particular method or technique is found to help one person, it may be useful in helping another who exhibits a similar set of problems. To judge the similarity of these two people, however, we need a system that allows us to document the nature and extent of their problems. Second, a classification system allows professionals to communicate with one another in an informed manner, which facilitates better understanding and treatment of problems and leads to new insights. In this way, the knowledge gained by one group of psychologists about the nature or the treatment of a particular problem can be shared with other psychologists, and this knowledge can be accurately and effectively

applied to new groups of people in need of help. In medicine, new disorders are often identified through a classification system long before they can be successfully treated. But the identification and classification of the symptoms, or syndrome, lays the foundation for research that may eventually result in an effective treatment.

Classification systems, although they offer many important benefits, are not also without costs. Foremost among these is the tendency for professionals to develop stereotypes based on their assumptions about the nature of the categories within the classification system. Thus, once someone is classified as depressed, as schizophrenic, or as having panic disorder, clinical psychologists may overlook information about that person that might have been helpful in determining a treatment plan. In this way, the use of classification systems can contribute to premature conclusions about the nature of certain problems and lead to unsuccessful treatment decisions. Nevertheless, it is apparent that the development of a taxonomy of psychopathology and its refinement are integral tasks in the field of clinical psychology. In the following section we describe the major approaches to the classification of psychopathology.

CLASSIFICATION IN CLINICAL PSYCHOLOGY

For centuries scientists have attempted to classify various forms of psychopathology. In fact, it is clear that virtually every culture over the past several thousand years has recognized differences among madness, depression, dementia (impairment of memory and mental function from brain injury or age), and criminality (Kendall & Hammen, 1998). But it is only in the last 75 years that the development of more refined classifications has become a major goal of mental health professionals. The origins of the systems for classifying psychopathology that are used most widely today are found in the work of **Emil Kraepelin,** a nineteenth-century German physician. Kraepelin assumed that identification and classification of specific psychological disorders was necessary in order to determine the particular cause of each. He further assumed that each form of "mental illness" was distinct from all other disorders, was exhibited with a particular set of symptoms, and followed a unique and predictable course. Moreover, as was becoming apparent in medicine, Kraepelin believed that different illnesses would require different treatments. Kraepelin made a fundamental distinction between **dementia praecox,** an early term for what is now referred to as schizophrenia, and manic-depressive illness, a syndrome now known as bipolar disorder. Although Kraepelin's original formulations and classification categories have been changed over the years, the current diagnostic systems developed by the World Health Organization and by the American Psychiatric Association are direct descendants of Kraepelin's work.

Current Diagnostic Systems

The two dominant systems for classifying psychopathology throughout the world are the **International Classification of Diseases,** 10th edition (ICD-10), developed by the World Health Organization (WHO, 1990), and the **Diagnostic and Statistical Manual of Mental Disorders,** 4th edition (DSM-IV), developed by the American Psychiatric Association (1994). Both these systems were developed shortly after World War II. In 1948, for the first time, the World Health Organization included mental disorders in the sixth edition of the ICD. This system was used primarily in Europe; in America, the American Psychiatric Association developed and published its own *Diagnostic and Statistical Manual* (DSM-I) in 1952. In response to criticisms leveled at DSM about the lack of consistency, or reliability, in diagnostic decisions (Spitzer & Fleiss, 1974), a second edition of DSM (DSM-II) was published in 1968, which coincided with a new and similar classification system published in Europe by the World Health Organization. Still, there was considerable opposition to these

systems. In particular, clinical scientists argued that terms and categories like *neurosis* and *hysteria* were based on theory rather than on empirical data and were too vague to permit accurate diagnosis. They maintained that until the classification systems had a stronger basis in science, there would continue to be problems involving reliability and validity of diagnoses.

In response to these criticisms, major revisions of the DSM were undertaken and published in 1980 (DSM-III), 1987 (DSM-IIIR [Revised]), and 1994 (DSM-IV); the ICD is now in its 10th edition. For diagnostic decisions, these classification systems now rely much more strongly on observable behavior and clinical descriptions (Widiger, Frances, Pincus, Davis, & First, 1991). The categories are also more "theoretically neutral." For example, instead of *neurosis* and *hysteria,* which have psychodynamic theoretical foundations, DSM-IV uses the term *anxiety disorders.* In its 1994 revision of the DSM, the American Psychiatric Association also turned to the results of empirical studies of psychopathology to a much greater extent than was the case with the earlier editions. For example, there is now a distinction between unipolar depression and bipolar affective disorder, based largely on research findings in which these two types of depression have been found to have different courses and to respond to different treatments. DSM-IV, in particular, relied heavily on the results of numerous field trials in which diagnostic criteria for different disorders were tested in clinics and research settings and then modified on the basis of the results of these trials. Other diagnostic categories have also undergone significant changes over the four editions of the DSM (see box 5.1). The DSM is now the most widely used and accepted diagnostic system, both in the United States and worldwide (Maser, Klaeber, & Weise, 1991). Therefore, we will focus on DSM-IV in our discussions in this chapter and throughout this book.

DSM-IV is a *multiaxial classification system* (see table 5.1) in that there are five broad dimensions, or **diagnostic axes,** on which individuals'

BOX 5.1

THE CHANGING FACE OF PSYCHOPATHOLOGY

The DSM-IV represents the fourth revision of the diagnostic and classification system of the American Psychiatric Association, with another revision anticipated by 2005. Changes have been made through the addition of new diagnostic categories, through alterations in the criteria of existing diagnoses, and through the deletion of other diagnoses.

Two changes that have occurred are relevant to the cases that we are following through this text. Our case example Alison meets the criteria for Bulimia Nervosa as detailed in DSM-IV. Bulimia Nervosa was not included as a category in DSM-I or DSM-II. The disorder first appeared in DSM-III in 1980 under the category of "Bulimia." The criteria in DSM-III were much more general than are those in DSM-IV and did not specify the presence of either binge eating episodes or "recurrent inappropriate compensatory behavior in order to prevent weight gain" (e.g., vomiting) for the diagnosis. Thus, bulimia has evolved considerably over the course of the revision of the DSM.

No category has gone through more changes, however, than the childhood disorder that has been labeled "Hyperactivity" or "Attention Deficit Disorder," the diagnosis assigned to our case example Jason. This category refers to a set of problems that usually emerge in early childhood and involve apparent difficulties in the regulation of motor behavior (being overactive) and attention (being inattentive). No reference was made to problems of overactivity or inattention in DSM-I. The publication of DSM-II in 1968 included a category of "Hyperkinetic Reaction of Childhood (or Adolescence)" under the general category of "Transient Situational Disturbances, Adjustment Disorder." This disorder was characterized primarily by motoric or physical overactivity. DSM-III in 1980 represented a major change in diagnostic thinking about these types of problems with the addition of the category "Attention Deficit Disorder with Hyperactivity (ADD-H) and Without Hyperactivity (ADD)." However, when the revision of the 1987 DSM-III was

current behavior and functioning may be classified. These dimensions refer to different aspects of individuals, their behavior, and their life situations. Two axes are concerned with diagnostic categories, while the remaining three axes permit the collection of additional relevant data about the individual. The use of **five axes in DSM-IV** reflects the recognition that a broad view of the person's life will contribute to more effective decisions about treatment than would result from a diagnosis alone.

What is considered a "mental disorder," according to DSM-IV? Here is the DSM-IV definition of mental disorder:

> [A mental disorder] is conceptualized as a clinically significant behavioral or psychological syndrome or pattern that occurs in an individual and that is associated with present distress (a painful symptom) or disability (impairment in one or more areas of

functioning) or with a significantly increased risk of suffering death, pain, disability, or an important loss of freedom. In addition, this syndrome or pattern must not be merely an expectable and culturally sanctioned response to a particular event, for example, the death of a loved one. Whatever its original cause, it must currently be considered a manifestation of a behavioral, psychological, or biological dysfunction in the individual. Neither deviant behavior (e.g., political, religious, or sexual) nor conflicts that are primarily between the individual and society are mental disorders unless the deviance or conflict is a symptom of a dysfunction in the individual, as described above (pp. xxi–xxii).

It is important to note that this definition is silent concerning the cause or etiology of mental disorder. We should also point out here that DSM-IV is careful to exclude culturally sanctioned behaviors of distress, like grief following the death of a loved one, as a mental disorder.

BOX 5.1 (concluded)

published, the disorder was relabeled as "Attention Deficit Hyperactivity Disorder" and the distinction between the disorder with and without hyperactivity was dropped. Finally, the DSM-IV used the label "Attention Deficit/Hyperactivity Disorder" (ADHD) and two subtypes of the disorder, "Predominantly Inattentive Type" and "Predominantly Hyperactive-Impulsive Type." Separate criteria are presented for inattention symptoms (e.g., "often fails to give close attention to details or makes careless mistakes in schoolwork, work, or other activities") and hyperactivity-impulsivity (e.g., "often fidgets with hands or feet or squirms in seat"; "often blurts out answers to questions before the questions have been completed").

Although these changes may be useful and may reflect ever-increasing knowledge about the nature of attentional and hyperactivity problems in children, the changing nature of this diagnostic category has represented a source of confusion to clinicians and researchers alike. More importantly, these changes have resulted primarily because of the evolving opinions of the panels of experts who have been responsible for this diagnostic category on each

of the successive versions of the DSM. Although research evidence has certainly been considered in the alterations of the diagnosis related to inattention and hyperactivity, it appears to have played a secondary role to the judgments of the committees. In fact, recent research continues to generate new information about the best way to construct this diagnostic category (e.g., Barkley, 1998; Farone, Biederman, Feighner, & Monuteaux, 2000). New collaborative effort, headed by the National Institutes of Health (NIH) have led to progress toward an understanding of ADHD that is more soundly based in research and reflects an integration of findings from psychology, psychiatry, and other disciplines (NIH, 2000). Perhaps the most important message here is that some of the categories represented in taxonomies such as the DSM are in a preliminary form and will continue to be subject to change. These changes should be based on research evidence and should be slow in coming to avoid premature shifts in the criteria that are presented. Finally, DSM categories should not be treated as pure diagnostic entities in the absence of definitive research evidence to support their validity.

Axis I in DSM-IV is the primary axis for diagnoses of psychopathology. Most diagnoses appear on Axis I, which includes conditions such as depression, anxiety, attention deficit/hyperactivity disorder, mental retardation, and schizophrenia. Many of the disorders that are classified on Axis I involve episodic disturbance, like depressive episodes or discrete panic attacks. In contrast, the second axis, Axis II, is concerned with more stable, long-standing problems, such as personality disorders. DSM-IV describes more than 200 specific diagnostic categories, arranged under 18 primary headings. Each category contains a varying number of subcategories with explicit criteria and decision rules to determine each diagnosis. These criteria include a specified set of symptoms and minimum standards for the number, severity, and duration of symptoms that must be present in order for a particular diagno-

sis to be made. For example, the diagnostic category of eating disorders includes anorexia nervosa, bulimia nervosa, and unspecified eating disorders with symptoms that do not meet the specific criteria for either anorexia or bulimia. Although anorexia and bulimia both involve severely disrupted patterns of eating, each has its own specified set of symptoms with its own defining features.

Individuals can (but do not have to) receive clinical diagnoses on both Axis I and Axis II. Personality disorders, diagnosed on Axis II, differ from Axis I disorders in that they reflect more long-standing problems in the person's style of behaving and interacting with the world. Personality disorders are assumed to develop during childhood or adolescence and continue into adult life, where they create difficulties in a person's interpersonal relationships and life situations

TABLE 5.1
Overview of DSM-IV Categories

Axis I: Clinical Syndromes

Disorders usually first evident in infancy, childhood, or adolescence (e.g., mental retardation; pervasive developmental disorders; disruptive behaviors and attention deficit disorders)

Delirium, dementia, amnestic, and other cognitive disorders (e.g., dementia of the Alzheimer's type; amnestic disorder)

Substance-related disorders (e.g., alcohol use disorders; caffeine use disorders; cocaine use disorders)

Schizophrenia and other psychotic disorders (e.g., schizophrenia, catatonic type; delusional disorder)

Mood disorders (e.g., depressive disorder; major depressive disorder, recurrent; bipolar disorder I)

Anxiety disorders (e.g., agoraphobia; post-traumatic stress disorder)

Somatoform disorders (e.g., hypochondriasis; body dysmorphic disorder)

Factitious disorders

Dissociative disorders (e.g., dissociative amnesia)

Sexual and gender identity disorders (e.g., sexual desire disorders; pedophilia)

Eating disorders (e.g., anorexia nervosa; bulimia nervosa)

Sleep disorders (e.g., primary insomnia; sleep terror disorder)

Impulse control disorders not elsewhere classified (e.g., kleptomania; pyromania)

Adjustment disorders (e.g., adjustment disorder with depressed mood)

Axis II: Personality disorders

paranoid; schizoid; schizotypal; antisocial; borderline; histrionic; narcissistic; avoidant; dependent; obsessive-compulsive

Axis III: General medical conditions

Axis IV: Psychosocial and environmental problems

Problems with primary support group

Problems related to the social environment

Educational problems

Occupational problems

Housing problems

Economic problems

Problems with access to health care services

Problems related to interaction with the legal system/crime

Axis V: Global assessment of functioning scale

(Widiger & Costa, 1994). The types of problems reflected in the specific personality disorders (e.g., antisocial personality, borderline personality) are presumed to be distinct from the types of problems represented on Axis I. The distinction between the two axes is not sharp as the authors of the DSM intended, however, because several Axis II personality disorders appear to differ from Axis I diagnoses primarily in degree (e.g., schizotypal personality and schizophrenia; obsessive-compulsive personality and obsessive-compulsive disorder; Widiger & Costa; Widiger & Shea, 1991).

The remaining axes (Axes III, IV, and V) are included to generate a more complete picture of individuals' psychosocial functioning and some information concerning the social context in which they function. True to the medical roots of the DSM, Axis III is designed to reflect general medical conditions that may be relevant to either the etiology of the individual's psychopathology or the proposed treatment program. Axes IV and V attempt to place the individual's psychiatric problems in a broader context by considering characteristics of the social and physical environment in which he or she is behaving as well as his or her overall level of functioning or competence. Axis IV is concerned with psychosocial and environmental problems that may be relevant to the individual's behavior. Finally, Axis V permits a global rating of the individual's adaptive functioning rated on a scale from 1 to 100 (see table 5.2). Axis V ratings are important because they serve to draw attention to the individual's strengths. In box 5.2 we demonstrate how DSM-IV would treat each of the four cases that we presented in chapter 1.

Criticisms and Limitations of DSM-IV

Despite its widespread use, there are a number of criticisms and limitations of DSM-IV (Clark et al., 1995; Kirk & Kutchins, 1994; Kutchins & Kirk, 1997). For example, patients often do not fit neatly into the circumscribed and well-defined categories of DSM-IV. For example, table 5.3 presents the DSM-IV diagnostic criteria for Generalized Anxiety Disorder (GAD). As you can see, the person must report excessive worry that occurs on most days for at least six months, as well as at least three additional symptoms. What would DSM-IV have a clinical psychologist do with an individual who reported excessive worry

---

BOX 5.2

MULTIAXIAL DSM-IV DIAGNOSES OF JASON, ALLISON, PHILLIP, AND MARIA

Jason, age 8, who presented with behavior problems:
Axis I: 314.01 Attention Deficit/Hyperactivity Disorder, Combined Type
313.81 Oppositional Defiant Disorder
Axis II: V71.09 (No Diagnosis on Axis II)
Axis III: Chronic Otitis Media (inner ear infections)
Axis IV: V62.3 (Academic Problem)
Axis V: Current GAF: 55

Allison, age 17, who presented with difficulties around eating:
Axis I: 307.51 (Bulimia Nervosa)
Axis II: 301.4 (Obsessive-Compulsive Personality Disorder)
Axis III: None (No Medical Conditions)
Axis IV: V62.3 (Academic Problem)
Axis V: Current GAF: 60

Phillip, age 43, who presented with symptoms of anxiety:
Axis I: 300.23 (Social Phobia)
Axis II: Possible 301.82 (Avoidant Personality Disorder)
Axis III: None (No Medical Conditions)
Axis IV: V62.2 (Occupational Problem)
Axis V: Current GAF: 51

Maria, age 73, who presented with symptoms of depression:
Axis I: 296.2 (Major Depressive Disorder)
Axis II: V71.09 (No Diagnosis on Axis II)
Axis III: None (No Medical Conditions)
Axis IV: V62.82 (Bereavement)
Axis V: Current GAF: 50

---

that was difficult to control, but reported experiencing only two, rather than three, additional symptoms? Because of its strict criteria and the

TABLE 5.2

Global Assessment of Functioning (GAF) Scale

Consider psychological, social and occupational functioning on a hypothetical continuum of mental health-illness. Do not include impairment in functioning due to physical (or environmental) limitations.

Code   (Note: Use intermediate codes when appropriate, e.g., 45, 68, 72.)

91–100   Superior functioning in a wide range of activities. Life's problems never seem to get out of hand, is sought out by others because of his or her many positive qualities. No symptoms.

81–90   Absent or minimal symptoms (e.g., mild anxiety before an exam), good functioning in all areas, interested and involved in a wide range of activities, socially effective, generally satisfied with life, no more than everyday problems or concerns (e.g., an occasional argument with family members).

71–80   If symptoms are present, they are transient and expectable reactions to psychosocial stressors (e.g., difficulty concentrating after family argument); no more than slight impairment in social, occupational, or school functioning (e.g., temporarily falling behind in schoolwork).

61–70   Some mild symptoms (e.g., depressed mood and mild insomnia) OR some difficulty in social, occupational, or school functioning (e.g., occasional truancy, or theft within the household), but generally functioning pretty well, has some meaningful interpersonal relationships.

51–60   Moderate symptoms (e.g., flat effect and circumstantial speech, occasional panic attacks) OR moderate difficulty in social, occupational, or school functioning (e.g., few friends, conflicts with peers or co-workers).

41–50   Serious symptoms (e.g., suicidal ideation, severe obsessional rituals, frequent shoplifting) OR any serious impairment in social, occupational or school functioning (e.g., no friends, unable to keep a job).

31–40   Some impairment in reality testing or communication (e.g., speech is at all times illogical, obscure or irrelevant) OR major impairment in several areas, such as work or school, family relations, judgment, thinking or mood (e.g., depressed man avoids friends, neglects family and is unable to work; child frequently beats up younger children, is defiant at home and is failing at school).

21–30   Behavior is considerably influenced by delusions or hallucinations OR serious impairment in communication or judgment (e.g., sometimes incoherent, acts grossly inappropriately, suicidal preoccupation) OR inability to function in almost all areas (e.g., stays in bed all day, no job, home, or friends).

11–20   Some danger of hurting self or others (e.g., suicide attempts without clear expectation of death, frequently violent, manic excitement) OR occasionally fails to maintain minimal personal hygiene (e.g., smears feces) OR gross impairment in communication (e.g., largely incoherent or mute).

1–10   Persistent danger of severely hurting self or others (e.g., recurrent violence) OR persistent inability to maintain minimal personal hygiene OR serious suicidal act with clear expectation of death.

0   Inadequate information.

(Reprinted with permission from the Diagnostic and Statistical Manual of Mental Disorders, Fourth Edition. Copyright 1994 American Psychiatric Association. Reprinted with permission.)

emphasis on discrete categories rather than dimensions, that individual would not be diagnosed with GAD, even though he or she is likely very similar to other individuals who do meet full criteria for that diagnosis. The general point here is that DSM-IV, like any categorical classification system, either excludes people who may in fact belong in a particular category, or includes people in the same category who may differ from each other in significant ways.

A second important criticism of DSM-IV involves the concept of **diagnostic comorbidity,** or the tendency of individuals to meet criteria for more than one diagnosis. It is now widely

TABLE 5.3
Diagnostic Criteria for Generalized Anxiety Disorder

A. Excessive anxiety and worry (apprehensive expectation), occurring more days than not for at least 6 months, about a number of events or activities (such as work or school performance).
B. The person finds it difficult to control the worry.
C. The anxiety and worry are associated with three (or more) of the following six symptoms (with at least some symptoms present for more days than not for the past 6 months). Note: Only one item is required in children.

    restlessness or feeling keyed up or on edge
    being easily fatigued
    difficulty concentrating or mind going blank
    irritability
    muscle tension
    sleep disturbance (difficulty falling or staying asleep, or restless unsatisfying sleep)

D. The focus of the anxiety and worry is not confined to features of an Axis I disorder, e.g., the anxiety or worry is not about having a Panic Attack (as in a Panic Disorder), being embarrassed in public (as in Social Phobia), being contaminated (as in Obsessive-Compulsive Disorder), being away from home or close relatives (as in Separation Anxiety Disorder), gaining weight (as in Anorexia Nervosa), having multiple physical complaints (as in Somatization Disorder), or having a serious illness (as in Hypochondriasis), and the anxiety and worry do not occur exclusively during Post-traumatic Stress Disorder.
E. The anxiety, worry, or physical symptoms cause clinically significant distress or impairment in social, occupational, or other important areas of functioning.
F. The disturbance is not due to the direct physiological effects of a substance (e.g., a drug of abuse, a medication) or a general medical condition (e.g., hyperthyroidism) and does not occur exclusively during a Mood Disorder, a Psychotic Disorder, or a Pervasive Developmental Disorder.

(Reprinted with permission from the Diagnostic and Statistical Manual of Mental Disorders, Fourth Edition. Copyright 1994 American Psychiatric Association. Reprinted with permission.)

recognized that, among both children and adults, different disorders tend to occur together in the same individuals. Comorbidities are common within the DSM diagnostic system. In a major epidemiological study, 56 percent of people who qualified for at least one DSM diagnosis at some point during their lifetime met criteria for two or more disorders (Kessler et al., 1994). In fact, depression, anxiety disorders, substance abuse disorders, and antisocial personality disorder are all more likely to occur with other conditions than to occur alone (Compas & Hammen, 1994; Kendall & Hammen, 1998). There is little acknowledgment in DSM-IV of these high rates of comorbidity; each disorder is treated as separate and distinct.

Some mental health professionals have also expressed concerns about the adverse effects of *labeling* an individual with a diagnosis. The argument here is that once a person is assigned a diagnosis and receives a diagnosis, we subsequently focus more on the label and the disorder than on the person. Indeed, the person may be viewed as if she or he *is* the diagnosis. Assigning a label may cut off further inquiry about the person and his or her situation. Indeed, Tucker (1998) has argued that diagnosing an individual with Major Depressive Disorder is likely to terminate any further investigation of the person's situation and lead quickly to a prescription for antidepressant medication. And once an individual receives a diagnostic label, they may be stigmatized by others in their social or professional networks (Fink & Tasman, 1992; Perlin, 1994), possibly leading to an exacerbation of their problematic behaviors.

Finally, a number of critics have argued that DSM-IV is not sensitive enough to diversity in culture and ethnicity or to the concerns of women (e.g., Eisenbruch, 1992; Fabrega, 1992; Tavris, 1992). The categories of abnormal behavior described in DSM-IV are largely based on the consensus of American mental health professionals, although DSM-IV does acknowledge that an individual's culture should be considered in making a diagnosis. Nevertheless, it is clear that some conditions are specific to particular cultural groups and that some disorders that occur in non-Western cultures do not correspond to any DSM categories (e.g., Liebowitz et al., 1994). Similarly, several observers have pointed to gender bias in the DSM-IV categories. Disorders with labels such as *premenstrual dysphoric disorder* and *self-defeating personality disorder* have been considered for inclusion in DSM to describe women who experience intense premenstrual distress, and women who stay in a relationship with a battering spouse (Goleman, 1994). As you can imagine, there are powerful social and political aspects to these categories in addition to whatever scientific evidence there may be for their existence.

An Alternative Approach to the Classification of Psychopathology

DSM-IV is a categorically based classification system: Individuals are classified and assigned to a particular category in which all members are assumed to share important features. An alternative to the classic categorical approach to the diagnosis of psychopathology involves the use of a quantitative, or dimensional, approach to taxonomy. Clinicians utilizing quantitative approaches do not a priori assume that there is a particular structure underlying psychological disorders. Rather, their position is that the pattern of symptoms and disorders is best understood by collecting data about the behavior in question from the most relevant informants. These sources could include adults reporting on their own behavior, clinicians' observations of individuals' behaviors, and parents and children reporting on the children's behavior. The clinician begins a quantitative approach to the development of a taxonomy of psychopathology by collecting large amounts of information on problematic behaviors, thoughts, and emotions, and then using powerful statistical methods (e.g., principal components analysis or factor analysis) to determine which behaviors, thoughts, and emotions are related to one another empirically in a systematic fashion. No assumptions are made about the underlying causes or course of any problems; these

must also be identified through careful empirical research.

Quantitative Taxonomic Systems   The most comprehensive **quantitative taxonomic system** of psychopathology has been developed for child and adolescent disorders by **Thomas Achenbach** and his colleagues at the University of Vermont (e.g., Achenbach, 1993; Achenbach, Howell, McConaughy, & Stanger, 1998; Hudziak, Wadsworth, Heath, & Achenbach, 1999). Achenbach's work is noteworthy for several reasons. First, the focus of initial phases of this research is on the nature of psychopathology during childhood and adolescence, an area of investigation that has been relatively neglected in the DSM until recently. Thus, the work has been important in

Thomas M. Achenbach, Ph.D., is a Professor of Psychiatry and Psychology at the University of Vermont. Through his research on behavioral and emotional problems in childhood and adolescence, Dr. Achenbach has developed a widely used, empirically based, system for the classification of psychopathology. (Photo courtesy of Tom Achenbach.)

providing much-needed information about psychopathology as it develops before adulthood. Second, Achenbach and his colleagues have provided the first comprehensive effort to actually develop a full taxonomy based on empirical data rather than on experts' preexisting ideas about what types of disorders and syndromes actually characterize the behavior of children and youth. Other quantitative approaches have focused more narrowly on specific types of psychopathology, most notably on the empirical identification of a syndrome of deviance or problem behavior (e.g., Costa, Jessor, & Turbin, 1999; Donovan, Jessor, & Costa, 1993; Farrell, Danish, & Howard, 1992; McGee & Newcomb, 1992).

What type of data or information could provide the basis for a quantitative taxonomy of child and adolescent psychopathology? The most relevant information on child and adolescent behavior comes from parents, who continuously observe their children's development; from teachers, who observe and compare the behavior of large numbers of children; and from the children themselves, who have access to internal thoughts and emotions that may not be available to observers such as parents and teachers. Achenbach and his colleagues collected reports from parents and teachers of a nationally representative sample of over 4,000 children and adolescents who had been referred for psychological or psychiatric services, and from the children themselves. These data were then used to identify clusters, or syndromes, of behaviors and emotions that consistently occurred together. A total of eight such syndromes have been identified across the reports of parents, teachers, and adolescents for both boys and girls between 4 and 18 years of age (Achenbach, 1991; see table 5.4).

These eight syndromes are subsumed within two broader behavior problem types: **Externalizing problems** (e.g., Delinquent Behavior, Aggressive Behavior), and **Internalizing problems** (e.g., Withdrawn, Anxious/Depressed). The two dimensions of Internalizing and Externalizing problems have been found empirically to be rec-

TABLE 5.4

Cross-Informant Syndromes of an Empirically Based Taxonomy of Child and Adolescent Psychopathology

Withdrawn
  (examples of problem behaviors include: would rather be alone; refuses to talk; is shy, timid)
Somatic Complaints
  (examples of problem behaviors include: feels dizzy; has aches, pains; has headaches; has nausea)
Anxious/Depressed
  (examples of problem behaviors include: is lonely; is nervous, tense; is fearful, anxious; unhappy, sad, depressed)
Social Problems
  (examples of problem behaviors include: is too dependent; gets teased; is not liked by peers)
Thought Problems
  (examples of problem behaviors include: can't get mind off certain things; hears things; repeats acts)
Attention Problems
  (examples of problem behaviors include: can't concentrate; can't sit still; is impulsive; is inattentive)
Delinquent Behavior
  (examples of problems behaviors include: runs away from home; sets fires; steals at home or outside of home; uses alcohol or drugs)
Aggressive Behavior
  (examples of problem behaviors include: is mean to others; fights; is stubborn, irritable; is disobedient at home or school)

ognizable in reports on children's behavior not only in the United States (Achenbach, Howell, Quay, & Conners, 1991), but in Holland (Verhulst, Achenbach, Ferdinand, & Kasius, 1993), Australia (Achenbach, Hensely, Phares, & Grayson, 1990), France (Stanger, Fombonne, & Achenbach, 1994), Thailand (Weisz et al., 1987), Puerto Rico (Achenbach, Bird et al., 1990), and Jamaica (Lambert, Lyubansky, & Achenbach, 1998; see Crijnen, Achenbach, & Verhulst, 1999, for an overview of this body of research).

Comparison With DSM It is instructive to compare the syndromes that have been identified through empirical analyses of the reports of parents, teachers, and youth with the diagnostic categories included in DSM-IV under the broad category of "Disorders Usually First Evident in Infancy, Childhood or Adolescence." Several of the empirically derived categories have counterparts in the DSM, suggesting that the two very different methods used to develop these taxonomies yield similar impressions of the types of psychological problems experienced by children and adolescents. For example, the empirically derived syndrome of Attention Problems is quite similar to Attention Deficit/Hyperactivity Disorder in DSM-IV; the Delinquent syndrome is similar to Conduct Disorder in DSM-IV; and the Aggressive syndrome is similar to the DSM-IV Oppositional Defiant Disorder.

Nevertheless, several of the empirical syndromes (e.g., Thought Problems; Somatic Complaints; Anxious/Depressed) do not have counterparts in the infancy, childhood, and adolescence section of DSM-IV. Moreover, a number of childhood disorders that are included in DSM-IV (e.g., Autistic Disorder; Enuresis; Selective Mutism) were not identified as unique syndromes in the analyses of parent, teacher, and youth reports. Indeed, many of the DSM-IV disorders that were not identified in the empirically derived taxonomy are either very rare in the population as a whole or are characterized by a single symptom that, even alone, is sufficiently problematic to be labeled a disorder in the DSM (Achenbach & McConaughy, 1996).

Extensions to Adult Populations   This quantitative approach has been extended to the development of an empirically based taxonomy of psychopathology in young adults ages 18 to 25 years (Achenbach, 1993; Wiznitzer et al., 1992) and, more recently, to a large national probability sample aged 15 to 54 years (Krueger, 1999). Young adults' self-reports and the reports by their parents concerning the behavioral and emotional problems of these young adults were used to identify syndromes of psychopathology in this age group. Interestingly, many of the syndromes

that were identified in analyses of data on children and adolescents were also identified in the young adult sample, including Withdrawn, Anxious/Depressed, Somatic Complaints, Delinquency, and Aggressive Behavior (Achenbach, 1993). It is also noteworthy that Attention Problems was not a clear syndrome in young adulthood, suggesting that problems related to attention and impulsivity may emerge most clearly when children and adolescents are attempting to comply with the demands and requirements of school. Finally, two syndromes that were not identified in the analyses of children and adolescents, Strange Behavior and Shows Off, were found in the young adult sample. These findings suggest that the structure of psychopathology and the expression of psychological problems change with development.

Robert Krueger, a clinical psychologist at the University of Minnesota, has recently examined whether the internalizing and externalizing dimensions obtained by Achenbach and his colleagues in studies of children and adolescents also characterize 18- to 21-year-old adults and older individuals. Krueger, Caspi, Moffitt, and Silva (1998) conducted a factor analysis on data obtained through structured diagnostic interviews (see chapter 7) with over 900 18-year-olds in New Zealand. The interviews yielded diagnostic information about 10 DSM categories that were found to have high prevalence rates within the sample: Major Depressive Episode, Dysthymia, Generalized Anxiety Disorder, Agoraphobia, Social Phobia, Simple Phobia, Obsessive-Compulsive Disorder, Conduct Disorder, Marijuana Dependence, and Alcohol Dependence. The use of a factor analysis permitted Krueger and his colleagues to examine whether there was any particular structure underlying or connecting these 10 different diagnoses. In fact, the investigators found that, consistent with Achenbach's work with children and adolescents, the forms of psychopathology exhibited by these young adults could be captured by two broad dimensions: Internalizing and Externalizing (see figure 5.1). Moreover, Krueger found considerable stability in this structure of psychopathology in this sample over a three-year period, from age 18 to age 21.

Finally, Krueger (1999) analyzed data collected by Kessler et al. (1994) as part of the National Comorbidity Survey of adults ages 15 to 54. Krueger examined the underlying structure of 10 mental disorders, similar to those assessed in the New Zealand sample, that were diagnosed using a structured clinical interview. Again, significant internalizing and externalizing factors were obtained in these analyses, indicating that the two dimensions of internalizing and externalizing problem behaviors are robust across different samples and different age groups. The findings of Achenbach and Krueger suggest that the major disorders diagnosed in DSM-IV may not be as categorically distinct and independent as many psychopathologists have assumed, but rather, may share common substrates of broad, higher-order internalizing and externalizing dimensions.

AN INSTRUCTIVE EXAMPLE: THE CASE OF DEPRESSION DURING ADOLESCENCE

The classification of depression provides an interesting and instructive example of the problems that have faced psychologists and psychiatrists in their efforts to develop reliable and valid methods to classify problems. As we observed in chapter 1, recognition of symptoms of grief, depression, and melancholia predate modern psychology and psychiatry. Several decades of research have greatly clarified the nature of depressive symptoms and disorders (e.g., Gotlib & Hammen, 1992, in press). Nevertheless, there is still considerable confusion surrounding the meaning of the term *depression,* both as it is used by mental health professionals and in its use by the general public. We will focus our discussion on depression occurring during adolescence because this is the problem presented by our adolescent client, Brian, and because adolescence represents an important developmental period for the emergence of depression (e.g., Compas & Oppedisano, 2000; Garber, 2000; Petersen et al., 1993).

Figure 5.1

A quantitative analysis by Krueger demonstrated that DSM disorders can be represented by the two broad factors internalizing and externalizing behavior problems.

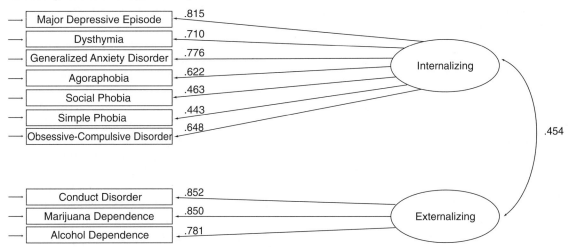

The term *depression* has been used to refer to three levels of depressive phenomena during adolescence: depressed mood; an empirically derived syndrome that includes depressive symptoms; and a categorical diagnosis as defined by DSM criteria (Angold, 1988; Compas, Ey, & Grant, 1993). At the level of depressed mood, depression refers to the occurrence of a single symptom, the presence of sad, unhappy, or dysphoric mood for an unspecified period of time. The occurrence of sad or depressed mood is fairly universal; indeed, research suggests that anywhere from 15 percent to 40 percent of adolescents experience significant levels of depressed mood at any given point in time (Achenbach, 1991). Sad and unhappy feelings are normative in adolescence and may occur in response to a variety of everyday experiences. Importantly, however, the presence of depressed mood is one of the most powerful symptoms in distinguishing adolescents who have been referred for mental health services from those who have not (Compas et al.), so it is important not to underestimate the potential significance of depressive symptoms during adolescence.

Depressive symptoms during adolescence are represented in a quantitative syndrome in the form of the Anxious/Depressed syndrome (Achenbach, 1991). The symptoms that occur together in the reports of parents, adolescents, and teachers, thereby forming an empirically derived syndrome, are presented in table 5.5. The syndrome includes sad, unhappy emotions, guilt, and feelings of worthlessness. Interestingly, it

TABLE 5.5
Symptoms of Empirically Derived Anxious/Depressed Behavior Syndrome

Lonely; fearful, anxious
Cries a lot; feels guilty
Fears own impulses; self-conscious
Needs to be perfect; unhappy, sad, depressed
Feels unloved; worries
Feels persecuted; tries to harm self
Feels worthless; thinks about suicide
Nervous, tense

also includes a number of symptoms that are more characteristic of anxiety than depression per se (e.g., nervousness, fears, anxiousness), raising the issue of symptom comorbidity that we discussed earlier in the chapter. The tendency of sadness, anxiety, and other unpleasant emotions to occur together has been widely recognized in children, adolescents, and adults and has been labeled as a general syndrome of "negative affectivity" (e.g., Watson & Pennebaker, 1989). The symptoms in the Anxious/Depressed syndrome are representative of negative affectivity in adolescence (Chorpita & Barlow, 1998; Compas & Oppedisano, 2000).

The symptoms in the categorical diagnoses in the DSM-IV that reflect depression are quite different from either depressed mood or the Anxious/Depressed syndrome. Under the broad category of mood disorders, the diagnostic criteria for Major Depressive Disorder (table 5.6) and the criteria for Dysthymic Disorder (table 5.7) are both relevant to understanding depression during adolescence. **Dysthymia** and **major depression** include similar types of symptoms but differ in the severity, duration, and degree of impairment in functioning that are associated with these symptoms. Whereas Major Depressive Disorder is viewed as an acute set of symptoms that must have been present for at least two weeks, in Dysthymic Disorder the symptoms must have been present to some extent for at least two years (at least one year when diagnosing children or adolescents). Both Major Depressive Disorder and Dysthymic Disorder differ from the symptoms in the Anxious/Depressed syndrome in that they exclude symptoms of anxiety and they include symptoms of disrupted appetite, sleep patterns, and impaired concentration. Further, although it is acknowledged that major depression and dysthymia can co-occur in the same individual, the separate categories for each implies that they are distinct disorders rather than different points on a single continuum of depressive problems.

These three different ways of thinking about depression (as a mood, a syndrome, or a

TABLE 5.6
DSM-IV Criteria for Major Depressive Episode

A. At least five of the following symptoms have been present during the same two-week period and represent a change from previous functioning; at least one of the symptoms is either (1) depressed mood or (2) loss of interest or pleasure.
  (1) depressed mood most of the day, nearly every day, as indicated by either subjective report (e.g., feels sad or empty) or observation made by others (e.g., appears tearful). Note: in children or adolescents, can be irritable mood.
  (2) markedly diminished interest or pleasure in all, or almost all, activities most of the day, nearly every day (as indicated by subjective account or observation made by others).
  (3) significant weight loss or weight gain when not dieting (e.g., more than 5 percent of body weight in a month), or decrease or increase in appetite nearly every day. Note: in children, consider failure to make expected weight gains.
  (4) insomnia or hypersomnia nearly every day.
  (5) psychomotor agitation or retardation nearly every day (observable by others, not merely subjective feelings of restlessness or being slowed down).
  (6) fatigue or loss of energy nearly every day.
  (7) feelings of worthlessness or excessive or inappropriate guilt (which may be delusional) nearly every day (not merely self-reproach or guilt about being sick).
  (8) diminished ability to think or concentrate, or indecisiveness, nearly every day (either by subjective account or as observed by others).
  (9) recurrent thoughts of death (not just fear of dying), recurrent suicidal ideation without a specific plan, or a suicide attempt or a specific plan, or a suicide attempt or plan for committing suicide.
B. The symptoms cause clinically significant distress or impairment in social, occupational, or other important areas of functioning.
C. Not due to the direct effects of a substance (e.g., drugs of abuse, medication) or a general medical condition (e.g., hypothyroidism).
D. Not occurring within two months of the loss of a loved one (except if associated with marked functional impairment, morbid preoccupation with worthlessness, suicidal ideation, psychotic symptoms, or psychomotor retardation).

(Reprinted with permission from the Diagnostic and Statistical Manual of Mental Disorders, Fourth Edition. Copyright 1994 American Psychiatric Association. Reprinted with permission.)

TABLE 5.7
DSM-IV Criteria for Dysthymic Disorder

A. Depressed mood (or can be irritable mood in children and adolescents) for most of the day, for more days than not, as indicated by subjective account or observation made by others, for at least two years (one year for children and adolescents).
B. Presence, while depressed, of at least three of the following:
  (1) low self-esteem or self-confidence, or feelings or inadequacy
  (2) feelings of pessimism, despair, or hopelessness
  (3) generalized loss of interest or pleasure
  (4) social withdrawal
  (5) chronic fatigue or tiredness
  (6) feelings of guilt, brooding about the past
  (7) subjective feelings of irritability or excessive anger
  (8) decreased activity, effectiveness, or productivity
  (9) difficulty in thinking reflected by poor concentration, poor memory, or indecisiveness
C. During the two-year period (one year for children or adolescents) of the disturbance, the person has never been without symptoms in A and B for more than two months at a time.
D. No major depressive episode during the first two years of the disturbance (one year for children and adolescents); i.e., not better accounted for by chronic Major Depressive Disorder, or Major Depressive Disorder in partial remission.
E. Has never had a manic episode or an equivocal hypomanic episode.
F. Does not occur exclusively during the course of a chronic psychotic disorder, such as Schizophrenia or Delusional Disorder.
G. Not due to the direct effects of a substance (e.g., drugs of abuse, medication) or a general medical condition (e.g., hyperthyroidism).

(Reprinted with permission from the Diagnostic and Statistical Manual of Mental Disorders, Fourth Edition. Copyright 1994 American Psychiatric Association. Reprinted with permission.)

disorder) have presented challenges to clinicians and researchers alike. When we use the term *depression,* to what constellation of symptoms are we referring? Specifically, when we consider Brian, how can we best conceptualize the problems that he is experiencing? In fact, Brian displays aspects of all three forms of depression: He clearly experiences depressed mood, he displays relatively high levels of many of the symptoms on the Anxious/Depressed syndrome, and he meets DSM-IV criteria for a Major Depressive Disorder.

It is likely that each of these three approaches have something important to offer about the depressive symptoms of Brian and of many other adolescents. Depressed mood, syndrome, and disorder may reflect three levels of a hierarchical and sequential model of depressive problems (Compas et al., 1993). Research has shown that there is considerable correspondence between adolescents who are identified by high scores on the Anxious/Depressed syndrome and those who meet DSM criteria for Major Depressive Disorder (e.g., Edelbrock & Costello, 1988; Gerhardt, Compas, Connor, & Achenbach, 1999; Rey & Morris-Yates, 1991). Similarly, the presence of depressed mood serves as a marker, or signal, that an adolescent is at high risk for experiencing a depressive episode in the future (Gotlib, Lewinsohn, & Seeley, 1995). It is possible that Brian's symptoms progressed along this continuum, beginning with sad and unhappy mood, expanding to a broader syndrome of depression and anxiety, and finally including social withdrawal, disrupted appetite and sleep, and suicidal ideation.

In summary, the lesson to be learned from research on adolescent depression is that the classical categorical diagnostic model and the quantitative or dimensional model are not incompatible. Both contribute information about the nature of depression and other forms of psychopathology. Further research is needed, however, to determine the best ways to try to understand depression and other forms of psychopathology.

KEY ISSUES IN THE IMPROVEMENT OF CLASSIFICATION SYSTEMS

Clinical psychologists are involved with classification systems in two important ways. First,

clinical psychologists are users or consumers of existing systems in their research and clinical practice. Second, clinical psychologists work as researchers to improve and enhance existing systems. Therefore, it is important to recognize the issues and concerns that face psychologists as they continue to try to improve their understanding of the nature and classification of psychopathology.

Linking Assessment and Taxonomy

The process of assessment, which is the focus of chapters 6 through 10, is closely linked to the classification system, or taxonomy, that one uses to classify psychopathology. That is, assessment is the process of identifying the key features of individual cases, and taxonomy involves the grouping of cases on the basis of these key features. The taxonomy and the assessment methods that a psychologist uses should reflect the same underlying assumptions about psychopathology. Further, changes in taxonomic systems should be reflected in commensurate changes in assessment methods, and data from comprehensive assessment procedures should be used to improve the quality of taxonomies. For example, the quantitative taxonomy developed by Achenbach and colleagues described in this chapter was developed from a set of standardized measures of children's behavior completed by parents, teachers, and adolescents (see chapter 10)—the taxonomy grew from the assessment tools. In contrast, as we will discuss in chapter 7, a set of structured diagnostic interviews have been developed for the assessment of symptoms of DSM-diagnosed disorders—in this case, the assessment methods grew out of the taxonomy. There is little question that the taxonomy that is used by a clinical psychologist plays an important role in the selection of his or her assessment methods.

Comorbidity and Covariation

Whether one follows a categorical or quantitative approach to taxonomy, there is now widespread recognition that different problems or disorders have a pervasive tendency to occur together in the same individuals. In the categorical approach, as we noted earlier, this tendency is referred to as *diagnostic comorbidity*. In the quantitative approach, this co-occurrence of different problems is referred to as the *covariation* of symptoms or dimensions. It is a striking fact that most psychological problems rarely occur alone. Depression, for example, has high rates of comorbidity during childhood and adolescence (Compas & Hammen, 1996) and adulthood (Kessler et al., 1994; Maser & Cloninger, 1991). Continued research is required to clarify both the patterns and the meanings of the co-occurrence of various symptoms and disorders. In particular, clinical scientists need to determine whether the disorders in a taxonomy such as DSM-IV are indeed distinct, or whether there are fuzzier boundaries (if any) between these psychological problems than is acknowledged in categorically based diagnostic systems. Finally, the recognition of comorbidity among different diagnoses or problems may lead to predictions of future difficulties in individuals who present with part of the "comorbidity package" and to prevention programs aimed at reducing the likelihood of an individual experiencing a normative comorbid disorder.

Developmental Patterns and Pathways

For much of the history of psychopathology, classification efforts have focused on problems and disorders in adults. Moreover, early attempts to understand and classify problems of childhood and adolescence assumed that problems in younger age groups were distinct from those experienced in adulthood. The emerging field of **developmental psychopathology** has shown, however, that it is essential to consider both the changes and the continuities of psychopathology throughout the life span. There are at least three distinct possible associations between psychopathology in childhood and psychopathology in adults. First, a problem or form of psychopathology may manifest itself in the same

way in childhood as it does in adulthood. For example, depression may be expressed with the same symptoms in children as it is in adults. Second, the same underlying problem may manifest itself in a different overt manner in childhood and adulthood. Thus, whereas difficulties in dealing with stress may result in an eating disorder in an adolescent, these same difficulties may lead to a series of panic attacks in an adult. Finally, a problem or disorder in childhood may lead to a different problem in adult life. Longitudinal research in which the same individuals are followed from childhood through adolescence and into adulthood is urgently needed to chart the course of various forms of psychopathology through the life span.

Gender

Earlier in this chapter we referred to the data collected by Kessler et al. (1994) as part of the National Comorbidity Survey of over 8,000 adults ages 15 to 54. In this major epidemiological study of mental health and illness in the United States, Kessler and his colleagues found that both major depression and alcoholism had profoundly different rates of occurrence (prevalence rates) among adult men and women. Women were found to have more than twice the lifetime rate of depression as men, while men had over five times the lifetime rate of alcoholism as women. We do not fully understand the meaning of these fundamental **gender differences in psychopathology,** but this area is a critically important one for clinical psychologists to examine. Although these gender differences may simply mean that women and men differ in the types of problems that they develop, it is more likely that these differences indicate that men and women show their reactions to stress in different ways (e.g., Nolen-Hoeksema, in press) or that men and women are at different genetic risk for particular forms of psychopathology (e.g., Merikangas & Swendsen, 1997). Currently, we do not know whether an episode of depression or an episode of alcoholism or other form of substance use has the same meaning when it is experienced by a man versus a woman in our society.

Ethnic Diversity

As our society becomes more diverse in its ethnic composition, increasing importance must be placed on understanding both commonalities and differences in the nature and rates of psychopathology in different ethnic groups, that is, **ethnic diversity** must be emphasized. Knowing that a particular form or degree of psychopathology is more prevalent in one group or another can help clinicians plan prevention and treatment programs for individuals in those groups that are most strongly affected. The limited data available on cultural consistencies and differences in psychopathology present a mixed picture of the role of culture in psychopathology. On one hand, there is evidence of differential rates of psychopathology among various ethnic groups. For example, depressive symptoms have been found to occur more often and at more severe levels in African American and Hispanic American youth than in Caucasian and Asian American adolescents (Dornbusch, Mont-Reynand, Ritter, Chen, & Steinberg, 1991; Hayward, Gotlib, Schraedley, & Litt, 1999), and Jewish people have been found to exhibit lower rates of alcohol abuse than have Catholics and Protestants (Yeung & Greenwald, 1992). And from a broader cultural perspective, children who are seen for mental health services in Thailand present with different types of problems than do children who are seen for mental health services in the United States (Weisz et al., 1987). On the other hand, some forms of psychopathology, such as schizophrenia, appear to be rather universal across different cultures and ethnic groups (e.g., Keith, Regier, Rea, & Matthews, 1991; Kendall & Hammen, 1998). Classification systems will need to be increasingly sensitive to possible cultural differences in the types of problems that people experience and the meaning of those problems in different cultural contexts.

SUMMARY AND CONCLUSIONS

Defining and classifying abnormal behavior is a major task for clinical psychologists. The debate about whether psychopathology should be classified in discrete categories has been ongoing for many years. Despite the concerns raised by critics, there is little question that classifying various forms of abnormal or problematic behavior can be helpful for clinicians both in making decisions concerning the treatment of an individual and in gaining a broader understanding of a person's difficulties.

The major classification system used in North America is the *Diagnostic and Statistical Manual of Mental Disorders,* 4th edition (DSM-IV). Using this system, individuals can receive diagnoses on any of five axes, or dimensions, that reflect different aspects of their functioning. A large body of empirical research leading up to this latest edition of the DSM has resulted in im-

proved reliability of classification and greater consistency within diagnostic categories. This classification system is not perfect, however, and some clinical scientists have argued for the use of quantitative dimensions rather than categories in descriptions of problematic behavior. Interestingly, findings from recent studies suggest that the two broad dimensions of internalizing and externalizing problems may underlie the major diagnostic categories of DSM-IV, although much more work needs to be done before strong conclusions can be drawn concerning the relative advantages and disadvantages of these two approaches to the classification of psychopathology.

Clinical psychologists continue to work actively to improve the classification and diagnostic process. They are critically involved in bridging classification and assessment procedures and in refining categories or dimensions along which individuals' problem behaviors can be described. Finally, recent changes in the cultural composition of the United States strongly underscore how important it is that clinicians consider factors that involve demographic and ethnic variables when they make diagnostic or classification decisions.

KEY TERMS AND NAMES

Thomas Achenbach
Classification
Dementia praecox
Developmental psychopathology
Diagnostic and Statistical Manual of Mental
   Disorders (DSM)
Diagnostic axes
Diagnostic comorbidity
Dysthymia
Ethnic diversity

Externalizing problems
Five axes of DSM-IV
Gender differences in psychopathology
Internalizing problems
International Classification of Diseases (ICD)
Emil Kraepelin
Major depression
Quantitative taxonomic systems
Syndrome
Taxonomy

RESOURCES

Books
American Psychiatric Association. (1994). *Diagnostic and Statistical Manual of Mental Disorders* (4th ed.).Washington, DC: Author.
Meehl, P. E. (1973). *Psychodiagnosis: Selected papers*. New York: Norton.
Kutchins, H., & Kirk, S. A. (1997). *Making us crazy—DSM: The psychiatric bible and the creation of mental disorders*. New York: Free Press.

Journals
Archives of General Psychiatry
Journal of Abnormal Psychology
Journal of the American Academy of Child and Adolescent Psychiatry
Psychological Assessment

PSYCHOLOGICAL ASSESSMENT

Psychological assessment is a major activity for clinical psychologists. Assessing a client's psychological functioning, including personality, intellectual functioning, psychopathology, and problematic behaviors, is a clinical psychologist's first step in deciding on the types of treatment that might be best for the client. In chapters 6 through 10 we describe how clinical psychologists measure and learn about psychological aspects of people and their problems. We discuss the general process of assessment (chapter 6) and then describe specific types of assessment procedures. Specifically, in chapter 7 we present interviewing strategies and formats for both children and adults, and we describe the skills that are necessary to conduct an effective interview. In chapter 8 we examine intellectual and neuropsychological assessment. We discuss the concept of intelligence, evaluate different tests that are used by clinical psychologists to assess intelligence, and describe the process of neuropsychological testing. In chapter 9 we turn to the assessment of personality. We describe the use of objective and projective personality tests and raise a number of issues concerning the use of these tests. In chapter 10 we describe the rationale and methods of behavioral assessment. We discuss several different procedures that are used in behavioral assessment and describe how two different disorders might be assessed using these procedures. Throughout these chapters we continue with our discussion of the four cases you read in chapter 1 by describing how each of the different approaches to assessment presented in this section would be used with these individuals.

CHAPTER SIX

ASSESSMENT: UNDERSTANDING INDIVIDUALS AND CONTEXTS

INTRODUCTION

Raymond was brought to the psychology clinic by his mother after he had been caught shoplifting in a local store. This was Raymond's first criminal offense, and as a 15-year-old he still qualified as a minor and would not be prosecuted for his actions. His mother was very concerned, however, because she felt that this problem was one of several for Raymond. When she called the clinic she reported that her son was frequently angry and could not control his extremely violent temper. He had recently punched a hole in the wall of their home during an argument with his mother. She further described him as sullen, withdrawn, and unhappy. He frequently missed school, spending his days alone at home playing video games, watching television, and sleeping.

Imagine that you are a clinical psychologist who has been assigned to work with Raymond. What would you want to know about him in order to help with these problems? A number of questions would be important to consider. What are his current problems and the possible resources he has for dealing with these problems? What information about his past might be relevant to understanding the present problems? What factors in his current environment might be contributing to Raymond's problems? Are there people in his life who might be able to help solve these problems? And what is Raymond's behavior likely to be in the future? You may have already formulated some hunches regarding Raymond's problems based on your own experiences and ideas. Clinical psychologists are uniquely equipped, however, to examine these issues *systematically* through procedures that have been carefully developed and evaluated by their field.

Your first step in helping any individual is to become informed and knowledgeable about that person—a process that clinical psychologists refer to as *assessment.* Answering the questions that we just raised is part of the process that you use to become informed about Raymond in order to make several important decisions. These decisions include whether Raymond is in need of psychological treatment, and if he is, what specific treatment might be the most helpful. Clinical psychologists make such important decisions only after collecting extensive information, only after conducting a thorough psychological assessment. Furthermore, clinical psychologists make these decisions based on the psychological theory and research that was presented in the introductory chapters. We will use two of our case studies, Jason and Maria, to provide examples of the assessment process (see box 6.1).

THE DEFINITION OF PSYCHOLOGICAL ASSESSMENT

We all form impressions of other people in our daily lives. We form images and we make judgments about people on a variety of dimensions, including aspects of their personalities and their competencies and weaknesses. This process of impression formation is often automatic, and people rarely think about the process. Clinical psychologists also form impressions of people, but in doing so, they follow an organized and systematic set of procedures—they conduct a psychological assessment. We define **clinical psychological assessment** as the process of systematically gathering information about a person in relation to his or her environment so that decisions can be made, based on this information, that are in the best interests of the individual. As shown in figure 6.1, this process is characterized by a series of six steps.

First, a psychologist formulates an initial question or set of questions. These questions are typically developed in response to a referral or request for help made by either an individual or by others on behalf of an individual (e.g., concerned family member, parent, physician). These initial questions provide a starting point for collecting information. Second, a psychologist generates a set of goals for collecting information—what the psychologist hopes to accomplish during the assessment process. The goals of assessment are influenced by the particular psychological theory that guides the psychologist's thinking (see chapter 4). These broad theories both guide the psychologist to collect certain types of information, and influence the decisions and judgments that are made on the basis of this

Figure 6.1
Steps in the assessment process

| Step 1: Deciding what is being assessed. | Step 2: Determining the goals of assessment. | Step 3: Selecting standards for making decisions. | Step 4: Collecting assessment data. | Step 5: Making decisions and judgments. | Step 6: Communicating information. |

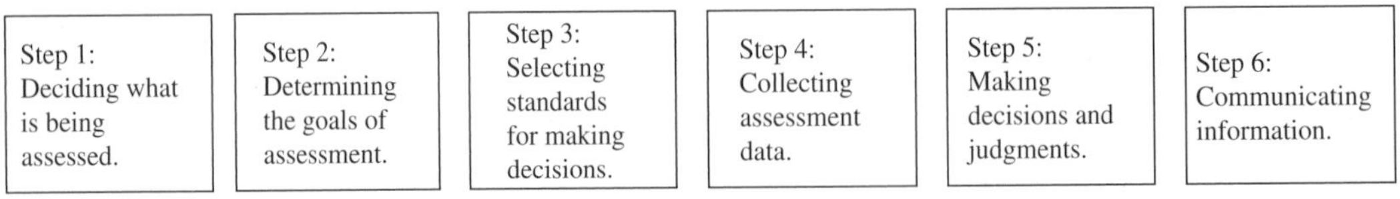

BOX 6.1

ASSESSMENT OF INDIVIDUAL CASES: JASON AND MARIA

JASON

Recall that Jason is an 8-year-old boy who was referred regarding problems with his behavior, attention, and performance in school. Assessment of Jason presents a number of interesting challenges. First, because of his age, Jason may not be able to provide reliable and valid reports on his own behavior. Therefore, it will be important to obtain information from other people who are familiar with and have raised concerns about his behavior. After conducting an initial interview with Jason and his mother, the psychologist would ask Jason's mother and his teacher to complete standardized behavior checklists to assess his behavior at home and at school. These measures will provide a broad view of Jason's behavior problems. Based on the responses on these measures, it will most likely be necessary to conduct a structured diagnostic interview with Jason's mother to determine if Jason meets criteria for one or more disorders that are suggested by his presenting behavior problems (e.g., Attention Deficit/Hyperactivity Disorder; Oppositional Defiant Disorder). Next, a standardized intelligence test will be administered to provide a measure of his current cognitive competencies and to estimate his potential for succeeding in school. Finally, the psychologist would have Jason respond to a continuous performance task, a computerized test, to measure his attention and distractability. The most challenging part of the assessment will involve the careful integration of the diverse data obtained from these various sources of information. Throughout the assessment process, the psychologist will need to determine the representativeness of the samples of children on which these measures are normed, paying careful attention to the inclusion of ethnic minority children in the normative samples.

MARIA

The assessment of Maria presents a different set of challenges than those presented in Jason's assessment. The primary task for the psychologist is to determine if Maria is suffering from Major Depressive Disorder. The psychologist will accomplish this task by administering a structured diagnostic interview to Maria and her son to determine if she is currently or has recently experienced an episode of major depression. If it is established that Maria is depressed, the psychologist will have to determine if her symptoms are exclusively a response to the death of her husband—an uncomplicated grief reaction. Alternatively, it may be that her symptoms exceed the level of grief that is typically experienced in response to the loss of a loved one in their frequency, intensity, duration, and quality. In addition to administering the diagnostic interviews, the psychologist would use other measures to obtain information about factors that research has shown to be related to depression. These methods could include questionnaires to measure perceptions of control, causal attributions, and sources of stress in her life. The psychologist will have to ensure that the measures are sensitive to both cultural beliefs that may relate to loss and grief, and to age differences in the experience of loss. Finally, as we will discuss in greater detail in chapter 8, when elderly individuals present with symptoms of depression, it is important to rule out the possibility that the symptoms are part of dementia, or deterioration of specific brain functions. In these cases, therefore, including the case of Maria, the psychologist will probably conduct an additional assessment of cognitive and neuropsychological functioning.

information. The third step in the assessment process involves the identification of standards for interpreting the information that is collected. In order to make decisions and judgments about a person, a psychologist must have a set of criteria for making such judgments. These standards may involve comparing the individual to a relevant sample of other people (normative standards) or comparing the person to himself or herself at another point in time (self-referent standards). Fourth, a psychologist must collect the relevant data. This step includes collecting information about the person and the environment and carefully describing and recording what is observed. Information can be obtained using any of dozens of different methods, including interviews, psychological tests, and direct observations of behavior. The fifth step in the assessment process involves making decisions and judgments on the basis of the data that have been collected. These decisions and judgments can include a formal diagnosis, a functional analysis of current behavior, or a prediction about future behavior. Finally, a psychologist must communicate these judgments and decisions to others, typically in the form of a psychological report.

Psychological theory and research are the two primary factors that shape the clinical assessment process and make it more systematic than the way that people form impressions of others in everyday life. Theories guide psychologists in forming certain types of questions or hypotheses and in looking for certain types of information. A theoretical framework shapes the type of information that is likely to be of interest, the tools or methods that are used to collect this information, and the way in which the information is interpreted or understood once it is obtained. For example, the types of assessment methods that will prove useful to a psychoanalytic psychologist will be quite different from the techniques that will be useful to a behavioral psychologist. Whereas a psychoanalytic psychologist will require information about unconscious dynamics that underlie behavior and the structure of personality (Exner, 1997), a behavioral psychologist will seek information about the antecedent stimuli and consequent conditions in the environment that precede and follow behavior (Beck, 2000). Regardless of their theoretical orientation, clinical psychologists need to use assessment procedures and measures that have been demonstrated in empirical research to provide accurate and

truthful information, that is, the assessment methods must generate information that is reliable, valid, and useful in making clinical decisions.

THE PROCESS OF PSYCHOLOGICAL ASSESSMENT

Step 1: Deciding What Is Being Assessed

The assessment process begins with a series of questions. Is there a significant psychological problem? What is the nature of this person's problem? Is the problem primarily one of emotion, thought, or behavior? What are possible causes of the problem? What is the course of the problem likely to be if it goes untreated? if it is treated? What types of treatment are likely to be the most helpful? In addition to the problems that are identified, what are the strengths and competencies that characterize this individual?

These questions come in part from the concerns presented by the client and are called the "referral questions"—questions that led the client to be referred to the psychologist. For example, in the case described at the beginning of this chapter, Raymond's mother specifically requested help for Raymond's aggressive behavior and his recent episode of shoplifting. She also questioned whether Raymond's aggression and thievery were related to his unhappiness and social withdrawal. As reflected in this example, clients' presenting concerns are often tied to a recent event (in this case, shoplifting). The recent event, however, may represent the final step in a more long-standing problem. For example, an individual who has experienced a fear of flying may seek treatment only when a change in job responsibilities requires frequent traveling as a part of a new position. Old methods used to avoid air travel are no longer effective, and the client is forced to cope with these fears in a different way. Or recall our case of Phillip, whose new job requires him to make oral presentations—something he had been able to avoid successfully at his former workplace. In Raymond's case, his shoplifting was only one of several problems. He was born with several birth defects, including a malformation of his spine and deformity in one of his legs. He missed a great deal of school when he was young because of several surgeries and hospitalizations. As a result, he failed to develop friendships with peers and became increasingly lonely and isolated. His current problems include his social isolation, school truancy, and difficulties in managing his sad and angry moods.

The questions and concerns that a client poses at the time of referral do not necessarily tell the whole story. A client is unlikely to be aware of all the information that may be relevant to a psychologist in formulating an understanding of the problem. Furthermore, the client may purposefully or unknowingly withhold information from the psychologist for a variety of reasons. It is important to recognize that clinical psychologists cannot simply use intuition and subjective judgment to identify the complex factors that lead to a referral or to a request for help. Rather, a clinical psychologist will need to turn to theory and research in formulating a more complete set of initial questions to guide a formal assessment.

What does a psychologist want to know about a person who is seeking help? Most current theories of human behavior recognize multiple levels of functioning that are relevant to understanding any behavior. For example, all emotions are associated with underlying biological processes, they exist within the conscious (but private) awareness of the individual, and they are linked to some type of observable antecedent and/or consequent event, either externally in the environment or internally within the experience of the individual (Cacioppo & Gardner, 1999). Further, many theories consider these processes to be interdependent and reciprocally related (e.g., Bandura, 1989, 1997; Lazarus, 1991, 1995, 1999; Zajonc, 2000). For example, biological processes are influenced by environmental events, thoughts are affected by underlying bio-

logical processes, and thoughts influence behavior. It is equally true, however, that biological states can lead to events in the environment, thinking can affect biology, and actions can influence how one thinks. In fact, some of the most exciting developments within psychological measurement involve the identification of intriguing and important relationships between physiology and thoughts, emotions, and behavior (e.g., Cacioppo, Bernston, & Anderson, 1991; Ito & Cacioppo, 2001).

The implication of these complex relationships for psychological assessment is clear—a psychologist may assess the client and his or her problems at a number of different levels, including aspects of both the person and the environment in which he or she functions. The primary aspects of the person that are possible targets for assessment are biological processes, cognitions, emotions, and behavior. Biological and psychophysiological processes include heart rate reactivity, blood pressure, galvanic skin response, muscle tension, sexual arousal, startle response, and eye tracking movement (Sturgis & Gramling, 1998). Cognitive processes include intellectual functioning, perceptions of the self, perceptions of others, beliefs about the causes of events, and perceptions of contingency and control (Kaufman, Kaufman, Lincoln, & Kaufman, 2000). Emotional processes that are the focus of assessment include current mood states, trait levels of emotions, and emotional reactivity (Merrell, 1999). Finally, measures of overt behavior include performance on standardized tasks, observations of behavior in simulated situations, and behavior observed in the client's natural environment (Beck, 2000).

In addition to these various aspects of the *person* that can be assessed, the *environment* is also multifaceted, confronting psychologists with a choice among several levels of focus. These levels of focus include distinctions among the proximal, intermediate, and distal environment (Bronfenbrenner, 1999; Friedman & Wachs, 1999) as well as objective versus subjective or perceived features of the environment. The proximal, or immediate, features of the environment include the client's family environment and the characteristics of the school or work setting. Intermediate levels of the environment include the geographic region in which the individual resides (e.g., urban versus suburban versus rural; the northeastern versus southwestern United States). Finally, the distal, or broader, environment includes the general geographic and sociocultural environment in which the client lives.

The distinction between the objective and subjective environment is also important. Consider for example, the characteristics of a family in which the mother is experiencing an episode of Major Depression. Members of this family are likely to report high levels of conflict and discord, especially between the parents (e.g., Goodman & Gotlib, 1999; Cummings & Davis, 1994; Gotlib & Goodman, 1999). The children in this family may describe their mother as emotionally distant and prone to periods of irritability and anger. Members of the family are unlikely to agree, however, about how often these behaviors occur or about their causes. The mother may be most discrepant from other family members in her perceptions of family interactions. Moreover, the reports of family members may not correspond with observations of family interactions made by an external observer.

Despite the potential importance of the different aspects of the individual and the environment, psychologists cannot assess all these factors for any single case. Both the time and the cost involved in conducting such an extensive assessment would be prohibitive. And even if it were possible, it would still be ill advised for the clinical psychologist to become overloaded with too much information about the client. The psychologist would find it difficult or impossible to distinguish information that is important for understanding the individual's problems from material that is superfluous or unnecessary. A psychologist's theoretical orientation plays a critical role in guiding the psychologist to obtain certain types of information and to disregard other aspects of the person or the environment.

Step 2: Determining the Goals of Assessment

The second step in the process of clinical assessment is the formulation of the psychologist's goals in a particular case. Once again, psychologists are confronted with a number of choices as they carry out the assessment process. Goals may include diagnostic classification, determination of the severity of a problem, risk screening for future problems, evaluation of the effects of treatment, and predictions about the likelihood of certain types of future behavior.

Diagnosis **Diagnosis** is perhaps a more familiar term than *assessment* is in the work of clinical psychologists. Although generating a diagnosis is one of the tasks in which a psychologist may engage, it is actually a subset of the broader process of assessment. Within the process of psychological assessment, the task of diagnosing implies that certain procedures or tests are administered to an individual in order to classify the person's problem and, if possible, to identify causes and prescribe treatment. As we discussed in chapter 5, psychologists typically make diagnoses based on the *DSM-IV* criteria.

Diagnoses are made for both clinical and economic reasons. Diagnostic decisions are often the first goal of the assessment process, because they can influence many of the other decisions that will follow. Optimally, a diagnosis should provide information about the specific features, or symptoms that the person shares with other individuals who have been identified as having the same pattern of symptoms. If the criteria for making a particular diagnosis are clear and have been carefully evaluated in this case, the psychologist will be able to draw on research and information about these other individuals. In addition, health care professionals are often required to supply a diagnosis for the problem being treated in order to be reimbursed from third party payers, such as insurance companies and managed care organizations. The strengths and weaknesses of the *DSM-IV* notwithstanding, it is the most commonly accepted classification system for generating diagnoses of psychological problems for the purpose of third party payment (Maser, Kaelber, & Weise, 1991).

There is a close link between assessment procedures and the diagnostic system that a psychologist uses for understanding and classifying psychopathology (see chapter 5). Specifically, assessment involves the identification of the features or characteristics that distinguish individual cases from one another, whereas a diagnostic system involves the grouping together of individual cases according to their identifying features (Achenbach, 1985, 1991; Achenbach & McConaughy, 1997). Any diagnostic system, such as the *DSM-IV,* should specify a method of assessment to measure and quantify the important symptoms or characteristics of the various categories or disorders within the diagnostic system. The assessment method is the way that the different categories or disorders are operationalized, that is, the way that the symptoms are judged to be present or absent. Similarly, any method for measuring the important features of people (or their environments) should specify how individuals are to be grouped based on the information that is generated from the assessment method. A diagnostic system represents one of the outcomes of assessment—the classification of individuals using the information that has been generated.

The initial versions of the *DSM* did not specify a particular assessment method for deriving diagnoses. Since *DSM-III* was introduced in 1980, however, several structured diagnostic interviews have since been developed to provide systematic ways to measure the presence or absence, severity, and duration of the symptoms specified in the *DSM*. These interviews include the Diagnostic Interview Schedule (DIS; Robins, Helzer, Croughan, & Ratcliff, 1981) and the

Structured Clinical Interview for the *DSM* (SCID; Spitzer, Williams, Gibbon, & First, 1992) as well as comparable diagnostic interviews for use with children and their parents (e.g., Schwab-Stone, Fallon, Briggs, & Crowther, 1994). If reaching a psychiatric diagnosis is one of the goals of the assessment, the psychologist must use assessment procedures that will generate information that can be used to evaluate the diagnostic criteria defined in the taxonomy. A useful diagnostic interview must include an assessment of the full range of symptoms that comprise the various diagnostic categories within the system as well as indices of the onset, duration, and intensity or severity of each symptom. We will discuss diagnostic interviews in detail in chapter 7.

The categorical nature of the *DSM-IV* leads psychologists to think about people and their problems in a particular way. The emphasis is on sets of symptoms that are judged as present or absent, either meeting or not meeting a predetermined set of criteria. If a psychologist is not directed toward generating a categorical diagnosis, the emphasis may be more on the description of the individual on a number of relevant dimensions. Rather than being judged as present or absent, these dimensions are measured and described as a matter of degree. As we noted in chapter 5 in our discussion of classification systems, categorical and dimensional systems are not mutually exclusive. Psychologists must be aware, however, that the generation of categorical diagnoses may come to dominate their thinking about their clients to the exclusion of thinking in more dimensional terms.

Severity　Arriving at a diagnosis is frequently an important first step in psychological assessment. However, it is not sufficient to know that an individual meets the criteria for a particular problem or disorder, because there can be substantial differences among individuals with a similar problem, a concept referred to as *heterogeneity*. To borrow an example from medicine, a positive diagnosis of breast cancer conveys a significant amount of information about a patient, yet there is enormous variability among women with breast cancer with regard to the severity and extent of the disease. Breast cancer can vary from a small, localized tumor (Stage I) to a carcinoma that has spread throughout other parts and systems of the body such as the lymphatic system and bone marrow (Stage IV). Similar distinctions can be made with regard to the various diagnostic categories in the *DSM-IV.*

Discrimination of the severity of problems or disorders requires assessment instruments and methods that are sensitive to variations in the frequency, intensity, and duration of specific symptoms. If a patient meets the criteria for Major Depression, the psychologist must gather additional information about the problem. Such information includes the number of symptoms (out of nine) that are present, the number of episodes of depression the client has experienced, how long the episodes have lasted, and which of the nine symptoms of depression are present during the episodes.

An important factor in determining the severity of a disorder is the degree of impairment that is present in the person's daily life (Elkin et al., 1995). For example, a patient with an eating disorder may have suffered from Bulimia Nervosa for several years, yet is still able to be successful in her college courses, work at a part-time job, and maintain her friendships. Another patient with bulimia, however, may find that her preoccupation with eating and her concerns about being overweight have become the predominant feature in her life. Her binge eating has become increasingly frequent, to the point that she often eats by herself out of fear that others will learn about her eating disorder. Her belief that she needs to be perfect in all that she does has made it difficult to continue with her schoolwork out of fear that she will fail, and her disordered eating patterns have begun to compromise her health. Thus, psychologists must consider the individual's overall life functioning and competence in

order to have a complete understanding of the scope of the problem.

The range of different types of problems that Raymond is experiencing presents a diagnostic challenge. Some of his symptoms appear to be characteristic of Major Depression, including his sad and dysphoric mood and his social withdrawal. On the other hand, he also exhibits behaviors that are associated with Conduct Disorder, including explosions of anger and violence, and stealing. It appears that Raymond may be experiencing two or more comorbid disorders (see chapter 5 for a discussion of comorbidity).

Screening   Not all psychological assessment takes place with individuals who have been referred for clinical services. Often clinical psychologists are called on to **screen** large groups of individuals, either to identify the presence of problems or to predict who is at greatest risk (who has the greatest likelihood) to develop a problem at some point in the future. For example, several interesting examples of screening related to depression have been developed (Muñoz, Le, Clarke, & Jaycox, in press; Muñoz, Le, & Ghosh Ippen, 2000). Depression is highly prevalent in the general population, but only a small portion of depressed individuals (less than 20 percent) seek treatment for the disorder. Efforts to screen for depression have been undertaken on a large scale. Initiated by the National Institute of Mental Health, the National Depression Screening Day represents an attempt to make it easier to identify individuals who suffer from depression but who, for any of a number of reasons, are not receiving treatment (e.g., Greenfield et al., 1997, 2000). The Depression Screening Day is publicized through the media (newspaper, television, radio) each year, and individuals are encouraged to go to a local site to complete a brief depression questionnaire that assesses their current level of depressive symptoms. Those who score above a certain cutoff level that is associated with increased risk for depression are then contacted for a diagnostic interview to determine if they are suffering from Major Depression. Results have indicated that over 50 percent of those who meet the risk criteria follow up and complete the interview (Greenfield et al., 1997). The National Depression Screening Day is a first step in providing access to treatment for those in need.

Children whose parents suffer from Major Depressive Disorder are much more likely to develop serious psychological and behavioral problems than are children whose parents do not exhibit an identifiable form of psychopathology (e.g., Cummings & Davis, 1994; Gotlib & Goodman, 1999). Psychologists may be called on to screen or identify early evidence of problems among children in these families in order to facilitate early interventions that may prevent the development of such problems. In the treatment of adult patients who have children living with them in their home, psychologists need to conduct a careful psychological assessment of the children to determine the degree to which they have begun to display early signs of problems or already meet criteria for a disorder themselves.

Depression in adolescence is also a prevalent problem that typically goes unrecognized. An avenue for screening has been identified through the co-occurrence of other symptoms. Specifically, depression in adolescents has been found to be associated with somatic problems, most notably with recurrent headaches. Although the reasons for this association are not clear, this finding suggests that it may be possible, and even advisable, to screen for depression when adolescents present with somatic problems, particularly headaches. One context in which this approach has been used involves the utilization of depression screening tools in medical emergency rooms (Porter et al., 1997). Brief depression questionnaires are administered to emergency room patients to identify those who may need treatment for depression.

Prediction   In addition to generating detailed descriptions of an individual's current function-

ing, psychologists are often called on to make **predictions** about how a person may behave at some point in the future. These predictions may span very short periods of time (e.g., whether this child is likely to encounter problems during the first few weeks of school) to long-term predictions about subsequent risk for disorder (e.g., whether this aggressive adolescent will become an antisocial adult).

One of the greatest challenges for psychologists is the prediction of violent behavior. Nowhere is this concern more pressing than in relation to the prediction of youth violence, especially in the aftermath of dramatic and tragic examples such as the shootings at Columbine High School in Colorado (see chapter 4). There is strong hope, or even an expectation, that psychologists should be able to predict which individuals are likely to engage in such extreme acts of violence (Verlinden, Hersen, & Thomas, 2000). The accurate prediction of violent behavior could then lead to attempts to prevent these acts before they occur.

Despite the extraordinary significance of predicting violent behavior, psychologists have been largely unsuccessful in this effort. This lack of success is due, in part, to the fact that we do not sufficiently understand the complex factors that lead to acts of violence such as the shootings at Columbine and at other schools in the United States. It is also important to realize, however, that our inability to predict incidents of school shootings may actually be inherent in the task. From 1990 to 2000, there were approximately a dozen incidents in the United States in which school-age children and adolescents have shot other children and schoolteachers. This number is staggering and is alarming in and of itself and in comparison to the relative absence of such acts in other countries. Any incident in which children murder other children is unquestionably unacceptable. However, school violence of this magnitude is in fact a very rare event when we consider the millions of school-age children and adolescents in the United States. Psychologists refer to an act that occurs this infrequently as a *low base rate event.* Thus, while school violence is extremely important when it does occur, the rate at which it happens in the general population is actually very low.

To make this point more concretely, imagine that you are a psychologist who has been hired by a school district to make predictions about students who might be likely to engage in violent acts. There are 1,500 students enrolled in this school district. In an effort to try to identify potentially violent individuals, you administer a psychological test to screen for violent thoughts and urges (no such test exists, but for the sake of this example, imagine that there is such a test). You decide on the basis of this test that only 5 percent of the students (or 75 students) are at risk to engage in a violent act. Conversely, you predict that the remaining 1,425 students are not at risk to perpetrate a violent act. Given how rare these incidents are, however, it is quite unlikely that an event of extreme violence will occur at all in this school district. Therefore, you will be 100 percent correct in predicting that the 1,425 students will not be violent. However, you will also be 0 percent correct in predicting that the other 75 students will be violent.

The accuracy of predictions of this type is understood in terms of rates of *sensitivity, specificity, false positives,* and *false negatives* (see table 6.1). Sensitivity refers to the portion of times that you predict that an event will occur out of the total number of times that it actually occurs. Specificity refers to the number of times

TABLE 6.1
Accurate and Inaccurate Predictions
in Clinical Psychology

Prediction	True case	True noncase
Case	True positives (A)	False positives (B)
Noncase	False negatives (C)	True negatives (D)

Sensitivity = A / (A + C)
Specificity = D / (B + D)
False positive rate = B / (B + D)
False negative rate = C / (A + C)

that you predict that event will not occur out of the total number of times that it actually does not occur. False positives occur when you predict that the event will occur and it does not, and false negatives occur when you predict that the event will not occur and it does. In the school district example, the sensitivity of your prediction method is 0 percent and the specificity is 95 percent. Your false positive rate is 5 percent and your false negative rate is 0 percent. Thus, you have made no errors by missing an act of violence that occurred; however, you have overpredicted the occurrence of violence by predicting that 75 individuals would engage in violence and they did not. Even if one act of extreme violence did occur, and you accurately identified the violent student by using your screening measure, you would still have been incorrect in predicting violence 74 out of 75 times.

Psychologists are actually effective in making predictions about certain problems, particularly if those problems have a reasonably high rate of occurrence in the population. For example, patterns of aggressive and disruptive behavior disorders in adolescence can be predicted with some degree of accuracy from information collected during early childhood. It is interesting that the single best predictor of aggressive and disruptive behavior problems in adolescence is the level of aggressive and oppositional behavior in the first years in school (Farrington & Loeber, 2000). Prior aggressive behavior is a better predictor than are other factors, including information about the child's family or any other individual characteristics of the child. In addition, clinical psychologist Terri Moffitt (1993) has shown that children who are aggressive and disruptive in early childhood have a much more persistent course of behavior problems in adolescence and into young adulthood than do those individuals who display aggressive or delinquent behavior for the first time during adolescence. That is, an early onset of problems predicts a much worse course than a late onset of problems. These predictions are generally more accurate and stronger than the prediction of incidents of extreme violence for two reasons. First, the base rate of aggressive and disruptive behavior problems is much higher (as high as 5 percent in the general population) than is the base rate of acts of extreme violence. And second, this task involves the prediction of stable patterns of behavior that occur over longer periods of time, rather than acts that occur only on a single occasion. In the prediction of violence and other low base rate behaviors, psychologists must carefully weigh the consequences of false positive and false negative predictions. If the consequences of wrongly predicting an outcome (a false positive) are small and the costs of missing an outcome that does occur (false negative) are great, then it will be acceptable to overpredict. However, if there are negative consequences to wrongly predicting an outcome, then even one instance of overprediction will be problematic.

Raymond's recent episodes of rage at home raise the concern that he may engage in more acts of violence in the future, perhaps behaviors that are even more serious. However, Raymond's mother reports that he has only recently become violent at home, and the recent shoplifting incident was the first time that he had ever committed a serious delinquent act. Thus, his pattern of behavior is consistent with a late onset of aggressive and disruptive behavior problems rather than an early onset of these problems, and the empirical literature suggests that Raymond has a better chance of changing these behaviors.

Evaluation of Intervention Assessment is often thought of as an initial step in formulating a sense of a client's problems or a diagnosis and in developing a plan for treatment. However, effective assessment does not end once treatment begins. Rather, assessment methods should be readministered at regular intervals to monitor and evaluate the effects of treatment. By obtaining pretreatment or baseline information on the nature and severity of a client's problems, follow-up assessments with the same instruments

can be conducted to allow for evaluation of changes that have resulted from treatment. Evaluating change requires a few essential steps. Obviously, the same instruments must be used at both the pretreatment and follow-up assessments so that exact comparisons can be made on these scales. Further, it is essential that the measures can be counted on to produce consistent or reliable information, that is, the measures must be minimally affected by error so that meaningful changes can be distinguished from random fluctuations (see the discussion of reliability in Step 4 of this chapter). Finally, criteria must be developed to distinguish clinically meaningful change from reliable but relatively trivial shifts in the target problems.

Step 3:
Selecting Standards for Making Decisions

Knowing what to measure is only part of the process of assessment. A psychologist must also know what to do with the information once it is collected. Making decisions about the information is essential, and decisions and judgments require points of reference for comparison. Standards are used to determine if a problem exists, how severe a problem is, and whether the individual has evidenced improvement over a specified period of time. Comparisons can be made to standards that involve other people (**normative standards**) or to the self at other points in time (**self-referent standards**).

Psychological assessment reflects the meeting point of two important functions of psychology—interest in the nature of people in general (the *normative*, or *nomothetic*, tradition) and concerns about a specific person (the individual, or *idiographic*, tradition). When working with an individual, a psychologist is drawing on the idiographic tradition. This process involves the discovery of what is unique about this person given his or her history, current personality structure, and present environmental conditions. In arriving at an impression of this individual, however, the psychologist is frequently required to make judgments about this person in comparison to most other people. In doing so, the psychologist draws on the nomothetic tradition of laws and rules that apply to the behavior of people in general.

The application of normative information to individual decisions is a complex process. No single individual is ever represented perfectly by data collected on large samples of people. Therefore, predictions made on the basis on data collected on large samples will not necessarily hold true for any particular individual, which means that psychologists are often involved in making educated guesses about an individual based on the knowledge base accumulated about people in general. In making normative comparisons, the psychologist must determine the degree to which a particular individual is similar to the normative sample on demographic characteristics such as age, sex, ethnicity, education, and economic status. For example, it would be inaccurate (and inappropriate) to make predictions about an inner-city African American adolescent's performance on a test if the normative sample that is used in deriving scores was composed only of middle and upper socioeconomic status Caucasian youth.

Normative Standards   To provide an understanding of normative comparisons, imagine that you administer an intelligence test (see chapter 8) to an 8-year-old child, who responds correctly to fewer than half the questions, and to a 16-year-old, who correctly answers approximately three-fourths of the questions. How can you interpret this information? Do these test scores indicate that the older child is brighter? Or should you expect 16-year-olds to know more and therefore perform better than 8-year-olds? If older children are expected to perform better on an intelligence test than are younger children, how can you evaluate the performance of these two individuals of different ages? The answer, of course, lies in obtaining information on how others of similar ages perform on the test. That

is, the relevant comparison for the 8-year-old is other 8-year-olds who have taken the test, just as the 16-year-old should be compared to others of that age.

Age is only one of many factors that must be considered in developing a *normative comparison sample* for a psychological measure (Anastasi, 1988). Typically the comparison sample should be *representative* of the general population, which includes, but is not limited to, representativeness with regard to age, gender, ethnicity, education level, income, and geographic region. In this way, the sample represents the distribution of these characteristics in the larger population. A representative sample offers a fair and meaningful criterion for evaluating the performance of a single individual. A normative comparison sample must be large in order to ensure that it reflects that population it is selected to represent. For most of the psychological characteristics that you measure, you can assume that the distribution of individuals in the population approaches a *normal distribution.* A curve with a normal distribution, also called a bell-shaped curve, is presented in figure 6.2. Any time a large group of individuals is sampled on a measure, they will differ, or show considerable *variability,* in their performance. Therefore, normative comparisons are used to determine where the individual falls within this variability or distribution.

The variability of a normative sample can be represented in several ways, but the most common is based on the *mean* as a measure of central tendency and the *standard deviation* as a measure of variability. The mean score for a population on a measure is determined by summing all the scores from a sample that is representative of the population and dividing by the number of individuals in the sample. The mean is what is typically thought of in lay terms as the average score that would be expected on the measure. But the mean says nothing about the variability that exists in the population. Therefore, an index is needed of the degree to which individuals' scores are distributed around (i.e., above and below) the mean. Assuming that the scores are

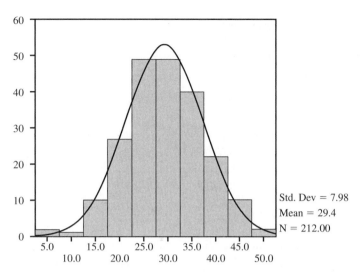

Figure 6.2
Normal distribution of scores.

normally distributed around the mean, the standard deviation corresponds to the points on either side of the mean that include approximately 68 percent of the scores for the sample; that is, by definition, approximately two thirds of the scores will fall within one standard deviation above and below the mean.

For use in psychological assessment, the mean and standard deviation are often converted to standard scores that allow for easy comparison across very different measures. One widely used metric is to convert scores to standardized *T scores* in which the mean score is converted to 50 and the standard deviation to 10. Therefore, you will know that regardless of the particular measure that was used, a *T score* of 50 indicates that an individual scored higher than 50 percent of the sample, and a *T score* of 60 indicates that an individual scored higher than 84 percent. Most standardized tests of intelligence are converted to standard scores that are based on a mean of 100 and a standard deviation of 15. Standard scores provide a useful shorthand method to describe the score of an individual relative to others in the population.

For many psychological measures it is important to determine if the person should be com-

pared to others with psychological problems or to others who represent the "normal" population. When the comparison sample is drawn from a clinical population, you do not necessarily expect the distribution of individual scores to approximate a normal curve. Rather, clinical samples may be highly *skewed* in their distribution on a measure (the scores are not evenly distributed around the mean). Further, the average score for a clinical sample is likely to be very different from that obtained in a sample drawn from the community. Scores obtained from normative community samples and those obtained from clinically referred samples are often compared to determine clinical criteria, or cutoffs, that are useful in distinguishing clinical and nonclinical groups on a measure. The bottom line on normative comparisons is this: Be sure you know to whom this individual is being compared and be sure you understand the representativeness of the comparison sample.

Self-Referent Standards   Some of the judgments that are made as part of the clinical assessment process do not involve comparisons to others. Rather, it is important to consider how much or how little this person has changed over time or across different situations. In such instances, the appropriate criterion is the person himself or herself. For example, if a client presents with complaints of persistent headaches, a psychologist may want to know how frequent and severe the current headaches are compared to the recent or more distant past. Have the headaches increased of late? If so, is the increase associated with any recent changes in the person's life, including work-related changes, changes in important interpersonal relationships, or changes in diet, exercise, sleep patterns, or exposure to noxious agents in the environment? If the client undergoes some form of treatment for the headaches, a psychologist will want to evaluate whether the headaches decrease as a result of the treatment. Although it may be useful to judge the person's headaches in comparison to a sample of similar individuals, it will ultimately be more useful to judge the degree of variability in headache frequency and severity for *this person* over time.

Self-referent standards can also be useful in determining the initial goals of a client and the degree to which he or she is satisfied with gains made in treatment. A client seeking help for a sleep disorder may report substantial satisfaction with being able to obtain a period of four to five hours of uninterrupted sleep on a nightly basis if the client who initiated treatment were unable to sleep for even a few minutes each night. Self-referent standards in this case would not be a replacement for normative standards, however, as it may still be important for health reasons to strive for greater gains in treatment until the client is able to achieve the expected seven to eight hours of sleep per night.

Step 4: Collecting Assessment Data

Methods to Be Used As psychologists make decisions about which aspects of the person-environment system are most relevant to measure, they must also decide which of many methods will be used to assess the targets that

have been selected. These choices include the use of structured or unstructured clinical interviews, reviews of the individual's history from school or medical records, measurements of physiological functioning, a wide array of psychological tests, self-reports from the individual, reports from significant others in the individual's life, and methods for the direct observation of behavior in the natural environment or in simulated conditions in the psychologist's office.

Interviews can be relatively open-ended, following the preferences or style of the individual psychologist, or highly structured in which a series of questions are asked in a prescribed manner and order regardless of who administers the interview. Physiological measures can include a device to monitor heart rate, blood pressure, skin temperature, or muscle tension in a particular area of the body (e.g., the muscles of the jaw). Literally hundreds of psychological tests have been developed, most of which are administered by a psychologist to a client on an individual basis; a smaller number are administered in a group format. Psychological tests include measures of intelligence (see chapter 8), assessments of neuropsychological functioning (see chapter 8), objective tests of personality (see chapter 9), and projective methods of assessing personality (see chapter 9). Self-report measures have been designed to assess symptoms of specific problems such as depression, stressful life events, current concerns and problems, or perceptions of relationships with others. Direct observation methods are used to assess specific behaviors as they occur either in the natural environment or under simulated conditions in the therapist's office (see chapter 10).

Typically a psychologist will draw on several of these methods in conducting a clinical assessment of a single case. The assessment process often begins with an interview as a means of obtaining general information about the individual and establishing rapport with the client. This initial interview may be followed by psychological testing, observations of behavior, and/or psychophysiological assessment. For example, the evaluation of a child referred for Attention Deficit/ Hyperactivity Disorder may include interviews with the parents, child, and teacher (Barkley, 1992); behavior checklists completed by parents and teachers (Chen, Faraone, Biederman, & Tsuang, 1994; Hinshaw & Nigg, 1999); and performance of the child on measures of intelligence, sustained attention on a continuous performance test, and neuropsychological function (Doyle, Biederman, Seidman, Weber, & Faraone, 2000; Nigg, Quamma, Greenberg, & Kusche, 1999).

The choice of methods is influenced by a number of factors. For example, the age of the client is an important consideration. Adult assessment typically involves tests and interviews administered to the individual, whereas child assessment often involves information obtained from other informants (e.g., parents, teachers) on the child's behavior. The referral question also plays a significant role in the assessment methods that are used. The procedures used with an adult referred for a sexual dysfunction will be quite different than those used in response to a referral for an anxiety disorder. The selection of methods is also strongly influenced by the psychologist's theoretical orientation and taxonomy of psychopathology.

Reliability and Validity   In chapter 3 we introduced the concepts of reliability and validity in the context of psychological research (see table 3.1 for a summary of the different types of reliability and validity in research). We now return to these issues in the context of psychological assessment. The most fundamental concern that a clinical psychologist must face when conducting a clinical assessment centers on the *accuracy* of the data she or he collects. Accuracy may be reflected in the consistency of the measure (reliability) and in the degree to which it reflects the construct of interest (validity).

The first way to determine accuracy is to consider the reliability of the information that is obtained. Reliability refers to the consistency of the observations or measurements that are made and provides a first step toward ensuring trustworthy information. Reliability is defined as the degree of consistency in measurement and is determined by using maximally similar methods to assess the same construct. The reliability of a measure is inversely related to the degree of random error in the instrument—high reliability indicates low error; low reliability provides a warning that the measure and the score are prone to a high degree of error. The importance of consistency in measurement can be seen easily in an example from outside the field of psychology. Imagine that you are a parent and you have taken your 3-year-old daughter to the pediatrician because she has been displaying a number of physical symptoms: vomiting, difficulty sleeping, crying much more than usual, and skin that feels hot and feverish. After asking you a series of questions about these symptoms, the nurse takes your child's temperature with a thermometer. The thermometer registers a temperature of 103.2 degrees. This reading would indicate a significantly elevated temperature above the "normal" level of 98.6 degrees, and a possible sign of a significant illness. As long as the thermometer is accurate, this information will form an important piece of data in forming a diagnosis of your daughter's condition. But how do you know that this instrument is accurate? What if the nurse took your child's temperature again 20 minutes later with the same thermometer and obtained a reading of 97.5 degrees? The second result would seriously undermine your faith in the use of this instrument to gauge whether your child was suffering from a fever as one of her current symptoms. Given that body temperature is very unlikely to change this much within 20 minutes, this second result would suggest that the thermometer is unreliable.

This example points to the problem that threatens accurate measurement—possible sources of error. To the extent that error affects the measures that are taken, one cannot be certain about the accuracy of these observations. Error can come in two forms—random and systematic. Random error occurs when factors influence measurements in ways that are unpredictable and unanticipated. Random error could occur when an individual responds randomly to an objective or multiple choice test, or when extraneous factors such as current mood, distractions present in the immediate environment, physiological states such as hunger or fatigue, and motivation interfere with the responses obtained on the measure. Whereas random error undermines the reliability of a measure, systematic error may be present and the instrument may still yield reliable results. Systematic error, which is reflected in a persistent bias in the test or in the interpretations made by the examiner, threatens validity without affecting reliability.

Reliability is determined in several different ways, depending on the type of assessment method that is being evaluated. As reflected in the example of the thermometer, the consistency of the measure over short periods of time may be important for some assessment techniques. This reliability is referred to as **test-retest reliability,** because the test or procedure is readministered and expected to produce identical or at least similar results over short periods of time. Tests of intelligence or personality characteristics, which are assumed to be stable personal characteristics, need to have high test-retest reliability. Test-retest reliability is typically expressed in the form of a correlation coefficient that can range from -1.00 to 0 to $+1.00$ (see chapter 3). Adequate reliability is typically accepted as a test-retest correlation of $+.80$ or greater. That is, most psychological measures are not perfectly reliable—there is some error reflected in a score on most tests or other assessment procedures. A reliability coefficient of $+.80$ or greater indicates that error is sufficiently low, however, that the score is primarily reflective of a consistent pattern of responding.

If you were asked to describe a person's character or personality, you would want to have the opportunity to observe or interact with that person on more than one occasion to obtain a good sample of his or her behavior. The more observations you were able to make, the more you would feel you had a chance to obtain a representative sample of this person's style of interacting with others and the world. Similarly, a psychological test or measure should contain many items or observations that are expected to reflect the same construct, such as many items on a test that serve as indices of anxiety. The degree to which these many items are related to one another reflects a second type of reliability, the **internal consistency reliability** of the measure. One approach to determining the consistency among items is to randomly split the items into two groups and determine the degree of correlation or correspondence between the two halves; this method is referred to as split-half reliability. A poor correlation between the two halves of the measure suggests that there is an unknown source of variability or error that leads to responses on some items that differ from responses on other items.

Because the splitting of a measure into two parts could result in a spuriously high or low correlation between the two parts because of a fluke in the way that the items were separated into two groups, a more thorough evaluation of this type of reliability can be obtained by determining the average of all of the possible ways that the measure could be split in half. This approach, referred to as *coefficient alpha* or *Cronbach's alpha,* is the most widely used method for determining the internal consistency of measures (Cronbach, 1951). The internal consistency reliability of a measure usually will increase as a function of the number of items included in the scale. In other words, the larger the sample that is obtained of any given behavior, the more representative and therefore more reliable the sample will be. The effect of one or two unreliable items will be reduced as the overall number of items is increased. Coefficient alpha is expressed, similar to indices of test-retest reliability, as a correlation coefficient (ranging from −1.00 to +1.00), and acceptable levels are expected to be greater than +.70.

A procedure that is developed to observe specific behaviors, such as the frequency of fidgeting and squirming by a child when seated at school, will need to reflect reliable observations regardless of who serves as the observer. This approach will need to have high reliability of a third type, **inter-rater reliability.** For example, a psychologist might be called on to observe a child's attention and disruptive behavior in a classroom. A list of specific behaviors could be developed, accompanied by a detailed definition of each behavior. It is important to determine, however, that the observations of these specific behaviors are not unduly affected by the perceptions of an individual observer and can be verified by more than one witness. The degree of correspondence between two observers or raters can be reflected in the percentage of observations on which they agree that a behavior was present or absent. Because raters can agree to a certain extent purely by chance, a *kappa* coefficient (Fleiss & Cohen, 1973) is often used to evaluate the extent of agreement above and beyond the level expected by chance.

As reflected in these examples, each form of reliability is not equally important for every assessment method. For example, inter-rater reliability is irrelevant in generating the scores for a personality test such as the MMPI (see chapter 9), because no raters are involved in evaluating a client's responses to this test. Test-retest reliability is not highly relevant to some forms of behavioral observation if the conditions under which the behavior is observed are known to change or fluctuate. On the other hand, this type of reliability is important if the environmental conditions under which the behavior is observed remain stable. Each type of psychological assessment procedure, however, must be shown to possess the appropriate type of reliability for that type of measurement.

Even if a measure produces consistent results, it still may be inaccurate. That is, it may be consistently in error in its measurement. Therefore, evaluating an assessment method's *validity* is as important as determining its reliability. Validity reflects the degree to which an assessment technique measures what it is designed or intended to measure. Validity is determined by using maximally different methods to measure the same construct. Several different types of validity exist.

The simplest form of validity does not require any statistical analyses. **Content validity** is the degree to which the measure covers the full range of the construct that is being measured as well as the degree to which the measure excludes factors that are not representative of the construct. In other words, do the items in the measure represent the features that are central to the definition of what is being measured? For example, if you were trying to develop an interview that could be used to determine if an individual met the *DSM-IV* criteria for Major Depressive Disorder, you would want to ensure that all nine core symptoms of depression were included in the questions in your interview. If you had omitted questions regarding sleep patterns and appetite, your interview would have poor content validity as a measure of depression.

Many or most of the factors that are measured by psychologists are hypothetical—they cannot be seen or touched, but they are conceptualized in particular ways in the minds and theories of psychologists. They represent constructs that have been defined as part of a psychological theory. Intelligence, personality, ego functioning, self-esteem, and attributional style are all hypothetical constructs. Psychologists, when they measure hypothetical concepts, must establish that their measure faithfully reflects what was outlined in the theory—they need to establish the measure's **construct validity.** Construct validity is the degree to which the measure reflects the structure and features of the hypothetical construct that is being measured. For example, many models of intelligence hypothesize that overall intelligence is comprised of two broad factors, one reflecting verbal skills and the other visiospatial abilities (Sternberg, 1999; Sternberg & Kaufman, 1998). An adequate test of this conceptualization of intelligence should contain items that assess verbal abilities that are highly correlated with one another and items that assess visiospatial abilities that are also highly correlated with each other. Further, items that are expected to measure verbal skills and those measuring visiospatial skills should correlate with each other to a lesser degree than with other items of the same type.

The pattern of correlations among items, and the degree to which this pattern reflects the hypothetical construct, is often evaluated through a statistical procedure of factor analysis (e.g., Cole, Hoffman, Tram, & Maxwell, 2000). This procedure is a way of examining the correlations among groups of items, referred to as factors. In Wechsler's test of intelligence, for example, two general factors, or groups of items, would be expected to be closely intercorrelated. Further, subtests that form the factor representing verbal intelligence should correlate more strongly with one another than with subtests that comprise the nonverbal factor.

Criterion validity is the most concrete of the various forms of validity. It is determined by the degree to which a measure of a particular construct is correlated with another construct that is hypothesized to be related to the construct of interest. These correlations may involve measures that are taken at the same time (**concurrent validity**), or a measure at one time may be correlated with another measure taken at a subsequent time (**predictive validity**). A classic example of criterion validity is the association between intelligence tests and indices of school performance or achievement. If scores on an IQ test reflect the underlying construct of intelligence, they should correlate with how well children are currently performing in school and should predict how well they will perform in future years as well.

Step 5: Making Decisions

The information obtained in the psychological assessment process is valuable only to the extent that it can be used in making important decisions about the person or persons who are the focus of assessment. The goals of assessment—diagnosis, screening, prediction, and evaluation of intervention—determine the types of decisions that are made. The decisions that are made on the basis of psychological assessments can have profound effects on people's lives. The outcomes can include the provision of special education services to a child who performs poorly on an intelligence test, the decision to place a child on medication following a diagnosis of Attention Deficit/ Hyperactivity Disorder, the administration of treatment for an anxiety disorder, the determination of the degree of neurological impairment as a result of a head injury, or the possible hospitalization for suicide risk, to name only a few examples. The process of making decisions is complex and the stakes are high. Therefore, it is important to understand the factors that influence the decisions and judgments made by clinical psychologists and ways to optimize the quality of these decisions.

Cognitive Aspects of Assessment and Clinical Judgment   The process of forming impressions of other people and trying to explain their behavior are central tasks for clinical psychologists. As noted at the beginning of this chapter, however, these tasks are not unique to psychologists. We are all involved in gathering information about people we encounter in our lives and attempting to generate sensible explanations for their behavior. The process that clinical psychologists follow should seem very familiar to all of us in many ways. **Information processing** involves gathering information about other people, forming impressions, and drawing conclusions. This process is also referred to as *person perception.*

Social psychologists have carefully studied the process of person perception—the ways in which human beings form impressions of and make judgments about other people (e.g., Berscheid, 1994). Basic research on the process of observing and learning about others provides a background and foundation for understanding the process of assessment in clinical psychology. This research has shown that human beings are prone to certain fundamental errors in processing information about the world, especially information about other people. People are imperfect information processors, and the types of errors that we make are important to the process of assessment in clinical psychology (Achenbach, 1985; Arkes, 1981). After all, clinical psychologists are human beings, albeit specially trained ones, who are making judgments about others.

The types of errors in information processing that are relevant to clinical assessment fall into three general categories: errors of selective attention to only certain parts of the information that is available to us, errors in retaining and accessing information once we have taken it in, and errors in the inferences or judgments that we make based on the information that we have retained or remembered. With regard to the first of these processes, our attention is selectively biased in several ways, most of which reflect the influence of our prior experiences and expectations that we bring to a situation. Confirmatory biases are those expectations and beliefs that lead us to give excess weight to data that tend to confirm our beliefs to the neglect of other types of information (Arkes & Harkness, 1983). Hypotheses formed very early in the clinical evaluation process, for example, may too readily be accepted because we continually seek evidence to confirm them (this process is also known as a primacy bias). Similarly, our confidence in our hypotheses increases the longer we hold them, even though the data to confirm them has not

been obtained. It is noteworthy that experienced clinicians have been found to be more susceptible to the biasing effects of initial information than are nonclinicians who placed much less confidence in their judgments (Friedlander & Phillips, 1984).

People are also biased in the ways that they encode or store information in their memories. One such bias is called the availability heuristic. Heuristics are strategies or rules for solving problems—they help people organize and simplify information but they may also bias judgment. The availability heuristic refers to the fact that the mental availability of previous cases to use in making judgments about a new case may be affected by such factors as the vividness, recency, and intensity of involvement with a particular case, or by similarities of the present case with other cases on dimensions that may not be relevant. Tversky and Kahneman (1974) point out that several errors can result from the availability heuristic: Clinicians can miss ways in which a new case differs from other cases it superficially resembles; they can match a case to an easily remembered pattern despite greater similarity to a less available pattern; they can infer correlations where none exist; and they can bias their estimates and predictions to reflect events most vivid to them rather than most representative of what is to be estimated or predicted.

Finally, people are prone to errors in the ways that they make inferences or judgments about information. Foremost among these errors is what is referred to as an illusory correlation—the tendency to infer associations between two variables that, in reality, are not correlated. Specifically, characteristics of people and responses on tests are often inferred to be related, and these inferences persist even when individuals are presented with data to the contrary (e.g., Chapman & Chapman, 1967, 1971; Garfield & Kurtz, 1978; Gyns, Willis, & Faust, 1995). Illusory correlation is related to problems in assessing covariation, or the ability to detect "what goes with what." People are often misled because cases that reflect covariation are typically given more weight and are more salient than cases in which two phenomena do not co-occur. Judgments of covariation are even more complex when the features are rated on dimensions rather than simple yes-no categories. There is an additional challenge in applying group level data to an inference about the co-occurrence and the meaning of the co-occurrence in an individual case. The representative heuristic is involved when people are trying to decide if one phenomenon (a child hits another child) is representative of a general class of phenomena (aggression). It is affected by insensitivity to base rates—low base rates of a phenomenon lead to overprediction that it is representative—and insensitivity to sample size—people often overestimate the degree to which a small sample is representative of the population (Achenbach, 1985).

Research on human information processing holds both bad news and good news for the understanding of assessment as conducted by clinical psychologists. The bad news is that the limitations in information processing place limits on clinical psychologists' abilities to develop impressions and make judgments about the people they serve. The good news is that a large number of procedures and methods have been developed to help clinical psychologists become more efficient and accurate in managing information about their clients.

Clinical Versus Statistical Prediction Because people, including clinical psychologists, are faced with a number of obstacles in the process of making judgments about the behavior of other people, how can the judgment process be improved? We return to an issue that we first raised in chapter 2—**clinical versus statistical prediction.** As you may recall, this issue was addressed by psychologist Paul Meehl in 1954 (Meehl, 1954/1996) and has continued to be a focus of research today (Grove et al., 2000). The debate centers on the relative efficacy of subjec-

Paul E. Meehl, Ph.D., is Emeritus Professor at the University of Minnesota. Dr. Meehl has had a profound impact on the field of clinical psychology. He was one of the first to question the validity of clinical judgment, and his continued focus on empiricism in clinical psychology has strengthened the training in this field. (Photo courtesy of Paul Meehl.)

tive judgments by the individual clinician versus the use of "actuarial" data collected on large samples and analyzed using statistical methods (Dawes, Faust, & Meehl, 1989).

The issue outlined by Meehl (1954/1996) is relatively straightforward. When clinicians use psychological assessment data, what is the best way for them to make judgments and predictions about individuals? Should the data be combined using statistical methods to make estimates of probability, or should the information be combined more subjectively by the individual clinician based on his or her experience? Statistical or actuarial judgments or predictions are made on the basis of data on large numbers of individuals that can be used to determine the rates at which certain events or relationships take place (base rates) and the probability that an event will happen in the future in light of current information. A classic example can be found in the actuarial tables used by insurance companies to estimate the probability that a given individual will die or have an automobile accident within a particular period of time. These predictions are important for insurance companies and customers, because they influence the amount of money the person will be charged for a policy—if the probability of a negative outcome is high, the cost of the policy goes up so that the company can cover its costs. If insurance companies were inaccurate in making these predictions, they would quickly go out of business by undercharging customers or they would lose customers by overcharging them. It is no surprise, then, that insurance companies do not rely on the subjective judgments of individual agents to make guesses about the likelihood that their policyholders are good or poor risks. Companies rely instead on data collected on hundreds of thousands of individuals to generate estimates of the probability that a particular individual with certain characteristics (e.g., being of a certain age, being a smoker, being a nondrinker, possessing a particular health history) will survive to age 75 or will have a car accident in the next year. Predictions that use the actuarial data are more accurate than predictions that depend on the judgments of individual agents.

Over 100 studies have compared the use of the clinical and statistical methods in making judgments in psychological assessment, including diagnostic decisions, evaluations of brain dysfunction, predictions of future violent behavior, predictions of work or school performance, and predictions of positive response to various forms of psychological and pharmacological treatment. The evidence clearly shows the superiority of statistical methods in making judgments (Dawes et al., 1989; Grove et al., 2000). One of the reasons for the relative superiority of statistically based judgments is that they are

perfectly reliable—they always combine the available information in exactly the same way. Human information processing, as we have already explained, is not perfectly reliable but is prone to a certain inherent level of inconsistency and error.

Findings from research comparing clinical and statistical methods do not mean that the clinical decision-making process should be cold and inhuman, carried out solely by computers. The role of the clinician is crucial for certain types of tasks that cannot be conducted adequately by purely empirical methods, including the generation of hypotheses and the use of theory in formulating questions (Dawes et al., 1989; Meehl, 1986). The important point is that statistical methods are superior for certain aspects of the process of psychological assessment, freeing psychologists to carry out other tasks for which they are uniquely suited.

The assessment process is much like the more general process of research. It begins with the generation of hypotheses, a process that is based partly on theory, partly on prior research, and partly on the creative hunches of the individual psychologist. After generating hypotheses, the psychologist must select the methods to be used to test these hypotheses. These methods should be selected based on their appropriateness for testing these hypotheses and on their psychometric characteristics (reliability, validity). Data are then collected and analyzed, steps that often require the use of computerized scoring techniques and comparisons to normative samples. Finally, judgments and predictions are made on the basis of these data, steps that are also best informed by normative or actuarial data.

Step 6: Communicating Information

After collecting information that is pertinent to the evaluation of an individual and the environments in which she or he functions, scoring the measures that were used, and interpreting the scores, the psychologist is faced with the final task of clinical assessment: communicating this information and interpretations to the interested parties. This communication typically takes the form of a written psychological report that is shared with the client, other professionals (physicians, teachers, other mental health professionals), a court of law, or family members who are responsible for the client. The challenges for psychologists in conveying assessment information are many, including the need to be accurate, to provide an explanation of the basis for their judgments, and to communicate free of technical jargon.

Just as the assessment process shares many features with the process of research, a good psychological report shares many features with a good research article. It should begin with an introduction to the case, including a description of the referral questions that were asked or the hypotheses that were tested. The methods or assessment procedures that were used should be described in sufficient detail so that the reader can understand and evaluate their quality. The results are reported next—a clear and succinct summary of the data. Finally, a discussion and interpretation of the results is provided, including recommendations for future assessment or intervention.

ETHICAL ISSUES IN ASSESSMENT

Psychologists are guided by a general set of rules or a code of conduct that includes rules for ethical conduct in the psychological assessment process (American Psychological Association, 1992). These guidelines have been developed to protect the best interests of the clients that are served by professional psychologists. Foremost among these guidelines are concerns for protecting clients from abuse by actions of psychologists, ensuring the **confidentiality** of information that is obtained, protecting clients' rights to privacy, ensuring the use of procedures that have well-established reliability and validity, and using the results of psychological assessment data in the best interests of clients.

Psychologists often obtain information about clients that reflects the most personal and intimate aspects of their lives. This information is shared with a psychologist in the strictest of confidence and with the expectation that no one has a right to access that information without the full informed consent of the client. Therefore, clients have the right to be aware of and to understand any and all information that has been obtained as part of the assessment process, to know where and how that information is stored, and to regulate who has access to that information.

The clearest example of the need to protect confidentiality centers on the disposition of the results of psychological tests and written psychological reports. How are test data and reports stored? How long are they retained? Who has access to test results and reports? Information from clinical assessments of individuals is always considered confidential, regardless of the length of time since the data were collected. Data that were collected from a person's past must be considered cautiously, because the characteristics that were measured may have changed significantly over time.

Although the concepts of reliability and validity may appear to be dry statistical abstractions, they are essential in the fair and ethical treatment of individuals. The use of a measure that has either poor or unknown reliability may produce information about a client that is not trustworthy. A lack of reliability in a measure indicates that if that test or procedure were used again it would not be expected to produce the same results. Therefore, an erroneous judgment could be made regarding a client's welfare on the basis of this unreliable information. If a test or procedure is not reliable it cannot be valid. Lack of validity indicates that the results are not an accurate representation of the psychological functioning of the individual.

Reliability is not the end of the story, however. Tests and procedures can produce information about a client that is highly reliable yet still wholly invalid as it pertains to a given individual. This situation is best exemplified in the inappropriate use of tests and inadequate normative data in the assessment of ethnic minority clients. In the 1970s, for example, the courts in California ruled that it was illegal to use standardized intelligence tests to classify minority children as mentally retarded because the tests were biased against these children (Mercer, 1988).

SUMMARY AND CONCLUSIONS

We have presented the process of psychological assessment as a series of six steps. The process commences with the formulation of questions that need to be asked, beginning with the questions that are raised by the referral made to the psychologist. Second, the psychologist formulates a set of goals for the assessment, which may include making a diagnosis, evaluating the severity of a problem, screening for the presence of problems, predicting future events or behavior, and evaluating the effects of an intervention. Third, it is necessary to establish standards that will be used in making decisions and judgments about the client. Fourth, the psychologist conducts the assessment by collecting the data. Assessment is accomplished through interviews, tests, and observations of behavior. Fifth, the psychologist evaluates the data to draw conclusions, make decisions, and arrive at judgments about the client. And finally, the psychologist communicates the information and decisions to others in the form of a psychological report.

Throughout the assessment process, priority is given to the collection of data that are both reliable and valid. The integration of information and the decision-making process are complicated by limitations in the ability of people to process and manage information. Therefore, statistical procedures are used to integrate complex data and draw conclusions that are less subject to error.

KEY TERMS AND NAMES

Clinical psychological assessment
Clinical versus statistical prediction
Concurrent validity
Confidentiality
Construct validity
Content validity
Criterion validity
Diagnosis
Information processing

Internal consistency reliability
Inter-rater reliability
Normative standards
Prediction
Predictive validity
Screening
Self-referent standards
Test-retest reliability

RESOURCES

Books

Achenbach, T. M., & McConaughy, S. H. (1997). *Empirically based assessment of child and adolescent psychopathology: Practical applications* (2nd ed.). Thousand Oaks, CA: Sage.

Anastasi, A. (1988). *Psychological testing* (6th ed.). New York, NY: Macmillan.

Mash, E. J., & Terdal, L. G. (Eds.). (1997) *Assessment of childhood disorders* (3rd ed.). New York, NY: Guilford Press.

Meehl, P. E. (1996). *Clinical versus statistical prediction: A theoretical analysis and a review of the evidence.* Northvale, NJ: Aronson. (Original work published 1954)

Journals

Psychological Assessment
The Journal of Personality Assessment
Behavioral Assessment
Assessment

ASSESSMENT: CLINICAL INTERVIEWING

INTRODUCTION

Phillip was embarrassed. Scheduling an appointment with a psychologist had made him feel that he was incompetent for being unable to overcome his anxiety and fear on his own. It had been complicated; it required leaving work early to make a 5:00 P.M. appointment, and he had to arrange for a sitter to take care of the children so that his wife could join him. As he drove to the psychologist's office, he became increasingly more worried about what this meeting would entail. He had never been to a psychologist before,

and the only images he had were based on characters portrayed in movies and television. What would she be like? He expected someone in tie-dyed clothes with incense burning in the office, asking him questions about his inner child. Would she try to unearth something from his unconscious? Grill him with questions about his childhood? As he continued on the drive, Phillip decided that seeing a psychologist seemed like a very poor decision. At the same time, he was fed up with feeling anxious all the time, tired of being afraid of giving a simple presentation at work, and tired of the burden that he felt he was placing on his wife and children.

He was pleasantly surprised when Dr. Marcus greeted him and his wife in the waiting room and invited them into her office. She was dressed conservatively but somewhat stylishly and seemed very at ease as she talked with them. Her office was not what he had expected either. There was a couch, but it looked more like the one in his own living room, not like the one he had seen in the picture of Sigmund Freud's office in his college psychology textbook. A desk was located in one corner of the room, but Dr. Marcus did not sit behind it; rather, she settled comfortably in a chair near the couch where Phillip and his wife sat.

He was relieved when Dr. Marcus began by summarizing the plan for the meeting. She would use the time to get to know Phillip and his wife, learn about their current concerns, and also give them the chance to ask questions about her background and how she planned to proceed in her work with them. After this short preamble, she asked simply, "So what brings you here today?" Phillip proceeded to unload his story about his recent bouts of anxiety, including his failed attempt to make a presentation at work and his recent experience on the telephone when he couldn't breathe and felt a pain in his chest. Dr. Marcus listened intently and asked questions to gain more of the details of these recent episodes. She had a way of rephrasing what Phillip said that made him feel that she understood what he was going through and that she was genuinely concerned about his feelings. She was skilled at drawing both Phillip and his wife into the conversation, allowing each of them to express their views without interrupting each other. The interview sped by much faster than Phillip had anticipated, and when it was over, he felt relieved and even hopeful that this person could help him.

As reflected in this glimpse of Phillip's initial visit to a psychologist, the first step in the process of clinical assessment typically begins with some form of interview of the client by the clinician. The clinical interview represents the first point of contact between the psychologist and the client and sets the direction for much of what will follow during the process of assessment. Psychologists can choose from among a number of alternative approaches to interviewing clients, ranging from unstructured methods based on the personal style of the psychologist to highly structured methods that prescribe that the same questions be asked, in the same order, for all clients. The particular interview method that is selected by any psychologist depends on the goals of the psychologist in working with a given individual. We will return to Phillip and another of our cases, Maria, when we discuss structured diagnostic interviews (see boxes 7.1 and 7.2).

The clinical interview has a long history in psychological assessment. Sigmund Freud relied almost exclusively on interviews to gather information and formulate diagnostic impressions of his patients. Although Freud came to rely on a process of asking his patients to report freely on their thoughts (free association) as part of his method (see chapter 12), he nonetheless provided significant structure to his interviews with his patients both through the types of questions that he asked and through other forms of verbal feedback. One of the first formally structured methods of psychological assessment was the Woodworth Personal Data Sheet, which was used in World War I as a kind of standardized psychiatric interview (Anastasi, 1988). The Woodworth Personal Data Sheet consisted of a series of questions about symptoms of psychopathology that had been developed for screening potential recruits for the armed services in the First World War. These early methods have evolved to the highly structured psychiatric interviews that are currently used in research and clinical practice to derive *DSM-IV* diagnoses.

The most widely used format for clinical interviews is relatively unstructured, with individual psychologists developing their style and format based on their personal experience. Psychologists bring to the interview their own style of establishing rapport with their clients; indeed, they may generate a set of questions that they ask of all clients. The nature of the questions, however, is often influenced by the characteristics of the client and the referral question. For example, an initial interview involving an adolescent boy referred for conduct problems may be quite different from the first interview with an adult woman who presents with concerns about generalized feelings of fear and anxiety. Certainly, the strength of personalized, unstructured interviews lies in their flexibility and responsiveness to the unique characteristics and concerns of each client (Beutler, 1996).

Nevertheless, the use of unstructured interviews also presents a number of problems. The lack of structure in many clinical interviews makes it impossible to evaluate the quality of the information that is obtained in these situations. When two psychologists use their own idiosyncratic methods for gathering information from the same client, they are unlikely to obtain similar information, that is, there is not likely to be high inter-rater reliability. The information that is obtained and the impressions that are formed based on this information are strongly influenced by the personal biases of the individual psychologist. Threats to the reliability of unstructured clinical interviews mean that validity is also difficult to establish.

Concern about the lack of reliability of unstructured clinical interviews provided part of the impetus for the development of structured interview protocols for use in research and clinical practice. The most extensive work in this area has focused on interviews that are used for obtaining information to make diagnoses based on the *DSM-IV* criteria (e.g., Spitzer, Williams, Gibbon, & First, 1992; Williams et al., 1992). While these efforts have led to interviews that are dramatically more reliable with respect to the information that is obtained, they have also resulted in concerns about the ability of the interviewer to establish rapport with the client. The highly structured nature of diagnostic interviews makes it difficult to respond to the unique features and concerns of each individual (Groth-Marnat, 1997). We will now discuss the purposes of clinical interviews and the strengths and weaknesses of the various interview protocols that have been developed.

CLINICAL INTERVIEWING

An effective interview is goal directed and purposeful. The interviewer enters the interaction with the client with a clear sense of what is to be accomplished during the course of the interaction and a plan or format for achieving these objectives (Ivey, 1994; Weins, 1991). Thus, while interviews share many features with day-to-day conversations, they differ in their goal directedness. Clinical interviews also differ from conversations in their unwavering focus on the client. Our daily interactions are typically bidirectional in emphasis, attending both to ourselves and to others with whom we interact. Clinical interviewers are not balanced in their focus—they are directed exclusively toward the client. In order to achieve this level of attention to the client, a successful interviewer must be, first and foremost, a good listener.

Clinical interviews have three primary goals: to *gather information* about the client; to obtain data needed to arrive at a *diagnosis* or make other important decisions; and to *establish a relationship* with the client to allow for continued assessment and intervention if it is warranted. While some interviews are designed to achieve all three of these goals, others are intended to accomplish only one of these objectives. The challenge for clinical psychologists is that the methods that are best suited to gather the most reliable and valid information and to help in generating a diagnosis are often the poorest for building rapport. In contrast, the methods that are most effective in establishing a good relationship with clients may yield information that is unreliable and, therefore, not valid for diagnostic or other decision-making purposes (Beutler, 1996).

Communication Skills

Regardless of whether a psychologist is attempting to gather detailed information about a client or to establish a strong working relationship, the success of any interview will depend on the psychologist's skills in communicating with the client. Through both verbal and nonverbal means of communication, the successful interviewer is able to put the client at ease, draw out information, and lay the groundwork for future assessment and intervention.

A variety of different frameworks have been developed to classify and understand the communication skills that are important in successful interviewing (e.g., Burnstein & Goodman, 1988; Goodman & Dooley, 1976; Maloney & Ward, 1976). The work of psychologists Allen Ivey, David Evans, and their colleagues offers a useful description of the "microskills" of successful interviewing—the specific verbal and nonverbal responses that can be used by the interviewer (e.g., Daniels, Rigazio-DiGilio, & Ivey, 1997; Evans, Hearn, Uhlemann, & Ivey, 1998; Ivey, 1994). Ivey and Evans organize communication skills into two general categories: *attending skills* and *influencing skills*. Whereas attending skills are important in building rapport, gathering information, and helping the client to feel understood, influencing skills are important in directing the interaction with the client and conveying specific information.

Attending Skills   Attending skills are those verbal and nonverbal methods of communication that are used to ensure the accurate monitoring of the client and to communicate sincere interest and concern on behalf of the interviewer. Through the use of active listening techniques, the interviewer not only learns about the client but also conveys a sense of concern, personal warmth, and understanding of the client's difficulties and situation. Attending skills are focused on the client and her or his concerns, wishes,

thoughts, and feelings (Ivey & Simek-Downing, 1980).

The nonverbal behaviors that are part of important attending skills involve eye contact, posture, and facial expression. Direct eye contact, leaning one's body slightly forward, facing toward the client, and gesturing in a manner appropriate to the content of the conversation are all nonverbal behaviors that convey interest in, and attention to, the client (Evans et al., 1998). Nonverbal behaviors are typically overlooked in day-to-day conversations, yet they have a significant influence on the nature of communication (Hall, Carter, & Horgan, 2000). The effects of nonverbal behaviors may be most noticeable when they are used ineffectively or inappropriately. When someone fails to make eye contact with you, sits slumped back in a chair, and is turned away from you, she or he conveys a message of distance and disinterest. Facial expressions have also been shown to be powerful and universal cues for conveying information about one's internal emotional state (Ekman, 1999). A furrowed brow and downturned mouth communicate a sense of anger and hostility and are not likely to foster feelings of comfort in another. A smiling, pleasant expression will convey appropriate emotions for some interactions, but is an inappropriate emotional response when listening to someone who is tearfully describing a tragic event in his or her life.

Although the importance of nonverbal factors cannot be overestimated, verbal behaviors form the central part of attending skills (Ivey, 1994). Verbal attending skills include the use of:

- closed questions
- open questions
- minimal encouragement
- paraphrasing
- reflection of feelings
- summarization

In addition, the ability to remain *silent* yet attentive to the client is also an important aspect of attending and active listening. Attending skills are important in the process of verbally tracking, or following, the client. Clients do not arrive at an interview with a careful script for all that they will say during the course of an interview; the content and emotions that they share are likely to change significantly over the course of an hour, or even from one moment to the next. A skilled interviewer is able to follow these shifts by attending to the content and meaning of the client's communication. Table 7.1 presents examples of verbal attending responses to a client (Phillip).

Closed questions are used for information gathering and clarification. Closed questions can often be answered with a "yes" or "no" or with very few words. For example, a psychologist may ask a client, "How old are you?" or "Is this the first time that you have spoken to anyone about this concern?" *Open questions,* as their name implies, are more broadly focused than are closed questions and are used to facilitate discussion and self-exploration by the client. Compared to closed questions, questions that begin with "what," "how," or "why" are more open and require more detailed, expansive answers. Examples of open questions include "How did you feel when that happened?" and "Why do you think you experience those feelings each time you go home?" Closed and open questions are the primary mechanism for gathering information from a client, because they require or demand a response in the form of information. In fact, questions are the primary means of communication in structured diagnostic interviews.

Despite the importance of questions in gathering information, a successful interviewer does not simply barrage a client with a series of questions. Overreliance on questions as a means of

TABLE 7.1
Examples of Attending and Influencing Communication Skills Used in Clinical Interviewing

Client statement (Phillip): "I feel anxious every time I have to give a presentation in front of others at work. I just completely panic; I'm terrified that I will make a fool of myself. And I don't even know why. It just feels automatic."

Attending skills	Examples of therapist responses
Open question	"Can you tell me more about the feelings?"
Closed question	"Where were you when this happened last?"
Paraphrasing	"So you are terrified of giving presentations at work but you don't know why."
Reflection of feeling	"You feel frightened, terrified, and confused."
Summarization	"So it sounds like you have an automatic reaction to having to make presentations at work—you become afraid and anxious, but you don't know why."

Influencing skills	Examples of therapist responses
Directive statements	"Tell me more about the fear you experienced when you stood up to give your presentation."
Self-disclosure	"I find myself beginning to feel anxious as you talk about your experience."
Interpretation	"Perhaps your fears about making presentations at work are just a part of a larger problem."
Advice or guiding information	"As part of the way we are going to deal with these fears, I'm going to have you spend time this week learning how to relax."

communication does not help a client feel understood. Effective interviewers use other communication tools to allow clients to share information and to offer a more complete sense of their concerns and experiences. *Minimal encouragement* takes the form of repetition to the client of a few of his or her own words, or the form of short comments such as "mmm-hmm" or "tell me more" or "so . . ." These responses can further discussion by encouraging the client to continue to express the same thought or feeling without the psychologist interrupting or disrupting the flow of what the client is saying. For example, after a lengthy disclosure by a client about an incident at work that led her to feel particularly frustrated and angry, minimal encouragement by the interviewer would involve a statement that reiterates a few of the client's words (e.g., "It sounds like you feel overwhelmed"). The full content of the client's disclosure is not repeated, but the main point or feeling is underscored.

Paraphrasing involves repeating back the essence or most salient aspects of the client's most recent statements. Paraphrasing can offer a sense of the direction of the client's statements, promote further discussion, and offer a check on the interviewer's understanding of what the client has said. If the interviewer has heard the client correctly, a paraphrase will be accurate and will provide the client with a sense that she or he has been listened to carefully. On the other hand, if the paraphrase is inaccurate the client can offer corrective feedback to the interviewer and ensure that his or her message has been correctly received.

Reflection of feeling serves the same function as a paraphrase, with the exception that reflection of feeling focuses attention on the emotional content of the client's verbalizations. Reflection of feeling involves a summary and repetition of what the interviewer perceives to be the central emotional tone of the client's message. This tone is inferred from both the content of what the client reports about his or her feelings ("I feel sad") as well as nonverbal information that is inferred from the tone of voice, facial expression, body posture, and displays of affect (e.g., crying). Reflection of feeling conveys to the client that the interviewer has understood the emotions of the moment and serves to draw out further information about the client's emotional experience.

Finally, *summarization* involves a synthesis of an entire segment or block of the client's communication. The goal of summarization is to provide the client with an integration of the content and emotion that they have conveyed over a period of several minutes or longer.

Although these skills are classified as means of attending to the client, they also influence the course of the interview. Encouragement, paraphrases, and reflections of feeling are made in response to only a portion of what the client presents during the interview, and they provide selective reinforcement to the client. The client is likely to continue to discuss or expand on those topics and feelings that are attended to by the interviewer and discontinue those areas that have not been noted. Thus, an interviewer's attention is always selective in nature and powerfully shapes the course of the interview.

Attending skills are used to gather information and learn about the client while conveying to the client that the interviewer is interested in and concerned about the client's concerns and experiences. The effective use of minimal encouragement, paraphrasing, and reflection of feeling are the primary means of conveying *accurate empathy* (Bohart & Greenberg, 1997). Empathy is the ability to accurately understand the perspective and experience of the client, to see the world from her or his vantage point, to experience to some extent the emotions that are felt by the client. Empathic responding by the interviewer may be the most important element in establishing rapport with a client, because it conveys concern for and interest in the client and recognition of his or her experience. Empathy may increase the amount of information that is obtained, the accuracy of that information, and the strength of the relationship that is built with the client (Bohart & Greenberg). However, high levels of empathy are not universally effective for interviewing all clients. For example, interpersonal warmth on the part of the interviewer does not elicit more information from all clients, and more reserved interviewers may be more effective with some individuals.

Influencing Skills   **Influencing skills** are used to guide and shape the responses made by the client (Evans et al., 1998; Ivey, 1994). The verbal responses that are used to direct and influence the interview include the following:

- directive statements
- expression of content
- expression of feeling
- summarizing in an attempt to influence the client
- interpretation
- self-disclosure
- provision of advice or guiding information

Although closed and open questions are classified as attending skills within Ivey's framework, they also exert an influence on the client and the interview by directing the course of the content of the interview.

The interviewer overtly guides the course of the interview through the use of *directives* (giving instructions, telling the client what to do), *expression of content* (providing feedback to the client, sharing information, giving instructions), and offering *influencing summaries* (selectively summarizing the main themes of what the client has said over an extended period of time). Directives involve specific commands or instructions to the client. Although directives are important when a clinician is trying to intervene and change some aspect of the client, they are also used to guide and influence the course of an initial interview. Expressions of content include offering an opinion, making a suggestion, pro-

viding feedback, or giving reassurance. Expression of content represents sharing information from the interviewer's point of view, rather than tracking what the client is saying. Influencing summaries are similar to paraphrases but they are broader in their focus. An influencing summary should occur after the client has had the opportunity to disclose a considerable amount of information and after the interviewer has attempted to selectively synthesize the main themes that have been expressed.

Other forms of communication more subtly influence and guide the interview, including the disclosure of feelings or personal information by the interviewer and the interpretation of what the client has said. *Disclosure of feelings or information* offers a model to the client for sharing personal experiences and emotions and provides information about the desired level of intimacy and openness that is desired by the interviewer. Although the focus is taken off the client and put onto an emotional or personal aspect of the interviewer, disclosure can still be useful in drawing additional information from the client. Disclosures that convey information about the interviewer at the present moment are most powerful for furthering rapport and eliciting more information. Finally, *interpretation* involves the renaming or relabeling of the client's thoughts and feelings from the perspective of the interviewer, typically based in the interviewer's theoretical perspective. Interpretations offered by a psychoanalytic interviewer will emphasize the meaning of behavior in terms of underlying personality dynamics, whereas interpretations offered by a behavioral interviewer will emphasize the current environmental context and contingencies and their influence on behavior. Interpretations are used to synthesize and analyze information once it has been obtained and to change the way that a client views himself or herself.

Through the combination of various attending and influencing skills, interviewers are capable of shaping and guiding the content, style, and rate of the interaction with the client (Groth-Marnat, 1997). The interviewer is able to use these skills best when he or she is aware of the impact of these responses on the client and can use them intentionally. Again, the use of attending and influencing skills speaks to the need for some degree of structure during clinical interviews to allow the interviewer to anticipate and understand her or his impact on the client.

Cultural Differences in Communication

Cultural and ethnic groups differ in their values and expectations regarding interpersonal relationships and communication (Sue, Ivey, & Pedersen, 1996; Tharp, 1991). These differences are important to consider when using communication skills in the context of clinical interviews with culturally diverse clients (Casas, 1995; Pedersen & Ivey, 1993). Cultural groups may differ on a number of dimensions that are relevant to communication within a clinical relationship, including values and beliefs about power and status, tolerance for uncertainty, emphasis on individualism, and emphasis on achievement and assertiveness (Sue et al.). These differences have implications for the ways that interviewers can obtain information and establish rapport with clients. Although it is important to take these cultural differences into account, it is equally important to avoid stereotypes about the preferred communication styles of individuals based solely on their ethnic heritage. In addition to considering cultural differences in communication, interviewers must also consider that the individual's experience with racial, economic, political, or legal prejudice may have a powerful effect on his or her ability and willingness to participate in an interview with a psychologist.

The cultural compatibility hypothesis suggests that mental health services will be more effective when they are congruent with the cultural patterns and values of a client (Tharp, 1991). Although the evidence in support of the importance of cultural compatibility between interviewer and client has been slow in coming, most authors agree that there is the need for some degree of matching between mental health professionals and ethnic minority clients (Tharp). There is evidence that what Tharp (1989) calls the "courtesies and conventions of conversation" exert an influence on the quality of the interviewer-client relationship. These factors include the length of pause between speakers, rhythm of speech, and patterns and conditions for speaking and listening. Matching of the ethnicity of the psychologist and the client appears to play an important role in establishing a working alliance (Sue, Fujino, Hu, Takeuchi, & Zane, 1991).

Interviews with Children

The process of interviewing children and adolescents presents a unique set of challenges. Because of differences in cognitive development, language skills, and interpersonal skills, the same techniques that are useful in interviewing adults may be ineffective in interactions with children. Bierman (1983) outlined several aspects of children's cognitive and social development that need to be considered in applying interviewing techniques with children. Children's thinking about themselves and their social world develops along several dimensions, including:

- from concrete thinking to more abstract and hypothetical thinking
- from unidimensional (good-bad) thinking to multidimensional thinking about the same person or relationship
- from thinking in rigid, black-white terms to more flexible types of thinking
- from egocentric thinking to being able to consider multiple perspectives simultaneously
- from a restriction to the present to being able to anticipate and consider the future

Therefore, interviews with very young children need to focus on concrete, here-and-now questions, and questions need to be asked in ways that allow children to offer simple, one-dimensional judgments.

Children are also much more accustomed to expressing themselves through nonverbal means, including art and play. Although some interviewers use drawing or dolls with children, their use is controversial, in part because clinicians vary in the degree to which they use drawings or dolls as means of communication as opposed to sources of information for interpretation. Interpretation of children's drawings and play during interviews has typically failed to meet minimal standards for reliability and validity and may reflect the biases and perspectives of the interviewer more than the experience of the child. Therefore, it is more conservative to assume that the use of play and art materials offers a means of communicating with children rather than serving as sources of inferences about underlying psychological processes. Recent advances in the use of pictures and puppets to children in clinical interviews have been shown to generate reliable information that can be used in deriving diagnoses (Ablow et al., 1999; Valla et al., 2000; see the section in this chapter titled "Diagnostic Interviews for Children and Adolescents").

Interviews with parents play a central role in the assessment of most child problems. Parents are assumed to be an important source of information on their children's behavior by providing information that children are either unable or unwilling to report. Children and their parents often disagree in their reports on children's adjustment and behavior problems (Achenbach, McConaughy, & Howell, 1987). Furthermore, interviewing children with their parents or interviewing parents and children separately will yield different information (McConaughy, 2000).

Clinical Interviews as a Means of Gathering Information

Clinical interviews are conducted for various purposes, including to serve as a screening or intake for clinical services, to obtain extensive background information in the form of a personal or family history, to be an initial contact in the context of managing a crisis, and to terminate an intervention. These different types of interviews are used at different points in the process of assessment and working with clients. A wide range of information is typically sought during an initial assessment interview as the psychologist strives to form an initial impression of the client, his or her current problems and resources for dealing with these problems, and aspects of the client's history that may have contributed to the current problems.

Information is often collected during the initial clinical interview for the purpose of screening and generating a diagnosis (Groth-Marnat, 1997). Screening interviews involve the collection of a broad range of background information that is useful in formulating an initial impression of the client and generating hypotheses to be evaluated at subsequent points in the assessment process. **Intake interviews,** screening interviews, and interviews conducted in crisis-oriented services all focus on identifying current problems and concerns. Interviewers are concerned with helping the client pinpoint and prioritize the problems that are the most pressing at the present time. This process is, in fact, often much more complex than it would first appear. When a client first calls a clinic to inquire about psychological services, a member of the clerical staff or an intake worker is likely to ask the caller briefly to identify the nature of the problem that led the person to call. The concerns offered by clients in an initial interaction of this type are often only vaguely related to problems that will eventually become the focus of assessment and treatment.

Clinical problems do not arise in the moment—they are the result of a series of events and processes that may extend over weeks, months, or years. Therefore, it is important for psychologists to obtain detailed information about the *background and history* of the client and, in many cases, of his or her family as well. The type of historical data that are relevant will depend in part on the theoretical orientation of the interviewer. For example, the psychoanalytic interviewer will want to have information on the client's memories of early childhood and relationships with parents in order to formulate interpretations about the client's psychosexual development and the gratification of basic needs and drives. The behavioral psychologist, on the other hand, will want to learn about the client's learning history—prior history of reinforcement and significant events that may have contributed to learned patterns of behavior.

Regardless of their theoretical orientation, most psychologists obtain a comprehensive personal and family history of the client. For children, this history includes an extensive interview with the parents to determine the events surrounding pregnancy, childbirth and early development, achievement of developmental milestones, school history, and significant stressors in the family. Documenting the history of any psychopathology in the family is critical in understanding the client's situation and possible early home experiences. Historical data are also important to obtain from adult clients, including their personal history of mental health problems, educational and work history, interpersonal relationship history, and significant stressful events.

Reliability and Validity of Interviews   Like all other forms of psychological assessment, clinical interviews need to be reliable and valid. Several forms of reliability are important with respect to interviews. First, if a clinician interviews the same client on two occasions, will he or she obtain the same information? This question represents the *test-retest reliability* of the interview. Research has shown that reliable information can be obtained from interviews conducted several weeks or even several months apart (Groth-Marnat, 1997). The reliability of the interview decreases, however, if clients are asked to provide retrospective reports or to recall information regarding events that occurred long ago (e.g., Olin & Zelinsky, 1991). Conversely, reliability increases when specific, factual information is

solicited as opposed to more vague or emotionally charged information (Beutler, 1996).

Second, if two different interviewers interact with the same client, will they obtain the same information? This type of agreement represents a form of *inter-rater reliability*. Inter-rater reliability of clinical interviews is typically calculated in the form of the **kappa coefficient.** *Kappa* reflects the degree of agreement between two raters after controlling for the rate of agreement that would simply occur by chance. Because diagnostic decisions are most often "yes" or "no," there is an inherent rate at which interviewers will agree simply by chance alone. The consistency of information obtained by different interviewers increases directly as a function of the degree of structure provided for the interview format and the level of training provided to the interviewers.

Third, if two clinicians are asked to evaluate and make judgments based on the same interview information, will they agree in their judgments? This type of inter-rater reliability is typically evaluated by videotaping an interview and having clinicians view the tape separately and provide their judgments and inferences about the client (e.g., Widiger, Frances, Pincus, Davis, & First, 1991). The level of training in a system for scoring the interview has the greatest impact on improving this type of inter-rater agreement. The development of structured diagnostic interviews has made a significant contribution to increasing the reliability of clinical interviews.

Establishing the reliability of any psychological procedure is necessary but not sufficient for determining whether the procedure is valid. Once clinical interviews have been shown to be reliable, they still must be found to generate accurate or valid information. Validity requires that the information obtained in the interview be compared to an external criterion to determine its accuracy. Considerably less research has been conducted on the validity of clinical interviews than on their reliability. Moreover, the judgments made on the basis of structured diagnostic interviews are often held as the "gold standard" against which other assessment procedures are judged. Like all other sources of assessment data, however, even highly structured clinical interviews are open to threats to their validity. Situational factors can affect the accuracy, and therefore the validity, of the information obtained in an interview. For example, the current mood or emotional state of the client can contribute to biases in recall of information about past history and events (e.g., Aneshensel, Estrada, Hansell, & Clark, 1987). Interviews designed to obtain lifetime histories may be especially vulnerable to errors and distortions as a function of current mood. However, highly structured diagnostic interviews have been shown to yield data that are related to information obtained using other methods such as tests and direct observations. These findings provide evidence for the validity of these interview methods.

Generating Hypotheses Versus Testing Hypotheses   If the reliability and validity of clinical interviews are threatened by so many factors, what role should interviews play in the process of gathering information about the client? It is best to view initial clinical interviews, especially unstructured interviews, as sources of information for *generating hypotheses* about clients but as poor sources of information for testing or confirming those hypotheses. Hypothesis generation is the process of developing well-informed hunches or initial impressions about the client that require further information. This additional information should be obtained using other methods to corroborate these hunches or prove them to be false. Using interviews to generate hypotheses means that the impressions formed by the interviewer are held as tentative, as requiring further validation. Hypothesis testing, on the other hand, involves the process of trying to reach conclusions about the client and his or her problems. Confirming or disconfirming a hypothesis requires the convergence of different types of information that are typically not available through an interview alone.

While the interview is best viewed as a starting point for the generation of hypotheses, it is important that interviewers fight the tendency to form lasting impressions too quickly and to reach premature closure about a client and about the nature of his or her problems. The subjective impressions that are developed during unstructured interviews may be particularly vulnerable to confirmatory biases in information processing (see chapter 6).

Confidentiality of Information   The interviewer has a professional obligation to protect the confidentiality of the information that is obtained during a clinical interview. Assurance of the private nature of this interaction will allow the client to disclose information that he or she may be unable to disclose in other contexts. The assurance of confidentiality will increase the likelihood that honest and accurate information will be obtained. Interviewers must assure the client that clinical interviews are conducted privately and without interruption and that the results of the interview, including any written records, are safely stored. The exceptions to the rule of confidentiality are when the client discloses information indicating that he or she is potentially harmful to himself or herself or others, or when the client offers material that suggests the possibility of child abuse or neglect. In these instances the interviewer is obliged to protect the welfare of the client or others who are in danger as a result of the client's behavior.

Clinical Interviews as a Means of Establishing a Relationship

There are a wide range of assessment tools and methods for gathering detailed information about a client. The clinical interview, however, is the only means of developing a strong relationship with a client—a relationship that is necessary for continued assessment and, when appropriate, intervention. In this sense, establishing rapport may be the most important function of the interview. The communication skills that are best suited to gather extensive information are not the same skills that are best to establish rapport between the psychologist and the client. Furthermore, the structure that is necessary to obtain accurate information may often undermine rapport and the development of a close working relationship (Beutler, 1996).

The solution to the dilemma lies in the balancing of structured and semiunstructured portions of the interview. A highly structured diagnostic interview can be both preceded and followed by more flexible interactions with the client that allow the interviewer to be more responsive to the unique concerns of the client and to ensure that the client feels that these concerns have been heard and understood by the interviewer.

INTERVIEW FORMATS

Clinical psychologists can choose from a variety of different interview protocols, ranging from semistructured formats that allow for some variation on the part of the interviewer to highly structured protocols that prescribe the responses of the interviewer in a step-by-step fashion. The more rigorously structured interviews were designed to be administered by nonprofessional interviewers after extensive training, whereas semistructured interviews were designed for use by mental health professionals who are able to use them with some flexibility to make clinical judgments during the course of the interview.

Although semistructured and structured interviews have been developed primarily for research purposes, it is important to extend their use to clinical practice. If the use of structured diagnostic interviews is limited to research, then the findings of extensive clinical studies cannot be generalized to clinical practice. Similarly, if only unstructured interviews are used in clinical practice, they cannot be used to reliably and validly make diagnostic decisions and other judgments that may be desired after an interview takes place.

Unstructured Clinical Interviews

Even interviews that are developed on the basis of the personal styles and experiences of different clinicians contain some similarities. It is recognized that interviews generally contain introductory, middle, and concluding phases that have certain features in common. Although to some degree these phases are characteristic of all interviews, they are most pronounced during the initial contact with a client. Before even beginning an interview, a skilled interviewer attends to the setting or context in which the interview is conducted. The interview should occur in a quiet and private setting, both to reduce interruptions or distractions that would interfere with interview process and to ensure that the exchange will be confidential. For example, it is inappropriate for a psychologist who works in a school to conduct a clinical interview in the back of a classroom where other students are present or in an office where other school personnel may overhear the interview.

The introductory phase of an interview is often characterized by uncertainty and discomfort on the part of the client. This interview may be the first occasion on which the client has disclosed information about a problem, and this discomfort may be compounded by a lack of familiarity with and uncertainty about the role of the psychologist. These concerns are particularly pronounced during an initial interview, when the client may be concerned that she or he will be judged to be crazy, or may be unsure about how the information that is discussed will be handled. These concerns dictate that the first phase of an interview be devoted to providing some basic information to the client about the nature and goals of the interview and to easing the client's discomfort to a manageable level. Therefore, the skilled interviewer begins not by asking for the reasons that the client is seeking services but by offering some basic information about the setting in which the interview is being conducted and the goals for the session. Offering the client the

Clinical interviewing is an important first step in the assessment of individuals, couples, and families. (Photo © *Stephen Simpson/FPG International.*)

opportunity to ask questions before moving into the main phase of the interview can facilitate both rapport building and information gathering.

The middle phase of unstructured interviews is devoted to gathering information. Interviewers differ in the order in which they use open and closed questions to achieve this goal. Some argue that it is best to begin with broad, open questions and follow with more specific questions in response to the information that is shared by the client. Others suggest that it is useful to initiate the interaction with more specific, closed questions to ease the client's uncertainty and to clarify for the client what information will be appropriate to disclose. The most frequent way to open this phase of the interview, however, is to simply ask the client, "What brings you here

today?" or "Tell me about the concerns or problems that led you to call for an appointment." These types of open questions allow the client some flexibility to begin the interview with a topic of his or her choice. The interviewer should not conclude prematurely, however, that the first issue discussed by the client is the most pressing or even the most important concern. It is a starting point from the frame of reference of the client rather than the point of view of the interviewer. The interviewer can follow the client's disclosures with more specific questions to fill in the necessary information about this problem. Attending skills are emphasized in this portion of the interview.

The third phase of an interview must provide some degree of closure for the session that is ending and a transition to subsequent sessions if they are warranted. The closing phase is likely to include an influencing summary and expression of content by the interviewer. Typically, the interviewer will provide a brief summary of the material that has been covered during the session as well as plans for the next meeting. An initial assessment interview will often be used to generate plans for psychological testing, behavioral observation, or other forms of assessment. The closing phase of the initial interview is used to provide the rationale for further assessment and to make specific plans for proceeding. The interview is also used to provide feedback when the assessment process is completed. Thus, a final assessment interview can be used to summarize the results of psychological tests and other assessment procedures in a language that the client can understand. The implications of assessment data for defining problems and planning future intervention are also covered in a final assessment interview.

Mental Status Examination

The **mental status exam** is one of the oldest forms of clinical interviews, dating back to the work of psychiatrist Adolf Meyer in the early 1900s. The mental status exam was developed as a part of psychiatric practice that is analogous to the physical examination in general medicine. (See table 7.2 for examples of the categories covered in the mental status exam). Drawing on the medical model for the development of a specific, differential diagnosis, the mental status exam typically includes an assessment of the patient's general appearance and behavior, speech and thought processes, consciousness, mood and affect, perception, orientation, memory, attention and concentration, general information, intelligence, insight, and judgment (Crary & Johnson, 1981; Groth-Marnat, 1997).

Assessment of general appearance and behavior includes observations of the client's dress, posture, gait, gestures, and personal hygiene and care. Symptoms of some disorders may be directly observable in behavior during the first interview (e.g., evidence of substance use, slow movement characteristic of depression). Assessment of speech and thought focuses on whether the client's speech is coherent, normal in progression, spontaneous, and understandable. It is important to note if speech is tangential, slowed or characterized by strange words or syntax and if delusional thinking is reported. Mood and affect are assessed by the content of the client's self-descriptions of current mood, and observations of posture and facial expression may provide additional information about the client's current affective state. Furthermore, the interviewer notes the appropriateness of the client's affect for topics being discussed and variations in affect during the interview. Questions are asked to determine if the client is oriented to time, place, and person (that is, does the client know the current date and time, where he is, and who he is?), functions that are usually intact except in severe cases of mental disorder. Memory is assessed by asking for accounts of recent or distant events that can be evaluated by comparisons with other records or informants. Deviations in attention and concentration are noted, including the degree to which the client is easily distracted or appears preoccupied. A rough estimate of intelligence is made from evidence obtained in the interview, including level of educational attainment, fund of general knowledge, and powers of reasoning.

Despite its wide usage, the mental status exam is not a single, well-standardized procedure—in fact, several versions of the mental status exam have been developed. Because it is not typically standardized, the mental status exam is subject to the personal predilections and idiosyncracies of the individual interviewer, and the reliability of this procedure may be questioned. In response to this concern, several efforts have been made to develop a standardized procedure for conducting this exam (e.g., Crary et al., 1981; Hedlund, Sletten, Evenson, Altman, & Cho, 1977).

TABLE 7.2
Examples of Items From the Mental Status Exam

			No data	Present	Absent
Appearance		1. unkempt, unclean, disheveled			
		2. clothing and/or grooming atypical			
		3. unusual physical characteristics			
Behavior	Posture	4. slumped			
		5. rigid, tense			
	Facial expression suggests:	6. anxiety, fear, apprehension			
		7. depression, sadness			
		8. anger, hostility			
		9. absence of feeling, blandness			
		10. atypical, unusualness			
	General body movements	11. accelerated, increased speed			
		12. decreased, slowed			
		13. atypical, unusual			
		14. restlessness, fidgetiness			
	Speech	15. rapid speech			
		16. slowed speech			
		17. loud speech			
		18. soft speech			
		19. mute			
		20. atypical quality, slurring, stammer			

Note: Adapted from Groth-Marnat (1997).

Structured Diagnostic Interviews

The increased precision in psychiatric diagnoses that is reflected in the evolution of the *DSM-IV* has been accompanied by the development of increasingly more explicit and structured forms of interviewing to obtain diagnostic information. Research on the development of diagnostic criteria and on structured interview protocols to accompany these criteria was initiated by re-searchers at the Medical School of Washington University in St. Louis. One of the first efforts to establish more precise diagnostic criteria was led by psychiatrist John Feighner. The Feighner criteria (Feighner et al., 1972; Woodruff, Goodwin, & Guze, 1973) provided the basis for one of the first diagnostic interviews, the Renard Diagnostic Interview (RDI; Helzer, Robins, Croughan, & Welner, 1981). Shortly after the publication of the Feighner criteria, a second set of diagnostic criteria was developed, known as the **Research Diagnostic Criteria** (RDC; Spitzer, Endicott, & Robins, 1978). The RDC provided a modification and elaboration of the Feighner criteria and included additional diagnoses. At the same time, Endicott and Spitzer (1978) published the Schedule for Affective Disorders and Schizophrenia (SADS), a structured interview designed to elicit information necessary for making RDC diagnoses.

The foremost goal in developing highly structured interview procedures was to have a method of obtaining information about specific diagnostic criteria. An equally important objective, however, was to improve the reliability of interviews by reducing the impact of interviewers' personal styles and idiosyncrasies (Edelbrock & Costello, 1984). Highly structured interviews specify the exact sequence and wording of questions; they provide clear rules for recording and rating responses, thereby limiting the role of clinical judgment in eliciting and recording information. Using highly structured interview protocols, different interviewers should obtain the same information from the same respondent. In contrast, semistructured interviews are less restrictive and permit the interviewer some flexibility in conducting the interview (Edelbrock & Costello). The interviewer has more latitude in deciding what is asked, how questions are phrased, and how responses are recorded. In using a semistructured interview, different interviewers should cover the same material when interviewing the same participant, but they may do so in different ways and may generate slightly different results. There are advantages to both types of interviews. Highly structured interviews reduce the role of clinical inference and interpretation in the assessment and diagnostic process and typically yield more objective and quantifiable raw data. Alternatively, semistructured interviews are less stilted and permit a more spontaneous interview that can be tailored to the client (Edelbrock & Costello).

Diagnostic Interviews for Adults

Although a number of diagnostic interview protocols have been developed for use with adults, they all share several features in common. Standardized interviews specify (a) the type of information that will be obtained (e.g., which symptoms and disorders will be covered); (b) the format of the interview (e.g., in person, over the telephone, computer-based interview); (c) the order of questions; (d) the wording of the questions; and (e) guidelines for additional questions used to probe for more information that may be needed before a response can be coded (Helzer, 1983).

Schedule for Affective Disorders and Schizophrenia The **Schedule for Affective Disorders and Schizophrenia (SADS)** is a semistructured interview developed by Endicott, Spitzer, and Robins (e.g., Endicott & Spitzer, 1978). The SADS was first used as a diagnostic instrument in a large, NIMH-sponsored collaborative study of depression. The first portion of the SADS is designed to obtain a detailed description of the current problem and the subject's functioning during the week prior to the interview. The second portion is concerned primarily with information regarding past psychiatric disturbance based on RDC criteria (Endicott & Spitzer, 1988). Each question is rated on a Likert scale with anchor points that define different levels of severity for the symptom in question. The interviewer is instructed to use all available sources of information (including chart notes and information from significant others) and as many general or specific questions as necessary to accurately score the items (Morrison, 1988). SADS items typically refer to the duration, course, or severity of symptoms or level of impairment. Several questions are suggested for each item to guide the interviewer in probing for information. The interview typically takes 1½ to 2 hours to complete, depending on the degree of pathology exhibited by the respondent. Endicott and Spitzer

(1978) suggest that because the types of judgments that are called for require knowledge of psychiatric concepts, the interview should be conducted only by carefully trained psychiatrists, clinical psychologists, and psychiatric social workers.

Diagnostic Interview Schedule The **Diagnostic Interview Schedule (DIS)** is a highly structured diagnostic interview that was developed for use by lay interviewers in conjunction with the Epidemiologic Catchment Area (ECA) study, the first national epidemiological study of psychopathology in the United States (Robins, Helzer, Croughan, & Ratcliff, 1981). To carry out the ECA study, researchers needed an interview that could be conducted by a large number of interviewers and that could be used to make diagnoses based on *DSM-III* criteria. The DIS does not require the interviewer to make any decisions concerning the existence or nonexistence of a psychiatric disorder. The interviewer reads specific questions and follows positive responses with additional prescribed questions. Each step in the sequence of identifying a psychiatric symptom is fully specified and does not depend on the judgment of the interviewers (Spiker & Ehler, 1984). Clinical judgment is held to a minimum through the use of highly explicit guidelines for administration (Groth-Marnat, 1997). Studies have generally indicated that results are comparable between trained clinicians and nonprofessional interviewers (Helzer, Spitznagel, & McEvoy, 1987).

The DIS utilizes a process similar to that employed by a physician interviewing a patient and assessing the nature and cause of a problem. First, the interviewer attempts to identify whether a symptom has been experienced, and second, whether it was of clinical significance. Clinical significance is ascertained by asking whether the individual has talked to a health professional about the symptom, has taken medication because of it, or feels that it has interfered

with his or her activities. The pattern of questions used to determine the clinical significance of the patient's endorsement of a symptom is specified and is the same for each item. In fact, the diagnosis based on the interview data can be made by computer using a scoring program developed for the DIS.

Reliability for the DIS was determined by comparing diagnoses made on the basis of the structured interview with those of a psychiatrist (Robins et al., 1981). For *DSM-III* diagnoses the mean *kappa* was .69, mean sensitivity was 75 percent, and mean specificity was 94 percent. The authors interpret these rates as reflecting the validity of nonprofessional interviewers' diagnostic judgments, using the judgments of psychiatrists as the criterion. As Groth-Marnat (1997) points out, however, this interpretation presupposes that the psychiatrist's diagnostic judgments are the benchmark against which the validity of an interview should be judged. As an alternative, he suggests that these figures be used as estimates of inter-rater reliability rather than of validity. Vandiver and Sher (1991) examined the stability of the DIS by administering the interview to 486 college students, administering it again 9 months later, and examining scores for 6-month, 12-month, and lifetime diagnoses for a number of disorders. Reliability estimates tended to be lower for 6- and 12-month diagnoses than for lifetime diagnoses. These findings indicate that the DIS is a moderately reliable instrument for assessing lifetime psychopathology over an extended time interval. Rubio-Stipec, Shrout, Bird, Canino, and Bravo (1989) administered the DIS to a large sample (N = 1,513) of community residents in Puerto Rico ranging in age from 18 to 64 to examine the structure of five clusters of symptoms (affective disorder, schizophrenia, phobic disorder, somatization disorder, and alcoholism). They compared these data with two other large samples, one of Mexican Americans and one of Anglo-Americans. Rubio-Stipec et al. obtained evidence for the cross-cultural stability of the DIS affective disorders and alcoholism scales, but weaker evidence for the stability of the schizophrenia, phobic disorder, and somatization disorder scales.

Structured Clinical Interview for *DSM-IV*
The most widely used structured diagnostic interview for adults is the **Structured Clinical Interview for *DSM-IV*** (SCID; First et al., 1995a, 1995b; Spitzer et al., 1992; Williams et al., 1992). The SCID was developed to provide direct assessment of *DSM-III* diagnostic criteria and has now been updated to mirror *DSM-IV* criteria (SCID-IV). Like the SADS, the SCID was developed for use by trained interviewers who are able to use considerable diagnostic judgment over the course of the interview. Slightly different forms are available for inpatients, outpatients, and nonpatients; diagnoses of personality disorders are enhanced by a series of 120 items that focus on *DSM-IV* Axis II disorders.

The SCID includes several open-ended questions as well as a "skip structure," which enables the interviewer to move into new areas depending on the client's previous responses (Groth-Marnat, 1997). The skip structure allows the interviewer to discontinue questions regarding a specific diagnosis once it becomes clear that the client will not meet criteria for the disorder. For example, if a client has responded negatively to the first five symptoms of major depression, then it is not necessary to ask the remaining four, since a minimum of five symptoms are required to meet the diagnosis. Thus, clinical judgment is important throughout the interview.

Reliability and validity of the SCID are well established. Several diagnostic categories that are often difficult to distinguish have been found to have relatively good levels of interrater agreement, including Generalized Anxiety Disorders (*kappa* = .79), Depressive Disorders (*kappa* = .72), Panic Disorders (*kappa* = .86), and Major Depression (*kappa* = .81); Reich & Noyes, 1987. In a validity study of the SCID, Skodol, Rosnick, Kellman, Oldham, and Hyler

(1988) compared SCID diagnoses of personality disorders with diagnoses by a panel of mental health professionals who relied both on their consensual judgments and on inpatient ward observations made over an extended period of time. Agreement was generally satisfactory, but was higher for personality disorders defined by specific behaviors (e.g., Antisocial and Schizotypal Personality Disorders) than for disorders requiring a greater degree of inference (e.g., Narcissistic and Self-Defeating Personality Disorders).

The results of SCID-IV interviews with Maria and Phillip are presented in boxes 7.1 and 7.2, and the format of the items for the depression module of the interview, including Maria's responses to the interview, is presented in figure 7.1.

Specialized Adult Structured Diagnostic Interviews   Other interview schedules have been developed to assess more specific disorders or to address specific referral or treatment decisions. For example, DiNardo, O'Brien, Barlow, and Waddel (1983) developed the Anxiety Disorders Interview Schedule (ADIS) as an instrument that would (a) permit differential diagnosis among the *DSM-III* anxiety disorder categories and (b) provide adequate information to rule out psychosis, substance abuse, and major affective disorders (see also Chorpita, Brown, & Barlow, 1998; DiNardo, Moras, Barlow, & Rapee, 1993). The Hamilton Rating Scale for Depression (HRSD; Hamilton, 1960, 1967) is the most widely used interviewer-based measure of depression. The HRSD combines observations made by the interviewer with the content of the client's responses to derive diagnoses of depressive disorders. Although the HRSD is widely used in clinical research, it is often modified from study to study, and Grundy, Lunnen, Lambert, Ashton, and Tovey (1994) have strongly recommended that it be used consistently, without such modifications.

BOX 7.1

STRUCTURED CLINICAL INTERVIEW: PHILLIP

The SCID-IV was used to conduct a clinical interview with Phillip to determine whether he met the criteria for any *DSM-IV* disorders. The results of the interview were consistent with Phillip's original description of symptoms of anxiety linked to making oral presentations at work. The interviewer administered the sections of the SCID that assess anxiety disorders, including Generalized Anxiety Disorder, Social Phobia, Agoraphobia, and Panic Disorder. Although Phillip endorsed a number of symptoms of anxiety, he met the specific criteria for Social Phobia. Phillip responded affirmatively to the question concerning whether he had a marked fear of speaking in front of a group of people, thereby meeting the first criterion for a diagnosis of Social Phobia. He stated that he felt this fear primarily in public-speaking situations, thus ruling out a diagnosis of Generalized Social Phobia. The interviewer continued by asking Phillip whether he has always felt anxious in a public-speaking situation ("yes"), whether he thought that he was more afraid of public speaking than he should be ("yes"), whether he went out of his way to avoid making public presentations ("yes"), whether this fear interfered significantly with his life ("yes"), and whether the effects

might be due to substance use or abuse ("no"). From Phillip's responses to the SCID, it was clear that he met *DSM-IV* diagnostic criteria for Social Phobia.

In addition to the symptoms of Social Phobia, Phillip had also recently experienced a Panic Attack. This occurred while he was on the phone at work; suddenly and unexpectedly he experienced a pain in his chest, shortness of breath, and extreme anxiety about the cause of these sensations. However, he did not meet the criteria for Panic Disorder on the basis of this single episode of a Panic Attack because he has not become preoccupied with the fear of these symptoms, nor has he experienced another attack.

From Phillip's responses to the Social Phobia section of the SCID, the interviewer thought it was possible that Phillip might meet *DSM-IV* diagnostic criteria for Avoidant Personality Disorder. Therefore, the interviewer also conducted a portion of the SCID with Phillip designed to assess personality disorders. Because Phillip met only three of the criteria for Avoidant Personality Disorder (where meeting a minimum of four criteria is necessary to make a diagnosis), he was not diagnosed with a personality disorder.

Diagnostic Interviews
for Children and Adolescents

The history and evolution of structured interviews for children has taken a somewhat different course than the development of interviews for adults. First, the development of specific diagnostic criteria for children in the *DSM* has lagged behind similar advances in diagnostic criteria for adult disorders. Consequently, there was not a strong impetus to develop structured interviews for children as the *DSM* evolved with the publication of the *DSM-II* and the RDC in the 1970s. Second, psychologists have long recognized the difficulties in relying on children as the sole informants about their own behavior. Thus, it was necessary to develop separate but parallel forms to interview children and others who could provide meaningful information about the children's behavior, typically their parents. The use of two sources of information (parents and children) presented the additional challenge that these two sources would not always agree on the problems that were being exhibited by an individual child (e.g., Achenbach et al., 1987). Indeed, resolution of such disagreements remains

BOX 7.2

STRUCTURED CLINICAL INTERVIEW: MARIA

Maria was interviewed by a psychologist using the SCID-IV to determine whether she met criteria for a *DSM-IV* diagnosis. Based on her initial presentation, the psychologist was concerned that Maria may be suffering from Major Depressive Disorder. Her son shared this concern but in addition was also concerned that some of Maria's symptoms may reflect a form of dementia, such as Alzheimer's disease. Based on the results of the SCID interview, it was clear that Maria met the criteria for a diagnosis of Major Depressive Disorder. Her responses to the depression portion of the interview are presented in figure 7.1. Specifically, Maria and her son reported that she is sad virtually every day, most of the day, and that she is unable to experience pleasure in her life. She is also troubled by sleep problems: She reports difficulty falling asleep at night and wakes very early in the morning (typically around 4:00 A.M.). Although Maria is physically healthy and is capable of walking independently, her son reported that she moves very slowly, even when trying to complete simple chores around the house. Her appetite has decreased, and she now eats very little unless her son is there to pressure her to eat. He reported that she has lost a significant amount of weight recently, so much so that most of her clothes no longer fit her. Although she is preoccupied by thoughts of death and wonders at times if she should "join" her late husband, she does not have thoughts of taking her life nor a plan for doing so. Given the clear link between the death of Maria's husband and the onset of her depression, the interviewer considered a diagnosis of Bereavement. According to *DSM-IV*, however, Maria's depressive symptoms were persisting far too long after her husband's death (i.e., two years) to be diagnosed as Bereavement, and the interviewer decided that a diagnosis of Major Depressive Disorder was appropriate.

one of the major challenges in conducting and interpreting child diagnostic interviews.

The earliest child diagnostic interviews were developed separately from adult interviews to provide epidemiological data on child psychopathology (Edelbrock & Costello, 1984). Lapouse and Monk (1958, 1964) worked to develop a structured interview for mothers and a parallel form for children to provide data for the first epidemiological study on child psychiatric disorders. In their research in London and England's Isle of Wight, Graham and Rutter (1968) were pioneers regarding the need to use structured methods to obtain information from children themselves. More recently, interviews for children and adolescents have actually been derived from adult interviews, including child versions of the RDI, the SADS, and the DIS.

Diagnostic Interview for Children and Adolescents Herjanic and colleagues (Herjanic & Campbell, 1977; Herjanic et al., 1975) developed the Diagnostic Interview for Children and Adolescents (DICA) based on the RDI described by Helzer et al. (1981); subsequent revisions to the DICA were based on *DSM-III* and on the adult DIS. Like the DIS, the DICA is highly structured and is designed to be administered by trained lay persons to children 6 to17 years of age. Initially, a joint interview is conducted with parent and child in order to obtain relevant history data. Next, parent and child are interviewed separately, with the same questions simultaneously asked of the parent and child (about the child) to assess *DSM* criteria. Finally, the third part of the interview, the Parent Questionnaire, contains information about developmental and medical history.

Schedule for Affective Disorders and Schizophrenia for School-Age Children The Schedule for Affective Disorders and Schizophrenia

SCID-I (DSM-IV) Version 2.0 Current MDE (Jan 1995 FINAL)   Mood Episodes A. 1

A. MOOD EPISODES

IN THIS SECTION, MAJOR DEPRESSIVE, MANIC, HYPOMANIC EPISODES, DYSTHYMIC DISORDER,
MOOD DISORDER DUE TO A GENERAL MEDICAL CONDITION, SUBSTANCE-INDUCED MOOD DISORDER,
AND EPISODE SPECIFIERS ARE EVALUATED. MAJOR DEPRESSIVE DISORDER AND BIPOLAR
DISORDERS ARE DIAGNOSED IN MODULE D.

CURRENT MAJOR DEPRESSIVE EPISODE	MDE CRITERIA		

Now I am going to ask you some more questions about your mood.

A. Five (or more) of the following symptoms have been present during the same two-week period and represent a change from previous functioning; at least one of the symptoms is either (1) depressed mood, or (2) loss of interest or pleasure.

In the last month...

...has there been a period of time when you were feeling depressed or down most of the day nearly every day? (What was that like?)

IF YES: How long did it last? (As long as two weeks?)

(1) depressed mood most of the day, nearly every day, as indicated either by subjective report (e.g., feels sad or empty) or observation made by others (e.g., appears tearful). Note: in children and adolescents can be irritable mood.   ?   1   2 (3)   A1

...what about losing interest or pleasure in things you usually enjoyed?

IF YES: Was it nearly every day? How long did it last? (As long as two weeks?)

(2) markedly diminished interest or pleasure in all, or almost all, activities most of the day, nearly every day (as indicated either by subjective account or observation made by others).   ?   1   2 (3)   A2

IF NEITHER ITEM (1) NOR ITEM (2) IS CODED "3," GO TO *PAST MAJOR DEPRESSIVE EPISODE,* A. 12

NOTE: WHEN RATING THE FOLLOWING ITEMS, CODE "1" IF CLEARLY DUE TO A GENERAL MEDICAL CONDITION, OR TO MOOD-INCONGRUENT DELUSIONS OR HALLUCINATIONS

During this (TWO-WEEK PERIOD)...

FOR THE FOLLOWING QUESTIONS, FOCUS ON THE WORST TWO WEEKS IN THE PAST MONTH (OR ELSE THE PAST TWO WEEKS IF EQUALLY DEPRESSED FOR ENTIRE MONTH)

..did you lose or gain any weight? (How much?) (Were you trying to lose weight?)

IF NO: How was your appetite? (What about compared to your usual appetite?) (Did you have to force yourself to eat?) (Eat [less/more] than usual?) (Was that nearly every day?)

(3) significant weight loss when not dieting, or weight gain (e.g., a change of more than 5% of body weight in a month) or decrease or increase in appetite nearly every day. Note: in children, consider failure to make expected weight gains.   ?   1   2 (3)   A3

Check if:
✓   weight loss or decreased   A4
    appetite
___ weight gain or increased   A5
    appetite

..how were you sleeping? (Trouble falling asleep, waking frequently, trouble staying asleep, waking too early, OR sleeping too much? How many hours a night compared to usual? Was that nearly every night?)

(4) insomnia or hypersomnia nearly every day   ?   1   2 (3)   A6

Check if:
✓   insomnia   A7
___ hypersomnia   A8

..were you so fidgety or restless that you were unable to sit still? (Was it so bad that other people noticed it? What did they notice? Was that nearly every day?)

IF NO: What about the opposite -- talking or moving more slowly than is normal for you? (Was it so bad that other people noticed it? What did they notice? Was that nearly every day?)

(5) psychomotor agitation or retardation nearly every day (observable by others, not merely subjective feelings of restlessness or being slowed down)   ?   1   2 (3)   A9

NOTE: CONSIDER BEHAVIOR DURING THE INTERVIEW

Check if:
✓   psychomotor retardation   A10
___ psychomotor agitation   A11

..what was your energy like? (Tired all the time? Nearly every day?)

(6) fatigue or loss of energy nearly every day   ?   1   2 (3)   A12

?=inadequate information   1=absent or false   2=subthreshold   3=threshold or true

FIGURE 7.1
Maria's responses to the Structured Clinical Interview for DSM-IV Axis I Disorders (SCID) for Major Depressive Disorder (adapted from First et al, 1997).

SCID-I (DSM-IV) Version 2.0 Current MDE (Jan 1995 FINAL)   Mood Episodes A. 3

During this time...

| ..how did you feel about yourself? (Worthless?) (Nearly every day?)

IF NO: What about feeling guilty about things you had done or not done? (Nearly every day?) | (7) feelings of worthlessness or excessive or inappropriate guilt (which may be delusional) nearly every day (not merely self-reproach or guilt about being sick) | ? 1 ② 3 | A13 |

NOTE: CODE "1" OR "2" IF ONLY LOW SELF-ESTEEM

Check if:
____ worthlessness   A14
____ inappropriate guilt   A15

| ..did you have trouble thinking or concentrating? (What kinds of things did it interfere with?) (Nearly every day?)

IF NO: Was it hard to make decisions about everyday things? (Nearly every day?) | (8) diminished ability to think or concentrate, or indecisiveness, nearly every day (either by subjective account or as observed by others) | ? 1 2 ③ | A16 |

Check if:
_✓_ diminished ability to think   A17
____ indecisiveness   A18

| ..were things so bad that you were thinking a lot about death or that you would be better off dead? What about thinking of hurting yourself?

IF YES: Did you do anything to hurt yourself? | (9) recurrent thoughts of death (not just fear of dying), recurrent suicidal ideation without a specific plan, or a suicide attempt or a specific plan for committing suicide | ? 1 2 ③ | A19 |

NOTE: CODE "1" FOR SELF-MUTILATION W/O SUICIDAL INTENT

Check if:
_✓_ thoughts of own death   A20
____ suicidal ideation   A21
____ specific plan   A22
____ suicide attempt   A23

AT LEAST FIVE OF THE ABOVE SXS [A (1-9)] ARE CODED "3" AND AT LEAST ONE OF THESE IS ITEM (1) OR (2)   1   3   A24

GO TO *PAST MAJOR DEPRESSIVE EPISODE,* A. 12

| IF UNCLEAR: Has (depressive episode/OWN EQUIVALENT) made it hard for you to do your work, take care of things at home, or get along with other people? | B. The symptoms cause clinically significant distress or impairment in social, occupational, or other important areas of functioning. | ? 1 2 ③ | A25 |

GO TO *PAST MAJOR DEPRESSIVE EPISODE,* A. 12

| Just before this began, were you physically ill?

IF YES: What did the doctor say?

Just before this began, were you using any medications?

IF YES: Any change in the amount you were using?

Just before this began, were you drinking or using any street drugs? | C. Not due to the direct physiological effects of a substance (e.g., a drug of abuse, medication) or to a general medical condition | ? 1 ③ | A26 |

DUE TO SUBSTANCE USE OR GMC. GO TO *PAST MAJOR DEPRESSIVE EPISODE* A. 12

IF GENERAL MEDICAL CONDITION OR SUBSTANCE MAY BE ETIOLOGICALLY ASSOCIATED WITH DEPRESSION, GO TO *GMC/SUBSTANCE* A. 43. AND RETURN HERE TO MAKE RATING OF "1" OR "3."

PRIMARY MOOD EPISODE

Etiological general medical conditions include: degenerative neurological illnesses (e.g., Parkinson's disease, Huntington's disease, cerebrovascular disease, metabolic and endocrine conditions (e.g., B-12 deficiency, hypothyroidism), autoimmune conditions (e.g., systemic lupus erythematosis), viral or other infections (e.g., hepatitis, mononucleosis, HIV), and certain cancers (e.g., carcinoma of the pancreas).

Etiological substances include: alcohol, amphetamines, cocaine, hallucinogens, inhalants, opioids, phencyclidine, sedatives, hypnotics, anxiolytics, and other or unknown substances (e.g., steroids).

CONTINUE BELOW

FIGURE 7.1 (continued)

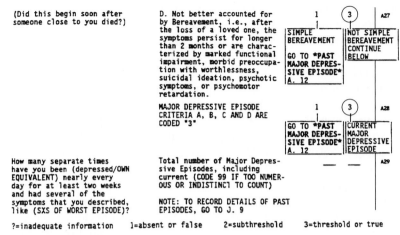

FIGURE 7.1 (concluded)

for School-Age Children (Kiddie-SADS, or K-SADS) (Chambers et al., 1985) was developed for youth 6 to 17 years of age and is based on the adult SADS. Although the SADS and K-SADS used the RDC for Major Depressive Disorders as a foundation, the current versions can also be mapped to *DSM-IV* criteria. The K-SADS is designed to be administered by a trained clinician to determine the onset, duration, and severity of current and past episodes of affective, anxiety, conduct, and psychotic disorders. Several versions of the K-SADS are available to assess a current episode, the most severe episode in the past, or a combination of the two.

The semistructured assessment format consists of separate one-hour interviews with the youth's parents and the youth. Questions include "Have you felt sad, blue, or moody . . ." and "What do you think is going to happen to you in the future?" Interviewers may use further questions to determine the severity and chronicity of the symptom. If responses to initial questions are negative with respect to symptomatology, the interviewer skips to the next section, thereby reducing the interviewing time for youth with no symptoms. Upon completion of the interview, interviewers use their clinical judgment to determine a summary diagnosis from the two sources

of data. When the parent and child accounts differ, interviewers may meet with both parent and adolescent to attempt to resolve the differences or make a judgment as to which information to use in making a diagnosis (Chambers et al., 1985).

The reliability of the K-SADS, like the reliability of the SADS for adults, is demonstrated more easily than its validity. Over a 72-hour period, test-retest reliability of the K-SADS, as reflected by the *kappa* statistic, with 52 psychiatrically referred 6 to 17-year-olds was established as .55 for individual items, .68 for summary scales, and .24–.70 for specific diagnoses (Chambers et al., 1985). Clinical syndromes and diagnoses were made based on the summary scores for particular symptoms. Agreement between parent and child or adolescent reports was .53 for symptoms (range −.08 to .96). The validity of the K-SADS is based on its ability to detect the prespecified diagnostic criteria and treatment effects (Edelbrock & Costello, 1988). For example, Puig-Antich, Perel et al. (1979) found that the K-SADS was sensitive to the effects of pharmacological treatment for depression in a sample of preadolescent children.

Diagnostic Interview Schedule for Children– Version IV In contrast to the K-SADS, the structure format of the Diagnostic Interview Schedule for Children (DISC) permits its administration by clinicians or lay interviewers (Costello et al., 1984; Schaffer et al., 1993). The DISC has been the focus of an intensive series of studies supported by NIMH in an effort to develop a standardized clinical interview for children and adolescents that can be used in both research and clinical settings (Shaffer et al., 1996; Shaffer, Fisher, Lukas, Dulcan, & Schwab-Stone, 2000). The DISC was developed as a youth version of the DIS for adults and is a comprehensive approach to detecting the presence, severity, onset, and duration of a broad range of symptoms in 6 to 18-year-olds. The results may be presented in two ways: (a) as the number and severity of symptoms; or (b) as *DSM-IV* diagnoses. *DSM-IV* diagnoses are developed from a set of operational rules on the level of symptoms needed to meet stringent criteria. Diagnoses are generated from computer algorithms of the DISC items, and the computer profiles are usually interpreted by trained clinicians.

The current version, the **Diagnostic Interview Schedule for Children–Version IV (DISC-IV),** is designed to assess *DSM-IV* diagnoses in children and adolescents (Shaffer et al., 2000; Schwab-Stone et al., 1996). Parallel versions are designed to be administered to children or adolescents and parents. Similar to the earlier versions of this interview, the DISC-IV has achieved adequate to excellent levels of both inter-rater and test-retest reliability for specific diagnostic categories (Shaffer et al.). The correspondence between parent and child reports is adequate, but agreement is higher between parents and adolescents than between parents and younger children (e.g., Edelbrock et al., 1986).

The question of the validity of the DISC has been addressed by examining the ability of the DISC to discriminate between pediatric- and psychiatric-referred youth, and by examining the correlation between the DISC and parent and

teacher ratings of behavior problems on standardized checklists. Costello, Edelbrock, and Costello (1985) found with the parent version of the DISC, 40 psychiatric-referred children (aged 7 to 11 years) scored significantly higher on all the symptom areas and total symptom score than did 40 pediatric-referred children. Significant correlations with behavior checklists provide some support for the concurrent validity of the DISC (Costello et al., 1984). For example, the total behavior problem score of a parent checklist correlated .70 with the total symptom score of the Diagnostic Interview Schedule for Children—Revised (DISC-R). Considering the evidence that there is often substantial parent-child disagreement on their measures (Achenbach et al., 1987), it is not surprising that the child version of the DISC correlated only .30 with the parent checklist.

More recent research with the DISC has addressed several challenges in conducting diagnostic interviews with children and adolescents. For example, there is a tendency for children (and parents) to endorse fewer symptoms as an interview progresses, or fewer symptoms on the second administration of an interview than on the first, a phenomenon known as attenuation (Piacentini et al., 1999). Attenuation was found to be greater in younger children, in children who were doing more poorly in school, and in mothers who themselves were younger (Piacentini et al.). Furthermore, attenuation is greater for longer and more complex interview items and for those items that require the assessment of timing, duration, or frequency of symptoms (Lucas et al., 1999). Edelbrock, Crnic, and Bohnert (1999) found that interview responses can be improved by using more common language in asking questions and by allowing respondents (parents and children) to select the order in which some of the questions are asked. Research of this type is important as psychologists continue to improve the reliability and validity of diagnostic interviews for children and adolescents.

BOX 7.3

DIAGNOSTIC INTERVIEWS WITH YOUNG CHILDREN

Conducting interviews with young children (under the age of 9) presents additional challenges to interviewers because children differ from adults in their cognitive development and language. Children are not accustomed to the type of face-to-face verbal exchange that is involved in traditional diagnostic interviews. To address this problem, researchers have developed alternative means of presenting questions to children. For example, Valla et al. (2000) developed a series of pictures in which a child (Dominic) is depicted either alone or with other children in situations that children encounter in daily life. The pictures represent emotions and behaviors that correspond to symptoms of child disorders on the *DSM-IV.* The interviewer asks the child if she or he has experienced these symptoms. The symptoms of specific disorders are presented in a mixed order to avoid problems with attenuation of responses. Drawings of happy children in normal situations are included to decrease the potential of overwhelming the child with negative questions. Valla and colleagues report adequate test-retest reliability of children's responses and good correspondence with diagnoses based on clinicians' ratings of *DSM-IV* disorders.

A second approach for interviewing children involves the use of puppets to present children with an engaging format for questions related to symptoms of *DSM* disorders (Ablow et al., 1999). In this novel approach, called the Berkeley Puppet Interview, the interviewer uses two puppets, one on each hand, who talk to each other and to the child. For example, one puppet says, "I'm a sad kid," and the second puppet responds, "I'm not a sad kid. How about you?" The child's response is then recorded with regard to the presence of sad affect. The puppets are highly engaging for young children and help sustain their attention. The forced choice format in which the child reports whether he or she is more like one puppet or the other helps simplify the response that is required of the child and decreases the likelihood that the child will simply deny any symptoms. Responses to the interview were found to correlate significantly with mothers' and teachers' ratings of children on a comparable set of symptoms (Ablow et al.).

The use of these and other methods show considerable promise for improving methods for interviewing children. This work is important for the assessment of emotions and thoughts of young children that are not readily observed by parents or teachers.

SUMMARY AND CONCLUSIONS

Clinical interviews form an important cornerstone in the process of assessment in clinical psychology. One-to-one interviewers are an essential step in initiating the process of gathering information about a client and in forming the necessary level of rapport for continued assessment and treatment. Interviews are used to gather information, generate diagnoses, and build rapport with clients.

Communication skills are at the core of effective interviewing. These include both skills used in attending to clients and the information that they present, and skills in guiding and influencing clients. Attending skills include open and closed questions, paraphrasing, and reflecting feelings. Influencing skills involve providing advice, interpretations, and self-disclosure by the interviewer.

Most clinical interviews are conducted using relatively unstructured formats. Unstructured interviews are useful in that they allow the client to shape the interview and are optimal for establishing rapport. Problems with the reliability and validity of unstructured clinical interviews, however, have led to the development and refinement of semistructured and highly structured diagnostic interviews. Structured diagnostic interviews have been developed for use with children, adolescents, and adults to reliably and validly establish *DSM-IV* diagnoses. These interviews are now being adapted for more effective use in clinical settings.

KEY TERMS AND NAMES

Attending skills
Diagnostic Interview Schedule for
   Children–Version IV (DISC-IV)
Influencing skills
Information gathering
Intake interview
Kappa coefficient

Mental status exam
Research Diagnostic Criteria
Schedule for Affective Disorders and
   Schizophrenia (SADS)
Structured Clinical Interview for *DSM-IV*
   (SCID-IV)

RESOURCES

Books
Evans, D. R., Hearn, M. T., Uhlemann, M. R., & Ivey, A. E. (1998). *Essential interviewing: A programmed approach to effective communication* (5th ed.). Pacific Grove, CA: Brooks/Cole.

Groth-Marnat, G. (1997). *Handbook of psychological assessment* (3rd ed.). New York: John Wiley.

Ivey, A.E. (1994). *Intentional interviewing and counseling: Facilitating client development in a multicultural society* (3rd ed.). Pacific Grove, CA: Brooks/Cole Publishing Co.

Shaffer, D., Lucas, C. P., & Richters, J. E. (Eds.). (1999). *Diagnostic assessment in child and adolescent psychopathology.* New York: Guilford Press.

Journals
Journal of Consulting and Clinical Psychology
Journal of Psychotherapy: Practice and Research
Psychological Assessment

CHAPTER EIGHT

ASSESSMENT: MEASUREMENT OF INTELLIGENCE AND NEUROPSYCHOLOGICAL TESTING

INTRODUCTION

What constitutes genius? What are the qualities that make it possible for some individuals to see unique and novel features of the world around them, to organize information in ways that no one before them has been able to do, or to create new ideas? A few examples from history may provide some clues. Science in the mid-seventeenth century was emerging from the Dark Ages, and the era was one of startling new discoveries. It was during this time that Sir Isaac Newton (1642–1727) developed a set of ideas that forever changed science and the way that people think about the earth and the universe. By age 22, with little formal education, Newton had formulated the binomial theorem of algebra, the elements of differential calculus, the basis of integral calculus, and his theory of gravitation.

He went on to develop a model for the spectrum of light, and he invented the reflecting telescope. Most astonishing to the people of his time, he unified all physical systems by postulating that a universal law of gravity (any body attracts every other body with a force directly proportional to their masses and inversely proportional to the square of the distance between them) that could explain phenomena that ranged from the swinging of pendulums to the motions of the planets around the sun.

The laws and rules that govern nature remained relatively unchanged for approximately 300 years until another young scientist, Albert Einstein, challenged the thinking of the scientific community. Although it's now almost cliché to describe Einstein's early struggles with formal education, it is true that throughout his elementary and secondary schooling in Germany, Einstein's teachers thought him to be unmotivated and unintelligent. From age 12, however, Einstein taught himself geometry, algebra, and calculus. Pursuing his scientific interests on his own while he worked in a patent office in Switzerland, Einstein by the age of 26 had revolutionized physics (and many of the laws developed by Newton 300 years earlier) by formulating quantum theory, the special theory of relativity, and the general theory of relativity. Among the startling leaps that he made was the observation that light, thought to exist only in waves, was actually composed of particles, or quanta, a discovery that laid the foundation for the development of photoelectric cells and eventually sound motion pictures and television. The theory of relativity was an example of his broad, integrative thinking: Einstein showed that the smallest subatomic particles and the largest bodies in the universe were all governed by the same physical laws.

A different type of intellect can be seen in the achievements of Wolfgang Amadeus Mozart. Mozart had composed a symphony by age 4, had written an opera by age 12, and went on to become one of history's most prolific and ac-

complished composers before his death at only 35 years of age. His style was completely unique, representing the synthesis of many different elements. The music he wrote as an adult was distinguished by its beautiful melodies, its technical flawlessness, an unmatched sense of joy, and unequaled complexity. Unlike Haydn and Beethoven, Mozart excelled in every medium current in his time, including sonatas, symphonies, and operas. As a result of the breadth, beauty, and technical quality of his music, he is regarded by many as the most brilliant composer in the history of western music.

There is little disagreement that Newton, Einstein, and Mozart were among the greatest geniuses to ever live. Based on their accomplishments, they serve as striking examples of what we mean by *intelligence*. Although these three individuals were extraordinarily intelligent, they did not express their intellect in the same way. These examples of brilliance reflect one end of the continuum of tremendous variability among people in their abilities, aptitudes, and motivations. Although we can achieve reasonable consensus that these individuals were highly intelligent, we have more trouble agreeing on what constitutes intelligence in general. That is, it is easy to recognize intelligence when we are dealing with extreme examples, but the nature of intelligence in the general population is much more challenging to define.

The concept of intelligence has presented clinical psychology with one of its greatest dilemmas. On the one hand, psychologists have been pressured for almost 100 years to quantify individual differences in intellectual functioning; on the other hand, intelligence has remained one of the most difficult and controversial psychological constructs to define and measure. The impetus to define and quantify intelligence comes from both practical and scientific forces. The practical significance lies in the potential use of measures of intelligence in predicting academic and work potential and achievement. From a scientific perspective, precise understanding of how to measure intelligence can contribute to our comprehension of an important aspect of human behavior and functioning. In spite of the significant role of intellectual assessment throughout the history of psychology, few issues have proven as volatile, both within psychology and in the perception of psychology by the general public. Much of the concern centers on several related issues. Can we accurately measure the true nature of intelligence? Can it ever be measured in a way that reflects a fair representation of all cultural groups? To what extent is intelligence the result of genetic versus environmental factors? If intelligence test scores are influenced by genetics to at least some degree, what implications does this influence have for the interpretation of differences between cultural groups on these tests? These broad social concerns provide the context in which the assessment of the intelligence of individuals is carried out.

GENERAL DEFINITION OF INTELLIGENCE

Intelligence is a *hypothetical construct*; that is, intelligence is a concept that exists only in the way that we (psychologists and the public) choose to define it. You cannot touch intelligence nor can you directly observe it. You can only observe the consequences of intelligence as they are reflected in the behavior and performance of individuals. Because of the hypothetical nature of the construct, it is essential to make a distinction between intelligence and what is measured by intelligence tests—these two are not one and the same. Intelligence tests are an attempt to operationalize or make observable a concept that is not observable. Intelligence is presumed to be an attribute of individuals that can be inferred or sampled from their performance on an intelligence test. Therefore, although intelligence tests represent the concept of intelligence, they do so in an imperfect way. It is possible that the con-

cept of intelligence is too broad to be used meaningfully as a single construct, and we must recognize that any test is a reflection of only a portion of the total concept.

Given the highly complex and hypothetical nature of intelligence, it is not surprising that psychologists have generated many different definitions of this concept. These definitions vary along several dimensions. First, they differ in the degree to which they view intelligence as the innate capacity of individuals (**genotypic intelligence**) as opposed to how individuals currently perform (**phenotypic intelligence**). This distinction has important implications for the measurement of intelligence, because it implies that tests may reflect a combination of what a person can do and what a person currently does. Second, some definitions view intelligence as a *single, global, general ability* whereas others view intelligence as a *set of specific abilities* that are related to one another but largely independent. At the one extreme, Spearman (1923) proposed that intelligence is characterized by a single general factor (g) that governs all aspects of intellectual functioning. In contrast, Guilford (1967) developed a three-dimensional model of intelligence that included four contents, six productions, and five operations. The result was a matrix of 120 separate aspects of intelligence. Third, definitions differ in their view of the relationship of intelligence to other, nonintellectual factors such as emotion, motivation, and personality. Some definitions view intelligence as relatively independent of these other factors, whereas other approaches conceptualize intelligence as closely tied to other aspects of individuals and their environments. For example, Piaget (1954) believed that no act of intelligence is without emotion, because emotion reflects the motivation and energy that drives intelligent behavior. In contrast, many intelligence tests have been developed with the intent of minimizing motivational and emotional factors in order to obtain a relatively "pure" index of the person's intellectual capabilities.

Specific Definitions of Intelligence

Because of the complex nature of intelligence, psychologists have generated a variety of definitions of this construct (see table 8.1 for several examples of definitions of intelligence). In one of the earliest attempts to define intelligence, Binet and Simon (1916) defined it as common or practical sense, the ability to adapt to one's circumstances, and skills in comprehending and reasoning. More recently, psychologist Howard Gardner (1983) emphasized the importance of skills in resolving problems encountered in real life. One of the current leaders in theory and research on intelligence, **Robert Sternberg** (1985, 1990), focuses on the ability to deal with real-world situations and problems. Finally, psychologist **David Wechsler** (1939), who developed the most widely used tests of intelligence, viewed intelligence as the broad capacity to think rationally, act purposefully, and deal effectively with one's environment.

These definitions reflect several common themes. All emphasize the ability to adapt to or interact with the environment and the capacity

TABLE 8.1
Definitions of Intelligence

Binet and Simon (1916): "judgment, otherwise called good sense, practical sense, initiative, the faculty to adapt one's self to circumstances. To judge well, to comprehend well, to reason well, these are the essential activities of intelligence" (pp. 42–43).

Gardner (1983): "a set of skills of problem solving—enabling the individual to resolve genuine problems or difficulties that he or she encounters, and, when appropriate, to create an effective product . . . the potential for finding or creating problems—thereby laying the groundwork for the acquisition of new knowledge" (pp. 60–61).

Sternberg (1990): "mental activity involved in purposive adaptation to, shaping of, and selection of real-world environments relevant to one's life" (p. 33).

Wechsler (1939): "The aggregate or global capacity of the individual to act purposefully, think rationally, and deal effectively with the environment."

for problem solving or reasoning in some form. Similar themes are reflected in a study in which over 1,000 professionals in the fields of psychology, education, sociology, and genetics were surveyed regarding their beliefs about the important elements of intelligence (Snyderman & Rothman, 1987). There was a high degree of agreement about the significance of the 13 behavioral descriptions that the researchers presented to the raters. Three characteristics received near unanimous agreement from these experts (96 percent or higher)—abstract thinking or reasoning, the capacity to acquire knowledge, and problem-solving ability. Six other descriptions were identified by a majority of respondents (60 percent to 80 percent)—adaptation to one's environment, creativity, general knowledge, linguistic competence, memory, and mental speed. Only three were rarely checked (less than 25 percent)—achievement motivation, goal directedness, and sensory acuity.

In addition to a broad definition, there is still a need to place specific skills into categories that reflect the structure of intelligence (Sattler, 1988). For example, Cattell and Horn developed a theory on the structure of intelligence that reflects two broad categories (Cattell, 1963; Horn, 1985; Horn & Cattell, 1967). Their theory holds that there are two broad types of intelligence: fluid and crystallized. **Fluid intelligence** includes nonverbal, relatively culture-free mental skills, whereas **crystallized intelligence** refers to skills and knowledge acquired through interactions that are specific to one's culture. Fluid intelligence involves the capacity to adapt to new situations and is represented in basic mental operations and processes; crystallized intelligence involves cognitive skills that are acquired through repeated exposure and practice and is reflected in the products and achievements of intellectual activity (Sattler).

Because the tests David Wechsler developed remain the most widely used intelligence tests in the United States today, it is important to give close consideration to his definition of intelligence (see table 8.1). Although his definition emphasizes a single, global aspect of intelligence, Wechsler acknowledged that global intelligence is not merely the sum of the component parts from which it is comprised. He emphasized the distinction between **verbal intelligence** and **performance intelligence,** a distinction that parallels the difference between crystallized and fluid intelligence. Wechsler also believed that factors other than mental ability, for example motivation and emotion, are involved in intelligent behavior. Finally, within Wechsler's definition, an excess of any particular ability was thought to add relatively little to the effectiveness of intelligence as a whole—no single component was more important than the others.

An issue that underlies all attempts to define intelligence is whether the same skills are needed to function competently in any environment or if the skills for intellectual competence differ significantly from one context or environment to another. Wechsler's definition begs this issue by proposing that intelligence involves the skills to "deal effectively with the environment" without specifying whether and how variations in the environment are reflected in variations in the skills and competencies that are required to be successful. How one answers this important question has a major influence on the interpretation that one gives to the performance of any individual in an intelligence test.

Theoretical Models: Metaphors of the Mind

If intelligence is something that cannot be directly observed or measured in a physical sense, then our theories of intelligence are metaphors for this construct. Theories of intelligence represent psychologists' best efforts to capture the essence of cognitive functioning and ability through symbols or allegories. Psychologist Robert Sternberg (1992, 1997) of Yale University has distinguished among several different *metaphors of the mind* that underlie current models of intelligence and, therefore, current tests

of intelligence. Psychological theories of intelligence are stories about how the mind operates, and intelligence tests are operationalizations of these stories.

Sternberg (1990) has identified seven modern metaphors for intelligence: geographic, computational, biological, epistemological, anthropological, sociological, and systems metaphors. These broad theories of the mind influence specific theories of intelligence. Theories of intelligence form the basis for the specific features of intelligence tests. The information that we collect on intelligence tests then becomes the basis for our judgments about differences between people in their intellectual ability—the tests become a major representation of our ways to observe and define intelligence. As Sternberg states, "The way in which intelligence is tested will depend upon a theory of intelligence, and this theory will in turn depend upon a metaphorical metatheory of mind" (1992, p. 5). Two of these metaphors deserve closer attention, because they have affected current approaches to intelligence testing.

The most widely used metaphor about the nature of intelligence is the *geographic metaphor*—the idea that a theory of intelligence provides a map of the mind. The geographic metaphor is reflected in many of the dominant theories of intelligence, including Spearman's (1927a) notion of general intelligence, Horn and Cattell's (1967) distinction between fluid and crystallized intelligence, and Wechsler's (1939) distinction between verbal and performance intelligence. These metaphors assume that different "regions of the mind" or even different parts of the brain are responsible for qualitatively different aspects of intellectual functioning (Sternberg, 1992). Much of the support for the geographic metaphor comes from the results of *factor analyses* of the performance of individuals on intelligence tests. Many or most factor analyses show that scores on tests that reflect the acquisition of knowledge within one's culture (e.g., vocabulary, arithmetic, analogies) are highly correlated with one another and that scores on tests of reasoning and problem-solving skills on more abstract tasks (e.g., solving complex puzzles with blocks, solving mazes) are highly correlated with one another (Sternberg). The development of intelligence tests, including the widely used Wechsler scales that are described in the section titled "Current Intelligence Tests," has been dominated by the geographic metaphor to such an extent that it is difficult to separate the two (Sternberg).

Many recent theories of intelligence reflect what Sternberg refers to as a *computational metaphor*—the brain is seen as analogous to a computer. These metaphors emphasize the ways that individuals process information about the world. The field of artificial intelligence (Boden, 1977; Stillings et al., 1987) was influential in describing the ways that computers function "intelligently" and using this description as a model for human intelligence. Cognitive psychologists have outlined the basic tasks that reflect the human ability to process information (e.g., translating sensory input into a representation of information, transforming one mental concept into another, or translating a mental concept into motor or behavior output) and the strategies that are used to carry out these steps. Measurement of these processes has focused on how quickly one can perform these tasks and the accuracy with which one performs them.

ORIGINS OF INTELLIGENCE: GENES AND ENVIRONMENT

Where does intelligence come from? What are the sources of the dramatic differences between individuals in their observable levels of intellectual functioning? Two broad sources of individual differences in intelligence have been considered: genes and environment. No issue related to intelligence testing, and perhaps no issue in all of psychology, has been more controversial than the debate about the relative contributions of genes and environment to the development of

intellectual abilities. To the extent that intelligence is considered to be the result of genes, differences between individuals are assumed to be unchangeable. In contrast, environmental explanations of differences in intelligence lead to a view that individual differences in intelligence can be reduced as a result of changes in environment and experience. Controversy around this issue was heated in the late 1960s, fueled by controversial positions on race and intelligence quotient (IQ) put forward by psychologist Arthur Jenson (1969). The debate subsided somewhat in the late 1970s and 1980s, only to be renewed by the publication of a highly controversial book, *The Bell Curve,* by Richard Herrnstein and Charles Murray in 1994. These controversies were stirred by assertions about inherited differences between racial groups in intelligence.

The investigation of genetic and environmental contributors to intelligence has often been portrayed as competition between these two factors, a test of whether genes or environment determines intelligence (e.g., Eysenck, 1981). This portrayal is a distortion of the issue, however. The real question is not whether intelligence is the result of genes or environment, but to what extent and in what ways do genes and environment combine to contribute to intelligence? All intellectual functions involve biological activity in the brain, activity that is shaped in part by the biological structure and capacity that is formed by information contained in one's genes. But cognitive development does not follow an immutable path that is set at birth. Intellectual activity equally reflects learning, the product of one's experiences with the environment. The challenge for psychologists is to understand how each of these factors influences the intellectual capacity of individuals.

The Research: Twin and Adoption Studies

The investigation of genetic and environmental contributions to intelligence has relied on the basic methodologies from the broader field of behavioral genetics—the comparison of individuals who are known to vary in the degree of similarity in their genetic makeup and in their environmental experiences (Plomin & Petrill, 1997). Studies of *monozygotic twins* and *dizygotic twins* and studies of biological and adopted children and their siblings and parents comprise the primary methods in behavioral genetics research. Twin studies compare the degree of similarity in IQ test performance of monozygotic twins, who are known to share 100 percent of the same genes, with the degree of similarity in IQ test performance of dizygotic twins, who on average share 50 percent of the same genetic information. Twins who are reared together not only share their common genetic makeup but also share certain aspects of the environment in which they are raised (the *shared environment)*. Twins raised in the same home also have experiences that are different and contribute to differences in their development (referred to as the *nonshared environment)*. In contrast, twins who are raised apart are presumed to have separate environmental experiences that would affect their performance on an intelligence test. Adoption studies, which can be combined with twin studies, compare the degree of correspondence in the IQ scores of adopted children with their adoptive parents and siblings to the similarity with the IQ scores of their biological parents and siblings. Adoption studies are unique in that they allow for comparisons of individuals who may have similar or different genetic makeups and similar or different environmental experiences.

The degree of correspondence, or similarity, of IQ scores of twins, siblings, and adopted siblings are examined using correlation coefficients to represent the degree of correspondence. As you will recall from chapter 3, a correlation of 1.00 would indicate perfect correspondence between the IQs of pairs of individuals, a correlation of .50 would reflect moderate correspondence, and a correlation of .00 would indicate that there was no association between IQs. In ac-

tuality, the correlations cannot reach a level of 1.00 because IQ tests are not perfectly reliable—there is always a certain degree of error in any test. This error places a limit, a ceiling, on the degree to which one person's score on an IQ test can correlate with the score of another person. Taking into account the rather high reliability of most standardized measures of intelligence, the highest correlation that could be obtained between the scores of two groups of individuals is approximately .80 to .90.

After correlations of scores from groups of matched pairs of individuals are derived, these correlations are used to derive a **heritability index**—a statistic that reflects the degree to which scores on intelligence tests (or any measure of a human trait or characteristic) are associated with a genotype. There are a number of ways to derive an estimate of heritability. For example, the correlation of monozygotic twins reared apart is taken as a direct index of the role of genetics, as these individuals are known to share all their genes and are presumed to share none of their environmental experiences. The correlation of dizygotic twins reared apart is multiplied by two to derive an index of heritability, because these individuals share on average only half their genes in common and none of their experience.

A surprisingly large number of studies have now been conducted in which the intelligence test scores of monozygotic twins, dizygotic twins, adopted siblings, and biological siblings and their parents are compared. Comprehensive reviews of these data have been provided by Bouchard (1984) and Plomin and colleagues (e.g., Plomin, 1990; Plomin & Petrill, 1997). The results of many of these studies are summarized in table 8.2. It should come as no surprise, perhaps, that the data indicate that both genes and environment make important contributions to individual differences in intellectual performance. Plomin (1990) concludes that approximately 50 percent of the variance in intelligence is due to genetic factors, with the remaining 50 percent of the variance distributed among shared and

TABLE 8.2
Heritability Estimates for IQ

Source of heritability estimate	Heritability estimate
Doubling the difference between correlations for identical and fraternal twins reared together	.52
Doubling the correlation for biological parents and their adopted-away offspring	.44
Doubling the correlation for biological siblings adopted apart	.48
Doubling the difference between correlations for nonadoptive parents and offspring and adoptive parents and adopted offspring	.46
Doubling the difference between correlations for nonadoptive siblings and adoptive siblings	.30
Correlation for identical twins reared apart	.72

Note: Adapted from Plomin (1990).

nonshared environmental factors and measurement error. Beyond this broad interpretation of the findings, however, it proves somewhat more difficult to discern the specific contributions of genetic and environmental factors to intellectual performance. Moreover, the different methods that are used yield quite varied estimates of these two factors. For example, heritability estimates range from .72 in studies of identical twins reared apart to .30 when comparing the difference between correlations for nonadoptive siblings and adoptive siblings. Deriving heritability estimates by comparing identical twins reared together and reared apart, biological parents and their adopted-away children, biological siblings adopted apart, and nonadoptive parents and children and adoptive parents and adoptive children all yield heritability estimates in the range of .44 to .52. Thus, although an exact estimate of heritability cannot be made, the convergence of evidence from a large number of studies indicates that intelligence, as measured by standardized intelligence tests, is influenced by genetic factors.

Studies of the degree of correlation between pairs of individuals do not tell us that these same pairs of individuals will actually achieve the same scores on an IQ test. Lewontin, Rose, and Kamin (1984) offer the hypothetical example of a group of fathers who have IQs of 96, 97, 98, 99, 100, 101, 102, and 103. Their daughters who were separated from their biological parents and raised by foster parents have IQs respectively of 106, 107, 108, 109, 110, 111, 112, and 113. There is a perfect correlation (+1.00) between the IQs of these fathers and their daughters, indicating that intelligence has a heritability coefficient of 1.00—the trait is perfectly heritable. That is, as the IQ scores of the fathers increase, the daughters' IQ scores show a corresponding and identical increase. However, it is also clear that the daughters are all 10 points higher in IQ than their fathers, indicating that the experience of being raised in a foster family had a powerful effect in increasing IQ. "There is thus no contradiction between the assertion that a trait is perfectly heritable and the assertion that it can be changed radically by environment" (Lewontin et al., p. 99). The heritability of intelligence, represented by the correlation between pairs of individuals, tells us about the genetic contribution to intelligence only under the current existing set of environmental conditions. Large differences in the environment can lead to large differences in the magnitude of IQ scores without changing their correlation (Dickens & Flynn, 2001). This distinction is essential to keep in mind when we consider the heated controversy that surrounds the social implications of the heritability of intelligence.

The Debate: Implications for Individual Differences in Intelligence

If the data are relatively clear in establishing the contribution of *both* genes and environment to intelligence, what is the source of the tremendous controversy surrounding this research? As is the case in many areas of scientific inquiry, the controversy lies in the interpretation of the data. The controversy in the study of genetic and environmental contributions to intelligence comes in the use of these studies for understanding differences between individuals (or groups of individuals). For example, if a group of children from a low socioeconomic background are found to score lower on a measure of intelligence than a group of children from a higher socioeconomic background, this difference demands an explanation. Do they differ as a result of their genetic endowment, because of their experiences as they grow in their different environments, or because of biases in the content of items on standardized intelligence tests? In fact, the data obtained from twin and adoption studies can tell us relatively little about the source of differences between groups of different cultural or socioeconomic backgrounds (Nisbett, 1998).

The point of controversy has centered on the finding that African American samples score on average 15 points (one standard deviation) lower on standardized IQ measures than do Caucasian samples (e.g., Flynn, 1999). Why has this persistent and large difference been observed? To what extent is this difference attributable to genetic differences between these two ethnic groups and to what extent is it due to environmental differences? The fathers and daughters example of perfect heritability offered by Lewontin et al. (1984) serves as a reminder that these between-group differences are independent of the correlations between individuals within similar cultural groups. That is, genetics may explain much or all of the variation among individuals within ethnic groups and none of the differences between individuals in the two groups. Research has shown that differences between the IQ test scores of black children and white children are greatly influenced by poverty and characteristics of the children's family environment (Brooks-Gunn, Klebanov, & Duncan, 1996). Furthermore, research on human genetics has shown that different "races" are in fact remarkably similar in their basic genetic characteristics. Once surface characteristics such as skin color and stature are taken into account, the genetic variability within racial groups is much greater than the differences between groups (Cavalli-Sforza, Menozzi, & Piazza, 1994).

The differences between racial groups that have been observed in performance on standardized intelligence tests is likely due to a variety of factors. One element is the difference between groups in their experience with the types of tasks that are included on standardized tests of intelligence. That is, tests reflect the types of experiences that are common for middle class children in our society and relatively less common for children from lower socioeconomic backgrounds. In this sense, the tests are biased in favor of the experience (and therefore preparation) of middle-class children (Gould, 1994). This is not to say that the tests are biased in the way that they predict performance on other measures of success in our society. For example, the correlations between IQ test scores and scores on standardized achievement tests are similar for Euro-American and African American children (Jensen, 1998). The tests actually reflect a broader social bias in access to experiences and resources that are important for the types of academic achievement that are reflected both in IQ tests and in standardized tests of school achievement (Gould). These facts notwithstanding, the role of genetics in the development of individual differences is likely to remain a heated political and social issue.

DEVELOPMENT OF INTELLIGENCE

Intelligence is assumed to change in two ways with development—in the amount of knowledge that is acquired, stored, and available to individuals as a function of age, and in the ways that information is processed. That is, both the *what* and the *how* of intelligence are assumed to change with age. The most comprehensive theory of developmental changes in the ways that children and adults process information about their world was offered by Jean Piaget, the renowned Swiss child development researcher. Piaget viewed intelligence as the result of biological maturation and environmental experience. Cognitive development enables the individual to manage information from the environment in progressively more independent ways. This progress is reflected in the development with age of increasingly more symbolic ways of thinking that replace cognitive processes that are dependent on concrete motoric actions. Thus, not only can adults store more information but they also think differently, more abstractly. In spite of the broad significance of Piaget's theory, standardized measures of intelligence are relatively insensitive to developmental changes in the ways that information is processed. Intelligence tests focus primarily on content and amount of information that is retained by comparing the performance of individuals of different ages on the same tasks.

Stability and Change in IQ Test Performance With Age

Although IQ tests may not adequately reflect developmental processes of intelligence, scores on these tests are related to age. If you were given an intelligence test when you were in the second grade, how well would we expect your score on that test to correlate with your performance on a test that you took today? Do we expect intelli-

gence, at least as it is reflected in scores on intelligence tests, to remain stable with age or to change with experience? Research indicates that intelligence is generally stable across the life span, with scores on tests becoming more stable with age. For example, tests for very young infants assess "intelligence" in terms of sensorimotor functions, but by 18 months of age, cognitively oriented skills can be measured (Sattler, 1988). The correlations of tests administered at 1 to 6 months of age, 7 to 12 months, 13 to 18 months, and 19 to 30 months, with tests administered to the same individuals many years later, are summarized in table 8.3. The correlations of early test scores with tests administered at a later age increase with the age at which the first test was administered and with shorter periods between the two test administrations. For example, tests administered at 1 to 6 months of age are modestly correlated with testing at 3 to 4 years of age (r = .21), but not correlated with testing at 5 to 7 or 8 to 18 years of age. Tests administered at 19 to 30 months of age, however, are moderately correlated with tests administered at ages 3 to 4 years (r = .59) and tests at ages 8 to 18 years of age (r = .49). These findings indicate that intelligence, or at least performance on IQ tests, becomes more stable with age.

Mental Age and the Intelligence Quotient

The significance of age is also reflected in the original approach that was used to generate

TABLE 8.3
Median Correlations of Infant Test Scores and Childhood IQ Test Scores

Age at childhood test (years)	Age at infant test (months)				
	1 to 6	7 to 12	13 to 18	19 to 30	Total
3 to 4 years	.21	.32	.50	.59	.40
5 to 7 years	.09	.20	.34	.39	.25
8 to 18 years	.06	.25	.32	.49	.28
Total	.12	.26	.39	.49	

Note: Adapted from Sattler (1988) and McCall (1979).

intelligence test scores. Lewis Terman, in his adaptation of the Binet-Simon intelligence test, developed the concepts of **mental age** and the **intelligence quotient (IQ)**. Scores on the Stanford-Binet were represented as a quotient, or ratio, of chronological age and mental age. (See "Measure of Intelligence" in this chapter for a complete explanation of the Binet-Simon and Stanford-Binet intelligence tests.) The concept of mental age was derived by determining those test items that were passed by a majority of children at each age level from 3 through 13 years. Certain tasks were selected as representative of each age level, based on the average number of children who solved the task correctly at each chronological age. An individual's IQ was then computed by dividing mental age (MA) by chronological age (CA) and multiplying by 100 (IQ = MA/CA × 100). A problem arises, however, in that the MA method inevitably limits the range of possible scores. These limits are reached when the mean scores for any given test cease to increase with advancing chronological age. Although this limit is actually reached in the mid to late twenties, the method begins to fail at age 13. Recognition of this problem led to an abandonment of this method for deriving an index of intelligence.

An alternative method is to determine a **deviation IQ.** This approach defines the IQ as the ratio between a particular score that an individual attains on a given intelligence test and the score that an average individual of his or her chronological age may be assumed to attain on the same test. Using the deviation method, IQ is one's actual score divided by the expected mean score for one's age. Deviation IQ is a measure of relative intelligence; it assumes constancy of IQ, particularly beyond childhood and particularly for those scores centered around the mean. Thus, deviation IQ scores are standard scores (see chapter 3). Most are based on a standard distribution with a mean of 100 and standard deviation of 15. An IQ score of 100 indicates that the individual performed at the average level for her or his age.

A score of 115 corresponds to 1 standard deviation above the mean for an individual's age, indicating that he or she scored higher than approximately 84 percent of others of the same age in the normative sample. All current intelligence tests rely on the deviation method for deriving scores. An IQ score merely states that a person's intelligence test score at any given time is defined by her or his relative standing among her or his peers. This statement assumes that although an individual's absolute fund of knowledge may change, his or her relative standing (IQ) will not change under ordinary circumstances.

MEASUREMENT OF INTELLIGENCE

Historical Background

We provided an overview of the history of intelligence testing in chapter 2. To review briefly, the work of Binet and Simon in France was particularly influential in the development of measures of intelligence. At the close of the nineteenth century in France, Alfred Binet and his colleagues tested school-age children with the goal of identifying those who were likely to encounter difficulties in school in order to provide them with the necessary experiences to help them succeed. Binet's theory of intelligence included the elements of direction (knowing what has to be done and how it is to be accomplished), adaptation (one's selection and monitoring of one's strategy during the course of task performance), and criticism (the ability to criticize one's own thoughts and actions; Anastasi, 1988; Sattler, 1988). From these early attempts to measure and quantify intellectual functioning, the work of Binet and Simon emerged as the approach that has dominated methods to test intelligence in western society to this day. The definition and operationalization of intelligence that dominates our field is still a direct result of Binet being asked to develop a method of predicting successful performance in school (Sternberg, 1990). Had Binet been asked to predict another criterion (e.g., work performance, creativity, artistic skills), the current definition and methods for the measurement of intelligence might be quite different.

Binet and his colleagues spent many years trying a variety of approaches to measuring intelligence, including even the measurement of cranial and facial features and the analysis of handwriting. The results, however, led to a growing conviction that the direct, even though crude, measurement of complex intellectual functions offered the greatest promise. It was in this connection that Binet, in collaboration with Simon, prepared the first Binet-Simon scale (Binet & Simon, 1905). The 1905 version of their test consisted of 30 problems or tests arranged in order of increasing difficulty. The difficulty level was determined by administering the tests to 50 normal children aged 3 to 11 years and to a small sample of mentally retarded children and adults. The tests were designed to cover a wide variety of functions, with special emphasis on judgment, comprehension, and reasoning (Sattler, 1988). In the second version of the scale, developed in 1908, the number of tests was increased and they were grouped into age levels on the basis of the performance of about 300 normal children between the ages of 3 and 13 years. The child's score on the entire test could then be expressed as a mental level corresponding to the age of normal children whose performance she or he equaled (Anastasi, 1988).

In order to be used in the United States, the Binet scale obviously needed to be translated from French into English and adapted for use in this country. Although a number of different versions were developed, the one carried out under the direction of psychologist Lewis Terman at Stanford University became the most widely used and known as the Stanford-Binet (Terman et al., 1916). Terman's work on the test included extensive modifications, extensions, and standardization. This test provided the impetus for the massive mental testing movement in the United States during the early 1900s (Sattler, 1988).

David Wechsler, Ph.D., was a pioneer in the field of intelligence testing. He developed the Wechsler intelligence scales for children and adults, the most widely used tests of intelligence today. (Photo courtesy *Archives of the History of American Psychology-The University of Akron.*)

The most widely used intelligence tests in the United States today are those originally developed by psychologist David Wechsler during the 1940s and 1950s. Building on existing tests of the day—including the Stanford-Binet, the Army Alpha and Beta tests, and the Bellevue Intelligence Scale—Wechsler first developed an individual test in intelligence for adults, followed by a similarly structured test for school-age children to age 16, and finally, a test for preschool-age children. These tests were influenced by Wechsler's belief that there is a total or global level of intellectual capacity that can be measured—thus, these tests yield a score that represents the person's overall intelligence. The tests developed by Wechsler also reflect the geographic metaphor of intelligence described by Sternberg (1990). Wechsler's tests more than any others have shaped psychologists' perceptions of intellectual functioning as comprised of separate but related *verbal* and *performance* (nonverbal) abilities.

Wechsler (1939) emphasized that an IQ test measures *functional intelligence,* not intelligence itself. Functional intelligence is influenced by nonintellectual factors including motivation, configuration of specific abilities, and emotional adjustment. According to Wechsler, a score on an IQ test is a reflection of what one has learned, which is a function of the opportunities to which one has been exposed and one's ability to take advantage of those opportunities. The subtests on Wechsler's tests represent samples of behavior but they are not exhaustive.

The need for continued adaptation of intelligence testing is represented in the history of the Wechsler scales, because all three versions have undergone substantial revisions since their inception and even after Wechsler's death. These changes have taken two forms: changes in the items of the tests to make them more current and appropriate for new generations, and the testing of new normative samples to provide up-to-date sources for normative comparisons in generating scores.

General Principles of Intelligence Testing

It comes as a surprise to some students of clinical psychology that there are literally dozens of intelligence tests from which to choose. How does a psychologist know which is the right test for a specific individual? First, the psychologist must understand the model or metaphor of intelligence that is reflected in the scale (Sternberg, 1992), which will ensure that the psychologist understands the meaning of the responses and scores for this individual. For example, the widely used Wechsler Intelligence Scale for Children–Third Edition (1992) is based on the geographic metaphor of mental functioning. Another intelligence scale for children, the Kaufman Assessment Battery for Children (1984), is based on the computational metaphor that is concerned with the

ways that individuals process information. Interpretation of the scores from these two tests requires a very different theoretical framework for understanding intelligence.

One of the goals of administering an individual intelligence test is to compare the performance of the examinee with the performance of a representative sample of others of the same age. In order to make such comparisons, it is essential that the test is administered to the individual in the same manner that it was given to those who were tested as part of the standardization sample. Therefore, standardized intelligence tests include detailed instructions for the administration of the instrument. These instructions include a specified order for the administration of all items and subtests, specific wording for all verbal items, a particular arrangement for the presentation of all nonverbal stimuli, and a scripted set of responses to deal with questions that an examinee may ask. A challenge for clinical psychologists is to develop a style of testing that is sufficiently warm and engaging to build rapport with the examinee while not violating the requirements of a standardized administration.

Deviations in the administration procedure can contribute to changes in the performance of the individual and result in a misinterpretation of the overall score. For example, all items and subtests are administered in a standardized order. It is likely that performance on the initial items on any test may be influenced by the individual's anxiety and unfamiliarity with the testing situation, whereas items later in the test may be affected by fatigue and in some cases boredom with the task. As long as the items and subtests are administered in a standard order, the effects of anxiety and fatigue are held relatively constant across individuals. If the order is changed, however, it is impossible to account for how these factors may have affected performance on items and subtests across individuals.

Rigorous efforts must be made to ensure that, like the administration of the test, the scoring and interpretation of the scores are also carried out in a standardized fashion. At issue is whether different examiners can establish high levels of inter-rater reliability (see chapters 3 and 6) in scoring a set of responses on an IQ test. In an effort to address this issue, all widely used IQ tests include detailed instructions for scoring responses to each item that is administered. It is easier to establish high agreement on responses to tasks that involve the use of physical materials (e.g., arranging a set of colored blocks to match a pattern that is presented) than to achieve consensus on responses to more complex verbal tasks (e.g., the exact definition of a vocabulary word).

Current Widely Used Intelligence Tests

We now briefly review the characteristics of four intelligence tests that are currently used in clinical assessment. The tests differ somewhat in their conceptual basis and the age groups for which they are used. The clinical use of intelligence tests is presented in reference to two of our case studies—Jason and Maria (see boxes 8.1 and 8.2 and figure 8.2).

Stanford-Binet (4th Edition)   The work of Binet, Simon, and Terman lives on today in a very real sense in the fourth edition of the Stanford-Binet Intelligence Test. The test has undergone many changes over the years in an effort to ensure that the instrument reflects modern developments in theories of intelligence and to provide current normative data for purposes of scoring and interpretation.

The Stanford-Binet is an individually administered test of intelligence that is comprised of a series of tasks reflecting both verbal and nonverbal functioning. Each task or subtest is composed of a series of questions or problems of increasing levels of difficulty. The same subtests are not all administered to all ages; several scales are added while others are dropped with increasing age. Since the original goal of this test was to distinguish mentally retarded from nonretarded

children, the focus was on generating a full scale IQ and not to generate subtest scores (although these divisions have been made subsequently). The first step is to establish basal level (highest level at which all tests are passed and no tests have been failed below that level), and then testing is continued until a ceiling level is established (lowest level at which all tests are failed when no tests have been passed above that level).

The original versions of the Stanford-Binet were heavily loaded with verbal subtests and items, with the vocabulary test asking for definitions of increasingly more difficult words as a prototypic example (Sattler, 1988). The fourth edition represents an expansion of the scope of the test, because many more nonverbal subtests and items are now included. The 15 subtests have been organized into four broader content areas: Verbal Reasoning (Vocabulary, Comprehension, Absurdities, Verbal Relations), Abstract/ Visual Reasoning (Pattern Analysis, Copying, Matrices, Paper Folding and Cutting), Quantitative Reasoning (Quantitative, Number Series, Equation Building), and Short-Term Memory (Bead Memory, Memory for Sentences, Memory for Digits, Memory for Objects).

Scoring of the fourth edition of the Stanford-Binet is based on a standardization sample of over 5,000 individuals between the ages of 2 and 23 from 47 U.S. states and Washington, D.C. The sample was stratified to match the 1980 U.S. census according to the distribution of the population by geographic region, sex, and ethnicity. Thus, performance of individuals on the current version of the Binet can be compared to a large representative sample of the U.S. population.

The internal consistency reliabilities (coefficient alphas; see chapter 6) for the Full Scale range from .95 to .99 depending on age. Subtest reliabilities vary from .80 to .97 for each of the four areas. For the subtests, most reliabilities fall between the high .80s and the low .90s. These

Clinical psychologists often administer tests to assess strengths and weaknesses in children's intellectual functioning. (Photo © *Bob Daemmrich/The Image Works.*)

data indicate that the Stanford-Binet is a highly reliable test. As is the case with the validity of most intelligence tests, the validity of the Stanford-Binet has been examined in two ways—correlations with other measures of intelligence and correlations with tests of school achievement or work performance/achievement. The Stanford-Binet has been shown to correlate moderately with other measures of intelligence, with school achievement and grades, and with adults' achievement in work (Sattler, 1988).

The Stanford-Binet is used primarily as an index of overall intellectual functioning. Individuals' full scale IQ scores are interpreted in terms of the degree to which they deviate from norms for one's age. Although determination of any clinical disorder or special condition requires more than information on a single measure such as an IQ test, the Stanford-Binet can provide important information in the identification of mental retardation or intellectual giftedness. Because the Stanford-Binet requires the examiner to administer a large number of items to establish the highest and lowest points of a child's functioning, it is more sensitive than other intelligence tests in discriminating among extreme scores at the high or low end of the distribution.

Wechsler Intelligence Scale for Children–Third Edition (WISC-III) Wechsler and colleagues developed two tests for use with children—the Wechsler Preschool and Primary Scale of Intelligence (WPPSI) for ages 2½ to 6, and the Wechsler Intelligence Scale for Children (WISC) for ages 6 to 16. The WPPSI has undergone one revision to its current version, the WPPSI-R (1989), and the **WISC-III** (1991) represents the second revision of this widely used measure. We will focus on the WISC-III here; more information on the WPPSI-R can be obtained from Sattler (1992). The WISC-III is the third version of the test for school-age children that was originally developed in 1949 and previously revised in 1974.

The WISC-III is an individually administered test that requires approximately 1 to 2 hours to administer, depending on the age and intellectual level of the child. It is comprised of 13 subtests that tap different aspects of intellectual functioning. Consistent with the geographic metaphor of intelligence that is reflected in Wechsler's work, these tests are divided into two broad categories of *Verbal subtests* and *Performance subtests*. The Verbal subtests assess basic knowledge that the child has acquired about the world and that is based in the processing and storage of verbal information. For example, one of these subtests is a list of vocabulary words that the child is asked to define. Performance tests examine the child's problem-solving skills on tasks that are less reliant on language and verbal skills. For example, one Performance subtest presents the child with a series of geometric designs and the child attempts to construct these designs using red and white blocks.

The WISC-III subtests have also been subjected to factor analysis (the examination of the correlations among the 13 subtests), and these results have provided partial empirical support for

Wechsler's original distinction between verbal and performance tasks (Sattler, 1992b). Factor analysis of the WISC-III identified the following four factors: *Verbal Comprehension* (information, similarities, vocabulary, comprehension), *Perceptual Organization* (picture completion, picture arrangement, block design, object assembly), *Freedom from Distractibility* (arithmetic, digit span), and *Processing Speed* (coding, symbol search). Thus, there are two factors (Verbal Comprehension, Perceptual Organization) that correspond to Wechsler's original conceptualization of verbal and performance skills. On the other hand, there are two other subgroups of tests that are not as highly correlated with these two broad factors, and it is useful to consider them separately when interpreting the test. (See figure 8.1 for examples of types of items from the WISC-III).

The reliability, validity, and normative sample of the WISC-III are exemplary within the realm of psychological tests. The 1991 standardization sample is comprised of 2,200 children and adolescents, 200 at each of 11 age groups—6 to 16 years old—based on 1988 U.S. census: 70 percent Anglo-American, 15 percent African American, 11 percent Hispanic American, and 4 percent other. The internal consistency and test-retest reliability coefficients for the WISC-III verbal, performance, and overall scales are as high as those obtained for any other psychological test (see table 8.4). The reliabilities of the individual subtests (e.g., vocabulary, block design) are generally lower, however, than the reliabilities for the broader scales that are the composite of the individual subtests. The lower reliabilities of the individual subtests are directly attributable to the fact that they are comprised of a smaller number of items than the broader scale scores are (reliability increases as a function of the size of the sample of the behavior that is taken). On those subtests that require judgments in scoring by the examiner (mazes, vocabulary, similarities, comprehension), inter-rater reliabilities on scoring range from .90 to .94.

The WISC-III can be used to address a number of important questions about the intellectual functioning of individual children. First and foremost, the test can be used as an index of the current cognitive functioning of a child on school-related tasks relative to his or her same-age peers. In this way, it can provide useful information in determining if a child is functioning at a level that is commensurate with expectations for a child of a given age in school. Is this 9-year-old's intellectual functioning at a level at which we should expect her or him to be able to succeed on tasks that are assigned to children in the fourth grade? Or does this child show deficiencies in current functioning to a degree that special services are needed to help this child succeed in school? In this way, scores on the WISC-III can be used as one piece of information (along with the assessment of adaptive functioning) in determining if a child meets the criteria for mental retardation.

In addition to providing information about the overall intellectual functioning of a child, the WISC-III can also be used to consider variations in a child's functioning in various aspects of intelligence. Is this child relatively more competent in verbal or performance-based tasks? Does this child show specific weaknesses on tasks requir-

TABLE 8.4
Reliability of the WISC-III

Scale or subtest	Internal consistency reliability	Test-retest reliability
Full Scale IQ	.96	.92 to .95
Verbal IQ	.95	.90 to .94
Performance IQ	.91	.87 to .92
Verbal Comprehension Index	.94	.89 to .93
Perceptual Organization Index	.90	.86 to .87
Freedom from Distractibility Index	.87	.74 to .86
Processing Speed Index	.85	.80 to .85

Note: Manual for Wechsler Intelligence Scale for Children–Third Edition. (Wechsler, 1991).

ing concentration or rapid processing of information? To address these questions, scores on the WISC-III are interpreted in a series of steps in which specific comparisons among the scales and subtests are guided by empirical data. Specifically, psychologists determine if a child's scores on scales or subtests on the WISC-III differ from each other in a way that is statistically significant and rare. The statistical significance of the difference between scales or subtests establishes whether the difference is reliable (i.e., would you expect to see a difference this large or larger if you gave the test to this child again?). Base rate information (see chapter 6) is used to determine if a difference between scores of this magnitude is relatively rare or frequent in the normative population. Careful use of significance and base rate data provides a sound empirical basis for the interpretation of WISC-III scores and helps psychologists avoid the types of inferential errors that they are prone to make when they interpret test data in a completely subjective manner (e.g., Lynman, Moffitt, & Stouthamer-Loeber, 1993).

Consider an 11-year-old girl who achieves a Verbal IQ of 127 and a Performance IQ of 112. The 15-point difference between her Verbal and Performance IQs appears to be considerable because it is equivalent to a full standard deviation on the WISC-III. Data generated in the standardization of the test and provided in the manual indicate that this difference is a significant difference, with less than a 5 percent probability that it occurred by chance. An examination of the base rate of this difference in the normative sample, however, indicates that a difference of this size between Verbal and Performance IQs can be expected in more than 25 percent of children who take the test. In contrast, consider an 8-year-old boy who achieves a Verbal IQ of 102 and a Performance IQ of 73. The 29-point difference in these scores is both reliable (less than a 1 percent probability that it occurred by chance) and quite rare, with less than 3 percent of the normative sample having a difference of this magnitude be-

tween their Verbal and Performance IQs. This type of careful quantitative approach to interpreting differences in scores on the WISC-III is consistent with the statistical approach to test interpretation (Dawes, Faust, & Meehl, 1989). (See figure 8.2 for a presentation of the results of the WISC-III with Jason).

Kaufman Assessment Battery for Children

In the late 1970s and early 1980s, Allen and Nadine Kaufman, two psychologists who had been actively involved in research on the WISC and the Stanford-Binet, developed a new measure of cognitive function. The primary goals in developing the Kaufman Assessment Battery for Children (K-ABC) were to measure intelligence from a strong theoretical and research base, to separate acquired knowledge from the ability to solve unfamiliar problems, to yield scores that translate to educational intervention, and to be sensitive to the diverse needs of preschool, minority, and exceptional children (Kaufman & Kaufman, 1984).

The K-ABC differs from the Wechsler scales in that it is based on a distinction between two styles of processing information—sequential and simultaneous processing, also labeled sequential and parallel processing, or analytic and gestalt/holistic processing (Kaufman, 1983). In *sequential information processing,* each test item presents a problem that must be solved by arranging information in sequential or serial order. Each idea is linearly or temporally related to the preceding one. Examples of tasks include repeating numbers in the order spoken by the examiner and reproducing an ordered series of hand movements made by the examiner. These tasks are presumed to be related to a variety of everyday, school-oriented tasks such as memorization of number facts or spelling words and learning associations between letters and the sounds they make. *Simultaneous information processing* tasks are spatial or organizational in nature. Information has to be integrated and synthesized simultaneously to produce the appropriate solution. Examples include recalling the spatial

Examples of Items Similar to the WISC-III

Paraphrased WISC-III-like questions

Information (30 Questions)

1. How many wings does a bird have?
2. How many nickels make a dime?
3. What is steam made of?
4. Who wrote "Tom Sawyer"?
5. What is pepper?

Comprehension (18 Questions)

1. What should you do if you see someone forget his book when he leaves a restaurant?
2. What is the advantage of keeping money in a bank?
3. Why is copper often used in electrical wires?

Arithmetic (24 Questions)

1. Sam had three pieces of candy and Joe gave him four more. How many pieces of candy did Sam have altogether?
2. Three women divided eighteen golf balls equally among themselves. How many golf balls did each person receive?
3. If two buttons cost 15¢, what will be the cost of a dozen buttons?

Similarities (19 Questions)

1. In what way are a lion and a tiger alike?
2. In what way are a saw and a hammer alike?
3. In what way are an hour and a week alike?
4. In what way are a circle and a triangle alike?

Vocabulary (30 Words)

This test consists simply of asking, "What is a _____?" or "What does_____ mean?" The words cover a wide range of difficulty.

Picture completion (30 Items)

The task is to identify the important or essential missing part of the picture (e.g., the stem of the flower in the picture below).

Digit symbol-coding (59 Items in coding A and 119 items in coding B).

The task is to copy numbers that correspond with symbols from the key.

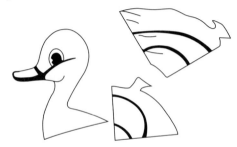

Object assembly (5 Items).

The task is to arrange the puzzle pieces to form a meaningful object.

Symbol search (45 Items in part A and 45 items in part B).

The task is to determine whether the target stimuli (on the left) appear in the array (on the right).

FIGURE 8.1

Examples of types of items from the WISC-III. (*Source:* Simulated items similar to those in the Wechsler Intelligence Scales for Children–Third Edition. Copyright© 1949, 1955, 1974, 1981, 1991 by The Psychological Corporation, a Harcourt Assessment Company. Reproduced by permission. All rights reserved. "Wechsler Intelligence Scale for Children," "WISC," and "WISC-III" are trademarks of the Psycholgical Corporation registered in the United States of America and/or other jurisdictions.)

location of stimuli, identifying the object in a partially completed drawing, and constructing an abstract design from several triangles. Simultaneous processing is hypothesized to be related to tasks that are primarily perceptual in nature, such as learning the shapes of letters and numbers, as well as to higher level intellectual functions because they involve the capacity to integrate information from different sources.

The K-ABC also contains a separate *achievement scale* that is intended to assess factual knowledge and skills typically acquired in school. Tasks that are assessed on the achievement scale rely primarily on verbal processes, much like the items on the verbal subtests on the WISC-III. The inclusion of separate scales of cognitive abilities and achievement was intended to provide a direct comparison of learning potential and learning experience. The focus of the K-ABC is on cognitive processes—how information is processed, not what type of information is processed. This focus is in contrast to the dichotomy underlying the Wechsler scales that is based on content of stimuli (verbal versus nonverbal content).

Much like the WISC-III, the K-ABC is strong in its reliability and standardization. The normative standardization sample consists of 2,000 children aged 2½ to 12½ years, equally distributed by age, sex, geographic location, and parents' socioeconomic status according to the U.S. census. Internal consistency reliability for the scales range from .96 for Simultaneous Processing to .93 for the Achievement subtests. Validity for the K-ABC has been evaluated in several ways. Kaufman and Kaufman (1984) report that factor analytic studies support the construct validity of the sequential-simultaneous processing and achievement subscales.

The K-ABC reflects a slightly different model of the structure of intelligence than do the Wechsler scales or the Stanford-Binet. The scores generated by the K-ABC represent competencies in the simultaneous and sequential processing of information as well as in current school-related achievement. These scores can be used to evaluate the child's preferred or stronger mode of in-

formation processing—managing information in a holistic, integrated manner versus in a serial, linear fashion (Kaufman & Kaufman, 1984). Furthermore, the K-ABC allows for comparisons between these information-processing skills and current achievement. For example, a child who scores significantly higher on the mental processing scales than on the achievement scales would be evaluated as underachieving and may be experiencing some form of a learning problem or learning disability (Kaufman & Kaufman, 1984).

Wechsler Adult Intelligence Scale–Third Edition (WAIS-III)   Fewer tests are available to measure intelligence in adults, and the vast majority of psychologists use the Wechsler Adult Intelligence Scale–Third Edition (**WAIS-III**), the third revision of Wechsler's intelligence scale for adults. The original version was published in 1939 as the Wechsler-Bellevue Intelligence Scale, and the WAIS-R was released in 1981. The WAIS-III reflects the same overall structure as the WISC-III, with subtests organized to generate Verbal, Performance, and Full Scale IQs. Although many of the tasks are similar to those on the WISC-III (e.g., vocabulary and block design), the items are more complex in order to distinguish between adults who vary in their intellectual functioning. The test is administered individually, following a standardized set of instructions for administration.

The WAIS-III, which was revised in 1997, was based on a normative sample of 2,450 adults ranging in age from 16 to 89 years and selected to be representative of the sociodemographic characteristics of the U.S. population as reflected in the 1995 census statistics. The reliabilities for the WAIS-III scale scores are very similar to those of the WISC-III. Internal consistency reliabilities are over .90 for Full Scale IQ, over .90 for Verbal IQ, and between .80 and .90 for Performance IQ. WAIS-III validity has been established by examining the correlations of scores on the test with other measures of intelligence and achievement. The Full Scale IQ on the WAIS-

III correlates highly with the Full Scale score on the Stanford-Binet, with number of years of education, and with scores on tests of reading, arithmetic, and spelling (correlations from .60 to .76; Groth-Marnat, 1997).

Interpretation of the WAIS-III follows the same general procedures as the WISC-III. The primary difference in the use of these two tests is the result of the different types of referral questions that are likely to lead to the use of intelligence tests in school-age children as opposed to adults. Whereas intelligence tests are most often used to shed light on school-related problems in children, school achievement is no longer a question for most adults. Instead, the WAIS-III is often used with adults as part of a test battery when there are questions concerning neurological impairment or brain injury as a result of trauma. (See box 8.2 for Maria's WAIS-III results).

NEUROPSYCHOLOGICAL ASSESSMENT

Although intelligence tests provide important information about cognitive functioning and, therefore, they reflect certain aspects of brain functioning, they do not tell the whole story. A number of other tests and procedures have been developed to assess *neuropsychological functioning* in a broader sense. Benton (1994) defines neuropsychological assessment in this way: "The primary purpose of neuropsychological assessment is to draw inferences about the structural and functional characteristics of a person's brain by evaluating an individual's behavior in defined stimulus-response situations" (p.1).

The term *neuropsychological testing* is frequently misinterpreted to reflect techniques that are used to obtain direct measurement of underlying functions in the brain (Sperry, 1961). This is not the case. Rather, neuropsychological tests are procedures that are used to measure observable behaviors that reflect or are influenced by underlying structure and function of the brain and central nervous system. Much like IQ tests are functional representations of the underlying (but unobservable) construct of intelligence, neu-

ropsychological tests are functional indications of the underlying processes in the brain and central nervous system. A battery of tests is typically administered to assess competencies and weaknesses on verbal and nonverbal tasks that could reveal specific patterns of underlying injury or dysfunction (Lezak, 1995). These tests could provide insight into receptive and expressive language, short- and long-term memory, processing of visual and spatial information, tactile functions, motoric functions, and higher order cognitive functions (Benton, 1994; Reitan & Wolfson, 1996).

Clinical neuropsychological testing is typically conducted to understand the effects of head trauma (head injuries incurred in accidents), stroke, brain tumors, degenerative diseases (e.g., Alzheimer's disease, Parkinson's disease), nutritional disorders, and the effects of chronic alcohol or drug abuse (e.g., Kaufman & Kaufman, 2000). Neuropsychological assessment is based on the relationship between the functions of specific areas of the brain and behavior. For example, in most people the left portion of the frontal cortex is responsible for language and the right frontal cortex is responsible for visual-spatial skills (Foundas, Eure, Luevano, & Weimberger, 1998; Goodglass, Kaplan, Weintraub, & Ackerman, 1976). Therefore, if a loss of language is observed after an accident or stroke, it can be hypothesized that the primary damage has occurred in the left hemisphere of the brain. Clinical neuropsychological testing has been described in terms of the *three Ls*: *lesion detection* (identifying lesions or injuries in the brain), *localization* (identifying where in the brain the damage exists), and *lateralization* (whether the damage is in the left or right side of the brain); (Groth-Marnat, 1997).

A wide range of tests have been developed to measure neuropsychological functioning. These include tests of intelligence, language, attention, abstract reasoning, short- and long-term memory, and visual-spatial processing. In addition to the administration of an intelligence test such as the age-appropriate form of the Wechsler scales,

BOX 8.1

JASON: WISC-III TEST RESULTS AND INTERPRETATION

As you will recall, Jason was brought to the clinic because of behavior problems that he had been exhibiting at school and home and because of questions about Attention Deficit/Hyperactivity Disorder (ADHD). In addition, his academic performance at school had declined even though his teachers felt he was a bright boy. As part of the assessment process, the psychologist thought that it would be important to obtain a measure of Jason's intellectual functioning. The WISC-III was administered in order to provide an index of Jason's current functioning and to provide additional data that may be related to the assessment for ADHD.

The results of Jason's WISC-III are presented in figure 8.1. At the time of the testing, Jason was 8 years, 6 months old. Therefore, his performance was compared with a sample of other children the same age from the normative comparison sample. He achieved a Full Scale IQ of 95, a Verbal IQ of 90, and a Performance IQ of 102. The 12-point difference between his Verbal and Performance IQs was statistically significant ($p < .05$), but it was not extraordinarily rare, because it occurred in 36 percent of the normative sample. The results suggest that Jason's overall intellectual functioning is average for his age, but he is significantly stronger on nonverbal tasks than on verbal tasks.

The Index Scores were also examined, because they may provide additional information relevant to the assessment of ADHD. His score on Verbal Comprehension was 95, his Perceptual Organization Index Score was 105, his Processing Speed Index Score was 88, and his Freedom from Distractibility Index Score (FD) was 69 (at the second percentile of the normative sample). His FD score was significantly lower than his other three Index Scores, and it fell more than two standard deviations below the normative mean. This score indicates that he did very poorly on two subtests that required him to listen to and repeat series of numbers (forward and backward), and to mentally solve (i.e., without writing the problem or the solution) a series of arithmetic problems. These tasks require attention to what the examiner is saying when the problems are presented and short-term memory to hold the problems in one's mind. Research has shown that children with ADHD score lower on the FD Index than non-ADHD children do, indicating that poor performance on these tasks may be associated with impairment in sustained attention (e.g., Anastopoulos, Spisto, & Maher, 1994; Mayes, Calhoun, & Crowell, 1998). Although a low score on the FD factor on the WISC-III is not diagnostic of ADHD, Jason's low score is consistent with the observations that he has difficulty in sustaining his attention, especially on school-related tasks.

neuropsychological testing typically includes test batteries (or portion of batteries) such as the **Halstead-Reitan Battery** (Horton, 1997; Reitan & Wolfson, 1996) or the Luria-Nebraska Neuropsychological Battery (Bradley, Teichner, Crum, & Golden, 2000; Golden, Moses, Graber, & Berg, 1981). An individual's performance is then compared to a normative sample of individuals as well as to clinical samples of individuals who had known brain injuries or disorders when they were tested. The goal of the clinician is to determine if the individual's responses on the test are similar to those of individuals with a known form of injury or disorder.

One example of neuropsychological assessment is found in tests of language skills that have been developed to use as measures of cerebral dysfunction in general and, in particular, to assess function in the left, or language dominant, hemisphere (Benton, 1994). An example is the Token Test (De Renzi & Vignolo, 1962; De Renzi & Faglioni, 1978), which was designed to evaluate oral verbal understanding in individuals with even very limited verbal abilities. The

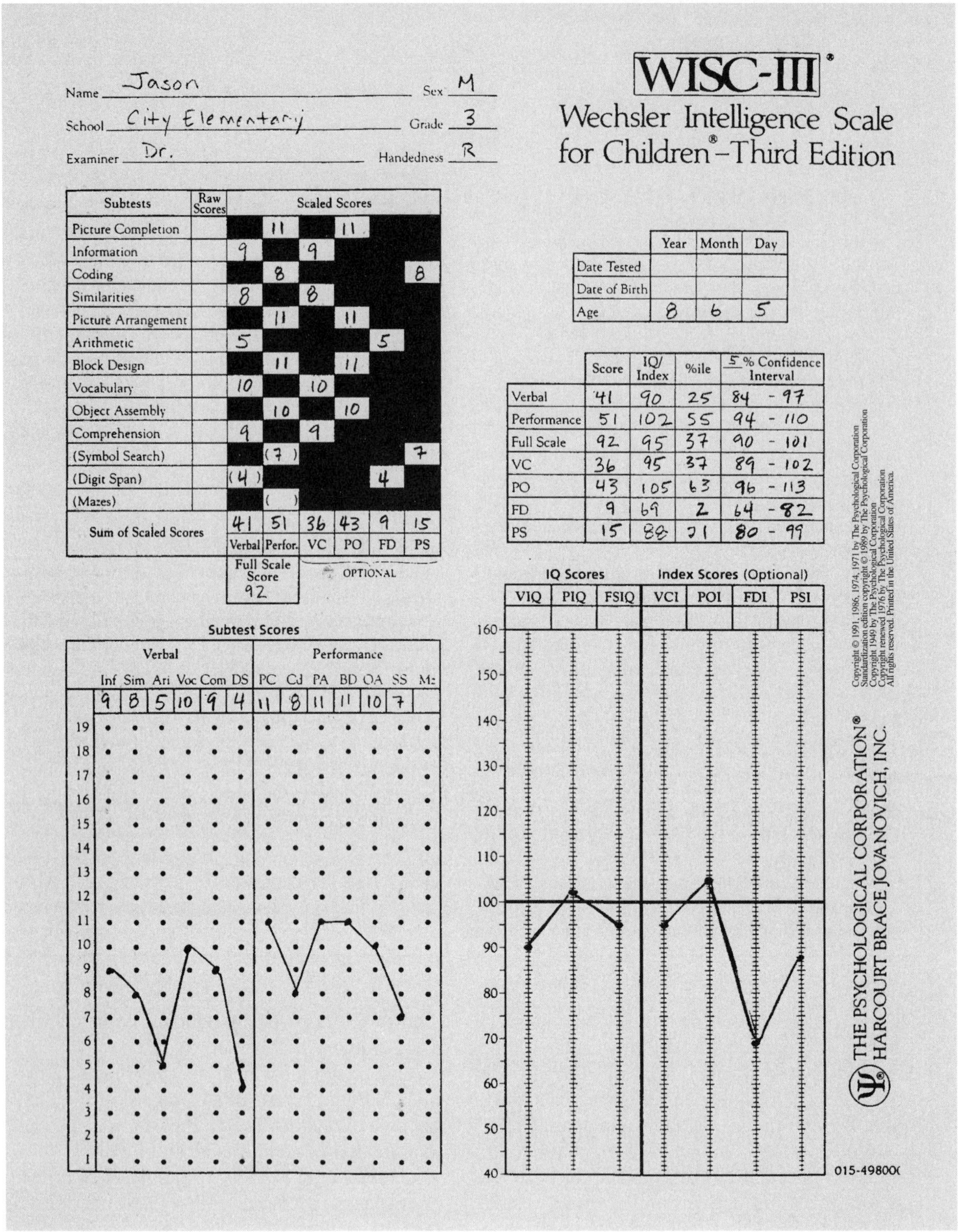

Name: Jason Sex: M

School: City Elementary Grade: 3

Examiner: Dr. Handedness: R

Subtests	Raw Scores	Scaled Scores					
Picture Completion		11		11			
Information	9		9				
Coding		8					8
Similarities	8		8				
Picture Arrangement		11		11			
Arithmetic	5					5	
Block Design		11		11			
Vocabulary	10		10				
Object Assembly		10		10			
Comprehension	9		9				
(Symbol Search)		(7)					7
(Digit Span)	(4)					4	
(Mazes)		( )					
Sum of Scaled Scores	41	51	36	43	9	15	
	Verbal	Perfor.	VC	PO	FD	PS	

Full Scale Score: 92 OPTIONAL

	Year	Month	Day
Date Tested			
Date of Birth			
Age	8	6	5

	Score	IQ/Index	%ile	5 % Confidence Interval
Verbal	41	90	25	84 – 97
Performance	51	102	55	94 – 110
Full Scale	92	95	37	90 – 101
VC	36	95	37	89 – 102
PO	43	105	63	96 – 113
FD	9	69	2	64 – 82
PS	15	88	21	80 – 99

Copyright © 1991, 1986, 1974, 1971 by The Psychological Corporation
Standardization edition copyright © 1989 by The Psychological Corporation
Copyright 1949 by The Psychological Corporation
Copyright renewed 1976 by The Psychological Corporation
All rights reserved. Printed in the United States of America.

Subtest Scores

Verbal						Performance					
Inf	Sim	Ari	Voc	Com	DS	PC	CJ	PA	BD	OA	SS	Mz
9	8	5	10	9	4	11	8	11	11	10	7	

IQ Scores | **Index Scores (Optional)**

| VIQ | PIQ | FSIQ | VCI | POI | FDI | PSI |

THE PSYCHOLOGICAL CORPORATION®
HARCOURT BRACE JOVANOVICH, INC.

015-498000

FIGURE 8.2

Scoring for Jason's responses to the Wechsler Intelligence Scale for Children–Third Edition (WISC-III). (*Source:* Wechsler Intelligence Scale for Children–Third Edition. Copyright © 1990 by The Psychological Corporation, a Harcourt Assessment Company. Reproduced by permission. All rights reserved.)

BOX 8.2

MARIA: WAIS-III TEST RESULTS AND INTERPRETATION

Maria presented at the clinic with symptoms characteristic of Major Depressive Disorder, including sad affect, sleep problems, and an inability to experience pleasure or positive affect. Her son also reported that Maria had difficulty concentrating and focusing her attention on activities such as reading or sewing, activities that previously occupied her for many hours each day. Her son was concerned that Maria's memory problems may be the result of dementia or Alzheimer's disease. The clinical psychologist chose to administer the WAIS-III as part of a battery of tests to determine if there were impairments in Maria's cognitive skills and if these impairments were more consistent with the effects of depression or dementia.

Research has shown that depression is associated with deficits in mental tasks that require high levels of effort and concentration, whereas mental activities that require relatively less effort are unaffected (Hartlage, Alloy, Vasquez, & Dykman, 1993). Thus, we might expect that Maria would have more difficulty (and score lower) on the Performance subtests of the WAIS-III than on the Verbal subtests. The Performance tasks require mental effort to solve

relatively novel and complex problems. In contrast, the Verbal subtests assess primarily the ability to recall information that has already been stored in memory.

Maria's scores on the WAIS-III were consistent with what we would expect in association with depression. Her Verbal IQ was 92, her Performance IQ was 83, and her Full Scale IQ was 88. When the Index Scores were examined, it was found that Maria had scored significantly low (an IQ score of 67, corresponding to the first percentile of the normative sample) on the Perceptual Organization Index, which is the combination of the block design and matrix reasoning subtests, both of which require substantial concentration and mental effort. In contrast, her Verbal Comprehension Index (vocabulary, similarities, and information) score was 98, placing her at the 45th percentile of the normative sample. Thus, her functioning was lowest on those tasks that require sustained mental effort and problem solving, while she performed well on tasks that required recall of previously learned information. These results were consistent with a diagnosis of depression (Hartlage et al., 1993).

Token Test uses stimuli that require knowing only the names of colors and familiar shapes and the meanings of such terms as *touch, large,* and *small.* The examiner records the accuracy with which commands of varying complexity (e.g., "touch the yellow circle and the red square") are carried out. Studies of patients with damage to one side of the brain have shown that impaired performance on this test is far more frequent among patients with lesions in the left hemisphere than in those with right hemisphere lesions.

An example of attention processes is the Trail Making Test (Reitan & Wolfson, 1992). This test requires the client to draw lines that connect consecutively numbered circles (see figure 8.3) and

is followed by a second task in which the client draws lines connecting alternating numbered and lettered circles (Groth-Marnat, 1997). Scores are based on the total time that it takes to complete each task. These tasks involve a number of skills in addition to attention, including complex scanning, motor coordination, visuomotor tracking, and speed of processing information (Groth-Marnat).

Understanding of brain functioning has increased greatly with revolutionary developments in cognitive science and in neuroscience (e.g., Davidson, 2000; Reiman, Lane, van Petten, & Bandettinni, 2000). The development of methods to measure brain activity using positron emission tomography (PET) scans and functional

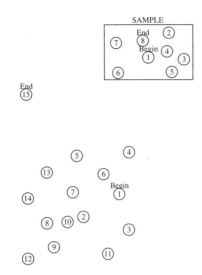

FIGURE 8.3
"Trail Making Part A": A measure of attention and speed of information processing.

magnetic resonance imaging (fMRI) has laid the foundation for understanding intellectual functioning on a level that was never before possible. Rather than replacing current functional measures of intelligence, methods of assessing brain activity will complement current measurement techniques (Raichle, 1994a, 1994b). Emission tomography produces an image of the distribution of a previously administered radionuclide in a desired section of the body (in this case, the brain). PET scans use the unique properties of the annihilation radiation that is generated when positrons are absorbed in matter to provide an image in a selected area of tissue (Raichle, 1997). PET has been used in humans to measure brain blood flow, blood volume, and metabolism of glucose and oxygen. The typical methodology is to have the individual perform a series of tasks that are hypothesized to involve different brain areas and to use PET scans to monitor brain activity during these tasks. fMRI measures the relative flow of oxygenated blood to areas of the brain that are activated in response to a task or stimulus—active areas of the brain are oxygen enriched compared with areas that are not active. It is likely that as PET and MRI technologies improve, they will become increasingly more integrated with current measures of cognitive performance to provide a more complete understanding of both the behavioral and biological components of cognitive functioning.

At the same time that advances are being made in measuring brain structure and functioning, the field of intelligence testing is coming to appreciate the significance of culture and environment in intelligent behavior. The future of intelligence testing and neuropsychological assessment will reflect the continued need to assess cognitive functioning in an environmental context and to consider the culturally dependent as well as the culturally invariant aspects of intelligence.

SUMMARY AND CONCLUSIONS

Intelligence is a central yet controversial concept in clinical psychology. It is a hypothetical construct, and intelligence tests are efforts to observe the behavioral expression of the underlying concept. A variety of definitions have been developed, with the work of David Wechsler being the most influential through the widely used intelligence tests that he developed. Intelligence is the result of both genetic and environmental factors, with evidence from twin and adoption studies setting the proportion of variance in IQ test performance explained by genetic factors at approximately 50 percent. However, this research does not account for the differences in observed IQ performance of cultural groups, which are strongly influenced by environmental factors.

The most widely used intelligence tests are the Wechsler scales for children (WISC-III) and adults (WAIS-III). These tests yield scores reflecting Verbal, Performance, and Full Scale IQ in addition to index scores of Verbal Comprehension, Perceptual Organization, Processing Speed, and, for children, Freedom from Distractibility. These tests are highly reliable, have adequate validity in predicting academic and work performance, and are scored in comparison with large, normative samples.

Neuropsychological assessment is related to intelligence testing in that it involves the measurement of behaviors that are linked to underlying brain functions. Neuropsychological tests include measures of language, abstract reasoning, short- and long-term memory, and visual-spatial processing. These tests are used to determine the presence, extent, and location of brain injuries, tumors, the results of chronic alcohol abuse, and other forms of brain lesions. The future of neuropsychological assessment offers exciting opportunities to link these measures with emerging technologies for the measurement of brain functions (e.g., PET scans and MRI techniques).

KEY TERMS AND NAMES

Crystallized intelligence
Deviation IQ
Fluid intelligence
Genotypic intelligence
Halstead-Reitan Neuropsychological Test
 Battery
Heritability index
Intelligence quotient (IQ)

Mental age
Performance intelligence
Phenotypic intelligence
Robert Sternberg
Verbal intelligence
WAIS-III
David Wechsler
WISC-III

RESOURCES

Books
Goleman, D. (1995). *Emotional Intelligence.* New York: Bantam Books.
Gardner, H. (1999). *Intelligence reframed: Multiple intelligences for the 21st century.* New York: Basic Books.
Sternberg, R. J., & Grigorenko, E. L. (Eds.) (1997). *Intelligence, heredity, and environment.* New York: Cambridge University Press.

Journals
Psychological Assessment
Intelligence
Child Development

ASSESSMENT: MEASUREMENT OF PERSONALITY

INTRODUCTION

Think back to your first-grade classroom and try to remember your classmates. Can you recall the most outgoing, sociable, and extroverted of the children in the class? The quietest, most withdrawn, and shy children? The most aggressive children? What do you imagine that those children are like today as young adults? If you are like most people, you expect that these children have maintained the basic characteristics that distinguished them as early as first grade. You expect that the shy and withdrawn children have remained somewhat reticent and unassertive as adults, while the outgoing children are now gregarious and extroverted young men and women. And the aggressive children are likely to still be relatively hostile and belligerent.

When we assume that people will display continuity in their behavior and emotional style over time, we are making assumptions about the continuity of their **personality.** Our assumptions about personality permeate the impressions we form of other people throughout our daily lives. We view others as relatively predictable in their behavior; in fact, we come to count on the predictability in their behavior in order to anticipate what they will do and how they will interact with us. The degree to which predictability rests in the behavior of people or is in the eye of the beholder is one of the key issues for psychologists who measure and study personality. Are people really consistent in their behavior, or do we perceive them as consistent because we have access only to a limited sample of their behavior under very similar types of circumstances? Your answers to these questions reflect a great deal about how you think about personality and human behavior.

The clinical implications of our assumptions about personality are far reaching. Considerable research has been devoted to determining if certain personality types or styles are prone to specific forms of psychopathology—for example, whether people who are perfectionistic are more likely to develop depression, or whether people who are angry are at increased risk to abuse alcohol. Researchers have also tested the notion that people with certain personalities are prone to developing specific physical diseases, such as cancer or coronary heart disease (e.g., Brandwin, Trask, Schwartz, & Clifford, 2000; Butow et al., 2000). The clinical significance of personality is reflected most strongly in *DSM-IV*, in Axis II diagnoses of personality disorders.

PERSONALITY THEORY AND PERSONALITY ASSESSMENT

Definition of Personality

When psychologists use the term *personality* they are referring to the observation that people display a certain degree of consistency and structure in the ways that they experience and interact with the world. There are two aspects to this consistency: stability across different situations, and consistency over time within similar circumstances or situations (Mischel, 1968, 1998). Personality theorists are concerned with stable, enduring characteristics of people, or what they refer to as **traits**—consistent ways of perceiving the self, the world, and other people; consistent

ways of experiencing and managing one's emotions; and consistent ways of behaving. These basic consistencies in behavior, thoughts, and feelings may be due to genetic factors, or they may be learned, ingrained patterns of behavior, or they may be both (e.g., Mischel 1998; Plomin, Defries, McClearn, & Rutter, 1997).

Psychologists who ascribe to a trait view of personality have developed psychological tests to assess the nature and structure of traits. Given the foundation of a trait perspective on personality, these tests largely assess constructs derived from psychoanalytic or humanistic theories. Thus, as we discuss in this chapter, personality tests have been developed to measure unconscious drives, ego defense mechanisms, self-actualizing tendencies, and object relations. Other personality tests have been guided by "mini-theories" that are variations on the larger models of personality described in chapter 4. Mini-theories do not meet the criteria for a true theory of personality or behavior because they are typically concerned with only a particular, circumscribed aspect of behavior. For example, psychologists Charles Carver and Michael Scheier have considered the processes involved in the self-regulation of behavior (Carver & Scheier, 2000, 2001). A central part of this model is the dispositional characteristic of optimism-pessimism, and Carver and Scheier have developed a measure of this specific trait that is widely used in research and practice (see box 9.1).

These approaches to the development of personality tests start with theory and construct tests to assess the traits described in the theory. A different approach to the development of personality tests does not begin with theory or with assumptions about the underlying structure of personality. Instead, this approach assumes that the structure of personality, including the major dimensions, or traits, on which people differ, is best determined empirically from the responses of large numbers of people to many different questionnaire items. The responses are then analyzed using factor analysis or similar statistical

BOX 9.1

MEASURING OPTIMISM

One of the most fundamental dimensions of personality is the tendency to perceive the world from a generally optimistic or pessimistic vantage point. When presented with a glass that is filled to the midpoint with liquid, dispositional optimists are expected to see the glass as half full whereas pessimists are expected to see the same glass as half empty. But can optimists and pessimists be reliably and validly distinguished based on their responses to a psychological test? Michael Scheier and Charles Carver set out to develop a measure that could tap the basic dimension of optimism-pessimism through a brief self-report questionnaire. The result was a short true-false test, the Life Orientation Test (LOT; Scheier & Carver, 1985; Scheier, Carver, & Bridges, 1994). The scale includes a set of face-valid items that when answered in one direction reflect optimism and when answered in the opposite direction indicate pessimism. This scale has strong internal consistency reliability (.75 to .82) and is quite stable over weeks or months (test-retest correlations range from .74 to .79).

Dispositional optimism appears to be a strong predictor of a variety of behavioral, psychological, and health outcomes. For example, responses to the LOT have been found to predict the course of patients' psychological adjustment to the stress of the diagnosis and treatment of breast cancer (Carver et al., 2000; Carver, Pozo, Harris, & Noriega, 1993; Compas, Worsham, Epping-Jordan, & Grant, 1994). Women who are relatively more optimistic report fewer symptoms of anxiety and depression at the time of their diagnosis and at follow-up assessments as much as one year after their diagnosis. The effects of an optimistic attitude on their adjustment is mediated by the type of strategies that they use to cope with their disease and its treatment. Optimistic women, compared to more pessimistic women, report that they use less disengagement and less wishful thinking and more humor and acceptance in coping. In a study of men recovering from coronary bypass surgery, Scheier et al. (1989) found that optimistic men make a more rapid physical recovery and reported a higher quality of life 6 months after their surgery. Thus, the trait of optimism may enable individuals to perceive stressful situations less negatively than those who are pessimistic, and it may contribute to the use of more active types of coping strategies. These findings contribute to a broader model of self-regulation in which positive expectancies about future outcomes are related to more active efforts to overcome adversity. Negative or pessimistic expectancies are related to the tendency to give up when important goals are threatened.

methods to identify sets of items that consistently cluster together, or intercorrelate. These sets of intercorrelated items are then used to identify and label the basic dimensions of personality.

A large body of research using this methodology converges on the identification of five empirically derived dimensions of personality, now known as the **Five-Factor Model of Personality,** or Big Five (John & Srivastava, 1999). These five dimensions of personality are: *Neuroticism* (Emotional Stability, Ego Strength); *Extraversion* (Assertiveness, Sociability); *Openness to Experience* (Inquiring Intellect, Curious); *Agreeableness* (Social Adaptability, Friendly Compli-

ance); and *Conscientiousness* (Dependability, Impulse Control). (The five factors can perhaps be best remembered by the mnemonic OCEAN.) Although proponents of the Big Five argue that it has provided an important integration of several different approaches to conceptualizing personality, critics are concerned that the Big Five is completely atheoretical and that its focus on broad, superordinate categories has resulted in a loss of much of the detail that is useful for both description and prediction (e.g., Block, 1995; McAdams, 1992).

Certainly, the notion of personality traits has not gone unchallenged in the field of psychology.

A major alternative to the trait perspective comes from behavioral theories, which hypothesize that consistency in people's behavior is actually due to consistency of situations (i.e., the environment) rather than to personality traits (see chapter 10). Still other theorists take a middle road, suggesting that the most comprehensive understanding of human behavior lies in the interaction, or combination, of personality traits and situational factors (e.g., Mischel & Shoda, 1995). The important point here is that each of these perspectives—the trait, the behavior, and the interaction perspective—are represented by very different approaches to assessment. In the remainder of this chapter and in chapter 10, we describe assessment procedures used by clinical psychologists to measure personality and behavior.

Assessment of Personality

According to Ozer and Reise (1994), "personality assessment, as a scientific endeavor, seeks to determine those characteristics that constitute important individual differences in personality, to develop accurate measures of such attributes, and to explore fully the consequential meanings of these identified and measured characteristics" (p. 357). The development of measures of personality raises a number of questions for psychologists. What *format* should be used? What *items* should be selected? How will the items be *scored*? How will the scores be *interpreted*? The most common approaches to personality assessment emphasize the measurement of traits (Wiggins & Pincus, 1992). Although individuals' motives, emotions, intentions, attitudes, and beliefs may also reflect important ways to conceptualize personality (Anastasi, 1997), the trait model remains the dominant approach to measurement (Tellegen, 1991). Based on the assumption that individuals will be consistent over time and across situations, psychologists have developed tests of personality that are used as general indices of the ways that people think, feel, and

behave in their everyday interactions with the world. The most important function of these tests is to be able to predict what people actually do in their daily lives.

What do we mean by a personality test? All psychological tests share certain fundamental characteristics (Anastasi, 1997). Psychological tests involve the use of standardized instructions and the presentation of stimuli that require subjects to respond in a prescribed manner. **Test standardization** is fundamental in all aspects of psychological testing—a test must be administered and scored and the results interpreted in the same manner regardless of who is taking the test or which psychologist is administering the test. Standardization is essential in order for comparisons to be made across many different individuals who may take the test. Standardization of administration and of scoring of a psychological test is also essential to establish the reliability of the test. The stimuli (usually, but not always, in the form of questions or items on a test) are assumed to be useful in predicting much more than how individuals respond to items on a test; they are presumed to predict behavior in daily living and in interactions with others. Data generated by psychological tests are then scored and interpreted in a standardized way, thereby reducing errors that may be due to characteristics of the psychologist who is scoring the test and interpreting the results.

Regardless of the specific measurement approach that is used, personality tests must meet accepted criteria for reliability and validity and must also generate appropriate norms. We discussed different forms of reliability and validity in chapter 6. Items on personality tests must be internally consistent (i.e., they must represent a homogeneous index of the trait they are measuring), and given the hypothesized stable nature of traits across time and situations, items should also have adequate test-retest reliability. Determining the validity of personality measures presents a challenge for psychologists. Personality traits, much like intelligence, are hypothetical constructs, and it is often difficult to establish clear external criteria for their validation. To the extent that scores on personality tests are expected to predict behavior, there must be clear external criteria for use in establishing their validity. When tests are used to measure underlying aspects of personality structures or processes (e.g., libidinal drives or ego defenses), which are not directly observable, it is difficult to establish external criteria for validation. In these cases, validity is typically established through comparison with other personality tests, a practice that unfortunately smacks of circular reasoning.

Personality tests can be grouped according to the methods that they use to obtain data. The broadest distinction is between what are termed **objective personality tests** and **projective personality tests.** Objective personality tests are essentially self-report measures: They rely on individuals' descriptions or accounts of their behavior, attitudes, emotions, and perceptions of themselves. The items are typically presented in the form of true-false questions or rating scales that refer to attributes of oneself. The items are typically grouped into scales based on theory, empirical analysis, or both. Projective tests, in contrast, are presented to the individual in a quite different form. They consist of ambiguous stimuli (e.g., abstract forms, vague or ambiguous pictures, incomplete sentences), and individuals are instructed to provide much more open-ended and subjective responses than are required for an objective personality test. Although there have been advances in recent years, it is still the case that scoring is more subjective for projective tests than for objective tests. We turn now to a discussion of these two types of personality tests.

OBJECTIVE PERSONALITY TESTS

The first of the two dominant approaches to measuring personality involves asking people to report directly on aspects of themselves. Generally referred to as *objective* measures of personality, these tests rely on a questionnaire format in which individuals are presented with verbal statements that they are asked to evaluate in terms of the degree to which the statements are true of themselves. Critics of this testing format contend that people may not have insight into the dynamics of their personality or may be more or less willing to report on different aspects of themselves. In response to this concern, psychologist Paul Meehl (1945) wrote,

> the verbal type of personality inventory is *not* most fruitfully seen as a "self-rating" or self-description whose value requires the assumption of accuracy on the part of the self. Rather, the response to a test item taken as an intrinsically interesting segment of verbal behavior, knowledge regarding which may be of more value than any knowledge of the "factual" material about which the item superficially purports to inquire. Thus, if a hypochondriac says that he had "many headaches" the fact of interest is that he *says* this. (p. 9)

Minnesota Multiphasic Personality Inventory

One of the most widely used and extensively researched psychological tests is the Minnesota Multiphasic Personality Inventory, or MMPI (Hathaway & McKinley, 1942). The MMPI was revised and restandardized in the 1980s; its revision, the MMPI-2, is currently used for the assessment of adults (Butcher, Dahlstrom, Graham, Tellegen, & Kaemmer, 1989), and a separate version, the MMPI-A, has been developed for use with adolescents (e.g., Butcher & Williams, 1992).

Starke R. Hathaway and **J. Charnley McKinley** began research in 1939 that eventually led to the MMPI. Their goal was to develop an instrument to assist in the assessment and diagnosis of patients in the Minnesota psychiatric hospitals in which they worked. These two psychologists believed that other objective personality tests available at that time were inadequate either because the tests were tied too closely to specific psychological theories about the structure of personality to be useful, or because they were developed with college students, or because they assessed variables that were unrelated to psychopathology and, therefore, were of little benefit in work with psychiatric patients (Butcher & Williams, 1992).

Hathaway and McKinley were interested in a direct and efficient method to distinguish individuals with psychiatric disorders from those without such problems. They constructed the MMPI based on the following assumptions: (a) the best way to obtain information for this purpose is to ask the person directly to respond to self-referent statements with which he or she can agree or disagree, using a true or false response; (b) patients who endorse similar symptoms or items in the MMPI pool are assumed to be diagnostically more alike than they are different; and (c) individuals endorsing more symptoms of a particular kind are experiencing a more serious problem than those reporting fewer symptoms.

To achieve their goal of distinguishing between groups of patients who differed in their diagnoses and to assess the severity of these problems, Hathaway and McKinley developed *scales* (groups of items endorsed in a defined direction) on which individuals could be compared. Hathaway and McKinley conceptualized the MMPI scales as dimensions that reflect particular problems or disorders such as depression, schizophrenia, or paranoia. One approach to developing these scales would have been to select items that were clearly linked to the symptoms of each disorder and ask individuals to report whether or not they had experienced those symptoms. However, Hathaway and McKinley did not believe that items should be selected for specific scales based on content that was obviously related to particular psychiatric diagnoses or clusters of symptoms. Instead, they developed the MMPI on the basis of item and scale validity; that is, they required that any item be assigned to a particular scale only if it empirically discriminated a given criterion group (e.g., individuals diagnosed with depression) from a normative sample, regardless of the content of the item. This approach was referred to as an empirical scale-construction strategy, or **empirical keying.**

Because in this approach deviation from the norm is used to define a high or low score on any particular scale, it is critical that the normative sample is truly "normal," that is, truly representative of the population. Unfortunately, the original normative sample for the MMPI was extremely weak in this regard—it was composed entirely of friends and relatives of patients at the University of Minnesota hospitals and several nonrandom samples of residents of Minneapolis and the surrounding area, all of whom were Caucasian. Indeed, the inadequacy of this original normative sample was a major impetus for the restandardization of the MMPI (Graham, 2000).

Hathaway and McKinley compiled a pool of over 1,000 potential items derived from a variety of sources, including previously published scales, symptoms of mental disorders or other problems treated on their psychiatric service, and clinical reports. They had no preconceived notion of whether a particular item would prove to be related to the constructs of interest. Instead, they empirically compared the responses of the normal subjects with those of groups of patients who had received specific psychiatric diagnoses (e.g., depression, schizophrenia) to determine which items would be included in a particular scale. They ended up with a final sample of 550 items—affirmative statements that could be answered true or false—across 10 clinical scales and 3 validity scales. Although Hathaway and McKinley's work is clearly a strong example of empirical test construction, it is important to recognize that the selection of items and the psychiatric diagnoses that were applied to the clinical groups in developing the MMPI were limited by the current state of knowledge of psychopathology and an inadequate psychiatric diagnostic system.

Since its inception the MMPI has become the most widely used and researched objective personality instrument in the world, with well over 10,000 published research references (Groth-Marnat, 1997). It is also the assessment instrument most frequently taught in graduate clinical psychology programs (Piotrowski & Zalewski, 1993). The MMPI has been used with psychiatric patients in inpatient and outpatient settings, patients in general medical contexts, adolescents in schools, inmates in correctional facilities, individuals in alcohol and drug treatment units, military personnel, and job applicants in industrial settings; it has also been translated into over 50 foreign languages.

Restandardization of the MMPI: The MMPI-2

Despite its remarkable popularity, the MMPI was not without its problems. The original MMPI was criticized for (a) its reliance on an outdated psychiatric diagnostic system that has been supplanted by several revisions of the DSM; (b) a normative sample that was not representative of the broader population in terms of socioeconomic diversity; and (c) items that became dated or that were objectionable or offensive in their content (Helmes & Reddon, 1993). These problems led to a large-scale effort, beginning in the 1980s, to revise the MMPI. Several major goals were established by a restandardization committee, including:

- revising and modernizing the MMPI items, including deleting obsolete or objectionable items (about 14 percent of the original items were changed)
- ensuring continuity with the original MMPI validity, standard, and supplementary scales
- developing new scales to address clinical problems not covered in the original MMPI
- collecting new, randomly selected samples of adults and adolescents who were representative of the U.S. population and developing age-appropriate norms
- developing new normative distributions for the adult and adolescent scales that would better reflect clinical problems
- collecting new clinical data to be used in evaluating and validating the new scales (Butcher et al., 1989).

The MMPI-2 normative sample consisted of 2,600 subjects, ages 18 to 85 years, randomly sampled from seven regions of the United States.

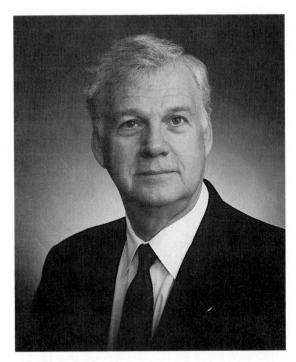

James Butcher, Ph.D., is a Professor at the University of Minnesota. Dr. Butcher is an authority on psychological assessment of personality and abnormal behaviors across different cultures. He played a leading role in the development of both the Minnesota Multiphasic Personality Inventory-2 (MMPI-2) and an adolescent version of this instrument (MMPI-A). *(Photo courtesy of James Butcher.)*

The normative sample was balanced for gender and demographic characteristics such as ethnic group membership to be representative of the U.S. population. The MMPI-A (adolescent version) was normed on over 1,600 14- to 18-year-old students across the United States. Scores on the MMPI-2 and MMPI-A scales were evaluated through comparison with the distribution of scores from these new samples; that is, an individual's score on the MMPI-2 is considered to be abnormal if it deviates significantly from the mean for this normative sample. Extensive new data were also collected from a variety of clinical samples.

The MMPI-2 contains 567 items, although it can be scored using only the first 370 items. Two broad categories of scales are generated from the items, both on the original MMPI and on the MMPI-2: validity scales and clinical scales. The validity scales are used to assess the test-taking style and attitude of the respondent, and as their name implies, they evaluate whether the examinee's responses to the items are valid. As Butcher and Williams (1992) note, the MMPI is a self-report measure, and if individuals wish to distort their responses, they can readily do so. A distorted presentation as the result of random responding or a motivated effort to look good or bad on the MMPI is a threat to both the reliability and the validity of the test. The validity scales were developed to evaluate the individual's openness, honesty, cooperativeness, and willingness to share personal information; the MMPI clinical scales were developed to evaluate the respondent's psychiatric status and personality characteristics.

Validity Scales　　The **MMPI-2 validity scales** were developed on the assumption that certain patterns of responding to the true-false items represent unreliable or biased responses that would invalidate the scores on the clinical scales. Therefore, items were included on the MMPI-2 that have extremely high or extremely low rates of occurrence in the normal population (i.e., high or low *base rates*). Individuals who endorse a disproportionately high number of such items are likely trying to present themselves in an overly favorable or overly negative light. There are four primary validity scales on the MMPI-2. The *Cannot Say (?)* scale is simply the total number of items left blank or rated as both true and false by the respondent. A high number of blank items will render the MMPI invalid. The *Lie Scale (L)* is a measure of the tendency to present oneself in an overly favorable light—claiming that one is far more virtuous, ethical, or moral than the population norms. While a single item may truly characterize an individual, the likelihood that a large number of these items would do so is extremely low. The *Infrequency Scale (F)* is a measure of the tendency to claim an inordinate number of psychological problems or exaggerate

one's adjustment problems. The *F* scale is composed of items that are rarely endorsed by either the normative or the patient samples. The Defensiveness *K* scale is an indicator of test defensiveness and is used to detect clients who are describing themselves in overly positive terms. Because a defensive test-taking approach will likely suppress scores on the clinical scales, a portion of *K* is added to some of the MMPI-2 clinical scales. Finally, several new validity scales or scores have been developed for use with the MMPI-2, including the tendency to respond inconsistently to items or to give indiscriminant true or false responses (Butcher et al., 1989).

Clinical Scales　　After determining that a valid profile has been obtained, the respondent's total score on each of the 10 **MMPI-2 clinical scales** is converted to a *T* score (scores with a mean of 50 and a standard deviation of 10) based on the normative sample. *T* scores over 65 (the 92nd percentile of the normative sample) are believed to be clinically meaningful—thus, clinical significance is defined in terms of deviation from the norm. The 10 clinical scales are described in table 9.1. Each of the clinical scales appears to be a stand-alone scale; that is, each could be interpreted by itself in reference to the original dimension of psychopathology that it was designed to represent. So, for example, a high score on the *Sc* scale could suggest a diagnosis of schizophrenia, and an elevated score on the *D* scale might suggest a diagnosis of depression. Decades of research with the MMPI and its revision have clearly indicated, however, that interpretation of single scale scores is not the most effective way to use this measure. Instead, examiners now consider the *profile* of scores on all 10 clinical scales in interpreting the MMPI-2.

Interpreting MMPI-2 Profile Types　　The **profile analysis** approach to interpreting responses to the MMPI-2 maximizes the amount of information that is used. Instead of considering one scale at a time, a clinical psychologist can

TABLE 9.1
Clinical Scales of the MMPI-2

Scale 1: *Hypochondriasis (Hs)*. This scale was designed as a measure of abnormal or "neurotic" concerns over bodily health. The original criterion group was patients who presented with concerns about physical ailments for which there were no organic bases. Personality descriptors that are associated with a high score on this scale: exhibiting excessive bodily concerns, numerous vague somatic symptoms, and undefined complaints such as gastric upset, fatigue, pain, and physical weakness; selfish; self-centered; pessimistic; defeatist; cynical.

Scale 2: *Depression (D)*. This scale measures symptomatic depression—a generally negative frame of mind in which the individual has reported poor morale, lack of hope for the future, dissatisfaction with life, and a low mood. Personality descriptors associated with elevated scores: depressed, unhappy, dysphoric, pessimistic, self-deprecating, guilt-prone, sluggish, lacking in self-confidence, introverted, shy, withdrawn from activities, exhibiting difficulty making decisions.

Scale 3: *Hysteria (Hy)*. This scale was originally developed as a measure of what was referred to as conversion hysteria, currently termed conversion disorder. Individuals who score high on this scale often manifest an unusual pattern of personality characteristics composed of denial and flamboyant social assertiveness, yet under stress in relationships the individual may become suddenly disabled by physical problems, usually of an unknown origin. Personality descriptors: reacts to stress by developing physical symptoms such as headaches, chest pains, weakness, and tachycardia; develops symptoms that appear rapidly and abate quickly; lacks insight about underlying etiology of symptoms or motives; does not report severe emotional turmoil; is self-centered; expects a great deal of attention and affection from others; engages in superficial and immature interpersonal relationships.

Scale 4: *Psychopathic Deviate (Pd)*. This scale is a measure of antisocial behavior or psychopathic behavior. Personality descriptors: antisocial activities, rebellious attitudes toward authority figures, stormy family relationships, a tendency to blame one's parents for one's own problems, a history of underachievement in school or work, impulsiveness and a striving for immediate gratification of impulses, an interest in others only in terms of how they can be used for one's own purposes. Individuals who score high on this scale act without considering the consequences of their actions, tend not to profit from experience, and engage in shallow and superficial interpersonal relationships but are likeable and make good first impressions.

Scale 5: *Masculinity-Femininity (Mf)*. This scale is different from other standard scales in several ways. The construct underlying its development is not a clinical syndrome. It was originally designed to identify personality features of "male sexual inversion" or homosexual men who had a feminine interest pattern. The Mf scale is not a symptom scale like most of the other standard scales are—elevations on this scale reflect interests, values, and personality characteristics. Males who score high have sexual problems and concerns; have conflicts in sexual identity; lack stereotyped male interests; have aesthetic and artistic interests; have an androgenous orientation; are clever, clear thinking, logical; show good judgment; are curious, creative, imaginative, sociable, sensitive to others. Females who score high reject traditional female roles; have interests that are more stereotypically male than female; are active, assertive, competitive, outgoing, uninhibited, self-confident.

Scale 6: *Paranoia (Pa)*. This scale assesses the behavior pattern of suspiciousness, mistrust, delusional behavior, excessive interpersonal sensitivity, rigid thinking, and externalization of blame commonly found in paranoid disorders. The personality descriptors associated with this scale change greatly with increased elevation, a pattern different from other scales. At highest scores individuals are frankly psychotic, engage in disturbed thinking, are delusional, utilize projection as a defense mechanism; whereas individuals with moderately high scores manifest a paranoid predisposition, are excessively sensitive and overly responsive to the opinions of others, rationalize and tend to blame others for their problems, are suspicious and guarded, are moralistic and rigid in opinions and attitudes.

Scale 7: *Psychasthenia (Pt)*. This scale was originally developed to assess a psychological disorder that today is described as anxiety disorder with obsessive-compulsive features. Personality descriptors: High scorers are anxious, tense, agitated; experience great discomfort, worry, and feelings of apprehension; are high-strung, depressed, jumpy; have concentration difficulties; experience obsessive thinking; engage in compulsive or ritualistic behaviors and ruminations; feel insecure and inferior; are self-critical, self-conscious; set high standards of performance for themselves and others; are perfectionistic and conscientious.

Scale 8: *Schizophrenia (Sc)*. This scale reflected an attempt to distinguish four subtypes of schizophrenia; this effort was unsuccessful, and the large items were grouped into a single scale. Personality descriptors: High

TABLE 9.1 (concluded)

scorers have a schizoid lifestyle; do not feel part of the social environment; are isolated, alienated, and misunderstood; are anxious, resentful, hostile, and aggressive; have difficulty separating fantasy and reality; have self-doubts; may manifest sexual preoccupation; react to stress by withdrawing into fantasy and daydreaming; are confused, disorganized, and disoriented; may report unusual thoughts or attitudes or hallucinations; are withdrawn, seclusive, secretive; avoid dealing with people and new situations.

Scale 9: *Hypomania (Ma).* This scale measures manic or hypomanic behavior or the tendency to act in euphoric, aggressive, and hyperactive ways. Personality descriptors: Very high scorers are viewed as hyperactive; have accelerated speech; may have hallucinations or delusions of grandeur; engage in excessive purposeless activity; make unrealistic self-appraisals; may have too many projects going at once; do not utilize energy wisely, often do not see projects through to completion; have little interest in routine and detail; have difficulty inhibiting expression of impulses.

Scale 0: *Social Introversion (Si).* This scale measures social discomfort, inferiority, low affiliation, interpersonal sensitivity, lack of trust, and physical complaints. Personality descriptors: High scorers are socially introverted; are more comfortable alone; are reserved, shy, retiring; are insecure and uncomfortable in social situations; lack self-confidence; are sensitive to what others think of them; are submissive and compliant in interpersonal relationships.

Note: Adapted from Butcher & Williams (1992) and Graham (2000).

TABLE 9.2
Examples of MMPI-2 Profile Interpretations

Butcher and Williams (1992) report the use of code types to gain information about symptoms and behaviors, personality characteristics, and predictions or dispositions. For example, a 2-7 code type (*Depression* and *Psychasthenia*) would "appear anxious, tense, nervous, and depressed. They report feeling unhappy and sad, and tend to worry excessively. They feel vulnerable to real and imagined threats, and typically anticipate problems before they occur—often overreacting to minor stress as though it was a major catastrophe. . . . appear docile and passive-dependent in relationships . . . They usually show a capacity for forming deep emotional ties and tend to lean on people to an excessive degree . . . usually diagnosed as depressive, obsessive-compulsive, or anxiety disordered." The 2-8 code type (*Depression* and *Schizophrenia*): "appear anxious, agitated, tense, and jumpy. They often report having a sleep disturbance and are unable to concentrate. Disturbed affect and somatic symptoms usually characterize the clinical picture. They are often clinically depressed, have soft and slowed speech, and thought . . . Problems with anger and interpersonal relationships are usually noted . . . They are overly sensitive to the reactions of others, suspicious of others' motivations, and may have a history of being hurt emotionally . . . . dependent, unassertive, irritable, and resentful . . . often fear losing control over emotions . . . guilt-ridden and self-punitive . . . . most common diagnoses are manic-depressive psychosis, schizophrenia, schizo-affective type, or severe personality disorder . . . often preoccupied with suicidal thoughts, and may have specific plans for doing away with themselves."

Note: From Butcher & Williams (1992)

interpret the full set of responses on the scales. Profile types are defined by the highest score or scores above 65 *T* on the clinical scales. Thus, a respondent who obtained *T* scores of 82 on the *D* scale (scale 2) and 76 on the *Pt* scale (scale 7) would have a 2-7 profile. Two general rules are used for interpreting profile types: The profile is clearly defined by two or more scales that reach interpretive significance (i.e., above 65 *T* score), and there has been sufficient research on the be-

havioral descriptions for the profile. Interpretation of profiles based on the highest two or three scales is the most widely used approach (Graham, 2000; see table 9.2). Clinicians can look up the profile (e.g., 2-7, 3-1-2) in any of a number of MMPI-2 codebooks that describe the personality and psychopathology characteristics of patients who obtained that particular profile. In figure 9.1 we present an MMPI-2 profile for Allison, one of the cases we described in chapter 1.

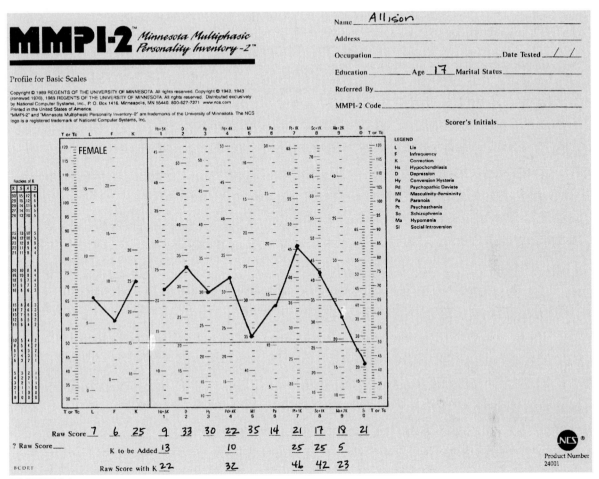

FIGURE 9.1

MMPI-2 profile representing Allison's responses.

Interpretation of MMPI Content Scales   A second approach to scoring and interpreting the MMPI-2 has been developed, based on an approach that differs from the original dustbowl empiricism that led to the development of the standard clinical scales. Items on the MMPI-2 have been grouped into scales according to their face valid content, and a second set of scales were developed that reflect a range of types of psychopathology. The content scales include items that directly reflect the core symptoms of clinical problems (e.g., anxiety, depression) as well as various aspects of daily living (e.g., family relations). For example, Ben-Porath, Butcher, and Graham (1991) examined the ability of the MMPI-2 content scales to distinguish between inpatients diagnosed with schizophrenia and those diagnosed with major depression. Their results indicated that both the original clinical scales and the new MMPI-2 content scales contain information that is useful in the differential diagnosis of these two disorders. More important, the content scales possess *incremental validity* with respect to this diagnostic question. That is, they yield information that is useful above and beyond what can be obtained from the profile scoring of the clinical scales.

Reliability and Validity   The reliability and validity of the MMPI clinical scales have been examined in hundreds, if not thousands, of studies. Both the internal consistency and the test-retest reliability of the clinical scales are reasonably high (e.g., Parker, Hanson, & Hunsley, 1988), particularly given the expected changes in patients' symptoms with treatment. There have been some concerns expressed that many of the clinical scales correlate too highly with each other because of shared items (e.g., Butcher et al., 1989). It is important to realize, however, that different forms of psychopathology are not neatly distinguished from each other. In particular, depression and anxiety have very high rates of co-occurrence, or comorbidity (see chapter 5). Consequently, it is reasonable to also expect item overlap among the 10 clinical scales of the MMPI-2. The validity of the MMPI scales has been tested primarily by studies that examine the ability of the test to discriminate between groups that are known to differ on some known criteria (i.e., discriminant validity). Evidence here is strong as well. Moreover, the MMPI-2 has been demonstrated to have incremental validity above and beyond information obtained with other assessment instruments (Barthlow, Graham, Ben-Porath, & McNulty, 1999).

Criticisms of the MMPI-2   The MMPI has a remarkable history within clinical psychology,

and the MMPI-2 represents a significant improvement over its predecessor. Despite the strengths of this instrument, however, it has been subject to a number of criticisms. Some of the concerns with the MMPI-2 are the result of the decision to retain many features of the original version for the sake of maintaining continuity; others involve problems that have arisen in the development of the new version. For example, no effort was made to bring the MMPI-2 into line with current theory in the area of personality and psychopathology. As a result of the use of the original clinical scales, the primary scores that are generated reflect an outdated conceptualization of psychopathology (Helmes & Reddon, 1993). Several of the scale names (e.g., *Hysteria, Psychasthenia*) refer to outdated concepts in psychopathology and may lack relevance for current diagnostic decisions. In addition, despite the effort that was expended to gather data on a more representative normative sample for the MMPI-2, concerns remain about the use of the new norms to generate and evaluate specific profile or code types (Helmes & Reddon). That is, much of the research on the characteristics of individuals with particular profile types was conducted using the MMPI and its original norms. It is not yet clear that the same profile on the MMPI-2 will necessarily warrant the same interpretations that were appropriate in the original version.

The Revised NEO-Personality Inventory

A more recently developed objective personality scale is the Revised NEO-Personality Inventory or **NEO-PI-R,** a test that differs from the MMPI in some important ways. Costa and McCrae (1992) developed the NEO-PI-R to assess the first three of the Big Five personality traits (Neuroticism, Extraversion, and Openness; hence, the name of NEO) and subsequently expanded the test to include all five factors (N, E, O, plus Agreeableness and Conscientiousness). The NEO-PI-R is a 181-item measure with both self-report and observer forms. Items are answered on a 5-point scale, from *strongly disagree* to *strongly agree.*

The format and content of the items on NEO-PI-R are quite different from that of the MMPI-2. Items on the NEO-PI-R are face valid or obvious in their content; that is, they ask respondents to report directly about the characteristics they are intended to measure. Costa and McCrae (1992) suggest that there are three major ways in which the resulting personality scale scores can be interpreted. The most straightforward is to view them as measures or estimates of what the individual is really like. A more subtle, second interpretation is that they represent the individual's self-concept, or how he or she sees himself or herself. Third, the scores can be seen as self-presentation, or the way in which the individual wishes to be viewed by others, either in general or on the specific occasion when the test is administered. It is probably the case that all three interpretations are correct to some extent.

Costa and McCrae (1992) report that the NEO-PI-R has reasonable internal consistency and test-retest reliability; they also report that the correlations between NEO-PI-R self-ratings and ratings by spouses ranged from .43 (conscientiousness) to .60 (openness). Trull, Useda, Costa, and McCrae (1995) administered the NEO-PI-R to a clinical sample and found substantial stability in personality scores over a 6-month period. There are also now a small number of studies linking particular forms of psychopathology to elevations on one or more of the NEO-PI-R scales (e.g., anxiety: Talbert, Braswell, Albrecht, & Hyer, 1993; alcohol use: Martin & Sher, 1994). Nevertheless, this measure has not escaped criticism in the context of its use as a clinical assessment tool (Butcher & Rouse, 1996). Ben-Porath and Waller (1992), for example, raised two concerns about the NEO-PI-R. First, they noted that five broad factors are unlikely to provide information that is sufficiently specific to meet the needs of clinical applications. And second, they criticized the absence of validity scales, such as those in the MMPI-2, in the NEO-PI-R. Costa and McCrae argued that self-reports of individuals are, in general, trustworthy. Given the nature of the samples and situations when the NEO-PI-R is used for clinical assessment, however, the lack of validity scales is clearly a major concern.

Other Objective Personality Tests

The MMPI-2 and the NEO-PI-R are two of many objective personality tests that are currently used in research and clinical practice. Other widely used tests include the Multidimensional Personality Questionnaire (MPQ; Tellegen & Waller, in press), the Millon Clinical Multiaxial Personality Inventory (MCMI; Millon, 1992, 1996), the Basic Personality Inventory (BPI; Jackson, 1989), and the California Personality Inventory (CPI; Gough, 1990). Although all these tests have adequate psychometric properties, the volume of empirical studies examining the validity of these measures is very small compared to the number of investigations of the MMPI-2 and, increasingly, the NEO-PI-R, and this disparity is likely to continue.

PROJECTIVE PERSONALITY TESTS

Projective tests represent the second broad approach to the assessment of personality, one that is radically different from the methods used in objective personality tests. The format, items, administration, and scoring of projective personality tests are all distinct from that of objective tests. Whereas objective tests require responses to explicit verbal questions or statements, projective tests ask for responses to ambiguous and unstructured stimuli. Indeed, a major distinguishing feature of projective techniques is the use of relatively unstructured tasks that permit an almost unlimited number of responses (Anastasi, 1997). This feature means that the instructions provided to the respondent and the stimuli themselves have a minimal level of structure, based on the assumption that the internal dynamics of the respondent's personality are more likely to be revealed in unstructured circumstances. These stimuli include inkblots, pictures that are ambiguous in nature, drawings of a person or objects made by the respondent, and incomplete sentences.

Although there are earlier examples of projective techniques, it was with Hermann Rorschach's publication in 1921 of *Psychodiagnostik* and the ink blot test that projective techniques began to receive attention from psychologists. Seventeen years later, in 1938, Henry Murray at Harvard University wrote *Explorations in Personality,* in which he introduced another major projective test, the *Thematic Apperception Test.* Human figure drawing techniques followed shortly afterward, in the 1940s (e.g., Buck, 1948; Machover, 1949). Over the next six decades, these approaches were subjected to intense criticism concerning their tenuous reliability and validity (e.g., Entwisle, 1972; Wood, Nezworski, & Stejskal, 1996; Lilienfeld, Wood, & Garb, 2000); in fact, in 1968 Walter Mischel, then at Stanford University, called into question the very existence of personality, let alone the need for projective measures of this "nonexistent" construct. Interestingly, these attacks did little to dampen many practitioners' enthusiasm for, and use of, projective tests.

The development and use of virtually all projective personality tests are based on the *projective hypothesis,* a term coined by Frank (1948), who wrote that projective techniques were essentially psychological X rays. According to the projective hypothesis, when faced with ambiguous stimuli, respondents will project aspects of their personalities onto the stimuli in an effort to make sense of them. The examiner then can work backward from the persons' responses to gain insight into their personality dispositions. The concept of projection comes from Freud's (1911) formulation of defense mechanisms. In using the defense mechanism of projection, people unconsciously attribute their own negative impulses and personality traits onto others

around them. Thus, projective tests are hypothesized to bypass the conscious defenses of respondents and to allow clinicians to gain access to important psychological information about individuals of which they themselves are unaware. Finally, because projective tests are believed to be sensitive to "unconscious" aspects of personality, whereas objective tests are not, proponents of projective tests maintain that these instruments provide incremental validity above and beyond the use of more structured procedures (e.g., Finn, 1996; Weiner, 1999).

Lindzey (1959) classified projective techniques into five broad categories (see also Aiken, 1999; Lilienfeld et al., 2000). *Association* techniques include inkblot and word association tests. *Construction* techniques include human figure drawing tests and story creation tests like the TAT. *Completion* techniques include sentence completion tests. *Arrangement or selection* techniques include the Szondi Test and the Luscher Color Test. Finally, *expression* techniques include projective doll play, puppetry, and handwriting analysis. The five major types of projective techniques in Lindzey's taxonomy are presented in table 9.3. We will now consider two of the most widely used and frequently studied projective assessment methods (Piotrowski & Belter, 1999): the Rorschach Inkblot Test and the Thematic Apperception Test.

The Rorschach Inkblot Test

The prototypic example of a projective personality test is the **Rorschach Inkblot Test,** developed by Swiss psychiatrist Hermann Rorschach in 1921. Indeed, as Hunsley and Bailey (1999) state, the Rorschach Inkblot Test "has the dubious distinction of being, simultaneously, the most cherished and the most reviled of all psychological assessment instruments" (p. 266). Rorschach experimented with a large number of inkblots, which he administered to different psychiatric groups and later to different groups of normals (e.g., scholars, artists). He then selected those cards and those response characteristics

TABLE 9.3
The Five Major Subtypes of Projective Techniques and Two Examples of Each Subtype

Subtype	Examples	Description
Association	*Rorschach Inkblot Test* (Rorschach, 1921)	Respondents are shown 10 symmetrical inkblots, 5 in black-and-white and 5 in color, and are asked to say what each inkblot looks like to them
	Hand Test (e.g., Wagner, 1962)	Respondents are shown various pictures of moving hands, and are asked to guess what each hand "might be doing"
Construction	*Draw-A-Person Test* (Machover, 1949)	Respondents are asked to draw a person on a blank sheet of paper, and are then asked to draw another person of the opposite sex from the first person
	Thematic Apperception Test (Morgan & Murray, 1935)	Respondents are shown pictures of ambiguous social situations and are asked to tell a story concerning the characters in each picture
Completion	*Washington University Sentence Completion Test* (Loevinger, 1976)	Respondents are presented with various incomplete sentence stems (e.g., "If my mother . . .") and are asked to complete each stem
	Rosenzweig Picture Frustration Study (Rosenzweig, Fleming, & Clark, 1947)	Respondents are shown cartoons of various frustrating situations (e.g., being accidentally splashed with water by a passing car) and are asked how they would respond verbally to each situation
Arrangement/ Selection	*Szondi Test* (Szondi, 1947)	Respondents are shown photographs of individuals with different psychiatric disorders, and are asked which patients they most and least prefer
	Luscher Color Test (Luscher & Scott, 1969)	Respondents are asked to rank order different colored cards in order of preference
Expression	*Projective puppet play* (e.g., Woltmann, 1960)	Children are asked to play the roles of other individuals (e.g., mother, father) or themselves using puppets
	Handwriting analysis (see Beyerstein & Beyerstein, 1992, for a review)	Individuals are asked to provide spontaneous samples of their handwriting

Note: From Lilienfeld, Wood, & Garb (2000).

that distinguished between groups. This process seems like an early example of the empirical keying method used in the selection of items for the MMPI—Rorschach selected those stimuli that did the best job in distinguishing between groups of people that were known to differ on certain characteristics. However, Rorschach's use of this approach was not empirical in that he did not collect and examine the data in a quantitative manner (Anastasi, 1997). Rorschach selected 15 cards for use in his test, but because his publisher did not have the funds to reproduce all 15 inkblots in the first edition of *Psychodiagnostik,* only 10 cards were published. These 10 cards

are used today. Five of the cards are achromatic (i.e., shades of gray and black), and five are chromatic (i.e., cards that include color). An inkblot similar to one of the Rorschach cards is presented in figure 9.2.

The use of these inkblots as a psychological test was profoundly affected by Rorschach's death due to complications of an appendicitis at age 38, only one year after he published his only major work on his approach to their use. As a consequence of his untimely death, it was up to others to expand on the use of Rorschach's method, resulting in the development of several competing approaches. In the 1930s and 1940s

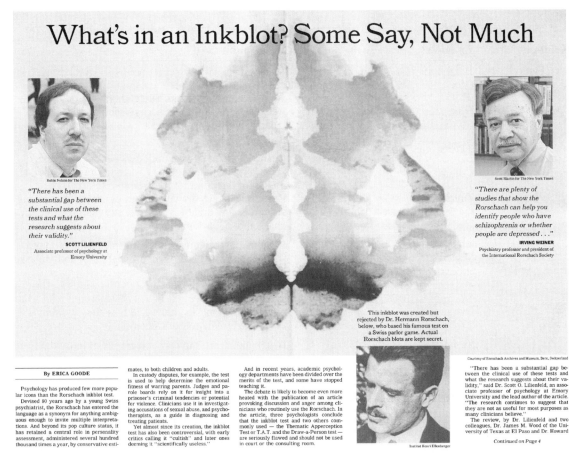

What's in an Inkblot? Some Say, Not Much

"There has been a substantial gap between the clinical use of these tests and what the research suggests about their validity."

SCOTT LILIENFELD
Associate professor of psychology at Emory University

"There are plenty of studies that show the Rorschach can help you identify people who have schizophrenia or whether people are depressed . . ."

IRVING WEINER
Psychiatry professor and president of the International Rorschach Society

This inkblot was created but rejected by Dr. Hermann Rorschach, below, who based his famous test on a Swiss parlor game. Actual Rorschach blots are kept secret.

Courtesy of Rorschach Archives and Museum, Bern, Switzerland

By ERICA GOODE

Psychology has produced few more popular icons than the Rorschach inkblot test. Devised 80 years ago by a young Swiss psychiatrist, the Rorschach has entered the language as a synonym for anything ambiguous enough to invite multiple interpretations. And beyond its pop culture status, it has retained a central role in personality assessment, administered several hundred thousand times a year, by conservative estimates, to both children and adults.

In custody disputes, for example, the test is used to help determine the emotional fitness of warring parents. Judges and parole boards rely on it for insight into a prisoner's criminal tendencies or potential for violence. Clinicians use it in investigating accusations of sexual abuse, and psychotherapists, as a guide in diagnosing and treating patients.

Yet almost since its creation, the inkblot test has also been controversial, with early critics calling it "cultish" and later ones deeming it "scientifically useless."

And in recent years, academic psychology departments have been divided over the merits of the test, and some have stopped teaching it.

The debate is likely to become even more heated with the publication of an article provoking discussion and anger among clinicians who routinely use the Rorschach. In the article, three psychologists conclude that the inkblot test and two others commonly used — the Thematic Apperception Test or T.A.T. and the Draw-a-Person test — are seriously flawed and should not be used in court or the consulting room.

Institut Henri Ellenberger

"There has been a substantial gap between the clinical use of these tests and what the research suggests about their validity," said Dr. Scott O. Lilienfeld, an associate professor of psychology at Emory University and the lead author of the article. "The research continues to suggest that they are not as useful for most purposes as many clinicians believe."

The review, by Dr. Lilienfeld and two colleagues, Dr. James M. Wood of the University of Texas at El Paso and Dr. Howard

Continued on Page 4

FIGURE 9.2
Clinical psychologists continue to disagree about the evidence for the reliability and validity of the Rorschach Inkblot Test, as evidenced by this February 20, 2001 *New York Times* article. (© 2001 *The New York Times Company, Reprinted by permission, Courtesy of Verlag Hans Huber.*)

five American psychologists—Samuel Beck, Marguerite Hertz, Bruno Klopfer, Zygmunt Piotrowski, and David Rapaport—developed methods for administering and scoring the Rorschach; these methods continue to be used to some degree today. All five of these approaches reflected psychoanalytic or psychodynamic assumptions regarding the nature of personality and the ways that internal dynamics are reflected in responses to the inkblots. They differed from one another, however, in the specifics of these assumptions and in how the test should be ad-

ministered and scored (none of the five systems used the same instructions to the respondent). Eventually, each system developed completely separate scoring procedures and nurtured separate groups of followers, leading to the fragmentation of the Rorschach as an assessment tool. Rather than a single test, during the decades following its inception the Rorschach came to be at least five different "tests."

Adding to this confusion are the results of a survey conducted by Exner and Exner (1972) indicating that 22 percent of clinicians had abandoned scoring altogether and that most of these respondents used their own personalized scoring rules, based on some combination of the five systems. Whereas some clinicians used the Rorschach as a perceptual-cognitive task, others used it as a "stimulus-to-fantasy" task (Erdberg, 1990). The perceptual-cognitive approach to the use of the Rorschach assumes that the task of the respondent is to organize his or her response to an ambiguous stimulus. The way that the individual goes about this task is presumed to be representative of the way that she or he responds to ambiguous stimuli in daily life, and the content of the response is secondary to the perceptual or structural aspects of the response. In contrast, the stimulus-to-fantasy approach is more consistent with the projective hypothesis: The person projects his or her inner need states onto the ambiguous blot in a symbolic fashion. The content of the response is interpreted as a symbolic representation of inner dynamics. Most of the scoring procedures that have been developed for the Rorschach include aspects of both these approaches.

To the extent that there is a standard procedure for the administration of the Rorschach, it is this: First the cards are presented to the subject in a set order and the individual is instructed to tell the examiner what he or she sees, what each card looks like or what the blot might be. The examiner is expected to record each response verbatim, although this task proves to be a very difficult one and is often not followed in clinical practice. Second, after responses to all 10 cards have been obtained, the examiner returns the first card to the respondent and asks him or her to explain the basis for each response—what made it look that way? The examiner records these responses as well, including what part or parts of the card were used in generating the response and what features of the blot (e.g., form, color, location) were important in forming the percept, or response.

Although systems for scoring the Rorschach differ in their specifics, the most common fea-

tures of responses that are coded and scored are *Location, Determinants, Content,* and *Popularity.* Location refers to the part of blot to which the respondent associates each response, which can include a portion or all of the inkblot—whether the respondent used the whole blot or only a part of the blot in forming her or his response. The Determinants of the response ("what made it look like a fox?") include the form or shape of the inkblot ("because it is the shape of a fox"), color ("because it has these two red eyes"), shading or variations of black and gray ("because this part looks like gray fur"), and the perception of movement in the stimulus ("it looks like the fox is running"). Scoring of the content of the response, or *what* the person sees, varies from one scoring system to another but often includes scores for the presence of human figures, human details (parts of human beings such as head, hands), animal figures, animal details (parts of animal figures), anatomical diagrams, inanimate objects, clouds, plants, maps, blood, sexual objects, and symbols. Finally, the popularity of responses is scored based on the relative frequency of different responses among people in general, that is, on the base rate of the response.

Many people who are unfamiliar with the Rorschach believe that the content of the responses is the most important aspect of the test—people who are disturbed or distressed see bizarre content in the Rorschach, which gives the clinical psychologist information about their diagnosis. So, for example, Allison (our 17-year-old case with bulimia nervosa) would be expected to see food or vomit on the Rorschach cards, giving the clinician insight into her eating disorder. In fact, that doesn't happen. Content is rarely used as a primary scoring indicator for the Rorschach.

One reason that we minimize the importance of content on the Rorschach, as well as on other projective tests, involves what Chapman and Chapman (1969) termed **illusory correlation.** Chapman and Chapman found that clinicians tend to rely on intuitive (but incorrect) associations to the Rorschach blots in making their interpretations. So, for example, a patient who saw eyes on the Rorschach blots would be described as suspicious or paranoid, and a patient who saw guns might be characterized as having violent tendencies. Although these interpretations seem credible, there is no empirical link between this content and these interpretations. People find it difficult to avoid making interpretations on the basis of illusory correlations, even when they are asked to be especially careful not to do so (Waller & Keeley, 1978) and particularly when they are trying to process a lot of information (Lueger & Petzel, 1979). Indeed, interpretation of content on projective tests, rather than a reliance on more empirically justified scoring criteria, contributes to the advantage of statistical method over clinical judgments in predicting behavior (e.g., Grove, Zald, Lebow, Snitz, & Nelson, 2000; Meehl, 1986).

The most ambitious effort to provide a comprehensive and psychometrically sound system for scoring and interpreting the Rorschach is the work of **John Exner** in developing the Comprehensive System for the Rorschach (e.g., Exner, 1978, 1986, 1993; Exner & Weiner, 1982). Exner's Comprehensive System emphasizes the structure of responses more than their content and utilizes the proportions and combinations of responses rather than single scores. Exner provided detailed rules for administering, scoring, and interpreting the Rorschach. He also provided a set of response norms for children and adults from both clinical and nonclinical populations, although there have been concerns expressed both that these norms overestimate the degree of maladjustment in the population (Wood, Nezworski, Garb, & Lilienfeld, in press) and that they are inappropriate for use with minority groups (Dana, 2000).

The results of Exner's efforts have met with mixed reviews. On the one hand his work is hailed as bringing order to the chaotic state of Rorschach administration and scoring that had existed previously (e.g., Anastasi, 1997). Indeed,

in 1998 the Board of Professional Affairs of the American Psychological Association commended Exner for his work on the Rorschach. On the other hand, critics have contended that the Exner's Comprehensive System still does not meet the standards for adequate reliability and validity (e.g., Lilienfeld et al., 2000; Wood, Lilienfeld, Garb, & Nezworski, 2000; Wood et al., 1996). These critics maintain that neither the inter-rater reliability nor the incremental validity of Exner's comprehensive system has been adequately demonstrated, that the clinical interpretations that are generated from specific patterns of responses have not been supported by research, and that much of the research that is purported to provide the basis for the system is unpublished and unavailable for examination by other researchers (see Lilienfeld et al., 2000). The criticisms of the Exner system have been most pointed in regard to the Egocentricity Index (EGOI), the oldest clinical index in this scoring system. The EGOI is used in the Comprehensive System as a measure of self-focused attention and narcissism and is presumed to be useful in assessing narcissistic personality disorder and depression. Nezworski and Wood (1995) evaluated the evidence for the use of the EGOI to assess these disorders and concluded that the scale lacks sufficient reliability and validity for these purposes.

Despite Exner's efforts to bring some degree of standardization to the administration, scoring, and interpretation of the Rorschach, alternative approaches to the use of the test continue to proliferate. Stricker and Healey (1990) cited several different procedures for scoring and interpreting the Rorschach based on object relations theory. Blatt and his colleagues (e.g., Blatt, Brenneis, Schimek, & Glick, 1976; Blatt & Lerner, 1983) drew from developmental psychoanalysis and cognitive developmental psychology to construct the Developmental Analysis of the Concept of the Object Scale. Using a content approach to analyze Rorschach responses, Blatt's system assesses seven dimensions of object relations (e.g., motivation of action, object-action integration, nature of interaction). Inter-rater reliability typically falls between 80 percent and 90 percent for the scales. The scales have been shown to distinguish between normal and psychiatric populations and among some diagnostic groups as well (e.g., Blatt et al., 1976; Farris, 1988). A second procedure, the Mutuality of Autonomy Scale (MOAS), was developed by Urist and colleagues based on the work of Kohut and of Kernberg reflecting self psychology, ego psychology, and object-relations theory. The MOAS focuses on the degree of the individual's separation-individuation from other people in the development of his or her identity or ego. Seven scales are scored in this approach, including reciprocity-mutuality, collaboration-cooperation, and anaclitic-dependent. Reliability is reported to be adequate—Urist (1977) reported inter-rater reliability scores ranging from .52 to .86 for the MOAS. Urist also reported construct validity based on correlations with autobiographical data and staff ratings of inpatients. In a study of a nonclinical child population, Ryan, Avery, and Grolnick (1985) reported significant correlations between grades and interpersonal functioning as measured by the MOAS and also provided evidence of discriminant validity of this measure. Finally, Strauss and Ryan (1987) used the MOAS to differentiate both restricting and bulimic anorexics from controls.

Based on data such as these, Stricker and Healey (1990) wrote:

> Considering the wide variety of approaches reviewed here, what can be concluded about the assessment of object-relations phenomena? At present, there is no single comprehensive system or approach to the assessment of object-relations phenomena, nor is there ever likely to be one . . . this is because different theoretical orientations have different conceptions of object-relations phenomena . . . The lack of a single system is not to be seen as a problem or a weakness of the tests but rather as a reflection of the diversity of theoretical interpretations of the construct relations. (p. 226)

After more than 80 years of use and thousands of studies, the controversy over the use of the Rorschach continues to rage. Dozens of reviews have summarized research on the Rorschach. Whereas some reviewers have concluded that the Rorschach is sufficiently reliable and valid for use in research and clinical practice (e.g., Hiller, Rosenthal, Bornstein, Berry, & Brunell-Neuleib, 1999; Parker et al., 1988), others have concluded that the systems currently available for scoring and interpretation of the Rorschach do not meet minimal criteria for reliability and validity (e.g., Wood et al., 1996, 2000). Still others take a middle ground, suggesting that some Rorschach variables are reliably related to the identification of some forms of psychopathology, most notably schizophrenia and borderline personality disorder (Lilienfeld et al., 2000). How can this unsettling state of affairs continue after so much effort has been put into scrutinizing this test? How can experts disagree so dramatically? It appears that the continued disagreement about the status of the Rorschach is based on differences in standards regarding what constitutes adequate reliability and validity, on differences between how the Rorschach is used in research and how it is used in clinical practice, and in part, on differences in the theoretical orientations of research psychologists and practicing psychologists who use the Rorschach Inkblot Test in their clinical practice.

The Thematic Apperception Test

Although the **Thematic Apperception Test** (TAT) is a projective test in the same broad sense that the Rorschach is, it presents more highly structured stimuli and requires more complex and meaningfully organized verbal responses (Anastasi, 1997). The respondent is presented with a series of pictures and is asked to create a story about each picture. Interpretation of the responses is usually based on a rather qualitative content analysis. Developed by Henry Murray and his colleagues at the Harvard Psychological Clinic (Murray, 1938, 1943), the TAT consists of 31 cards containing vague pictures in black and white and one blank card. Murray believed that the TAT is a "method of revealing to the trained interpreter some of the dominant drives, emotions, sentiments, complexes, and conflicts of personality. Special value resides in its power to expose underlying inhibited tendencies which the subject is not willing to admit, or cannot admit because he is unconscious of them" (Murray 1943, p. 1). He chose the term *apperception* rather than *perception* precisely because he believed that respondents actively interpret the TAT stimuli in accord with their personality traits and drives (Anderson, 1999).

Usually only 8 to 12 of the 31 cards are administered to a respondent, selected on the basis of the person's presenting problem. The respondent is asked to make up a story to fit the picture on each card, telling what led up to the event shown in the picture, describing what is happening in the moment and what the characters are thinking and feeling, and giving an outcome for this scene. An example of a TAT card is presented in figure 9.3. The following are Murray's (1943) original instructions to the respondent:

> This is a test of imagination, one form of intelligence. I am going to show you some pictures, one at a time; and your task will be to make up as dramatic a story as you can for each. Tell what has led up to the event shown in the picture, describe what is happening at the moment, what the characters are feeling and thinking; and then give the outcome. Speak your thoughts as they come to your mind. Do you understand? Since you have fifty minutes for ten pictures, you can devote about five minutes to each story. Here is the first picture (p. 3).

The examiner records the individual's complete responses for later scoring. Each response is interpreted by determining who the "hero" is in the story—the character of either sex with whom the respondent has presumably identified. The original scoring system then continued to analyze content in terms of the 17 needs from Murray's model of personality. Anastasi (1997) reports that normative data have been accumulated and structured scoring systems that achieve adequate reliability have been developed, but

FIGURE 9.3

An example of a card from the Thematic Apperception Test (TAT). *Reprinted by permission of the publishers from Henry A. Murray,* Thematic Apperception Test, *Cambridge, Mass: Harvard University Press, Copyright 1943 by the President and Fellows of Harvard College, 1971 by Henry A. Murray.*

they are sufficiently cumbersome that examiners most often use their own subjective norms and standards. In fact, most clinicians also vary the methods of administration and the number, sequence, and types of cards that they give (Keiser & Prather, 1990), and only 3 percent report using any standardized scoring system (Pinkerman, Haynes & Keiser, 1993). As you can imagine, such an approach to testing is highly problematic because it is impossible to evaluate the reliability and validity of the scoring and interpretation methods used by individual examiners in clinical practice. As Ryan (1985) stated, "Practitioners interpreting the TAT are likely to use different systems, an idiosyncratic combination of systems, or no system at all. This is the bane of the psychometrician, and it also suggests that in common usage the interpretation of the TAT is based on strategies of unknown and untested reliability and validity, a potentially dangerous outcome" (p. 812).

Several scoring systems have been developed for the TAT. Bellack (1993), for example, rates each story on several scoring categories, including unconscious structure and drives of the subject, relationship to others, significant conflicts, defenses used, and ego strength. Westen and his colleagues (e.g., Westen, 1991; Westen, Lohr, Silk, Gold, & Kerber, 1990) have developed a scoring system for the TAT designed to assess object relations, that is, respondents' mental representations of other people. Westen assesses four dimensions of object relations: complexity of representations of people, affect-tone of relationships, capacity for emotional investment in relationships and moral standards, and understanding of social causality. As Lilienfeld et al. (2000) note, however, various studies examining Westen's system have used different TAT cards, making comparisons across studies difficult. Nevertheless, this system may be useful in distinguishing individuals who are diagnosed with borderline personality disorder from both nonpsychiatric controls and individuals with other forms of psychopathology (e.g., Ackerman, Clemence, Weatherill, & Hilsenroth, 1999; Westen et al.).

The most extensive research on the TAT, spearheaded by McClelland and Atkinson in the 1960s and 1970s, utilized a subset of the original TAT cards to measure Murray's (1938) **need for achievement,** or power motivation (e.g., McClelland, 1985; McClelland, Atkinson, Clark, & Lowell, 1976). McClelland and Atkinson defined achievement, or power motivation, as needs for power and to have an impact on or to affect other people. Individuals who are high in achievement motivation are typically assertive, argumentative, and competitive; they tend to collect prestige items or join organizations in order to have an enhanced sense of interpersonal impact (McClelland). McClelland was also interested in affilia-

tion motivation, defined as a strong need to be accepted by and to be around other people. Individuals who score high in affiliation motive want to be friendly with and liked by others, not as a means to an end, as is the case with people high in achievement motivation, but as an end in itself. A series of studies by Jemmott, McClelland, and their colleagues has focused on the association of power motivation with two important and highly objective external criteria: cardiovascular dysfunction and immune function. McClelland and Jemmott (1980) found that college students high in power motivation had greater self-reported illness than did students high in affiliation motivation. To examine the underlying biological processes that could contribute to differential illness rates among people who differ in power and affiliation motivation, McClelland, Alexander, and Marks (1982) focused on salivary immunoglobulin A (S-IgA), a measure of immune function that reflects susceptibility to disease. Using a sample of male prison inmates, McClelland et al. found that high power motivation was related to lower S-IgA. This finding could have considerable practical significance, because S-IgA reflects hormonal immune function and is the body's first line of defense against many forms of infection.

Jemmott and his colleagues expanded this research by focusing on natural killer cell activity, a measure of cell-mediated immunity. Natural killer cell activity reflects the extent to which natural killer cells destroy target cells. Natural killer cells act without prior sensitization and appear to be an important component of the body's defense against many viruses and neoplasms. Jemmott et al. (1990) assessed levels of power motivation and affiliation motivation based on responses to four pictures from the TAT in samples of college students, middle-class men, and patients at a health maintenance organization. Importantly, their results indicated that whereas power motivation, as assessed by response to the TAT, was associated with relatively low natural killer cell activity, affiliation motivation was related to higher natural killer cell activity.

Similar research was reported by McKay (1991), who exposed subjects to a film that aroused feelings about relationships and then measured responses to TAT-like pictures on the Affiliative Trust-Mistrust scale. McKay conceptualized this scale as measuring aspects or qualities of object relations and their associations with immune function (S-IgA concentration). He found that subjects who produced benevolent descriptions in response to the TAT pictures had increases in their immune function after viewing the film, whereas those who described negative relationships had decreases in their immune function. In general, McKay found that high Mistrust scores based on the TAT responses were significantly associated with poorer immune functioning.

Research linking TAT responses to parameters of immune function is important for two reasons. First, these studies provide evidence for the link between emotional factors and the body's resistance to disease. This association underscores the likelihood that psychological factors play a role in the onset, course, or recovery from infectious diseases. Second, these studies provide evidence for the association between responses to a projective test and hard, objective, external criteria. That is, they suggest that if a projective test such as the TAT can be scored in a reliable manner, it can prove to be a valid predictor of external criteria that are clear and observable. More research of the type carried out by Jemmott and McKay is needed to provide a clear scientific basis for the use of projective tests in making predictions to highly specific somatic and behavioral criteria.

In sum, as Lilienfeld et al. (2000) note, there is modest support for the construct validity of a number of TAT scoring themes, particularly those assessing object relations and need for power, achievement, and affiliation. There are also unresolved issues, however, concerning the appropriateness of the TAT for clinical use. Even with the most reliable of the TAT scoring systems, there are typically not adequate norms available to compare respondents with the profiles of individuals from different diagnostic groups or from different cultural groups (Hibbard et al., 2000). Moreover, there are other measures that assess object relations and achievement or affiliation motivation (e.g., Barends, Westen, Byers, Leigh, & Silbert, 1990; McClelland, 1961). It is not clear, therefore, that the TAT is necessary to assess these constructs.

Other Projective Methods

A number of other projective tests and methods are available to psychologists. Perhaps not surprisingly, the use of these tests, like the Rorschach and the TAT, is also characterized by controversy. For example, having individuals draw human figures has a long history as a projective technique. Like other projective tests, the **projective drawing test** has its basis in psychoanalytic theory: It represents indirect access to the person's unconscious personality characteristics and conflicts. There are several versions of projective drawing tests, including the Draw-A-Man test (Goodenough, 1926), later revised by Harris (1963) and again by Naglieri (1988). Machover (1949) developed the Draw-A-Person test, and Buck (1948) extended the required drawings in his House-Tree-Person test. Hulse (1951) developed the Draw-A-Family test, which was used by Burns (1987) as the basis of the Kinetic Family Drawing test, in which the family is to be drawn "doing something." In all these versions, the individual is required to draw one or more people (and a house and tree in the House-Tree-Person test), and the drawings are interpreted by the clinician.

The reliability and validity of drawing techniques are hotly debated, with advocates contending that "figure drawing tests have enormous potential that should be cultivated" (Riethmiller & Handler, 1997, p. 460), and critics arguing that the drawing test "more properly belongs in a museum chronicling the history of simple-minded assessment practices" (Gresham, 1993, p. 185). Despite this controversy, projective drawings were the second most popular tests used in clinics and hospitals in the 1950s (Sundberg, 1961), and even today surveys indicate that projective drawings are among the top 10 most frequently administered tests (e.g., Piotrowski & Zalewski, 1993; Watkins, Campbell, Nieberding, & Hallmark, 1995). In their recent comprehensive review, Lilienfeld et al. (2000) described the scientific status of scores derived from human figure drawings as "weak." They reported that although test-retest reliabilities are sometimes high, there is considerable variability across studies. Moreover, there is no consistent association between scores on figure drawings and aspects of personality and psychopathology. Finally, Lilienfeld et al. describe evidence indicating that experts in the interpretation of drawings are less accurate in differentiating normal from abnormal children than are individuals without any psychological training.

Another projective test that is frequently used is the Sentence Completion Test. Although there are many different versions of sentence completion tests, the most commonly used are Rotter's (1954; Lah & Rotter, 1981) Incomplete Sentences Blank and the Washington University Sentence Completion Test (Loevinger, 1998). Sentence completion tests are somewhat more structured than the Rorschach, TAT, and figure drawing tests. Respondents are simply asked to complete sentence stems such as "I wish _____," "My mother _____," "I hate _____," and "Most women _____." Proponents of sentence completion tests contend that the tests help clinicians identify individuals' problems, symptoms, and attitudes through the content of their responses. Critics, of course, argue that interpretation of sentence completion tests is subjective and unreliable. It is interesting to note that sentence completion tests are among the least disguised, or most direct, of the projective tests; therefore, it is possible that the information gleaned from these tests could have been obtained more simply from direct questioning of the respondent. Nevertheless, sentence comple-

tion tests are used in clinical practice. Holaday, Smith, and Sherry (2000) recently surveyed psychologists who were members of the Society for Personality Assessment and reported that the most common reasons for using a sentence completion test were "(a) to use it as part of an assessment battery . . . , (b) to determine personality structure . . . , and (c) to elicit quotable quotes" (p. 371).

ISSUES IN THE CLINICAL USE OF PERSONALITY TESTS

Uses of Personality Tests

How are personality tests used by psychologists in clinical practice? It is important to point out that the models of personality and the scales that are generated by some of the measures (e.g., the Big Five dimensions of personality) do not correspond to the categories in the *DSM* used to classify various forms of psychopathology. And even those measures that do yield labels that bear some relationship to diagnostic categories do not necessarily correspond to the *current* system of psychiatric classification. For example, the MMPI-2 scale labels do not match the diagnostic categories in *DSM-IV*. Given this situation, can personality tests be used to diagnose individuals?

The answer to this question is a qualified "yes." While individual scales do not correspond to distinct diagnostic categories, it is possible to compare the overall test *profile* obtained by an individual to norms generated from samples of patients with different diagnoses. Thus, knowing that an individual obtained a profile on the MMPI-2 similar to that obtained by patients diagnosed with bulimia nervosa gives the clinician some confidence that his or her client may warrant the same diagnosis (see figure 9.1 for the MMPI-2 profile of Allison, which matches the MMPI-2 profile generated by patients with bulimia nervosa, e.g., Cumella, Wall, & Kerr-Almeida, 2000; Lipson, Stevens, Graybill, & Mark, 1995).

But testing has other goals besides diagnosis. Having a client complete the NEO-PI-R may offer the clinician important information concerning the client's emotional and interpersonal functioning and can identify the client's emotional strengths and weaknesses. As long as the objective or projective personality test that is being used has incremental validity with respect to the purpose it is intended to serve, the information it yields will be of use to the clinician.

Ethics and Testing

Psychologists have been administering, scoring, and interpreting tests for over 80 years. During this time **ethical principles** have evolved in the interest of protecting the client and maintaining an appropriate professional relationship between the client and the psychologist. The American Psychological Association has recently revised its Ethical Principles of Psychologists and Code of Conduct (American Psychological Association [APA], 1992), and according to some psychologists, this revision is the most significant revision in a decade (e.g., Keith-Speigel, 1994). The new code of conduct requires that clinical psychologists be formally trained in the use of assessment instruments and should only use those techniques or procedures that are within their competence. Acquiring competence generally entails pursuing graduate coursework in clinical psychology combined with appropriate supervised experience. Although most publishers of testing materials ask to see proof of the educational degree and licensure status of psychologists who request copies of tests, these qualifications alone do not guarantee competence in psychological testing (Butcher & Rouse,

1996). Clearly, therefore, although the revised ethical principles represent an important step, there is still much work to be done to ensure that all tests are administered in an ethical manner.

Test Bias

The revised APA code of ethics now also carries a mandate for psychologists to use assessment procedures that are appropriate to an "individual's gender, age, race, ethnicity, national origin, religion, sexual orientation, disability, language, or socioeconomic status" (APA, 1992, p. 1603). The possibility of **test bias** in psychological testing, particularly with respect to cultural, ethnic, and minority groups, has a long and controversial history. Many psychological tests have been criticized on the grounds of being heavily biased in favor of individuals from European American, middle-class samples. As we saw in chapter 8, this controversy has raged most vehemently in the area of intelligence testing. Nevertheless, personality tests have not remained unscathed. For example, as Groth-Marnat (1997) observed, some populations of African Americans have obtained significantly higher scores than European Americans have on the MMPI scales F, 8, and 9, and it is not at all clear how these differences should be interpreted. Initial reports offered substantive interpretations to these MMPI differences, but psychologists later found that the differences were eliminated when African Americans and European Americans were comparable in age, education, and other relevant characteristics (Timbrook & Graham, 1994). These findings clearly suggest that differences on at least some of the test scores are due to factors such as socioeconomic status rather than to ethnicity.

SUMMARY AND CONCLUSIONS

Personality testing remains a major activity for clinical psychologists. In this chapter we described two broad categories of personality tests: objective tests and projective tests. Objective personality tests use structured stimuli and require a limited range of responses. Projective tests, in contrast, use unstructured or ambiguous stimuli and allow a virtually unlimited range of responses.

The most frequently used objective personality test is the MMPI-2. This questionnaire, now built on a foundation of more than 10,000 research articles, is generally used by matching the profile of scale scores generated by a client with the scale scores of a large, normed sample. The MMPI-2 is likely to continue to serve as the benchmark against which all other personality tests are measured. The most commonly used projective tests are the Rorschach Inkblot Test and the Thematic Apperception Test. These tests do not have the strong empirical foundation that characterizes the MMPI-2, but despite perennial predictions of their forthcoming demise, they continue to be used in clinical practice.

We concluded the chapter by discussing issues in the clinical use of personality tests. We noted here that although tests do not often map easily onto *DSM-IV* diagnostic categories, there are other goals of personality testing, including identifying individuals' emotional strengths and weaknesses and describing their emotional and interpersonal functioning. We outlined ethical issues regarding personality testing and highlighted the importance of being aware of potential biases in personality tests when they are used with individuals who do not come from a European American, middle-class background.

KEY TERMS AND NAMES

Empirical keying
Ethical principles
John Exner
Five-Factor Model of Personality
Starke Hathaway
Illusory correlation
Charnley McKinley
MMPI-2
MMPI-2 clinical scales
MMPI-2 validity scales
Need for achievement

NEO-PI-R
Objective personality tests
Personality
Profile analysis
Projective drawing tests
Projective personality tests
Rorschach Inkblot Test
Test bias
Test standardization
Thematic Apperception Test
Traits

RESOURCES

Books
Anastasi, A. (1997). *Psychological testing* (7th ed.). Upper Saddle River, NJ: Prentice-Hall.
Dana, R. H. (Ed.). (2000). *Handbook of cross-cultural and multicultural personality assessment.* Mahwah, NJ: Lawrence Erlbaum.

Groth-Marnat, G. (1997). *Handbook of psychological assessment* (3rd ed.). New York: John Wiley.
Journals
Assessment
Psychological Assessment
Journal of Personality Assessment

CHAPTER TEN

BEHAVIORAL ASSESSMENT: MEASUREMENT OF BEHAVIOR, COGNITION, AND PSYCHOPHYSIOLOGY

INTRODUCTION

"How often do you force yourself to vomit?" It seemed like such a simple question to Allison when the psychologist asked it. But she couldn't give an easy answer. She felt so ashamed about her binge eating and vomiting that she tried to forget each episode as soon as it happened. "I honestly don't know," she responded. "Maybe a couple of times a week." This answer led to an even more challenging question from Dr. Marcus: "And what do you think leads to your binge eating and vomiting? What seems to set off an episode?" Allison had no reply. She began to cry as she sensed how much these behaviors were out of her control, even out of her own awareness.

In the previous four chapters, we described various approaches used by clinical psychologists to assess intelligence, psychopathology, and personality. In this final chapter in the assessment section of the book, we discuss a fundamentally different approach to assessment in clinical psychology: behavioral assessment. Traditional approaches to assessment, particularly personality and intelligence assessment, are based on the assumptions that much of human behavior is characterized by enduring traits and that these traits (and accompanying problematic behaviors) are influenced by underlying psychological processes such as needs and drives or by genetic or biological factors that are often outside the individual's awareness. These assumptions about the nature of intelligence and personality led to the development of intelligence tests and objective and projective personality tests, which were designed to measure intelligence and personality as enduring characteristics of individuals. Projective personality tests, in particular, focused on the assessment of "internal" processes. Responses on these tests were considered to be *signs* of underlying psychological processes, and the clinician made inferences about the traits beneath the signs.

In contrast, behavioral assessment makes no assumptions about the existence of traits, enduring characteristics of people, or underlying intrapsychic phenomena. Rather, behavioral assessment focuses on obtaining *samples* of behavior; there are no inferences about traits beneath the behavior. In this approach, behavior is viewed as resulting from a combination of an individual's learning history and current environmental conditions that are maintaining the behavior (or preventing its occurrence). Consequently, behavioral assessment focuses primarily on observable behavior and its context, that is, on preceding events and environmental consequences of the behavior.

Behavioral assessment is concerned with precisely what people do and with the situational determinants, or **contextual determinants,** of the behavior. Behavioral assessment evolved from learning theories of behavior. As we discussed in chapter 4, operant and classical conditioning theories focus on environmental conditions that are linked to specific behaviors—conditions that precede the behavior and conditions that follow it. Behavioral assessment is based directly on behavioral theory: For example, if anxiety is conceptualized as a classically conditioned response to specific stimuli in the environment (e.g., Mineka & Zinbarg, 1996), then assessment of anxiety will focus both on observable behaviors that comprise anxiety (e.g., trembling, sweating, rapid breathing, avoidance of feared stimuli) and on the specific conditions in the environment that elicit or reinforce an anxious response (e.g., exposure to certain stimuli or situations such as heights, public speaking, or germs; reinforcements gained from avoiding particular situations). (See the accompanying cartoon.) The results of a comprehensive behavioral assessment, perhaps more than the results of any other form of assessment, have direct implications for how therapy will be conducted with the client.

HISTORY AND FOCUS OF BEHAVIORAL ASSESSMENT

From the 1920s through the 1950s, psychological assessment was dominated by the use of objective and projective personality tests. Psychologists used these tests to understand the motives and instincts underlying an individual's functioning. The emergence in the 1950s of behavioral models of psychopathology and the development of the first treatment methods based on theories of learning represented the first serious challenge to the use of personality tests. An important event in the emergence of behavioral assessment came with the publication in 1968 of a now-classic book by psychologist **Walter Mischel,** *Personality and Assessment.* Mischel attacked the very existence of personality traits and, consequently, the need to assess them. Mischel offered three main reasons to explain psychologists' continued belief in the existence and structure of personality traits:

THE FAR SIDE® By GARY LARSON

Behavioral assessment involves the measurement of behaviors and environmental factors through direct observations. (*Source:* The Far Side® by Gary Larson © 1986 FarWorks, Inc. All Right Reserved. Used with permission.)

1. Our language is replete with terms that describe behavior as stable and traitlike, and traits are a fiction based on biases in our language.
2. Consistency of behavior is not due to internal characteristics of individuals but rather to consistency in features of the environment and in the person's societal roles.
3. Our strong need to see the behavior of others as predictable leads us to infer the presence of traits.

Mischel's powerful arguments highlighted difficulties with the trait view of personality and psychopathology and contributed to the emer-

gence of behavioral methods as a viable alternative approach to clinical assessment. We should point out here that Mischel's criticisms of traits and personality assessment have been tempered considerably in recent years. Indeed, Mischel now acknowledges that there is consistency in people's behavior across a range of situations (e.g., Mischel & Shoda, 1995). Moreover, as behavioral theories evolved, behavioral assessment increasingly expanded beyond its initial exclusive focus on overt behaviors and came to consider and integrate other aspects of individuals' functioning, such as cognitions, feelings, and psychophysiology (e.g., Bandura, 1997; Lazarus, 1973, 1989; Mahoney, 1989).

In sum, although early forms of behavioral assessment focused solely on the observation of overt behaviors and the evaluation of environmental contingencies that may be maintaining the behavior, more contemporary forms of behavioral assessment take a considerably broader perspective. As we will see throughout this chapter, behavioral assessment now includes, in addition to different types of observations of overt behavior, such methods as self-reports, ratings by significant others, diaries of thoughts and feelings, and assessment of psychophysiological responses to environmental stimuli.

GOALS OF BEHAVIORAL ASSESSMENT

There are four major goals of behavioral assessment:

1. identification and operationalization of problem behaviors and of the contextual variables that are controlling or maintaining the behavior
2. evaluation of the relationship between the problem behaviors and the controlling variables
3. design of an appropriate treatment based on the results of the behavioral assessment
4. evaluation of the effectiveness of the treatment

The first goal is to complete a detailed assessment of the client's problem behaviors and of the environmental or contextual factors that may be eliciting or reinforcing these behaviors. The second goal is to identify and evaluate the nature of the relationship between the problem behaviors and the controlling variables. We will describe these two goals in detail in the sections that follow. The third and fourth goals underscore the strong link between assessment and treatment from a behavioral perspective. As Peterson and Sobell (1994) point out, behavioral assessment is regarded by behavioral scientists as the cornerstone of treatment. From a behavioral perspective, assessment and treatment are interrelated processes: Assessment should lead to treatment decisions, which should be evaluated as treatment progresses. Moreover, some information may not be available or accessible before the start of treatment and may need to be assessed during the treatment process. Because we discuss behavioral approaches to treatment in detail in chapter 14, we will spend less time in this chapter on the third and fourth goals.

Identifying and Operationalizing Problem Behaviors and Contextual Variables

The first goal of behavioral assessment is to identify precisely and to quantify the client's problem behaviors and the environmental variables that are controlling the behaviors. These descriptions are known as **operational definitions** of the problem behaviors and controlling factors (Haynes & O'Brien, 2000). In a behavioral assessment the clinician will attempt to quantify, or measure, behaviors and situational variables along a number of dimensions. These dimensions most often include ratings of magnitude, or intensity (e.g., how anxious does Phillip become before having to make a presentation; how sad does Maria feel when she is alone in her house), and frequency and duration (e.g., how many times per week does Allison binge and purge; how many times per day, and for how

long, is Jason out of his seat inappropriately in class). The clinician will also attempt to quantify possible controlling variables in the environment. Thus, for example, is Jason's out-of-seat behavior followed consistently by attention from the teacher? Does Phillip's anxiety lead him to cancel presentations and avoid speaking in front of others? Does Maria's depression result in an increase in the number of visits she receives from friends? Is Allison receiving support and acceptance from her peers because of her bulimic behaviors?

Evaluating the Relationships Among the Problem Behaviors and the Contextual Variables

Once the problem behaviors and the possible controlling factors have been identified and operationalized, the clinician must assess the nature of the relationship between these two sets of variables. This assessment will provide information about the function of the behavior—what purpose does the behavior serve in terms of the contextual variables, and how do the situational variables function to exert control over the behavior? Behavioral assessment methods are designed to identify the covariations between changes in stimulus conditions and changes in behavior. The information obtained from this assessment is critical in developing an intervention that will be effective in altering the frequency of the problematic behavior.

The evaluation of the function of behaviors and situational variables is known as a **functional analysis of behavior** (Haynes & O'Brien, 2000). In a functional analysis, the clinician identifies significant, controllable, and causal functional relationships between specified target behaviors and situational characteristics. Functional analysis is also referred to as establishing the ABCs of behavioral assessment, that is, identifying *A*ntecedents, *B*ehaviors, and *C*onsequences. Importantly, functional analysis of behavior helps clarify the nature of the relation between assessment and intervention. In this sense, behavioral assessment is clearly utilitarian—identifying precisely both behaviors that need to be changed and environmental contingencies that must be altered to achieve these changes is directly relevant to the development of an effective intervention.

Before we describe the various methods of behavioral assessment, we should say a few words about the nature of the relation between behavioral assessment and the *DSM* taxonomy. Initially, the strict behavioral approach to assessment stood in stark contrast to the nature and structure of the *DSM*. Whereas behavioral assessment was concerned with discrete behavior and environmental contingencies that maintained the behavior, the early versions of the *DSM* stemmed from a psychiatric nosology that was based largely on psychoanalytic or psychodynamic theories of psychopathology (see chapter 5). The most recent revisions of the *DSM,* however, now include clear, operationally defined criteria for many disorders, and behavioral assessment can be used to identify and evaluate these criteria in individual patients. Moreover, as we described in chapter 5, the focus of Axis IV on specific psychosocial stressors is consistent with the emphasis of behavioral assessment on environmental factors.

In fact, because of the growing influence of *DSM-IV,* many behavioral assessment methods have now been designed to assess specific *DSM* diagnoses. Behavioral assessment techniques have been developed for adult diagnostic categories such as anxiety disorders (Beck & Zebb, 1994), depression (Persons & Fresco, 1998), eating disorders (Kerwin, Ahearn, Eicher, & Burd, 1995), and addictive behaviors (Stasiewicz, Carey, Bradizza, & Maisto, 1996); and for childhood disorders, including attention deficit/hyperactivity disorder (Willcutt, Hartung, Lahey, Loney, & Pelham, 1999) and conduct disorder (Donohue, Van Hasselt, Hersen, & Perrin, 1998). For example, the results of a structured diagnostic interview may indicate that a young adoles-

cent meets *DSM-IV* criteria for a conduct disorder (e.g., lying, stealing, destroying property, frequent fighting). Identification of this general pattern of behaviors (or syndrome) offers important information about the scope of this adolescent's behavior problems. Nevertheless, it is important to realize that a *DSM* diagnosis does not provide information about when and under what conditions these specific behaviors occur (Kazdin, 1994). Behavioral assessment is designed to provide this detailed level of information about the circumstances that are associated with, that might control, the adolescent's lying, cheating, and destructive behaviors.

We will now consider several methods of behavioral assessment, including behavioral interviewing, naturalistic and analog behavioral observation, self-monitoring, the use of rating scales, cognitive-behavioral assessment, and psychophysiological assessment.

METHODS OF BEHAVIORAL ASSESSMENT

A wide range of methods and measures has been developed for use in behavioral assessment. These methods and measures can be implemented across the age range from children to adults and can be used to examine different areas of functioning (e.g., classroom performance, marital communication, psychopathology, social skills, psychophysiological functioning; Bellack & Hersen, 1998; Craighead, Craighead, Kazdin, & Mahoney, 1994). Assessment information can be drawn from different sources, including observations by clinicians or other trained observers, reports by the clients themselves, and ratings by significant others (e.g., parents, spouses, teachers). Information can also be obtained about behavior in different settings (e.g., home, school, work, community). Regardless of the specific method or measure that is used, however, or the particular area of functioning that is assessed, a critical distinguishing feature of this approach is the emphasis on samples of behaviors (or cognitions, or physiology) that occur in specific situations. In the following sections we will describe three broad classes of behavioral assessment methods: behavioral interviewing, behavioral observation, and self-report inventories.

Behavioral Interviewing

In chapter 7 we described various approaches to interviewing, including the use of structured diagnostic interviews. In contrast to many forms of interviewing in clinical psychology, **behavioral interviewing** is used to obtain information that will be helpful in formulating a functional analysis of behavior (Haynes & O'Brien, 2000). That is, behavioral interviews focus on describing and understanding the relationships among antecedents, behaviors, and consequences. Behavioral interviews tend to be more directive than other, nonbehavioral interviews, allowing the interviewer to obtain detailed descriptions of the problem behaviors and of the patient's current environment. Kratochwill (1985) suggests that behavioral interviews follow a four-step problem-solving format:

1. problem identification, in which a specific problem is identified and explored and procedures are selected to measure target behaviors
2. problem analysis, conducted by assessing the client's resources and the contexts in which the behaviors are likely to occur
3. assessment planning, in which the clinician and client establish an assessment plan to be implemented, including ongoing procedures to collect data relevant to assessment and intervention
4. treatment evaluation, in which strategies are outlined to assess the success of treatment, including pre- and postassessment procedures.

Thus, behavioral interviewing focuses not only on obtaining information within the interview session, but also on making plans to obtain information on behavior outside the interview, in the environment in which the behavior naturally occurs.

One important reason that behavioral interviews are more directive than most other kinds of interviews is that clients will often describe their difficulties in trait terms. That is, they will speak of being "anxious," or "depressed," or "angry." The behavioral clinician must then work with the client to translate these broad terms into more specific and observable behaviors. For example, "being anxious" may mean breathing rapidly, sweating profusely, experiencing an increase in heart rate, having cognitions about danger and threat, and avoiding specific types of situations. In the following example, the interviewer helps quantify a client's difficulties in behavioral terms:

Interviewer: It sounds like you have been having difficulty in a number of areas, but your conflicts with your roommate are the most trouble right now.

Client: Yes, he's inconsiderate and I can't stand being around him.

Interviewer: I'd like to ask some more questions about what happens when you are the most bothered about it. Can you pick a particular disagreement and tell me how you felt at the time?

Client: He really pissed me off when I came in last night and wanted to go to sleep. He wouldn't turn the TV off, and I couldn't sleep with the light and the noise.

Interviewer: How angry were you? Can you rate it from 1 to 10, with 10 being the most angry you've ever been?

Client: I guess about a 6. What does that matter?

Interviewer: Well, I'm wondering if you also felt anything else, like tension, nervousness, anxiety, apprehension? If so, how much?

Client: I was tense, too. About a 6, I guess. We don't really talk much except about the TV and superficial things about school.

Interviewer: When do you feel the most angry, and also the most tense? For example, when you were walking into the room, before? After he didn't turn down the TV?

Client: I was getting tense coming into the room, thinking what a drag this roommate situation was, and then when he kept watching TV, I was so angry I couldn't sleep. (Adapted from Sarwer & Sayers, 1998, p. 70)

As this example makes clear, the client and therapist will work together to describe and understand the problem behaviors, where and when they occur, and the impact that they have on the client's relationships. The information obtained in a behavioral interview should be helpful to the clinician both in generating hypotheses about what specific behaviors or contextual factors to target in an intervention and in developing further plans for additional behavioral assessment procedures, such as direct observation or self-monitoring.

An excellent example of behavioral interviewing is found in the work of psychologist **Russell Barkley** and his colleagues, who have developed extensive interview protocols for use in the behavioral assessment of attention deficit/hyperactivity disorder, or ADHD (e.g., Barkley, 1998; Barkley & Murphy, 1998). One portion of the interview generates information on the nature of specific parent-child interactions that are related to the defiant and oppositional child behaviors often associated with ADHD. The interviewer reviews a series of situations that are frequent sources of problems between children and parents and solicits detailed information about those situations that are particularly problematic (see table 10.1). For example, parents may report that their child has temper tantrums, during which the child cries, whines, screams, hits, and kicks. A behavioral interview will be used as a first step in determining precisely what these behaviors look like when they occur, in which situations the behaviors occur (e.g., while the parent is on the telephone, in public places, at

Russell Barkley, Ph.D., is a clinical psychologist at the University of Massachusetts Medical School. Dr. Barkley has demonstrated the important role that clinical psychologists can play in increasing our understanding of Attention Deficit/Hyperactivity Disorder. He has made major contributions to the assessment and treatment of this disorder. *(Photo courtesy of Russell Barkley.)*

bedtime), and in which situations they do not occur (e.g., when the child is playing alone, playing with other children, at mealtimes). Additional information is then sought regarding the sequence of events, including the behaviors of the parents and the child, that unfold during a tantrum. This type of situationally focused interview provides a detailed picture about how the parent perceives the antecedents and consequences that surround the child's problematic behaviors. In box 10.1 we describe the results of a behavioral interview with the mother of Jason, one of the cases we presented in chapter 1.

In sum, behavioral interviewing is the first step in conducting a comprehensive behavioral assessment of a problem behavior and the contextual variables that may be controlling the behavior. A behavioral interview is more direct than are unstructured clinical interviews and focuses explicitly on the occurrence (or

TABLE 10.1

Parental Interview Format for Assessing Child Behavior Problems at Home and in Public

Situations to be discussed with parents	*If* a problem, follow-up questions to ask

General—overall interactions
Playing alone
Playing with other children
Mealtimes
Getting dressed in the morning
During washing and bathing
While parent is on telephone
While watching television
While visitors are in the home
While visiting others' homes
In public places (supermarkets,
  shopping centers, church, etc.)
While mother is occupied with
  chores or activities
When father is at home
When child is asked to do chores
At bedtime
Other situations
	1. Is this a problem area? If so, then proceed with questions 2–9.
	2. What does your child do in this situation that bothers you?
	3. What is your response likely to be?
	4. What will your child do in response?
	5. If the problem continues, what will you do next?
	6. What is usually the outcome of this situation?
	7. How often do these problems occur in this situation?
	8. How do you feel about these problems?
	9. On a scale of 1 to 9 (1 = no problem; 9 = severe problem), how severe is this problem to you?

Note: From Barkley, R. A. (1998). *Attention deficit hyperactivity disorder: A handbook for diagnosis and treatment* (2nd ed.). New York: Guilford Press.

BOX 10.1

JASON, AGE 8: BEHAVIORAL ASSESSMENT OF ATTENTION DEFICIT/HYPERACTIVITY DISORDER AND OPPOSITIONAL DEFIANT DISORDER

"His teacher says he's hyperactive; that he has an attention deficit disorder. The guidance counselor thinks he should be on medication. I don't know what to think anymore." The psychologist listens patiently as Mrs. Newman relates the problems she is having with her 8-year-old son. She reports that she feels overwhelmed by his behavior, unable to manage him or get him to comply with the simplest request. She is afraid that he will be expelled from school if his problems continue to escalate, and as a

working single parent she is at a loss for how to care for him if he is not in school.

As you will recall from information presented in chapters 1 and 5, an initial intake interview was conducted with Jason and his mother, and it was followed by a structured diagnostic interview to determine whether he meets criteria for a *DSM-IV* diagnosis. Based on the results of the diagnostic interview with his mother, it was established that Jason meets criteria for attention deficit/hyperactivity dis-

BOX 10.1 (continued)

order–combined type (ADHD) and oppositional defiant disorder. Establishing these diagnoses was an important step in gaining an understanding of Jason's problems; a diagnosis, however, does not provide details concerning the specific aspects of Jason's behavior that are most problematic, when these problems occur, and how others in his environment respond. To obtain this type of detailed understanding of Jason's behavior, the psychologist turns to methods of behavioral assessment.

The first step in conducting a behavioral assessment of Jason involves administering a behavioral interview to Mrs. Newman. Following a structured interview protocol developed by Russell Barkley, one of the leading experts in the assessment and treatment of ADHD, the psychologist asks Mrs. Newman a series of questions about specific situations to determine whether Jason's behavior is a problem at these times (Barkley & Murphy, 1998). These situations include when Jason gets up in the morning, at meals, when she is talking on the telephone, when Jason is asked to do his homework, when he is asked to do chores around the house, when they are in the car, when they out in public, and at bedtime. Mrs. Newman indicates that Jason is most difficult for her to manage whenever she asks him to comply with a request; she reports that Jason refuses to obey her and that the more she demands that he cooperate, the angrier and more oppositional he becomes.

To gain a comprehensive picture of the types of problem behaviors that Jason exhibits at home and at school, the psychologist asks Mrs. Newman to complete the Child Behavior Checklist (CBCL; Achenbach, 1991) and sends a copy of the Teacher Report Form (TRF; Achenbach, 1991) to Jason's teacher for her to complete. Once these forms are completed, the psychologist scores them by computer and is able to compare the responses of Jason's mother and his teacher to those of more than 1,000 mothers and teachers of boys Jason's age. The results are analyzed in terms of a profile of eight problem syndromes (see figure 10.1 for a presentation of Mrs. Newman's responses on the CBCL). Mrs. Newman's mother's responses to the CBCL place Jason in the clinical range (greater than 98 percent of

the normative sample of boys) on the Attention Problems and Aggressive scales. The responses of his teacher on the TRF corroborate Mrs. Newman's responses, placing Jason in the clinical range on the Attention Problems and Aggressive scales. In addition, however, the teacher's responses also place Jason in the clinical range on the Withdrawn and Social Problems scales. This pattern of results indicates that Jason exhibits consistent problems related to inattention, overactivity, impulsivity, aggression, and noncompliance both at home and at school. Jason also appears to have significant problems in peer relationships at school, and he is withdrawn and sullen in class.

The psychologist wants to obtain more information on the nature and severity of Jason's problems with inattention and impulsivity. He has Jason respond to a series of tasks on the Gordon Diagnostic System (GDS), one of several standardized continuous performance tasks that are available for the assessment of ADHD symptoms (Rielly, Cunningham, Richards, Elbard, & Mahoney, 1999). This computerized test presents the child with a series of standardized tasks, including a measure of sustained attention. The child views a series of random numbers that flash on the computer screen and is instructed to press a button every time she or he sees a *1* followed by a *9*. It is possible to make two types of errors on this task: error of omission (failing to press the button when the target sequence *1, 9* has occurred), and errors of commission (pressing the button when the target sequence *1, 9* did not occur). A child who has difficulty sustaining attention is more likely to commit errors of omission. Jason scores very poorly on this test and, in fact, commits an extremely high number of omission errors, indicating that he failed to accurately monitor the sequence of numbers as they appeared on the computer.

The information obtained through these methods has provided a more detailed picture of Jason's problem behaviors than would be possible through a sole reliance on interviews or broad questionnaires. It is apparent that Jason is noncompliant with his mother in most situations and that she is not able to exert even minimal control over his behavior. The results of Jason's performance on the GDS, along with his

BOX 10.1 (concluded)

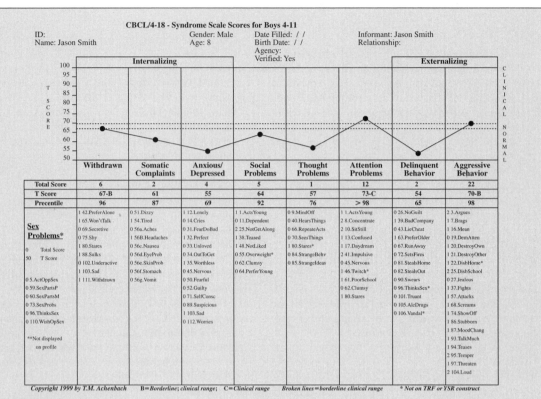

FIGURE 10.1
Jason's mother's report of his behavioral and emotional problems on the Child Behavior Checklist (CBCL).

performance on the Freedom from Distractibility scale on the WISC-III (see chapter 8) provide direct evidence of his problems in sustaining attention on tasks that require concentration. Finally, it is clear that Jason is experiencing difficulties involving noncompliance and lack of concentration both at home and at school; the test results indicate further that Jason is also experiencing problems with his peers at school and a tendency to withdraw from those around him.

The psychologist will use the information about the specific problem behaviors that were identified through this behavioral assessment to develop a treatment program for Jason. We will describe this program in detail in chapter 14.

nonoccurrence) of specific behaviors. It is important to point out that, despite the relatively narrow focus of the behavioral interview, we know little about its reliability and validity. In fact, there is evidence indicating that behavioral interviews are only moderately reliable (Haynes & O'Brien, 2000; Nezu, Ronan, Meadows, & McClure, 2000; F. E. Wilson & Evans, 1983). Therefore, although we clearly need further research to understand and increase the reliability and validity of behavioral interviews, it is important to use other behavioral assessment methods to supplement the information obtained through the behavioral interview.

Behavioral Observation

The most fundamental method of behavioral assessment involves the direct observation of behavior. **Behavioral observation** allows the psychologist to document the frequency and intensity of specific behaviors as well as contextual variables that may be eliciting and maintaining the behaviors. This dual focus on behavior and the environment permits an examination of the situational antecedents and consequences of the problem behavior. Behaviors can be observed either in the environment in which they naturally occur (e.g., home, work, school) or in simulated (analog) situations created in the psychologist's office or laboratory. Moreover, behaviors can be observed by trained raters or by observers who are typically present in the client's natural environment (e.g., family members, teachers, co-workers, nursing staff, etc.).

Defining the Behavior   Regardless of where the behavior is observed and by whom it is observed, it is critical that the target behaviors be carefully selected and operationalized. In selecting the behaviors to be observed, every effort should be made to ensure that the observers do not need to make inferences about the behavior. Thus, yelling, hitting, striking, and pushing can be observed and rated; it is more difficult to rate "anger." Similarly, speaking out of turn, getting out of seat, fidgeting in the chair can be observed and rated; "poor attentional control" is too abstract a term and is clearly more difficult to rate. In general, the behavior and the context need to be defined in such a way that two observers rating the same behavior will exhibit high inter-rater reliability, thereby demonstrating that the behavior has been adequately operationalized.

In choosing and defining a behavior to be observed, it is helpful to be aware of Lindsley's (1968) discussion, over 30 years ago, of the **"dead man test."** Lindsley pointed out the importance of selecting an active behavior as a target for change. As Lindsley said,

How many experts, people who have never really tried to count behavior, have sat up here and looked at seas of behaving organisms from university towers? Many of these people will advise you to record behavior that isn't behavior—that doesn't pass the movement cycle test. They say record school phobia. Well, that doesn't even pass the dead man test. So don't try to teach a child something that the dead do better.

What do we mean? Let's be very specific. A teacher decides to record number of minutes spent doing arithmetic. She's going to count how often the clock goes around while Billy is in arithmetic position. Could we have a corpse in arithmetic position? Of course! It wouldn't be very pleasant but we COULD do it. Now if the teacher pays Billy off for every ten minutes he's in arithmetic position, he may not be dead, but he may go into arithmetic position while he plots her destruction. You see, she thinks she's teaching arithmetic. She's not. She's teaching staying in arithmetic position. What Billy does in arithmetic position is up to HIM not HER.

We have Sandra, ten years old, and we say, "Go upstairs in your room and study for a half an hour before you go out and play." Does that pass the dead man test? No! Going upstairs does, yes, she'll go upstairs, and the dead won't, but "sit at your desk?"—the dead can sit at a desk in arithmetic position. Most experienced teachers know how to require a movement cycle. They say, "Go upstairs and study until you can bring me down 22 correct addition facts. When you have 22 correct, you can go out and play. And zip, zip, no child plots teacher's destruction in arithmetic position, they all add two plus two is four and three plus three is six. They come down and have two wrong, go back and make two right, and they're free to play. That's the difference. The dead man test will rule out recording non-behaviors. (Lindsley, 1968, pp. 6–7)

In sum, it is important that the behavior that is selected for observation is an active, rather than a passive, behavior.

Obtaining the Data: Strategies   Once the behaviors to be observed have been defined, the clinician must decide *how* the observations will be conducted. Clearly, it is not possible to observe all behavior all the time in all situations. A strategy must be developed that will "minimize costs and maximize representativeness, sensitivity, and reliability" of the data obtained through behavioral observation (Hartmann, 1984, p. 114). Behavior analysts have developed a number of different systems to observe, code, and record target behaviors. Two of the most commonly used systems are **interval recording** and **event recording.**

In interval recording, the clinician records whether or not the target behavior occurred within each of a number of specific time intervals. For example, a 15-minute observation period may be divided into 60 intervals of 15 seconds. For each interval, the observer codes whether the behavior occurred or not. Interval recording is most appropriate when the target behavior occurs with moderate frequency (e.g., once or more per minute) or when there are no clear beginning and end points for the behavior. For example, in coding social interaction for a child, an observer might rate for each 15-second interval whether the child was interacting with another person.

In contrast to interval recording, in which the units of measurement are time based, in event recording the observer records each discrete occurrence of a target behavior during the observation period. Thus, the occurrence of the behavior—rather than the end of a time interval—is the signal for the observer to make a rating. As you might expect, event recording is most appropriate for behaviors that have a distinct beginning and end, such as hitting, swearing, talking, and smoking. A clinician investigating a child's hyperactivity might, for example, use event recording to record each instance of the child's out-of-seat behavior that occurs during the observation period, say, between 10:30 A.M. and 11:30 A.M. It is important to recognize that event recording does not necessarily provide information about the environment or about responses to the behavior and so is difficult

to use when conducting a functional analysis of behavior.

Obtaining the Data: Locations   Once the target behaviors have been identified and the sampling method for data recording and collection has been selected, the next decision involves the setting in which the behavior will be observed. There are two broad choices here: Observe the behavior in a natural setting, or **naturalistic observation;** or observe the behavior in a more controlled setting like a clinic or laboratory, referred to as **analog observation.** These two types of settings have distinct advantages and disadvantages.

Naturalistic, or in vivo, observations generate information that has greater ecological validity because they reflect the ongoing conditions under which the behavior actually occurs. Naturalistic settings include school, home, and work and are effective when the behaviors to be observed occur with relatively high frequency. For example, a clinical psychologist might observe a socially withdrawn child on the playground; an adult with agoraphobia (fear of open spaces) as he leaves his house; or a client with acrophobia (fear of heights) as she climbs a fire escape (see figure 10.2).

There are several limitations to the use of naturalistic observation. For example, the presence of an observer or other recording methods (e.g., an audio or video recorder) may inadvertently affect the behaviors that are being observed. That is, people may react to the process of being observed by intentionally or unintentionally altering the frequency and magnitude of the target behavior (Christensen & Hazzard, 1983). Steps can be taken to try to reduce reactivity by making the observer less intrusive, by eliminating the cues that signal the collection of data, and by extending the number and length of data collection sessions and discarding the data from the initial observations. Direct observations are also often

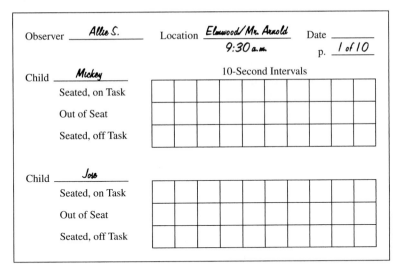

FIGURE 10.2
Naturalistic observation of behavior rating form.

very costly, because observers or measurement devices must be placed outside the clinic or laboratory. Finally, the psychologist does not have direct control over the contingencies in the natural environment, making it difficult to predict whether the behavior will occur during any single observational session.

Because of the difficulties and limitations of naturalistic observation, most behavioral assessments are conducted using some form of analog observation. Although they are obviously not as natural as in vivo assessments, analog observations allow the clinician to control the contextual factors and systematically examine their effects on the target behavior. There are several different kinds of analog assessment, ranging from the highly contrived settings used in conducting behavioral avoidance tests (see next paragraph) to the almost naturalistic research barroom settings used by Marlatt and Thomas and their colleagues to examine situational factors that affect alcohol intake (e.g., Nelson et al., 1998; Nelson, McSpadden, Fromme, & Marlatt, 1986) and to the living room settings used by Barkley to assess

the effects of Ritalin on interactions of hyperactive children and their families (e.g., Barkley, 1998; Barkley, Fischer, Newby, & Breen, 1988).

All analog observation settings are structured to permit a reliable assessment of the target behavior and an evaluation of the effects of controlling variables on the behavior. For example, a clinician may instruct a couple who present with complaints of marital distress to discuss a problem situation in front of her (or behind a one-way mirror) so that she may observe the sequence of negative comments and behaviors in the two spouses. Analog observation is frequently used in assessing behaviors associated with anxiety. For instance, in a version of the behavioral avoidance test, clients who present with specific phobias might be requested to approach the feared object (e.g., snake, mouse, spider) or to stay in the same room as the feared object while the assessor measures how close the client is able to approach the object or how long the client is able to stay in the room. In an analog observation of a client with obsessive-compulsive disorder that involves a fear of contamination combined with immediate hand washing, the clinician might bring together in a room a set of objects that the client would not want to touch (e.g., a particular doorknob, a small pile of dirt, a used book). The client would be asked to rate his discomfort in attempting to touch each object, and the clinician might measure how close the client could come in approaching each object and how long the client could refrain from washing his hands after touching the objects.

Analog observations have an advantage over naturalistic observations in that they are relatively cost effective. Analog methods are also useful in documenting the effectiveness of interventions, because they allow the clinician to quantify the target behaviors both pre- and post-treatment. Thus, in treating marital distress, the number of negative or hostile comments made by the spouses in an analog observation session prior to treatment can be compared to the same situation following treatment. It is important to be aware, however, that analog assessments are still subject to the reactive effects of observation. Furthermore, many of the important situations in which the target behaviors occur are impossible to represent accurately in the office or laboratory. For example, a child's noncompliance about bedtime or bathing is difficult to simulate in the office, as is a withdrawn adult's behavior at a social gathering. Despite these concerns, direct observations remain a cornerstone of behavioral assessment.

Self-Monitoring

In **self-monitoring,** clients are instructed to observe and record their own behavior as it occurs. This approach to behavioral assessment differs from the use of questionnaires, which typically require individuals to make retrospective ratings or judgments (e.g., "How often do you feel anxious?" "How many stressors have you experienced in the past month?"). Self-monitoring is particularly useful in obtaining information about the rate and magnitude of a behavior and the circumstances surrounding its occurrence in cases where the behavior occurs relatively infrequently and an observer cannot follow the subject around all day. For example, self-monitoring can be used effectively to assess frequency of smoking, rate and amount of alcohol intake, time spent studying, and similar behaviors. Self-monitoring has also recently been extended to include the client's observation and recording of his or her negative thoughts (e.g., Hollon, Haman, & Brown, in press), particularly in the behavioral assessment of anxiety and depression. As we describe in box 10.2, self-monitoring can be an informative assessment method in assessing Allison's problematic eating behaviors.

BOX 10.2

ALLISON, AGE 17:
BEHAVIORAL ASSESSMENT OF BULIMIA NERVOSA

We began this chapter with a segment from one of Allison's initial sessions with her psychologist, Dr. Marcus. During a previous session, Dr. Marcus had conducted a diagnostic interview with Allison and determined that she meets *DSM-IV* criteria for bulimia nervosa. Allison and Dr. Marcus are now faced with a dilemma. How can they measure a problem that Allison keeps hidden from everyone else, even

BOX 10.2 (continued)

her parents and her closest friends? Dr. Marcus has no reason to doubt Allison's report that she binges frequently on cookies, chips, and other fattening foods while she is alone in her room and then steals into the upstairs bathroom and forces herself to vomit. But Dr. Marcus needs to know more about Allison's bingeing and purging episodes: How often do they happen? When do they occur? What seems to set off an episode? And what happens afterward? These questions are at the heart of behavioral assessment, which focuses on the frequency and the context of specific behaviors. The private nature of these behaviors presents a problem, because Allison is the only person in a position to provide this information about her bingeing and purging. As we saw in the opening passages of this chapter, Allison reports that she cannot recall the details of these episodes, in part because of her feelings of embarrassment and guilt.

The solution to this problem lies in the use of self-monitoring methods to assess these behaviors. Dr. Marcus provided Allison with a form (see figure 10.3) developed by psychologist G. Terrance Wilson for monitoring binge-purge episodes (e.g., G. T. Wilson & Vitousek, 1999). Allison was instructed to record all food and liquids she consumed during the day, the time of day and location that she ate/drank, the circumstances (how she was feeling, what she was doing), and whether or not she purged or took laxatives after eating. Self-monitoring can be a reliable and valid method to assess behaviors as long as the specified behaviors are well-identified and the client is provided with a clear method for recording the behavior. As you can see from figure 10.3, Allison reported two binge episodes on this day. In both instances, she felt depressed and out of control. After completing the self-monitoring form for a week, Allison's records showed that she had binged at least twice each day; on one day she had four bingeing and purging episodes. Allison reported to Dr. Marcus that it was helpful to keep these records, because she had difficulty remembering when and what she had eaten until she began to write it down. On the other hand, she also disclosed that reading over the record

was upsetting, because it forced her to confront how frequent these episodes had become.

Dr. Marcus supplemented these self-monitoring records with additional behavioral assessment methods. Allison completed the Binge Eating Scale (BES; Gormally, Black, Daston, & Rardin, 1982) to provide a broader picture of her thoughts and feelings associated with her binge episodes. Questions on the BES are answered by selecting from four alternative responses on each question. For example, Question 11 is "(a) I usually am able to stop eating when I want to. I know when 'enough is enough;' (b) Every so often, I experience a compulsion to eat which I can't seem to control; (c) Frequently, I experience strong urges to eat which I seem unable to control, but at other times I can control my eating urges; (d) I feel incapable of controlling my urges to eat. I have a fear of not being able to stop eating voluntarily." This measure has been shown to be a reliable method of assessing attitudes and experiences related to binge eating. Allison scored very high on this scale and endorsed items indicating that she felt she could not control her eating.

Allison reported to Dr. Marcus that she was very concerned, even obsessed, about her weight. To obtain a better understanding of how Allison felt about her body and her weight, Dr. Marcus conducted the Body Dysmorphic Disorder Examination, a semi-structured clinical interview designed to diagnose body dysmorphic disorder and to measure symptoms of severely negative body image (Rosen & Reiter, 1996). This interview assesses preoccupation with and negative evaluation of appearance, self-consciousness and embarrassment, excessive importance given to appearance in self-evaluation, avoidance of activities, body camouflaging, and body checking. Allison's responses indicated that she was clearly self-conscious about her appearance, felt that she was overweight, spent a great deal of time looking at her body in the mirror in her room and checking the size of her thighs and other areas of her body, and avoided activities that would allow others to see her body (e.g., swimming, gym class).

BOX 10.2 (concluded)

DAILY FOOD RECORD

NAME___Allison_____   DAY____Tuesday_____   DATE____10/14_____

TIME	FOOD AND LIQUID CONSUMED	PLACE	MEAL (M) SNACK (S) BINGE (B) PURGE (V, L)	CIRCUMSTANCES
7:30am	2 cups of coffee with skim milk & equal half a bagel	on way to school	M	rushing, but feel okay- in control
1:00pm	1 pear	school	S	
3:30pm	large bag potato chips large blueberry muffin bag M&M's salad 4 slices bread 2 cereal bars peanut butter & jelly sandwich	room	B V	Just got home from school; hungry and anxious, feeling depressed and hopeless - why do I keep doing this to myself? I had tried so hard to be good about eating
11:00pm	3 slices bread 15 graham crackers raisins 1/4 jar peanut butter	room	B V	automatic - time of day already binged & purged earlier- still depressed; out of control
1:00am	15 pretzels 6 oz. Orange juice	room	S	woke up; felt empty after purges

FIGURE 10.3
Self-monitoring chart for Allison's eating behavior.

These behavioral assessment methods provided Dr. Marcus with important information that gave her a more comprehensive understanding of the nature of Allison's problem and that allowed her to develop a cognitive-behavioral treatment protocol to help Allison overcome these symptoms.

In self-monitoring procedures, as in other methods of behavioral assessment, the target behaviors and situational variables must be defined clearly so that it is easy for clients to make accurate observations and recordings of their behaviors. Even if the target behaviors are clearly defined, however, it is important that the therapist be aware of possible attempts by individuals to distort the record of their behavior, making themselves look either better or worse than is actually the case. Usually, this distortion will be evident through discrepancies between the self-monitoring record and the client's situation (e.g., recording a low caloric intake while continuing to gain weight). As you might expect, self-monitoring is usually based on event sampling; that is, clients record the behavior (smoking, drinking, eating, bingeing) when it happens rather than, say, each hour. Because clients are recording their behaviors, self-monitoring tends to increase their awareness of the situational factors that may be related to their behavior and facilitates the subsequent development of an effective treatment program (Haynes & O'Brien, 2000).

Rating Scales

Direct observation of behavior, either by external observers or by the client, represents one important approach in behavioral assessment. Nevertheless, because of the constraints that we have described in this chapter, these methods may not generate a sufficiently broad sample of a client's behaviors. In part to address this limitation, clinical psychologists have developed a number of **rating scales** and behavior checklists. These measures are intended to provide information on a wider range of an individual's behavior over a longer period of time than is possible with direct observation.

Rating scales have been developed to assess problem behaviors in children, adolescents, and adults. The importance of assessing the behavior of children and adolescents in their natural environments is widely recognized (e.g., Franz & Gross, 1998; Silverman & Serafini, 1998). Children's behavior may differ in critical ways depending on whether they are at home, at school, alone, or with peers, and it is important to obtain samples or reports of their behaviors in these different settings. It is also important that ratings of children's behavior be obtained from different people, or informants, in the children's lives, most typically from parents, teachers, and peers. In fact, numerous studies have found only modest levels of agreement among different informants with respect to ratings of the children's behavior (e.g., McAuley, 2000; Mitsis, McKay, Schulz, Newcorn, & Halperin, 2000), and only modest agreement between the informants and the children themselves (e.g., Achenbach, Mc-Conaughy, & Howell, 1987; DiBartolo, Albano, Barlow, & Heimberg, 1998; see Modestin & Puhan, 2000, for similar findings with adult psychiatric patients). These findings highlight the importance of situational factors in rating chil-

dren's behavior and underscore the need for assessments in different contexts. The findings also indicate that different informants may offer unique perspectives or judgments regarding children's behavior.

A number of different rating scales have been developed to assess problem behaviors in children and adolescents (e.g., the Revised Behavior Problem Checklist, Quay, 1983; the Revised Conners Parent Rating Scale, Conners, Sitarenios, Parker, & Epstein, 1998; the Conners/Wells Adolescent Self-Report of Symptoms, Conners et al., 1997; the Sutter-Eyberg Student Behavior Inventory, Rayfield, Eyberg, & Foote, 1998). The most widely used rating system for child and adolescent psychopathology, however, are the checklists developed by Achenbach and his colleagues (e.g., Achenbach, 2000; Wadsworth, Hudziak, Heath, & Achenbach, 2001). This system empirically integrates data obtained from parents (the Child Behavior Checklist or CBCL), teachers (the Teacher Report Form or TRF), and adolescents (the Youth Self-Report; see box 10.1 for a description of how the Achenbach checklists were used in the behavioral assessment of Jason). Indeed, as we described in chapter 5, Achenbach has utilized data from these three groups of informants in generating an empirically based taxonomy of child and adolescent psychopathology (e.g., Achenbach, 1995).

Rating scales have also been developed to assess behavior problems in adults. Typically, ratings on these scales are made on the basis of information collected during an interview with the client. While some rating scales focus on a particular disorder (e.g., the Hamilton Rating Scale for Depression, Hamilton, 1967; the Yale-Brown Obsessive-Compulsive Scale, Goodman et al., 1989), other scales are broader (e.g., the Brief Psychiatric Rating Scale, Overall & Gorham, 1962; the Global Assessment Scale, Endicott, Spitzer, Fleiss, & Cohen, 1976). For example, interviewers using the Yale-Brown Obsessive-Compulsive Scale (e.g., Halmi et al., 2000) are required to make a rating from 0 to 4, indicating the client's level of distress or impairment around obsessions and compulsions. Similarly, interviewers who rate clients on the Hamilton Rating Scale for Depression rate several depressive symptoms, such as insomnia, depressed mood, and behavioral slowness, on 3- to 5-point scales. As is the case with most rating scales, the total score of all items can be used as an index of the severity of the particular disorder.

In part because they focus so explicitly on behaviors, all these rating scales have sound psychometric properties. Both the child and the adult measures have good internal consistency and test-retest reliability. As we noted earlier, there is not always perfect agreement among informants for the child rating scales. Consequently, Achenbach and McConaughy (1997) have formulated a decision tree, or flowchart, for assessors to follow based on the rating scale responses of different informants (see figure 10.4). Currently, these behavioral rating scales are used more frequently in clinical research than they are in clinical practice (Silverman & Serafini, 1998), but as more data accrue, demonstrating the scales' utility in formulating effective treatment plans, this situation should change.

Cognitive-Behavioral Assessment

The early development of behavioral assessment was characterized by strong adherence to the principles of radical behaviorism, which meant an exclusive focus on overt behavior and observable external events. Internal events, including thoughts and unobservable aspects of emotions, were viewed as hypothetical constructs that were irrelevant to the task of developing a scientific understanding of behavior and behavior change. As we noted earlier in this chapter, behavioral theories slowly began to recognize the importance of other aspects of individuals' functioning. In particular, a growing body of research was demonstrating a strong association between behavior and cognitions (e.g., Bandura, 1986;

Gotlib & Hammen, 1992). An important consequence of this demonstration was that behavioral procedures began to be applied to the assessment of cognitions, leading to the development of cognitive-behavioral assessment.

Linscott and DiGiuseppe (1998) describe four broad categories of methods that are used to assess cognitions. *Expressive methods* require the client to think aloud while he or she is performing a task, for example, imagining participating in a social interaction. Thus, the psychologist tries to access the client's thoughts directly as they occur. A promising adaptation of this procedure is the Articulated Thoughts in Simulated Situations paradigm developed by Davidson and his colleagues (Davidson, Navarre, & Vogel, 1995). In this task clients listen to brief audiotapes that are relevant to their problems and then verbalize their thoughts when the tape stops. *Production methods* require clients to record their thoughts about a particular event. This assessment procedure is widely used in cognitive therapy to identify dysfunctional or maladaptive cognitions that clients have about events that happen in their lives. Clients are encouraged to keep a record of events and their thoughts about the event (see figure 10.5).

Inferential methods for measuring cognitions are used most often in research rather than in clinical practice. These methods attempt to assess cognitive schemas, or expectancies that guide the client's perceptions and interpretations of experiences in his or her environment. Cognitive schemas are hypothesized to function outside the individual's awareness, which makes them particularly difficult to measure. Such inferential methods as the Stroop color naming task and the self-referential encoding task (Gotlib & Neubauer, 2000) are promising in delineating schematic functioning in clients who are experiencing depression and anxiety, but these procedures have yet to be incorporated into clinical practice. Finally, *endorsement methods* are those that present the individual with a predetermined set of items (written statements on a

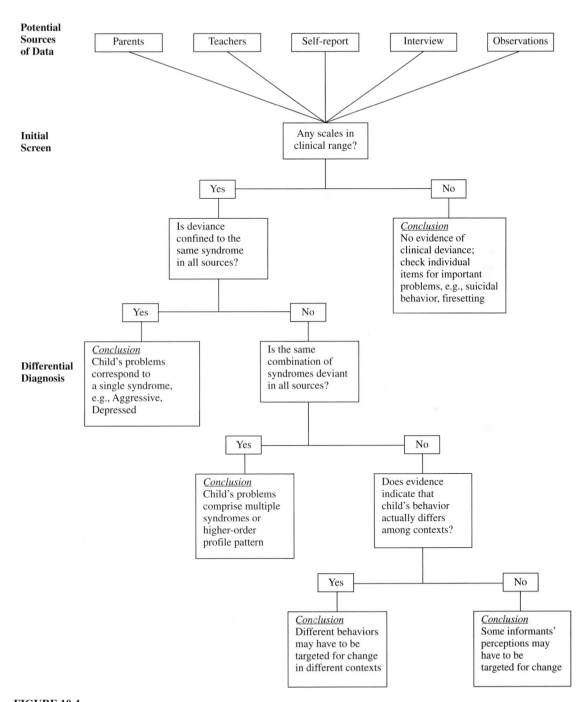

FIGURE 10.4
Flow chart for making clinical decisions based on checklist ratings of children's behavioral and emotional problems.

DATE	EMOTION(S) What do you feel? How bad was it (0-100)?	SITUATION What were you doing or thinking about?	AUTOMATIC THOUGHTS What exactly were your thoughts? How far did you believe each of them (0-100%)?	RATIONAL RESPONSE What are your rational answers to the automatic thoughts? How far do you believe each of them (0-100%)?	OUTCOME 1. How far do you now believe the thoughts (0-100%)? 2. How do you feel (0-100)? 3. What can you do now?
Sat.	Sad 80 Empty 80 Guilty 90	Evening out with ex-husband	We're never going home together again, because of the stupid way I've handled my life. Things are never going to be as good again. I don't deserve any happiness because of the hurt I've caused him. 90%	There's nothing I can do to alter what has happened in the past. 100% There is no point dwelling on what might have been. 70% I don't know that things will never be as good again because I can't see into the future. 90% I'm still young and there are lots of people in my situation who end up having a happy life and do lots of things they never would have done if things hadn't changed. 75% In fact, the future could be better for me than the past—if I'm honest with myself, the marriage just wasn't working out for either of us. 70%	1. 60% 2. Sad 50 Empty 50 Guilty 70 3. Don't dwell on the past. Put your energy into planning future pleasures.

FIGURE 10.5
Daily record of dysfunctional thoughts diary for the assessment of depression.

questionnaire) and ask the client to rate each statement in terms of its applicability. Endorsement methods have been used to assess a broad range of functioning. This category of assessment methods is often referred to as *questionnaire assessment,* or as assessment by *self-report inventories.*

Endorsement methods for the assessment of cognitions are likely the most widely used assessment procedure in clinical practice. Questionnaire and self-report measures of cognitions differ significantly in two important ways from the more rigidly "behavioral" assessment measures that we have discussed in this chapter. First, rather than focusing on specific, overt behaviors, self-report measures of cognition are typically more global and also assess clients' attitudes and emotions. And second, rather than assessing behaviors as they occur (as is the case with direct observation and self-monitoring), self-report measures of cognitions are typically retrospective accounts that are summed over relatively long periods of time, usually days or weeks (e.g., "I tend to think about negative things").

Despite these important departures from strict behavioral assessment procedures, self-report inventories continue to be developed and widely used (Linscott & DiGiuseppe, 1998). As Groth-Marnat (1997) observed, many of these inventories have poor, or even nonexistent, psychometric properties (i.e., reliability and validity), and very few have normative data. Nevertheless, there are a number of self-report inventories that do have acceptable psychometric properties. To assess cognitive aspects of depression, for example, psychologists use such scales as the Automatic Thoughts Questionnaire (Hollon & Kendall, 1980), the Dysfunctional Attitudes Scale (Weissman & Beck, 1978), and the Explanatory Style Questionnaire (Buchanan & Seligman, 1995). To assess anxiety disorders, clinicians frequently administer the Fear Questionnaire (Marks & Mathews, 1979) and the Anxiety Sensitivity Index (Reiss, Peterson, Gursky, & McNally, 1986). And assessment of eating disorders includes the use of the Eating Disorder Inventory-2 (Garner, 1991), the Eating Disorder Examination Questionnaire (Wilfley, Schwartz, Spurrell, & Fairburn, 1997), and the Binge Eating Scale (Gormally et al., 1982).

Psychophysiological Assessment

In addition to measuring overt behavior in the form of actions, behavioral assessment can also include **psychophysiological assessment,** or the measurement of psychophysiological reactions to situational demands. *Psychophysiology* refers to responses or reactions by the body that are governed by the sympathetic and parasympathetic portions of the autonomic nervous system (ANS), (Haynes, 1991; Sturgis & Gramling, 1998). These responses include heart rate, blood pressure, respiration, skin conductance, muscle tension, and electrocortical activity. Changes in these physiological response systems are an important source of information about an individual's psychological adjustment or functioning.

A fundamental principle of psychophysiology is that social, behavioral, cognitive, and emotional reactions are intimately tied to physiological processes (Haynes, 1991). Therefore, psychophysiological assessment is a natural extension of assessments in other areas of people's functioning. Indeed, Ax's (1953) pioneering demonstration that fear and anger were characterized by different patterns of physiology paved the way for assessments of emotional states to move beyond questionnaires and include psychophysiology. We now know that the ANS is highly reactive to environmental events. As individuals become aroused, for example, the changes in their ANS are reflected by changes in heart rate, respiration, skin conductance, and so on. Consequently, psychophysiological assessment can provide important information about a person's internal state (Miller & Kozak, 1993).

Psychologists have shown a growing interest in utilizing psychophysiological assessment in their understanding of different forms of psy-

chopathology and behavioral problems. For example, physiological assessment has been used extensively in the evaluation and treatment of sexual disorders (e.g., Freund & Watson, 1991). Investigators are also utilizing psychophysiological assessments in the study of anxiety, both in children (Waters, Lipp, & Cobham, 2000) and adults (Wilken, Smith, Tola, & Mann, 2000), and in understanding the emotional dysregulation in depression (e.g., Marshall & Fox, 2000; Rottenberg, Gross, Wilhelm, Najmi, & Gotlib, 2001). Finally, psychophysiological assessment has been used in studies of patterns of marital interaction and divorce. Gottman and his colleagues (e.g., Gottman & Levenson, 1992; Levenson, Carstensen, & Gottman, 1994) have found that husbands who report being dissatisfied in their marriages have higher levels of physiological arousal during interactions with their spouses than do more satisfied husbands, even though this arousal is not apparent in their verbal behavior. Gottman also found that this pattern of psychophysiological functioning predicts subsequent divorce, underscoring the importance of psychophysiological assessment in understanding behavior.

BEHAVIORAL ASSESSMENT OF SPECIFIC DISORDERS

The use of behavioral assessment methods is best exemplified by considering the techniques that are used to assess specific problems or disorders. We will consider two disorders that have a high prevalence rate, that offer a broad range of techniques in their assessment, and that involve both adults and children: anxiety disorders and attention deficit/hyperactivity disorder.

Behavioral Assessment of Anxiety Disorders

The behavioral assessment of anxiety disorders utilizes multiple methods to obtain different types of information. McGlynn and Rose (1998) suggest that the responses recorded during the behavioral assessment of anxiety occur in three domains: verbal reports, motor acts, and physiological events. In the sections that follow, we will describe procedures for the assessment of anxiety that include all three of these domains.

Interviews   The first step in the behavioral assessment of anxiety begins with the use of a structured diagnostic interview to evaluate the client according to *DSM-IV* criteria (Street & Barlow, 1994). A structured interview is used to distinguish among the various types of anxiety disorders, including social phobia, panic disorder, agoraphobia, generalized anxiety disorder, and obsessive-compulsive disorder. More specialized interviews such as the Anxiety Disorders Interview Schedule–Revised (DiNardo & Barlow, 1988) and the more recent Anxiety Disorders Interview Schedule for *DSM-IV* (Brown, DiNardo, & Barlow, 1994) are used to obtain more detailed information about the history and course of the disorder, the client's methods for coping with anxiety, and the client's level of avoidant responding (Street & Barlow, 1994).

Questionnaires   Numerous questionnaires are available for a quick and efficient assessment of various aspects of anxiety. The questionnaires can be completed in the psychologist's office or at home and require minimal instruction or training. These include the Fear Questionnaire to assess changes in phobic severity over time (Marks & Mathews, 1979), the Body Sensations Questionnaire and Agoraphobic Cognitions Questionnaire to measure physical sensation and catastrophic thoughts (Chambless, Caputo, Bright, & Gallagher, 1984), the Yale-Brown Obsessive-Compulsive Scale (Goodman et al., 1989), and the Anxiety Sensitivity Index to measure the belief that anxiety symptoms have harmful consequences (Reiss et al., 1986). These and other questionnaires provide global measures of anxiety symptoms that can be administered before, during, and after treatment to efficiently monitor and evaluate changes in symptoms. Fur-

thermore, most questionnaires can be used to generate scores that reflect specific aspects of anxiety disorders, including specific fears, avoidant behavior, and sensitivity to physical symptoms associated with anxiety and panic.

Self-Monitoring   Self-monitoring methods are used to assess the frequency, intensity, and context of anxiety symptoms by having the client make the ratings. McGlynn and Rose (1998) made the following observations about self-monitoring with anxious clients:

- Accuracy is highest when the client knows that accuracy is being checked.
- Accuracy can be enhanced by providing accuracy-based incentives.
- Descriptions of the to-be-recorded behaviors should be as concrete as possible.
- Negatively valenced target behaviors might be self-recorded less accurately than positively valenced ones.
- Accuracy is likely to suffer when the self-recorder must attend simultaneously to tasks other than self-assessment.
- Accuracy is enhanced by instructions to record each and every instance of the target behavior, and can be enhanced by training in self-monitoring activities (p. 187).

Psychologist David Barlow and his colleagues at the Center for Stress and Anxiety Disorders in Albany, New York, and now at Boston University (Street & Barlow, 1994), have developed a set of self-monitoring forms for the assessment of several aspects of anxiety disorders. The Panic Attack Record is completed during or immediately after an episode of panic symptoms and includes the intensity and duration of the attack, the situation and time when the attack occurred, and the specific symptoms that were experienced. The Weekly Record of Anxiety and Depression is completed by clients in the evening just prior to going to bed. Clients reflect on the events of the day and record average and maximum levels of anxiety and depression experienced during the day during various activities they performed during the day (e.g., staying home alone, going to work, shopping, driving).

Behavioral Measures The avoidance of anxiety-provoking stimuli and situations is one of the primary features of most anxiety disorders—as anxiety increases in response to exposure to a situation, highly anxious individuals withdraw from or avoid the situation in an attempt to reduce their anxiety. Consequently, measures of overt behavior related to anxiety have focused on the assessment of avoidance behaviors. The most common measure is what is generally referred to as the behavioral avoidance test (BAT). In these tests, a fear-eliciting stimulus is placed in a standardized environment and the client is instructed to approach the stimulus and to engage in progressively closer or more direct interactions with it (McGlynn & Rose, 1998). For example, a client who presents with a fear of snakes may be asked to approach a snake by, in sequence, entering the room where the snake is present, in a glass case standing next to the glass case, looking down into the case, reaching in and touching the snake, picking up the snake, holding the snake, and sitting passively in a chair while the snake is placed in his or her lap.

The logic of the BAT is that the more intense the anxiety that is elicited, the earlier in the approach sequence the person will avoid or escape from the provocative stimulus. Other examples of BATs include the distance ventured from home or other safe place by a client experiencing agoraphobia, and the number of procedures in a routine dental exam that dental phobics can complete. Therapists can also assess clients' fears of social interactions by asking them to engage in imaginary role playing such as giving a speech in front of a large audience or in asking someone out on a date.

Psychophysiological Measures All the standard methods of psychophysiological assessment have been applied to the assessment of anxiety, including electromyography (EMG), cardio-

vascular measures, and electrodermal measures. For example, EMG measures of the frontalis muscle have shown it to be sensitive to anxiety-provoking stimuli (Nietzel, Bernstein, & Russell, 1988). Cardiovascular measures, including heart rate, blood pressure, and peripheral blood flow, are the most frequently used index of physiological arousal in anxiety research. Heart rate is often used because it can be monitored continuously, and relative to other physiological measures, it is reasonably error free (McGlynn & Rose, 1998). Skin conductance and resistance are influenced by sweat glands innervated by the sympathetic nervous system. Therefore, increased sweating will be reflected by decreased resistance (increased conductance) to the electrical flow between electrodes. Skin conductance is often measured before and after presentation of a threatening stimulus and the difference between the pre- and postrates (the elicited or evoked responses) is calculated (Nietzel et al.).

Summary The use of these various assessment methods will provide a comprehensive picture of the features of anxiety symptoms, the contexts in which they occur, and the individual's reactions to the symptoms when they occur. The results of such a comprehensive assessment are then used to develop an appropriate intervention for the client.

Behavioral Assessment of Attention Deficit/Hyperactivity Disorder

One of the most common referral problems encountered by clinical child psychologists is attention deficit/hyperactivity disorder (see the case of Jason in chapter 1). Epidemiological surveys estimate that 3 percent to 5 percent of school-age children evidence clinically significant problems of inattention, hyperactivity, and impulsivity (Barkley, 1998; DuPaul, Guevremont, & Barkley, 1994). Because ADHD is frequently treated with psychostimulant medication, assessment of the disorder is often carried out in collaboration with a pediatrician or child psychiatrist to evaluate the child's medical history and current functioning (Barkley).

Interviews Structured diagnostic interviews for children (e.g., the DISC, DICA, CAS; see chapter 7) are used to derive *DSM-IV* diagnoses of ADHD. These interviews include both a review of the symptoms that comprise the diagnostic criteria for ADHD and information about the age at which the symptoms were first observed and their current intensity. Behavioral assessment of ADHD also includes behavioral interviewing to assess the specific situations in which the symptoms occur, the environmental precipitants that precede the symptoms, and the responses of significant adults (parents and teachers) to the symptoms when they occur (Barkley, 1998). An example of a widely used behavioral interview for problems associated with ADHD was presented in table 10.1.

Behavior Rating Scales Standardized behavior checklists completed by parents and teachers form the core of behavioral assessment of ADHD. The CBCL and TRF (Achenbach, 1991) are the most commonly used measures of this type. These scales can be used to generate scores on an Attention Problems syndrome, which closely corresponds to *DSM* criteria for ADHD (e.g., Biederman et al., 1994). Each symptom is rated by the parent or teacher as *not at all true, somewhat or sometimes true,* or *very or often true* with regard to the child's behavior over the previous six months. Because many of the items that comprise the Attention Problems syndrome are on both the parent and teacher forms, these scores can be used to compare the severity of these symptoms at home and at school. Additional items that reflect behaviors that are only observed by teachers allow for more specific assessment of inattention, impulsivity, hyperactivity, and other school-related problems. Because these scales are broad in their focus, they provide

information on the presence of other problems and disorders that frequently co-occur with ADHD, including conduct disorder and oppositional defiant disorder (Hinshaw, 1992).

Direct Observation of Behavior More detailed information on problem behaviors and environmental contingencies that surround these behaviors is provided by direct observation of behavior at home and school. For example, observation schemes have been developed for use in assessing the amount of time off task and the number of disruptive behaviors in the classroom (Abikoff, Gittelman-Klein, & Klein, 1977; Milich, Loney, & Landau, 1982). Coding systems have also been developed to observe behavior in analog settings such as a clinic playroom in which children are instructed to work on academic tasks or respond to parental commands (e.g., Barkley et al., 1988; Mash & Barkley, 1986).

Intelligence Tests Although deficits in intellectual skills are not a component of diagnostic criteria for ADHD, there are two reasons why standardized intelligence tests are frequently part of a comprehensive behavioral assessment of ADHD. First, an evaluation of the child's general cognitive competencies is important because children referred for assessment of ADHD are often experiencing academic problems or failure. An evaluation of the child's overall intellectual skills is critical in determining whether school failure is due to problems other than inattention, impulsivity, and hyperactivity. Second, the most widely used measure of children's intelligence, the WISC-III, can be used to generate a factor analytically derived score that represents problems with distractibility and inattention. Although its usefulness in the assessment of ADHD has been controversial, the Freedom from Distractibility scale from the WISC-III has shown some utility in distinguishing problems of distractibility in children with ADHD (Anastopoulos, Spisto, & Maher, 1994).

Performance Measures   A special group of measures, referred to as **continuous performance tests,** have been developed to assess the inattention component of ADHD. These measures are typically computer tasks that involve the presentation of a series of letters or numbers and require the child to respond selectively to certain stimuli and not to others. These tasks are used to assess sustained attention and vigilance under rather monotonous conditions. One of the most widely used of these tasks is the Gordon Diagnostic System (GDS; Rielly et al., 1999). The GDS is a portable computerized continuous performance task in which the child must press a button each time a specified, randomly presented numerical sequence appears on the screen (e.g., a *7* followed by a *2*). Scores are computed for the number of correct responses, the number of errors of omission (failure to respond when the designated sequence appears), and the number of errors of commission (responding when the designated sequence has not appeared). The child's scores are then compared with the scores of a normative sample of more than 1,000 children.

Summary   As was the case with anxiety disorders, the use of these assessment methods will provide the clinical psychologist with a comprehensive and integrative picture of a child diagnosed with ADHD. Information from structured interviews, combined with data derived from rating scales, intelligence tests, performance measures, and direct observations of behavior, can be utilized in developing or selecting the most effective treatment for the child.

SUMMARY AND CONCLUSIONS

Whereas traditional approaches to assessment emphasize the importance of traits, or enduring characteristics of individuals, behavioral assessment focuses on obtaining samples of behavior. Behavioral assessment grew out of a learning theory foundation and initially focused solely on the assessment of overt, observable behaviors and situational antecedents and consequence of the behavior. As behavioral theories evolved, behavioral assessment expanded beyond this circumscribed focus on overt behaviors and began to include measurement of other aspects of individuals' functioning, such as cognitions, feelings, and psychophysiology.

In this chapter we examined the goals of behavioral assessment and then described a number of distinct methods used in behavioral assessment. We discussed behavioral interviewing, naturalistic and analog observations, self-monitoring procedures, the use of rating scales of behavior for both children and adults, cognitive-behavioral assessment, and psychophysiological assessment. We then presented a range of behavioral assessment procedures for adult anxiety and child attention deficit/hyperactivity disorder. Within each of these disorders we described interviews, observational procedures, cognitive assessment methods, and psychophysiological measurement procedures that are commonly used in behavioral assessment.

The results of a behavioral assessment, perhaps more so than those of all other forms of assessment, have clear and concrete implications for treatment of the problem behavior. At the present time, not all of the behavioral assessment methods have found their way from the laboratory to the clinic, but there are clear signs of progress on this front. There is a strong relation between assessment and intervention from a behavioral perspective. As cognitive therapies and behavior therapies continue to be shown effective in the treatment of specific disorders, it is likely that behavioral assessment methodologies will be developed and refined to measure those variables found to impact treatment.

KEY TERMS AND NAMES

Analog observation
Russell Barkley
Behavioral interviewing
Behavioral observation
Cognitive-behavioral assessment
Contextual determinants of behavior
Continuous performance tests
Dead man test
Event recording

Functional analysis of behavior
Interval recording
Walter Mischel
Naturalistic observation
Operational definitions of behavior
Psychophysiological assessment
Rating scales
Self-monitoring

RESOURCES

Books:

Bellack, A. S., & Hersen, M. (Eds.). (1998).
    Behavioral assessment: A practical handbook
    (2nd ed.). Elmsford, NY: Pergamon Press.
Ciminero, A. R., Calhoun, C. S., & Adams, H. E.
    (Eds.). (1986). *Handbook of behavioral assessment*
    (2nd ed.). New York: John Wiley.
Hersen, M., & Bellack, A. S. (Eds.). (1988).
    Dictionary of behavioral assessment techniques.
    New York: Pergamon Press.

Shapiro, E. S., & Kratochwill, T. R. (Eds.). (2000).
    *Behavioral assessment in schools: Theory,
    research, and clinical foundations* (2nd ed.).
    New York: Guilford Press.

Journals:

Behavioral Assessment
Journal of Consulting and Clinical Psychology
Journal of Applied Behavior Analysis

PSYCHOLOGICAL INTERVENTION: PROMOTION, PREVENTION, AND PSYCHOTHERAPY

In chapters 11 through 15 we discuss the broad area of psychological intervention. We begin in chapter 11 with an overview of intervention, which includes promotion of health and positive behaviors, prevention of psychopathology and physical illness, and psychological treatment of psychopathology and illness. In chapters 12 through 14 we describe in detail three different approaches to treatment of psychopathology. In chapter 12 we describe psychoanalytic, psychodynamic, and interpersonal approaches to psychotherapy. In chapter 13 we present humanistic, existential, and experiential psychotherapies, and in chapter 14 we describe behavioral and cognitive approaches to psychotherapy. In these chapters we discuss theory and research related to each approach, present the application of each therapy to specific psychological disorders, and illustrate how the therapies would be applied to the four cases that we first presented in chapter 1. In chapter 15 we discuss research on the effectiveness of psychotherapy and discuss similarities and differences across the various approaches to psychotherapy that are presented in chapters 12 through 14. Finally, in chapter 16 we provide a summary of the past and present of the field of clinical psychology, and our thoughts about its future.

CHAPTER ELEVEN

PSYCHOLOGICAL INTERVENTION: PROMOTION, PREVENTION AND TREATMENT

INTRODUCTION

At least if they get a divorce, then maybe the yelling and the fighting will stop. That was

Brian's first reaction when his mother told him that she and his father were splitting up. Their arguments had escalated dramatically over the last

6 months. Perhaps the most significant change was that they no longer tried to hide their fighting from Brian and his younger sister, Jessica. They now yelled openly at one another, and their rage often spilled over toward the two children. Relief from the anger and tension in their home would be worth the pain of his parents getting divorced, or so Brian thought. But his parents' separation and divorce had not brought relief. Instead, his life had been turned upside down.

We first introduced you to Brian in chapter 1 and revisited him in chapter 5. He is 16 years old, and it has been a little over 1 year since his parents went through a very difficult divorce. Following the divorce, Brian, his mother and younger sister moved to a new town for his mother to begin a new job. Because Brian's father did not provide regular financial support, the family was faced with significant money problems. Brian has struggled with his parents' divorce and the move to a new school and town. He has had difficulty making new friends at school and has become increasingly withdrawn and lonely. He has problems sleeping, has lost his appetite, and has become sullen and angry. Three months before coming to see a psychologist, Brian became severely depressed and made a serious, but uncompleted, suicide attempt by taking an overdose of sleep medication he had found in his mother's medicine cabinet.

In the previous chapters we discussed how a clinical psychologist would classify Brian's problems and would measure important aspects of the behavior, emotions, personality, and current environment of clients such as Brian. We will now consider perhaps the most important contribution that clinical psychology can make to Brian and others who suffer from psychological problems—how can we help people to *change*? We will draw on Brian's case to exemplify three approaches to change: programs to promote positive development during adolescence, interventions to prevent the adverse effects of divorce, and methods to treat depression during adolescence.

Much of the work carried out by clinical psychologists is based on the conviction that people can change their behavior, their thoughts, and their emotions. The assumption that people can change, that people can better themselves and the quality of their lives through perseverance and self control, is deeply rooted in American culture (Seligman, 1994). The methods developed by psychologists to help people change exemplify the American belief in the malleability of human nature. Furthermore, the methods used by psychologists to deal with mental health problems offer an important alternative to the methods developed by biologically oriented psychiatry that produce change through the use of psychoactive medication (Seligman). Clinical psychologists assist people in bringing about change by, among other methods, altering the contingencies in their environment, by helping them change the ways that they think, by helping them regulate their emotions in different ways, and by altering the ways that they relate to others.

Psychologists are involved in *intervention* whenever they purposefully try to produce change in the lives of others. In this chapter and the ones that follow, we will consider three types of interventions that are intended to produce change in people's lives. First, there has been a recent emphasis in clinical psychology (and, indeed, in psychology in general) on "positive psychology," including the *promotion* of health and positive behaviors (Seligman & Csikszentmihalyi, 2000). This approach typically targets broad populations and is exemplified by programs that teach, for example, stress management, exercise and healthy eating, and social competence skills. Second, programs designed to *prevent* psychopathology and disease have a longer history (Coie, Miller-Johnson, & Bagwell, 2000). These programs typically target groups who are at elevated risk for developing disorder (e.g., low-birth-weight infants, children of depressed mothers, victims of assault) and are designed to reduce the probability of adverse outcomes in these samples. Third, the most common form of intervention in clinical psychology is psycho-therapy, the process used to *treat* various types of disorders once they have occurred. Many different forms of psychotherapy have been developed to treat depression, anxiety, personality disorders, and other psychological problems. We briefly introduce the nature of psychotherapy in this chapter and then discuss therapy in more detail in the four chapters that follow.

Interventions carried out by clinical psychologists have a remarkably wide range of goals and take a variety of different forms. Psychological interventions have been developed to change behaviors in order to reduce the risk for AIDS (Ross & Kelly, 2000), prevent violent behavior (Stoolmiller, Eddy, & Reid, 2000), promote healthy patterns of diet and exercise (Perry, Story, & Lytle, 1997), improve children's learning and performance in school (Adelman, 1995), control alcohol abuse (Marlatt & George, 1998), treat the victims of trauma (Resnick, Acierno, Holmes, Kilpatrick, & Jager, 1999), manage problems of inattention and aggression in children (Barkley, 1998), alleviate major depression (Hollon, DeRubeis, & Evans, 1996), and prolong the lives of patients with serious illness (Fawzy et al., 1993). These are only a few examples of the wide range of psychological interventions that have been developed within the realm of clinical psychology and other mental health professions.

In spite of the apparent diversity in psychological interventions, they share a number of common factors. Foremost among these is the role of psychological theory and research—interventions in clinical psychology are based on comprehensive models of human behavior and the science of psychology (Borkavec, 1997; Davison, 1997). The link with the science of psychology is what sets interventions in clinical psychology apart from a multitude of other interventions that have emerged as part of our popular culture. Programs for self-improvement and overcoming serious emotional problems abound in the popular literature and are often labeled as

"psychology." Bookstores are filled with self-help manuals, workshops to solve psychological problems are widely available, and infomercials for self-improvement programs fill the television airways. However, programs that are not based in sound psychological theory and research and have not undergone careful empirical evaluation of their effectiveness are not part of clinical psychology. Although some of these "pop" interventions may be effective, the absence of controlled scientific data on their effectiveness is highly problematic. Self-help and self-improvement programs cannot be assumed to be effective, and they must provide data to show that they are. The goal of this chapter is to provide an overview of the nature and process of interventions in clinical psychology and to provide some direction for the more specific examples of interventions that will be considered in the chapters that follow.

ETHICAL PRINCIPLES IN PSYCHOLOGICAL INTERVENTION

All efforts to help people change, indeed all the activities performed by clinical psychologists, are guided by a set of principles that protect the welfare and interests of the individuals that they serve. Interventions must be conducted in a manner that places the best interests of the client and society as the highest priorities. As we first noted in chapter 2, the profession of clinical psychology is based on a set of ethical principles (American Psychological Association, 1992). We now return to ethical guidelines as they relate to intervention.

Participants in any psychological intervention have a right to be fully aware of the nature of the intervention prior to participating; that is, patients have the right to **informed consent.** The decision to enter into and to continue psychotherapy must be made knowingly, intelligently, and voluntarily (O'Neill, 1998; Pope & Vasquez, 1998). Psychologists have an obligation to fully inform their clients about the characteristics and parameters of an intervention prior to treatment.

In psychotherapy, therapists are obligated to tell a prospective client what to expect will happen in the course of treatment, how long it will take, possible risks, and alternative methods (O'Neill). Unfortunately, this information is not always transmitted. Consumers of psychological services are frequently naive about the specific nature of psychological treatment, and some therapists are reluctant to fully inform clients about what to expect in the process. This reluctance stems in part from the assumption, held by some psychologists, that unconscious processes and defense mechanisms prohibit clients from understanding the source of or the solution to their problems. Ensuring informed consent for children and adolescents who enter psychological treatment is further complicated because younger clients are limited in their ability to understand the nature of psychotherapy (Jensen, McNamara, & Gustafson, 1991; Taylor & Adelman, 1998). However, these concerns do not change the right of clients to be fully informed about the nature and potential benefits and risks of the procedures that will be used.

As part of many psychological interventions, clients are likely to disclose some of the most intimate and private aspects of their lives. Disclosure of intimate emotional concerns requires the assurance of privacy and **confidentiality**—that information disclosed during any intervention will be treated with respect and will remain private (Smith-Bell & Winslade, 1994; Vasquez, 1994). Psychologists must maintain a client's privacy except in certain instances specified by law. This guideline means that psychologists must ensure that information about the person's identity and what is disclosed in therapy remains private between the client and the therapist. Only with the specific consent of the client can information be given to insurance companies, schools, employers, and the like. Confidentiality also means that a family member cannot gain access to information about a client's treatment from the therapist (only when a child is a minor does a parent have a right to such information).

In these and many other ways, the therapist must provide a secure and private place for disclosure. The exceptions to confidentiality involve instances in which there is a threat to the welfare of the client or the client is a threat to the welfare of another (see box 11.1). A therapist may be obligated to disclose confidential information related to suicidality, threats of violent behavior against another, and physical or sexual abuse of a child. In these instances, a psychologist is required by law to disclose this information to specified legal or social agencies (e.g., police or social welfare agencies).

Clinical psychologists are obligated to define their areas of **competence** and expertise and to operate within these domains (Overholser & Fine, 1990). Therapists cannot perform professional services beyond the boundaries of their competence based on their training and education, the supervision they have received from other trained professionals, or their own professional experience. For example, a psychotherapist who has received her or his training in clinical social work cannot represent herself or himself as a clinical psychologist. A clinical psychologist who has not been trained in the use of clinical hypnosis or biofeedback technology cannot ethically use these methods in clinical practice. Moreover, clinical psychologists may not misrepresent themselves or what they do. Psychologists cannot make false or overstated claims about the efficacy of their methods or their personal areas of competence. In most states, licensing laws require clinical psychologists to maintain their expertise by staying aware of and properly trained in new developments in the field. This training is accomplished through participation in continuing professional education activities regulated by the APA and other professional groups. Unfortunately, clear standards for what is current knowledge have not been developed. For example, the APA does not require that continuing education courses and workshops should teach empirically validated methods of assessment and treatment. Therefore,

BOX 11.1

ARE THERE LIMITS TO CONFIDENTIALITY?

One of the hallmark characteristics of any helping relationship is the protection of privacy and confidentiality. Protecting clients' rights to privacy is central to the relationship between physicians and patients, lawyers and clients, and psychologists and clients. Assurances of confidentiality and privacy allow clients to disclose aspects of themselves that they may be unable to address in the context of other relationships out of fear that the information might in some way be misused. Given the importance of this issue, would there ever be circumstances in which the need to protect clients' confidentiality is outweighed by other concerns? A case in the 1970s presented psychology with just such a challenge.

On October 27, 1969, University of California student **Tatiana Tarasoff** was stabbed and shot to death on the front porch of her home by Prosensit Poddar, a UC student from India. Mr. Poddar had become romantically obsessed with Ms. Tarasoff and pathologically jealous of her after a brief dating relationship. As his obsession with her had increased, a friend had urged Poddar to seek help through the student health service at the university. Mr. Poddar was evaluated by a staff psychiatrist and then referred to a psychologist at the health center for counseling. During the course of therapy, Poddar disclosed that he might kill Tarasoff, and his friend informed the

psychologist that Poddar had a gun. The psychologist informed the police that Mr. Poddar might be a threat to Ms. Tarasoff's safety, and the police subsequently detained and interviewed Poddar. They judged that he was thinking rationally and that his mood was normal, and they subsequently allowed him to go. He then proceeded to murder Tarasoff. Subsequently, Ms. Tarasoff's parents sued the university, the psychiatrist, and the psychologist for failing to warn their daughter that she was in grave danger. Eventually the California Supreme Court ruled in favor of the Tarasoffs, declaring that there are limits to the privilege of confidentiality between a client and a psychologist.

The court ruled that the duty to protect another person from potential harm supersedes the right of the client to privacy within a relationship with a psychologist. The court recognized the difficulties in predicting violent behavior, but deemed that the potential negative effects of overpredicting violence do not outweigh the rights of a potential victim to be informed of a threat that has been made against him or her. This ruling has changed the nature of the therapist-client relationship, because in many states therapists must now inform clients that they are required to breach confidentiality if they judge the client to be a threat to the safety and welfare of another person.

---

some of the regulations designed to ensure the public that psychologists are maintaining the highest of professional standards function more in name than in reality (Dawes, 1995).

Guidelines have been set regarding the nature of the relationships that can be formed between clinical psychologists and their clients (Pope et al., 1995; Pope, Sonne, & Holroyd, 1993). Psychologists may not engage in any other relationships with their clients outside the therapeutic relationship; in other words, *multiple or dual relationships* such as a friendship or business relationship with a client are unethical. Most importantly, psychologists are prohibited from

engaging in sexual contact or relationships with their clients. This professional standard is designed to guard against exploitation of the client, to protect the client's welfare, and to encourage the therapist's objectivity. Thus, a therapist should not engage in business or other professional relationships, friendships, social activities, or intimate relationships with clients. Such relationships are assumed to be inherently harmful to clients by causing conflicts of interest or by blurring lines between therapeutic and nontherapeutic encounters.

Individuals who seek psychological services have the right to maintain their fundamental liberties and to function in a setting that provides the fewest restrictions on these liberties. For example, individuals with developmental disabilities such as mental retardation have the right to live, learn, and work in settings that provide opportunities to live in the community with as much independence as they are capable of managing. Clinical psychologists work to ensure that their clients are not coerced or manipulated into receiving treatment.

CHARACTERISTICS OF INTERVENTIONS

All psychological interventions share the ethical principles we have discussed in this book. However, interventions in clinical psychology differ along a number of dimensions, the most salient of which are the goals and targets of the interventions, the means for producing change, and the timing of interventions.

Goals of Intervention: What Are We Trying to Change?

Psychological interventions differ in the aspects of human functioning that they are designed to change. Just as psychologists can choose to assess and measure thoughts, feelings, behavior, biology, or the environment, so too can psychologists help people change in one or more of these various levels of functioning (Kanfer & Goldstein, 1991). Some interventions are intended to change what people do, to change particular problem *behaviors*. For example, an intervention may be designed to reduce the amount and frequency of the consumption of alcohol or cigarette smoking. Other interventions are designed to change *emotions* by decreasing emotional distress and increasing emotional comfort, as when an intervention is used to reduce feelings of anxiety and worry. Still other interventions are intended to change the ways that people *think*; for example, to stop persistent thoughts about a traumatic experience or to help individuals develop

more positive and optimistic beliefs about the future. Psychological interventions also may be designed to change underlying *biological processes*. Examples include the use of psychological techniques to reduce blood pressure, lower resting heart rate, or decrease headache pain. Finally, interventions can be designed to change the *environment* rather than the person, such as changing the structure and resources of a junior high or middle school to ease the often stressful transition of students from the primary grades. Most interventions are, in fact, designed to produce change in more than one of these levels of functioning.

Much of the work carried out by clinical psychologists is concerned with the prevention or treatment of specific forms of psychopathology as defined in the *DSM-IV*. But clinical psychological interventions are also concerned with broader social problems and problems in living that are not included as specific diagnostic categories in the *DSM-IV* (Adelman, 1995). These include problems in learning and development, difficulties in daily living, and problems in interpersonal relationships. Furthermore, advances in clinical health psychology and behavioral medicine have expanded the focus of interventions in clinical psychology to include a number of physical disorders and diseases—psychologists contribute directly to the prevention and treatment of, among other diseases, cancer, diabetes, hypertension, and AIDS (see box 11.2).

The goals of an intervention may not be the same for all parties involved. For example, the parents and the teachers of an adolescent boy who is referred for treatment of disruptive behavior and conduct problems may not share the same goals for improving his behavior. The adolescent may have radically different goals than either his parents or his teachers, or he may not wish to change at all. Similarly, a client may have different goals from those that are formulated by a psychologist. A framework for understanding differences in goals for intervention has been outlined by psychologist Hans Strupp

BOX 11.2

OUTCOMES OF PSYCHOLOGICAL INTERVENTION: IMPROVING HEALTH AND PROLONGING LIFE

Interventions in clinical psychology were originally limited to problems of behavior, problems in living, and psychopathology. In recent years, however, the continued development of clinical health psychology and behavioral medicine has seen increased involvement of clinical psychologists in medical settings. The goals of interventions in clinical psychology have increasingly grown to include physical health and disease in addition to mental health and psychopathology (Andersen, Kiecolt-Glaser, & Glaser, 1994; Belar, 1997).

Recent research on the relationship between psychological factors and disease has provided the impetus for interventions to change health-related behaviors. Examples of recent research include the following:

- Stress decreases the body's ability to ward off the virus that causes the common cold (Cohen, Doyle, & Skoner, 1999; Cohen et al., 1998) and the ability of the body to heal wounds, including the course of recovery from surgery (Kiecolt-Glaser, Page, Marucha, MacCallum, & Glaser, 1998).
- A personality style characterized by hostility, competitiveness, and time urgency (referred to as Type A personality) is a significant risk factor for coronary heart disease (Friedman, Fleischmann, & Price, 1996), with the strongest increase in risk associated with hostility (Iribarren et al., 2000).
- Symptoms of depression in the weeks following a heart attack significantly increase the risk for a second heart attack (Frasure-Smith, Lesperance, & Talajic, 1995; Frasure-Smith et al., 1999).

Based on these and other findings, interventions employed by clinical psychologists are now intended not only to improve the quality of people's lives, but also to increase the length of survival and to decrease mortality in individuals with serious disease. Two studies of the effects of psychological interventions for cancer patients are especially noteworthy (Fawzy et al., 1995; Spiegel et al., 1989). Psychologists, psychiatrists, social workers, and other mental health professionals originally were enlisted in the treatment of cancer patients to help patients cope with the stress of the diagnosis of a life-threatening disease, to help patients manage the negative side effects of chemotherapy treatments, and to improve the quality of patients' lives as they either lived with the uncertainty about a future recurrence or coped with a terminal diagnosis. However, research has shown that psychological interventions may increase the length as well as the quality of patients' lives (Fawzy et al., 1993; Spiegel et al.). Evidence suggests that one way in which psychological interventions may contribute to enhanced survival of cancer patients is through the effects that these interventions have on improved functioning of the immune system and its ability to fight against cancer (Andersen et al., 1998). This exciting research will be discussed in more detail in chapters 13 and 14.

(Strupp, 1996; Strupp & Hadley, 1977). Strupp's tripartite model distinguishes among the criteria for successful interventions that are held by clients, society, and mental health professionals. Clients are typically concerned with achieving change in their personal sense of well-being and with reducing their subjective sense of distress. Alternatively, society is most often concerned with interventions that bring about change in disruptive or harmful behavior. Finally, mental health professionals are concerned with change that can be evaluated according to criteria that are specified as part of a model of personality or psychopathology. Therefore, the goals of interventions and the evaluation of success in achieving these goals involve the measurement of different perspectives and frequently use different criteria of success.

Process of Intervention:
How Do We Produce Change?

The goals of an intervention are often distinct from the processes or mechanisms that are used to achieve these objectives. Many interventions are designed to produce change in one level of functioning as a way of altering another level. Research on the mechanisms responsible for the changes that are produced by psychological interventions supports a general model of *reciprocal determinism* (Bandura, 1986, 1997). The concept of reciprocal determinism implies that the various levels of human functioning (cognition, emotion, behavior, biology) and the environment all influence one another, and a change in any one of these factors will lead to change in other components (Lazarus, 1991). Interventions initiate a complex set of processes in which the person's thoughts, behaviors, emotions, and biology as well as the surrounding environment all influence one another in reciprocal paths. Here are some examples:

- Changes in cognition lead to changes in biology, emotions, and behavior. Interventions have been developed to help individuals alter maladaptive ways of thinking in order to change their emotions, behavior, and physiology. A prominent example is the cognitive therapy for depression developed by psychiatrist Aaron Beck that we will discuss in detail in chapter 14 (Beck, Rush, Shaw, & Emery, 1979). A central component of this treatment involves systematic steps to identify and change dysfunctional ways of thinking (e.g., blaming oneself for problems; expecting the worst to happen; focusing attention on only the negative aspects of a situation).
- Changes in behavior lead to changes in biology, cognitions, and emotions. Psychologists often help individuals change their actions in order to help change their emotions, cognitions, and underlying biological processes. For example, an important element in behavior therapy for anxiety disorders involves preventing clients from engaging in behaviors that al-

low them to escape or avoid the source of the anxiety (e.g., Franklin, Abramowitz, Kozak, Levitt, & Foa, 2000). Preventing behavioral avoidance leads to extinction of feelings of anxiety and to changes in one's beliefs about the source of the anxiety (Tarrier & Humphreys, 2000).

- Changes in the environment lead to changes in biology, thoughts, emotions, and behavior. Changes in either the stimuli that serve as antecedent cues for behavior (classical conditioning) or the stimuli that are contingent on specific behaviors (operant conditioning) will result in changes in those behaviors. For example, classical conditioning approaches to change can involve the pairing of a stimulus that has been conditioned to produce aversive emotional responses with a stimulus that is associated with more positive responses. Operant conditioning processes involve systematic rewards for desired behaviors and the extinction of maladaptive behaviors through withdrawal of positive reinforcement. Environmental factors can also have an indirect impact on behavior via processes of learning through the observation of salient models in one's environment.

These examples suggest that the processes by which psychological interventions lead to change in behavior, emotion, and cognition are complex and multifaceted. We will consider these issues in more detail in our discussion of different forms of psychotherapy and the ways they work in chapter 15.

Timing of Intervention:
When Should We Intervene?

When is the best time to intervene with the goal of changing a person's patterns of behavior, thinking, and emotions? Perhaps it is important to have evidence that a problem exists before professional psychologists invest their time and expertise, and the time and money of their clients, in bringing about change. Even more specifically, evidence of a diagnosable psychiatric disorder that meets the criteria spelled out in the *DSM-IV* may be needed before the services

Ricardo Muñoz, Ph.D., is a Professor of Psychology in the Department of Psychiatry at the University of California, San Francisco, and is the Director of the Clinical Psychology Training Program there. Dr. Muñoz has played a leading role in research on preventive interventions for depression, and has developed effective programs to help people stop smoking. *(Photo courtesy of Ricardo Muñoz.)*

of a clinical psychologist are enlisted (e.g., Nathan & Gorman, 1998). Alternatively, once a disorder is present it may be too late for an intervention to be most useful and efficacious—an ounce of prevention may in fact be worth a pound of cure when it comes to serious behavioral and emotional disorders (Muñoz, Mrazek, & Haggerty, 1996; Price, Cowen, Lorion, & Ramos-McKay, 1988). The best time for intervention may be when there is evidence that an individual is at high risk to develop a problem or may have evidenced early precursors of a serious problem, but the problem itself is not fully manifested. And a third position is represented in the belief that psychological interventions are best used to promote and develop healthy styles of behavior and thinking (Kaplan, 2000). We may all be at risk to develop serious health problems ranging from cancer to AIDS if we fail to follow a set of fundamental guidelines for a healthy lifestyle. Similarly, we may all be at risk for developing psychological problems such as depression and anxiety if we fail to develop a healthy style of thinking and behavior. Therefore, the optimal use of psychological interventions may be to promote healthy development as a means of improving the overall quality of human functioning.

The effective management of psychological problems involves all three levels of intervention. Furthermore, promotion, prevention, and treatment form a sequence of intervention strategies (see figure 11.1). Health promotion represents the first line of intervention with the goal of building and developing adaptive behaviors, attitudes, and lifestyles in all members of a population. However, it is unlikely that even the most

FIGURE 11.1.
Sequential model of promotion, prevention, and treatment as interventions in clinical psychology.

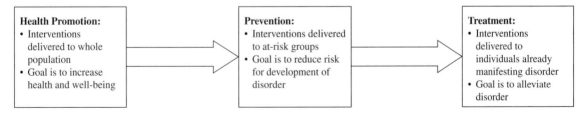

Health Promotion:
- Interventions delivered to whole population
- Goal is to increase health and well-being

Prevention:
- Interventions delivered to at-risk groups
- Goal is to reduce risk for development of disorder

Treatment:
- Interventions delivered to individuals already manifesting disorder
- Goal is to alleviate disorder

BOX 11.3

DIET AND WEIGHT LOSS: SHOULD WE INTERVENE?

Interventions to help people change are a major part of clinical psychology. However, it is not clear that we should always intervene. An example can be found in interventions for dieting and weight loss. Concerns about weight and physical appearance have become a source of tremendous debate within psychology and in the American culture as a whole. On one side of the debate are strong advocates of dieting and weight control who argue that excess weight and obesity are significant health risks (Brownell & Rodin, 1994). On the other side of the debate are individuals who question the value of weight control programs because weight may be strongly influenced by biology and beyond the control of the individual (Stunkard, 1991). Furthermore, some who argue against dieting believe that concerns about the health risks of weight are overstated and that overweight individuals in our society are a target of social stigma (Cogan & Ernsberger, 1999). Clinical psychologists are in the middle of this debate. Many psychologists have been actively involved in the development of programs to change eating habits and produce weight loss. More recently, psychologists have begun to help overweight individuals change their attitudes about their bodies

and feel less negatively about themselves (Rosen, Orosan, & Reiter, 1995). The question now is whether psychologists should be involved in efforts to help people lose weight or in programs to help individuals accept themselves regardless of their weight.

The argument in favor of dieting and weight loss typically centers on the health risks associated with obesity. Obesity is associated with adult-onset diabetes, hypertension, cardiovascular disease, and some forms of cancer. Moreover, 31 percent of men and 24 percent of women in America are considered overweight based on actuarial standards, with 12 percent of both men and women considered severely overweight. Perceptions of being overweight are also informative, because 37 percent of men and 52 percent of women consider themselves to be overweight. Further concern comes from statistics indicating that the percentage of individuals who are overweight has risen considerably since 1900. This rise in obesity in the population has been accompanied by steady increases in the proportion of both men and women who are dieting at any given time. Data collected between 1950 and the mid-1960s indicated that 7 percent and men and 14 percent of

effective programs to promote healthy behavior will be able to protect all individuals from factors that contribute to psychopathology and illness. Prevention programs offer a second set of resources for those individuals who are exposed to conditions of high risk. Preventive interventions are likely to be most effective in warding off problems if they are delivered selectively to those in greatest need. But similar to interventions designed to promote healthy behavior, preventive interventions are unlikely to be completely effective in averting the onset of problems and disorders in all individuals who are at high risk. At the third level, treatments are needed to remediate problems that are fully or

partially manifested. Comprehensive approaches to intervention suggest that all three levels are important in coordinating clinical psychology's contribution to managing problems of mental and physical health (Adelman, 1995; Compas, 1993; Kaplan, 2000).

These three levels of intervention are exemplified in the need for multileveled interventions for alcohol abuse and dependence (alcoholism) in our society. The lifetime prevalence rates for alcohol abuse and dependence in the United States are staggering—approximately 5 percent for women and over 20 percent for men (Grant et al., 1994). The social, emotional, and economic costs of alcoholism are equally overwhelming in

BOX 11.3 (concluded)

women were dieting to lose weight, whereas in studies conducted in the 1990s, 24 percent of men and 40 percent to 45 percent of women reported that they were dieting. The general pattern suggests that Americans are becoming heavier, less healthy and dieting more. One solution is the use of dieting to regulate weight and, indirectly, other health problems.

Concerns about the possible negative consequences of dieting and attitudes toward obesity have increased beginning in the 1970s to the point that there is now a strong and vocal backlash against concerns with weight and dieting programs. Several concerns have been raised. First, dieting may not be effective. Reviews of research on dieting programs have suggested that only a portion of participants lose weight and only small percentage are able to maintain their weight losses. Second, critics suggest that the tendency to regain lost weight has led to yo-yo dieting—a pattern of dieting, regaining weight, dieting again, and regaining weight again. Third, critics have argued that weight is determined primarily by genetics and is beyond the control of the individual. Dieting holds individuals responsible for their weight and gives them the false belief that they can reduce their weight by changing their behavior.

Given this debate, what role should clinical psychologists play? There are, in fact, many contributions that clinical psychologists can make in this arena (e.g., Brownell & Rodin, 1994; Rosen et al., 1995). First, more research is needed on the efficacy of weight loss programs. Most prior studies have evaluated the effects of dieting among individuals who have sought help from professional weight loss programs, and these individuals are only a small subset of people who diet. The effectiveness of weight loss programs with this group may not generalize to the effectiveness of dieting among the general population. Second, decisions about dieting cannot be made globally with regard to all individuals. For example, decisions about dieting are different for obese individuals than for those who are normal weight or slightly overweight. Third, the benefits of modest weight loss may be substantial, particularly in severely overweight individuals. Fourth, dieting may disrupt weight gain, even when the weight lost during a diet is regained. Finally, an alternative form of intervention is to help individuals develop more positive feelings about themselves by changing their body image. Decisions about dieting and weight loss programs reflect the complex issues involved in psychological interventions. It is not sufficient to develop techniques to help people change. Numerous factors have to be considered in deciding whether an intervention is warranted at all.

terms of the disrupted lives, conflict and discord within families, and lost job productivity associated with this problem. Furthermore, children of alcoholic parents are at risk for a wide range of behavioral and emotional problems (Chassin, Pitts, DeLucia, & Todd, 1999). On the one hand, efforts to treat identified cases of alcoholism cannot keep up with the emergence of new cases. On the other hand, programs to prevent alcohol-related disorders could decrease the incidence of new cases but have nothing to offer to the millions of currently afflicted individuals and their families. Therefore, multiple levels of intervention are called for. First, the promotion of healthy alternatives to alcohol use can be taught to young people during childhood and adoles-

cence (Leventhal & Keeshan, 1993; Marlatt & George, 1998). Second, evidence that alcoholism runs in families is clear (Schuckit, 2000), making children of alcoholic parents a group at particularly high risk to develop the disorder. Thus, preventive interventions can be used to target children of alcoholics in an effort to reduce their risk for developing the disorder (Short, Roosa, Sandler, & Ayers, 1995). Finally, treatment programs can be delivered to individuals who abuse and are dependent on alcohol in order to facilitate abstinence and to reduce the risk for relapse once they have stopped drinking (Marlatt & George, 1998). As an example of how the continuum of interventions can come full circle, the treatment of a problem in one individual (an alcoholic parent) may be an effective component of the prevention of the development of the problem in another person (the child of an alcoholic parent; Short et al.).

PROMOTION AND PREVENTION

We now turn our attention to the first two broad categories of intervention—the promotion of positive behavior and health, and the prevention of problems and disorder. We first consider the need for health promotion and preventive interventions. Next we examine some of the key concepts that underlie these interventions.

The Increasing Incidence of Problems

The incidence rates are increasing steadily for many types of mental health problems and a number of infectious diseases. The increased **incidence** (the occurrence of new cases in a specified period of time) of any disorder has clear implications for interventions to address such problems. Treatment typically cannot reduce the incidence of new cases, because the focus of treatment is on problems that are already manifested. Only promotion and prevention efforts can decrease the onset of new cases of any disorder or problem. Prevention of disorders that are increasing in frequency represents one of the greatest challenges facing clinical psychology and other behavioral sciences. Three selected examples are particularly sobering.

HIV and AIDS   The epidemic of the human immunodeficiency virus (HIV) and acquired immunodeficiency syndrome (AIDS) continues to rage in the United States and worldwide. Epidemiological data indicate that 250 cases of AIDS were reported in the United States in 1982, a total that had grown to nearly 300,000 cases by 1993, and more than 750,000 cases by 2000 (Centers for Disease Control, 2001). As of the year 2000, over 430,000 deaths due to AIDS had been reported in the United States. The rates of

new cases of AIDS underestimate the magnitude of this epidemic, however, because AIDS occurs an average of 10 years after initial HIV infection. The statistics for AIDS worldwide are almost incomprehensible—there are now more than *36 million* cases of AIDS reported in the world, with 95 percent of all cases occurring in developing nations.

Major Depressive Disorder   Determining the incidence rates of psychopathology has proven more difficult than for physical disease because of changes in the criteria for psychological disorders and the use of retrospective interviews to assess lifetime history of psychopathology. In spite of these challenges, there is evidence to suggest that the rate of at least one form of psychopathology, major depression, increased in several countries over the course of the twentieth century (Cross National Collaborative Group, 1992; Klerman & Weissman, 1989). Klerman and Weissman examined differences in rates of depression as a function of the decade in which individuals were born (1905–1915, 1915–1925, etc.), referred to as different birth cohorts. For example, the cohort born between 1945 and 1955 (aged 30 to 40 years old at the time of the interview) had almost twice the probability of a depressive episode in their lifetime, as compared with a cohort of those born between 1925 and 1935 (aged 50 to 60 years old when interviewed). These findings stimulated a cross-national study in which similar data were collected from the United States, Canada, Puerto Rico, France, Lebanon, and Italy. Data from all these locations, with the exception of Italy, showed the same pattern—higher rates of depression were reported by age 25 for the group born after 1955 than for any other cohort, and generally high rates for younger subjects (Cross National Collaborative Group).

Violence Against Women   Violence against women represents a public health concern of enormous proportions (Acierno, Resnick, &

BOX 11.4

THE LIFE OF BRIAN:
EXAMPLES OF PROMOTION, PREVENTION, AND TREATMENT

How should a clinical psychologist try help Brian, who is currently depressed and struggling with the effects of his parents' divorce? His situation provides an excellent example of the role of all three levels of intervention that we have described in this chapter. Let's begin with the *treatment* of Brian and his current problems. He currently meets criteria for major depression as defined by the *DSM-IV*, including symptoms of depressed affect, irritability, sleep disruption, feelings of hopelessness, and suicidality (American Psychiatric Association, 1994). There are well documented treatments available for treating depression during adolescence (Lewisohn & Clarke, 1999). Specifically, a cognitive behavioral treatment developed by psychologists Greg Clarke of the Kaiser Permanente Center for Health Research in Portland, Oregon, and Peter Lewinsohn of the Oregon Research Institute has been shown to be effective (Clarke, Rohde, Lewinsohn, Hops, & Seeley, 1999; Lewinsohn & Clarke). This treatment addresses negative ways of thinking that are characteristic of depression and offers behavioral techniques to alter the withdrawn behavior that is associated with depression.

It is possible that Brian's depressive episode could have been prevented, however, if the adverse effects of his parents' divorce were addressed early on. Several researchers have developed *prevention* programs to help children and adolescents cope with the stress of parental divorce (e.g., Wolchik et al., 2000). These programs are typically based in schools and provide support and coping skills instruction to children and adolescents in a group format. Participants share their experiences related to

their parents' breakup and are taught specific ways to solve divorce-related problems and to cope with the negative emotions that they are experiencing. The rationale of these programs is to provide support and skills to children to help them cope with parental divorce and to prevent the onset of problems such as depression and disruptive behavior that might result from the stress of the divorce. Thus, the goal in this case would have been to prevent Brian's episode of depression by enhancing his ability to cope.

At an even broader level, programs to *promote* healthy psychological development during adolescence may have provided Brian with the skills that he needed to manage the experience of his parents' divorce even before it occurred. Programs that teach children and adolescents social competence skills are aimed at all students, regardless of their exposure to risk or evidence that they have developed a psychological problem (Weissberg, 2000). Social competence promotion programs emphasize social and emotional learning by teaching children basic problem-solving skills, social skills to form relationships with others, and skills to manage and regulate their emotions. A program of this type could have prepared Brian for the problems he would face as a result of his parents' divorce before it occurred.

Clinical psychologists are involved in all these levels of intervention. Psychologists provide therapy directly to adolescents who are suffering from depression. Prevention and health promotion programs are typically delivered in school settings, and clinical psychologists are often involved as consultants to schools to help develop and implement these programs.

Kilpatrick, 1997; Koss, 2000). It is estimated that 15 percent of women in the United States have been raped and over 20 percent have been physically assaulted in an intimate relationship in their lifetimes (Tjaden & Theonnes, 2000). The rates of violence against women are even greater

worldwide, because one in every three women has been physically beaten, forced into sex, or abused in her lifetime (Koss, 2000). In addition to the obvious physical harm, there are emotional and psychological consequences. The threat of male violence is a major source of fear and stress among women, a fear that cuts across age, ethnicity, socioeconomic status, and sexual orientation (L. A. Goodman, Koss, Fitzgerald, Russo, & Kieta, 1993; Kilpatrick, Resnick, & Acierno, 1997). Post-traumatic stress disorder (PTSD) has been documented as the primary psychological response to these events, with estimates as high as 95 percent of victims suffering PTSD immediately after rape and 45 percent to 50 percent continue to suffer from PTSD 3 months later (Koss, 1993). Although it is essential that the consequences of violence are treated effectively, the answer to this pervasive problem lies in the prevention of violent acts against women.

Reducing the Incidence of These Three Problems   To the extent that the causes of the problems of HIV and AIDS, Major Depressive Disorder, and violence against women are associated with human behavior, clinical psychology can take a leading role in changing the behaviors that contribute to the increased incidence of HIV infection, major depression, and violence against women, among many other problems. Risk factors (see section titled "Risk and Protective Factors") that can be changed through psychological interventions include high-risk behaviors, exposure to conditions of stress and adversity, and societal values and beliefs. Clinical psychology can contribute to changing all these factors.

There is as yet no vaccine to prevent the spread of HIV and AIDS. The suffering associated with AIDS could be eliminated, however, through the prevention of behaviors that are related to the transmission of this highly communicable disease. Specifically, the reduction of high-risk sexual behavior is the target for psychological interventions to reduce the risk for HIV (Ross & Kelly, 2000). Sexual behaviors can be modified, most notably through limitations in the number of sexual partners and in the use of condoms to protect against the spread of HIV. The rate of new reported cases of AIDS reached a peak in the United States in 1992–1993 and has declined since then (Centers for Disease Control,

2001). This decline can be directly attributed to changes in high-risk sexual behavior.

Depression is responsive to several different types of treatment, including at least two forms of psychotherapy and several types of psychoactive medication (see chapter 15). However, effective means to prevent depression will be required to reduce the trend for increases in depression in recent birth cohorts. The tendency for initial episodes of depression to increase significantly among adolescents suggests that intervention early in the life span will be important to deter the onset of the disorder. For example, Hankin et al. (1998) found that the rate of clinical depression increased dramatically after age 15 (see figure 11.2). This finding suggests that early adolescence is an optimal time for preventive interventions to reduce the incidence of new cases of depression.

Violent acts against women reflect the broader values and attitudes of society, including dehumanizing attitudes toward women and the condoning of violence. Psychology can contribute to changing these attitudes that are socialized in families, schools, and other formal and informal structures in society. Such actions include changing societal responses to crimes against women in order to protect victims and decrease recidivism of offenders, and changing public policy as well as individual behavior (Koss, 2000).

Key Concepts in Promotion and Prevention

Health and Wellness   The promotion of positive development, functioning, and mental health requires a clear definition of the central concepts. Several terms have been used to capture optimal psychological functioning, including psychological wellness (Cowen, 1991, 1994), social and emotional competence (Weissberg, 2000), and **positive mental health** (Compas, 1993). It is unlikely that a single definition can be generated to satisfy the multiple, divergent perspectives that are needed to understand optimal psychological health. Rather, a multidimensional framework is

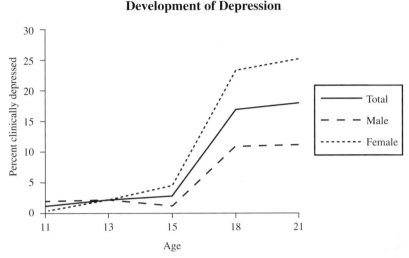

FIGURE 11.2.
Longitudinal data on the rates of depressive disorder by age during adolescence (from Hankin, Abramson et al., 1998).

needed to account for differences in positive mental health as a function of the perspectives of individuals and others in their lives (spouses, children, parents, teachers, peers, mental health professionals), the developmental level of the individual, and sociocultural factors (Compas).

The two primary dimensions of positive mental health include the development of skills and resources to (a) *protect* oneself from stress and adversity and (b) *involve* oneself in personally meaningful activities in order to generate a sense of personal mastery and competence (Compas, 1993; Weissberg, 2000). The protective functions of positive mental health center around the ability and motivation to adequately cope with stress and adversity (e.g., Compas, Connor-Smith, Saltzman, Thomsen, & Wadsworth, 2001). Effective coping contributes to positive mental health by providing ways to deal with adverse effects of acute and chronic stress. The second dimension of positive mental health is characterized by generative functions that include the ability and motivation to involve oneself in personally meaningful instrumental or expressive activities that are goal directed, that are experienced by the individual as autonomous, and

that are initiated by the self. Personal commitments to meaningful activities and relationships have been central to a number of theories of human functioning, development, and adaptation (e.g., Diener & Suh, 2000; Fredrickson, 2000; Ryan & Deci, 2000).

Risk and Protective Factors   Risk factors are defined as characteristics of the person or the environment that, if present for a given individual, make it more likely that this individual, as compared with others in the general population, will develop a disorder (NIMH, 1993). Research supports several generalizations about risk factors. First, risk exists in multiple domains. For example, in the case of drug abuse, risk factors have been identified within individuals, family environments, school experiences, peer or social interactions, and community contexts. Second, individuals who are exposed to a greater number of risk factors have a higher degree of risk for psychopathology; in other words, risk factors are additive in their input. Third, a given risk factor can increase the probability of a variety of disorders. For example, marital discord as characterized by high levels of parental conflict has been related both to depression among young women and conduct problems among children.

Risk factors serve as markers that an individual or group of individuals have a greater probability of developing a disorder. However, markers of risk fail to provide information about how or why a disorder is likely to develop. For example, depression in a mother or father is a significant risk factor for psychopathology in children (Gotlib & Goodman, 2000). In spite of the clear evidence for the risk associated with parental depression, there are several possible mechanisms that account for the increased risk among children of depressed parents (S. H. Goodman & Gotlib, 1999). Biological mechanisms are plausible, because the risk for psychopathology, or more specifically the risk for depression, may be genetically passed on to children. Social risk processes are also possible, because depressed parents are more withdrawn, less responsive, and more irritable and hostile in their interactions with their children than are nondepressed parents. Cognitive mechanisms may also contribute, because children of depressed parents may acquire maladaptive ways of thinking through observation of and interactions with their parents. Preventive interventions for children of depressed parents would differ based on whether some or all these mechanisms are important in explaining the transmission of problems from depressed parents to their children.

The flip side of risk factors are those features of individuals and their environments that are associated with a decreased likelihood of psychopathology and other psychological problems in spite of exposure to sources of risk. **Protective factors** are defined as characteristics of the person or the environment that increase an individual's resistance to risk and, therefore, strengthen the individual against the development of psychological disorder (Coie et al., 1993; NIMH, 1993). There is increasing evidence that exposure to risk can be mitigated by a variety of individual and social characteristics operating as protective factors. These factors decrease psychological problems in a number of ways: in a direct, straight-line fashion; by interacting with given risk factors to buffer against dysfunction; by disrupting the chain of events through which risk factors operate to cause dysfunction; or by preventing the initial occurrence of the risk factor. Each of these protective processes can be used to design strategies for intervention that can then be implemented at the level of the individual, the group, the community, or at multiple levels.

Approaches to Prevention

Knowledge of risk and protective factors is used to formulate preventive interventions to reduce the adverse effects of exposure to risk and to enhance the beneficial effects of protective factors. Preventive interventions are intended to counteract risk factors and build protective factors in order to disrupt processes that contribute to human dysfunction (Coie et al., 2000). Three levels of preventive interventions have been described: universal, selective, and indicated (Mrazek & Haggerty, 1994). **Universal preventive interventions** are directed to the general population and address factors that contribute to increased risk in the population as a whole. For example, depression occurs at a relatively high rate in the population from adolescence onward, and preventive interventions can be directed to the whole population to teach cognitive and behavioral skills that may reduce one's risk for experiencing a depressive episode. **Selective preventive interventions** are targeted to subgroups of the population whose risk is greater than for the population as a whole but who have not yet manifested the problem or disorder. For example, children whose parents are clinically depressed are at dramatically increased risk for developing depression themselves; therefore, preventive interventions can be delivered to families in which one or both of the parents has suffered an episode of major depression. **Indicated**

preventive interventions focus on high-risk individuals identified as having minimal but detectable signs of or symptoms foreshadowing mental disorder. Elevated levels of depressive symptoms have been found to increase the risk for a clinical depression. Screening methods can be used to identify individuals in the population who are experiencing high levels of depressive symptoms, and those individuals can receive interventions to reduce the likelihood that they will experience an episode of major depression.

Preventive interventions have historically been a part of community psychology—a branch of psychology that is committed to understanding people in relation to their communities and their social context, to empowering people and communities to identify and address the problems that they face, and to preventing psychopathology and social problems. Community psychology emerged in the 1960s and 1970s as the result of several factors (Rappaport & Seidman, 2000). These included the deinstitutionalization of psychiatric patients, the federally funded effort to make mental health services available to all members of society through the establishment of community mental health centers, the increasing acceptance of the assumption that mental health problems are rooted in social problems and forces and not solely within individuals, and a commitment to prevention as the most efficacious way to meet the mental health needs of society.

There is mutual benefit to a close link between community and clinical psychology. Community psychologists draw on methods and techniques developed in clinical psychology for many preventive interventions. Conversely, clinical psychologists need to be cognizant of the limits of treatment of psychopathology as a method of truly meeting the mental health needs of society. The distinction between clinical and community psychology, like the distinction among most divisions within psychology, is more counterproductive than beneficial. There is an ever-increasing need for psychologists—whether they identify themselves primarily as clinical or community psychologists—to combine their efforts to increase the scope and effectiveness of preventive interventions.

EXEMPLARY PROMOTION AND PREVENTION PROGRAMS

Health Promotion

The promotion of a healthier lifestyle has become pervasive in American culture. Programs and centers that promote a healthier diet, regular aerobic exercise, stress management, and an optimistic outlook on life permeate our society. Many of these programs reflect little more than fads that are aimed at capturing a portion of the huge market for these activities. However, the field of psychology, including clinical psychology, has contributed extensive research and program development that has led to a number of empirically validated programs to achieve these goals.

Lifestyle is comprised of expressive behaviors of the individual, that is, behaviors over which one has some degree of choice and control, that establish a distinctive mode or pattern of living (Kaplan, 2000). Research has established certain lifestyles as **health enhancing** and others as **health compromising.** Health-enhancing lifestyles are those patterns of behavior that are associated with lower morbidity and disease and higher levels of fitness and competence. For example, research on the lifestyles of adolescents has shown that certain health-promoting behaviors tend to be correlated with one another, including exercise, sleep, healthy diet, dental care, safe driving, and positive social activities (Jessor, 1998). There is also evidence that certain health-compromising or health risk behaviors also occur together, including substance abuse, delinquent behaviors, unsafe sexual activity, and drunk driving (Jessor). Health promotion interventions are designed both to increase behaviors that enhance health and reduce those that compromise health.

Most interventions typically target a specific aspect of a healthy lifestyle, although some are broad in scope and address many health-enhancing behaviors. The following sections offer salient examples of health promotion programs.

Diet and Exercise   Extensive research has shown that diets that are low in fat content and high in dietary fiber, in combination with regular aerobic exercise, are related to a variety of positive health outcomes. The challenge for psychologists is how to help people adhere to good dietary practices. Interventions have been effective in the development of positive dietary practices and exercise in school-age children (e.g., Lytle, Stone, Nichaman, & Perry, 1996; Sallis et al., 2000) and in adults (Ornish et al., 1998). Simple education about nutrition alone seems to be ineffective in promotion of healthy diet and has to be accompanied by specific methods to bring about behavioral change. Several successful dietary interventions that involve structured behavioral programs have been reported, but these interventions have been very brief, typically only five to six sessions. For example, the Child and Adolescent Trial for Cardiovascular Health (CATCH) program modified the food served in school cafeterias, increased the quality of physical activity in physical education classes, and campaigned against cigarette smoking. The program resulted in significant changes in children's diet, exercise, and smoking (Perry et al., 1997).

Stress Management   It can be said that we live in an era of stress. Adults and children report that they experience high levels of stress in their lives, including major events that involve significant loss and disruption as well as the minor chronic stresses and hassles that characterize daily living in our highly technological society. Pressures at work and school, disruptions and conflict in families, economic problems, the threat of violence in our communities, and the fast pace of life all contribute to the experience of high stress. The consequences of stress are well documented and include increased risk for physical disease, anxiety, and depression (e.g., McEwen, 1998; Sapolosky, 1998). To combat the effects of stress, individuals can choose from an array of programs. Most stress management programs rely on a single intervention technique—methods to increase relaxation. Relaxation methods are used to decease emotional and physiological arousal in response to stress and to help prevent the adverse emotional and physical consequences of stress (e.g., Kabat-Zinn et al., 1998).

Optimism, Personal Control, and Self-Efficacy   Positive mental health is characterized by a set of beliefs or a cognitive style that includes an optimistic outlook on the future, a sense of personal control over one's life, and a sense of self-efficacy (e.g., Bandura, 1997; Carver & Scheier, 1998; Ryan & Deci, 2000). These attitudes and ways of thinking are associated with more positive emotions and better physical health, even in the face of stress. Interventions have been successful in facilitating the development of these adaptive cognitive styles. For example, Seligman and colleagues have shown that more optimistic ways of thinking can be taught to school-age children as part of an effort to prevent the development of depressive symptoms (e.g., Gillham, Shatte, & Freres, 2000).

Promotion of Social Competence   What are the features of positive development during childhood and adolescence? What do children need to become happy and productive adults? In addition to needing the basic skills for learning, children need to acquire skills and competencies in forming and maintaining social relationships and in solving problems in daily living (Caplan, Weissberg, Grober, & Sivo, 1992; Weissberg,

2000). Clinical and community psychologists have developed programs to promote **social competence** that have become part of the regular school curricula in many parts of the country. The most widely used programs have been aimed at the enhancement of a set of positive outcomes variously labeled social competence or life skills (Weissberg). These programs share a common set of concerns centered around the development of the adaptive skills of the individual adolescent.

Multi-Component Programs   The most comprehensive health promotion programs have involved multiple components to develop many of the elements described above, such as teaching stress management skills, increasing optimism, and enhancing social competence. For example, Ornish and colleagues (1998) have tested the effects of a multicomponent program in an effort to reduce the risk for heart disease. This lifestyle program included a 10-percent-fat vegetarian diet, aerobic exercise, stress management training, smoking cessation, and group psychosocial support. Results indicate that participants reversed their signs of coronary heart disease as compared to a control group. Programs that include multiple elements of health-enhancing behaviors may very well lead to beneficial effects in both physical and psychological health.

In spite of the promise offered by programs to promote both mental and physical health, these programs are still in their early stages of development and application. Several factors have worked against the widespread application of health promotion efforts. One impediment has been clinical psychology's history of focusing on people's problems rather than on their strengths. There are also economic barriers, because our health care industry is designed to pay for the treatment of problems but not for the development of health. This problem is even greater for psychology because of the ambiguities in defining and measuring psychological health. In spite

of these barriers, promoting health and positive development warrants continued and increased investment as a first step in psychological intervention.

Prevention of Psychopathology and Disease

Preventive interventions are designed to counteract risk factors and reinforce protective factors in order to disrupt processes that contribute to psychological dysfunction (Coie et al., 1993). We will now consider prevention programs that have an established record of efficacy at different points in the life span. These programs reflect the changing nature of risk factors and problems that emerge at different points in development—the problems that need to be prevented in infancy differ from those of childhood and adolescence and from those of adulthood. Preventive interventions typically reflect the notion that early intervention is the best intervention. As such, they have tended to focus on interventions during childhood and adolescence on the premise that it is possible to prevent some of the problems found in adults by preventing the precursors at an earlier point in development. However developmental changes and processes continue throughout the life span, and adults face significant stressors that can exert effects independent of risk factors during childhood and adolescence. Therefore, it is important to consider examples of preventive interventions that have been developed to meet the unique needs of adults.

Intervening During Pregnancy   Certainly the earliest interventions in terms of developmental course are those that aim to enhance the prenatal environment and development of children. A number of programs have been developed to enhance the health and behavior of pregnant women in order to prevent a number of problems and disorders that can develop in their unborn babies. An excellent example of such a program is the Prenatal/Early Infancy Project for women in poverty, developed by psychologist David Olds (e.g., Olds, 1988, 1989; Olds, Henderson, Kitzman, & Cole, 1995; Olds, Henderson, & Tatelbaum, 1994). This program is interdisciplinary and involves home visitations by nurses to prevent a wide range of maternal and child health and behavioral problems that are associated with poverty. The overall objectives of the program are to improve child health and development by enhancing maternal prenatal health practices, improving the quality of maternal caregiving during early development, and increasing formal and informal community social support for pregnant women and new mothers (Olds, 1986). These interventions have been shown to increase children's IQs (Olds et al., 1994); they also lead to fewer childhood injuries, fewer behavioral and parental problems, and fewer visits to the emergency department for child-related problems. Intervention mothers were also observed to be more involved with their children and to use more effective means of discipline and punishment (Olds et al., 1994). These researchers also showed that the intervention led to thousands of dollars in reductions on government spending per family for intervention mothers by the time their children were 3 to 4 years old (Olds, Henderson, Phelps, Kitzman, & Hanks, 1993).

Substance Abuse Prevention   Cigarette smoking, alcohol use, and drug use emerge as significant health and behavioral problems in late childhood and early adolescence. Patterns established during these years have immediate implications both for health and other behavioral problems and for lifelong patterns of substance use and abuse. Prevention programs for adolescents have targeted cigarette smoking, drug abuse, and alcohol dependency (Botvin, 1999; Dusenbury & Falco, 1997). Two approaches have been used: the provision of information, and efforts to change specific behaviors. Informational strategies were guided first by educational research and later by social psychological theories of communication and attitude change, whereas behavioral approaches were informed

first by behavior therapy and later by social learning theory. The general consensus from years of research is that programs that rely solely on provision of information alone are unsuccessful (Leventhal & Keeshan, 1993). Behavioral interventions have been shown to be more effective and typically include multiple components and often combine information, decision making, coping with stress, enhancing self-concept, and refusal skills (Botvin).

Prevention of Aggression, Violence, and Delinquency   Few problems may be more pressing in our society than violence and aggression among youth (e.g., Margolin & Gordis, 2000). The incidence of violent behavior rises rapidly during adolescence, peaking between the ages of 17 and 19, and powerful gender differences in violent crime arrests also appear in late adolescence, with males being 10 times more likely than females to be arrested (Farrington, 2000). One of the most comprehensive efforts to prevent aggressive and violent behavior is a large-scale, multisite intervention study called the FAST Track (Families and Schools Together) program (Conduct Problems Prevention Research Group, 1992). Research has indicated that it is possible to identify children at a very young age who are likely to develop an enduring pattern of delinquent and even violent behavior by adolescence. The FAST Track program is designed to identify children who are at risk for this persistent pattern of aggressive and antisocial behavior at preschool age and to intervene with the children, their families, their schools, and communities in a large-scale effort to reduce the likelihood of these negative behaviors. The intervention includes five components: (a) parent training; (b) home visiting and case management; (c) social skills training; (d) academic tutoring; and (e) teacher-based, classroom intervention (Coie et al., 2000).

Prevention of PTSD in Victims of Sexual Assault   The number of women in the United States who are victims of sexual assault is staggering (National Victim Center and Crime Victims Research Center, 1992). One of the most prominent psychological consequences of such victimization is the presence of symptoms of PSTD, including intense fear and anxiety, re-experiencing of the traumatic event through flashbacks and intrusive thoughts, avoidance of trauma-related situations and stimuli, and increased emotional arousal (Kilpatrick, Resnick, Dansky, & Saunders, 1993; Rothbaum, Foa, Riggs, Murdock, & Walsh, 1992). Edna Foa and her colleagues have reported on the effects of a four-session cognitive-behavioral intervention for victims of assault (Foa, Hearst-Ikeda, & Perry, 1995). The program included education about the common reactions to assault, relaxation training, reliving the assault through imaginal exposure, confronting fearful but safe situations related to the assault, and changing negative thoughts about the assault. Compared to a sample of women who did not receive treatment, participants in the intervention had significantly less severe PTSD symptoms; only 10 percent of the intervention group as compared with 70 percent of the controls met criteria for PTSD at 2 months post-trauma. Five and one-half months later, the participants in the intervention were significantly less depressed and had significantly fewer symptoms of reexperiencing the trauma than did the controls (Foa et al.). These initial findings are encouraging—early interventions with victims of assault can be effective in preventing the longer term emotional costs that occur in many victims.

Job Loss and Unemployment The loss of one's job and sustained periods of unemployment are significant sources of stress in the lives of many adults. Even during economically prosperous times, it is estimated that 3 percent to 4 percent of eligible workers in the United States are unemployed. Furthermore, significant mental health problems are related to unemployment, the most significant of which is depression. Given that the loss of jobs and unemployment

are inevitable even in the best of times, an important target for psychologists is to prevent the adverse mental health consequences of job loss and to promote the skills and behaviors that are important in reemployment. Richard Price, Amiram Vinokur and their colleagues at the University of Michigan have conducted two large-scale prevention trials to evaluate a program that is designed to achieve these goals (Caplan, Vinokur, Price, & Van Ryn, 1989; Vinokur, Price, & Schul, 1995). The JOBS intervention program taught participants effective strategies to help them find appropriate new positions and to enhance their job search skills. Additionally, the program aimed to reduce negative mental health outcomes by enhancing participants' self-esteem and sense of personal control, their sense of self-efficacy in the job search process, and their sense of personal mastery. The findings were encouraging for the whole sample and more positive for a high-risk subgroup. Participants in the program, compared with a control group who received only a three-page pamphlet on job search strategies, experienced a greater sense of mastery, reported fewer depression symptoms, and experienced better reemployment outcomes (Vinokur et al.).

Prevention of HIV Infection The only methods available to stop the spread of HIV and AIDS involve changing behavior. Several promising efforts have been reported in this important arena of preventive interventions (Carey, 2000; Kelly et al., 1993; Ross & Kelly, 2000). Research has identified several high-risk populations: gay men, intravenous drug users, women in third-world countries, African American youth, and runaway adolescents. Interventions have focused on these high-risk populations with varied but encouraging results (Coates & Collins, 1999). Allen et al. (1993) report a study of 1,458 women in Rwanda assigned to intervention or control groups. Intervention participants received AIDS education counseling, educational video-tapes, HIV testing, and condoms and spermicides.

Women participating in the intervention increased the use of condoms and had decreased rates of gonorrhea and HIV infection through the 2-year follow-up. St. Lawrence et al. (1995) conducted a study in which African American adolescents were randomly assigned to an educational program for an 8-week intervention that combined education with behavior skills training, including correct condom use, sexual assertion, refusal, information provision, self-management, problem solving, and risk recognition. Skill-trained participants reduced their unprotected intercourse, increased their condom-protected intercourse, and displayed increased behavioral skills to a greater extent than did participants who received information alone. Risk reduction was maintained one year later for skill-trained youths: It was found that 31.1 percent of youths in the education program who were abstinent at baseline had initiated sexual activity one year later, whereas only 11.5 percent of the skill-trained participants were sexually active.

Kelly and associates have reported a series of studies with gay men, including several studies of men patronizing gay bars in an intervention community and several control comparison communities (Ross & Kelly, 2000). The researchers identified, trained and contracted with popular opinion leaders among gay men in the intervention city to serve as behavior change endorsers and diffusion agents to their friends and acquaintances. The researchers found reductions in reports of unprotected sex in intervention communities compared to the unchanged levels of risk behavior in comparison communities.

Coping With Divorce   Parental discord, conflict, and divorce represent significant risk factors for emotional and behavioral difficulties in children and adolescents (e.g., Emory & Forehand, 1996). Although a small but significant effect on children's adjustment can be directly attributed to parental divorce itself, the evidence is clear that far greater adverse effects can be attributed to parental conflict and fighting. Because of the risk associated with divorce and accompanying parental conflict and discord, preventive interventions have been developed to help children cope with the stress of divorce and reduce their risk for emotional and behavioral problems (Alpert-Gillis, Pedro-Carroll, & Cowen, 1989; Pedro-Carroll & Cowen, 1985; Stolberg & Mahler, 1994; Wolchick et al., 2000). Prevention programs for children of divorce have concentrated on teaching children coping skills to handle the stress of parental divorce and conflict, with additional efforts aimed at teaching parents behavioral skills that will reduce levels of interparental conflict and provide greater resources to their children in coping with the experience. The results of these programs have been promising. In controlled trials, children who receive the intervention are found to function better in terms of their emotions and behaviors than do control children. Controlled studies have shown that the program leads to reductions in anxiety, noncompliance, and learning problems, and increases in assertiveness, sociability with peers, and overall behavioral adjustment (e.g., Wolchick et al.).

Prevention of Depression   Several different models have emerged to explain the increased risk for depression during the adolescent period, and as a result, different models of intervention have emerged (Compas, Connor, & Wadsworth, 1997; Sandler, 1999). One approach to the prevention of depression in young people directly targets the negative cognitive processes that may contribute to the development of depressive symptoms (Gillham & Revich, 1999). The Penn Prevention Program at the University of Pennsylvania uses cognitive-behavioral techniques proactively to teach children coping strategies in the face of negative life events and to enhance their sense of mastery and competence across a variety of situations (Jaycox, Reivich, Gillham, & Seligman, 1994). The intervention program led to significant reductions in children's depressive symptoms as compared to control children who did not participate in the program (Jaycox et al.). The effects of the intervention were greater for children who reported high levels of parental conflict at home than for children who reported low levels of conflict. Thus, the intervention achieved its strongest effects for those children who were at greatest risk as a function of exposure to parental conflict, and achieved these effects at least in part by changing the ways that children interpreted the causes of negative events in their lives. The effects of the intervention were maintained at follow-up assessments at 12, 18 and 24 months (Gillham, Reivich, Jaycox, Seligman, 1995). Clarke, Lewinsohn, and colleagues have conducted an important series of studies illuminating the nature and course of depression during adolescence, the treatment of depression in young people, and most recently, the use of an indicated preventive intervention among adolescents at risk for depression (Clarke, 1999; Clarke et al., 1995). Across a 12-month follow-up period, 27.5 percent of the control group (18 of 70) experienced an episode of Major Depressive Disorder or Dysthymia, whereas 14.5 percent (8 of 55) of the intervention group had experienced an episode, a statistically significant difference.

Although the programs to prevent depression during childhood and adolescence represent an important first line of preventive interventions, they must be accompanied by similar efforts aimed at adults (Price & Johnson, 1999; Seligman, Schulman, DeRubeis, & Hollan, 1999). In one of the first documented efforts to prevent depression in adults, Muñoz et al. (1995) conducted a selective preventive intervention—they pinpointed a subgroup at increased risk for depression. These researchers reasoned that adults at early stages of depression and thus at high risk for developing clinical episodes of depression

could be identified through primary care facilities. The preventive intervention consisted of a course on cognitive-behavioral methods to gain greater control of one's mood carried out by doctoral-level psychologists who followed a specified protocol (the Depression Prevention Course; Muñoz, Ying, Perez-Stable, & Miranda, 1993). Results of the study found that participants in the intervention reported significantly lower levels of depressive symptoms compared to the control group at postintervention, 6 months, and 1 year. The effects of the intervention on depressive symptoms were largely attributable to changes in negative cognitions among the participants in the intervention.

To summarize, a wide array of interventions have been employed to prevent psychological problems and physical disease. Many of these programs share the approach of teaching individuals cognitive and behavioral skills to manage stress and adversity and teaching individuals to engage themselves in activities and relationships that are personally meaningful. Prevention researchers have tackled some of our most pressing public health problems. In spite of progress that has been made, significant impediments still remain. The greatest challenge for prevention lies in the record to date—psychology has yet to effectively prevent any major form of psychopathology. This record is in part due to the complex causal processes for any psychological disorder. Disorders are most likely the result of multiple different risk factors that contribute their development, and these multiple contributing risk factors may interact in complex ways in each individual case. As a result, prevention programs need to be broad in scope to address all possible sources of risk in a population. Furthermore, prevention research is a painstaking and lengthy process, because evidence for prevention effects requires sufficient time for problems to develop in an untreated group while their incidence is shown to be lower in a treated group. This process often requires studying large samples of individuals over long periods of time, in many instances for years. These challenges notwithstanding, preventive interventions play a critical role in the arsenal of clinical psychologists in their battle against psychological disorder.

PSYCHOTHERAPY AS TREATMENT

Although clinical psychologists are involved in a wide range of different forms of intervention, the majority are involved in conducting psychotherapy with individuals, groups, or families. With the range of different psychological treatments that have been developed, the term **psychotherapy** has come to represent a field so broad as to render the label almost useless or misleading. The breadth of the field has made it extremely difficult to define psychotherapy or to determine whether it is an effective means of treating psychopathology. To ask questions about psychotherapy is similar to asking questions about medicine. One cannot define the broad field of medicine in a way that captures the enormous range of treatments that it encompasses, nor can one ask whether "medicine works." Similarly, it is difficult to define psychotherapy and whether or not it works. In spite of these challenges, there are enough common elements that hold the concept of psychotherapy together that we can start by considering it at a broad level. In defining psychotherapy it is helpful to consider the features that all approaches to psychotherapy have in common as well as the dimensions on which specific approaches can be distinguished from one another.

All approaches to psychotherapy are based on a unique human interaction between two people. Within this interaction, a trained and certified professional attempts to help a client or patient to think, feel or behave differently. It is presumed that the verbal and nonverbal interactions between the therapist and the client, as well as the unique relationship that is formed, are important

elements in facilitating change in the client. The relationship between therapist and client is characterized by confidentiality, trust, and respect. Within the context of this relationship, the therapist typically follows a set of procedures that are, to a greater or lesser extent, prescribed by a certain theory or school of thought (Davison & Neale, 1998).

Psychiatrist **Jerome Frank** (1982; Frank & Frank, 1991) described four characteristics of the therapist-client relationship that may be common to all forms of psychotherapy. He believes there are important parallels between psychotherapy and other forms of socially accepted healing that have existed in other cultures throughout history. The four characteristics are (a) a therapeutic relationship that is highly emotional and private; (b) a setting or context for this relationship that is believed to promote healing of psychological problems; (c) a theory or set of principles (which Frank refers to as a shared or cultural "myth") that provide a reasonable explanation for the client's problems and for procedures used in therapy; and (d) a set of procedures (or in Frank's terminology, a "ritual") that both the therapist and client believe to be the means of solving the client's problems and restoring psychological health. All forms of psychotherapy are conducted within the framework of a private and confidential relationship between the client and therapist. The underlying belief systems and the specific techniques that are used are different for various forms of therapy. However, Frank argues that the important feature of all approaches is that there are a set of procedures, rituals, and beliefs that provide structure to the interaction between the client and therapist.

Kanfer and Goldstein (1991) have identified characteristics of helping relationships that distinguish them from other social relationships: Helping relationships are unilateral, systematic, formal, and time limited. Whereas most social relationships attend to the concerns and needs of both parties, helping relationships are unilateral in that they involve a contract to focus on solving the problems of the client. Helping relationships are systematic, because the therapist and client agree at the outset to follow a set of procedures in an organized manner in order to meet a mutually agreed upon goal. Formality is introduced into helping relationships in the limits that are placed on the relationship—contact will be limited to specific times and places, and these limits and boundaries are respected by both parties. Finally, helping relationships have a specified time limit, typically defined by the resolution of the client's problems.

Other researchers have attempted to identify a common set of steps or stages that characterize most forms of psychotherapy. Psychologist Ken Howard of Northwestern University and his colleagues have presented a phase model of psychotherapy that delineates three steps in the psychotherapeutic process (Howard, Lueger, Maling, & Martinovich, 1993). The phase model of psychotherapy involves progressive improvement of the client's subjective sense of well-being, reduction in psychological symptoms, and enhancement of overall life functioning. These authors argue that a client must make progress in each prior level before moving to the next phase. The first phase of psychotherapy involves **remoralization** or overcoming a sense of demoralization (Howard et al.). Frank and Frank (1991) describe demoralization as a state wherein patients "are conscious of having failed to meet their own expectations or those of others, or of being unable to cope with some pressing problem. They feel powerless to change the situation or themselves and cannot extricate themselves from themselves or their predicament" (p. 35). The second phase involves **remediation** of current problems, resolution of patients' underlying symptoms or life problems, or both. Treatment is concerned with mobilization of the patient's coping skills, encouragement of more effective coping skills, or both. The final phase of psychotherapy involves **rehabilitation,** in which the process is focused on the unlearning of troublesome, maladaptive, longstanding patterns and the

establishment of new ways of dealing with various aspects of self and life. Howard et al. have presented data from studies of psychotherapy processes that support their three-phase model. Remoralization typically occurs rapidly (within the first two sessions) and is reflected in increased subjective well-being. Remediation occurs next as reflected in decreased symptoms and must be preceded by increased subjective well-being. Rehabilitation (improved current life functioning) occurs last and must be preceded by both enhanced subjective well-being and symptom reduction.

In addition to attempts to identify the common elements in the various approaches to psychotherapy, it is equally important to recognize the differences among the diverse models of therapy. One important dimension on which approaches differ is the degree to which they emphasize insight versus action as their primary goals (e.g., London, 1986). Insight-oriented therapies assume that behavior, emotions, and thoughts become disordered because people do not adequately understand what motivates them, especially when their needs and drives conflict. Insight therapy tries to help people discover the true reasons for behaving, feeling, and thinking as they do. The premise is that greater awareness of motivations will yield greater control over and subsequent improvement in thought, emotion, and behavior. Behavioral therapies, in contrast, focus on changing overt behavior and do not regard insight as a necessary ingredient of therapy.

A second dimension on which therapies differ is the emphasis that they place on events that occur within versus outside the therapy sessions. Psychodynamic and humanistic therapies emphasize the importance of the therapy sessions themselves, specifically what transpires in the relationship between the client and the therapist. In contrast, behavioral and cognitive therapies, while recognizing the importance of the client-therapist relationship, place much greater importance on what takes place outside the therapy sessions in the client's daily life. This approach is most clearly reflected in the prescription of specific homework assignments in cognitive and behavioral therapies. The emphasis on events outside the therapy sessions is consistent with the greater action-orientation of these therapies.

We will examine the three most influential approaches to psychotherapy (psychodynamic, humanistic, and cognitive-behavioral) in chapters 12 through 14, emphasizing the unique features of each. We will return to the issue of possible common elements in different forms of psychotherapy, as well as their effectiveness, in chapter 15.

SUMMARY AND CONCLUSIONS

Clinical psychology has an important role to play in the promotion of mental and physical health and in the prevention of psychopathology and disease. Techniques and methods that have been found to be effective in treating problems can be used to prevent these problems as well. Efforts to promote health and prevent disorder need to be considered within a broader context as well, however—one that includes not just the skills and competencies of individuals but also the broader social context in which individuals live and function. Several principles can be drawn from current research and knowledge of health promotion and disease prevention that will help shape the future of clinical psychology.

We have sufficient knowledge of risk factors and processes to predict the risk for a variety of psychological and health problems. This knowledge can be used to inform the development of well-planned preventive interventions to address sources of risk or to enhance protective mechanisms. By using empirical research on risk and protective factors and processes, clinical psychologists can develop preventive interventions with greater precision and increased confidence that interventions are indeed addressing those factors that contribute to the development of problems and disorders. Unfortunately, knowledge of risk and protective factors is incomplete with regard to some problems and disorders. Continued basic research is needed to provide a better foundation for the prevention of a wider range of important psychosocial problems and psychological disorders.

The most effective preventive interventions have focused on developing adaptive cognitive and behavioral skills that will reduce risk for pathology and increase the likelihood of positive outcomes even in the face of exposure to known risk factors. The characteristics of these interventions are similar to those in cognitive-behavioral approaches to psychotherapy. Individuals and those in their social network are taught to manage and regulate emotions, to develop positive and adaptive ways of thinking, to solve problems, and to develop and maintain satisfying interpersonal relationships. Furthermore, individuals are taught important skills to avoid high-risk behaviors and situations. Through these interventions, people are able to increase their personal competence and cope more effectively with the stress and strain of everyday life as well as with more traumatic and severe forms of life stress.

Psychotherapy is the form of intervention most widely practiced by clinical psychologists. All forms of psychotherapy share a set of common factors and follow a sequence of stages of change. However, various approaches to therapy differ in the specific techniques that are used, in their emphasis on insight versus action, and in their focus on events within versus outside the therapy session.

KEY TERMS AND NAMES

Competence
Confidentiality
Jerome Frank
Health-compromising behaviors
Health-enhancing behaviors
Incidence of problems
Indicated preventive interventions
Informed consent
Positive mental health
Prevention
Promotion

Protective factors
Psychotherapy
Rehabilitation
Remediation
Remoralization
Risk factors
Selective preventive interventions
Social competence
Tatiana Tarasoff
Universal preventive interventions

RESOURCES

Books
Frank, J. D. & Frank, J. B. (1991). *Persuasion and healing: A comparative study of psychotherapy.* Baltimore: Johns Hopkins University Press.
Seligman, M. E. P. (1994). *What you can change and what you can't.* New York: Knopf.
Weissberg, R. P., Gullotta, T. P., Hampton, R. L., Ryan, B. A., & Adams, G. R. (Eds.). (1997).

Healthy children 2010: Enhancing children's wellness. Thousand Oaks, CA: Sage.
Journals
Journal of Primary Prevention
American Journal of Community Psychology
Health Psychology
Psychotherapy: Research and Practice

CHAPTER TWELVE

PSYCHOTHERAPY: PSYCHOANALYTIC AND PSYCHODYNAMIC APPROACHES

INTRODUCTION

Most forms of psychotherapy practiced today are in some way affected by the work of Sigmund Freud. Many current psychotherapies are either derived from Freudian psychoanalysis or, in some sense, are a reaction against Freud's ideas. Freud's theorizing and writings have permeated contemporary society, influencing not only psychiatry and psychology but also literature, film, and even accounts and interpretations of history. One unfortunate consequence of the far-reaching influence of Freudian theory is that many of the representations of his ideas have become caricatures, often bearing little resemblance to his original ideas. An accurate understanding of the theory and practice of psychoanalysis must move beyond these superficial representations of Freud's ideas to the basic concepts and principles of this approach in the treatment of psychological problems.

A significant number of mental health practitioners, including psychologists, still adhere to the original theory and methods outlined by Freud during his career, practicing what is generally referred to as "orthodox psychoanalysis" (e.g., Karon & Widner, 1995). Not surprisingly, however, there have been many variations and derivations of Freud's original ideas. Beginning with Freud's own students and contemporaries and continuing to the present, psychologists, psychiatrists, and other mental health practitioners have adapted Freud's work in developing a wide range of therapeutic methods that are grouped together as "psychodynamic" psychotherapies as well as a less closely related group of "interpersonal" psychotherapies. These variations of orthodox psychoanalysis are now more widely practiced than is the original therapy. They have also spawned intensive research efforts aimed at understanding whether and how psychodynamic psychotherapy works, that is, whether it helps people deal more effectively with life's circumstances.

In chapter 4 we presented an overview of Freud's psychoanalytic theory. We described Freud's views of the origins and structure of personality and the importance he accorded the roles of anxiety and defense mechanisms in the development and experience of psychological distress. We begin this chapter by describing the practice of psychotherapy that Freud developed, known as psychoanalysis. Following our discussion of psychoanalysis, we turn to the development and

practice of psychodynamic psychotherapies and interpersonal psychotherapies. Throughout this chapter and over the next three chapters as well, we will underscore the importance of research results that examine not only the active ingredients of these and other psychotherapeutic methods but also their efficacy and effectiveness in helping people. We will describe this research in greater detail in chapter 15.

FREUDIAN PSYCHOANALYSIS

Based on the reports provided by Freud's patients during intensive sessions of psychotherapy, Freud formulated a theory of the development of personality and of psychopathology. We described this theory in detail in chapter 4, and here we will briefly turn our attention to those aspects of the theory that are most important for understanding the principles and techniques of Freudian **psychoanalysis.** Freud emphasized the principle of psychic determinism (all our thoughts, feelings, and behaviors are determined by prior mental activity) and the primary role of the unconscious in explaining the way we function. Essentially, Freud postulated that we are largely unaware of the powerful underlying forces that shape and direct our thoughts and behaviors. He believed that emotional and biological drives and needs are satisfied or not satisfied to different degrees during childhood. To defend ourselves against the pain that would be caused by remembering experiences of frustration in getting our needs met or by remembering early unacceptable feelings of love, disappointment, or resentment toward one or both of our parents or other significant figures in our lives, we relegate these memories and feelings to our unconscious. Even though we are not aware of this material, it nevertheless affects our day-to-day behaviors and feelings. We develop defense mechanisms, such as repression, projection, and reaction formation, to keep ourselves from consciously recognizing or facing this material. Unfortunately, although defense mechanisms serve the useful and adaptive (at least in the short term) function of keeping us from experiencing anxiety, they are also costly. For example, defense mechanisms require a considerable expenditure of psychic energy (libido), which, in the context of Freud's view of people as closed energy systems, means that there is less energy available for use in dealing adaptively with life stress. Moreover, because defense mechanisms keep us from being aware of unacceptable thoughts, memories, and feelings, we cannot learn from these early experiences.

These concepts of the unconscious and the use of defense mechanisms lie at the heart of the practice of psychoanalysis. Indeed, Karon and Widener (1995) stated that "According to Freud, there are four concepts so basic that, if one accepted them, one would be practicing psychoanalysis even if one disagreed with Freud in every other respect. These concepts are the unconscious, repression, transference, and resistance" (p. 25). We have already presented Freud's views regarding the unconscious and defense mechanisms such as repression and projection; in the following sections of this chapter we will describe how these constructs come into play in the process of Freudian psychoanalysis.

Goals of Psychoanalysis

Virtually all approaches to psychotherapy have as their broad, ultimate goal improvement in the quality of the patient's day-to-day functioning. As we will see, however, each form of psychotherapy also has more specific objectives derived primarily from the theoretical foundations on which the therapy is built. With respect to psychoanalysis, a major goal of therapy is to help patients achieve insight into the sources and origins of their difficulties. This objective is based on Freud's formulation of the importance of the unconscious in contributing to our experience of anxiety and general distress. Because it is unacceptable material in our unconscious that leads us to experience anxiety, psychoanalysis attempts to help us become aware of this unconscious material and information and bring it to a

conscious level, to help us make the unconscious conscious. Indeed, Freud believed that we can change only what is conscious—conflicts and unacceptable drives and impulses that remain in the unconscious cannot be faced and managed in a psychologically mature and effective manner. This "transfer" of material from the unconscious to the conscious level not only represents a gain in insight on the part of the patient and facilitates the process of change, but it also reduces or eliminates the need for the patient to continue to use defense mechanisms to keep this unacceptable material in the unconscious. And this reduction in the use of defense mechanisms frees up libido, energies that can now be used for more adaptive functioning.

Training

For many years psychoanalytic training was restricted to psychiatrists, even though Freud himself was trained originally as a neurologist and supported the practice of analysis by nonphysicians. More recently, however, psychoanalytic training centers have been broader in their acceptance criteria, and now mental health practitioners from a variety of professional backgrounds apply and are accepted to be trained in psychoanalysis. One of the hallmarks of training in psychoanalysis is the frequent requirement that the trainees undergo analysis themselves as part of their training, an endeavor that may take four to six years. Training in the more recent variations of psychodynamic and interpersonal therapy can be obtained as part of graduate training in some doctoral training programs in clinical psychology and is not regulated in the manner that psychoanalytic training has been.

Logistics

When psychotherapy is portrayed in cartoons or movies, more often than not the patient is lying on a couch with the therapist sitting in a chair off to the side with a notepad (and a beard and pipe!). This perception of the structure of the psychotherapy session comes from the practice of orthodox psychoanalysis. Freud had his patients lie on a couch in a darkened room while he sat in a chair behind their heads, out of their line of sight. There are several reasons for this arrangement. From a purely practical perspective, Freud saw patients in his practice for very long stretches of time and did not want to have to continually monitor his facial expressions. Indeed, some historians have suggested that Freud simply was uncomfortable in face-to-face encounters. Of greater theoretical importance, the patient lying on a couch in a darkened room with the analyst out of sight serves two purposes. First, Freud believed that having the patient lie on a couch inhibits the patient's motor movement and, consequently, encourages the patient to engage in mental activity. The darkened room also serves to reduce the influence of stimulation from external sources and facilitates the patient's experience and production of fantasies and projections. Second, an important aspect of psychoanalysis (and, indeed, of most psychoanalytically oriented psychotherapies) is the development and analysis of the patient's transference. Having the analyst seated behind the patient, out of the patient's sight, lessens the likelihood that the patient's feelings about the analyst are based on the analyst's nonverbal expressions or behaviors and increases the probability that these feelings represent a "transference neurosis," emanating from the patient's unconscious feelings about significant people early in his or her life.

Psychoanalysis involves frequent sessions over a long period of time. It is not unusual, for example, for patients to attend hour-long sessions of psychoanalysis three to four times per week for up to three to five years. Although this may seem like a long time to be in therapy, particularly in light of current managed care practices, it is important to recognize that, in contrast to other forms of treatment that might focus on changing such circumscribed behaviors as smoking or overeating, psychoanalysis attempts to bring about significant and long-lasting changes

in the patient's personality more globally. Because patients may have had problematic patterns of personality difficulties and dysfunction that have been ingrained and strengthened for many years or even decades, the process of effecting lasting change in personality is understandably a time-consuming endeavor. And to further compound this process, the patient is, at least at an unconscious level, ambivalent about making changes in his or her personality and is using defenses to work against the efforts of therapy. More contemporary derivations of psychoanalysis have worked hard to reduce the length of standard psychoanalysis without losing its unique characteristics.

Methods

Hypnosis   The primary goal of psychoanalysis is to help patients become aware of unconscious feelings and memories that are causing them anxiety and interfering with their day-to-day functioning, that is, to make the unconscious conscious. Two observations that Freud made during his collaborations with Breuer and Charcot led him to begin to use **hypnosis** to achieve this goal by delving into the patient's unconscious. First, Breuer and Freud used hypnosis to treat a young woman, Anna O., and found that her symptoms disappeared while she was hypnotized. Second, when Anna O. expressed strong emotions under hypnosis, the intensity of her symptoms following the hypnotic session appeared to be reduced. On the basis of these observations, Freud believed that hypnosis might hold the key to unlocking the secrets of the unconscious.

Freud began to use hypnosis with his patients but found the results to be disappointing. He continued to believe in the importance of gaining access to unconscious material but felt that if patients are to become aware of this material, the ego needs to be actively involved in this process. Freud thought that hypnosis did not have lasting effects because it essentially bypassed the ego in accessing unconscious materials. Patients had contact with information in the unconscious only while under hypnosis; after they emerged from the hypnotized state, their defense mechanisms continued to ensure that they would be unaware of this material. And if patients have no memory of talking about feelings or materials that are in their unconscious, they will make no therapeutic gains outside the hypnotized state. So Freud was faced with the problem of trying to gain access to the patients' unconscious while at the same time circumventing the defense mechanisms to allow the patients to become aware of this material.

Free Association   The solution that Freud hit upon was to develop and use a procedure that has come to be known as **free association.** In free association the patient, lying on the couch, is encouraged to say everything that comes into her or his mind during the course of a therapeutic session. Freud (1913) instructed the patient to "Act as though . . . you were a traveler sitting next to the windows of a railway carriage and describing to someone inside the carriage the changing views which you see outside" (p. 135). Essentially, Freud wanted patients to learn to be passive recipients and reporters of their trains of thoughts, eliminating conscious control over their mental processes. The therapist is a careful and attentive listener but does not guide the patient's verbalizations. In fact, the therapist tries not to interrupt the patient's thoughts and speech unless it will serve to help the process of discovery. Freud assumed that under these unstructured and ambiguous conditions, the defense mechanisms would be relaxed and unconscious processes would emerge. More important, because the patient is awake and aware throughout this process (in contrast to hypnosis), any material that is uncovered from the unconscious becomes part of the patient's conscious experience and memories.

The analyst's task in this process is to try to make sense of the patient's sequences of associations. Based on the principle of psychic determinism, the analyst works from the assumption that each association is related in some way to the content of the previous verbalization. It is only because the patient's defense mechanisms are relaxed or weakened by the structure of the psychoanalytic environment that unconscious material begins to emerge with free association. The patient may not be aware of the meaning or significance of what she or he is saying at any given moment; it is the task of the analyst to understand and interpret the importance of the patient's somewhat rambling talking.

Dream Analysis   Freud believed that a similar process is involved in **dream analysis.** He believed that, during sleep, the normal ego controls are more relaxed than is the case while the patient is awake and, consequently, unconscious processes are freer to operate and be expressed in dreams. In fact, Freud (1900, p. 647) referred to dreams as "the royal road to . . . the unconscious." He believed that dreams represent the fulfillment of wishes. Freud made a distinction between two levels of content in dream analysis: **manifest content** and **latent content.** Whereas manifest content refers to the actual content of the dream, latent content refers to what the manifest content symbolically represents. For example, the manifest content of a dream about a train entering a dark tunnel is the train and the tunnel. In contrast, the latent content might involve the patient's feelings about engaging in sexual activity.

The difference between manifest and latent content is also illustrated in the following example:

> Tom, a midlevel business executive, has sought out help in psychotherapy to deal with his vague feelings of unhappiness and frustration in his life. Tom is unable to identify the source of his unhappiness; he says he feels satisfied with his job, his family, and with his accomplishments. Tom observes, however, that even though he often feels frustrated, he virtually never expresses his anger toward others. As the only exception to this pattern, Tom reports

that he frequently loses his temper at home with his wife and his children. Tom then describes a dream that he has had about wolves. In this dream, a pack of gray and black wolves is roaming together through the woods. One of the wolves stands out because he is bright yellow. When the wolves are hunting, the yellow wolf often stays to himself, outside the pack. Although he is able to hunt and catch rabbits, deer, and other sources of food, the other members of the pack eat what he catches before he has the chance. Tom is puzzled by this dream; he lives in Boston, and he has never been hunting or ever seen a wolf or any animal in the wild. Thus, the manifest content of the dream appears to have little significance. The analyst notes that wolves are strong and powerful animals, but that the color yellow denotes cowardice and fear. After continued discussion about Tom's feelings of frustration, the analyst offers the interpretation that the yellow wolf in Tom's dream represents strong feelings of power and strength that he is afraid to express. It is at this point that Tom begins to describe his extreme feelings of frustration in his work where he often feels angry with his superiors, who do not work as hard as he does yet take all of the credit for his efforts and successes. From the perspective of the analyst, the yellow wolf symbolized Tom's ambivalent and conflicted feelings of anger that he was afraid to express.

Freud recognized that the wishful ideas in dreams do not emerge easily. We keep these ideas and fantasies that make up the latent content of dreams stored in our unconscious because they are unacceptable to us. It is only because the latent content of our dreams is sufficiently disguised in the form of more neutral or acceptable manifest content that we are able to continue our dreams and to recall them when we are awake. If the latent content were too easily recognizable to us, we would become anxious and awaken. In fact, Freud believed that this defense mechanism is precisely what leads us to have and to wake up from nightmares—the unacceptable and anxiety-inducing latent content of our dream has emerged without being changed enough to be innocuous and is so threatening to the ego that the anxiety awakens us.

Given the high rate at which we dream (see box 12.1) and the relatively low rate at which most of us are awakened by nightmares, psychoanalysts would conclude that we are obviously reasonably successful in disguising the latent content of our dreams. The process of transforming the latent content of our dreams into manifest content is referred to as **dream work.** Dream work takes place, of course, at an unconscious level. It is a self-protective process that allows us to express our unacceptable wishes and feelings to a relaxed ego, but in a disguised form.

In analyzing dreams, the psychoanalyst will often ask the patient to free associate to the manifest content of the dream, which is the only content of which the patient is aware. The patient's associations to this content in turn provide additional material for further analysis. It is unlikely that a single dream (or a single association) will provide the answer to the puzzle of the patient's problems. Rather, analysis of many dreams and associations is necessary to reveal consistent patterns of latent content that will bring the analyst and patient closer to understanding the patient's unconscious motivations, memories, and impulses.

Resistance   Why does it take so long to uncover latent content in free associations and dreams? In large part, the reason for this lengthy process is due to the patient's use of defense mechanisms. We use defense mechanisms to keep from experiencing unacceptable drives, impulses, feelings, and memories that would cause us anxiety if we were to become aware of them. The major goals of psychoanalysis, paradoxically, run completely counter to this purpose. In fact, the process of psychoanalysis actually activates and strengthens the patient's use of defense mechanisms. That is, while the patient and therapist are attempting to bring the patient's unconscious material into awareness, the patient's defenses are working (unconsciously) to prevent this from happening. Although it is not considered a classic defense mechanism like repression or projection, the concept of **resistance** clearly operates against the efforts of the patient and therapist to uncover unconscious material. Resistance, in the context of psychoanalysis, may be defined as "the trend of forces within the patients which oppose the process of ameliorative change" (Menninger, 1958, p. 104).

Freud recognized that resistance is an inevitable part of psychoanalysis: "The resistance accompanies the treatment step by step. Every single association, every act of the person under treatment must reckon with the resistance and represents a compromise between the forces that are striving toward recovery and the opposing ones" (Freud, 1912, p. 103). The patient has had many years of practice and experience using defense mechanisms to keep unacceptable unconscious material from reaching consciousness, and these defenses do not stop operating simply because the patient is now in therapy. Resistance can show itself in any number of ways. For example, a patient might be inexplicably late for a session or may forget to attend a session altogether (an especially interesting lapse if the patient had been coming to therapy sessions faithfully three times per week for the past three years). In the session itself, resistance might be seen in slowed-up production or blocking in the patient's free associations, or in the patient's relaying of bland or minute details of her or his day. Resistance might also be seen in the patient's dream content, as in the following example offered by Menninger (1958):

> A young man had achieved a reputation for brave and dashing military exploits. For this, and because he was handsome and well-to-do, he was a romantic figure. But his physical relations with his wife were a disappointment to both him and her, and he began psychoanalytic treatment for this and some other symptoms. The early weeks of his analysis brought a sincere contrasting of the world's impression of him with his own realization of weakness. This encouraging phase was succeeded by a period of slowed up production culminating in a dream. He was exploring a house which looked very good on the outside. But as he went further

through the halls of this interesting and handsome building he came to a corner of one room where he stopped short, horrified. For on the floor in that corner lay something dreadful, disgusting, terrible — 'too awful to look at. Perhaps it was a decaying dog—a cur—a beast—something of mine.' He did not dare to look at it but turned and fled from the building. A few days later the patient wrote that he was feeling better and believed he would discontinue his analysis. (pp. 101–102)

At its strongest, as we saw in this example, resistance might even lead the patient to discontinue therapy prematurely. It is important to remember that, as is the case with all defense mechanisms, resistance operates at an unconscious level, outside the patient's awareness. Therefore, the patient will not realize that the motivation underlying his termination of therapy is an avoidance of dealing with conflict-laden issues. Rather, he will believe that he discontinued therapy because he is "cured"; he believes that he is now significantly healthier psychologically than he was when he began therapy and that he has benefited from therapy enough that he can now terminate treatment. This premature termination of psychoanalysis, triggered by the patient's motivation to avoid dealing with conflictual issues that were activated during therapy, is referred to as a "flight into health." More accurately, of course, this action is a flight away from dealing with troublesome feelings or memories.

If the patient does terminate treatment in this way, the defense mechanisms have "won": They have served their purpose by preventing the patient from becoming aware of unconscious conflicts and feelings that would cause him greater anxiety than he is already experiencing. Unfortunately, this victory is only short term. The issues and problems that initially brought the patient to therapy will continue to plague him once the immediate relief of not having to deal with these difficulties passes.

Transference and the Therapist-Patient Relationship   At the core of psychoanalysis is the relationship or alliance between the patient and

BOX 12.1

THE MEANING AND FUNCTION OF DREAMS

Freud was by no means the first person to focus on the importance of dreams. Indeed, throughout recorded history we have sought to understand the meaning and function of dreams. As far back as the Bible's Book of Genesis, for example, we read that Joseph interpreted a dream reported by Pharaoh, an ancient Egyptian leader, as predicting seven years of feast followed by seven years of famine. The classic Greeks used dreams as a basis to make medical diagnoses. Ill patients were required to sleep in a temple, and during sleep, they were awakened by priests who elicited and recorded reports of their dreams. These dreams were then used as part of the basis for the patients' diagnoses.

But it was Freud who offered the first systematic psychological explanation of the function and meaning of dreams. In 1900 Freud published *The Interpretation of Dreams,* in which he proposed that dreams were the royal road to the unconscious. Essentially, Freud believed that dreams represent a disguised form of our deepest (and most unacceptable) impulses and wishes. For Freud, dreams are constructed in order to allow these wishes to be expressed in an acceptable form (manifest content),

and we must work to keep the underlying (latent) content of the dream unrecognizable in order to preserve our sleep.

Since Freud's formulation, there has been a good deal of empirical research examining both psychological and physiological aspects of dreams. This amount of attention should not be surprising given that in a life span of 70 years we devote some 30,000 hours (over 3 full years) to dreaming. And in fact, today there are a number of theories about dreaming, anchored on one extreme by the view that dreams serve an adaptive function by helping us deal with stressors in our lives and on the other extreme by the position that dreams are essentially meaningless entities, the results of random nerve cell activity that occurs with greater frequency during a stage of sleep known as rapid eye movement (REM) sleep.

Dreams occur primarily during REM sleep. Typically, four periods of REM sleep occur each night, beginning about 90 minutes after sleep onset, occurring about 90 minutes apart, and increasing in length from about 10 minutes to 20 to 30 minutes. If we remember dreams at all, they are usually from this last REM period.

the analyst. This relationship is unlike any other that the patient has encountered in her or his life, and its unique features are hypothesized to contribute greatly to how psychoanalysis works. Part of the reason that the analyst sits behind the patient's head, out of sight, is so he or she may serve as a "blank screen" onto which the patient can project or transfer unconscious feelings and desires. Freud's emphasis on this aspect of the relationship led to the widely held (but mistaken) assumption that the psychoanalyst must remain distant and detached from the patient. Although the therapist is not highly active or directive, it is critical that the patient form an attachment or working alliance with the therapist in order for treatment to proceed (Horvath & Luborsky, 1993). And to foster this alliance, the therapist

must convey both an understanding of the patient's emotions and a concern for the patient's welfare.

A critical aspect of this therapeutic alliance or relationship is the **transference** process. Freud observed that patients would experience feelings toward him (e.g., anger, dependency, sexual attraction) that were disproportionate to the actual nature of his relationship with them. He hypothesized that this was because patients were reliving experiences and feelings from the past as if they were occurring in the present, that is, patients were "transferring" their unconscious feelings onto their relationship with Freud. As Kubie (1950) wrote,

In psychoanalysis the word *transference* is used for the fact that in adult years our relationships to

BOX 12.1 (concluded)

There is a growing consensus among dream researchers that dreams are not meaningless, that they do serve important psychological and biological functions (Braun et al., 1998). Investigators who have studied dream content have demonstrated quite convincingly that dreams are related to issues and content with which we are dealing in our daily lives. Dream content, for example, can be directly manipulated by giving subjects presleep suggestions to dream about certain topics, by introducing stimuli during REM sleep, or by altering the environment. Depriving people of water increases the frequency of thirst-related dreams. Subjects exposed to subliminal presentations of pictures leads them to dream about parts of the pictures that they could not report seeing before they fell asleep. From a more naturalistic perspective, clinical researchers have found that the dream content of depressed people changes as their depression improves, moving from dreams of masochism, hostility, and anxiety to dreams of intimacy and sexuality. And similar findings have been obtained with patients diagnosed with post-traumatic stress disorder.

So it does not seem that dreams are meaningless or random. In fact, recent work by Jonathan Winson suggests that dreams may serve an evolutionary function of helping the individual process information necessary for survival. Winson (1990) notes that a brain wave called theta rhythm is found in all animals during REM sleep, the stage of sleep in which dreaming occurs. Based on these findings, he suggests that dreams are the "nightly record of a basic mammalian memory process: the means by which animals form strategies for survival and evaluate current experience in light of those strategies . . . With the evolution of REM sleep, each species could process the information most important for its survival" (p. 86–94).

Finally, although recurrent dreams have not been the focus of a lot of study, they are relatively common, occurring in 50 percent to 65 percent of people. Recurring dreams are most often reported to begin in childhood or adolescence and are typically negative in content. These dreams are more likely than ordinary dreams to include only the dreamer and to involve themes of being attacked or chased. Given the negative nature of these themes, it is not surprising that researchers have found recurrent dreamers to score significantly lower on measures of well-being than either former recurrent dreamers or nonrecurrent dreamers (Brown & Donderi, 1986).

others are compounded of both conscious and unconscious elements, and that the unconscious elements consist largely of attitudes, needs, feelings, and purposes which are carried over (i.e., "transferred") unconsciously from the attitudes and needs and feelings and purposes towards others which we developed in infancy and early childhood. (p. 57)

Freud believed that transference was an unconscious process for managing inner conflicts. Therefore, the patient's relationship with the analyst is a representation of his or her unconscious conflicts. Everything about this relationship provides clues to the patient's unconscious and must be analyzed and interpreted to help the patient understand his or her underlying problems.

Transference occurs at an unconscious level and, therefore, is not a logical process. Transference does not respect logic, time, or place. Consequently, the patient may respond to a male analyst as if he were the patient's rejecting mother or to a female analyst as if she were the patient's jealous brother. Freud recognized that transference is not unique to the psychoanalytic situation but rather occurs in any human relationship in which the individual projects his or her own conflicts, desires, attributes, and so on onto another person. What is unique about transference in the psychoanalytic relationship is that only in this situation is it analyzed and used to promote change. The transference relationship is critically important in psychoanalysis because it brings the patient's unconscious needs and conflicts into the present, making them visible and accessible to the patient's conscious awareness. The following example illustrates this point:

> A young woman reacts to my keeping her waiting for two or three minutes by becoming tearful and angry, fantasizing that I must be giving extra time to my favorite woman patient. This is an inappropriate reaction in a thirty-five-year-old intelligent and cultured woman, but her associations lead to a past situation where this set of feelings and fantasies fit. She recalls her reactions as a child of five waiting for her father to come to her room to kiss her good night. She always had to wait a few minutes because he made it a rule to kiss her younger sister good night first. Then she reacted by tears, anger, and jealousy fantasies—precisely what she is now experiencing with me. Her reactions are appropriate for a five-year-old girl but obviously not fitting for a thirty-five-year-old woman. The key to understanding this behavior is recognizing that it is a repetition of the past, i.e., a transference reaction (Greenson, 1967, pp. 151–152).

Because the transference relationship was both immediate and evident in the patient's behavior during the therapeutic session, Freud believed that analysis of the transference relationship was the most powerful technique for making the unconscious conscious and resolving unconscious conflicts. Transference did not require the recollection of dreams, nor did it rely on a special technique such as hypnosis. As long as the analyst was a sensitive yet relatively passive listener, the patient would inevitably reexperience, or transfer, repressed feelings and conflicts onto the therapist. This relationship was made even more compelling because the analyst represented a figure of authority to the patient, which was a powerful recreation of the authoritarian aspects of the parent-child relationship. Because the most important conflicts and problems were rooted in parent-child relationships, Freud believed, the therapist-patient relationship became a natural context in which a patient could reexperience these past conflicts.

Psychoanalysts themselves are not necessarily immune to transference; when the analyst experiences transference feelings toward the patient, it is referred to as *countertransference*. Counter-

transference can take the form of the analyst dreaming about a patient, forgetting an appointment, coming late to a session. If it is not recognized and dealt with early on, countertransference can impede the progress of therapy.

Catharsis   As Karon and Widner (1995) note, Freud believed that an unemotional, intellectual knowledge of previously unconscious feelings and material is not sufficient to produce lasting personality change. The unconscious will not be affected by the sterile knowledge of the conflict. Rather, the patient must deeply *experience* these feelings and conflicts and come to see them in a new way. This experiencing of feelings may take the form of the release of powerful emotions that have been repressed or blocked from direct expression—a process known as **catharsis.** Knowl-

Catharsis involves the release of powerful emotions in the context of psychotherapy. (*Source:* The Far Side® by Gary Larson © 1990 FarWorks, Inc. All Rights Reserved. Used with permission.)

edge of the power of catharsis dates back to the early Greeks, who believed that evoking emotions was an effective means of providing relief from emotional distress. Interestingly, more recent research conducted by professor James Pennebaker at the University of Texas provides empirical validation of the ameliorative effects of emotional expression (see box 12.2).

BOX 12.2

THE IMPORTANCE OF CATHARSIS

Professor James Pennebaker at the University of Texas has conducted an impressive series of studies documenting the impact of "emotional expression"—similar in many respects to the concept of catharsis—on psychological and physical health and well-being. Indeed, consistent with a psychoanalytic perspective, the assumption underlying these investigations is that holding emotions in, or not expressing emotions, is a form of inhibition, is hypothesized to affect autonomic and central nervous system activity, and represents a long-term, low-level stressor. Pennebaker reasoned that just as constraining the expression of thoughts and feelings that are linked to an emotional experience is stressful and upsetting, letting go and talking about these experiences should reduce the stress of inhibition.

Pennebaker had subjects write about assigned topics for three to five consecutive days, for 15 to 30 minutes per day. Subjects randomly assigned to the experimental group were asked to write (or talk into a tape recorder) about their deepest thoughts and feelings about an extremely important emotional issue or event that has affected their lives. Control subjects, in contrast, were asked to write or talk about more superficial topics, such as how they spend their time and what they did when they woke up that morning. Pennebaker (1997) describes this emotional expression paradigm as exceptionally powerful:

> Participants, from children to the elderly, from honor students to maximum-security prisoners, disclose a remarkable range and depth of traumatic experiences. Lost loves, deaths, incidents of sexual and physical abuse, and tragic failures are common themes in all of the studies. (p. 162)

In well over a dozen different studies, Pennebaker and his colleagues have documented remarkable effects of expressing emotions in writing. For example, compared with writing about superficial control topics, writing or talking about emotional experiences has been found to be associated with significant drops in the number of visits to physicians. Emotional expression, although painful in execution, has also been found to produce long-term improvements in mood and reductions in emotional distress. Students who wrote about emotional topics have been found to show improvements in their subsequent grades, professionals who have been laid off from their jobs have been found to get new jobs more quickly after writing, and university staff members have been found to have lower rates of absenteeism following emotional expression.

The range and diversity of these effects of expressing deep thoughts and emotions are consistent with the importance accorded the concept of catharsis in psychoanalytic therapy. The question that remains, of course, is *how* emotional expression results in these changes. That is, what are the mechanisms underlying emotional expression's impact on these behaviors? Although the answer to this question is not yet clear, two promising possibilities have been raised. First, emotional expression appears to affect physiology. For example, writing about emotional topics has been found to have beneficial influences on immune function, including T-helper cell growth, killer cell activity, and antibody response to hepatitis B vaccination and to the Epstein-Barr virus, which has been implicated in chronic fatigue syndrome. Emotional expression has also been found to produce changes in autonomic and muscular activity. Any of these effects might lead to changes in mood or health-related behaviors. Second, Pennebaker has argued that the act of translating experiences into language is important for behavioral changes, particularly if the individual's writing shows evidence of increased insight over the course (days) of the study. This latter explanation certainly underscores the importance of *both* catharsis and gains in insight as critical mechanisms involved in adaptive change in psychotherapy.

Interpretation and Working Through In psychoanalysis, the patient must achieve a new level of both intellectual and emotional insight into and understanding of his or her behavior. This insight and understanding requires the analyst to **interpret** the patient's previously repressed material. A therapeutic interpretation often involves restating the patient's behavior or feelings in a new language and from a new frame of reference. In this case, the frame of reference is that of psychoanalytic theory. Interpretations are what the analyst tells the patient about her conflicts in order to help the patient increase her knowledge of herself and her experiences (Brenner, 1995). Interpretations convey the underlying meaning of a behavior to the patient. Among the most important interpretations are those that focus on the transference relationship between the patient and the therapist (Piper, Joyce, McCallum, & Azim, 1993). For example, a psychoanalyst may interpret how the therapist represents an authority figure for the patient and how the patient seems to be reenacting unresolved earlier conflicts within the therapeutic relationship.

In making an effective interpretation, the analyst must consider whether the client is able to accept the interpretation. If the interpretation is made too early, that is, before the client is ready to hear it, it will be rejected and it will be even more difficult for the client to hear it and accept it later in treatment. It is important, therefore, that interpretations be well timed. In general, the analyst should start from the "surface," that is, with material that is already close to conscious awareness and then go only as deep into the unconscious as the patient is able. The analyst also tries to make interpretations concerning the patient's defenses or resistance before interpreting the conflicts or emotions that lie beneath them.

As you might expect, it is typically difficult for the patient to accept a single interpretation of the use of a defense mechanism or of an underlying conflict. After all, the patient has spent most of a lifetime defending against unconscious issues and conflicts and avoiding dealing with the defenses. Therefore, a single interpretation that the patient's helplessness is really an unconscious form of aggression is unlikely to have much impact. Consequently, various interpretations of the same issue or conflict must be made, repeated from a number of different perspectives and contexts, in order to bring home to the patient how the conflict pervasively and adversely affects the patient's life in a variety of domains. The patient must become aware of how the conflict affects her or his life with respect to interpersonal relationships, work, home, social life, play, and so on. This process—the analyst making repeated interpretations of the patient's unconscious wishes, feelings, and memories and the patient experiencing and rediscovering these interpretations in many contexts—is referred to as *working through*. It is this process that is largely responsible for the considerable length of psychoanalysis.

In box 12.3 we describe the case of 17-year-old Allison as it might be conceptualized and treated from a psychoanalytic perspective.

DERIVATIONS OF PSYCHOANALYTIC THEORY AND THERAPY

We have spent a considerable amount of time describing the foundations of psychoanalytic thought and treatment because without this background it is difficult to understand and appreciate the writing of Freud's followers and colleagues or more current approaches to treatment that have grown from Freud's model. Mitchell and Black (1995) note that one of the myths regarding Freud and psychoanalytic theory and therapy is that contemporary psychoanalysis is virtually the same as it was in Freud's day. While Freud was unquestionably the founder of psychoanalytic theory and practice, the development of the principles and practice of psychoanalysis did not end with his death in 1939. From the early stages of the development of psychoanalysis, Freud's students and colleagues disagreed with certain aspects of his theory or techniques. This disagreement was not surprising, because Freud's followers were an exceptionally bright and thoughtful group that included, among others, Carl Jung and Alfred Adler. In fact, Jung's and Adler's disagreements with Freud led to their expulsion from his "inner circle" of followers.

Carl Jung

Carl Jung (1933, 1956) argued that Freud placed too great an emphasis on sexuality. Although, like Freud, Jung believed that personality is shaped by psychic energy, Jung disagreed that this energy was necessarily sexual or aggressive. Rather, Jung postulated that psychic energy led to behavior designed to actualize and fulfill the person's needs, a position that foreshadowed subsequent humanistic theories of personality (see chapter 13).

Jung did agree with Freud, however, about the importance of unconscious determinants of behavior. But whereas Freud discussed a single unconscious, Jung believed that the unconscious was composed of two parts: the **personal unconscious** and the **collective unconscious.** The personal unconscious is probably most similar to the unconscious envisioned by Freud. It holds repressed memories, wishes, and feelings from infancy and early childhood, and its contents are unique to each individual. In contrast, the collective unconscious is composed of latent memory traces shared by all human beings. Jung believed that this shared storehouse of memories explains the universality of symbols and mythologies.

Symbols are important in treatments derived from Jung's theory, as they are in Freudian psychoanalysis. The Jungian analyst leads the patient to explore his or her dreams, fantasies, and use of symbols, with the goal of helping the patient gain insight into his or her inner world. Thus, although there are certainly differences between Jung's and Freud's view of personality and psychotherapy, it is not difficult to discern Freud's influence on Jung's thinking and practice.

Alfred Adler

Like Jung, **Alfred Adler** disagreed with Freud's emphasis on sexual and aggressive instincts. But unlike Jung, Adler also disagreed with Freud's emphasis on the unconscious as a primary motivator of behavior. Adler believed that people are motivated by social interests and urges, and he focused on conscious rather than unconscious functioning. In this context, Adler believed that we invoke defenses not only in response to internal threats, such as those from the id and the superego as Freud suggested, but in response to external threats as well.

Adler placed great importance on the uniqueness of each person. Reflecting this position, Adler called his system *individual psychology.* Adler had a particular interest in children and family functioning and believed that to truly understand a person, it is important to understand the nature of their family of origin and the quality of their interactions with other family members. In fact, Adler is credited with being the first to examine issues of sibling rivalry and the effects of birth order on personality formation.

Perhaps because he had rickets as a child, which prevented him from walking until he was four years of age, Adler also emphasized the importance of feelings of inferiority. He believed that all individuals experience these feelings; whereas some people compensate for feelings of inferiority and go on to achieve a great deal, others fail to compensate for these feelings and consequently develop negative personality characteristics. These personality characteristics, as well as feelings of insecurity or grandiosity, are part of what Adler called an **inferiority complex.**

Adlerian psychotherapy follows from Adler's theory. In contrast to Freud's use of the couch in psychoanalysis, in Adlerian therapy both the patient and the therapist sit in chairs. The therapist

BOX 12.3

THE CASE OF ALLISON FROM A PSYCHOANALYTIC PERSPECTIVE

Dr. Washington listens intently as Allison tells her story. The doctor has worked with many patients with eating disorders before and is not surprised when Allison describes her preoccupation with her weight and appearance and her pattern of bingeing and purging. From Dr. Washington's perspective as a psychoanalyst, Allison's eating disorder is not itself the primary problem—rather, it is a symptom, a manifestation of a deeper, underlying psychological conflict. The symptoms of an eating disorder are an ineffective way for Allison to manage the internal conflicts that she is experiencing. As a psychoanalyst, Dr. Washington's task is to help Allison become aware of these deeper conflicts and develop more adaptive ways of resolving them.

As you have learned in this chapter, psychoanalytic theory and therapy emphasizes the importance of early experience, the role of the unconscious, and the use of defense mechanisms in understanding the origin of current difficulties in functioning. Allison is a 17-year-old girl who has been diagnosed with bulimia nervosa. She binges on junk food and then purges what she has eaten by forcing herself to vomit. A psychoanalyst would recognize that Allison is unaware of why she binges on fattening food when, at the same time, she is acutely sensitive to her weight and appearance. The source of this pattern of self-defeating behavior is buried deep in Alli-

son's unconscious. Her pattern of bingeing and purging serves as a defense against strong feelings or urges that she cannot allow herself to experience consciously; as long as Allison can focus on the eating problems, she does not have to deal with the underlying emotions and urges.

In working with Allison, a traditional psychoanalyst would have Allison relax and engage in free association. The analyst would likely also work with Allison in analyzing her dreams, searching to understand their meaning. The most important aspect of the therapy would center on Allison's transference reactions to the therapist, that is, on the feelings that she develops toward the therapist that have been transferred from feelings that she harbors toward other important people in her life. The specific nature of her transference reaction will depend on the specific source of conflict in her life (e.g., with her mother versus with her father). Analyzing the transference relationship will allow the psychoanalyst to gain access to the conflicts and emotions that are underlying Allison's eating-disorder symptoms.

From a psychoanalytic perspective, there are several possible explanations for the development of bulimia nervosa. These explanations primarily involve difficulties in early experiences with parents or parental figures. For example, it is possible that Allison has not adequately resolved the Electra com-

---

typically focuses on strengthening the patient's social interest by using the therapeutic relationship as a model. The importance of the family constellation is also apparent in Adlerian therapy. The patient and therapist focus on early childhood recollections, the patient's birth order, and the quality of the patient's interactions with his or her family. In fact, Adler often worked with children, and he would invite family members to attend and participate in the sessions. Adler believed that improvement in therapy would reduce

the patient's feelings of inferiority and lead to better day-to-day functioning.

Contemporary Psychodynamic Therapy

The practice of what is now referred to broadly as *psychoanalytically oriented therapy,* or *psychodynamic psychotherapy,* has evolved throughout the twentieth century, as successive generations of theorists, researchers, and therapists continue to build on or alter both the theory

BOX 12.3 (concluded)

plex in the phallic psychosexual stage and has under-identified with her mother and overidentified with her father. These difficulties in parental identification may lead Allison to want to stay boylike in her appearance. Her desperate attempts to be thin are a part of her effort to deny her physical development as a woman. Psychoanalysts might hypothesize further that Allison is not comfortable thinking about her sexuality and may see her need to stay thin as an unconscious defense against intercourse. One might expect, therefore, that Allison's unresolved feelings about her mother or her father would be transferred onto the therapist.

An alternative psychoanalytic explanation for Allison's eating disorder is that she experienced difficulties as she progressed through the oral psychosexual stage. In general, eating disorders represent an oral problem, and the emotional issue during this stage is dependency and trust. The conflict between being dependent on parents and becoming independent reaches its height during adolescence, the developmental period when eating disorders typically first appear. Thus, Allison's struggle with being emotionally dependent on her parents is hypothesized to be played out in her bulimia. Again, Allison might transfer these feelings onto Dr. Washington by becoming strongly dependent on her.

In both these formulations, it is assumed that Allison would not be conscious, or aware, of these issues. Indeed, Allison would be using one or more defense mechanisms to keep herself from becoming aware of these unacceptable issues. For example, Allison may be using repression to keep these issues from entering consciousness, or she may be using projection and see sexual behavior and sexual issues in others in her social network. In fact, Allison's bulimic behavior may be seen as a defense against her sexual feelings, allowing her to expunge these feelings as she purges and to slow down or avoid her sexual development.

Through psychoanalysis, Allison would gradually become aware of these issues and of the defenses that she uses to deal with them. Over the course of treatment, which may last for three or four years, Allison would gain insight into the roots of her disturbed eating behavior. By instructing Allison to engage in free association, by analyzing Allison's dreams, and by analyzing Allison's transference reactions, Dr. Washington would help Allison come to understand the difficulties she had with early parental identification, or dependency, or control. With Dr. Washington's interpretations, Allison would work through these issues and conflicts. The interpretations would help make Allison's unconscious feelings and conflicts more acceptable to her and would allow Allison to consciously experience them without needing to use defense mechanisms. If Allison is able to resolve these issues through therapy, the fact that she will no longer need to use defense mechanisms to deal with these issues will leave her with more energy to deal adaptively with her environment and will free her from her eating disorder.

and methods that were originally laid out by Freud. As we discussed in chapter 4, there are several derivations of psychoanalysis that have theoretical underpinnings that differ in significant ways from Freud's psychoanalytic theory. These theoretical derivations gave rise to therapies with shorter time frames and greater flexibility than psychoanalysis has.

The acceptance of more flexible forms of psychoanalytic therapy as viable alternatives to psychoanalysis is due in large part to the work of Franz Alexander and his colleagues at the Chicago Psychoanalytic Institute. Alexander and French (1946) argued that orthodox psychoanalysis had been developed by Freud with the dual purposes of gathering general knowledge about personality and dysfunction and treating emotional disorder (remember that the intensive case study was Freud's approach to research). They contended that because the relation between personality and psychopathology had now been established, therapy could focus more exclusively on psychological change than on information gathering. To this end, they suggested, therapists could conduct psychoanalytic therapy that fit the patient's needs, rather than trying to fit the patient to an inflexible standard regimen of psychoanalysis. Thus, while using Freud's theoretical framework, Alexander and French advocated flexibility in treatment and a shorter regimen of therapy. In fact, they described treating 600 patients with psychoanalytic therapy that ranged from 1 to 65 sessions (remember that orthodox psychoanalysis was often conducted three to five times per week for three to six years) and reported improvements that were previously believed to be attainable only through protracted long-term orthodox psychoanalysis.

In general, more contemporary psychodynamic approaches to therapy differ from orthodox psychoanalysis in at least three ways (Binder, Strupp, & Henry, 1995). First, they have replaced much of the language and complex constructs of Freudian theory with more parsimonious explanations of behavior (see chapter 4 for a discussion of the importance of parsimony). Second, they emphasize the significance of interpersonal relationships as much as they do internal, intrapsychic processes. And third, treatments have been developed that are briefer and more clearly defined than are treatments in traditional psychoanalysis. There are a number of different categories of current psychodynamic approaches to treatment, including ego psychology, object relations, brief psychodynamic psychotherapy, and interpersonal psychotherapy. We will consider each of these categories throughout the rest of this chapter. However, we will give particular attention to brief psychodynamic psychotherapy and interpersonal psychotherapy because they have been the subject of the most intensive empirical research.

Ego Psychology As we described in chapter 4, one of the first derivations or offshoots of psychoanalytic theory was actually developed in part by Freud's daughter Anna and is referred to as **ego psychology.** Ego psychology is represented in work that emphasizes the relative im-

portance of the ego over the functions of the id and the superego. Freud had emphasized the importance of biological factors in understanding human behavior and wrote in great detail of the role of instincts, which were housed in the id. He relegated the ego to the role of a servant to the id and its drives and minimized the role of the environment in affecting people's functioning.

Ego psychologists felt that the ego could play a more important role in therapy than Freud had theorized, and they had a considerable impact on the field of psychotherapy, both with children and with adults. As Mitchell and Black (1995) state, ego psychologists believed that patients could call on their ego capacities to

> reveal to the analyst the "inside story" on crucial psychic terrain, enabling the analyst to more effectively discern the competing psychic claims and crafty defensive strategies of neurosis. As a consequence, techniques were developed aimed at encouraging the patient to enter into what would eventually be called a "working alliance," within which analyst and patient could share the work . . . Although cure itself was still understood in terms of making the unconscious conscious, the process was now envisioned as occurring within a dyadic context, within a metaphoric partnership rather than a battle. (pp. 58–59)

Treatment based on the tenets of ego psychology is certainly not a quantum leap away from orthodox psychoanalysis; it does differ, however, in its focus. Instead of concentrating on deeply rooted instincts and needs and targeting early childhood experiences, ego analysis focuses more directly on current difficulties and conflicts and strives to strengthen the functioning of the ego. These goals are achieved, in part, by enlisting the patient's cooperation actively and directly in fortifying the effective and adaptive aspects of the ego and its interaction with the environment, by attempting to help patients recognize and build on their strengths. Ego analysis is, in some sense, more of a reparenting or reeducative process than is psychoanalysis, which Freud saw as reconstructive. Consequently, treatment from an ego analytic perspective is considerably shorter than more orthodox forms of psychoanalysis are.

Importantly, it was Anna Freud's (1928, 1946) focus on the ego, defense mechanisms, and the environment as important determinants of behavior that led her to play a major role in developing psychoanalytic treatment for children. With Melanie Klein (1932, 1955), a British psychoanalyst, Freud was instrumental in focusing attention on the application of psychoanalytic principles to helping disturbed children. Both Freud and Klein used play instead of free association as a technique to understand the nature of the difficulties experienced by children and to help them in treatment. Whereas Freud believed that, for children, play was essential in strengthening their relationship to the therapist, Klein focused more explicitly on the symbolic meaning of play. In fact, as Klein developed her practice with children, she began to emphasize the importance of the first year of life and postulated that the quality of the infant's relationship with his or her caretaker in that first year is enormously important in determining how well the infant will function psychologically in later years. This focus on the relationship of the infant with another person (or "object," as Klein referred to the caregiver) contributed to the growth of object relations theory and to treatment based on this perspective.

Object Relations   A second derivation of psychoanalysis is the therapy based on the work of object relations theorists such as Otto Kernberg, Heinz Kohut, Margaret Mahler, and John Bowlby. We presented a detailed description of object relations theory in chapter 4. Essentially, object relations theorists disagreed with Freud that people are motivated by instincts of sex and aggression. Rather, they postulated a more positive view of human nature, that people are motivated to seek social contact and bond with another person, or "object." In particular, the relationship between an infant or young child and his or her caregiver is extremely important in shaping both the characteristics of the self and the quality of the individual's subsequent relationships. Given this focus, therapy based on object relations theory explores the nature of the patient's interpersonal relationships and reasons for possible shortcomings in these relationships that might stem from early interpersonal experiences.

From an object relations perspective, therefore, a major aim of treatment is not only to understand childhood interpersonal relations and how these patterns are repeated in adult life but also, and equally important, to help the patient recognize problematic interpersonal behaviors and attitudes by using the transference relationship with the therapist as a prototype, or prime example, of these interpersonal difficulties. Other therapists have drawn on object relations theory to formulate a more explicitly interpersonally focused treatment, a form of therapy to which we will return later in this chapter when we discuss interpersonal psychotherapy.

Short-Term Dynamic Therapy   Brief or time-limited methods of psychodynamic psychotherapy first emerged from the dissatisfaction of several of Freud's followers, who felt that the process of psychoanalysis had become unnecessarily long and cumbersome (see box 12.4). They argued that it was possible to encourage the development of transference in the therapeutic relationship, to bring unconscious conflicts into conscious awareness through analysis of the transference relationship, and to offer interpretations much more quickly than Freud had allowed.

The more contemporary beginnings of current short-term dynamic therapies took place in the 1970s, when several groups of clinicians began to experiment systematically with psychoanalytic techniques in the context of short-term psychotherapy. Malan (1976, 1979) in England, Sifneos (1972, 1987) and Mann (1973) in Boston, and Davanloo (1978, 1980) in Montreal

BOX 12.4

PSYCHODYNAMIC PSYCHOTHERAPY IN THE AGE OF MANAGED CARE: THE NEED FOR BRIEF TREATMENT

As we observed in chapter 2, the history of clinical psychology has been influenced profoundly by factors within both the science and the profession of clinical psychology as well as by factors in the broader society in which psychology functions. Nowhere is this influence more evident than in the evolution of psychodynamic approaches to psychotherapy. Freud's original treatments took years to complete, and this time frame became the working model for orthodox, or traditional, psychoanalysis. From the outset, however, some psychoanalytic theorists and therapists questioned the need for lengthy treatment. For example, Ferenczi and Rank (1925) challenged the belief that therapy needed to involve the intensive reconstruction of childhood conflicts. Although they agreed with Freud that childhood experiences were the source of the patient's presenting problems, they felt that treatment could move directly and rapidly to the way that these experiences were represented in the transference relationship (Binder et al., 1995). Similar themes were reflected in the work of Alexander and French (1946) in their focus on the therapeutic relationship as the source of a corrective emotional experience.

The shift to brief forms of psychodynamic therapies was given a major impetus, however, by pressure from societal factors. Specifically, third-party payers of health care (insurance companies and government insurance) have demanded more cost-effective means of treating psychological problems. This economic imperative exerted much greater pressure for the advancement of brief forms of treatment than did any theoretical developments within the field. Managed care companies typically require that a specific diagnosis be generated for each patient in order for treatment to be reimbursed. More significantly, managed care organizations further place a limit on the number of sessions that they will reimburse for each disorder. Therefore, for those patients who are paying through insurance or other forms of third-party coverage, the therapist is no longer free to allow therapy to continue without time limits. To remain competitive in the therapeutic marketplace, psychodynamic psychotherapies have been forced to become more brief and problem focused.

all developed briefer forms of psychoanalytically oriented therapies that, while still based on Freud's model of psychopathology, permitted the therapist to be more active in interpreting the patient's emotional experiences with the therapist (i.e., the transference relationship). These therapies ranged from 12 to 50 sessions and were more explicitly problem focused than was orthodox psychoanalysis. Collectively, they demonstrated that patients suffering from what would be conceptualized as long-standing neurotic and characterological problems could exhibit enduring change following treatment with psychodynamically oriented therapy in a much shorter

time frame than was previously believed possible.

More recently, researchers and clinicians have adapted and improved on these short-term therapies in developing psychodynamic treatments that are applicable to a wider range of patients and that are more explicitly interpersonal and present oriented in their focus. Among the most prominent of these approaches is **Time-Limited Dynamic Psychotherapy (TLDP),** developed by psychologist Hans Strupp and his colleagues at Vanderbilt University (e.g., Binder et al., 1995; Strupp & Binder, 1984). TLDP attempts to modify the way a person relates to others and to himself or herself, primarily by analyzing the (transference) relationship between the patient and the therapist. From the perspective of TLDP, psychopathology is understood as emerging from recurrent interpersonal patterns in the patient's life that create and maintain dysfunctional relationships. This pattern is referred to as the *cyclical maladaptive pattern,* which is essentially a formulation of a vicious cycle: patients' inflexible interpersonal behaviors, negative feelings about themselves, and self-defeating expectations of others interact with each other and lead to problematic relationships and to psychopathology.

Levenson (1995) describes the four categories of information that make up the cyclical maladaptive pattern (see also figure 12.1):

a. *Acts of the self.* These include the patient's thoughts, feelings, wishes, and behaviors of an interpersonal nature. For example, "when I meet strangers, I can't help thinking they wouldn't want to have anything to do with me" (thought) . . . "I yell and scream at my kids when they get in my way" (behavior). Sometimes these acts are conscious . . . and some-

times they are outside awareness, as in the case of the woman who does not realize how jealous she is of her sister's accomplishments.

b. *Expectations of others' reactions.* This category pertains to all the statements having to do with how the patient imagines others will react to him or her in response to some interpersonal behavior (act of the self). "My boss will fire me if I make a mistake." "If I go to the dance, no one will ask me to dance."

c. *Acts of others toward the self.* This third grouping consists of the actual behaviors of other people, as observed (or assumed) by the patient . . . "When I went to the dance, guys asked me to dance, but only because they felt sorry for me."

d. *Acts of the self toward the self.* In this section belong all of the patient's behaviors or attitudes toward herself or himself—when the self is the object of the interpersonal dynamic. How does the patient treat himself or herself? "When no one asked me to dance, I told myself it's because I'm fat, ugly, and unlovable." (p. 49)

In essence, therefore, patients are hypothesized to behave in ways that evoke particular reactions from others, which, in turn, affect the

FIGURE 12.1
Time Limited Dynamic Psychotherapy emphasizes the cyclical maladaptive pattern of clients' behavior toward the self and others.

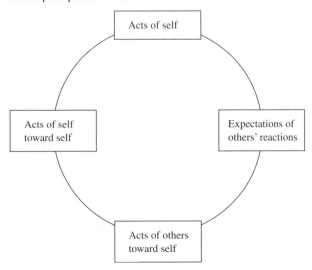

patients' self-views. TLDP assumes that the interpersonal problems that emerge in treatment with the therapist are similar in form to the chronic, maladaptive interpersonal patterns that underlie the patient's difficulties in living, difficulties that are expressed through symptoms such as anxiety and depression. That is, TLDP therapists assume that the patient will unintentionally and unknowingly respond to the therapist as if she or he were a significant other (typically a parent) in the patient's life and will act out maladaptive patterns of behavior that characterize his or her other relationships. As you can see, this process is a direct parallel to the concept of transference in original Freudian psychoanalysis. Thus, TLDP uses the therapeutic relationship to understand and change the patient's current relationships with the assumption that these interpersonal changes will lead to symptomatic improvement.

The most important mechanism of change in TLDP is the recognition (or insight) by the patient of patterns of interactions with others that continuously reinforce maladaptive attitudes and feelings about the self and others (Binder et al., 1995). The patient learns new patterns of behavior by enacting previously ingrained patterns of interaction with the therapist but experiencing different results. To help attain this goal, the therapist listens attentively to the patient but also facilitates an examination of the therapeutic relationship with careful guided questioning. The following interaction, described by Strupp and Binder (1984), illustrates this process:

Therapist (T): Why don't you tell me some more about you in general. I've asked some specific questions and I want to get back with some more I want to ask you too, but tell me more about you.
   Patient (P): I don't know what to tell you. It's just not—
   T: Whatever you feel is important.
   P: There's just not a whole lot to tell.
   T: You mean you're just present?
   P: Yeah.

T: Well tell me what you did and—well, let me ask you about that. What do you mean there's not a whole lot to tell, you're thirty-two years old, lived for thirty-two years! Nothing to tell about all that?
   P: Nothing I consider interesting or—
   T: Nothing you consider interesting?
   P: I can't see that anybody else would consider it interesting either.
   T: Why not?
   P: It's just a very average life.
   T: You know what's happening now sounds very similar to what you described happens when you're out with people. That you feel you have nothing to say. There's nothing that you can say that you think about what's happened with you that would be of any interest to anybody else.
   P: It's true.
   T: I wonder why you feel that so strongly?
   P: I don't know, I've always been—I've not found myself an interesting subject of conversation.
   T: Do you wonder about that? Why you feel that way?
   P: I have.
   T: What have you concluded?
   P: I don't know. I say I wonder about it on occasion but it's not something I've reached a conclusion about.
   T: Have you come up with anything?
   P: No, not really.
   T: Do you think it's realistic?
   P: No. But yet my experience with others, it does seem to be.
   T: So it seems like something worth looking at. As you've been talking with me today what's your—how do you imagine I'm reacting to you? My attitude toward you, things you're saying about yourself?
   P: I really can't imagine that you're the least bit interested.
   T: I'm bored to death?
   P: Basically.
   T: How does that leave you feeling? If that's the way you see me—my attitude toward you? (Pause)
   P: Just that I'm here and answering questions. That's about all.
   T: That we know. It doesn't bother you at all?
   P: No.
   T: Why do you think that's the case?

P: I think that it's something I've built up over the years. And I don't care whether—

T: You've sort of steeled yourself to it?

P: Right. (pp. 122–123)

In this sequence, the patient has described a core experience in her relationships with others—she believes others are not interested in her or her welfare. This central belief is being played out in the context of the therapeutic relationship, as she expresses her belief that, like others in her life, the therapist does not find her interesting. It is the therapist's use of direct questioning that brings this belief to light. The goal in TLDP is for the therapist to respond to the patient in a way that is inconsistent with her previous experiences and with her expectations of others. In this example, the therapist would accomplish this goal by exhibiting genuine interest in the patient. The patient's recognition that this relationship is fundamentally different from others that she has experienced will contribute significantly to her ability to change her expectations of others and, subsequently, both her pattern of interacting with others and her sense of self. Thus, the patient learns that relationships do not need to lead inevitably to the same negative outcomes that have been the case in the past, and her symptoms of anxiety and depression should dissipate.

Interpersonal Therapy   Within the development of psychodynamic approaches to psychotherapy, perhaps the most dramatic departure from original Freudian concepts and methods is found in interpersonal approaches to psychotherapy. Psychiatrists Harry Stack Sullivan (1953, 1956) and Adolf Meyer (1957) offered the first systematic interpersonal theories of psychopathology and psychotherapy. Like Freud, Sullivan believed that the roots of interpersonal relationships lie in early childhood experiences. Unlike Freud, however, Sullivan felt that the most important manifestations of these experiences, and ultimately their resolution, were in the person's current social relationships and inter-

actions. Therefore, according to Sullivan, the emphasis of treatment needed to shift from the individual and the resolution of past relationships to the successful development of current interpersonal interactions. Sullivan advocated that the analyst, rather than wait patiently and silently for hidden wishes to appear through free association and then make interpretations, instead actively inquire about the patient's interpersonal interactions and relationships, although the focus was still on making a link to the childhood origins of these interpersonal patterns.

Recent research on the importance of social relationships and social stress in psychopathology (e.g., Dohrenwend, 2000; Eaton, 2001) and the role of interpersonal attachment bonds throughout the life span (e.g., Roberts, Gotlib, & Kassel, 1996) have provided further support for the significance of interpersonal approaches to the treatment of depression and other disorders. For example, depressed persons, individuals with eating disorders, patients with panic disorder, and persons experiencing difficulties with substance abuse have been found to have smaller and less supportive social networks than do normal controls (e.g., Henirch, Blatt, Kupermine, Zohar, & Leadbeater, 2001; Rorty, Yager, Buckwalter, & Rossotto, 1999; Westermeyer & Specker, 1999). People suffering from depression, anxiety, or alcoholism have also been found to experience significant marital difficulties (e.g., Da Costa, Larouche, Dritsa, & Brender, 1999; Kelly, Halford, & Young, 2000; Kung, 2000). In fact, there is now research suggesting that living with a spouse or parent who is very critical or negative in their comments and behavior places both depressed and schizophrenic patients at increased risk for relapse or recurrence of the disorder (Hooley & Gotlib, 2000).

Empirical findings such as these provide the impetus for investigators to continue to develop and refine interpersonally focused approaches to psychotherapy. These approaches typically do not make any assumptions about the underlying causes of psychopathology (e.g., Mufson,

Moreau, Weissman, & Klerman, 1993; Weissman & Markowitz, in press), but rather they focus on the interpersonal context in which current symptoms are developed and maintained. The therapist's primary goal is to change the patient's patterns of self-defeating interpersonal interactions. The therapy is brief, and the therapist is more directive and active than in other forms of psychodynamic psychotherapy. Similar to TLDP, however, the therapist uses his or her relationship with the patient as an important means to identify maladaptive behaviors and patterns of communication.

Probably the most systematic and extensive application of interpersonal psychotherapy is the **interpersonal psychotherapy (IPT)** developed by Gerald Klerman and Myrna Weissman for the treatment of depression (Weissman & Markowitz, in press; Weissman, Markowitz, & Klerman, 2000). IPT is conducted primarily as a short-term therapy (approximately 16 weeks) but has also been modified for use as a maintenance therapy for the longer term treatment of patients with recurrent or chronic depression. IPT is designed to reduce depressive symptoms by educating the client about the nature and course of depression. A major goal of IPT is to change the patient's interpersonal functioning by encouraging more effective expression of emotions, clearer communication with significant others, and increased understanding of the patient's behavior in interpersonal interactions. The rationale for IPT is that by solving interpersonal problems in therapy, the patient will improve his or her life situation and simultaneously relieve the symptoms of the depressive episode. Although many of the techniques used in IPT are similar to those used in other forms of psychodynamic psychotherapy, IPT also includes specific techniques for selecting a focus for the treatment of depression. In box 12.5 we describe the case of Maria as it might be conceptualized and treated from the perspective of IPT.

A somewhat different version of interpersonal psychotherapy for depression was developed by

Myrna M. Weissman, Ph.D., is Chief of Psychiatric Research in the Department of Clinical and Psychiatric Epidemiology at Columbia University. With Dr. Gerald Klerman, Dr. Weissman developed Interpersonal Psychotherapy, now a major approach in the treatment of depression. Dr. Weissman is also recognized for her research examining the impact of maternal depression on children. *(Photo courtesy of Myrna M. Weissman.)*

David Shapiro and his colleagues as part of the Sheffield Psychotherapy Project in Great Britain (e.g., Barkham et al., 1996; Hardy, Sharpiro, Stiles, & Barkham, 1998; Shapiro et al., 1995). This approach is based on Hobson's conversational model of psychotherapy (Davenport, Hobson, & Margison, 2000; Hobson, 1985) and uses psychodynamic, interpersonal, and experiential concepts by focusing on the therapist-client relationship as a means for revealing and resolving interpersonal difficulties. The method empha-sizes negotiation between therapist and client, a language of mutuality, and the use of statements rather than questions (Shapiro et al., 1995). Sim-ilar to the classic approach to the analysis of transference, this method views the therapist-client relationship as a reflection of the interper-sonal problems that are seen as the primary source of depression.

APPLICATION TO SPECIFIC PROBLEMS AND DISORDERS

Classical Freudian Psychoanalysis

Throughout the early phases of the development of psychoanalytic and psychodynamic psycho-therapy, little emphasis was placed on devel-oping different methods for the treatment of specific problems and disorders. There are two reasons for this. First, Freud and those who fol-lowed him assumed that all forms of psycho-pathology share common underlying dynamics; therefore, the same methods could, and should, be used for uncovering these underlying dy-namics and treating the presenting symptoms. Second, when Freud developed his theory and treatment, there was no extensive taxonomy, or classification system, comparable to the current version of the *DSM* for differentiating forms of psychological disorder. Consequently, there was little need to develop highly specific techniques for different disorders.

Specificity in the conceptualization and treat-ment of problems can be found, however, in the Freudian perspective of what are currently re-ferred to as anxiety disorders and major de-pressive disorders. From a psychoanalytic perspective, both anxiety and depression are viewed as failures by the ego to successfully manage libidinal drives, the demands of the superego, and unconscious conflicts. Despite these shared features, however, depression and anxiety are postulated to have different underly-ing psychological dynamics and conflicts and to have different implications for treatment with psychoanalysis.

Anxiety Disorders   Anxiety disorders are rep-resented at a conscious level as fear or anxiety about an object, event, or circumstance. For ex-ample, phobias are represented by fears of a par-ticular setting (e.g., heights), event (e.g., giving a public speech, flying in an airplane), or object (e.g., snakes). From a patient's perspective, these tangible objects and events are the source of the fear—the patient is unaware of any deeper sig-nificance or source of these fears. According to psychoanalytic theory, however, these objects and events are merely conscious representations of the real source of anxiety. The conscious tar-gets or objects of an underlying fear are devel-oped through defense mechanisms, which help convert a fear that cannot be consciously admit-ted or tolerated into one that is more manageable and acceptable to the ego.

The underlying source of anxiety disorders is presumed to be an unconscious conflict re-garding unacceptable aggressive or sexual drives and wishes. Typically, these conflicts are rooted in early development and have been defended against since childhood. In psychoanalysis, treat-ment of an anxiety disorder consists of searching for the underlying sexual or aggressive conflict, bringing that conflict into the patient's conscious awareness, resolving the conflict, and strength-ening the patient's ego to be able to deal effec-tively with the previously unacceptable and unmanageable feelings. From the time of his early collaborations with Breuer, Freud believed that unconscious conflicts, particularly about sexuality, will be manifested in the form of anxi-ety about other concerns and will be translated into inappropriately strong feelings about the therapist. Thus, one of the major psychoanalytic techniques in the treatment of anxiety disorders involves first allowing the unresolved feelings to be transferred onto the therapist and then having the analyst interpret the true nature of those feel-ings to the patient.

BOX 12.5

THE CASE OF MARIA FROM AN INTERPERSONAL PSYCHOTHERAPY PERSPECTIVE

Maria is 73 years old. She speaks slowly, interrupted by long silences, and talks mostly about her husband who passed away two years ago. Dr. Fitzpatrick listens patiently, asking very focused questions that require concrete answers. Dr. Fitzpatrick is experienced in treating elderly patients for psychological difficulties. She has a PhD in clinical psychology and has specialized in her training in clinical geropsychology, an area that focuses on psychological assessment and treatment in older populations. In addition, Dr. Fitzpatrick attends clinical training workshops every year to keep abreast of the latest developments in the field. She conducted a structured diagnostic interview with Maria, and it was clear that Maria is experiencing an episode of major depression.

Dr. Fitzpatrick had to rule out two other possibilities before arriving at this diagnosis. First, it is difficult in elderly people to distinguish, or differentiate, depression from dementia. But Dr. Fitzpatrick

reasoned that because Maria was active and alert before the death of her husband and because she reports doing crossword puzzles, her symptoms are unlikely to be caused by dementia. Second, because Maria's depression seems to be strongly linked to the death of her husband, Dr. Fitzpatrick had considered the possibility that Maria's symptoms could be attributed to bereavement rather than depression. According to *DSM-IV,* however, symptoms of bereavement do not typically last beyond a few months, and Maria has been depressed for two years. The results of neuropsychological testing were consistent with this diagnosis (see chapter 8).

There are relatively few approaches to psychotherapy that have been demonstrated to be effective in treating depression in the elderly. One approach that has been shown to reduce depression in this population, however, is interpersonal psychotherapy (IPT). In fact, there is a version of IPT, interpersonal psychotherapy—late life (IPT-LL;

Depressive Disorders   Although the psychoanalytic treatment of depression is similar to that of anxiety disorders, Freud (1917) believed that the underlying dynamics are quite different. He conceptualized depression as emerging from the interaction of an early vulnerability to depression and a recent stressor that activates that vulnerability. In this sense, the psychoanalytic conceptualization of depression is similar to the more general diathesis-stress model described in chapter 4. From a psychoanalytic perspective, the underlying diathesis or vulnerability is the dependency on others that results from inadequate gratification of needs early in childhood. Needs are either overgratified (the infant's needs are appeased too rapidly and the infant fails to develop a sense of autonomy), or under-gratified (the infant's needs are ignored and the infant experiences the world as nonresponsive and un-

supportive). Failure to have one's needs gratified increases dependency on others for the development of a sense of one's self, one's identity. This dependency on others leaves the individual vulnerable to the loss of sources of dependency— the individual has failed to develop a sufficiently strong sense of self (ego) to function independently if the source of the dependency is lost.

Depression develops from two psychological processes that result from a loss. The loss can be either real (a relationship that ends, the death of a loved one) or symbolic (the person feels rejected by another even in the absence of a real rejection or loss). In an attempt to ease the loss, the individual internalizes parts of the lost person or relationship into his or her sense of self. At the same time, the individual feels anger at the lost other for leaving and abandoning him or her. However, because the other has been incorpo-

BOX 12.5 (concluded)

Frank et al., 1993), that has been developed specifically for use with older clients. Dr. Fitzpatrick has attended workshops on the use of IPT-LL and believes that this approach is the best treatment for Maria. IPT-LL is a time-limited therapy (12 to 16 weeks) with a broad focus on the link between depression and life events. The overall strategy of IPT-LL is that by solving an interpersonal problem—such as dealing with interpersonal loss or grief—the patient will improve her or his life situation and simultaneously relieve the symptoms of the depressive episode.

IPT-LL is divided into three phases. In the first phase, usually one to three sessions, Dr. Fitzpatrick conducts a diagnostic evaluation and obtains a psychological history from Maria, and then describes the treatment to her. She educates Maria about depression, letting her know that depression often results from changes in relationships, such as the passing of a spouse. In IPT-LL the therapist and patient focus on one of four interpersonal problem areas: grief, interpersonal role disputes, role transitions, or interpersonal deficits. In Maria's case, Dr. Fitzpatrick decides to work with Maria primarily on her grief at the death of her husband and to also touch on Maria's difficulties accepting her transition from the role of spouse to widow.

In the middle phase of IPT-LL, therefore, Dr. Fitzpatrick pursues strategies relevant to Maria's grief. She facilitates Maria's experience of feelings of mourning, encourages her to talk with her family about their memories of her husband, and gradually helps Maria find new activities and relationships. Dr. Fitzpatrick also works with Maria to help her master her role as a widow rather than a spouse, while at the same time recognizing how important Maria's husband was to her.

In the final phase of IPT-LL, the last two to four sessions, Dr. Fitzpatrick supports Maria's newly gained sense of independence and competence by recognizing and consolidating her therapeutic gains. Dr. Fitzpatrick also helps Maria anticipate possible difficulties in the future and develop ways of countering depressive symptoms should they arise. She helps Maria express her sad feelings about the end of treatment—but is clear to distinguish this sadness from depression—and at the same time underscores Maria's accomplishments during therapy.

rated into the sense of self, the anger at the other is now also anger at the self. And to make matters worse, Freud postulated that the individual's superego generates feelings of guilt for being angry with the lost other; thus, guilt and self-retribution compound the anger and self-derogation that are already present. This "anger turned inward" lies at the core of the psychoanalytic conceptualization of depression.

What should the analyst expect in the treatment of depression? Rather than the transference of sexual or aggressive feelings, the psychoanalyst would expect to encounter feelings of dependency followed by anger transferred onto the therapist. For example, during the initial phases of treatment the depressed patient would be expected to develop a strong sense of dependency on the therapist for advice and support. Because of the dynamics underlying depression, however,

the patient would also interpret any slights by the therapist as signs of rejection or disapproval and would consequently experience anger. Once the anger is apparent in the transference relationship with the therapist, the true source of the anger can be clarified through interpretations. Whereas initial interpretations would likely focus explicitly on the anger toward the therapist, as treatment progressed interpretations would deal with the link between this transferred anger and the patient's deeper-rooted anger toward others in his or her past.

Thus, the psychoanalytic treatment of both anxiety and depression involves the development of transference, open display or catharsis of previously repressed emotions in the context of the transference, and interpretation of the true meaning of these feelings. Treatment of these two problems differs, however, in the nature of the feelings that are transferred onto the therapist.

BRIEF PSYCHODYNAMIC PSYCHOTHERAPY AND INTERPERSONAL PSYCHOTHERAPY

As psychodynamic and interpersonal theories have evolved and as the taxonomy of psychopathology has become increasingly complex and differentiated, psychodynamic and interpersonal approaches to psychotherapy have been developed for the treatment of specific problems or difficulties. And with these developments have come detailed treatment manuals to guide therapists through the process in a prescribed and standardized manner. Perhaps the greatest strides in this area have occurred in the application of interpersonal psychotherapy to major depressive disorder (Cornes & Frank, 1996; Weissman & Markowitz, in press) and bulimia nervosa (Agras, Walsh, Fairburn, Wilson, & Kraemer, 2000). In contrast, TLDP has not focused as much on the nature of the patient's psychopathology or diagnosis as it has on identifying patients who can form a collaborative relationship with the therapist (Strupp & Binder, 1984). Evidence for this capacity is gathered from observations of how well the patients handle trial interventions made in the first few sessions.

Depressive Disorders

The application of IPT to depression reflects the assumption that many of the important aspects of depressive symptoms center on the nature of the current interpersonal relationships of the depressed patient. Clinical researchers have found the onset of depressive episodes to be strongly associated with the occurrence of social stressors, difficulties, and disruptions (e.g., Monroe & Hadjyannakis, in press). The impact of the depressed person on others in his or her social world and the effects of others' behaviors on the depressed individual are conceptualized as an ongoing negative cycle that contributes to the maintenance of depression. The techniques of IPT have been tailored specifically for the problems faced by depressed patients (Weissman & Markowitz, in press).

IPT for depression is divided into three phases. In the initial phase of treatment (the first three sessions), the therapist conducts a diagnostic evaluation for depression, educates the patient about depression, and evaluates the quality of and conflicts in the patient's current interpersonal relationships. The therapist then establishes which of four interpersonal problem areas are most strongly related to the patient's current depressive episode: grief, interpersonal role disputes, role transitions, or interpersonal deficits (Weissman & Markowitz, in press; Weissman et al., 2000). In the middle phase of treatment (sessions 4 through 13), the therapist uses specific techniques (outlined in a treatment manual) that are designed to address these four problem areas. For example, if the depressive episode is related to grief and complicated bereavement over the loss of a loved one, the therapist helps the patient mourn the loss and subsequently find new activities and relationships that will compensate for the loss. The final phase of treatment (sessions 14 through 16) focuses on consolidation of changes made in therapy and helps the patient recognize and counter depressive symptoms should they arise again in the future. Unlike traditional psychodynamic therapies, in IPT "therapists take an active, nonneutral, supportive, and hopeful stance" (Weissman & Markowitz, in press).

Eating Disorders

IPT for bulimia nervosa resembles IPT for depression in its style and structure (Agras et al., 2000; Fairburn, 1998; Wegner & Wegner, 2001), involving fifteen to twenty 50-minute sessions of individual therapy conducted over four to five months. The treatment has three stages. In the first stage (three to four sessions), the goal is to engage the patient in treatment, identify current interpersonal problems, and establish a treatment contract. Three sources of information are used to identify the problems: (a) an evaluation of the interpersonal context in which the eating problems developed and, more importantly, in which they have been maintained; (b) an assessment of the quality of the patient's current interpersonal functioning; and (c) an examination of the interpersonal context of individual bulimia episodes. This stage ends with the therapist and patient deciding which of the identified problems will be the focus of the remainder of treatment. As originally developed, the second and third phases of the treatment are identical to IPT for depression except that the patient is put under more pressure to change. Interestingly, the eating disorder per se is not addressed directly: If it is mentioned by the patient, the therapist promptly shifts the focus onto its interpersonal context.

RESEARCH ON PSYCHODYNAMIC AND INTERPERSONAL PSYCHOTHERAPY

Research on the process and outcome of psychodynamic psychotherapy has been a source of considerable controversy. Much of the controversy involves differences of opinion about what constitutes empirical research on psychotherapy. Freud and his students believed that intensive case studies constituted the basis for a scientific approach to the study of personality, psychopathology, and psychotherapy, a stance reflected in Karon and Widener's (1995) statement that "the most important (and sometimes the only) criterion of scientific truth is your own observations; whether or not other scientists accept these observations is irrelevant" (p. 24). As a consequence of this position, much of the published literature on psychoanalytic methods has appeared in the form of detailed case studies. Certainly, case studies can be extremely illuminating and can serve as an important form of hypothesis generation. They cannot, however, be used to *test* hypotheses (see chapter 5). Thus, regardless of the effects that they may imply, uncontrolled case studies cannot be used as evidence in support of the efficacy of any form of psychotherapy.

Fortunately, research on current psychodynamic and interpersonal approaches to psychotherapy has moved well beyond the case study method to include controlled clinical trials and careful empirical studies of the therapy process. Landmark studies have included careful evaluations of the outcome of psychodynamic and interpersonal psychotherapy compared to waiting list or placebo treatments and to other forms of psychotherapy or medication. Although we will discuss research evidence relevant to all forms of psychotherapy in depth in chapter 15, we provide here an overview of research examining psychodynamic and interpersonal therapy.

Treatment Outcome Research

Psychoanalysis and Psychodynamic Psychotherapy The effectiveness of traditional, long-term psychoanalytic treatment has not been the subject of extensive empirical research. The original proponents of this approach were satisfied with case studies as evidence for its effects and, consequently, did not invest their time and energy in the types of carefully controlled, empirically based methods that are now considered the standard in psychotherapy outcome research. Long-term psychoanalysis also presents a number of problems for evaluation using traditional controlled clinical trials. In particular, it is difficult to utilize control groups in studies of psychoanalysis, because doing so would require assignment of patients to a no-treatment or a waiting-list control condition for periods of what might be several years. As a result, most evaluations have focused on briefer forms of psychodynamic therapy. There has, however, been one major study of the effects of psychoanalysis.

Kernberg et al., (1972) reported on the Psychotherapy Research Project, conducted at the Menninger Foundation in Topeka, Kansas, over a 20-year period. Kernberg et al. collected data from 42 adult patients who received either psychoanalysis (an average of 835 hours of treatment, or about 4 years of 4 sessions per week) or psychoanalytic psychotherapy (an average of 289 hours, or about 3 years of 2 sessions per week). Kernberg et al. did not focus so much on comparing the effectiveness of psychoanalysis versus psychoanalytic psychotherapy but rather on identifying what characteristics of patients were associated with positive therapeutic outcome. Perhaps not surprisingly, the patients who benefited the most from therapy were those with higher initial ego strength, defined in part as the ability to tolerate anxiety, form relationships, and control their impulses. In fact, the best predictor of success in psychoanalysis and psychoanalytic psychotherapy was the quality of the patient's interpersonal relationships.

We cannot tell from this study, of course, how effective psychoanalysis is compared with other forms of therapy or even what proportion of patients improve significantly with psychoanalytic treatment. Indeed, even after decades of work, research on the effects of psychodynamic therapy have been mixed and present a confusing picture. Several authors have argued that there is clear evidence for the efficacy of psychodynamic therapy or that its effects are comparable to other forms of therapy, including behavior therapy, cognitive therapy, and Rogerian therapy (e.g., Heine, 1953; Sloane et al., 1975). On the other hand, the results of efficacy studies indicate that the effects are modest at best and have been disappointing to advocates of psychodynamic treatment. For example, Shapiro and Shapiro (1982), Crits-Christoph (1992), and Svartberg and Stiles (1991) all concluded that although psychodynamic therapies may be more effective than no treatment at all, they are not more effective (and may even be less effective) than other forms of supportive psychotherapy. Perhaps most generously, Prochaska (1994) has suggested that the effectiveness of psychoanalytic psychotherapy has not yet been adequately tested—a troubling conclusion given that a century has now passed since the development of psychoanalysis.

Interpersonal Psychotherapy   In contrast to research on psychoanalytic psychotherapy, the results of research examining the effects of interpersonal models of psychotherapy have been clear and very encouraging. Over the past 20 years, IPT has been carefully studied in many research protocols and has been demonstrated to be successful in the treatment of patients with depression, including adolescents, the elderly, and patients in primary medical care facilities (e.g., Elkin et al., 1989; Mason, Markowitz, & Klerman, 1993), and patients with eating disorders (e.g., Agras et al., 2000; Fairburn, 1998). With respect to depression, IPT has been found to be effective both in treating acute episodes of depression and in preventing or delaying the onset of subsequent episodes.

IPT was one of the treatments examined in the NIMH multisite Treatment of Depression Collaborative Research Program. This project compared IPT with cognitive therapy for depression, pharmacotherapy (imipramine hydrochloride) plus clinical management, and placebo plus clinical management (see Elkin et al., 1989, for an overview of this project). Two hundred and forty depressed outpatients were randomly assigned to one of these four conditions and were followed for 16 weeks. One of the most important aspects of this study was its careful selection and training of therapists. Each therapist received months of intensive training, ensuring standardization of the therapy administered in each condition (see Hollon, Shelton, & Davis, 1993).

The results of this project indicated that IPT was an effective treatment for depression. Those patients who received IPT demonstrated a substantial decrease in their depressive symptomatology over the 16 weeks of the study. Interestingly, differences between IPT and the other conditions in the study (cognitive behavior therapy, imipramine with brief supportive clinical management, and placebo pill with clinical management) were minimal. Elkin et al. (1989) concluded that, although IPT appeared to be highly effective, it did not appear to offer specific or additional effectiveness over the other treatments. Shea, Widiger, & Klein (1992) reported a similar pattern of results over an 18-month naturalistic follow-up of these patients.

In a more recent investigation of IPT, Frank, Kupfer, Perel et al. (1990) followed a sample of depressed patients who had responded to a combination of antidepressants and IPT over three years. Frank, Kupfer, Perel et al. concluded from their results that IPT is an effective therapeutic tool for patients who do not respond to other forms of treatment. IPT has also been demonstrated to be effective in the treatment of depressed adolescents (Mufson, Weissman, Moreau, & Garfinkel, 1999) and depressed elderly patients (e.g., Reynolds et al., 1999; Sloane, Staples, & Schneider, 1985).

IPT appears to be effective in the treatment of bulimia nervosa (Fairburn, Marcus, & Wilson, 1993). Several studies conducted by Fairburn's group at Oxford provide the empirical support for using IPT to treat patients with bulimia nervosa. These studies compared IPT with cognitive therapy and behavior therapy (see chapter 14) in the treatment of bulimia. Patients who received interpersonal therapy or cognitive therapy improved substantially and showed greater improvement than did patients who received behavior therapy. In addition, their improvement was maintained without further treatment over the subsequent year (Fairburn et al., 1991; Fairburn, Jones, Peveler, Hope, & O'Connor, 1993; Fairburn et al., 1995).

Treatment Process Research

Based on the assumption that psychodynamic therapy has at least small to moderate positive effects, researchers have attempted to examine the factors or processes that account for the beneficial effects of this type of therapy. **Treatment process research** on psychodynamic therapy, in comparison to **treatment outcome research,** focuses on those characteristics of therapists, patients, and therapeutic techniques that may account for positive changes in patient functioning. Several factors have been found to be associated with better outcomes in psychodynamic therapy. First, specific characteristics of the therapist-patient alliance have been found to be related to more positive effects in therapy (e.g., Horvath & Luborsky, 1993). In particular, the alliance between the therapist and the patient, which reflects both a positive working relationship between the two individuals and a shared commitment to the therapeutic process, has been found to explain a significant proportion of the variance in the outcome of psychodynamic therapy (Horvath & Luborsky; Horvath & Symonds, 1991). Second, the nature and frequency of interpretations made by the therapist are related to the outcome of short-term dynamic therapy (Piper et al., 1993). Specifically, interpretations that focus on the transference relationship and that are provided in low concentrations (i.e., not too frequently) are related to more positive outcomes, although the effects of these interpretations are modified by characteristics of the patients' attachment relationships (Piper et al.). Third, the way that patients think about and develop representations of their relationship with the therapist have been found to be related to therapy outcomes, with more positive representations of the therapist and the therapeutic relationship being associated with more positive outcomes in dynamic therapy (Orlinsky, Geller, Tarragona, & Farber, 1993).

SUMMARY AND CONCLUSIONS

In this chapter we presented the foundations of psychoanalysis and psychodynamic therapies. Freud's belief that material stored in the unconscious contributes to psychopathology led him to develop psychoanalysis, with the goal of helping patients become aware of these unconscious feelings and memories. Freud used free association, dream analysis, and analysis of the transference relationship with the patient to gain access to this unconscious information. Psychoanalysis typically lasted for several years, primarily because the patient had to work through this unconscious material and resolve unconscious conflicts.

More recent derivations of psychoanalysis, known broadly as psychodynamic psychotherapies, are generally shorter and more flexible in their execution and have a stronger focus on interpersonal relationships. Psychodynamic psychotherapies, such as Time-Limited Dynamic Psychotherapy, also have a stronger empirical foundation than does psychoanalysis. One of the most widely practiced of the psychodynamic psychotherapies is Interpersonal Psychotherapy, a short-term therapy currently used primarily in the treatment of depression and eating disorders.

Although much of the published literature concerning the effectiveness of psychoanalysis was in the form of uncontrolled case studies, there is a growing body of empirical research examining the effectiveness of more contemporary psychodynamic and interpersonal therapies. In particular, Interpersonal Psychotherapy has been found to be an effective treatment for depression and bulimia nervosa. In chapter 15 we compare in greater detail the effectiveness of psychodynamic therapies with other forms of psychological treatment.

KEY TERMS AND NAMES

Alfred Adler
Catharsis
Collective unconscious
Dream analysis
Dream work
Ego psychology
Free association
Sigmund Freud
Hypnosis
Inferiority complex
Interpersonal psychotherapy (IPT)
Interpretation

Carl Jung
Latent content
Manifest content
Object relations
Personal unconscious
Psychoanalysis
Resistance
Time-Limited Dynamic Psychotherapy (TLDP)
Transference
Treatment outcome research
Treatment process research

RESOURCES

Books
Freud, S. (1933). *New introductory lectures on psycho-analysis*. London: Hogarth.

Freud, A., & Sandler, J. (1985). *The analysis of defense: The ego and the mechanisms of defense revisited*. New York: IUP.

Bowlby, J. (1988). *A secure base: Parent-child attachment and healthy human development*. New York: Basic Books.

Strupp, H. H., & Binder, J. L. (1984). *Psychotherapy in a new key: A guide to Time-Limited Dynamic Psychotherapy*. New York: Basic Books.

Weissman, M. M., Markowitz, J. C., & Klerman, G. L. (2000). *Comprehensive guide to interpersonal psychotherapy*. New York: Basic Books.

Journals
The International Journal of Psychoanalysis
Journal of Consulting and Clinical Psychology
Archives of General Psychiatry
Journal of the American Psychoanalytic Association

CHAPTER THIRTEEN

PSYCHOTHERAPY: HUMANISTIC, EXISTENTIAL, AND EXPERIENTIAL APPROACHES

INTRODUCTION

Acts of extreme violence represent human nature at its worst. We saw this in chapter 4 when we discussed the mass shootings and suicides that occurred at Columbine High School in April of 1999. Eighteen-year-old Eric Harris and 17-year-old Dylan Klebold planned and carried out the cold-blooded murder of their classmates and then their own suicides. What could have led them to their actions? And what does this event tell us about the basic nature of people? The factors that led to Harris and Klebold's acts are not yet understood, and there was little in their past that would have led anyone to expect they were capable of these murders. Violent acts such as these lead many people to assume that there is a fundamentally dark and frightening side to human nature.

In this chapter we will address a second approach to psychotherapy that has been deeply concerned with questions about the fundamental characteristics of human nature. This perspective takes the position that there is something fundamentally good in all people, even when they act in terrifying and unconscionable ways. Consider the following assumptions about people:

- We are all free to determine our own lives and destinies; we are not shaped and constrained by internal drives or forces in the external environment.
- There is no external, valid truth to the world; we each possess our own perspective that is unique and valid in its own right.
- Problems arise when we lose contact with our own internal experience and our own emotions. Positive growth will occur so long as individuals focus on and become more aware of their own emotions and experiences.

These assumptions are at the core of a somewhat diverse set of therapies that emerged during the 1940s through the 1960s. These therapies include models that are variously labeled humanistic, person-centered, existential, experiential, supportive, or expressive models of psychotherapy; as a shorthand method, we will refer to the early versions of these approaches here as *humanistic-existential* models and to more recent versions of these therapies as *process-experiential* models.

Humanistic-existential approaches to psychotherapy comprise a group of related models and methods that share many features with psychodynamic psychotherapy yet also reflect a strong reaction against principles embodied in psychodynamic, and more specifically psychoanalytic, approaches. Similar to psychodynamic psychotherapy, humanistic-existential approaches are *insight*-oriented approaches to psychotherapy; that is, they emphasize the importance of gaining increased awareness or understanding of oneself, one's motives, and one's emotions in order to resolve problems and to change behavior. Insight and awareness are achieved through the experiencing and release of intense, personal emotions, a process that in psychodynamic and psychoanalytic psychotherapy is referred to as *catharsis*. These two principles, the importance of insight and emotional experience, link humanistic-existential approaches with psychodynamic models of psychotherapy.

Humanistic-existential models of therapy also differ in several important ways from psychodynamic methods that were described in chapter 12. Most importantly, whereas psychoanalytic theory presents a relatively negative and pessimistic view of human nature, humanistic-existential models are based on a much more positive view of what it means to be human. These theories emphasize the inherent potential and tendency of people to grow and develop in positive ways and the capacity of people to determine the direction of their own lives. Rather than requiring an expert therapist to offer interpretations of the client's experience, these methods emphasize the importance of *allowing* individuals to draw their own conclusions about their experience (Greenberg & Paivio, 1997). These different assumptions about human nature, personality, and psychopathology have led to techniques and processes in psychotherapy that are quite distinct from those used in psychodynamic psychotherapy (and different from the cognitive and behavioral therapies that we will discuss in chapter 14). The central difference between psychodynamic psychotherapies and humanistic-existential therapies involves the role of the therapist in interpreting the client's experience. In psychodynamic therapy, the interpretations that are made by the therapist are crucial in helping the client achieve insight; the therapist offers an explanation for the client's behavior that is based in the perspective and point of reference of the therapist, not the client. In humanistic-existential therapy, it is assumed that the client can achieve insight without interpretations from the therapist.

HISTORICAL BACKGROUND

Humanistic Psychotherapy

As we discussed in chapter 4, the roots of **humanistic psychotherapy** can be traced to the writings of William James in the early 1900s. However, the most influential figure in the development of humanistic, existential, and experiential models of psychotherapy is the American psychologist **Carl Rogers.** Beginning in the 1940s, Rogers developed a theory of personality and an approach to psychotherapy, and initiated research to better understand the process of therapy and to evaluate its efficacy. Originally called *nondirective psychotherapy*, later termed *client-centered psychotherapy,* and finally *person-centered psychotherapy,* Rogers's method of psychotherapy was one of the first distinct alternatives to Freudian psychoanalysis. The most pronounced difference between the approaches offered by Freud and Rogers involved their basic views of human nature. Rogers countered the Freudian view of the human condition with an inherently more positive and optimistic view of humanity. These differences have major ramifications for how these two theorists thought about psychopathology and methods of treatment. It is important to recognize that many of the differences in the theories offered by Freud and Rogers were rooted in their personal experiences.

Sigmund Freud's views on personality, psychopathology, and psychotherapy were deeply affected by his experiences as a Jewish physician in Europe in the late nineteenth and early twentieth centuries. In contrast, Carl Rogers's thinking was shaped by his experiences growing up in a conservative Christian family in the midwestern United States in the early 1900s. Spending the latter part of his childhood growing up on a farm, Rogers was drawn to agriculture and the ministry as possible careers. As his personal views developed, however, he found that he disagreed with

Carl Rogers, Ph.D., developed what is known today as client-centered therapy. Over the course of his career, Dr. Rogers has had a major impact both on the training of clinical psychologists and on the empirical evaluation of psychotherapy. (Photo © *Bettmann/CORBIS.*)

many of the tenets of fundamental Christianity, first during a missionary experience in China and later while enrolled in the Union Theological Seminary in New York City. Rogers (1961) described his participation in a discussion group with other seminary students as a significant experience in the development of his basic ideas about helping others. This group had no instructor and allowed the student participants to develop and freely express their own ideas. Rogers and others in the group came to question what they perceived as the authoritarian and controlling methods that characterized both traditional education and religion. With this group experience as an impetus, Rogers left the seminary after two years and enrolled in Teachers College at Columbia University to begin studying psychology.

During his education and training as a psychologist Rogers was influenced strongly by theories that emphasized humans' capacity for free will and self-determination. From the realm of education, he was strongly affected by the writings of John Dewey, who believed that optimal learning occurred when students were allowed to engage in the process of discovering knowledge for themselves rather than being taught within an authoritarian structure. During his early experiences as a clinical psychologist, Rogers was influenced by the writings of psychiatrist Otto Rank, who maintained that therapy must occur without control on the part of the therapist—that the goal of therapy was to allow the individual to pursue his or her capacity for free will (Rank, 1936, 1945).

Rogers's early experiences as a clinical psychologist involved work with children in Rochester, New York, at the Society for the Prevention of Cruelty to Children and subsequently as the director of the Rochester Child Guidance Clinic. Although he had received training in psychoanalytic treatment of children, he gradually broke with that tradition and was later appalled by his own early use of these methods (Rogers, 1961). He came to see the psychoanalytic method as an authoritarian approach to treating individuals, one that provided the therapist with an inappropriate level of power and authority, not only in defining the patient's problem but also in literally defining the patient's own experience through the use of psychoanalytic interpretations of the patient's memories, emotions, and motives. He believed that the patient, rather than the therapist, is the expert, in that the patient knows her or his own experience, the nature of the problem, and even the best ways to solve the problem. These beliefs are reflected in his choice of the word *client* rather than *patient* to refer to those whom he helped in therapy.

By 1940, when Rogers accepted a position as a professor of psychology at the Ohio State University, he had developed the first comprehensive version of his nondirective approach to psycho-

therapy. This development led to the publication of his landmark book *Counseling and Psychotherapy* in 1942. Two major themes were evident in this early version of his theory that remained important throughout his work. First, Rogers had become convinced that a supportive, permissive, nondirective relationship between the therapist and the client was at the core of facilitating the resolution of emotional suffering and fostering personality change (Rogers, 1949a). And second, based in his early interest in agricultural science, Rogers expressed a commitment to empirical research in attempting to understand both the process and outcome of psychotherapy (Rogers, 1949b). Until this time, the only record of what occurred during psychotherapy sessions came from the recollections and notes of therapists, which Rogers argued could be biased. Rogers initiated the audio recording of psychotherapy sessions as a way to better understand and analyze the content and process of what took place during these sessions. And perhaps most importantly, Rogers was one of the first to suggest that the effectiveness of psychotherapy should be evaluated empirically.

Existential Psychotherapy

Existential psychotherapy, although closely aligned with Rogers's humanistic and client-centered views, has separate origins and contains several features that distinguish it from the humanistic perspective. The existential approach derives from writings of such European philosophers as Sartre, Kierkegaard, and Heidegger and psychiatrists such as Viktor Frankl from Austria (e.g., Frankl, 1963, 1967). The existential tradition emphasizes the human potential for free will as well as human limitations and the troubling and tragic dimensions of existence—the belief that we are all ultimately alone in our experience and face the inevitable anxiety and uncertainty that comes from recognizing our own mortality. Whereas humanistic models reflect fundamental American principles of growth, potential, optimism, and unlimited possibilities, existential theories reflect Europeans' greater experience with geographic and ethnic conflict, war, death, and uncertain existence (Yalom, 1980). Existential theories highlight two contrasting sides that characterize free will—the positive sense of **self-determination** that is accompanied by the *existential anxiety* that is inevitable in making important choices, especially the choices upon which our existence depends, such as choosing a partner, selecting a career, or even choosing to live or die. Among the sources of existential anxiety that were outlined by Tillich (1952) are the awareness that one day we will die; we are helpless against chance circumstances that can permanently change our lives; we must ultimately make decisions, act, and live with the consequences of our decisions and actions; and we must create meaning and purpose in our lives.

A mixture of the humanistic and existential traditions is reflected in *Gestalt therapy* as developed by Fritz Perls in the 1950s and 1960s. Perls received a medical degree in Germany in 1921 and trained to become a psychoanalyst. However, Perls strongly challenged some of the basic principles of psychoanalysis, particularly the importance of the id and its role in the development of neurosis (Perls, 1947). Perls left Germany in 1933 shortly after Hitler came to power and moved first to the Netherlands, then to South Africa in 1934, and finally to the United States in 1946. He eventually settled at Esalen, a center for humanistic-existential psychotherapy in Big Sur, California. Perls was similar to Rogers in his belief in the innate goodness of human beings, but he placed even greater emphasis than did Rogers on the role of the individual to take responsibility for his or her own behavior.

The primary goal of Gestalt therapy is to help clients understand and accept their needs, desires, strengths, and fears in order to increase their awareness of how they prevent themselves from reaching their goals and satisfying their needs. Perls believed one of the primary mechanisms to achieve personal growth was to become

more aware of what one was thinking and feeling *in the moment;* to become aware of the *here and now* of existence and to avoid concerns and worries about the future. Perls felt that therapy was intended to help individuals become more integrated and whole by increasing their awareness of unacknowledged feelings and having them reclaim the parts of their personality that they had denied or disowned (Perls, 1973).

MAJOR THEORETICAL FOUNDATIONS

The central components of humanistic-existential theory were outlined in chapter 4; we will briefly summarize them here as they pertain to these models of psychotherapy. First, these approaches are **phenomenological**—people can be understood only from the vantage point of their own unique perceptions and feelings, from their phenomenological world. The phenomenological world includes all that is within the sensory awareness of the individual at a given moment in time. Each person's phenomenological world is the major determinant of her or his behavior and serves to make that person unique. Second, people have the capacity to be *aware* of their own behavior and what motivates them; indeed, greater awareness of one's motives is a desirable and important goal of therapy. Third, people are *innately good and effective.* They become ineffective and disturbed only when faulty learning or traumatic experiences disrupt normal development. Fourth, people are capable of achieving *control* over their lives and their destinies. Healthy people are able to accept and act on the capacity for personal control. Fifth, psychologically healthy people are *purposeful and goal directed.* They do not respond passively to their environment or inner drives; rather, they are self-directed. Sixth, therapists should not attempt to manipulate events for the individual. Rather, therapists should create conditions that will *facilitate* independent decision making by the client. When people are no longer concerned with the evaluations, demands, and preferences of others, their lives are guided by an innate tendency toward positive growth.

Rogers's Theory of the Self

Self-concept (one's conception of oneself) and self-esteem (one's affective evaluation of oneself) are central notions in most humanistic and existential models. According to Rogers (1961), for example, individuals develop both a real and an ideal sense of themselves. The **real self** refers to perceptions of the self as the individual is currently functioning—aspects of the self that are currently included in awareness. The **ideal self,** in contrast, refers to perceptions of the self to which the individual aspires. The ideal self is often based on the internalized values and goals of others—what others expect and want from us rather than what we want for ourselves. Rogers assumed that most individuals experience some degree of discrepancy between the real and ideal selves. An optimal degree of discrepancy will serve as a source of motivation for growth and change. However, when the discrepancy between these two aspects of the self is too great, the result is general dissatisfaction with oneself and the emergence of emotional suffering, unhappiness, and distress (see box 13.1 for current research on the real and ideal self).

Psychopathology is viewed as the consequence of blocks to positive growth that are encountered in the environment and the individual's experience. In the most general sense, blocks to positive growth and development are the result of interactions with other people that lead individuals away from their own experience. Psychopathology occurs when individuals try to live their lives based on the goals and values that other people hold for them rather than following their own motives and goals. The result is a discrepancy between the self and experience or between the real and ideal selves. Furthermore, focusing on the reactions of others will lead individuals to mistrust their own experience and their own emotions and to become anxious and preoccupied with meeting the expectations of others rather than their own goals.

Existential Theory

The word *existential* refers to existence and more specifically to human existence and life. The term has come to have a more limited meaning with reference to psychotherapy, however. In this context, it refers to theories that give a central role to the importance of human beings' awareness of their own existence and to the capacity for awareness itself, that is, consciousness (Bugental & McBeath, 1995). The roots of existential psychotherapy are in philosophy, and this approach has been described as a form of "clinical philosophy" (Koestenbaum, 1978). This description implies that the fundamental aspects of this model are not testable via empirical research. Proponents of existential psychotherapy argue that it does not involve or imply the treatment of disease or disorder; rather, it assists individuals to face the fundamental tasks in their lives, whether they do so consciously or not. The goal of existential psychotherapy is not to address symptoms, although symptoms of distress may be alleviated as a consequence of helping the individual recognize and negotiate life tasks (Bugental & McBeath, 1995; May & Yalom, 1989; Schneider & May, 1995).

According to the existential-humanistic approach, each individual is presented with an infinite range of possibilities in her or his life (Bugental & McBeath, 1995). To develop a personal identity and to form a direction for one's life, one must reduce this range of possibilities and select a direction to follow. Personal identity and life direction are reflected in the concept of a **self-and-world construct system** (SAWC; Kelly, 1955). The SAWC is a way of defining oneself and the world in such a way that one is protected from the anxiety that would come from recognizing all of life's possibilities. The SAWC involves the development of answers to the crucial, existential questions of life. These questions include: What is my essential nature? Am I a good person? What are my strengths? What are my failings? What do I need to change? What is valuable in me that must be protected? The SAWC also includes questions about the outer world: What is the nature of the world? Is it safe or dangerous? What are the good things worth pursuing or sacrificing? These questions and their answers are only partly conscious; they are mostly implicit and vary widely in the firmness with which they are held. These questions and their answers are more a part of philosophy than the science of psychology.

The concept of destiny is central to existential psychotherapy (May, 1981). Destiny refers to external influences and circumstances that shape the developing person. The influential conditions described by psychologist **Rollo May** include *cosmic* factors of birth and death; *genetic* factors of race, gender, and innate talents; *cultural* factors of society and family; and *circumstantial* factors of economic, political, and social conditions in the time in which one is born (May, 1990). Each of these circumstances affects the possibilities that are open to the individual in her or his life. The effects of destiny are assumed to be strong but not inevitable. It remains the responsibility of each person to develop a personal identity and a conception of the world in order to be alive and to grow (May). Because the rate of change in culture and society has increased dramatically in the late twentieth and early twenty-first centuries, an expectation of change, uncertainty, and unpredictability is now assumed to be a part of the SAWCs of many people (Bugental & McBeath, 1995).

Psychological problems develop when the SAWC is not functional—when it fails to generate a sense of satisfaction or leads to too much frustration or pain. The level of psychological distress that develops when the SAWC is not functional may be relatively incidental and easily overcome, or it may be catastrophic (Bugental & McBeath, 1995). The psychological distress that results from dysfunction of the SAWC is what leads a person to seek help through psychotherapy. The existential-humanistic view of psychotherapy requires that the SAWC be explored so that it can become more effective in generating satisfaction and preventing frustration.

GOALS OF THERAPY

Humanistic and existential approaches to psychotherapy share common goals with psychodynamic and psychoanalytic therapies, but they also differ in fundamental ways. Similar to psychodynamic and psychoanalytic psychotherapy, humanistic and existential approaches emphasize the goal of facilitating greater insight and self-understanding in the client in order to bring about personality change. Humanistic-existential approaches depart radically from psychodynamic and psychoanalytic approaches, however, in that they emphasize that the concrete goals for psychotherapy must be set by the client. As Rogers (1961) noted,

> it is the client who knows what hurts, what directions to go, what problems are crucial, what experiences have been deeply buried. It began to occur to me that unless I had a need to demonstrate my own cleverness and learning, I would do better to rely upon the client for the direction of movement in the process. (p. 28)

The goals of humanistic-existential psychotherapy are to offer support and empathy in order to help clients explore the true nature and meaning of their behaviors, emotions, and relationships with others. The therapist strives to allow clients to confront and clarify past and present choices that they have made; to enable clients to relate authentically, openly, honestly, spontaneously, and lovingly to others; to allow clients to accept their own aloneness in the world; and to provide clients with a genuine and authentic encounter or relationship with another person

BOX 13.1

CONTEMPORARY RESEARCH ON THE REAL AND IDEAL SELF

The themes outlined by Carl Rogers in his original model of the components of the self have been the subject of continued research. Much of this work has been based on **self-discrepancy theory** outlined by social psychologist E. Tory Higgins and his colleagues (e.g., Higgins, 1987; Higgins, Roney, Crowe, & Hymes, 1994; Moretti & Higgins, 1999a, 1999b). A central premise of self-discrepancy theory is that individuals develop and hold particular types of self-standards. Within this model, there are three main domains of the self that influence a person's emotional experience: *the actual self* (the cognitive representation of the attributes that a person believes he or she actually possesses), *the ideal self* (the cognitive representation of the attributes that a person believes he or she would ideally like to possess), and *the ought self* (the cognitive representation of the attributes that a person believes he or she ought to possess). The ideal and ought selves are referred to as self-guides, and the actual self consists of what is usually meant by the term *self-concept*. The actual self, therefore, would be composed of perceptions of the important, self-defining attributes that individu-

als believe they currently possess. According to self-discrepancy theory, self-guides serve as standards by which the self is evaluated. People may evaluate themselves from their own standpoint (how they see themselves) or from the standpoint of a significant other (e.g., how their parents might see them).

According to the self-discrepancy model, discrepancies between the actual self and the self-guides (ideal and ought selves) can contribute to a person's vulnerability to experience negative emotions. More specifically, greater discrepancies between the actual self and self-guides are hypothesized to be associated with higher levels of emotional distress. Whereas discrepancies between the actual self and the ideal self (A:I discrepancies) are predicted to increase vulnerability to dysphoric emotions such as dissatisfaction, sadness, and disappointment, discrepancies between the actual self and the ought self (A:O discrepancies) are hypothesized to increase vulnerability to anxious symptoms such as agitation, worry, and fear. Theoretically, individuals with A:I discrepancies experience dysphoric emotions because they believe that they have not

---

(the therapist) in the context of therapy (Patterson, 2000).

Although the specific goals of humanistic-existential therapy are set by the client, they include the general goals of the development of authenticity and self-actualization. Therapy is intended to help clients learn to live their lives more fully and genuinely and to find a sense of meaning and purpose to their existence (Bugental, 1981; Frankl, 1965). Thus, one of the major goals of humanistic-existential therapy is to facilitate the client's movement toward increasingly greater self-actualization (Scharf, 1996). The process of self-actualization is to become all that one is capable of being and thus to live a life that is full of meaning and accomplishment (Goldstein, 1959; Maslow, 1987).

TRAINING

Systematic training in the core skills of humanistic-existential psychotherapy began with Rogers's (1957) graded training experiences and was continued by Truax and Carkhuff's (1967) didactic-experiential training (Greenberg & Goldman, 1988). In Rogers's graded experiences, students listened to tape-recorded interviews, experienced live demonstrations by a supervisor, participated in group and personal therapy, conducted individual psychotherapy, and recorded their own sessions with clients for discussion with a supervisor. More recently, Allen Ivey and his colleagues have designed a comprehensive microcounseling training program that is similar in format (e.g., Daniels,

BOX 13.1 (concluded)

fulfilled important hopes and wishes, whereas individuals with A:O discrepancies experience anxious symptoms because they believe that they have not lived up to appropriate obligations (Higgins, 1987). Essentially, A:I discrepancies are hypothesized to be associated with the loss of positive outcomes, whereas A:O discrepancies are predicted to be associated with the presence of negative outcomes.

A number of studies using college analog populations (e.g., Higgins, Klein, & Strauman, 1985; Strauman & Higgins, 1987) and clinically diagnosed samples (e.g., Scott & O' Hara, 1993; Strauman, 1989) have reported correlations between self-discrepancies and various forms of emotional distress. As predicted by the theory, high A:I discrepancies have been found to be correlated with depressive mood and symptoms, whereas high A:O discrepancies are correlated with anxious mood and symptoms. For example, Scott and O'Hara and Strauman reported that A:I discrepancies are associated specifically with major depressive disorder, whereas A:O discrepancies are associated with anxiety disorders. In addition to these correlational investigations, several experimental studies have examined the affective impact of activating particular

self-discrepancies. Higgins, Bond, Klein, and Strauman (1986) demonstrated that an individual's larger self-discrepancy (A:I or A:O) appears to determine whether he or she experiences depressive or anxious symptoms after imagining a negative event. Similarly, Strauman and Higgins found that increasing the accessibility of ideal and ought self-discrepancies results in depressive and anxious affect, respectively. Finally, Strauman (1992) demonstrated that activating discrepant self-guides enhances retrieval of negative childhood memories that appear to be associated with the developmental origins of the discrepancy. Considered collectively, this correlational and experimental evidence suggests that particular self-discrepancies contribute to specific negative emotional states. More recently, Hankin, Roberts, and Gotlib (1997) found that A:I discrepancies and self-oriented perfectionism were associated specifically with depressive symptoms after controlling for anxious symptoms, whereas A:O discrepancies were associated specifically with anxious symptoms after controlling for depressive symptoms. Thus, some aspects of Rogers's original conceptualization of the self have been borne out in empirical research.

Rigazio-DiGilio, & Ivey, 1997; Ivey, 1994, 1995). This program teaches a set of skills through a sequence of instruction, practice, and feedback provided to the student therapist. Training includes observation of live or videotaped demonstrations of experienced therapists, followed by role-playing experiences to practice interpersonal skills and communication skills, and finally, supervised experiences working with clients. This approach focuses on teaching basic listening and communication skills that form the basis for a person-centered approach to counseling and therapy. It includes the use of questions, paraphrasing, reflection of feelings expressed by clients, helping clients to explore their values and beliefs, and helping clients understand the meaning of their emotions and experience.

Humanistic and existential approaches to psychotherapy achieved a high level of popularity within clinical psychology during the 1960s and 1970s. Many doctoral training programs in clinical psychology included opportunities for training in these techniques during this time. However, the popularity and level of influence of these approaches has declined in subsequent years. In a recent survey of members of the Division of Clinical Psychology of APA, only 4 percent identified themselves as humanistic-existential in their orientation, and only 1 percent described themselves as client-centered in their approach (Bechtold, Norcross, Wyckoff, Pokrywa, & Campbell, 2001). This decline is attributable in part to the relative lack of research on these methods of psychotherapy in the treatment of serious forms of psychopathology (see chapter 15 for a more detailed discussion of this concern). Training in humanistic and existential psychotherapy continues to play a role in counseling programs that emphasize methods that foster the development of self-awareness and personal growth rather than the treatment of psychopathology.

KEY ASPECTS OF TECHNIQUES

Client-Centered Psychotherapy

Rogers described the central techniques of his model of psychotherapy in two critical papers. The first, entitled "The Processes of Psychotherapy," appeared in the *Journal of Consulting Psychology* in 1940. The second, with the provocative title, "The Necessary and Sufficient Conditions of Therapeutic Personality Change," appeared in the same journal in 1957. In these two influential but surprisingly brief papers (the first was 3 pages and the second 12 pages in length), Rogers described the six conditions that he believed were essential for effective psychotherapy. Consistent with his view of personality and psychopathology, Rogers focused on the conditions that must be established by the therapist in order to *allow* the client's innate tendency for positive growth to emerge.

Rogers's ideas evolved and changed over his career based on his clinical experience and research that tested some of the central components of his theory. Although he identified six elements of his therapeutic approach in both his 1940 and 1957 papers, it is noteworthy that the six elements in these two papers were quite different. We will focus here on the second version of these elements, because they became the enduring structure of the client-centered approach. Rogers believed that six specific elements or conditions must be present in the client, in the therapist, and in the relationship between the client and the therapist in order for positive change to occur in psychotherapy. As implied in the title of the second of these papers, Rogers be-

lieved that these six conditions were both *necessary* for personality change to occur (i.e., they must be present) and *sufficient* for personality change (i.e., no other techniques or conditions were required to facilitate positive growth and relieve emotional distress and suffering).

Rogers's (1957) six core conditions are as follows.

1. The client and the therapist must be in "*psychological contact.*" Rogers hypothesized that significant positive personality change does not take place except in the context of a close interpersonal relationship.
2. The client is in a state of psychological or emotional *incongruence*, being vulnerable or anxious. Rogers defined incongruence as a discrepancy between the actual experience of the client (i.e., the client's emotions and feelings) and the view that the client holds of herself or himself. Incongruence, therefore, essentially describes the discrepancy between the real self and ideal self.
3. The therapist is *congruent*, integrated, or genuine in the relationship. Within the context of the relationship with the client, the therapist is accurately aware of his or her own experience on a moment-to-moment basis. The emphasis is on the therapist's ability to be aware of what she or he is feeling during sessions with the client and to behave in ways that do not contradict these feelings.
4. The therapist experiences **unconditional positive regard** for the client. Rogers defined unconditional positive regard as warm acceptance of the client's experience, no matter what it is. There are no conditions or qualifications on the therapist's acceptance of the client. Unconditional positive regard entails accepting both the good and the bad characteristics of the client. The therapist cares for the client in a nonpossessive way or in a manner that focuses on the needs of the client and not the needs of the therapist.

5. The therapist acquires an **empathic** understanding of the client's internal experience and strives to communicate this understanding to the client. Accurate, empathic understanding of the client's experience includes the therapist's capacity to sense the client's private world as if it were her or his own world. The therapist stands with one foot in the client's frame of reference and one foot outside the client's perspective. This view allows the therapist to sense the client's emotions (e.g., anger, fear, confusion) without the therapist's own feelings becoming caught up in the moment. Rogers felt that accurate and deep empathy allowed therapists both to communicate their understanding of the client's experience and, hopefully, to identify aspects of the client's experience of which the client is unaware. Thus, Rogers believed that accurate empathy may go beyond the client's current awareness and reflect aspects of the client's experience that are outside conscious awareness at that moment.

6. Finally, communication to the client of the therapist's empathic understanding and unconditional positive regard must be achieved, at least minimally. It is not enough for the therapist to experience these reactions to the client—they must be effectively communicated to the client in order to have an impact on the client's awareness and to facilitate change. Rogers believed that unless a minimal level of communication of these attitudes has been achieved, the client will not experience their beneficial effects.

Can positive change occur in the absence of these conditions? And are these conditions actually sufficient to facilitate positive change in all clients and to relieve all problems and disorders? Despite his formulation of the all-encompassing nature of these conditions, Rogers included several significant qualifiers to the six conditions. He observed, for example, that clients must bring some level of dissatisfaction with their present level of adjustment to the therapy, some fundamental need for help. Rogers also felt that therapy would not be effective if a client was faced with adverse social conditions that would make adjustment impossible except through radical alteration of these circumstances. Finally, Rogers believed that it was necessary for the client to have intellectual skills above the "borderline level" in order to benefit from verbal psychotherapy (Rogers, 1940). Rogers (1957) noted that these conditions were open to validation—that is, to be proven or disproven—through empirical research. As we shall see in this chapter's section on research on humanistic psychotherapy, Rogers was proven only partly correct at best.

Specific techniques are important in this model only to the degree that they serve as mechanisms for fulfilling the six conditions. Warmth, empathy, and genuineness, for example, are conveyed through communication skills such as the use of open-ended questions. Open-ended questions provide an opportunity for clients to expand on their thoughts and feelings (e.g., "How do you feel about yourself as a student?"). Reflection of the content of what the client has said, as well as the emotion that the client has conveyed, is another important communication skill (Bohart & Greenberg, 1997). Reflection involves the reiteration of the content (e.g., "So you think that you are going to fail the test") or the emotion (e.g., "You sound very worried about how others will react if you fail the test") that is conveyed by the client. Another important communication skill in therapy is self-disclosure by the therapist of her or his moment-to-moment reactions to the client (e.g., "When you talk about the test, I find myself beginning to feel anxious and concerned"). Communication skills that involve the use of play have been applied to therapy with children (see box 13.2).

Existential Psychotherapy

In existential psychotherapy, the therapist helps clients become increasingly aware of the ways

BOX 13.2

HUMANISTIC PSYCHOTHERAPY WITH CHILDREN

Although the focus of much of the work on humanistic-existential therapy has been on adults, beginning with the work of Virginia Axline (1955), this approach has also been applied to children. The most common application of humanistic psychotherapy with children has been through client-centered (or nondirective) **play therapy** (e.g., Goetze, 1994). In this approach, the basic principles of Rogerian therapy are followed—all feelings on the part of the child are considered valid, the child is accepted as she or he is, and the child is allowed to set the directions for therapy (Carroll, 1995). However, instead of a reliance on verbal interactions between the therapist and client, as in adult psychotherapy, play is used as the primary vehicle for communication and interaction between the therapist and client. The therapist makes available to the child an array of toys, games, stuffed animals, dolls, and drawing materials. The child is allowed to choose freely among these various play mediums, and the therapist either joins in or observes the child in the play activities. It

is assumed that the child will choose activities that will allow for the experiencing and expression of important emotional themes. The therapist's task is to reflect and support the expression of these emotions and provide the child with acceptance and valuing, regardless of what feelings are shared. The experience of understanding, acceptance, and positive regard during play is assumed to provide the child with a context in which his or her natural tendencies toward positive growth and self-understanding will emerge. Unfortunately, research evaluating the effects of nondirective or client-centered child therapy has failed to support its efficacy. Client-centered therapy with children has been found to be less effective in the treatment of a number of childhood disorders than are other methods of therapy, especially behavioral and cognitive-behavioral methods, and to differ very little from no treatment (see reviews by Weiss & Weisz, 1995; Kazdin & Weisz, 1998).

---

that they think about and experience the self and the world. Clients are encouraged to look deeply into their own experience; to express their emotions, goals, and fears; to become increasingly open to their own experience; and to modify self-defeating aspects of their self and world construct system. This method is referred to as "searching," a way of tapping into less conscious aspects of one's experience that is similar to the psychoanalytic process of free association. The existential psychotherapist encourages clients to develop a sense of concern for the self, a recognition of what truly matters in their lives in this precise moment (Bugental & McBeath, 1995). In this way, the existential approach shares an emphasis with Rogerian therapy on the present, the here and now (Bugental, 1999; see box 13.3).

Existential therapy involves the therapist and client working together to help the client main-

tain a focus on her or his own inner struggle for greater awareness of the self and the world (Bugental, 1999). The therapist facilitates the client's self-discovery by encouraging the client to be persistent, by supporting the confrontation of threats and fears, and by facilitating the verbal expression of the client's inner experience. The existential therapist highlights resistance to therapy as it is encountered, that is, in the immediate moment in the therapeutic sessions, by continually drawing the client's attention to the factors that interfere with his or her searching for a sense of identity and direction, and by identifying repetitive patterns in the client's life (Bugental & McBeath, 1995).

In a manner similar to the Rogerian perspective, existential therapy views the *alliance* or *relationship* between the client and therapist as one of the primary resources for achieving change

BOX 13.3

MINDFULNESS MEDITATION: FOCUSING ON THE HERE AND NOW

Humanistic-existential models of psychotherapy all emphasize the importance of focusing on present experience, on being aware of one's current experience. The importance of focusing on the here and now is also central to Eastern philosophies, including Zen Buddhism. An interesting variation of humanist-existential therapy can be found in the application of Zen beliefs and principles in the context of therapy. Jon Kabat-Zinn has applied the principles of Zen in teaching methods of stress management for medical patients (e.g., Kabat-Zinn, Lipworth, & Burney, 1985; Kabat-Zinn, Massion, Kristeller, Petersen et al., 1992; Kabat-Zinn et al., 1998; Miller, Fletcher, & Kabat-Zinn, 1995).

A central concept in Kabat-Zinn's approach is the importance of living in and appreciating the present moment, a notion that is similar to the emphasis on the here and now in existential and humanistic psychotherapy. One of the techniques used in Kabat-Zinn's approach is the body scan, in which patients are taught to focus their attention on their bodies and to increase their awareness of physical sensations in the moment. Patients are taught to appreciate the moment, as reflected in the mantra, "This is it." That is, rather than focusing thoughts and attention on the future, on what one does not have, and on unfulfilled wishes, the individual is taught to focus on being in

and appreciating the present moment. This approach also shares another belief or value with the humanistic-existential approaches in the emphasis on the active role of the patient in decision making with the therapist. This model has been applied in medical settings and has involved patients as participants in managing their health and treatment, has recognized the importance of treating the patient as a person rather than as a "case," and has offered the patient more participation in her or his own treatment (Salmon, Santorelli, & Kabat-Zinn, 1998).

Several studies have shown that this program (also called "Full Catastrophe Living") is associated with positive outcomes for medical patients who are coping with a variety of different illnesses. For example, Kabat-Zinn et al. (1985) found that a 10-week meditation and stress reduction program was related to decreased pain, reductions in the use of pain medications, and increased feelings of self-esteem. Kabat-Zinn et al. (1998) found that patients suffering from the skin condition psoriasis who were randomly assigned to use mindfulness meditation along with ultraviolet light treatments recovered more quickly that did patients who received light treatments only, as reflected in ratings by physicians who were blind to the type of treatment that the patients received.

---

and growth. This relationship is viewed as "a bond between what is best and most dedicated in the therapist and what is most health-seeking and courageous in the client" (Bugental & Bugental, 1978). Also consistent with the Rogerian approach to therapy is the existential therapist's emphasis on genuineness and openness with the clients, making sure that they do not withdraw behind a protective wall of objectivity (Bugental & McBeath, 1995, p. 72).

Existential therapy emphasizes the process of how clients express their emotions and their ex-

perience rather than the content of what they express. The therapist monitors the client's facial expressions, gestures, breathing patterns, body language, and other nonverbal behaviors in addition to what the client is saying. Existential therapists acknowledge that a process similar to transference in psychoanalysis occurs in treatment—clients bring to therapy their ways of interacting with others, their way of presenting themselves, their way of trying to win approval, and their needs in relationships (Bugental & McBeath, 1995). These patterns are expected to be acted out with the therapist, and much of these transference interactions are assumed to be out of the conscious awareness of the client. The power to bring about change is assumed in existential psychotherapy to reside in the client, not in the therapist or in the techniques of therapy. All humans realize only a small part of their potential—psychotherapy is a process of helping individuals recognize more of their own potential and put it into action.

CONTEMPORARY APPROACHES: PROCESS-EXPERIENTIAL PSYCHOTHERAPY

The early work and writings of humanistic and of existential psychotherapists have provided the foundation for current applications of this approach to psychotherapy. The most fully developed and widely used of the current approaches is represented by the **process-experiential** approach of psychologists **Leslie Greenberg** of the York University in Toronto, **Robert Elliott** of the University of Toledo, and others (e.g., Elliott & Greenberg, 1995; Greenberg & Watson, 1998; Greenberg, Rice, & Elliott, 1993). This approach reflects an integration of Rogers's client-centered therapy, Gestalt therapy, and existential therapy, with current research and theory on the nature of emotions (Greenberg & Paivio, 1997; Greenberg, Van Balen, 1998; Safran & Greenberg, 1987). This integration reflects a greater commitment to link the process-experiential approach with psychological research than was evident in earlier existential and humanistic approaches.

Theory

The process-experiential model is phenomenological and emphasizes that clients have unique access to information about their emotional and personal experiences and that therefore they are experts about their own experience. Consequently, processes that involve personal choice and discovery are emphasized over methods that involve interpretation or advice by the therapist.

Leslie Greenberg, Ph.D., is a Professor of Clinical Psychology at York University in Canada. Dr. Greenberg is a leader in contemporary research on the development and the process of psychotherapy that emphasizes importance of the expression of emotions. *(Photo courtesy of Leslie Greenberg.)*

Clients are encouraged and allowed to explore and describe their inner experience rather than having the therapist offer interpretations about their internal conflicts, motives, or possible connections between clients' present and past experience. The individual is seen as an active participant in therapy, and the therapeutic process is one of facilitating choice by clients who are exploring their own experience (Bohart & Tallman, 1998). Similar to client-centered and existential therapy, process-experiential therapy focuses on the client's present experience and on the current moment-by-moment process that occurs in the therapy session (Leijssen, 1998).

The process-experiential model also emphasizes a belief in an inherent growth tendency in the individual that can contribute to positive development if the person trusts his or her own growth tendency. Drawing on the existential approach, clients are helped to confront their own freedom and to accept responsibility for determining their own lives (Elliott & Greenberg, 1995). An authentic relationship between client and therapist is seen as central to growth in therapy. There are hypothesized to be two types of barriers to healthy psychological functioning: (a) difficulties in finding words or images to represent or communicate one's experiences; and (b) dysfunctional **emotion schemes** that affect how individuals interpret their experiences (Elliott & Greenberg, 1995; Greenberg & Paivio, 1997). Emotion schemes are the basic units of emotional experience and are comprised of emotional memories, hopes, expectations, and fears. Therefore, one goal of therapy is to help clients access their dysfunctional emotion schemes in the context of a therapeutic relationship that will lead to change in these problematic emotions.

The process-experiential approach differs from traditional Rogerian therapy in several ways. Most notably, in process-experiential therapy the therapist takes a much more active role in directing the process of the therapy sessions. The therapist encourages or directs the client to engage in activities during sessions that will facilitate a deepening of emotional experience. However, as in client-centered therapy, in process-experiential therapy the therapist does not direct or determine the content of what the client chooses to talk about. As described by Greenberg, Elliott, and Lietaer (1994), "This distinction can be characterized as *being* with the client in the client-centered view, or *doing* something with the client, in the experiential" (p. 510). The therapist directs the process of the session (how the client experiences emotions) by encouraging the client to engage in actions that

will lead to the experiencing of emotions without directing the content of the session (what the client talks about or expresses).

Techniques

The basic aspects of treatment in the process-experiential approach are divided into those factors that are concerned with the client-therapist relationship and those that involve facilitation of the central tasks of therapy. The optimal relationship is described as one of mutual collaboration in which the client and the therapist work together to help the client explore his or her experience more deeply (Elliott et al., 1995). When disagreements or differences in perspective are encountered, the therapist is expected to defer to the opinion of the client—the client is the expert on her or his experience. Therefore, the therapist offers ideas as suggestions in an open and nonauthoritarian manner rather than as statements of truth (Elliott et al., 1995).

Three basic principles characterize the client-therapist relationship in the process-experiential approach. The first principle involves *empathic attunement* between the client and therapist. The therapist continually tries to maintain a genuine understanding of the client's internal experience and frame of reference without evaluating the client's statements in terms of their truth or appropriateness. There is also no attempt on the part of the therapist to interpret patterns, drives, or defenses or to challenge irrational beliefs (Elliott et al., 1995; Greenberg, 1996; Greenberg & Elliott, 1997). The second relationship principle refers to the *therapeutic bond* between the therapist and the client. The therapist responds to the client from an attitude characterized by empathy and acceptance of the client. These characteristics are intended to help foster a relationship in which the client feels understood and accepted. The therapist communicates that the client is a worthwhile person whose value is not contingent on performing certain behaviors or having certain feelings. The third relationship principle refers to task *collaboration* between the therapist and client. The therapist facilitates mutual involvement of the therapist and client in formulating the goals and tasks of therapy. The therapist accepts the goals and tasks presented by the client and helps the client engage in the process of experiencing and exploring feelings.

The process-experiential approach also emphasizes **experiential processing,** which involves facilitating the client's awareness of her or his experience. In this process, the client becomes aware of internal physical sensations and external stimuli, both of which are essential components of making clear contact with reality. The therapist attempts to facilitate a greater sense of self-awareness by calling attention to some visible aspect of the client's expression (e.g., "Are you aware that you are clenching your fists?"). The therapist further encourages the client to actively and spontaneously express her or his own emotional reactions. The focus is on helping the client become more aware of and able to express his or her emotions. Methods for focusing on emotions are presented in table 13.1. A key technique involves responding empathically to the client's expression of emotions (Bohart & Greenberg, 1997). It is essential for a process-experiential therapist to be able to accurately identify the nature of the emotions that are experienced by the client (Machado, Beutler, & Greenberg, 1999).

These processes are observable in transcripts of therapist-client interactions from process-experiential therapy presented by Elliott and Greenberg (1995). They offer the following statement by a client (p. 128):

> *Client (C):* My mother had high blood pressure and a bad heart, but I think she was a hypochondriac. And once us girls got old enough, she didn't do anything and it was left up to us. I had to do it or else it didn't get done.

As an example of empathic reflection, the therapist might respond (Elliott & Greenberg):

TABLE 13.1
Framework for the Process of Emotionally Focused Therapy

Therapist's specific intentions	Therapist's actions
1. Direct attention	Respond empathically.
2. Refocus attention	Redirect client's attention to his or her internal experience.
3. Focus on present	Bring clients' attention to present experience.
4. Analyze expression	Comment in a supportive manner on and create awareness of nonverbal expression. Focus on *how* things are said by the client.
5. Promote ownership and agency	Promote client's use of "I" language instead of speaking as disowned parts. Help client to "reown" experience.
6. Intensify	Use vivid imagery and expressive enactments. Suggest exaggerations and repetition of expressions and actions.
7. Evoke memories	Promote reentry and reliving of concrete events of the past from the client's point of view. Focus on emotional content of memories, personal perceptions, and meanings.
8. Symbolize	Put feelings into words mainly by empathic responses. Conjecture about what the client might feel. Promote reflection and creation of new meaning.
9. Establish intents	Focus on wants, needs, and goals by asking what the client needs. Promote planning and action in the world.

Note. Adapted from Greenberg, L. S., & Paivio, S. C. (1997). *Working with emotions in psychotherapy.* New York: Guilford Press.

[Therapist] (T): Uh-huh. So it was either you did it or it didn't get done, just a sense of "I have to do it."

Alternatively, the therapist could try to facilitate greater exploration through a reflection that goes beyond a reiteration of the content of what the client said. This approach can be achieved by a number of different summaries and reflections of what the client has said and what the client feels. Here are some empathic explorations in response to the example statement by the client (Elliott & Greenberg, 1995) (pp. 128–129):

> *T:* Almost like she would say "Oh, my *heart*— you do it!" and you would just feel this tremendous weight of responsibility being put into your hands.
> *T:* (with a pondering quality): So I guess it was sort of a sense of being left with all that responsibility . . . or something like that?
> *T:* So it was having all that put on you. What was that like for you then?
> *T:* I'm not sure, but as you talk about this right now, it seems almost as if you're feeling some of what that was like. Does that fit?

As part of the therapeutic process, the client may experience a moment of intense vulnerability and share this feeling with the therapist. This experience helps the client to confront a feared aspect of the self that she or he has kept hidden and to share this feeling with another person (the therapist). The therapist's task is to reply with empathic understanding and genuine caring for the client. The therapist doesn't push or demand but rather tries to understand and accept.

One technique used in the process-experiential approach, drawn from Gestalt therapy, is the empty chair dialogue, used to deal with the client's "unfinished business." This technique addresses problems in which emotional memories of significant others continue to trigger the reexperiencing of unresolved emotional reactions—when the client thinks of the other person, bad feelings ensue (Paivio & Greenberg, 1995). The empty chair technique involves reexperiencing the unresolved feelings in the safety of the therapeutic environment, with the immediacy and intensity of the original situation, in order to allow the emotional expression to run its course and be experienced in a different way. The therapist instructs the client to imagine that the other person is seated in an empty chair, and the client is asked to express his or her feelings to the other person. Here is a continuation of the example provided by Elliott and Greenberg (1995) of the client discussing her feelings about her mother's illness behaviors that focuses on the empty chair technique (p. 129):

> *T:* I wonder if it would be okay with you to imagine your mother sitting in this chair here. Can you tell your mother what this was like for you?

The goal is to help the client bring these unresolved feelings about her mother into the present and to either forgive her mother or hold her accountable for her behavior. By talking to her mother as if she were present, the feelings are brought to the surface and more directly into her current experience. In this case, the client may express feelings of resentment and anger toward her mother for failing to do more to care for the client and her sisters. Additionally, the client may express guilt for feeling angry toward her mother, who presented herself as helpless and in need of care. Regardless of the nature of the specific emotions, the therapist's goal is to help bring the emotion into the client's current experience and to overcome the client's efforts to repress or push the feeling out of awareness.

The process-experiential approach to psychotherapy is illustrated with two of our continuing cases—Phillip and Maria (see boxes 13.4 and 13.5).

APPLICATION TO SPECIFIC PROBLEMS AND DISORDERS

Proponents of humanistic and existential approaches to psychotherapy have generally resisted developing specific techniques for use with particular problems or disorders or with particular types of clients. Rogers believed that the six conditions for effective client-centered

BOX 13.4

PROCESS-EXPERIENTIAL THERAPY: PHILLIP

Phillip's anxiety felt like it was snowballing—the frequency and intensity of his anxious feelings seemed to increase by the day. When he arrived for his appointment with Dr. Miller, the only thing he was sure that he wanted was some way to calm down and feel less anxious. Dr. Miller's office had a warm and welcoming feel to it. Phillip sat on a comfortable couch that was filled with colorful pillows. The room was softly lit and filled with plants; the walls decorated with art in pleasant, pastel colors. The session began with Dr. Miller simply asking Phillip to start by explaining why he came to therapy. Phillip began to unload his story, telling about his recent panic episode and going on to describe his overwhelming anxiety about public speaking. *Unloading* was really the best term to describe the process, because his feelings came pouring out while Dr. Miller listened intently and encouraged Phillip to describe his feelings in detail.

Dr. Miller practices process-experiential psychotherapy, the contemporary version of humanistic-existential therapy, based on the original work of Carl Rogers and the more recent work of Greenberg, Elliott, and other contemporary psychologists. Her perspective on Phillip's anxiety focused on the importance of Phillip's experience of himself, or more accurately, Phillip's difficulty in focusing on his own experience (Wolfe & Sigl, 1998). Anxiety, according to Greenberg and Paivio (1997), is "a response to symbolic, psychological, or social situations rather than immediately present physical danger" (p. 194). The goal of the therapy was to help Phillip become increasingly more aware of his own emotions and his own experience in the moment. This awareness would allow Phillip to become less preoccupied with what others thought of him and what he thought others wanted from him. Dr. Miller would pursue these goals through the use of emotion-focused techniques (see table 13.1) that involve empathy and the promotion of emotional expression.

Over the course of therapy, Phillip became increasingly aware of how he felt in the session. He spent less time trying to recall how he felt during his daily life and more focused on his emotions in the present. As he did this, he became aware of how frustrated he was in his job and that even if he were successful in his work, it would leave him feeling empty and dissatisfied. He began to explore what he wanted from his life, both in his work and in his relationships with his family and his friends. Phillip came to recognize the sometimes subtle ways that Dr. Miller would help him realize his feelings by pointing out something that Phillip was doing physically (clenching his fists while he talked, a tremor in his voice, tightness in his jaw). As Phillip focused on these sensations, he would often recognize an emotion that he had not been aware of. Throughout the sessions, Dr. Miller would convey a genuine sense of concern and understanding for what Phillip was going through. Phillip never felt judged and never felt pressured by Dr. Miller, but he most certainly felt understood. Through her careful use of reflections of feeling, open-ended questions, and encouragement to explore deeper levels of emotion, Dr. Miller helped Phillip to trust his feelings more and to set new and different priorities in his life. Phillip felt fortunate to have found a therapist who he felt was a "world class listener," something Phillip had not encountered before.

Dr. Miller guided Phillip to recall memories of experiences from his past in which he had felt anxious as a way of helping him understand the full intensity of his feelings and their meaning. As he explored his past, Phillip came to realize that his feelings were rooted deep in a fear of being rejected by others. Process-experiential therapy helps clients understand the meaning of long-held feelings and bring them into the present so that they can be experienced and then resolved.

therapy applied universally to all clients, regardless of the type of problem they presented. Rogers argued against the need for specific treatments for specific problems or diagnoses. He did not believe that it was necessary for the therapist to have an accurate diagnosis of the client in

BOX 13.5

PROCESS-EXPERIENTIAL THERAPY: MARIA

Maria was skeptical as she began therapy with Dr. Warren. She had never seen a psychologist before, and she was not sure what to expect. She had little hope that it would be helpful and only came to the session because her son insisted that she do so. Dr. Warren asked Maria to begin by describing why she felt she was in therapy. When Maria referred to her son's insistence that she come for the appointment, Dr. Warren gently encouraged Maria to describe how she felt about her son's concern for her. She expressed how much she loved him and appreciated his concern for her welfare, but she also did not want to be a burden to him or to anyone. As she talked, it became clear that her son's worries were centered on Maria's functioning since the death of her husband. When Dr. Warren asked Maria to describe her husband, what their relationship had been like, and how she felt about him, Maria was overcome with feelings of sadness and grief.

Working from a process-experiential approach, Dr. Warren set out to help Maria experience her deepest feelings about her husband, his death, and her life on her own. The doctor began with the assumption that Maria's depression was in part a result of her disconnection from her true feelings about this overwhelming loss in her life and her efforts to avoid or suppress these feelings. As described by Greenberg and Paivio (1997) from the perspective of process-experiential therapy, "Sadness emerges from parting, separation, or loss of attachment" (p. 163). The primary goal of therapy with a client suffering from depression is "allowing and accepting the pain, and experiencing and expressing it, in order to live through it and come out the other end" (p. 167). Therefore, Dr. Warren encouraged Maria to allow herself to experience the pain, to recall what she missed most about her husband and how she felt in the moment when she recalled aspects of their life together.

To help Maria experience her feelings about her late husband in the present, Dr. Warren used the empty chair technique (Paivio & Greenberg, 1995). Maria was encouraged to imagine that her husband was with her, seated in an empty chair in Dr. Warren's office. Dr. Warren then encouraged Maria to tell her husband what was on her mind, to tell him how she felt. In doing this exercise, Maria felt sadness and an acute sense of grief as she struggled with her sense of loss over her husband of 34 years, a man whom she loved dearly. However, she was surprised to find that she felt a great deal of anger toward him, both because he had left her and because she felt so lost without him. Maria felt intense guilt for expressing anger at her late husband, because she believed that anger was an inappropriate emotion to feel toward someone who had died and because she had worked hard to contain any angry feelings in their relationship while he was alive. With Dr. Warren's support, she came to realize that feelings of anger were genuine and legitimate emotions to feel toward someone who was gone and that to try to deny these emotions would only intensify the pain she felt.

One of the primary methods used to evoke emotions in process-experiential therapy is to encourage the client to recall important memories. Dr. Warren used this technique frequently to help Maria become aware of memories and emotions that she had about her husband and come to accept and embrace these memories.

order to conduct psychotherapy. Indeed, with respect to diagnostic testing and assessment, Rogers (1957) wrote that "such diagnostic knowledge is not essential to psychotherapy" and may even be "a colossal waste of time."

In a shift from this original position taken by Rogers, more recent work using the process-experiential approach has examined the development and adaptation of different types of therapy for different types of clients. This approach includes applications for *DSM-IV* disorders such as anxiety and depression, for personality disorders, and for medical problems (e.g., Elliott, Davis, & Slatick, 1998; Greenberg, Watson, & Goldman,

1998; Paivio & Greenberg, 1998; Wolfe & Sigl, 1998). Elliott and Greenberg (1995) suggest that process-experiential therapy is most appropriate for use in an outpatient clinic or private practice setting with clients who are experiencing mild to moderate clinical distress and symptoms. Some clients may enter therapy with emotion-processing styles that allow them to engage almost immediately in the empathic exploration and experiential search processes so critical to experiential treatment. Clinically, such clients may have a range of diagnoses and problems, including depression, anxiety, low self-esteem, and lingering resentments and difficulties with others. Perhaps not surprisingly, process-experiential therapy appears to be more difficult with clients who enter treatment with processing styles that focus on external factors and with clients who are seeking advice. With these clients a process-experiential therapist needs to gradually create and nurture an internal focus. Proponents of process-experiential therapy note that it is also not suited for clients with major thought disorder or schizophrenia, impulse control or antisocial personality disorders, or for those in need of immediate crisis intervention (Elliott & Greenberg).

Recent work has also described existential approaches to specific problems, including depression, anxiety, post-traumatic stress disorder, and other problems and disorders defined by the *DSM-IV* (Elliott et al., 1998). For example, Bugental (1987) outlines the practice of existential therapy for depression, a condition he refers to as "dispirited." Dispiritedness refers to the anhedonic quality of depression, the lack of motivation and inability to experience positive emotion. Bugental outlines three phases in existential therapy for depression. First, when patients report inactivity or try to dismiss their depression, the therapist deals directly with this detachment by bringing it to the patients' awareness. Second, as people become less detached, the therapist calls attention to and reduces the guilt or blame patients feel for their own depres-

sion or dispiritedness. Third, clients are helped to accept their own dispiritedness. When this happens, they are likely to feel the existential anxiety, and fears of death, meaninglessness, or aloneness that underlie their depression; and issues of responsibility are addressed.

Lukas (1994) describes the use of one form of existential therapy, logotherapy (Frankl, 1969, 1992), as it was applied to a client suffering from obsessive-compulsive disorder. Logotherapy is intended to help clients find meaning in what may seem to be a meaningless world. A technique known as paradoxical intention was used to help the client learn that she would experience no adverse consequences if she did not engage in her compulsive behavior. The following excerpt concerning the use of logotherapy comes from Lukas (1994):

> One of my patients had mirror compulsion that prompted her to run to a mirror up to 20 times a day to make sure that her hair was sufficiently well-groomed. She resisted paradoxical intention until I offered to participate with her in a game of "hair rumpling": We would see who could rumple our hair more thoroughly by attacking it with all ten fingers. Afterwards we ran hand in hand around the block, all the while paradoxically intending to show all passers-by just how wildly our hair "stood on end." When someone passed us by without paying any attention, we roughed up our hair a bit more because it obviously was not disheveled enough. . . . Who nowadays cares whether someone's hair is well groomed? My patient realized this and was able to overcome her compulsion to go the mirror by paradoxically wishing, "Let my hair stand on end. Let it be a mess!" After eight weeks her mirror compulsion was gone. (p. 24)

Although there may be several explanations for the change that Lukas observed in this client, it is noteworthy that the most compelling one may come from the perspective of behavior therapy (see chapter 14). That is, the therapist may have facilitated exposure to the source of anxiety (allowing others to see her when she did not feel she looked her best), and that exposure resulted in the extinction of the anxiety. Interestingly, one recent study found that client-centered therapy for agoraphobia was effective only when coupled with behavioral exposure treatment (Teusch & Boehme, 1999). We will consider research on the mechanisms through which therapy works in chapter 15.

These examples notwithstanding, humanistic-existential approaches to psychotherapy do not place a strong emphasis on the development of specific techniques for use with particular forms of psychopathology. It is still generally assumed that the basic qualities of the client-therapist relationship and the core skills developed by the therapist are necessary and sufficient for the effective treatment of virtually all problems with which clients present.

RESEARCH ON HUMANISTIC, EXISTENTIAL, AND PROCESS-EXPERIENTIAL PSYCHOTHERAPY

Early Research

Carl Rogers was a pioneer in research examining the process and outcome of psychotherapy. Despite this early commitment to research, however, many proponents and practitioners of humanistic-existential psychotherapy have expressed ambivalence about the value of empirical research. This lack of enthusiasm for empiricism is in part due to some of the fundamental philosophical tenets of these approaches, because many leading figures in the humanistic-existential movement have argued that the essential aspects of therapy cannot be measured or quantified (e.g., Perls, 1973). Furthermore, there is also opposition to the logical-positivism perspective that underlies empirical research. Nevertheless, in spite of this overall resistance to conducting research on the nature and effects of humanistic-existential therapy, there have been a number of noteworthy studies and an accumulating body of research on the effects of these approaches to therapy.

One of the early significant studies involved the analysis of excerpts from tape recordings of a therapy case handled by Carl Rogers (Truax, 1966). The tapes of Rogers's sessions with a client in long-term psychotherapy were analyzed to determine if he indeed responded to the client in a nondirective way as he had outlined in the original model of nondirective psychotherapy. Contrary to the major principles of non-directive therapy, Truax found that Rogers was not unconditional in his behavior with the client. Indeed, Rogers was found to respond to the client in a contingent manner, paying significantly greater attention to, and "rewarding," certain types of client behaviors and providing less attention to other types of behavior. A subsequent study of the interactions of four different therapists conducting Rogerian therapy with 30 patients provided further evidence that therapists provide contingent positive reinforcement for behavior that is seen as involving self-exploration (Truax, 1968). Perhaps more important, Truax found that this process of contingent reinforcement was associated with better client outcomes. These two studies played a central role in leading Rogers to redefine his therapy as client centered (focused or centered on the experience of the client) rather than nondirective.

Putting aside the issue of whether therapists can actually be nondirective, considerable research has addressed the role of the six core conditions outlined by Rogers as necessary and sufficient conditions for successful therapeutic change. The results of these investigations have been mixed. In an early review, Truax and Mitchell (1971) cited evidence suggesting that these conditions were in fact both necessary and sufficient for effective therapy. However, subsequent reviews of this body of research offered a less positive interpretation of the findings. For example, Beutler, Crago, and Arezmendi (1986) concluded that there is no clear evidence that the core conditions (especially therapist warmth, empathy, and genuineness) are either necessary or sufficient for producing client change. We should note here that although these conditions do not appear to be sufficient to produce change, they may nevertheless represent important communication and relationship skills that are valuable for therapists working from a variety of theoretical approaches. Characteristics such as empathy and warmth may help establish a trusting and safe relationship between the client and therapist that enables the therapist to employ other specific techniques that can help bring about change (Bohart & Greenberg, 1997). In particular, therapist empathy and warmth are emphasized as important skills in several other approaches to therapy, including the widely used cognitive therapy for depression developed by Aaron Beck (Beck, Rush, Shaw, & Emery, 1979; see chapter 14).

Treatment Outcome Research

With the continued development of the process-experiential approach to therapy and its increased commitment to research, a body of evidence has accumulated on the efficacy of this approach. In a review of studies on the effectiveness of humanistic, existential, and process-experiential therapy that were published from 1978 to the early 1990s, Greenberg et al. (1994) reported a generally favorable picture of the effects of these various types of therapy. Based on the results of 37 studies that reported data on clients before and after treatment, Greenberg et al. concluded that humanistic-existential therapy was associated with significant improvement from pre- to posttreatment. They also found that gains made immediately following therapy were maintained in follow-up evaluations ranging from 9 months to 2 years after the end of treatment. However, these studies did not include control groups for comparison purposes. Studies of the effects of therapy that do not include control or comparison groups are limited in what they can tell us about the effectiveness of therapy (see chapters 3 and 15).

Greenberg et al. (1994) also reported on the results of 15 studies that compared the effects of humanistic-existential or process-experiential therapy to no-treatment or waiting-list controls. These studies found significant improvement as a result of therapy compared to no treatment. These results suggest that the improvement associated with therapy was not simply the result of the passage of time or improvement that would have occurred even in the absence of treatment. However, the magnitude of the effect of therapy, as measured by effect sizes (see chapter 15) was quite variable across the 15 studies, indicating that some forms of humanistic-existential or process-experiential therapy may be more effective than others.

Finally, Greenberg et al. (1994) reviewed the results of studies in which humanistic-existential or process-experiential therapy was compared to an alternative form of treatment. The results of these studies show that this type of therapy did not differ significantly from other forms of therapy in the magnitude of the effects that they produced. Again, however, the size of the effects of therapy varied widely across the studies, suggesting that some humanistic-existential and process-experiential therapies may be stronger than some alternative forms of therapy and weaker than others. For example, cognitive-behavioral therapy generally produced larger effects than did humanistic-existential and process-experiential therapy (Greenberg et al.; see Weiss & Weisz, 1995, for a review of similar research with children). Box 13.6 summarizes the results of an intriguing study of a variation of process-experiential therapy—supportive-expressive group therapy—with cancer patients.

Some of the strongest effects of process-experiential therapy have been reported for a version of this therapy that has been developed for use with couples who are experiencing marital distress (e.g., Johnson, Hunsley, Greenberg, & Schindler, 1999). Emotion-focused couples therapy is a brief approach to therapy designed to

BOX 13.6

SUPPORTIVE-EXPRESSIVE
GROUP PSYCHOTHERAPY AND CANCER

Another variation of current approaches to process-experiential and emotionally focused therapy can be found in supportive-expressive group therapy. Supportive-expressive groups are designed to allow for the provision and receipt of social support among members of the group, with an emphasis on the expression of deeply felt emotions. An interesting application of supportive-expressive therapy involves the use of group therapy for cancer patients. Psychiatrist David Spiegel of Stanford University has developed and evaluated a supportive-expressive group therapy approach for women with metastatic breast cancer (i.e., cancer that has spread through the body and is incurable). Patients meet in a group format with other patients and a therapist on a weekly basis for as long as one year. In the groups, patients receive *support* from fellow patients facing a similar prognosis and *express* their fears, dread, anger, and hope associated with terminal illness. The therapy is designed to counter patients' sense of isolation, help them deal with their fears of death and dying, and help them to more effectively manage their relationships with family, friends, and one another as well as with physicians, nurses, and other health care staff (Spiegel & Classen, 2000). A primary goal is to help patients live as fully and as richly as possible, reorder their life priorities, and take advantage of what is available to them given the constraints that their illness puts on their lives.

In a landmark study of the outcomes of this approach to supportive-expressive therapy with women with metastatic breast cancer, Spiegel, Bloom, Kraemer, and Gottheil (1989) compared patients who were randomly assigned to group therapy versus those assigned to a control condition in which they did not participate in group therapy. The researchers found that, compared with patients who did not participate in a support group, patients who participated in the groups lived an average of 18 months longer. Combined with findings that participation in the groups reduced patients' symptoms of anxiety and depression (Spiegel, 1991), these results suggest that participation in supportive-expressive group therapy may actually enhance both the quality of life and the survival of terminally ill patients.

These exciting findings raise interesting questions about how participation in supportive groups that emphasize the expression of emotions could help patients live longer. First, an important finding such as this requires replication to ensure that it is a reliable effect (Spiegel et al., 1999). Second, what might be the pathway through which support and emotional expression lead to an improved ability of the body to fight off cancer? Current research is examining the possibility that the effects of supportive-expressive group therapy on survival are achieved through changes in the immune system and through the immune system's ability to control cancer cells in the body (e.g., Andersen et al., 1998).

modify distressed couples' patterns of interaction with one another, alter their emotional responses, and foster the development of a more secure emotional bond. This therapy targets negative emotions, such as anger or fear, which tend to be associated with distress in relationships. In this approach, couples learn to express newly formulated emotional responses in such a way as to create changes in the emotional bond in their relationship and increase contact and caring between partners. This therapy has been found to produce substantial reductions in marital distress and to improve the quality of the marital relationship (e.g., Johnson & Greenberg, 1985; Johnson & Talitman, 1997).

Other research has examined the effects of specific techniques that have been used in process-experiential psychotherapy. For example, Paivio and Greenberg (1995) conducted a controlled study of the effects of the use of the empty chair technique to help clients resolve "unfinished business" in relationships with others; unfinished business reflects unresolved feelings and conflicts in interpersonal relationships. Results indicated that most patients who received experiential therapy achieved clinically meaningfully gains and demonstrated significantly greater improvement on all measures than did patients in a psychoeducational group. Importantly, treatment gains for patients in the experiential group were maintained at the follow-up assessments.

Finally, there has been increasing emphasis on the use of qualitative research methods in the study of process-experiential therapy (Elliott, 1999; Elliott, Fisher, & Rennie, 1999). Qualitative, as contrasted with quantitative or empirical research, does not involve the use of controlled research designs or the statistical analysis of data for hypothesis testing. Qualitative data emphasizes the description of therapist-client interactions in order to identify themes and patterns that may emerge. This approach emphasizes the discovery of new and unexpected information rather than the testing of predetermined hypotheses (Elliott). It is well suited to many researchers interested in process-experiential psychotherapy, because it does not involve measuring and quantifying those aspects of therapy that they believe cannot be quantified.

SUMMARY AND CONCLUSIONS

Humanistic-existential approaches to psychotherapy are based in a perspective on human nature that emphasizes (a) the capacity for free will, (b) self-determination, and (c) an innate tendency toward positive growth. The pioneering work in this area was conducted by Carl Rogers, who developed client-centered therapy. This approach emphasizes six conditions for effective therapy that include empathy and warmth on the part of the therapist and the creation of an accepting and nonevaluative relationship with the client. Existential therapy is based more in the work of European philosophers and psychotherapists and focuses on the fundamental existential dilemmas faced by all people, including the meaning of free will, responsibility for one's life, and facing one's own mortality.

Current approaches, labeled process-experiential therapy, have built on the work of Rogers and others and have given the therapist a more active role in the process of therapy. These approaches emphasize the importance of helping clients focus on their emotions and on their present experience. Techniques are used to help clients increase their awareness of emotions and express them in the context of therapy.

Research on humanistic-existential psychotherapy has a long history, beginning with the seminal research conducted by Rogers and his colleagues. Early research showed that Rogers's techniques were not nondirective, because the therapist selectively reinforced the client for certain types of behavior. Furthermore, research failed to show that the core conditions outlined by Rogers were necessary and sufficient for client change. More recent research has focused on the outcomes of process-experiential therapy and on the specific methods that are associated with positive outcomes.

KEY TERMS AND NAMES

Robert Elliott
Emotion schemes
Empathy
Existential psychotherapy
Experiential processing
Leslie Greenberg
Humanistic psychotherapy
Ideal self
Rollo May

Phenomenological
Play therapy
Process-experiential psychotherapy
Real self
Carl Rogers
Self-and-world construct system
Self-determination
Self-discrepancy theory
Unconditional positive regard

RESOURCES

Books
Axline, V. M. (1965). *Dibs: In Search of Self.* Boston: Houghton Mifflin.

Bohart, A. C., & Greenberg, L. S. (Eds.). (1997). *Empathy reconsidered: New directions in psychotherapy*. Washington, DC: American Psychological Association.

Greenberg, L. S., & Watson, J. C. (Eds.). (1998). *Handbook of experiential psychotherapy*. New York: Guilford Press.

Patterson, C. H. (2000). *Understanding psychotherapy: Fifty years of client-centered theory and practice*. Ross-on-Wye, England: PCCS Books.

Perls, F. F. (1969). *Gestalt Therapy Verbation*. Lafayette, CA: Real People Press.

Rogers, C. R. Kirshcenbaum, H., & Henderson, V. L. (Eds.). (1989). *The Carl Rogers Reader*. Boston, MA: Houghton Mifflin.

Journals
Humanistic Psychologist
Journal of Counseling Psychology
Journal of Humanistic Psychology
Psychotherapy Research

CHAPTER FOURTEEN

PSYCHOTHERAPY: BEHAVIORAL AND COGNITIVE APPROACHES

INTRODUCTION

It was much harder to fall asleep now. When he was very young, Brian would gaze at the stars that his mother had painted on the ceiling of his room, painted so that they would glow in the dark after the lights were off. As he grew older he would lie in bed and think comfortably about the things that mattered to him most. Would this be the year that the Red Sox finally won the World Series? What would he and his friends do together this weekend? What would it be like to go out with the beautiful girl in his algebra class? Now it could take hours of anguish before he finally fell asleep. And the biggest source of his suffering came from this burning question about his parents' divorce: "What did I do to cause it?"

When his parents first began fighting Brian just felt anger and frustration. When they yelled at one another, he would yell too. But as he grew older and things began to worsen at home, he started to question why it was happening. As the hostility in the house increased, Brian's grades suffered and his performance in sports, which had long been a source of great pride to him and his father, also declined. The worse he did, the more his parents fought, and the more they fought, the worse he did. He can't remember when he first began to blame himself for his parents' fighting, but soon he was overcome with guilt over his role in breaking the family apart. The thought that he caused their divorce ate away at him, and it was most painful when the lights went out and he had nothing to distract himself from his blame.

As his parents' relationship worsened, other things changed profoundly in Brian's life. His father spent more time at work and less time with Brian and his sister. When he was young, Brian's father coached his Little League teams in the summer and his youth basketball teams in the winter. Now his dad didn't even attend Brian's games, much less serve as his coach. Brian felt this was just as well—he was playing horribly in all sports anyway. The things that used to bring Brian so many rewards and such a sense of accomplishment—school and sports—were now sources of failure and frustration. And he didn't see how things could ever get better.

These passages highlight an important aspect of people who are struggling with depression—the way that they think about themselves, their world, and their future. As we will learn in this chapter, changing these negative ways of thinking lies at the core of one of the most effective means of treating depression: cognitive therapy. The methods of cognitive therapy have grown out of, and are used in conjunction with, another major form of psychological therapy—**behavior therapy.**

In chapters 12 and 13 we have described orthodox and contemporary approaches to psychoanalysis and psychoanalytic psychotherapy and therapies conducted from the perspective of humanistic and phenomenological frameworks. In this chapter we present a set of therapies developed from a different perspective. In fact, behavior therapy was developed originally in large part as a reaction against the practice of psychoanalysis. Psychologists felt both that the empirical foundation of psychoanalysis was nonexistent, and that claims for its efficacy were unwarranted. In those early years, there was no love lost between psychoanalysts and behavior therapists. Here, for example, is Andrew Salter's introduction to his 1949 book on behavior therapy, entitled *Conditioned Reflex Therapy:*

> It is high time that psychoanalysis, like the elephant of fable, dragged itself off to some distant jungle graveyard and died. Psychoanalysis has outlived its usefulness. Its methods are vague, its treatment is long and drawn out, and more often than not, its results are insipid and unimpressive. Every literate non-Freudian in our day knows these accusations to be true. But we may ask ourselves, might it not be that psychotherapy, by its very nature, must always be difficult, time-consuming, and inefficient? I do not think so. I say flatly that psychotherapy can be quite rapid and extremely efficacious. I know so because I have done so. And if the reader will bear with me, I will show him how by building our therapeutic methods on the firm scientific bed rock of Pavlov, we can keep out of the Freudian metaphysical quicksands and help ten persons in the time that the Freudians are getting ready to "help" one. (p. 1)

There are two aspects about this statement by Salter that are particularly noteworthy. First, it is clear that Salter's opposition to and dissatisfaction with Freudian psychoanalysis is quite strong. He has criticized psychoanalysis in terms of its conceptualization, its practicality, and its effectiveness. Second, Salter formulated this critique over 50 years ago, underscoring the fact that efforts to generate an alternative to psychoanalysis that is based in the scientific study of behavior have been long-standing.

Since the 1920s, when Pavlov and Watson demonstrated the power of conditioning to affect behavior, there has been a steady increase in the use of learning-based procedures developed to reduce patients' levels of emotional distress and eliminate their maladaptive behaviors. As we will see in this chapter, early approaches to behavior therapy, or behavior modification as it was referred to then, completely denied the importance of cognitions in the process of clinical improvement. Cognitions were not directly observable and could not be measured reliably; consequently, advocates of behavior therapy felt that a focus on cognitions was irrelevant to a science of behavior change. The 1970s however, brought the beginnings of a dramatic reversal of this position. Psychologists began to integrate cognitive procedures with behavioral techniques in the practice of what came to be known as cognitive-behavior therapy. And more recently, theorists and therapists have made notable developments in a form of psychotherapy referred to as cognitive therapy.

In this chapter we will describe the development and effectiveness of behavioral and cognitive approaches to the practice of psychotherapy. We begin by briefly presenting the historical foundations of behavior therapy. We then describe a variety of behavioral procedures and techniques that have been developed to reduce anxiety and improve functioning. Following this presentation we discuss the integration of behavioral and cognitive perspectives in the treatment of emotional distress, and then turn our attention to the more recent practice of cognitive approaches to psychotherapy. Finally, we describe the literature examining the efficacy of behavioral, cognitive-behavioral, and cognitive treatment of psychopathology.

HISTORICAL FOUNDATIONS OF BEHAVIOR THERAPY

Pavlov, Watson, and Classical Conditioning

As we will see throughout this chapter, the practice of behavior therapy is closely tied to principles of learning theory. In chapter 4 we described the development of learning theory, beginning

with the Russian physiologist **Ivan Pavlov**'s observation that dogs learned to salivate in anticipation of food, a response he referred to as a conditioned reflex. Pavlov's work was refined and expanded in the United States by psychologist John Watson. While other American psychologists at the time were studying internal processes like thoughts, introspection, and emotional states, Watson worked to develop principles of learning, focusing instead on overt, observable behavior.

Watson believed that we are born with three basic emotions: fear, rage, and love. He also recognized, however, that there are wide differences among people in the stimuli that elicit these emotions. To explain this variability in emotional responsivity, Watson posited that we all learn different stimulus-response associations through conditioning. In chapter 4 we described Watson's famous experiment conducted with his graduate student, Rosalie Rayner. Briefly, Watson and Rayner (1920) used principles of classical conditioning to condition fear in an 11-month-old infant, now known as "Little Albert." Watson and Rayner presented a slightly positive stimulus (a white rat) to Albert and then startled the infant by clanging heavy steel bars above his head. After only five pairings of the white rat with the aversive noise, Albert began to exhibit signs of distress and soon showed fear to the rat.

Watson and Rayner's experiment was the first empirical demonstration that emotions can be learned. Furthermore, as we pointed out in chapter 4, this experiment was also the first laboratory demonstration of an "experimental neurosis" in a human—the acquisition of anxiety in response to a stimulus that does not represent a realistic threat to the individual. But this was just the first step. As Watson (1924) wrote, "Finding that emotional responses could be built in with great readiness, we were all the more eager to see whether they could be broken down, and if so by what methods" (p. 132). Watson wanted to be able to apply learning and conditioning principles to changing problematic or maladaptive behaviors. However, because he was forced to leave Johns Hopkins University following a sensationally publicized divorce suit involving Rayner (whom he later married) and join the J. Walter Thompson advertising company in New York, it did not seem likely that Watson would have the opportunity to continue his research. But four years after his Little Albert experiment, Watson was asked by a former student, Mary Cover Jones, to supervise her in the use of conditioning procedures to treat a fear of rats, rabbits, and other furry objects in a 3-year-old boy, "Peter."

Jones (1924) treated Peter slowly, gradually bringing a caged rabbit near Peter while he was eating a favorite food, a little closer with each presentation. After two months of this reconditioning procedure, Peter no longer exhibited fear of the rabbit. Conducting the first study demonstrating that a child's fear could be reduced significantly through conditioning procedures was clearly important to Jones. As she wrote in 1974,

> It has always been of the greatest satisfaction to me that I could be associated with the removal of a fear when I came in contact with this three-year-old in whom a fear of animals was already well established . . . I could not have played the role of creating a fear in a child, no matter how important the theoretical implications. When my own children came across the case of Peter in their college textbooks, they too were relieved to find that I had functioned in this benign capacity in the psychological experiments with children and children's fears. (p. 581)

Despite the significance of this research, it is important to acknowledge that Watson's work with both Little Albert and Peter were case studies—provocative examples that emotions could be learned and changed through associative conditioning. It was several years before investigators obtained more carefully controlled evidence based on a large number of subjects. Nevertheless, Watson's studies planted the seeds for the development of subsequent interventions based

on principles of conditioning. It would be 14 more years, however, before another scientific report of the use of conditioning procedures in the treatment of problematic behaviors appeared in the literature. In 1938, O. H. Mowrer, a learning psychologist at Yale, and his wife, W. M. Mowrer, a human development specialist, described a conceptualization of nocturnal enuresis (nighttime bed wetting) as a child's failure to respond to bladder distension (onset of urination) by waking up and contracting the sphincter. They reported the use of an electrical bell-and-pad procedure to treat enuresis in children. A pad connected to a bell was placed on the child's bed, and the bell was set off whenever the pad became wet. After several trials of this procedure, the child associated bladder distension with sphincter contraction, and enuresis was prevented. This procedure, based on principles of classical conditioning, was important in providing an early clinical demonstration of the utility of behavioral approaches to treatment. Interestingly, extensive research has been conducted on the bell-and-pad procedure since its development, and the results of recent reviews indicate that this procedure is still the most effective method of treatment for enuresis (e.g., Murphy & Carr, 2000; Rajigah, 1996).

It would be another 15 years before the next step in the evolution of behavior therapy was taken. With World War II came an increased need for psychologists, functioning in their roles both as developers of psychological tests and procedures to aid in personnel selection and as therapists to treat the thousands of veterans returning from the war with significant symptoms of trauma and distress. Recall from chapter 2 that the vast majority of these psychologists had been trained in experimental psychology (which, at the time, was largely behavioral). This surge of behaviorally trained psychologists entering the workforce set the stage for a wider emergence of interventions based on behavioral principles.

After the war, three groups of investigators and therapists made major contributions to the development of behavior therapy: B. F. Skinner in the United States, Joseph Wolpe in South Africa, and Hans Eysenck in England.

Skinner and Operant Conditioning

With the publication of *Science and Human Behavior* in 1953, Skinner changed the focus of learning studies from classical conditioning to operant conditioning and opened the door to a different way of conceptualizing psychopathology. As we saw in chapter 4, operant conditioning involves administering a consequence to a behavior that alters the frequency of the recurrence of the behavior. Either administering positive consequences or removing negative stimuli following the occurrence of a behavior will increase the likelihood of the behavior being exhibited again (positive reinforcement). Similarly, administering negative consequences following a behavior will reduce the probability that the behavior will be emitted in the future (punishment).

In *Science and Human Behavior*, Skinner proposed that much of human behavior could be explained by principles of operant conditioning. More important in the context of clinical psychology, Skinner strongly criticized the predominant psychoanalytic approach to psychotherapy and, in its place, offered a behavioral conceptualization of therapy, behavior modification. He argued that the focus of psychoanalysis on internal mechanisms, defenses, and motivations was not defensible scientifically. As Watson had contended 30 years earlier, Skinner argued that psychologists should limit their focus and practice to the association of objectively measured behaviors and the environmental factors that control those behaviors. In 1968, a specialized journal, *The Journal of Applied Behavior Analysis*, which was based strongly on Skinner's operant conditioning perspective, began to publish scientific articles reporting successful applications of this "radical behaviorism" approach to the treatment of mentally retarded individuals, to the management of persons with chronic mental illnesses like schizophrenia, and to the treatment of addictive behavior like smoking and overeating.

Wolpe and Reciprocal Inhibition

Joseph Wolpe was a psychiatrist in South Africa who was trained originally in classical Freudian psychoanalysis. He became disenchanted with Freud's view of the development of neuroses and began to conduct his own experiments by first inducing, and then treating, experimental neuroses in cats. Wolpe induced fear in cats by administering shocks to them in a specific cage. He observed that the cats refused to eat in the cage in which they had been shocked; instead, they exhibited marked behaviors of distress and anxiety. Wolpe believed that the cats' anxiety was preventing them from eating. If conditioned anxiety could inhibit eating, he reasoned, then under the right conditions, the opposite could also happen: the cats' eating response could be used to inhibit the anxiety. Wolpe tested this hypothesis by having the cats begin to eat at a considerable distance from the cages in which they had been shocked and gradually bringing their food bowls closer and closer to the cages (recall the similar procedure used by Mary Cover Jones to treat Peter's fear of rabbits). Wolpe succeeded in using the cats' eating responses to inhibit their anxiety through the use of this procedure, called *counterconditioning*, which was based on a principle that Wolpe referred to as **reciprocal inhibition:** "If a response antagonistic to anxiety can be made to occur in the presence of anxiety-evoking stimuli so that it is accompanied by a complete or partial suppression of the anxiety response, the bond between these stimuli and the anxiety responses will be weakened" (Wolpe, 1958, p. 71).

Wolpe suggested that there is a wide variety of antagonistic responses, including muscle relaxation, assertive behaviors, and sexual behaviors; in fact, any response or behavior that is incompatible with anxiety is a possible candidate for this category of response. Wolpe developed a behavioral procedure for the treatment of anxiety and phobias that was based on the principle of reciprocal inhibition and that was called systematic desensitization. As you might expect, in this procedure responses that are incompatible with anxiety, such as relaxation, are "brought" in some way closer and closer to the anxious stimuli in order to reduce the patient's experience of anxiety and distress.

In 1966 Wolpe joined Cyril Franks, Andrew Salter, and Dorothy Susskind in forming the Association for the Advancement of Behavior Therapy (AABT). What began as a small group of behavior therapists and behavioral psychologists has grown now into an organization with an international membership of over 4,500. AABT holds an annual convention, supports a newsletter (*The Behavior Therapist*), and since 1970, has published a scientific journal focusing on behavioral approaches to the assessment and treatment of psychopathology (*Behavior Therapy*).

Eysenck and Behavior Therapy

Hans Eysenck was a clinical psychologist who worked at the Maudsley Hospital in London, England. As we discussed in chapter 2, Eysenck wrote in 1952 what is undoubtedly one of the most controversial scientific articles in the history of clinical psychology, in which he challenged the effectiveness of traditional (that is, psychodynamic) psychotherapy. This article spurred clinical psychologists to develop new forms of treatment. Given the emerging focus on behaviorism in America, these new treatments were based soundly on behavioral principles. In 1959 Eysenck coined the term *behavior therapy,* and a year later he edited an influential book titled *Behaviour Therapy and the Neuroses.* In 1963, with his student S. J. Rachman (now at the University of British Columbia in Canada), Eysenck founded the first exclusively behavioral

scientific journal, *Behavior Research and Therapy,* a journal in which behavior therapists continue to publish today.

Throughout this history of behavior therapy, from Watson to Skinner and Wolpe, it is clear that although there are significant differences in approach (e.g., classical conditioning, operant conditioning, counterconditioning), all the early behavioral approaches were united in two convictions: first, that it is unnecessary to posit the existence of unconscious drives and processes and, second, that therapy is more likely to be effective if it focuses on discrete maladaptive behaviors rather than on more diffuse psychiatric diagnostic categories. Even though theorists like Julian Rotter and Albert Bandura subsequently integrated cognitive processes and constructs with these behavioral approaches, the nature of this focus on cognitions was very different from the emphasis on mental processes postulated by Freud. Whereas Freud's views of mental processes and constructs were not easily operationalized, contemporary integrations of cognitive methods with behavior therapy emphasize the importance of clear definitions of cognitions and of antecedents and consequences of problematic cognitions and behaviors, which lead to reliable and readily quantifiable assessment and treatment procedures. Finally, all these behavioral approaches were based on principles that had been validated in the laboratory and extended in an effort to change maladaptive human behavior. This strategy had already been proven to be effective in other sciences, such as medicine and engineering; it was also being demonstrated to be a powerful tool for change in psychology.

BEHAVIOR THERAPY

There are many different procedures and approaches to psychotherapy that can be (and often are) included under the heading of behavior therapy. Despite differences in the techniques associated with various forms of behavior therapy, they are virtually all characterized by a common philosophy and set of underlying principles. All forms of behavior therapy focus to a large extent on providing learning experiences designed to change the patient's maladaptive behaviors. O'Leary and Wilson (1987) list a number of principles that apply to most forms of behavior therapy. The following five principles are those that we believe represent the strongest foundation on which behavior therapies are built:

1. All behavior, normal and abnormal, is acquired and maintained according to the same basic principles of learning.
2. It is not necessary to infer an underlying cause or motive for maladaptive behaviors; the behaviors are the disorder; they are not a manifestation or *sign* of an underlying disorder or disease process.
3. It is usually not necessary to know how a specific problem behavior was learned; the focus of treatment should not be on historical issues but rather on those factors that are currently maintaining the behavior.
4. Most abnormal behavior can be modified through the application of learning principles, by which maladaptive behaviors can be unlearned and replaced by new, more adaptive, learned behaviors.
5. Treatment methods are precisely specified and replicable and are tailored to the needs and strengths and situation of each client; treatment progress is assessed continually, and treatment outcome is evaluated objectively.

These principles highlight the importance of first, the focus of behavior therapy on overt behaviors rather than on underlying conflicts and motivations and, second, of the scientific evaluation of the effectiveness of each treatment program. It is not difficult to see that both these concepts represented a significant change from the psychoanalytic perspective that was prevalent at the time behavior therapy was being developed.

Goals

Given the focus of behavior therapy on the patients' maladaptive behaviors, an important general goal of this form of psychotherapy is to reduce or eliminate the patient's problematic behaviors and to increase the frequency of more adaptive behaviors. The emphasis on overt behaviors, rather than on more vaguely defined intrapsychic conflicts, means that the goals of behavior therapy will generally be both clear and specific. Furthermore, in contrast to psychoanalytic and psychodynamic therapists, behavior therapists work actively and collaboratively with their patients in planning the goals of therapy and executing the procedures designed to attain these goals. Because behavior therapists assume that maladaptive behavior is a consequence of specific antecedents and consequences in the patient's natural environment, much of the important work in behavior therapy takes place outside the therapist's office, either through therapy conducted directly in the patient's environment (in vivo therapy) or through homework assignments carried out by the patient between sessions. The rationale underlying the selection of the specific objectives and techniques is generally made explicit to the patient, and the therapist and patient together carry out the therapy, evaluate the patient's progress, and if necessary, modify the treatment plan.

Training and Supervision

Unlike psychoanalysts, behavior therapists are not required to undergo therapy themselves. Behavior therapy, as we have noted, is a strongly empirical approach to psychotherapy that is based solidly on principles of learning. Therefore, behavior therapists must have a thorough understanding of the major theories of learning, including classical and operant conditioning and social learning theory. Because of this requirement, it is generally (though not always) the case that behavior therapists are psychologists by training. In fact, the high proportion of behavior therapists who are psychologists stands in contrast to orthodox psychoanalysis, which is composed primarily of individuals who are trained in psychiatry. Finally, the strong focus on overt behavior and the importance of behavior change also extends to supervision in behavior therapy. Not surprisingly, therefore, behavior therapists who are being supervised are frequently observed by their supervisors as they conduct therapy and are rated on scales that assess their skills and their progress as behavior therapists.

The Importance of Assessment in Behavior Therapy

The link between assessment and therapy is stronger for behaviorally oriented therapies than is the case for virtually any other approach to psychotherapy, including psychoanalysis and phenomenological therapies. We described in chapter 10 the nature of behavioral assessment and the assessment procedures used most commonly by behavior therapists. We would like to underscore here that, from a behavioral perspective, assessment has profound implications for therapy. In fact, many behavior therapists would argue that one cannot begin behavior therapy without first conducting a comprehensive behavioral assessment, or functional analysis, of the patient's difficulties.

Mueser and Liberman (1995) outline a behavioral approach to assessment and therapy that describes the interdependence of these two endeavors. Mueser and Liberman note the importance of identifying the problem behavior or behaviors as objectively and precisely as possible by using a variety of assessment procedures that includes self-report questionnaires, structured interviews, self-monitoring, and behavioral observation. In chapter 10 we discussed the functional analysis of behavior, in which problematic behaviors of the patient are identified along with antecedents and consequences of the behaviors.

This operationalization of the patient's maladaptive behaviors permits the behavior therapist to develop and carry out a treatment program aimed specifically at changing the frequency or intensity of the problematic behaviors in as efficient a manner as possible.

Methods

Behavior therapists have available to them a wide variety of techniques for teaching or increasing adaptive behaviors and eliminating maladaptive behaviors. Because of the large number of techniques available for changing behavior, it is tempting to view behavior therapy as simply an assortment or arsenal of procedures. As Kalish (1981) states, however, this view is not an accurate perception of this approach to psychotherapy:

> The inclination to regard the methods of intervention in behavior modification as a collection of standardized techniques is especially misleading. It tends to obscure one of the most important contributions to the understanding of behavior change made by the advent of behavior modification procedures: namely, that for every so-called technique, there is a more fundamental and more general principle of behavior derived from research with animals and/or humans which can be applied to the solution of a problem in human functioning. This means, among other things, that those who intend to use behavior modification to help solve human problems should be aware of these principles and resourceful enough to propose treatment strategies which fit the case after a thorough analysis of the conditions which initiate and maintain the behavior. (p. 3)

In the following sections we will present and discuss the application of a number of behavioral methods and procedures used in the treatment of various forms of psychological distress. We will begin with behavioral procedures that are used to reduce high levels of fear (most commonly phobias) and will then discuss procedures used to teach and maintain new behaviors.

APPLICATIONS OF BEHAVIOR THERAPY TO SPECIFIC PROBLEMS

Fear Reduction Procedures

We know from recent epidemiological studies that fears and phobias are among the most common forms of psychological distress (Brunello et al., 2000; Curtis, Magee, Eaton, Wittchen, & Kessler, 1998; den Boer, 2000). Watson's experiments with Little Albert demonstrated that fears can be learned through experience, that is, through classical conditioning. Fears can also be learned indirectly, through observation. It should not be difficult to imagine, for example, that a child can learn to be afraid of snakes by watching a parent exhibit overt signs of pain (like screaming and writhing) after being bitten by a snake. Given that this fear is aversive, the individual understandably avoids coming into contact with the feared object or situation. From a behavioral perspective, however, this avoidance of the feared object means that the individual will never have an opportunity to extinguish the fear, that is, to approach a snake and find that nothing happens. In the absence of any new learning experience, the fear or phobia will persist indefinitely.

Most behavioral approaches to fear reduction involve some type of exposure of the feared stimulus to the patient. Sometimes this exposure is done using the patient's imagination; that is, the patient is instructed to imagine himself or herself in coming in contact with the feared object or situation. Other times the exposure is actual, or in vivo, in which the individual actually confronts the target of his or her fear. We will begin our discussion of these procedures with a description of systematic desensitization.

Systematic Desensitization Systematic desensitization is one of the most widely studied and commonly applied behavioral procedures for the reduction of fears and phobias. It is generally used when a patient has the skills or ability to engage in appropriate or adaptive behaviors but instead avoids the feared stimulus or situation. Typically, this avoidance takes the form of a phobia, which is a fear of a particular object or situation that is out of proportion to any actual danger. In addition, however, the fear or phobia must present a serious problem in functioning or daily living for the individual. For example, a diabetic patient who is unable to inject herself with insulin because she is afraid of needles will be far more likely to seek treatment for her needle phobia than will an accountant living in Manhattan who has a phobia that keeps him from being able to approach and handle snakes.

Systematic desensitization was among the first clearly defined and tested behavioral techniques designed to reduce anxiety in humans. Systematic desensitization was developed and first described by Wolpe (1958) in his book *Psychotherapy by Reciprocal Inhibition.* The principle of reciprocal inhibition simply means that we cannot be both anxious and relaxed at the same time, that these two states mutually inhibit one another. Thus, we cannot experience both the physiologic components of anxiety (e.g., racing heart, increased respiration, high arousal) and the physiologic components of relaxation (e.g., decreased heart rate, slowed respiration, low arousal) at the same time—they are incompatible with each other. Wolpe reasoned that if he could teach anxious patients to remain relaxed in the presence of increasingly aversive or phobic stimuli, they could not at the same time feel anxious.

There are three distinct steps in systematic desensitization. First, because the patient cannot be anxious when she or he is relaxed, the patient is trained in one or more specific relaxation techniques. The relaxation procedure that is used most frequently in systematic desensitization is based on E. Jacobson's (1938) progressive muscle relaxation technique. This procedure involves alternately tensing and relaxing groups of muscles systematically throughout the body. The therapist will often give the patient an audiotape of the relaxation instructions so that the patient can practice at home. If the patient or the therapist prefers, however, there are several other procedures available for teaching the patient how to relax. Many patients, for example, prefer to use a technique known as autogenic relaxation, in which they use imagery to relax. Thus, rather than alternately tensing and relaxing specific muscles, patients listen to the therapist (or to an audiotape) describe relaxing scenes (e.g., "imagine lying on a warm, sandy beach listening to the breeze pass through the palm trees and feeling the warmth of the sun on your skin"). Still other patients prefer to use hypnosis, biofeedback, or meditation to relax.

The second stage in systematic desensitization involves the construction of an anxiety hierarchy. An anxiety hierarchy is a list of related scenes or situations that vary in the amount of anxiety they elicit when the patient imagines or visualizes them. The patient works with the therapist to construct an initial large list of scenes related to the feared object or situation that cause the patient to feel anxious when imagining them. The patient then rates each scene to indicate how anxious he or she feels when imagining or visualizing the scene. Based on the patient's ratings,

the patient and therapist select approximately 15 to 20 of the scenes that best span the range of ratings. Examples of anxiety hierarchies for two patients are presented in table 14.1.

The final step in systematic desensitization is really the heart of this procedure: the successive pairing of relaxation with each of the stimuli in the patient's anxiety hierarchy. The patient begins the session by becoming relaxed, which, because the patient has already learned to completely relax relatively quickly, takes only 10 to 15 minutes. Then, beginning with the lowest ranked stimulus in the hierarchy, the patient is instructed to imagine or visualize the scene for about 10 seconds while remaining relaxed. If the patient begins to feel anxious while visualizing the scene, he or she signals this anxiety to the therapist, who then instructs the patient to stop imagining the scene and to regain a state of relaxation. When the patient has achieved this relaxed state, the therapist presents the same scene again. When the patient can visualize this scene while remaining relaxed, the therapist repeats this procedure for the next stimulus in the hierarchy. This procedure is repeated until the patient

TABLE 14.1
Sample Desensitization Hierarchies

Systematic desensitization is used most frequently and successfully in the treatment of specific fears and phobias. A major component of this treatment is the development of one or more stimulus hierarchies that cover the range of anxiety experienced in the presence of the phobic object or situation. Here we present two such hierarchies, one constructed with a patient to treat a fear of flying and the other constructed to treat a patient's fear of spiders.

Fear of Flying	Fear of Spiders
Seeing an airplane flying overhead	Walking outside with no spider in sight
Hearing an airplane flying overhead	Seeing a spider on the sidewalk in front of you
Driving past an airport	Seeing a spiderweb in the corner of a room
Driving to the airport	Seeing a spider on the floor in front of you
Seeing an airplane on the ground	Seeing a spider on your shoe
Walking into an airline terminal	Seeing a spider on your shirt
Waiting to board a plane	Seeing a spider crawling toward you
Entering an airplane	Seeing a spider crawling on your hand
Buckling the seatbelt in an airplane	Feeling a spider crawling on your leg
Feeling the airplane beginning to move	Feeling a spider crawling on your face
Feeling the wheels leave the ground	Walking into a spiderweb
Feeling the airplane beginning to descend	

can remain relaxed while visualizing the most anxiety-inducing scene in the hierarchy.

When the patient can visualize the most intense anxiety-inducing scene in the hierarchy without experiencing anxiety, systematic desensitization is complete. Most therapists who practice this procedure, however, also advise the patient to search for real-life equivalents of the imagined scenes in the hierarchy to ensure that the relaxation generalizes to the actual scenes. In fact, there is a variant of systematic desensitization, called in vivo desensitization, in which the patient is actually exposed to anxiety-inducing stimuli. For example, an individual with acrophobia (a fear of heights) may accompany the therapist to a second-floor balcony while attempting to remain relaxed. This procedure would be repeated until the patient could relax while standing on the balcony, at which point the patient and therapist might proceed to looking out a third-floor window.

Because any state that is incompatible with anxiety can be used in desensitization, the therapist is not limited to having the patient try to relax using muscle tensing or meditation. Bryntwick and Solyom (1973), for example, reported the successful treatment of a person with a fear of elevators by having him eat gourmet meals (which brought him great pleasure) while riding in an elevator. The positive affect experienced by the patient because of the quality of the food was incompatible with any feelings of anxiety. Of course, as in Jones's (1924) treatment of Peter, the order of presentation of the elevator and the food is critical. With the wrong order of presentation in this example case, the patient might have learned to associate his anxiety with eating gourmet meals, leading to an aversion to some foods rather than to an association of relaxation and pleasantness to elevators.

Does desensitization work? Since Wolpe (1958) first proposed systematic desensitization as a treatment for fears and phobias, literally hundreds of studies have been conducted, virtually all attesting to the efficacy of this intervention in the treatment of fears and phobias (see

David Barlow, Ph.D., a professor at Boston University, is best known for his seminal work in clinical research methodology and the treatment of anxiety disorders. Dr. Barlow founded clinical psychology internships at both the University of Mississippi Medical Center and Brown University, and in 2000 was awarded the Distinguished Scientific Award for the Applications of Psychology by the American Psychological Association. *(Photo courtesy of David Barlow.)*

Emmelkamp, 1994 for a review of these studies). Desensitization procedures have also been found to be effective in the treatment of sexual dysfunction. For example, Cranston-Cuebas and Barlow (1990) found that 50 percent to 70 percent of patients who receive sexual dysfunction treatments that are based on a reduction of anxiety through systematic desensitization procedures show some immediate improvement. More broadly, Berman, Miller, and Massman (1985) conducted a meta-analysis (see chapter 15) of studies comparing systematic desensitization with cognitive therapy in the treatment of anxiety disorders. Berman et al. concluded that systematic desensitization and cognitive therapy are both effective and are roughly comparable to each other in efficacy. Interestingly, the authors concluded further that therapies that combine both cognitive and desensitization procedures are no more effective than one of the treatments alone.

Although it is apparent now that systematic desensitization is an effective treatment for the reduction of fears and phobias, it is less clear how systematic desensitization achieves its effects. More than 25 years ago, Kazdin and Wilcoxon (1976) conducted a component analysis of systematic desensitization and concluded that none of the three primary steps of this treatment (relaxation, the use of an anxiety hierarchy, and the pairing of relaxation and the hierarchy) is necessary for the reduction of fears and phobias. More recently, Bouton (1994, 2000) demonstrated that the new pairing of the feared stimulus with relaxation in systematic desensitization does not replace the original association between the stimulus and the patient's fear response. Rather, both associations are now available, and the patient may react to the stimulus with either fear or relaxation, depending on a number of different factors (see box 14.1). Indeed, this recent perspective may go a long way in explaining why some patients who respond favorably to systematic desensitization in the short term display the original fearful avoidant behavior months later. Most theorists and researchers now agree that the most important feature of systematic desensitization appears to be the patient's exposure to the feared stimulus (Marks, 1987; Rachman, 1990). Based on this formulation, researchers have now begun to examine the efficacy of simply exposing individuals to the feared objects or situations.

Exposure Treatments As is the case with many procedures in behavior therapy, **exposure treatments** have their roots in animal models of psychopathology. For example, psychologist

THE FAR SIDE® By GARY LARSON

"Bedtime, Leroy. Here comes your animal blanket."

Behavior therapy for fears and phobias can often involve exposure to the feared objects. (The Far Side® by Gary Larson © 1984 FarWorks, Inc. All Rights Reserved. Used with permission.)

Martin Seligman of the University of Pennsylvania demonstrated in the 1960s that one effective way of teaching a dog to reenter a cage that had previously been associated with shock is to force the dog into the cage and prevent its escape. Although the dog initially shows signs of considerable distress, in time the anxiety and emotionality dissipate (extinguish) and the dog is able to enter the cage to obtain food, something it had not been able to do prior to its exposure to the anxiety-provoking situation (Seligman, 1975; Seligman, Maier, & Greer, 1968).

Behavior therapists drew on these scientific findings, which demonstrate the effectiveness of forcing dogs back into cages in which they had initially experienced fear, in developing exposure therapies for the treatment of fears and phobias. The earliest example of such a therapeutic approach is **implosive therapy,** or flooding

BOX 14.1

DOES EXTINCTION DESTROY THE ORIGINAL LEARNING?

The concept of extinction is an integral part of classical conditioning and, to some extent, operant conditioning as well. In classical conditioning, a stimulus that was conditioned to produce a response by being paired with a biologically significant event loses its ability to do so if it is presented alone, without that event. So, for example, a snake that was paired with pain from a bite to produce fear should lose its ability to evoke fear if it is presented repeatedly in the absence of a painful bite. Similarly, in operant conditioning, withholding reinforcement from a behavior that has been reinforced in the past should ultimately reduce the frequency of that behavior to zero. The ability to change behaviors in response to alterations in environmental contingencies, as Pavlov long ago noted, are vital to successful adaptation.

For many years, psychologists believed that the decrease or elimination of a behavior through extinction was a reflection of the destruction of the original learning (see Rescorla, 1988, 2001). Similarly, counterconditioning, or making a new association to the original stimulus, as is the case with systematic desensitization in which the feared stimulus is reconditioned to a relaxation rather than an anxiety response, was believed to work by replacing the original association with a new association (see Bouton, 2000). Indeed, Wolpe (1958) thought that the relaxation responses conditioned in systematic desensitization "weaken" the bond between the anxiety-evoking stimuli and the anxiety response. More recent research, however, casts serious doubt on this perspective and is helping us gain a better understanding of the fact that, even after it is extinguished or reconditioned, a response can occur again to the original stimulus, a phenomenon known as *spontaneous recovery*.

The results of these investigations, which have important implications for behaviorally oriented approaches to clinical treatment, suggest that instead of destroying the learned basis of the conditioned behavior, extinction and counterconditioning leave at least part of the original learning and associations in place (Bouton, 1994, 2000). Bouton (1994) argues that both learning and extinction are strongly affected by the context in which they take place. For example, behavioral methods for the treatment of fear and anxiety often involve exposing patients to the threatening stimulus until their fear dissipates or is extinguished. However, the fear-provoking stimulus can still elicit fear under certain conditions. To explain this finding, Bouton and Swartzentruber (1991) contend that extinction or counterconditioning does not cause unlearning of the fear. Rather, the stimulus takes on a second meaning; it is now more ambiguous than it was originally (because it has been paired, for example, with both fear and relaxation), and whether it evokes anxiety or relaxation will depend on the context in which it is presented. Context includes both the physical environment as well as internal states such as emotions and physiological states produced by drugs.

In fact, Bouton (1994) has demonstrated in a number of studies that the original anxiety responses can be retrieved relatively easily when the original context is presented again. He observes, consequently, that because extinction and counterconditioning do not necessarily involve unlearning of an association, there is always the possibility that patients will relapse following clinical treatment. Based on the concept of generalization, Bouton suggests that the likelihood of relapse or recurrence of maladaptive behavior can be reduced by broadening the range of contexts in which the new associations (brought about either through extinction or counterconditioning) are learned.

(Stampfl & Levis, 1967; Wanderer & Ingram, 1990). Implosive therapy attempts to extinguish the fear response by exposing anxious individuals to fear-eliciting situations and forcing them to remain in those situations until their arousal is reduced or eliminated.

It is important to recognize that this approach to fear reduction differs dramatically from desensitization procedures. In systematic desensitization or in vivo desensitization the individual is taught to relax and is exposed in slow, gradual, steps to situations that elicit an increasing level of anxiety; the individual is never allowed to experience more than a low level of anxiety before the situation is withdrawn. In contrast, implosive therapy involves in many respects the opposite approach, essentially starting at the top of the anxiety hierarchy. The individual is not taught relaxation methods; she or he is immediately either exposed to or instructed to imagine herself or himself in the most anxiety-inducing situations for a prolonged period of time. Moreover, the patient is instructed to dwell on the worst possible outcome of the situation in order to elicit the greatest level of anxiety. For example, a claustrophobic patient might be instructed to imagine staying in a small room for two hours and to imagine that the room is getting smaller. In implosive therapy, the individual learns that there are no long-term aversive consequences to approaching the feared object or to remaining in the anxiety-inducing situation. People see that they can survive their worst fears, and the feared stimuli lose their potency to elicit anxiety.

The results of a number of studies attest to the effectiveness of exposure-based treatments for fears and phobias. In their reviews of studies examining the efficacy of implosive therapy, Marks (1987) and Spiegler (1998) concluded that exposure is an effective procedure for the treatment of a variety of anxiety disorders and is generally more effective than systematic desensitization. Supporting its effectiveness, DeRubeis and Crits-Christoph (1998) included exposure therapy as an empirically supported treatment for social phobia, agoraphobia, panic disorder, and post-traumatic stress disorder.

As you might expect, implosive therapy initially causes more distress among patients than does systematic desensitization, and for that reason alone many therapists are more comfortable using systematic desensitization. In response to this concern, graduated exposure has been used increasingly in behavior therapy. In this procedure, patients are initially exposed to situations that evoke only minimal levels of anxiety and then gradually progress to more stressful and anxiety-producing stimuli. Interestingly, there is now evidence that graduated exposure may be more effective than intensive exposure (Spiegler, 1998).

A variant of implosive therapy, known as **response prevention,** has been used successfully in the treatment of obsessive-compulsive disorder (e.g., Salkovskis & Kirk, 1989). Patients with obsessive-compulsive disorder (OCD) are characterized by unwanted thoughts and behaviors that they cannot stop. In response prevention, patients are exposed to the stimuli that elicit their obsessive thoughts but are prevented from engaging in the compulsive behavior that they use to reduce the anxiety associated with the stimuli. For example, in the case of an obsessive-compulsive hand washer, response prevention treatment might consist of exposing the patient to dirt and then preventing the patient from washing his or her hands. Typically, exposure and response prevention sessions are continued for extended periods of time (e.g., 2 hours per day over several weeks) and are combined with homework assignments.

A number of studies have documented the effectiveness of exposure and response prevention in the treatment of OCD. For example, in an early study Foa and Goldstein (1978) demonstrated that the combination of exposure and response prevention is more effective than is either component alone. Subsequent positive results were also reported by Foa, Kozak, Steketee, and McCarthy (1992), Marks (1987), and Rachman and Hodgson (1997). Moreover, in a recent review, Abramowitz (1996) reported that therapist-supervised exposure is more effective than self-controlled exposure in the treatment of OCD and that the addition of response prevention to exposure therapy yields better results than does exposure alone.

This technique has also been applied to patients suffering from bulimia nervosa, based on the assumptions that eating fattening foods leads to anxiety and to fears of gaining weight and that purging reduces the anxiety. From this perspective, bulimia is treated by having bulimic patients eat fattening foods in the therapist's office (exposure) and then having them remain in the office with the therapist until both the urge to vomit and the associated anxiety have dissipated (response prevention). Early studies have reported success using exposure plus response prevention in the treatment of bulimia (e.g., Cooper & Steere, 1995; Leitenberg, Rosen, Gross, Nudelman, & Vara, 1988; G. T. Wilson, Rossiter, Kleifield, & Lindholm, 1986). The results of more recent studies suggest that it is the exposure component of cognitive-behavior therapy and not response prevention that is effective in treating bulimia. G. Terence Wilson, a clinical psychologist at Rutgers University, has conducted several elegant studies over the past decade demonstrating that, although cognitive-behavior therapy is the most effective treatment for bulimia, response prevention does not enhance the effectiveness of this therapy (Wilson, Eldredge, Smith, & Niles, 1997; see also Agras, Schneider, Arnow, Raeburn, & Tekh, 1989). G. T. Wilson and Fairburn (in press) present a comprehensive discussion of the effectiveness of cognitive-behavior therapy in the treatment of eating disorders, clearly supporting the use of this approach to treatment for bulimia.

One interesting question concerns how exposure, relaxation, and systematic desensitization fare in the treatment of anxiety when compared with pharmacotherapy (treatment by medication). Gould, Otto, Pollack, and Yap (1997) recently examined this question by conducting a meta-analysis of 35 studies that included a total of 61 separate treatment interventions for gener-

G. Terence Wilson, Ph.D., is a clinical psychologist at Rutgers University. Dr. Wilson is a major figure in the profession of clinical psychology. In 1994, Dr. Wilson received the Award for Distinguished Scientific Contributions to Clinical Psychology from the American Psychological Association. Dr. Wilson is especially well known for his research on the etiology and treatment of eating disorders. *(Photo courtesy of Terry Wilson.)*

alized anxiety disorder (GAD), including systematic desensitization, exposure, relaxation, cognitive restructuring, and treatment by anti-anxiety medication. On the basis of their analysis, Gould et al. arrived at two major conclusions: First, both cognitive-behavioral therapy and pharmacotherapy are effective treatments for GAD, and second, there are no substantial differences between these two types of treatment. It will be important in future research to examine whether the combination of cognitive-behavioral therapy and antianxiety medication is more effective than either treatment alone.

Difficulties in Social Functioning

Social Skills and Assertion Training   Behavior therapists have used **social skills training** to treat disorders that are characterized by difficulties in social or interpersonal functioning. Over the past two decades, a large psychological research literature has demonstrated a consistent association between problematic social functioning and psychopathology, most typically depression and anxiety (e.g., Gotlib, Lewinsohn, & Seeley, 1998), but also social phobia (Chambless & Hope, 1996) and schizophrenia (Bellack & Mueser, 1994). Individuals suffering from these disorders report having fewer close friends and, in general, smaller social networks than do persons who are not experiencing elevated levels of psychopathology. Many investigators have interpreted these findings to indicate that people with these particular forms of psychopathology are deficient in their social skills (Segrin & Flora, 2000).

Behavior theorists and therapists have identified a number of verbal and nonverbal components of social skills. For example, patients who report problems in social situations often have difficulty maintaining eye contact, matching the tone of their voice to the content of the conversation, accurately perceiving others' emotions, smiling at appropriate times, correctly interpreting others' nonverbal behaviors, and timing their responses appropriately (e.g., not interrupting the other person or finishing their partner's sentences). Depending on the specific situation, individuals may also have difficulty in initiating or maintaining conversations, in making requests of other people, or in standing up for their rights. All of these deficiencies in basic social skills interfere with developing and sustaining social relationships.

In helping a patient to become more socially skilled or assertive, behavior therapists use a number of procedures. Bellack and Mueser (1994) reviewed the research that examined social skills training, and they concluded that the most effective programs include many of the following components:

1. Assessment of the patient's behavioral assets, deficits, and excesses in social situations
2. Selection of specific social behaviors for modification
3. Modeling of appropriate behaviors by the therapist
4. Instruction or coaching of appropriate behaviors and role playing and rehearsal by the client
5. Feedback and positive reinforcement of small steps leading to the desired behavior
6. Homework assignments, most often to engage in particular social behaviors outside the therapy

Other investigators have advocated the inclusion of problem-solving skills in protocols of social skills training (e.g., Nezu & Nezu, 1993; O'Reilly, Lancioni, & O'Kane, 2000). All these training components are designed to help the patient learn from the therapist exactly what behaviors are appropriate in various situations and to become more comfortable and adept at engaging in those behaviors. The increased level of social skill, in turn, should lead to a reduction in the patient's level of anxiety and depression in social situations.

This approach to the treatment of social skills deficits and increasing assertiveness has been used successfully in the treatment of shyness, social isolation, schizophrenia, and social phobia and in reducing outbursts of anger and violence in psychiatric patients. It has also been used to treat interpersonal problems in children (Spence & Donovan, 1998). And, in conjunction with other procedures, social skills training has been used to treat marital conflict, depression, and alcohol abuse and dependence. Interestingly, in a recent review, Emmelkamp (1994) concluded

that the improvements in functioning obtained through social skills training are comparable to those attained through systematic desensitization and in vivo exposure.

Contingency Management　Contingency management is a broad term used to describe a class of procedures based on principles of operant conditioning that change behavior by controlling its consequences. As you no doubt realize, clinical psychologists were not the first to use contingency management techniques. Indeed, every time parents say to their children, "Clean up your room, and then I'll take you to the mall" or "You shouldn't have hit your sister: Go to your room and no television for you tonight," they are using contingency management procedures. The primary contribution of clinical psychology in this area has been to systematize and evaluate a number of these procedures so they may be used more effectively to change maladaptive behaviors. There are many forms of contingency management (see, for example, Masters & Burish, 1987). In the following sections we discuss three of the most common techniques: shaping, contingency contracting, and token economies.

Shaping　At its simplest, the concept of strengthening a behavior through reinforcement requires that the behavior be emitted and then be reinforced. In practice, however, the process is not that simple—there are many behaviors that are not emitted spontaneously. For example, young children do not spontaneously emit grammatically correct sentences, people who are afraid of dogs do not spontaneously hug the next dog they see, and smokers find it difficult to stop "cold turkey." In these cases the desired behavior cannot be reinforced because it will not occur naturally; therefore, shaping is used to develop a final behavior by reinforcing successive approximations, or gradual steps, toward the ultimate goal. Initially, behaviors that represent the first step toward exhibiting the desired behavior are reinforced, and then the standard for what represents a reinforceable behavior is gradually raised until the individual is emitting the final desired behavior. Shaping is generally used in cases in which the person is capable of emitting the desired behavior but has not been able to do so. For example, a shy person whose ultimate goal is to interact easily with people at parties may begin by simply attending a party without any expectation or pressure of talking with anyone, then saying "hello" to one person at the next party, increasing that to two people at the next party, and so on until he or she is comfortable interacting with people in a party situation.

Contingency Contracting　Contingency contracting typically involves constructing and signing a formal agreement describing exactly the behaviors that are expected of each participant and the precise consequences of the behaviors. Contingency contracts can be made between the therapist and patient, describing in detail both the target behaviors and the consequences of engaging or not engaging in the behavior. For example, a patient who is trying to stop smoking may enter into a contract with the therapist to smoke fewer than 30 cigarettes during the next week or else donate a specified sum of money to an organization he or she dislikes intensely. Contracts frequently are also made between two patients being seen in therapy together, typically spouses, or among family members participating in therapy. It is critical in this technique that behaviors and contingent consequences are spelled out in precise detail for all participants.

One of the most widely used interventions based on operant conditioning and contingency contracting principles is called a parent training program for the treatment of oppositional defiant disorder, which is characterized by noncompliant and aggressive behavior in children (e.g., Barkley, 1998; Forgatch & Patterson, 1998; Long, Forehand, Wierson, & Morgan, 1994). These interventions are used to decrease problematic behaviors in young children (typically

from ages 2 to 10 years) that involve willful defiance of parents, teachers and other adult authorities and aggressive behavior toward peers and adults. Oppositional, noncompliant, and aggressive behaviors are hypothesized to be initiated and maintained by stimuli and consequences in the social environment. Patterson and his colleagues, for example, have described a pattern in which these behaviors have been negatively reinforced by the child's parents (e.g., Forgatch & Patterson, 1998). Recall that negative reinforcement involves increasing the frequency of a behavior by withdrawing a negative or aversive stimulus. For example, a parent who, in exasperation, stops making requests of a child and lets the child continue to engage in a problem behavior has negatively reinforced that behavior. Behavioral interventions typically include training the parent in consistent punishment and reinforcement behaviors and developing contingency contracts between the parents and the child. An example of such an intervention in the case of Jason is presented in box 14.2.

BOX 14.2

COGNITIVE-BEHAVIORAL TREATMENT OF ADHD AND ODD: JASON

What surprised Mrs. Newman most was that Dr. Marcus wanted *her* to come to therapy sessions, not Jason. She had expected that Dr. Marcus would meet individually with Jason and provide some type of counseling to make him less angry and help him control his behavior. The more Dr. Marcus explained her approach, however, the more sense it made to Mrs. Newman. And so the treatment plan was laid out—Mrs. Newman would participate in a 12-week treatment program with Dr. Marcus, and she would also take Jason to his pediatrician to be evaluated for medication for the treatment of attention deficit/hyperactivity disorder (ADHD).

The approach outlined by Dr. Marcus is based on extensive research on the treatment of ADHD, oppositional defiant disorder (ODD), and other disruptive behavior disorders. These problems can be conceptualized as deficiencies in children's capacity for self-regulation (Barkley, 1997a). Importantly, interventions designed to teach children self-control skills directly have generally been ineffective in the treatment of ADHD and ODD (Abikoff, 1991). In fact, only two specific treatments have been found to be effective in treating ADHD and ODD: psychostimulant medication and parent training. Indeed, working with parents to help them better manage their child's noncompliant, oppositional, and aggressive behavior has been shown to be an effective treatment of ODD (Forgatch & Patterson, 1998) and to be a useful supplement to medication in the treatment of ADHD (Hinshaw et al., 2000).

Dr. Marcus followed a standardized treatment protocol developed by psychologist Russell Barkley (1997b; 2000) to help Mrs. Newman manage Jason's behavior. After completing a careful behavioral assessment of Jason's problems (see chapter 10), they met on a weekly basis. Dr. Marcus outlined tasks for Mrs. Newman to complete each day at home with Jason, and when they met for each session they reviewed Mrs. Newman's progress and made necessary adjustments in the treatment. Because research has demonstrated that disruptive behavior disorders are associated with highly negative and aversive interactions between parents and children (Patterson, 1997), the first component of the treatment focused on reestablishing positive interactions between Jason and his mother. Mrs. Newman scheduled 30 minutes of "special time" each day to spend with Jason, playing games and participating in activities that he selected. Second, Dr. Marcus taught Mrs. Newman to be more effective in making requests and giving commands to Jason. Parents of noncompliant chil-

BOX 14.2 (continued)

dren often have difficulty delivering clear directives to their children, and their children then fail to comply with these requests. Third, Dr. Marcus and Mrs. Newman developed and implemented a point system whereby Jason would be rewarded with poker chips for positive behavior, which he could cash in for specific rewards (e.g., small toys or activities such as going to a movie; this contract is presented in table 14.2). Jason's teacher also completed a daily report on his behavior at school, and he could earn additional points for good behavior at school. Finally, Dr. Marcus taught Mrs. Newman to use time-out as a response to Jason's noncompliance and his other negative behaviors. After receiving a warning from his mother for a specific misbehavior, Jason would have to sit in a time-out chair for one minute.

None of these steps was easy for Mrs. Newman to implement, because the pattern of negative behavior between her and Jason was well established by the time she sought help. Based on her experience, Dr. Marcus warned Mrs. Newman that Jason's problem behaviors might increase initially before they improved, especially when she implemented the time-out procedure. Mrs. Newman kept records of Jason's problem behaviors and reviewed them with Dr. Marcus each week. They discussed difficulties that Mrs. Newman encountered and charted the slow but steady reductions in Jason's noncompliant and aggressive behaviors.

At the same time that Mrs. Newman was participating in this parenting program, she followed through with the referral to Jason's pediatrician. The

TABLE 14.2
Jason's Contingency Contract

Home Point System

Jason can earn points at home for the following activities:

Activities	Points	Rewards	Points
Getting up on time for school	5	Playing on the computer for 30 minutes	10
Making his bed in the morning	5	Watching 30 minutes of TV	10
Completing homework after school	5	Riding bike after school	10
Emptying the kitchen wastebasket	5	Renting a movie or video	20
Feeding the cats at dinnertime	5	Buying a toy for $5 or less	15
Clearing the table after dinner	5	Going to the movies	30
Washing the dinner dishes	10	Having a friend for a sleep-over	35
Mowing the lawn	15		
Taking a bath in the evening	5		
Brushing teeth	5		
Getting to bed on time (8:30)	5		

Jason's Record

Activity or reward	Points earned	Points spent	Balance
Got up on time	5		5
Made bed	5		10
Fed cats	5		15
Cleared table	5		20
Played on computer		10	10
Brushed teeth	5		15
Mowed lawn	15		30
Rented movie		20	10

BOX 14.2 (concluded)

pediatrician reviewed Dr. Marcus's report describing the results of her behavioral assessment of Jason. Based on the diagnosis of ADHD, the pediatrician prescribed methylphenidate, a psychostimulant medication. This medication works by stimulating those portions of the brain that are responsible for sustained attention and self-control. Extensive research has demonstrated that stimulant medication is effective in managing symptoms of ADHD; in fact, a recent large-scale study of over 500 children has shown that medication combined with behavior therapy is the most effective approach to the treatment of ADHD (Arnold et al., 1997; Hinshaw et al., 2000). Thus, the dual approach of behavioral parent training conducted by a psychologist in combination with medication prescribed and monitored by a physician is the most effective treatment protocol for ADHD currently available.

Numerous controlled outcome studies have demonstrated that parent training is superior to no treatment and to other forms of nonbehavioral child therapy in decreasing noncompliant and oppositional behavior and in increasing more positive social behaviors (e.g., Patterson & Chamberlain, 1994; Stoolmiller & Patterson, 1997; Wierson & Forehand, 1994). These studies highlight the importance of contingency contracts in improving child noncompliance and oppositional behavior. Contingency contracts have also been used successfully in the treatment of substance use (e.g., Saxon, Calsyn, Kivlahan, & Roszell, 1993), family dysfunction (Blechman, 1980), and marital distress (Bennun, 1987). As table 14.2 illustrates through examples based on Barkley's (1997b) work, an important component of contingency contracts may be the use of tokens or points gained and lost from engaging in specific behaviors, points that can be exchanged for goods or privileges. Nowhere is this system more explicit than in the development of token economy programs.

Token Economy Programs   **Token economy programs** represent applications of contingency management principles to groups of people rather than individuals. In fact, much of our society is essentially a token economy system based on principles of contingency management: People are rewarded with tokens (money, grades) contingent on their performance or behavior. There are several aspects to the construction and implementation of token economy programs. For example, the behaviors that are to be changed (most often, increased) must be operationalized, and the tokens or other symbolic reinforcers must be selected. Participants must be able to exchange these tokens for goods, services, or privileges. For example, patients may be allowed to exchange tokens for specific privileges (e.g., an extra hour of television, an out-of-hospital trip) or for goods, such as magazines; children may be offered snacks or book time in exchange for tokens they have earned by engaging in the specified behaviors. In all cases, the precise rate of exchange must be specified before the tokens are earned.

Token economy programs have most typically been developed and used with institutionalized populations. In fact, one of the first reports of a systematically organized token economy program described the use of tokens and reinforcements to increase socially desirable behaviors in a sample of hospitalized chronic psychiatric patients (Ayllon & Azrin, 1965). Since that report, there have been numerous studies of the effectiveness of token economy systems in both psychopathological samples (e.g., Foxx, 1998; Mohanty, Pati, & Kumar, 1998) and "normal" populations (e.g., Swain & McLaughlin, 1998). Importantly, there is empirical evidence that the behaviors that have been learned and reinforced in a token economy system do generalize outside that specific environment. Paul, Redfield, and Lentz (1976), for example, found that patients

who had been in a token economy program were more able to stay out of the hospital following discharge than were patients who received traditional hospital care.

Reducing Unwanted Behaviors: Aversive Conditioning

The goal of **aversive conditioning** is to reduce the occurrence of unwanted behaviors, such as excessive drinking, smoking, or eating, by pairing the behavior with a noxious stimulus. Thus, a behavior that was initially associated with pleasure or reward, like smoking, is conditioned to be associated instead with negative emotions and feelings, such as anxiety or nausea. As you might imagine, these procedures are often unpleasant and may involve noxious chemicals or shock. Consequently, aversive conditioning is typically used only when more positive procedures have failed to reduce or eliminate the problematic behavior.

Most frequently, aversive conditioning is used to eliminate addictive or destructive behaviors. For example, to treat a patient's heavy cigarette smoking, a therapist may pair each inhalation of smoke with an aversive stimulus, such as a noxious odor blown in the patient's face or a mild electrical shock administered to the patient's finger. After a number of such pairings, the patient begins to associate cigarette smoking with the unpleasant feelings evoked by the noxious odor or shock. Similarly, to reduce or eliminate excessive alcohol consumption, a therapist might mix a nausea-inducing drug into an alcoholic drink so that the patient will become nauseous and vomit after ingesting the drink. Again, a number of such pairings leave the patient feeling sick simply at the sight of the alcoholic drink. Finally, aversive conditioning has been used when the behavior to be reduced is self-injurious or destructive. For example, some severely disturbed psychiatric patients and some autistic children gouge their skin, punch themselves, or bang their heads against the wall, sometimes causing irreversible bodily damage. Although such patients are often kept in restraints, these solutions unfortunately also prevent the patients or children from engaging in adaptive behaviors. Aversive electric shock, administered contingent on the self-injurious behavior, has been demonstrated to successfully reduce this maladaptive behavior (e.g., Lovaas & Buch, 1997).

In general, the outcome research on aversion therapy has yielded equivocal results. For example, although the drug Antabuse (Disulfiron), which interacts with alcohol to produce nausea, has been found to temporarily reduce alcohol intake, its long-term effectiveness has been called into question (e.g., Barrera, Osinski, & Davidoff, 1994). Electric shock has also been assessed in the treatment of alcoholism and has not fared particularly well (e.g., E. O. Wilson, 1978). Interestingly, although electric shock has been reported to temporarily suppress smoking and overeating (e.g., Johnson, 1997), it is much less effective in the long-term treatment of these problems (Russell, Armstrong, & Patel, 1976), a conclusion that applies to most forms of aversive conditioning (e.g., Lichtenstein, 1982). Finally, we must emphasize here that, even in situations in which aversion therapy has been found to be successful, therapists typically recommend that these methods not be used unless other, less painful methods have failed.

COGNITIVE BEHAVIOR THERAPY

Historical Foundations

Behaviorism and the behavior therapy procedures we have described in this chapter dominated the thinking and practice of clinical psychology from the 1930s, when Watson and then Skinner developed their behavioral theories, to the early 1970s. In 1974 Dember described what he referred to as a "cognitive revolution" in clinical psychology, reconceptualized more recently by Meichenbaum (1995) as a "cognitive evolution." Regardless of whether the movement was a revolution or an evolution, there is no question that clinical psychology, and indeed psychology as a whole, was becoming more concerned with cognitive processes. Increasing attention was being given in psychology to information-processing models of cognition, and there was growing dissatisfaction with the simple behaviorist stimulus-response learning model. As Mahoney (1984) stated, "By the late 1970s . . . behavior therapy, like psychology in general, had 'gone cognitive' " (p. 9).

The first efforts to include an explicit cognitive focus in behavior therapies attempted to incorporate cognitive factors into existing behavioral treatments. Bandura's work on observational learning represented a major step in the integration of cognitive and symbolic processes into behavior therapy. In his 1969 volume, *Principles of Behavior Modification*, Bandura emphasized the importance of modeling, or observational learning, in understanding the development of some forms of anxiety and in the treatment of these problems. Bandura argued that all learning that could occur through direct experience could also take place vicariously through observation of another's behavior and its consequences. In suggesting that behavior change can be mediated by cognitions, Bandura developed one of the first forms of cognitive-behavior therapy.

Modeling

Albert Bandura, a professor at Stanford University, has been a major figure in psychology for more than 40 years. He pioneered the therapeutic use of **modeling,** or observational learning, to treat fears and phobias as well as to teach positive skills and behaviors. Bandura noted that modeling can be used not only to teach individuals adaptive behaviors that were not previously in their repertoire but also to facilitate or inhibit the expression of behaviors that they are already capable of performing. It is difficult to imagine

how some forms of learning could occur without the use of modeling. As Bandura (1977) stated, "One does not teach children to swim, adolescents to drive automobiles, and novice medical students to perform surgery by having them discover the appropriate behavior through the consequences of their successes and failures" (p. 12). Thus, rather than through learning that takes place exclusively by operant conditioning, in which novel behaviors would be broken down into small components and each gradually shaped to form a final complex behavior, modeling allows more complex behaviors to be learned relatively rapidly by observation.

Bandura has found that behaviors that are rewarded are more likely to be modeled than are behaviors that are either punished or that are not followed by a consequence. This finding forms the theoretical foundation for the use of treatments that rely on modeling procedures to increase rates of adaptive behaviors. For example, in one of the earliest studies in this area, Bandura, Grusec, and Menlove (1967) found that simple modeling was effective in treating a group of preschool children who were afraid of dogs. Bandura subsequently demonstrated that stronger results could be obtained using a procedure called participant modeling, essentially having a live model guide the participant in emitting the desired response. Using participant modeling, Bandura, Blanchard, and Ritter (1969) reported the successful treatment of snake phobia in a sample of young adults. Modeling has now been used successfully not only to reduce fears and phobias but also to treat social phobia or shyness, obsessive-compulsive disorder, impulsivity, and attention deficit/hyperactivity disorder and to reduce physical aggression (e.g., Hollon & Beck, 1994; Rosenthal & Steffek, 1991; Salkovskis & Kirk, 1989).

How does modeling, or observational learning, work? Bandura (1997) has argued persuasively that the positive effects of modeling treatments are due to the increase in the individual's self-efficacy that is brought about through modeling. Self-efficacy refers to "beliefs in one's capabilities to organize and execute the courses of action required to produce given attainments" (p. 3). Bandura posits that modeling promotes a sense of mastery or competence in the individual, and it is this sense of mastery that leads to the beneficial effects of modeling. In support of this position, several studies have now demonstrated that behavioral improvement can be predicted directly from change in level of self-efficacy (see Bandura, 1997, 2000).

The Transition to Cognitive Therapy

Bandura's theory and studies of observational learning provided the foundation for subsequent integrations of cognitive and behavioral aspects of therapy. Michael Mahoney's 1974 book, *Cognition and Behavior Modification*, and Donald Meichenbaum's 1977 volume, *Cognitive-Behavior Modification: An Integrative Approach*, both further developed the role of cognition as a mediator of change in behavior therapy and strengthened the practice of cognitive-behavior therapy. At about the same time, **Albert Ellis** and Aaron Beck were refining their development of therapies for emotional disorders that not only included a strong cognitive component but, more important, gave primary emphasis to dysfunctional cognitions, or problematic patterns of thinking, as a direct cause of psychological distress and as a critical focus in bringing out therapeutic change. The greater emphasis on cognition in these theories and treatments led them to be referred to not as cognitive-behavior therapies but, more simply, as cognitive therapies.

COGNITIVE THERAPY

Both Albert Ellis's **rational-emotive therapy** and Aaron Beck's **cognitive therapy** have had a profound impact on the practice of clinical psy-

chology. Ellis and Beck were trained as psychoanalysts but were frustrated at the relatively passive role of the therapist in psychoanalysis and the slow progress of therapy. Both Ellis and Beck moved away from psychotherapy's psychoanalytic focus on unconscious drives and psychosexual stages and developed a strong interest in the importance of cognitions, or thoughts, in affecting mood and behavior. Based on their view of the central role of cognitions in contributing to problems in emotions and behaviors, Ellis and Beck developed therapeutic interventions aimed at changing the way people think in order to improve their emotional and behavioral functioning.

Ellis's Rational-Emotive Therapy

Ellis (1962, 2000) formulated what has come to be known as an A-B-C theory of dysfunctional behavior. Contrary to the prevailing view at the time, Ellis argued that stressful life events, referred to as *activating events (A)*, do not cause psychopathology or emotional *consequences (C)* such as depression and anxiety. Instead, Ellis contends that it is the *irrational beliefs (B)*, or unrealistic interpretations, that people have about events in their lives that lead them to become depressed or anxious. Ellis believes that when we experience a negative or unpleasant event, we have logical and rational beliefs about that event; in addition, however, we also "automatically" engage in a series of irrational or dysfunctional beliefs about the event. For example, if we fail a midterm examination we may have such logical thoughts as "it's unfortunate that I failed—I didn't study hard enough and I must make sure that I study harder for the final exam" or "I don't seem to understand this material—maybe I had better seek extra help in this course." Ellis argues that while these logical, rational thoughts may lead to disappointment or sadness, they will not lead to more severe emotional states such as depression or anxiety. According to Ellis, if we are experiencing these more dysfunctional emotions we must also be holding a number of irrational beliefs about failing the midterm, such as "I'm stupid—I'll never be able to pass this course and I will fail my year" or "If I can't pass an easy exam like that I'm not worthy of being at this university."

Ellis believes that there are a number of irrational beliefs that are common to many of us. These beliefs are presented in box 14.3. In rational-emotive therapy, Ellis focuses on identifying the patient's specific irrational beliefs that are contributing to his or her experience of depression, anxiety, hopelessness, or despair. Once these irrational beliefs are identified, Ellis adds a D and an E to his A-B-C theory. Ellis teaches patients to *dispute (D)* their irrational or illogical beliefs. In this process, patients learn to argue with their irrational beliefs and to substitute more rational and adaptive beliefs in their place. And finally, Ellis has the patients evaluate the *effects (E)* of disputing their irrational beliefs. If the treatment is successful, the effects should be evident in reductions of feelings of depression, anxiety, or malaise. These reductions of negative affect serve to reinforce the patient's identification and disputation of irrational beliefs and ideas as well as the substitution of more adaptive cognitions.

Beck's Cognitive Therapy

Perhaps because Beck formulated his cognitive theory of psychopathology in more clearly testable terms than did Ellis, it is Beck's ideas about the role of cognition in emotional disorders that have been examined most systematically in clinical research. In the remainder of this chapter, therefore, we describe the foundations of cognitive therapy and how it has been applied to a number of psychological disorders.

As we described in chapter 4, Beck (1967) developed cognitive therapy from his clinical experience with depressed patients. Beck's obser-

Aaron T. Beck, M.D., is considered to be the founder of cognitive therapy. Over the past 40 years Dr. Beck has conducted empirical investigations of the psychopathology of depression, suicide, anxiety disorders, panic disorders, and substance abuse, and has developed cognitive therapy approaches for these disorders. Dr. Beck has received Distinguished Scientists Awards from the American Psychological Association and the Society for Psychotherapy Research. *(Photo courtesy of Aaron T. Beck.)*

vations that the dreams of depressed patients were full of negative content led him to posit that negative thoughts play a central role in the onset and course of depression. He postulated that depressed people have a negative view of themselves and the world and are hopeless about the future. Beck further theorized that depressed people have negative cognitive schemas, or structures through which they perceive and interpret their experiences. These negative schemas are always part of a person who is vulnerable to becoming depressed, but they are essentially unconscious; they become activated when the individual experiences a stressful event. Thus, a person who has a negative schema involving rejection and abandonment will become depressed when a partner leaves him or her. Similarly, individuals will become anxious if they have a schema involving threat or danger and are faced

BOX 14.3

ALBERT ELLIS'S LIST OF COMMON IRRATIONAL IDEAS

Albert Ellis (Ellis, 1994; Ellis & Grieger, 1977) has offered a number of irrational beliefs or ideas that he contends are held by many people in our society. Ellis maintains that the greater the degree to which people ascribe to these beliefs, the greater the likelihood that people will exhibit problematic or debilitating functioning.

1. I absolutely must have sincere love and approval almost all the time from all the significant people in my life.
2. I must be thoroughly competent, adequate, and achieving in all respects, or I must at least have real competence or talent at something important; otherwise I am worthless.
3. People who harm me or who do a bad thing are uniformly bad or wicked individuals, and I should severely blame, damn, and punish them for their sins and misdeeds.
4. When things do not go the way I would like them to go, life is awful, terrible, horrible, or catastrophic.
5. Unhappiness is caused by external events over which I have almost no control. I also have little

ability to control my feelings or rid myself of feelings of depression and hostility.
6. Some things are dangerous or fearsome, so I must become terribly occupied with them and upset about them.
7. I will find it easier to avoid facing life's difficulties and responsibilities than to face them.
8. My past remains all-important, and because something once strongly influenced my life, it must continue to determine my feelings and behavior today.
9. People and things should turn out better than they do; it is awful and horrible for me if I do not quickly find good solutions to life's hassles.
10. I can find happiness by being passive and noncommittal in life.
11. There is always a single correct solution to human problems, and if that solution is not found, I must be quite upset.
12. I give myself a global rating as a human, and my general worth and self-acceptance depend on the goodness of my performance and the degree that people approve of me.

---

with a relevant stressful event that activates the schema.

 ### Cognitive Therapy for Depression and Anxiety

Based on his theoretical formulations, Beck developed cognitive therapy for the treatment of depression and anxiety. Beck, Rush, Shaw, & Emery (1979) describe cognitive therapy in the following way:

> Cognitive therapy is an active, directive, time limited, structured approach used to treat a variety of psychiatric disorders . . . It is based on an underlying theoretical rationale that an individual's affect and

behavior are largely determined by the way in which he structures the world . . . His cognitions (verbal or pictorial "events" in his stream of consciousness) are based on attitudes or assumptions (schemas), developed from previous experiences. For example, if a person interprets all his experiences in terms of whether he is competent and adequate, his thinking may be dominated by the schema, "Unless I do everything perfectly, I'm a failure." Consequently, he reacts to situations in terms of adequacy even when they are unrelated to whether or not he is personally competent. (p. 3)

As you might expect given this conceptualization, cognitive therapy focuses primarily on identifying and changing maladaptive thoughts or cognitions, with the belief that these changes will lead to a reduction in symptoms of distress. In addition, however, cognitive therapists may also assign behavioral homework to patients and give them training in problem-solving skills (it may be more accurate, therefore, to call it cognitive-behavior therapy). Cognitive therapy is time-limited: it rarely exceeds 30 weekly sessions and typically ranges from 15 to 25 sessions.

In the first few sessions of cognitive therapy, the therapist explains the cognitive theory of emotional disorders to the client, emphasizing how negative cognitions contribute to distress. The client is taught the importance of being able to identify, evaluate, and replace negative automatic thoughts with more positive cognitions. The therapist attempts to engage the client as a collaborator, or a fellow scientist in therapy, a process referred to as collaborative empiricism. Working together, the therapist and client test the logic and consistency of each identified negative thought, and the client is encouraged to change her or his cognitions to be more consistent with the available evidence and logic. The therapist teaches the client behavioral coping strategies, such as problem-solving skills and assertiveness training, to help her or him in using these more positive cognitions.

The middle sessions of cognitive therapy are devoted to helping the client identify and modify the basic underlying beliefs that lead him or her to have negative thoughts. These beliefs may include, "I am not a worthwhile person," "I do not deserve to be loved," "I will fail when I try to do something new," or other, similar beliefs. It is important to note that the underlying beliefs that are the focus of the middle sessions of cognitive therapy are more general and all-encompassing than are the more specific negative automatic thoughts that were identified in the first sessions. Cognitive therapists theorize that these underlying global beliefs lead to the more specific beliefs that trigger an episode of depression or anxiety. In cognitive therapy, therefore, the specific negative cognitions are identified first, be-

cause they are closer to the surface. Then, when the client has had some experience with the process of therapy, the deeper and more global beliefs are examined and, in collaboration with the client, challenged.

In the final sessions of cognitive therapy (typically sessions 12 through 16), the therapist has two major goals. First, the therapist works with the client to solidify the gains the client has already made in therapy. Thus, the therapist attempts to broaden the range of negative cognitions that the client has identified as problematic and to strengthen the more positive cognitions and behaviors that the client has used to improve his or her functioning thus far. Second, because many emotional disorders like depression and anxiety have a high rate of recurrence, or relapse, the therapist focuses in the final sessions of cognitive therapy on trying to prevent recurrence of the disorder. Here, the therapist makes sure that the client has adequately identified the underlying dysfunctional attitudes and beliefs that gave rise to the negative cognitions and works with the client to anticipate the kinds of life stressors that he or she may encounter in the future. Indeed, many cognitive therapists role-play adaptive responses and cognitions to these anticipated adverse events and help their clients become aware of subtle emotional cues that they are under stress and should engage in positive cognitions. An example of cognitive therapy is presented in box 14.4, describing the treatment of Phillip, who is experiencing social anxiety.

Evaluation of Cognitive Therapy

Given that cognitive theory and therapy originated in an attempt to understand and treat depression (e.g., Beck, 1967), it is not surprising that the majority of studies examining the effectiveness of cognitive therapy have focused on depression. In fact, cognitive therapy and cognitive-behavior therapy for depression have now been evaluated in over 80 controlled studies (American Psychiatric Association, 2000). The

BOX 14.4

COGNITIVE THERAPY FOR SOCIAL ANXIETY: PHILLIP

Dr. Marcus had considerable experience helping clients who presented with problems like Phillip, people who had an unreasonable fear of social or performance situations. Having administered a structured clinical interview to Phillip, Dr. Marcus was able to confirm her initial impression that he was suffering from diagnosable social phobia. She knows from her training as a clinical psychologist that cognitive-behavior therapy is an effective treatment for social phobia, and she proceeds to share with Phillip her understanding of social phobia from this perspective. Dr. Marcus tells Phillip that his negative thoughts are a major source of his difficulties. Individuals with social phobia believe that some or all social situations are dangerous because of their potential for negative evaluation, which leads to feelings of embarrassment, rejection, and low self-esteem. Dr. Marcus continues by informing Phillip that his negative thoughts become increasingly powerful as the day of his presentation looms closer and become overwhelming when he is actually presenting. She suggests that Phillip misperceives members of the audience as viewing him critically and that these thoughts interfere with his presentation, leading to a poorer performance. This poor performance leads to more negative thoughts and to physical symptoms of anxiety, such as increased heart rate and shortness of breath, which further impair his performance. This, Dr. Marcus explains to Phillip, is the vicious circle of negative thoughts affecting performance, which in turn leads to more negative thoughts and other symptoms of anxiety. Dr. Marcus also points out that Phillip may not be aware of these negative thoughts. It is likely that he has experienced these thoughts so often that they have become automatic.

Phillip had never thought about his fear of presentations and his physical symptoms in these terms before. He hadn't heard about "dysfunctional thoughts" before meeting Dr. Marcus, but her explanation of his difficulties made sense to him, and he was eager to work with her to put his fears behind him. Dr. Marcus explained that she was going to use a combination of relaxation techniques, exposure to the source of his anxiety, cognitive techniques, and extinction techniques in treating Phillip. She explained that Phillip was also going to have homework assignments to help him practice the skills he would learn in the therapy sessions. To prepare him for the exposure procedures, Dr. Marcus gave Phillip a relaxation audiotape and asked him to follow the instructions on the tape twice each day. She gave Phillip a self-monitoring log to record his relaxation sessions (see figure 14.1). She emphasized that it would be important for Philip to practice the progressive muscle relaxation procedure regularly to enable him to cue himself into a relaxed state whenever he needed to.

Dr. Marcus then worked with Phillip to identify his dysfunctional thoughts about giving presentations at work. Over the course of two sessions, Phillip identified the following thoughts: "I know I will be anxious in the presentation"; "My coworkers will see that I am anxious and think I am ridiculous"; "I will make a fool of myself"; "I really don't know what I am doing at this job." Phillip was afraid that he would not be able to control overt signs of anxiety such as blushing and his voice cracking and that he would have difficulty thinking clearly. And his greatest fear was that he would have another panic attack like the one he experienced recently when he was unable to breathe and felt as if he was having a heart attack. Because of his fears, he thought, the presentation would go badly and he would be evaluated as being incompetent.

Dr. Marcus began the exposure component of the treatment by having Phillip first relax, as he had learned to do from the audiotape, and then had him imagine giving a presentation to his coworkers. She had Phillip imagine starting off well, but then fumbling with his papers and losing his place in the presentation. It was important for the treatment that Phillip continue imagining this experience even though he was starting to become anxious. In preventing Phillip from avoiding the situation, Dr. Marcus was using a procedure known as exposure plus

BOX 14.4 (continued)

		Relaxation Record Rate relaxation and concentration at the end of each practice, using the scale below: 0------1------2------3------4------5------6------7------8 none mild moderate strong excellent	
DATE	PRACTICE	RELAXATION AT THE END OF THE EXERCISE	CONCENTRATION DURING THE EXERCISE
	In Session		
	1		
	2		
	1		
	2		
	1		
	2		
	1		
	2		
	1		
	2		
	1		
	2		
	1		
	2		
	1		
	2		
	1		
	2		

FIGURE 14.1
Phillip's self-monitoring log for recording his relaxation practice sessions at home.

response prevention, which has been found to be effective in treating anxiety because it leads to extinction of the anxiety in the presence of the source of threat.

Phillip was able to continue imagining himself in the situation, and his anxiety level slowly started to subside. Over the next few sessions, Dr. Marcus had Phillip imagine giving presentations under increasingly difficult circumstances, each time encouraging him to continue imagining himself in the situation even as he was becoming increasingly anxious. Importantly, each time Phillip's anxiety level rose, it

BOX 14.4 (concluded)

fell by the end of the session even though he was continuing to imagine himself in the situation. Phillip continued to practice relaxation, and during the treatment sessions, Dr. Marcus began to work with Phillip to identify his dysfunctional thoughts as he was imagining himself giving a presentation. Dr. Marcus and Phillip identified more adaptive thoughts, and Phillip practiced these thoughts as he gave presentations in Dr. Marcus's office. Dr. Marcus also assigned Phillip homework of giving brief presentations to his staff and monitoring his thoughts

and anxiety level. Phillip was able to identify specific cognitive distortions that he was making during the presentations, but he was also able to formulate and substitute more rational and adaptive thoughts. By the end of treatment (15 sessions), Phillip was able to give presentations at work without experiencing debilitating anxiety. At a 6-month follow-up session with Dr. Marcus, Phillip reported that, while he did not enjoy making the presentations, he had not avoided a single event and thought that he was doing a good job.

results of these clinical trials are consistent: It is clear now that cognitive therapy is an effective treatment for unipolar depression. Indeed, cognitive therapy was identified by the Task Force on Promotion and Dissemination of Psychological Procedures of Division 12 of the APA (Chambless & Hollon, 1998) as a "well-established treatment" (see chapter 15). Although there are exceptions (e.g., N. S. Jacobson et al., 1996; Shapiro, Barkham, Rees, & Hardy, 1994), cognitive therapy has generally been found to be as effective as (and sometimes more effective than) alternate forms of treatment for depression, including antidepressant medication (DeRubeis, Gelfand, Tang, & Simons, 1999; Hollon, Haman, & Brown, in press). At the same time, however, it is important to realize that, despite the explicit focus of cognitive therapy on the prevention of relapse, about two-thirds of depressed patients who receive cognitive therapy have another episode of depression within two years (Gortner, Gollan, Dobson, & Jacobson, 1998), a problem that also plagues other forms of psychotherapy. We will examine this research in more detail in chapter 15.

Because not all depressed clients respond to cognitive therapy, investigators have begun to examine whether there might be particular client characteristics that are associated with better outcomes. Put another way, the question these researchers are asking is, "Do some types of clients

respond better to cognitive therapy than other types of clients?" Although this research has not yet yielded consistent results, there are a few unexpected findings that have emerged. For example, even though cognitive therapy requires clients to use logic to evaluate their beliefs, level of intelligence is not associated with outcome of cognitive therapy for depression (Haaga, DeRubeis, Stewart, & Beck, 1991). Similarly, because cognitive therapy is posited to work by reducing the level of dysfunctional cognitions, it would be reasonable to think that depressed patients with the highest levels of dysfunctional thinking would benefit the most from this form of treatment. Paradoxically, it appears that just the opposite is the case: Patients with lower levels of dysfunctional thinking have been found to respond best to cognitive therapy (e.g., Jarrett et al., 1991). Interestingly, patients with the most dysfunctional cognitions also tend to have the most severe depressions (Whisman, 1993) and are also relatively unresponsive to antidepressant medication as well (Sotsky, Glass, Shea, & Pilkonis, 1991). Finally, Barber and Muenz (1996) found that patients who engage in avoidance behaviors in relationships do better in cognitive therapy than in interpersonal psychotherapy, whereas patients with a more obsessive style show the opposite pattern of response.

Finally, it is important to point out here that cognitive therapy has been found to be effective

BOX 14.5

COGNITIVE-BEHAVIOR THERAPY FOR CHRONIC PAIN

One of the broadest and most successful applications of cognitive therapy, or cognitive-behavior therapy, has been in the treatment of chronic pain. Millions of individuals suffer from chronic pain associated with a variety of conditions, including headache, various forms of stomach and abdominal pain (e.g., colitis, irritable bowel disorder), back pain, arthritis and other rheumatoid diseases, AIDS, and cancer. Although a number of medications are effective in managing chronic pain, most have negative side effects, including being addictive. As a result, cognitive-behavioral researchers and therapists have employed and evaluated methods to help patients learn to better manage and cope with their pain and its consequences for their daily functioning. A large body of empirical research has demonstrated that these methods are highly effective in managing chronic pain (Compas, Haaga, Keefe, Leitenberg, & Williams, 1998; Morley, Eccleston, & Williams, 1999).

Behavioral, cognitive, and cognitive-behavioral interventions for chronic pain typically include several elements. For example, some treatments are based on principles of operant theory and focus on reducing the social reinforcements and attention that are often contingent on both pain behavior and the loss of functioning that often accompanies chronic pain (e.g., Fordyce, 1988, 1993). These methods have been used successfully in the treatment of chronic low back pain, an often debilitating condition that affects millions of Americans. Behavior therapy approaches to the treatment of pain involve reinforcing adaptive or healthy behaviors, such as regular exercise, and talking about topics that are unrelated to the pain (in an attempt to reduce the preoccupation with pain that often characterizes the interactions of chronic pain patients). At the same time, reinforcement is withdrawn for those behaviors that serve to maintain the pain and reduce normal activities. These maladaptive behaviors may include spending time in bed or lying down, moving in an excessively guarded or cautious manner, and talking or complaining about pain. This operant behavior therapy approach has been shown to be effec-

---

in the treatment of disorders other than depression. In their recent review of empirically supported psychotherapies for adults, DeRubeis and Crits-Christoph (1998) noted that cognitive therapy has been used successfully to treat generalized anxiety disorder, obsessive-compulsive disorder, and panic disorder. There are also growing literatures documenting the effectiveness of cognitive therapy in the treatment of eating disorders such as bulimia and anorexia nervosa (e.g., Kinoy, 2001; Ricca, Mannucci, Zucchi, Rotella, & Faravelli, 2000; Whittal, Agras, & Gould, 1999), marital difficulties (e.g., Emanuels-Zuurveen & Emmelkamp, 1996; Epstein, Baucom, & Daiuto, 1997), and sexual dysfunction (Nobre & Gouveia, 2000). Furthermore, cognitive therapy and cognitive-behavior therapy have also been found to be effective in the treatment of difficulties that have a significant physi-cal as well as psychological component. Because the treatment of chronic pain represents an excellent illustration of this point, we describe cognitive and cognitive-behavioral approaches to this problem in greater detail in box 14.5.

In addition to these studies demonstrating that cognitive therapy is effective in the treatment of various forms of psychopathology in adults, there is a rapidly evolving literature indicating that cognitive therapy is also effective in treating emotional disorders in children. For example, several investigators have examined the efficacy of cognitive-behavior therapy in the treatment of child anxiety and have reported beneficial effects both at immediate posttreatment and at one- to three-year follow-up assessments (e.g., Barrett, Dadds, & Rapee, 1996; Kendall, Flannery-Schroeder, Panichelli-Mindel, & Southam-Gerow, 1997). Other researchers have reported

BOX 14.5 (concluded)

tive in the treatment of chronic low back pain (e.g., Nicholas, Wilson, & Goyen, 1991; Turner, Clancy, McQuade, & Cardenas, 1990).

A second approach to the treatment of pain utilizes biofeedback, a procedure that involves increasing patients' awareness of and their ability to control physiological processes that are related to pain. The feedback is provided via electronic devices that can be used to measure muscle tension, skin conductance, heart rate, blood pressure, or other indications of physiological tension or arousal. Biofeedback has been shown to be effective in the treatment of several pain conditions, most notably migraine headaches (e.g., Blanchard, Peters, & Hermann, 1997; Kropp, Gerber, Keinath-Specht, Kopal, & Niederberger, 1997; Sarafino & Goehring, 2000).

A third psychological approach to the treatment of pain involves systematic efforts to enhance the ways that patients cope with their pain. This approach includes the use of methods to distract the patient's attention from the pain, the use of relaxation methods to decrease physiological arousal that frequently accompanies pain, and the development of other coping strategies to manage emotional distress. In these interventions patients are typically educated about the behavioral, psychological, and biological aspects of pain. They are taught a variety of skills to cope with pain, and they learn to apply these pain management skills in increasingly more difficult situations (e.g., Gil et al., 2000; Keefe & France, 1999; Moore, Von Korff, Cherkin, Saunders, & Lorig, 2000).

In learning to cope with pain, patients are taught relaxation techniques (progressive muscle relaxation, guided imagery, deep breathing) and how to pace their activities; they are taught to schedule pleasant activities, to change the way they think about pain, and to refocus their attention on stimuli other than pain. These methods have been demonstrated to be effective in the treatment of pain associated with rheumatic diseases (e.g., Keefe & France, 1999), migraine headaches (e.g., Blanchard et al., 1997), and irritable bowel syndrome (e.g., Boyce, Gilchrist, Talley, & Rose, 2000; Blanchard, 2001).

---

similar positive results for coping skills training in the treatment of child depression. This approach has a significant cognitive focus on identifying and modifying depressogenic or maladaptive schemas and attributions and has been found to be effective in the treatment of depression in both children (Stark, Swearer, Kurowski, Sommer, & Bowen, 1996) and adolescents (Lewinsohn, Clarke, Rohde, Hops, & Seeley, 1996; Weisz, Rudolph, Granger, & Sweeney, 1992). In fact, there is now recent evidence to suggest that targeting maladaptive cognitions may help prevent the occurrence of depression in children who are at elevated risk for this disorder (e.g., Gillham, Shatte, & Freres, 2000). Finally, a number of investigators have reported the successful use of cognitive problem-solving skills training in the treatment of oppositional and aggressive behavior in children (e.g., Durlak, Fuhrman, & Lampman, 1991; Kazdin & Weisz, 1998).

SUMMARY AND CONCLUSIONS

Behavioral approaches to the treatment of psychological disorders grew out of learning theory. Whereas Pavlov and Watson emphasized classical conditioning procedures, in which stimuli evoke responses, Skinner focused on operant conditioning and the consequences of behavior. While the specifics of the theories may have differed, they all emphasized the examination of overt, observable behavior rather than underlying conflicts and motivation.

Behavior therapists assume that the same principles of learning apply to both normal and abnormal behavior. Consequently, the methods developed to change behaviors are based explicitly on laws of learning. Behavioral procedures have been used in the treatment of fears and phobias (systematic desensitization, exposure-based treatments like implosive therapy), and obsessive-compulsive disorders and eating disorders (exposure plus response prevention). Behavior therapy has also been used to train patients in social skills and assertiveness, and contingency management techniques have been utilized in parent training and token economy programs. Finally, aversion conditioning procedures have been developed to eliminate problematic behaviors like smoking and engaging in self-injurious behaviors.

The strong focus of behavior therapy on overt, observable behavior was challenged by theorists such as Bandura, Ellis, and Beck, who wrote persuasively about the important role played by cognitions in affecting behavior. These theorists paved the way for the development of both cognitive and cognitive-behavioral therapeutic procedures. Today, cognitive therapy enjoys strong empirical support in the treatment of a wide range of psychological disorders in both children and adults, including depression, anxiety, and eating disorders; it is also now used increasingly to help clients deal more effectively with physical pain.

Cognitive-behavior therapy represents an excellent example of the interplay of science and practice. As more investigations assess the effectiveness of cognitive and cognitive-behavior therapy in the treatment of particular psychological disorders, specific aspects of the treatment are refined on the basis of the results of the studies. The refined treatment protocol is then tested, and if necessary, further changes are made. Because of this iterative process, there are now a number of empirically supported versions of cognitive therapy for the treatment of specific disorders.

KEY TERMS AND NAMES

Aversive conditioning
Albert Bandura
Behavior therapy
Cognitive therapy
Contingency contracting
Albert Ellis
Exposure treatments
Implosive therapy
Modeling

Ivan Pavlov
Rational-emotive therapy
Reciprocal inhibition
Response prevention
Shaping
Social skills training
Systematic desensitization
Token economy programs
Joseph Wolpe

RESOURCES

Books

Bandura, A. (1997). *Self-efficacy: The exercise of control.* New York: W. H. Freeman.

Graham, P. J. (1998). *Cognitive-behaviour therapy for children and families.* New York: Cambridge University Press.

O'Donohue, W., & Krasner, L. (Eds.). (1995). *Theories of behavior therapy: Exploring behavior change.* Washington, DC: American Psychological Association.

Salkovskis, P. M. (Ed.). (1996). *Frontiers of cognitive therapy.* New York: Guilford Press

Journals

Behavior Modification
Behaviour Research and Therapy
Behavior Therapy
Cognitive Therapy and Research
Journal of Cognitive Psychotherapy

CHAPTER FIFTEEN

PSYCHOTHERAPY: EFFECTIVENESS, EVALUATION, AND INTEGRATION

INTRODUCTION

The pain of seeing her son so despondent and in such anguish was more than Brian's mother could bear. She had tried to talk with both Brian and his sister, Jessica, about the divorce. Jessica was open about her feelings and often expressed and shared her sadness, anger, and fears with her mother. Brian was different. He said little or nothing about his feelings and quickly became impatient with his mother whenever she tried to talk with him. As the weeks passed, Brian's mother could see the toll that her divorce from his father was taking on him.

Brian had become more sullen and irritable, and the slightest problem brought a flare of his anger. He no longer wanted to eat, frequently refusing to join her and Jessica for meals and picking at his food when he did eat with them. She knew he was also not sleeping well—most nights the light was still on in his room when she went to bed well after midnight. Most heartbreaking of all for her was that the joy that she was so accustomed to seeing in Brian was gone. He no longer took pleasure in the things he had loved so much; most notably, he had lost his passion for sports, the greatest source of enjoyment in his life since he was a little boy.

Knowing that she wanted to get help for her son, Brian's mother looked in the Yellow Pages of her telephone book under "psychologist." She was shocked to find more than 200 names listed. Some were listed individually, and others were part of groups with names such as The Center for Growth, Associates in Psychology, and Psychotherapy Networks. The advertisements that appeared in the Yellow Pages indicated that they could offer help with depression, anxiety, stress, low self-esteem, and relationship problems. How was she to choose? The process of getting help became more frustrating when she contacted her insurance company to learn about coverage for mental health services. She was told that she could select a psychologist only from a list of providers who had been approved by the insurance company for reimbursement. They did not offer her guidance, however, in how she should go about selecting someone from their list. And finally, her most nagging questions remained: How will I know if the person I choose will be able to help Brian? Will psychotherapy help him?

Concern over the likely effectiveness of psychotherapy is no different than concern about the effectiveness of other health care practices. In seeking medical care, you want to know that your physician will use state-of-the-art methods to diagnosis and treat any problems that you may have. If your physician prescribes medication, you want to be confident that the effects of that medicine have been tested in controlled clinical studies and that any negative side effects of the medication have been carefully examined and judged to be minimal. In fact, the beneficial effects and side effects of any medication prescribed by a physician were most likely carefully evaluated by the U.S. Food and Drug Administration, the agency responsible for monitoring the safety and effectiveness of medications, before the drug was approved for use.

People seeking help through psychotherapy deserve the same level of assurance that the treatment they receive has been held to the highest standards of effectiveness. That is, the form of psychotherapy that a client receives should be proven, through the best available scientific methods, to be more beneficial than not receiving treatment; if a higher standard is used, the treatment should be at least as effective as, if not more effective than, alternative treatments.

In chapters 11 through 14 we examined a number of aspects of the practice of psychotherapy. We discussed the importance of the prevention and treatment of mental and emotional disorders and of the promotion of positive mental health. We outlined both general and specific goals of psychotherapy and highlighted the role of theory in the development of approaches to prevention, intervention, and promotion. We then described in detail several different approaches to psychotherapy, including psychoanalytic therapies, humanistic-existential therapies, and behavioral and cognitive therapies. In this chapter we conclude our discussion of intervention in clinical psychology by examining issues and findings in the area of psychotherapy evaluation. We will address three broad questions in this chapter: (a) Why is it important to evaluate psychotherapy? (b) How do we evaluate psychotherapy? (c) How effective are different approaches to psychotherapy?

WHY SHOULD WE EVALUATE THE EFFECTIVENESS OF PSYCHOTHERAPY?

Given the strong scientific orientation of this book, it may seem self-evident by now that psychotherapy must be evaluated empirically in order to assess its effectiveness. It might surprise you to learn, however, that there has been considerable controversy about whether psychotherapy should be evaluated. Some practitioners have argued that it is impossible to study psychotherapy scientifically. Freud (1917) long ago maintained that psychotherapy patients are too heterogeneous to be analyzed statistically, a sentiment echoed more recently by Guntrip (1973), who contended that psychotherapy is too individualized to be submitted to empirical investigation. This position maintains that it is impossible to operationalize, quantify, and measure the process of therapy and that the issues and outcomes of treatment are different for every patient. As we noted in chapter 13, this position is also characteristic of some approaches to humanistic-existential psychotherapy, especially Gestalt therapy (e.g., Perls, 1969). At the other end of the pendulum are therapists who are so convinced that therapy is effective that they believe no further scientific study is required (e.g., Arlow, 1984). In fact, until recently the position that psychotherapy cannot be evaluated scientifically had been so powerful that Bergin and Garfield (1971) stated in the preface to the first edition of their handbook on empirical studies of psychotherapy that "For most of its history, the field of psychotherapy has appeared to rely almost exclusively on clinical reports, case studies, and theoretical accounts" (p. ix).

What accounts for this resistance to subjecting psychotherapy to empirical study? Both therapists and clients may be resistant to having psychotherapy evaluated scientifically in part because of cognitive dissonance, a phenomenon with a long history in social psychology (e.g., Cooper, 1998; Festinger, 1957). Dissonance occurs when there is a conflict between the beliefs that one holds and one's actual behavior. To reduce this dissonance, people tend to bring their attitudes and beliefs in line with their behavior. In the case of psychotherapy, it would be highly dissonant to believe that psychotherapy is ineffective at the same time that one is practicing as a psychotherapist or receiving psychotherapy as a client. Thus, therapists want clients to improve in order to justify their belief that their professional activities are important and effective. Similarly, clients want to believe that they must be improving in order to justify the large amount of time and money they are spending in the therapy.

Clearly, both therapists and clients *want* the client to improve in therapy. We believe that it is imperative that we use controlled experimental methods and procedures to examine whether particular therapies offer benefits beyond nonspecific motivational effects, such as those that may result from cognitive dissonance. Indeed, there are at least four major reasons why the enterprise of psychotherapy evaluation is critically important. First, by some estimates (e.g., Craighead, Craighead, Kazdin, & Mahoney, 1994; Mahoney, 1998), there are more than 400 different forms of psychotherapy. Thus, in purely practical terms, we must be able to determine which of the many available forms of therapy are the most effective in the treatment of psychological distress. Ideally, we must try to address the question of *specificity* or *matching*; that is, we must be able to determine which therapy or therapies are most beneficial for the prevention or treatment of particular problems or disorders.

Second, clinical psychologists have an ethical responsibility to their clients to treat them using methods or procedures that have been demonstrated to be effective in controlled research studies. Clients typically come to therapy having little, if any, knowledge of which specific treatments have been found in clinical studies to be effective in alleviating the types of difficulties they are experiencing. They rely, most often blindly, on the expertise of the therapist to provide them with an effective intervention. It is unethical for a clinical psychologist to offer a treatment to a client without having any knowledge of whether it is likely to alleviate the client's difficulties. This practice is especially problematic if there is an available treatment that the therapist is not using that has been found in research studies to be effective for the client's problem. Certainly, the more information clients have before they first meet with a therapist, the better able they will be to make an informed decision about undertaking any proposed treatment.

The third major reason for evaluating the effectiveness of psychotherapy is that it moves the field of clinical psychology forward to continue to develop and refine approaches to the prevention and treatment of psychological distress.

Indeed, it is *only* by empirically evaluating the impact and benefits of various forms of psychotherapy for different disorders that we can be sure of offering the most effective interventions possible to our clients. And as a related point, as managed health care organizations become increasingly concerned about **accountability** and cost efficiency—about how their money is spent—they will undoubtedly begin to reimburse only procedures or approaches that have been demonstrated empirically to be effective.

This movement toward greater accountability by psychologists will become even more salient over the coming decades as we continue to learn more about the societal costs of emotional distress. We know now that mental health is related to economic variables such as work productivity, number of sick days, and job turnover (e.g., Druss, Rosenheck & Sledge, 2000); in fact, the World Health Organization Global Burden of Disease Study recently ranked depression as the single most burdensome disease in the world in terms of total disability-adjusted life years among people in the middle years of life (Murray & Lopez, 1996). We also now know that particular kinds of emotional distress are strongly related to physical health. For example, both depression and anxiety have been found to predict subsequent heart disease or a second heart attack (e.g., Barefoot et al., 2000; Jonas & Mussolino, 2000; Kubzansky & Kawachi, 2000). Finally, emotional distress is strongly related to increased health care utilization: Persons who are emotionally distressed are more likely to seek out not only mental health services but all types of health care (e.g., Schraedley, Gotlib, & Hayward, 1999). All these findings strongly underscore the importance of identifying approaches to psychotherapy that can alleviate or even prevent these difficulties.

Fourth, psychotherapy evaluation can provide insights into the validity of the theory or theories that underlie the therapy under investigation. As we have seen in chapters 12 through 14, therapeutic strategies and procedures are typically developed on the basis of a particular theory of psychopathology. For example, the practice of free association in psychoanalysis or psychoanalytic therapy is based on the assumption in psychoanalytic theory of psychic determinism. Similarly, client-centered therapists provide their clients unconditional positive regard because of Rogers's conceptualization of the importance of eliminating perceived conditions of worth. And perhaps the strongest examples of therapeutic procedures being derived directly from theory are seen in techniques developed by cognitive and behavior therapists. Virtually all procedures in behavior and cognitive therapies that utilize principles of reinforcement, punishment, or modeling are based strongly on theories of learning. Studies in which patients are randomly assigned to a condition in which they receive a specific treatment or in which they receive an alternative treatment or no treatment, provide direct *experimental* evidence of the effects of changing specific cognitive, emotional, or behavioral factors.

We believe it is clear, therefore, that evaluating the effectiveness of different forms of psychotherapy is a critically important endeavor, perhaps the most important task facing clinical psychology today. How have clinical psychologists approached this enterprise, and what have they discovered? In the remainder of this chapter we discuss methods that clinical psychologists use to evaluate the effectiveness of psychotherapy, and we examine the results of studies designed to examine the efficacy of different forms of treatment for specific emotional difficulties and disorders.

HOW DO WE EVALUATE PSYCHOTHERAPY?

How do we determine whether psychotherapy is effective? The requirements for making such a determination are really no different than the fundamental requirements of all scientific inquiry in psychology (we discussed the basic principles of research in clinical psychology in chapter 3). Strong studies of psychotherapy effectiveness require stringent experimental methods, including randomly assigning patients or participants to treatment groups, using appropriate control groups, selecting valid measures of psychological functioning, monitoring the conduct of psychotherapy, and conducting assessments both prior to and following treatment. Without stringent scientific inquiry it is impossible to know with any degree of certainty, first, whether patients have improved substantially from the beginning to the end of therapy and, second, whether the improvement was due to the treatment or to other factors that are independent of the therapy. We now describe three different methodological approaches to the study of psychotherapy effectiveness: **within-subject designs, between-subjects designs,** and meta-analysis, a procedure for statistically combining the results of many studies.

Within-Subject Designs

Given the history of clinical psychology, it may not be surprising to learn that early claims regarding the effectiveness of psychotherapy focused intensively on the therapeutic experiences of a single case. For example, we saw in chapters 4 and 12 that Freud wrote extensively about the psychoanalytic treatment of specific individuals, like Anna O. In fact, Breuer and Freud's (1895) *Studies on Hysteria* contained five detailed case descriptions of psychoanalysis. But Freud was not the only therapist to use case studies in an attempt to evaluate the effectiveness of treatment. In 1924, Mary Cover Jones, one of John Watson's students, published a case study of the behavioral treatment of "Peter," a young boy who was treated by counterconditioning to reduce his fear of rabbits. And more recently, Enrico Jones and his colleagues (e.g., Jones & Windholz, 1990; Jones, Ghannam, Nigg, & Dyer, 1993) have described a single-case method

for more formally assessing psychoanalytic psychotherapy.

Even with the most detailed case description of therapy, however, it is impossible to determine scientifically whether the therapy per se was responsible for the client's changes. It may be, for example, that the client got a more satisfying job or entered into a more fulfilling personal relationship; indeed, sometimes feelings of depression or anxiety simply dissipate with the passage of time. Depression, in particular, is a time-limited disorder, and many depressed individuals will improve over the course of a few months even without receiving therapy (Hankin & Locke, 1983). Thus, case studies cannot be used to evaluate the effectiveness of psychotherapy.

To address some of these limitations but continue to focus on the individual patient, researchers and clinicians turned to **single-case experimental designs.** This methodology was developed by behavior therapy researchers (e.g., Barlow & Hersen, 1973; Leitenberg, 1973) but has been applied to other types of therapy as well (e.g., Jones et al., 1993; Warrington & Leff, 2000). In single-case experiments, the individual is exposed systematically to different conditions, and changes in the patient's functioning are assessed as these conditions are changed (Kazdin, 1998). Two of the most frequently used single-case experimental designs are the **A-B-A-B design** and the **multiple baseline design.** In the A-B-A-B design, an outcome of interest (e.g., a child's noncompliant or aggressive behavior; an adolescent's bulimic behavior) is assessed continuously during a baseline condition (the A phase), in which no treatment is in effect, followed by a condition in which treatment is implemented (the B phase). The A and B phases are then repeated to complete the A-B-A-B design. That is, treatment is withdrawn in the second A phase and then reintroduced in the second B phase. The effectiveness of therapy is demonstrated in this design if the outcome level varies systematically with the introduction and withdrawal of the treatment. Thus, if treatment is effective *and* is responsible for improvement in the patient, the patient's behavior would be expected to improve when treatment is first introduced (i.e., from the first A to the first B), to return to initial levels when treatment is withdrawn (the second A phase), and finally, to improve with the reintroduction of treatment (the second B phase). As you can see clearly in figure 15.1, this is exactly the pattern of results reported by Friman and Vollmer (1995), who demonstrated the effectiveness of a urine-sensitive alarm to treat nighttime enuresis (bed wetting, which is a *DSM-IV* diagnosis) in a 15-year-old girl.

Although in the A-B-A-B design the reversal or withdrawal of treatment is necessary to demonstrate that the treatment is responsible for the patient's change, one of the drawbacks of this design is that outside the research setting it is not clinically desirable to withdraw treatment or to cause deterioration in the patient's functioning. Indeed, with some approaches to treatment, withdrawal is simply not possible. For example, it is difficult to imagine reversing a patient's insight

into his or her difficulties. To address this issue, clinical psychologists often use a second type of single-case experimental design, the multiple baseline design, which has the advantage of not requiring a withdrawal or reversal of treatment to demonstrate effectiveness (Kazdin, 1998). In a typical multiple baseline design, two or more treatment components targeting different outcomes or behaviors in the same individual are begun at different times. Data are collected continuously on all behaviors throughout treatment. When an intervention is begun, it is applied to only one of the behaviors and not to the others. If the intervention is specific, only the behaviors to which it is applied should change when that treatment is begun. For example, Chorpita, Vitali, and Barlow (1997) used a multiple baseline design to examine the effectiveness of an exposure-based treatment for a choking phobia in a 13-year-old girl. These authors conducted 14 sessions of exposure therapy to different foods and assessed the girl's anxiety regarding swallowing food, her rate of eating and size of the bites of food she ate, and the variety of food she ate. The

FIGURE 15.1

Results of an A-B-A-B behavioral treatment for nocturnal enuresis using a urine sensitive alarm

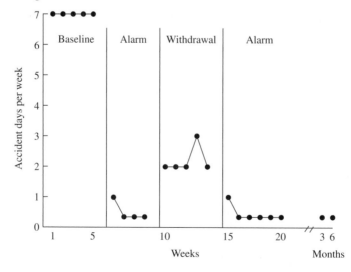

exposure was presented sequentially to different foods. Chorpita et al. found that the girl improved on all these measures from pretreatment to posttreatment. More important, however, the girl's improvement with respect to each specific food or food group was related specifically to the exposure treatment implemented for that particular food, documenting the specificity of the exposure treatment.

Although these A-B-A-B and multiple baseline designs clearly represent an improvement over case studies, they do have significant limitations. For example, because the treatment is typically applied only to a single case, it is not clear whether the results of the treatment will generalize to other clients. Furthermore, it is extremely rare in these studies for the data to be analyzed statistically. Most commonly, investigators simply present graphs of the results, and if the graphs are visually striking, the results are discussed as if they are statistically significant. Therefore, the degree of confidence that we can have in the results is not supported by traditional statistical standards.

In part because of these limitations, researchers have extended within-subject designs to the study of groups rather than individual subjects. Most commonly, the functioning of a group of patients is assessed once before they begin treatment and again after they complete therapy. This simple design has the advantages over the single-case experimental design of including data from several participants rather than from just a single individual, and of ensuring that every participant has essentially the same therapy experience. Nevertheless, it is still possible that factors other than the treatment were responsible for any improvement over the course of therapy. For example, we noted earlier that many depressed individuals will recover within a few months, even without receiving treatment. Therefore, patients in a within-subject study of the effectiveness of therapy for depression may have improved in the time from pretreatment to posttreatment anyway, even if they had not been treated.

Between-Subjects Designs

A more powerful design for determining whether the treatment is actually responsible for the patients' improvement involves the use of control groups or control conditions. A critical function of control groups is to ensure that the improvements that are exhibited by patients who receive a particular treatment are in fact due to the treatment and not to other factors or changes that may have occurred in the patients' lives or, more simply, to the passage of time.

Nonrandomized Control Group Studies   Perhaps the simplest version of the between-groups design is the **nonrandomized control group study,** in which two "naturally occurring" groups are compared. Recall Eysenck's (1952) study of "neurotic," or anxious, individuals described in chapter 2: One group had sought and received psychotherapy, while the other group was treated "by their own physicians with sedative, tonics, suggestion, and reassurance" (p. 320). Eysenck found that 72 percent of the individuals who did not receive psychotherapy recovered from their problems, compared with only 54 percent of those who received psychotherapy. Based on these data, Eysenck concluded that psychotherapy was not effective in the treatment of emotional difficulties.

The major problem with this nonrandomized design is that we have no way of knowing whether the two groups differed in any way before one group began receiving therapy. People who seek and receive psychotherapy often differ systematically from people who seek other forms of treatment, not only with respect to such demographic variables as social class and education level, but more important, in the severity of their dysfunction. In fact, individuals who seek or receive psychological treatment are typically more severely impaired or demoralized than are people who do not (Wells, Manning, Duan, & Newhouse, 1986; Young, Klap, Sherbourne, & Wells, 2001). Given this situation, it is possible that the patients who received treatment and were worse off at the end of Eysenck's study were also worse off at the beginning.

There are also other reasons why one group might show greater improvement at the end of treatment. One common explanation, for example, is that greater improvement in one group might have nothing to do with the effects of therapy, but rather might be a statistical artifact known as "regression to the mean." That is, individuals who obtain scores on a measure of psychological problems that are furthest away from the group mean at the beginning of treatment (e.g., those who have the highest depression scores, or the lowest adaptive functioning scores) are very likely to score closer to the mean on that measure at a second assessment, even in the absence of any intervention. Thus, subjects with the highest scores on a measure of depression at the beginning of treatment would be expected to have lower scores at the end of treatment because of regression to the mean, even if treatment is ineffective.

Randomized Clinical Trials   Because of the problems with nonrandomized control group studies, true experiments represent a stronger method in which participants are *randomly assigned* to different conditions, or treatments. This design is referred to as a **randomized clinical trial** (RCT; Haaga & Stiles, 2000). Rather than having the participants choose their treatment, the investigator randomly assigns some of the participants to one condition (e.g., receiving a particular treatment) and other participants to a different condition (e.g., receiving a different treatment or being put on a waiting list to receive the treatment). Although random assignment of participants does not guarantee that the groups will be equivalent on every variable prior to the beginning of therapy, it is the best procedure for

maximizing the likelihood that the groups will not differ systematically. The assumption underlying random assignment of subjects to treatment groups is that any prior differences that might affect the outcomes will be more or less evenly distributed across the groups. And the larger the sample size, the more likely it is that random assignment will make the groups equivalent.

Three common variations of a between-subjects design with random assignment differ in terms of the control group to which the treatment group (the experimental group) is compared: a no-treatment control group, a wait-list control group, and a placebo control group. In the no-treatment control group design, one group receives the treatment and one group does not. A study using this design would address the question of whether a particular therapy is more effective than no treatment at all. If the therapy is effective, patients in the experimental group should demonstrate significantly greater improvement from pretreatment to posttreatment than do patients in the control group.

The major issue with this design involves the ethics of deliberately withholding treatment from participants in a no-treatment control group. Most investigators deal with this issue by placing these participants on a waiting list for treatment, known as a wait-list control condition. Participants in this condition do not receive treatment until after participants in the experimental group have been treated (typically 2 to 4 months). Those patients who receive treatment first are compared with those on the waiting list, which provides a comparison of treatment and no treatment that is limited to the waiting list period. Because many treatment clinics normally have a waiting list of two to three months before a patient can begin therapy, a wait-list control condition helps resolve the ethical dilemma.

At the same time, however, this condition does have constraints. For example, patients will not wait indefinitely to receive treatment, so this condition is far more appropriate for briefer therapies, such as cognitive-behavior therapies, than it is for more lengthy treatments, such as psycho-analysis or other long-term psychodynamic therapy. Furthermore, even over short periods of time patients in a wait-list control group may seek treatment from another therapist or from other sources such as friends or clergy. Indeed, it is reasonable to expect that participants who remain on the waiting list for the full period may be less disturbed than participants who drop out of the study, which raises an additional problem in interpreting the results of the experiment.

To deal with these problems, some investigators use a **placebo** condition instead. Placebo conditions are used routinely in treatment studies in medicine. In that context, a placebo is generally an inert substance that has no direct effect on the outcome in question. Studies examining the effects of medications on outcomes as diverse as cancer and the common cold almost universally include a placebo condition (Shapiro & Morris, 1978). To the extent that the treated group demonstrates greater improvement than the placebo group, the medication under study is effective. Any improvement in the placebo condition is believed to be a result of such indirect factors as the patients' motivation to improve, attention paid to them from the therapist, and their belief in the treatment or in the therapist. However, it is noteworthy that in medical research, both patients and health professionals who administer the treatments are typically not informed (i.e., they are kept "blind") as to who is receiving the active medication and who is receiving the placebo. This arrangement is referred to as a "double blind" design, because both the patient and the person providing the treatment are blind to the conditions.

As you might imagine, it is more difficult to develop a placebo condition in a study of psychotherapy than it is in a study of the effectiveness of medication. Most placebo conditions in psychotherapy research have patients meet with a therapist to receive nonspecific support, making sure that the "active ingredients" of the therapy under scrutiny (e.g., focusing on changing the patient's cognitions; conveying deep empathic understanding of the patient's experience; exposing the patient to feared stimuli) are absent in the placebo condition. The more closely the placebo condition matches the treatment condition in all other respects (e.g., length and number of sessions, meeting with a therapist), the more likely it is that differences between the experimental and control groups are due to the specific characteristics of the therapy being evaluated. Interestingly, Klein (1998) has made an elegant argument that a pill-placebo may be the optimal placebo in both psychotherapy and pharmacotherapy, or medication, studies.

Comparing Two or More Treatments A more complex version of a between-subjects design is typified by studies that compare the effectiveness of two or more different treatments or treatment conditions. In these studies, different treatments are compared not only with a control condition, but with each other as well. For example, Bouvard, Mollard, Guerin, and Cottraux (1997) compared the effectiveness of two therapy conditions for the treatment for Panic Disorder. Forty-eight patients who were diagnosed with panic disorder were randomly assigned to receive cognitive-behavioral therapy (CBT) for panic disorder combined with medication (buspirone) or CBT combined with a pill placebo. At the end of treatment, Bouvard et al. found that patients who received CBT plus buspirone showed greater improvement in their panic symptoms than did patients who received CBT plus placebo (see also Barlow, Gorman, Shear, & Woods, 2000). Interestingly, however, both groups continued to improve following termination of treatment, so that at a one-year follow-up, the two groups no longer differed. Bouvard et al. suggested that adding medication to CBT for the treatment of panic accelerates improvement only in the short term. Using this design, in which two or more active treatments are compared with each other, allows the investigator to attribute changes in the patients' symptoms to a particular intervention as opposed to the nonspecific effects of simply being in treatment. In fact, Davidson and Parker (2000) recently examined the findings of 34 studies of EMDR and concluded that while EMDR is as effective as other exposure techniques in the treatment of anxiety, there is little evidence that eye movements are a necessary component of the treatment.

Comparing the Components of Treatments
Once researchers have demonstrated that a particular intervention is effective in the treatment of a specific disorder, it becomes important to determine how that intervention might be offered most effectively and efficiently. In particular, most cognitive and behavioral therapies are actually composed of several components, all of which are typically combined in delivering the therapy to the patient. For example, we saw in chapter 14 that systematic desensitization involves three steps: training in relaxation, constructing an anxiety stimulus hierarchy, and learning to pair the stimuli with relaxation. Similarly, cognitive therapy often involves identifying dysfunctional beliefs or cognitions and then implementing various procedures designed to alter these patterns of thinking. Although these treatments have been demonstrated to be effective as a "package," it is not clear that each component is necessary for the effectiveness of the treatment. Indeed, it is possible that the treatments could be shortened considerably without a loss of effectiveness. This issue is the primary question that investigators who are interested in analyzing components of treatment try to answer.

An excellent example of a **components analysis** is a study conducted by Agras, Schneider, Arnow, Raeburn, and Telch (1989), who examined the additive effects of the major components of cognitive-behavior therapy for bulimia. Agras et al. randomly assigned 77 female participants who met diagnostic criteria for bulimia nervosa to one of four groups: wait-list control, self-monitoring of caloric intake and purging behaviors, cognitive-behavioral therapy (CBT), and CBT plus response prevention of

vomiting. Participants were assessed with respect to purging, dietary intake, and psychological symptoms before, during, and after the 4-month treatment and again at a 6-month follow-up. As expected, participants in all three of the active treatment conditions, particularly the CBT condition, showed significant improvement; participants in the wait-list control condition did not. In addition, however, there were two other important findings from this study. First, adding behavior-change elements to simple self-monitoring led to greater improvement compared with self-monitoring alone. Second, and perhaps more important, not only did adding response prevention of vomiting to the treatment protocol not lead to greater improvement than CBT administered without this component, but further, participants who received response prevention did worse than those who received CBT alone. As Agras et al. state, response prevention seems to have a "deleterious effect" in the treatment of bulimia nervosa (pp. 215).

These findings clearly highlight the utility of component analysis studies. Another example of a component analysis is a study conducted by Feske and Goldstein (1997). These investigators drew on a growing but controversial literature suggesting that symptoms of panic can be reduced in patients diagnosed with panic disorder if they are instructed to move their eyes rapidly back and forth while they think about the trauma. This treatment, known as eye movement desensitization and reprocessing (EMDR), was developed by psychologist Francine Shapiro (1995) and has been tested in a large number of studies. Feske and Goldstein designed a study to examine whether eye movements are a necessary component of this treatment. They randomly assigned 43 patients diagnosed with Panic Disorder to (a) 6 sessions of EMDR, (b) the same treatment without the eye movements, or (c) a wait-list control group. At the end of treatment, EMDR was found to be more effective in alleviating panic and panic-related symptoms than was the waiting-list procedure. And compared with the same treatment without the eye movements,

EMDR also led to greater improvement on 2 of 5 primary outcome measures. At a 3-month follow-up assessment, however, there were no longer any advantages of EMDR over the condition without eye movements, thereby raising questions about the usefulness of the eye movement component in EMDR treatment for Panic Disorder.

These studies represent excellent examples of how the between-groups design with random assignment of participants can be used to examine the effectiveness of different treatments or of different components of the same treatment. This basic design can be made more complex by adding additional treatment conditions, by adding additional patient groups, and even by conducting the study in multiple sites or settings. For example, in a large-scale study of the effectiveness of psychotherapy in the treatment of depression, Elkin et al. (Elkin, Parloff, Hadley, & Autry, 1985; Elkin et al., 1989; Shea, Elkin, & Sotsky, 1999) compared four different treatment conditions: cognitive-behavioral therapy, interpersonal therapy, clinical management with antidepressant medication, and clinical management plus drug placebo. Moreover, this study was conducted in three different sites, with 28 therapists and 250 patients. And in several analyses of the results of this study, patients were subcategorized on the basis of their initial levels of severity of depressive symptoms. We will discuss the results of this study in the section titled "How Effective Is Psychotherapy?" but for now it is important to recognize that the between-subjects design in psychotherapy research has a wide range of complexity.

Aggregating Findings Across Multiple Studies: Meta-Analysis

In the approaches to psychotherapy evaluation that we have already discussed, each investigator or team of investigators typically conducts a single study and draws conclusions based on the obtained results. Any single study, however, is almost certain to have one or more methodological limitations, such as small sample size and low statistical power, limited outcome measures, or limited control or comparison groups. Even review articles, in which researchers compare the results of several studies in a single article, typically combine results from stronger and weaker studies and from studies with larger and smaller samples; in many cases, the author of the review article gives roughly equal weighting to the results of each study. As you can imagine, there is considerable room for the author's interpretation and qualitative judgment in writing review articles. As a striking example of this drawback, Munsinger (1975) and Kamin (1978) both wrote review articles examining the effects of the environment on children's intelligence, and reached opposite conclusions.

To circumvent some of these limitations, investigators increasingly have used the procedure of **meta-analysis** to examine the effects of psychotherapy outcome studies. Meta-analyses are, in essence, studies of studies. Meta-analysis is a procedure that statistically pools, or combines, the results of existing studies on a particular topic. Researchers conducting a meta-analysis begin by searching for all published (and even unpublished) empirical studies that have examined the question in which they are interested. For example, a researcher planning to conduct a meta-analysis on the effectiveness of cognitive-behavior therapy in the treatment of bulimia nervosa would search for and collect all the studies he or she could locate that have included a condition in which cognitive-behavior therapy was administered to treat bulimia. Then, for each of the studies, an **effect size** is calculated based on the standard deviations of scores on measures that were included in each study. The effect size expresses the difference between the means of the treated group and the comparison group in terms of the standard deviation of the groups on the dependent measure. For example, if the mean of the treated group was $1\frac{1}{2}$ standard deviations above the mean of the comparison group, the effect size would be 1.5. The effect size, therefore, is used to estimate how much difference receipt of treatment makes for the average participant. Importantly, in a meta-analysis the effect size of each separate study is weighted by the sample size of the study. This procedure ensures that studies with larger samples, and therefore with more reliability and statistical power, contribute proportionally more to the overall conclusions than do studies with smaller samples.

Another advantage of meta-analysis is that the studies included in a single meta-analysis are not required to have used the same measure to assess change. This advantage is an especially important consideration given Lambert and Hill's (1994) observation that 1,430 different measures were used to assess therapy outcome in studies published between 1983 and 1988. Interestingly, 840 of these different measures were used in only one study! The ability to include studies with different outcome measures provides the investigator with a larger number of studies in the meta-analysis, again increasing both the power of the meta-analysis and the reliability of the results. Once the investigator has calculated the effect size for each study, all the effect sizes can be combined to yield a single overall effect size for the meta-analysis. In our bulimia research example, this overall effect size would be used to determine from a large sample of studies whether cognitive-behavior therapy has a significant effect on bulimia nervosa. The effect size would allow the investigator to assess statistically how much better off (if at all) the average bulimia patient who received cognitive-behavior therapy is compared to the average untreated control patient. And to put closure on this example, the results of meta-analyses do indicate that psychotherapy is more effective than medication in the treatment of bulimia (Laessle, Zoettl, & Pirke, 1987; Whittal, Agras, & Gould, 1999) and, more specifically, that cognitive-behavior therapy is superior to other types of psychotherapy in treating this disorder (Whitbread & McGown, 1994).

HOW EFFECTIVE IS PSYCHOTHERAPY?

Now that we have reviewed the most important reasons for evaluating psychotherapy and the major research designs used in this endeavor, we can turn to a discussion of the results of studies examining the effectiveness of psychotherapy. We begin this presentation with a brief historical overview of psychotherapy research and then discuss the current status of research that examines the effectiveness of psychotherapy.

Early Research Efforts

Although psychotherapy has existed now as a formal practice for over 100 years, it is only in the last 50 years that attention was paid to whether psychotherapy worked, that is, to whether this enterprise actually was beneficial to patients. One of the first people to try to examine whether psychotherapy is effective and, further, what components or mechanisms contributed to its effectiveness, was Carl Rogers. In the 1940s, Rogers began recording and analyzing the tapes and transcripts of therapy sessions. He concluded on the basis of his analyses of these therapy sessions that the therapist's characteristics of congruence and empathy and the therapist's expression of unconditional positive regard for the client all contributed to the success of client-centered therapy. Although, as we saw in chapter 13, more recent analyses have tempered these conclusions, Rogers's work was important nevertheless both for his insistence on subjecting his treatment to scientific scrutiny and for his focus on the *process* of therapy. In fact, Rogers's process orientation in many ways provides the basis for our understanding of why particular treatments may be effective for specific problems and why several different therapies might be indistinguishable in terms of their effectiveness.

The event in the area of psychotherapy evaluation that had the most powerful impact on psychotherapy research, and arguably on the field of clinical psychology in general, occurred in 1952. We noted in chapter 2 that **Hans Eysenck,** a British psychologist, published a landmark study examining the efficacy of psychotherapy. Eysenck statistically examined outcome data from over 7,000 patients who were experiencing various forms of psychopathology. Most of the patients who received psychotherapy were treated with psychoanalysis or "eclectic" therapy. As a comparison group, Eysenck used data from neurotic patients who did not receive formal psychotherapy; these patients were either treated by general practitioners or were discharged from New York state hospitals. Based on these data, Eysenck concluded that the rate of recovery from psychopathology for patients who did not receive psychotherapy was no worse than the improvement rate for patients who did receive psychotherapy. In fact, the data Eysenck presented indicated that improvement rates were higher for patients who received no psychotherapy than for patients who received psychoanalysis or some form of eclectic psychotherapy: Whereas just over half the treated patients seemed to improve, almost three-quarters of the untreated patients showed improvement.

Eysenck's data and his conclusion that there was no evidence that therapy worked had an immediate and profound impact on clinical psychologists around the world. After all, most clinical psychologists spent the majority of their time practicing psychotherapy, and now Eysenck was telling them not only that what they were doing was not effective but that their patients might actually be worse off for being treated. As you might expect, there was a strong reaction from clinical psychologists to Eysenck's report, which set off a flurry of investigations. In fact, there is now more research examining the effectiveness of psychotherapy than there is for any medical treatment (Messer, 1994). Although several therapists and researchers agreed with Eysenck's conclusions, the vast majority disagreed vehemently. Indeed, many clinical psychologists conducted their own reviews of the psychotherapy outcome literature and, interestingly, reached more optimistic conclusions than Eysenck did. For example, Allen Bergin (1971), a noted psychotherapy researcher, acknowledged that while there may be "deterioration effects" of psychotherapy for a small proportion of patients (i.e., a small number of patients get worse), the majority of individuals benefit from psychotherapy. In fact, Meltzoff and Kornriech (1970) reported that over 80 percent of psychotherapy outcome studies yield positive results.

Contemporary Research

General Meta-Analyses Reviews conducted since Eysenck's original study have tended to support the position that psychotherapy generally produces more positive outcomes for patients than does receiving no treatment (e.g., Kazdin & Wilson, 1978; Lambert & Bergin, 1994; but also see Dawes, 1996, for a less positive perspective). Indeed, the results of several large-scale analyses of psychotherapy outcome demonstrate that psychotherapy is effective in reducing emotional distress. For example, in the first widely cited meta-analysis of psychotherapy outcome, Smith, Glass, and Miller (1980) located over 475 studies in which some type of psychotherapy was compared with some type of control group. Smith et al. found an average effect size for psychotherapy of 0.85. A score that is .85 standard deviations above the mean falls at the 80th percentile of a distribution, which means that the average treated person is better off at the end of therapy than 80 percent of the untreated people (see figure 15.2).

To give you some perspective on this effect size of 0.85, it may be helpful to know the magnitude of some effect sizes from other areas of research. The effect size for nine months of instruction in reading in elementary school is 0.65 and for computer-based instruction in mathematics, 0.40 (Smith et al., 1980); the effect size for cigarettes increasing risk for lung cancer is 0.60

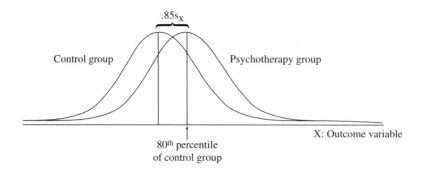

FIGURE 15.2
The results of a meta-analysis demonstrating that receiving psychotherapy is more effective than not receiving psychotherapy.

(American Psychiatric Association Commission on Psychotherapies, 1982); and the effect size for aspirin preventing heart attacks is 0.034 (Steering Committee of the Physicians Health Study Research Group, 1989). Indeed, even though this last effect size of 0.034 appears to be very small, it was considered to be so substantial that the study was discontinued because investigators felt that it would now be unethical to withhold aspirin from the control participants (Rosenthal, 1991). Seen against this backdrop, therefore, the 0.85 effect size for psychotherapy effectiveness is considerable.

Several meta-analyses have been conducted since Smith et al. (1980) reported their seminal findings (see Lambert & Bergin, 1994). Although the effect sizes vary somewhat from one study to another, Smith et al.'s general conclusion remains intact: Receiving psychotherapy is significantly more beneficial than not receiving treatment. In fact, the results of several meta-analyses indicate further that receiving an active psychotherapy is also more effective than receiving a placebo treatment for adults and children (e.g., Prout & Prout, 1998; Shadish, Navarro, Matt, & Phillips, 2000; Svartberg & Stiles, 1991; Weisz, Weiss, Han, & Granger, 1995). Importantly, these meta-analyses also indicate that the beneficial effects of therapy are maintained over

a period of 6 to 18 months (e.g., Andrews & Harvey, 1981; Taylor, 1996). You undoubtedly will have noticed that this conclusion regarding the effectiveness of psychotherapy is strongly at odds with Eysenck's (1952) proclamation that psychotherapy is ineffective. This difference could be attributable to several factors, including the methodological limitations of Eysenck's use of naturally occurring samples rather than randomized clinical trials, changes in the measures used to assess the outcomes of therapy, and perhaps most importantly, changes in the types of psychotherapy that have been examined.

Comparisons of Effectiveness of Different Psychotherapies   It is reasonably clear from these meta-analyses, therefore, that psychotherapy is more effective than both placebo and waitlist controls. What was not as clear early on, however, was whether some forms of psychotherapy were more effective than other approaches. In 1967, **Gordon Paul** wrote that the important question is not whether psychotherapy works but rather what treatment, by whom, is most effective for people with what specific problems under which set of circumstances. In essence, Paul believed that to ask the question, "Is psychotherapy effective?" is analogous to asking whether education is effective. Certainly, in general, education is "better" than no education. But just as there are better and worse teachers, better and worse students, and better and worse educational methods, Paul believed that there were ranges of therapists, patients, emotional difficulties, and therapeutic approaches. In posing the question that he did, Paul was raising the possibility that particular therapeutic approaches might be more effective for patients with specific problems.

There were a number of early attempts to address aspects of Paul's question, most of which compared the relative effectiveness of different types of therapies. For example, in one of the largest such studies, Sloan, Staples, Cristol, Yorkston, and Whipple (1975) randomly assigned 90 predominantly "neurotic" patients to receive behavior therapy, short-term psychoanalytically oriented therapy, or to a minimal-treatment wait-list control condition. Although all the patients in the study improved over the 4-month study period, patients in the two treatment conditions improved more than did patients in the wait-list condition. Importantly, there were virtually no differences in outcome between patients who received behavior therapy and patients who received psychoanalytically oriented therapy.

This pattern of findings was highlighted by Luborsky, Singer, and Luborsky (1975) in a highly influential review of this body of research. Luborsky et al. concluded that receiving most forms of psychotherapy is more beneficial than receiving no treatment. Equally important, however, Luborsky et al. also concluded that there are very few differences among various types of therapies with respect to their effectiveness. This lack of differential efficacy among therapeutic approaches led Luborsky et al. to invoke the **dodo bird verdict,** taken from Lewis Carroll's book *Alice's Adventures in Wonderland*, in which the dodo bird presides over a race and, after it is over, proclaims that "Everyone has won and all must have prizes."

It is important to recognize two limitations to Luborsky et al.'s (1975) "all are equal" conclu-

sion about psychotherapies. First, this conclusion applies only to therapies that have been subjected to empirical scrutiny. More than 400 different types of psychotherapy have been identified, and only a small number of these have been examined empirically. Second, the "all are equal" proclamation is based on a subjective judgment about the relative efficacy of therapies. That is, Luborsky et al. looked at the results of a collection of individual studies and tried to discern a pattern in the findings. This process is fraught with potential biases and errors in judgment because of the subjective task of trying to integrate findings from studies with different sample sizes and measures. As you might anticipate, more recent attempts to examine the differential effectiveness of psychotherapies have used meta-analysis to yield a more objective verdict.

Lambert and Bergin (1994) reviewed the results of a large number of meta-analyses of the effectiveness of psychotherapy. Many different types of psychotherapies were examined in these meta-analyses, including cognitive therapy, cognitive-behavior therapy, behavior therapy, short-term dynamic psychotherapy, marital and family therapy, and rational-emotive therapy. Considered collectively, these meta-analytic reviews represent summary data for thousands of patients treated by hundreds of therapists from many different therapeutic orientations. Consistent with one of Luborsky et al.'s (1975) conclusions, the results of these meta-analyses indicate quite clearly that patients who receive psychotherapy are better off than patients who do not receive therapy. Importantly, however, these meta-analyses are not consistent with Luborsky et al.'s conclusion that all psychotherapies are equally effective. In fact, the majority of the meta-analyses demonstrate a greater effect size for cognitive and behavioral therapies than for more traditional verbal or relationship-oriented therapies, both with adults (Lambert & Bergin) and with children (Weisz et al., 1995).

The meta-analyses reviewed by Lambert and Bergin (1994) address the question of whether, in general, some therapies are more effective than other therapies. The conclusion of these meta-analyses concerning the superiority of cognitive and behavioral therapies is based largely on the results of studies that assessed the outcome of different types of psychotherapies without particular regard to the type or diagnosis of patients who received the treatment. Remember, however, that an important component of Paul's (1967) statement involved the question of whether we can effectively "match" the type of therapy offered to a patient with the type of problem or disorder. That is, are certain therapies more effective than others in the treatment of specific disorders?

The Relative Effectiveness of Different Therapies for Different Disorders   There are now sizable (and growing) empirical literatures assessing the effectiveness of different types of psychotherapy in the treatment of specific problems. Interestingly, the pattern of findings of these studies is generally consistent with the findings of the broader meta-analyses that we have described. The two largest bodies of investigations are those examining the effectiveness of different therapies for depression and anxiety. This finding should not be surprising, perhaps, in light of the fact that depression and anxiety have been found in epidemiological studies to have the highest prevalence rates of all emotional disorders. Moreover, given the extraordinary societal costs of depression and anxiety (e.g., Judd, Paulus, Wells, & Rapaport, 1996; Murray & Lopez, 1996; Wells, Golding, & Burnam, 1989), it is crucial that we identify the most effective therapies to treat and ultimately prevent these debilitating disorders.

A large number of studies have now been conducted that compare the relative effectiveness of different psychotherapies for depression. The largest and most rigorous of these investigations is the **National Institute of Mental Health Collaborative Depression Research Project**

(Elkin, 1994; Elkin et al., 1985, 1989; Shea et al., 1999). This study was conducted with 250 depressed patients across three different sites (Pittsburgh, Oklahoma City, and Washington, DC). The investigators randomly assigned patients to one of four treatment conditions: Beck's cognitive-behavioral therapy (CBT; see chapter 14); Weissman and Klerman's interpersonal psychotherapy (IPT; see chapter 12); imiprimine (an antidepressant medication) plus clinical management (IMI-CM); and drug placebo plus clinical management (PLA-CM). Therapists received extensive training in CBT or IPT, and therapy sessions were monitored throughout treatment. Patients were seen for an average of 16 treatment sessions, and a wide range of measures of psychological and psychosocial functioning were administered before, during, and following treatment.

This investigation has resulted in a number of analyses and scientific reports, but here we will describe the major findings concerning the relative effectiveness of the study's treatments. At the termination of treatment, patients in all four groups, including the PLA-CM group, had improved from their pretreatment levels of depression. Perhaps more important, there were few significant differences in improvement and functioning among patients in the three active treatment groups (CBT, IPT, and IMI-CM). In some analyses, IPT and IMI-CM were found to be significantly more effective than the placebo condition, particularly for those depressed patients who were the most severely impaired at the beginning of treatment. As Steve Hollon, a clinical psychologist at Vanderbilt University and an expert in cognitive-behavior therapy, has eloquently argued, however, this study may be alone in finding that medication is more effective than CBT in the treatment of severe depression (Hollon, Haman, & Brown, in press). In general, the data from this project indicate similar effectiveness of CBT and IPT in the treatment of depression, even at an 18-month follow-up assessment.

Steven D. Hollon, Ph.D., a clinical psychologist at Vanderbilt University, has been active in the development and evaluation of cognitive therapy as an empirically supported treatment for depression. Dr. Hollon is also a leading figure in the integration of cognitive and biological factors in affective disorders. *(Photo courtesy of Steve Hollon.)*

A similar but smaller-scale study is the Second Sheffield Psychotherapy Project, conducted by Shapiro and his colleagues in England (e.g., J. P. Shapiro, Leifer, Martone, & Kassem, 1990; Startup & Shapiro, 1993). In this investigation cognitive-behavior therapy was compared with psychodynamic interpersonal therapy in the treatment of depression. One hundred and seventeen mildly, moderately, and severely depressed patients were randomly assigned to receive either 8 or 16 weekly sessions of one of these two therapies. Across all three levels of depression, Shapiro et al. found that the cognitive-behavioral treatment led to greater improvement in symptoms than did psychodynamic interpersonal therapy. Interestingly, Shapiro et al. also found that the more severely depressed patients derived greater benefit from the longer duration of treatment than did the mildly or moderately depressed patients, suggesting that patients should be offered different amounts of treatment according to the severity of their depression.

Considered together, the pattern of findings reported in these two large investigations indicates that cognitive-behavior therapy and interpersonally oriented therapy are both effective in the treatment of depression, with cognitive-behavior therapy enjoying a slight advantage in effectiveness. The findings of recent meta-analyses of psychotherapy for depression are consistent with this position. For example, Dobson (1989); Robinson, Berman, and Niemeyer (1990); and Gloaguen, Cottraux, Cucherat, and Blackburn (1998) demonstrated that cognitive-behavior therapy is more effective than placebo, medication, and traditional verbal psychotherapies in the treatment of depression in adults, a result replicated by Reinecke, Ryan, and DuBois (1998) for the treatment of depressed children. DeRubeis, Gelfand, Tang, and Simons (1999) concluded that cognitive therapy for depression is at least as effective as antidepressant medication. Gloaguen et al. went further, stating that the results of their meta-analysis suggest that cognitive therapy is more effective than antidepressant medication in preventing relapse of depression. At this point, therefore, there is little doubt that structured cognitive-behavior therapy and, perhaps to a lesser extent, interpersonal therapy are effective in the treatment of depression.

A similar pattern of results has been reported for the treatment of anxiety disorders. As Lambert and Bergin (1994) note, across a large number of empirical studies and meta-analytic reviews and across a range of anxiety disorders such as agoraphobia, obsessive-compulsive disorder, and Panic Disorder, the clear conclusion is that psychotherapies are more effective than are wait-list and no-treatment control conditions. As was the case for depression meta-analyses, however, more recent anxiety disorder meta-analyses have compared the effectiveness of different forms of treatment for specific anxiety disorders. For example, Clum, Clum, and Surls (1993) and Gould, Otto, and Pollack (1995) conducted meta-analyses comparing the effectiveness of psychological and pharmacological treatments for Panic Disorder. In both reports, treatment was found to be more effective than no treatment or placebo. More specifically, however, cognitive-behavioral treatments that included an exposure component were more effective than medication and were the most successful in maintaining treatment gains over time.

Similar results have been obtained in meta-analyses examining treatment for social phobia (Feske & Chambless, 1995; Gould, Buckminster, Pollack, Otto, & Yap, 1997; Taylor, 1996) and obsessive-compulsive disorder (Abramowitz, 1996). For both social phobia and obsessive-compulsive disorder, the results of these analyses indicate that cognitive-behavioral treatments with exposure are more effective than other treatments, including medication. In addition, Abramowitz found that therapist-supervised exposure was more effective than self-controlled exposure and that the addition of complete response prevention to exposure therapy resulted in better outcome for obsessive-compulsive disorder.

Although depression and anxiety continue to be the largest literatures in the area, the use of meta-analysis to examine the effectiveness of psychotherapy has expanded to cover a wider range of psychopathology. For example, in an early report, Laessle et al. (1987) demonstrated that psychotherapy is more effective than medication in the treatment of bulimia. Subsequent investigations present a more refined version of this conclusion, demonstrating that cognitive-behavior therapy in particular is effective in treating bulimia (e.g., Ghaderi & Andersson, 1999; Lewandowski, Gebing, Anthony, & O'Brien,

1997). Meta-analyses have also documented the effectiveness of psychotherapy in general, and of behavioral self-control training more specifically, in reducing alcohol consumption among individuals being treated for alcohol use or dependence (e.g., Agosti, 1995; Walters, 2000).

Statistically Versus Clinically Significant Change The results of individual studies and meta-analyses are critical in telling us whether receiving psychotherapy leads to better outcomes than not receiving therapy or whether one therapy is more effective than another treatment in producing change. In making those determinations, we use statistics to assess whether a change in one group is significantly larger than a change in a comparison group. So, for example, in a study comparing the relative effectiveness of cognitive therapy and medication in the treatment of depression, patients would be randomly assigned to one of the two treatment groups (and perhaps to a no-treatment control group) and would complete measures of depression before and after treatment. Statistics would be used to determine whether the improvement from pretreatment to posttreatment is significantly greater in one group than in the others.

Although this information is certainly important, these comparisons do not tell us whether any of the changes from pretreatment to posttreatment, even if they are **statistically significant,** are **clinically significant.** That is, even if patients improve as a result of therapy, are they now indistinguishable from nonpatients, or are they still functioning at a level below that of others in their social networks? To continue with our example, if treated depressed patients move from a pretreatment score of 35 on the Beck Depression Inventory to a score of 15 following therapy, these scores indicate a statistically significant improvement in their depression level, but these patients are still at a higher level of depression than is the general population, whose mean score on the Beck Depression Inventory is about 8.

The treatment outcome studies that we have reviewed in this chapter and in chapters 12 through 14 clearly demonstrate that people with psychological problems do benefit from receiving psychotherapy. But do they benefit enough to put them in the "normal" range of psychological functioning following therapy? This question has not typically been examined in the psychotherapy literature, but we believe that it should be. Most research data, particularly from meta-analyses, gauge improvement or change in effect sizes or standard deviations. Sechrest, McKnight, and McKnight (1996) note the difficulty in interpreting such data:

> Suppose you were talking to a jeweler about buying a diamond ring, and the jeweler told you that for an extra $2,000 you could buy a diamond one-half standard deviation larger than the one you were looking at? Or suppose you were negotiating to purchase a health care plan and were told that for a 20% larger premium you could buy into an HMO that on a service quality scale scored seven points higher than its competitors. We think that in either case you would, at best, be uncertain as to what you should do; at worst, you would be completely mystified. (p. 1066)

Sechrest et al. (1996) suggest a number of different real-life measurements that should be included in studies of psychotherapy outcome. For example, do patients who received therapy for panic attacks or depression miss fewer days of work? Are patients treated for agoraphobia able to perform more of the ordinary chores of life, such as shopping for food and running errands? A slightly different approach to this problem was taken by Jacobson and Truax (1991), who actually defined clinically significant therapeutic change as a statistically significant change in a person's standing on a dependent variable that is also large enough to move the person to within two standard deviations of the mean for a normal population. Put more simply, Jacobson and Truax felt that clinically significant change should move a patient from dysfunction into the "normal" range of functioning. In fact, using this definition, a number of investigators have now demonstrated clinically significant changes as a result of psychotherapy in the treatment of depression (Nietzel, Russell, Hemmings, & Gretter, 1987; Ogles, Lambert, & Sawyer, 1995), anxiety (Nietzel & Trull, 1988), and marital difficulties (Snyder & Wills, 1989).

The Dose-Response Question   It is clear from our review that, for most disorders, receiving psychotherapy is definitely more beneficial than not receiving psychotherapy. Moreover, cognitive-behavior therapy has consistently been found to be more effective than other types of psychotherapy in the treatment of depression, anxiety, and eating disorders. Because we have established that psychotherapy can be an effective treatment for a number of psychological disorders, an intriguing next question is whether the amount of improvement exhibited by patients is related to the amount of therapy they receive. This question is known as a **dose-response question**—is the patient's response (i.e., improvement) proportional to the dose (i.e., length of treatment)? Shapiro et al. (1990) found that for severely depressed patients, clinical improvement seemed to be related to the duration of their treatment. Several investigators have examined whether this finding is a general rule, or principle, in psychotherapy. As you might imagine, given what you have learned in chapters 12 through 14, psychoanalytically oriented therapists would argue strongly that longer treatment is indeed related to greater improvement—after all, there must be a reason for patients to spend 3 to 4 years in intensive psychoanalysis. In contrast, cognitive and behaviorally oriented therapists would argue that most gains made in therapy would be made in 16 to 20 sessions, after which there would be diminishing returns.

Studies examining the dose-response relationship in psychotherapy have found that if therapy is going to be effective at all, it will usually be effective relatively quickly. Howard, Kopta, Krause, and Orlinsky (1986) conducted a meta-analysis on more than 2,400 patients in studies published over a 30-year period. They examined the relation between the number of therapy sessions and the proportion of patients who had improved at each session. A graph of their results is presented in figure 15.3. As you can see from this graph, approximately 40 percent of patients are improved by the 8th session of psychotherapy, and about 75 percent of patients are improved within 6 months of weekly psychotherapy. Importantly, Howard et al. also demonstrated that the amount and the rate of improvement in patients who are untreated are both significantly lower than is the case for the treated patients. Therefore, in addition to underscoring the benefits of receiving psychotherapy, the results of this meta-analysis indicate that most patients improve after a relatively brief course of psychotherapy and that the gains that are made beyond 6 months of therapy appear to be modest.

Howard, Moras, Brill, and Martinovich (1996) found a similar dose-response relationship in their analysis of data collected in a survey

FIGURE 15.3

A dose response curve demonstrating the rapid rate of improvement during the initial sessions of psychotherapy.

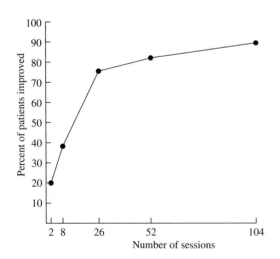

conducted by Consumer Reports (CR; Seligman, 1995). In that **Consumer Reports psychotherapy survey,** 186,000 randomly selected CR subscribers were sent a questionnaire asking about their experiences with mental health problems and therapy. Seven thousand people responded, about 4,100 of whom reported having sought professional help. Of these 4,100 people who consulted a mental health professional, 37 percent saw a psychologist, 22 percent saw a psychiatrist, 14 percent saw a social worker, and 9 percent saw a marriage counselor. Importantly, almost half these respondents said that they were in a "very poor" or "fairly poor" emotional state when they sought help.

The major results of this survey, reported in the November 1995 issue of *Consumer Reports*, were the following:

1. Fifty-four percent of individuals who reported receiving psychotherapy felt that it had helped "a great deal," and almost 90 percent reported that psychotherapy had helped them at least "somewhat."

2. There were few differences in consumer satisfaction among the various types of mental health professionals or types of psychotherapy; people who saw a marriage counselor were least likely to report having benefited from therapy.

3. People who were treated by a family physician did not benefit as much as people who were treated by a mental health professional.

4. Psychotherapy alone worked as well as combined psychotherapy and medication.

5. Respondents reported that the longer they stayed in therapy, the greater their improvement.

This last point warrants some attention, because it appears to contradict the results of Howard et al.'s (1986) earlier meta-analysis of the dose-response relationship in psychotherapy. This meta-analysis indicated that about 75 percent of patients are improved by 6 months of treatment, whereas the CR data seem to indicate that the more psychotherapy, the better. In fact, Howard et al. (1996) were able to conduct a dose-response analysis of the CR data, which paints a more refined picture than the CR summary indicates. Consistent with the results of their earlier meta-analysis Howard et al. (1996) found that improvement was rapid during the first 10 to 20 sessions of treatment and then, although it continues to increase somewhat with additional sessions, the slope, or speed of improvement, drops off rather sharply. The results of this analysis provide support, therefore, for proponents of brief forms of psychotherapy that are typically limited to fewer than 20 sessions, such as cognitive-behavior therapy, interpersonal psychotherapy, and brief dynamic psychotherapy.

The data from the CR survey paint a very positive picture of the benefits of psychotherapy—after all, almost 90 percent of the respondents reported that psychotherapy had helped them. But is this picture too rosy? Some critics suggest that it is. The CR report is a correlational study, in which scores on some questionnaire items are correlated with scores on other items. Not only are there inherent problems in the interpretation of correlational data, but also some psychologists think that the CR study is more a study of consumer satisfaction than of psychotherapy effectiveness. As Nathan, Stuart, and Dolan (2000) state,

> In our view, too many essential elements . . . including information on the nature and severity of patents' diagnoses; therapists' training and experience; form, length, and nature of outcomes of the treatment; and a reliable metric for reflecting therapeutic change—were lacking to justify considering the study one of effectiveness research. The absence of an untreated comparison group and concerns over possible sampling bias add to our conviction that this study ought not to be held up as an exemplar of (psychotherapy) effectiveness research. (p. 973)

Certainly, therefore, there are good reasons to be concerned about *figures* presented in the CR re-

port. Nevertheless, the *pattern* of findings from this project is consistent with previous data, that psychotherapy is effective in helping people deal more effectively with their problems. The growing number of meta-analyses is helping us identify the most effective treatments for specific disorders. One of the limitations of meta-analysis is that it does not take into consideration how many different investigators have conducted the studies that make up the meta-analysis. For example, it is possible that a single investigator conducted all the studies of exposure therapy for the treatment of agoraphobia that comprised the larger meta-analysis. Should this matter? Actually, yes. Robinson et al. (1990) presented data suggesting that the theoretical allegiance of the investigator might influence his or her findings. Spurred in part to address this issue, clinical psychologists have developed guidelines for the identification of what are referred to as **empirically supported treatments.**

Empirically Supported Treatments   We noted at the beginning of this chapter that one important reason for evaluating psychotherapy empirically is that literally several hundred different forms of psychotherapy are being offered to consumers and these therapies are certainly not equally effective. In an effort to distinguish those therapies that have received empirical support from those that have not, Division 12 (Clinical Psychology) of the APA recently formed a task force to identify therapies that had been shown to be effective in controlled research studies (Task Force on Promotion and Dissemination of Psychological Procedures, 1995). This task force was chaired by Dianne Chambless, a clinical psychologist at the University of North Carolina at Chapel Hill. The task force published the criteria it used to determine the effectiveness of therapies as well as a list of treatments that met these criteria (Chambless, 1996; Chambless et al., 1998; Chambless & Hollon, 1998). These criteria are presented in table 15.1, and the list of

Dianne Chambless, Ph.D., is a professor of clinical psychology at the University of North Carolina at Chapel Hill. Dr. Chambless is a leading researcher on the treatment of anxiety disorders. Dr. Chambless serves as the Chair of the American Psychological Association Task Force on Promotion and Dissemination of Psychological Procedures, establishing criteria for identifying empirically supported psychological treatments. *(Photo courtesy of Diana Chambless.)*

TABLE 15.1
Criteria for Empirically Supported Treatments

Well-Established Treatments

I. At least two good between-group design experiments demonstrating efficacy in one or more of the following ways:
    A. Superior (statistically significantly so) to pill or psychological placebo or to another treatment.
    B. Equivalent to an already established treatment in experiments with adequate sample sizes.

OR

II. A large series of single case design experiments ($n > 9$) demonstrating efficacy. These experiments must have:
    A. Used good experimental designs and
    B. Compared the intervention to another treatment as in IA.

FURTHER CRITERIA FOR BOTH I AND II:
III. Experiments must be conducted with treatment manuals.
IV. Characteristics of the client samples must be clearly specified.
V.   Effects must have been demonstrated by at least two different investigators or investigating teams.

Probably Efficacious Treatments

I. Two experiments showing the treatment is superior (statistically significantly so) to a waiting-list control group.

OR

II. One or more experiments meeting the Well-Established Treatment Criteria IA or IB, III, and IV, but not V.

OR

III. A small series of single case design experiments ($n \geq 3$) otherwise meeting Well-Established Treatment.

Note: Adapted from Chambless, Baker et al. (1998) (page 4)

treatments that met these criteria are presented in table 15.2.

As you can see from table 15.1, a therapy that is labeled a well-established treatment must have been demonstrated in at least two between-subjects studies from at least two different laboratories (or in at least nine single-case experiments) to be either superior to medication or psychological placebo or equivalent to an already established treatment. Therapies must also have accompanying treatment manuals available to investigators and practitioners. Although all

therapies are eligible for inclusion in the list, it is perhaps not surprising, given these criteria, that the majority of well-established treatments, called empirically validated treatments or empirically supported treatments, are cognitive and

TABLE 15.2
Well-Established
Empirically Validated Treatments

Anxiety and Stress:

Cognitive-behavior therapy for panic disorder
Cognitive-behavior therapy for generalized
  anxiety disorder
Exposure treatment for agoraphobia
Exposure/guided mastery for specific phobia
Exposure and response prevention for
  obsessive-compulsive disorder
Stress inoculation training for coping with
  stressors

Depression

Behavior therapy for depression
Cognitive therapy for depression
Interpersonal therapy for depression

Health Problems

Behavior therapy for headache
Cognitive-behavior therapy for bulimia
Multicomponent cognitive-behavior therapy for
  pain associated with rheumatic disease
Multicomponent cognitive-behavior therapy with
  relapse prevention for smoking cessation

Problems of Childhood

Behavior modification for enuresis
Parent training programs for children with
  oppositional behavior

Marital Discord

Behavioral marital therapy

Note: Adapted from Chambless, Baker et al. (1998)

behavioral therapies. In fact, cognitive and behavioral therapies are also identified when one examines empirically supported therapies for children and adolescents (Kazdin & Weisz, 1998), for health problems (Compas, Haaga, Keefe, Leitenberg, & Williams, 1998), and for marital difficulties (Baucom, Shoham, Mueser, Daiuto, & Stickle, 1998). As expected, the task force has also recommended that these empirically supported therapies be taught in clinical psychology graduate programs. (See box 15.1 for

a discussion of how we would apply empirically supported therapies to each of our four cases.)

Although many clinical researchers and practitioners applauded the process and the implementation of these criteria, there were a number of critical reactions to the publication of empirically supported treatments. Several writers argued that humanistic and psychodynamic therapies are at a disadvantage in this rating system because they are open ended and do not typically have manuals, which they feel destroy spontaneity in treatment (e.g., Silverman, 1996). Other writers took issue with the task force's requirement that researchers carefully specify the patient sample under investigation, maintaining that this requirement is irrelevant to how psychotherapy is typically practiced in the real world (e.g., Garfield, 1996). This concern is an important one, particularly in light of findings reported by Weisz, Weiss, and Donenberg (1992) that psychotherapies with children as they are practiced in real clinical settings do not appear to be as effective as the same therapies examined under carefully controlled research settings. Nevertheless, it is our position that the field of clinical psychology would be better served by trying to enhance the effectiveness of empirically supported psychotherapies as they are practiced in real-life settings than it would by diluting the criteria required for the scientific identification of effective therapies. As Kendall (1998, pp. 4–5) has eloquently stated,

> Consider what the mental health field would be like for psychologists if we did not use criteria for making evaluative decisions and if we did not consider scientific research evaluation to be a cornerstone of our clinical applications. To what category would the professional practice of clinical psychology be assigned: to philosophy, psychic reader, advisor? Our empirical basis sets and maintains a preferred high standard for the profession, and our practice of professional psychology benefits from this foundation . . . As you contemplate your position with regard to the empirical evaluation of psychological therapies, consider whether there is an acceptable alternative.

BOX 15.1

TREATMENT OUTCOME RESEARCH: IMPLICATIONS FOR JASON, ALLISON, PHILLIP, AND MARIA

Using the findings from the treatment outcome studies presented in chapters 11 through 14, we can judge which therapy or therapies are most likely to be effective with each of our cases.

JASON

As you will recall, Jason was diagnosed with two psychological disorders, attention deficit/hyperactivity disorder (ADHD) and oppositional defiant disorder (ODD). Extensive research has been conducted on both these disorders, and the results are quite clear. The most effective intervention for ADHD is the use of a nonpsychological treatment: psychostimulant medication. Psychostimulant medication has been shown to be more effective than control treatments in multiple studies, including a number of well-controlled, double-blind, placebo-controlled investigations. In addition, however, a recent large-scale study found that behavior therapy produced additional beneficial effects beyond those attributable to medication (Arnold et al., 1997; Hinshaw et al., 2000). Extensive research on ODD has established the efficacy of behavior therapy involving parents of children with ODD (e.g., Kazdin & Weisz, 1998). No other psychological treatments

have been found to produce documented beneficial effects for either ADHD or ODD. Thus, the use of behavior therapy in conjunction with medication that has been prescribed and monitored by a physician is likely to produce the best effects for Jason.

ALLISON

Allison was diagnosed with bulimia nervosa, a disorder characterized by a severe disturbance of eating in which attempts to restrict food intake are punctuated by episodes of uncontrolled overeating, commonly followed by self-induced vomiting or the misuse of laxatives. Allison binges on junk food and then, to prevent weight gain, purges what she has eaten by forcing herself to vomit. The results of both individual studies and meta-analyses clearly document the effectiveness of cognitive-behavior therapy (CBT) and, to a somewhat lesser extent, interpersonal psychotherapy (IPT) in the treatment of bulimia. Although some studies support the use of antidepressant medication in treating bulimia, CBT has been found to be more acceptable than medication to bulimic individuals and, importantly, also has a lower drop-out rate than does treatment with medication (Wilson & Fairburn, in press). Interestingly,

SUMMARY AND CONCLUSIONS

For many reasons, it is critically important that we evaluate the effectiveness of psychotherapy. Consumers deserve to receive effective psychotherapy, and clinical psychologists have an ethical obligation to treat their clients using methods that have been demonstrated to be effective in controlled research studies. But how do we evaluate the effectiveness of psychotherapy? In this chapter we describe in detail different research strategies that are used by clinical psychologists to evaluate the effectiveness of different forms of

psychotherapy. Although psychologists have used single-case experimental designs to evaluate the effectiveness of a specific intervention, a more powerful research design is a randomized clinical trial. In this design, some patients are randomly assigned to receive one or more different treatments and others are typically assigned to placebo or to wait-list control conditions.

Individual studies of the effectiveness of psychotherapy are clearly important in demonstrating that a specific therapy might be effective in

BOX 15.1 (concluded)

adding antidepressant medication to CBT does not improve treatment effectiveness over CBT alone. By treating Allison with CBT, we can expect rapid improvement in her symptoms of bulimia; we can also expect her improvement to be long-lasting (Fairburn et al., 1995).

PHILLIP

Phillip has been experiencing what are likely panic attacks, and he becomes fearful when he has to give presentations at his workplace. Phillip meets *DSM-IV* diagnostic criteria for social phobia. The results of treatment efficacy studies indicate that cognitive-behavior therapy (CBT) with exposure is the most effective form of treatment for this disorder. As we saw in chapter 14, a therapist using CBT for social phobia would explain to Phillip the importance of his negative cognitions, both about his presentations and about the meaning of his physical symptoms of anxiety, such as racing heart and rapid breathing. For the exposure component of CBT, the therapist would provide Phillip with either imaginal or actual exposure to giving presentations to coworkers and would likely train Phillip to deal with the increased anxiety that would accompany these presentations. Finally, if Phillip's feelings of panic persisted, they could be treated separately using CBT for panic disorder (Sanderson & Rego, 2000).

MARIA

Maria is a 73-year-old woman who was widowed two years ago. Since the loss of her husband, she has had little interest in activities that she used to enjoy. She has become increasingly despondent and isolated, to the point where her children are concerned about her health. Maria meets *DSM-IV* criteria for Major Depressive Disorder. As we have seen throughout in this chapter, there is a large literature examining the effectiveness of psychotherapy for depression. Two forms of psychotherapy have been identified in this literature as effective treatments for depression: cognitive-behavior therapy (CBT) and interpersonal psychotherapy (IPT). In treating Maria with CBT, the therapist would work with her to identify her negative or maladaptive thoughts that are maintaining her depressed mood. The therapist would also have Maria complete behavioral assignments aimed at increasing her involvement in pleasant activities. In contrast, as we saw in chapter 12, the therapist who treats Maria with IPT would educate her about depression, help her work through her grief surrounding her husband's death, and work with her to facilitate her transition to widowhood. Given Maria's age, IPT may be a more effective treatment for her than CBT because there is a late-life version of IPT that has been developed and evaluated specifically for the treatment of depression in the elderly.

the treatment of a particular disorder. But each study will have its limitations, such as a small patient sample, limited outcome measures, or few control groups. To address these shortcomings, clinical psychologists have increasingly used meta-analysis to examine the effectiveness of psychotherapy. This statistical procedure allows the investigator to combine, or aggregate, data from many studies that examine the same question, even if they used different outcome measures. In general, the results of contemporary meta-analyses of psychotherapy effectiveness strongly indicate that cognitive-behavior thera-

pies are the most effective treatment for a broad range of disorders, including depression, anxiety, eating disorders, and substance use difficulties.

Recently, the Clinical Psychology division of the APA formed a task force to develop strict criteria to identify therapies that have been shown to be effective in controlled research studies. Among other factors, these criteria stipulate that the therapy must have an accompanying treatment manual and that the treatment must have been found to be effective in controlled studies conducted in at least two laboratories. Treatments that meet all the criteria developed by the task force are referred to as empirically supported treatments. Quite appropriately, we believe, the task force suggested that empirically supported treatments be taught in clinical psychology graduate training programs.

KEY TERMS AND NAMES

A-B-A-B design
Accountability
Between-subjects designs
Components analysis of psychotherapy
Consumer Reports psychotherapy survey
Dodo bird verdict
Dose-response question
Hans Eysenck
Effect size
Empirically supported treatments
Meta-analysis

Multiple baseline design
National Institute of Mental Health
   Collaborative Depression Research Project
Nonrandomized control group studies
Gordon Paul
Placebo
Randomized clinical trials
Single-case experimental designs
Statistically versus clinically significant change
Within-subject designs

RESOURCES

Books

Hersen, M., & Bellack, A. S. (1999). *Handbook of comparative interventions for adult disorders* (2nd ed.). New York: John Wiley.

Nathan, P. E., & Gorman, J. M. (Eds.). (1998). *A guide to treatments that work.* New York: Oxford University Press.

Seligman, M. E. P. (1994). *What you can change and what you can't.* New York: Knopf.

Journals

Behavior Therapy
Cognitive Therapy and Research
The Journal of Abnormal Child Psychology
The Journal of Consulting and Clinical Psychology

CHAPTER SIXTEEN

CLINICAL PSYCHOLOGY: OUR PAST, OUR FUTURE, AND YOUR OPPORTUNITIES

INTRODUCTION

Psychology is a relatively young science, with a much shorter history than biology, chemistry, or other physical and life sciences. Similarly, clinical psychology is a young profession, having begun much more recently than professions such as medicine or law. As a developing science and profession, clinical psychology is at a critical point in its growth. The first decades of this century are likely to be a time of significant change in this field and therefore present the next generation of clinical psychologists with exciting opportunities.

Throughout this book we have described both the science and practice of clinical psychology. At this point, you should have a clear understanding of the development of clinical psychology and of the scientific foundations underlying the practice of assessment, prevention and promotion, and psychotherapy. In this final chapter of the book we first highlight some of the accomplishments that have been achieved since the origins of clinical psychology more than 100 years ago. Many professionals within the field are often critical of clinical psychology for not having moved far enough in many respects. As we will see in this chapter, however, clinical psychology has actually come a long way since the founding work of Lightner Witmer in 1896. In making this point, we will focus specifically on growth and accomplishment in the areas of psychopathology, assessment, and intervention. Following this discussion, we present some of the major challenges and issues that confront clinical psychology at the outset of the twenty-first century. The ways in which clinical psychologists address and resolve each of these issues will affect both the role and the direction of research in clinical psychology and the nature of the practice of clinical psychology in the coming years. We conclude this chapter (and this book) by discussing what we believe are important new areas of opportunity for clinical psychologists over the next decades. We believe that these areas will continue to gain prominence within the field of clinical psychology and will open up exciting new avenues for research and the application of science to practice. As you read this chapter, we encourage you to consider your own thoughts both about where clinical psychology has come as a field and, perhaps more important, how you as a clinical psychologist might deal with the

challenges that we raise and the opportunities that we describe.

ADVANCES IN THE AREAS OF PSYCHOPATHOLOGY, ASSESSMENT, AND INTERVENTION

Psychopathology

At the end of the nineteenth century and the dawn of the twentieth century, as the new field of clinical psychology was in its earliest stages, there was no comprehensive diagnostic system for the classification of psychopathology. Emil Kraepelin (1883) had only recently coined the term *dementia praecox* (essentially, "premature dementia") to refer to a group of disorders that we now know as schizophrenia. Sigmund Freud had just begun his work on neuroses, or what are now referred to as anxiety disorders. Thus, the level of understanding of the nature and causes of psychopathology was extremely primitive. Since the time of Kraepelin and Freud, we have witnessed significant advances in our knowledge of psychopathology, including the development of systems for the differentiation and classification of psychological disorders, the course and correlates of many disorders, and factors that place individuals at risk for the development of psychopathology.

One major advance in knowledge to which clinical psychologists have contributed is the *DSM-IV* (American Psychiatric Association, 1994), which has provided clinical psychologists with a system for classifying psychological disorders that is significantly more refined than the four preceding versions of this taxonomy. With *DSM-IV*, adequate levels of reliability have been achieved for many diagnoses, there is a stronger research base, and this classification system has proven useful as a guide to the diagnosis and treatment of many forms of psychopathology. Although *DSM-IV* is published by the American Psychiatric Association, clinical psychologists have made significant contributions to both the overview of *DSM-IV* and the diagnostic criteria for a number of specific disorders. For example, David Barlow, a clinical psychologist at Boston University, was a prominent member of the *DSM-IV* task force as well as the Anxiety Disorders Work Group. Indeed, clinical psychologists were members of several of the work groups that developed the criteria for certain diagnoses, including Childhood Disorders, Eating Disorders, Mood Disorders, Substance Use Disorders, and Personality Disorders. Clinical psychologists also played important roles in designing and conducting field-trial projects in which the reliability of the *DSM-IV* diagnoses was evaluated. David Barlow, Thomas Widiger, Benjamin Lahey, Edna Foa, Dean Kilpatrick, and Linda Cottler were all project directors for different field trials for *DSM-IV.*

Clinical psychologists have also played a leading role in virtually all areas of research on the nature, course, and causes of psychopathology (see chapter 5), including both descriptive and experimental research:

- Descriptive research has contributed to the understanding of the rates and course of psychological disorders as they occur in the community. Examples of longitudinal studies of psychological disorder include research on aggression and disruptive behavior disorders in early childhood by Mark Greenberg of Pennsylvania State University and his colleagues (Greenberg et al., 1999); the study of the incidence, course, and correlates of depression in adolescence by Peter Lewinsohn of the Oregon Research Institute (Lewinsohn, Allen, Seeley, & Gotlib, 1999); and research by Laurie Chassin at Arizona State University that has shown the long-term effects on adult mental health among children of alcoholic parents (Chassin, Pitts, DeLucia, & Todd, 1999).
- Descriptive research has also contributed to our understanding of important risk and protective factors associated with different psychological disorders. For example, clinical

psychologists such as Scott Monroe at the University of Oregon have shown the importance of life stress in the etiology and course of emotional disorders (e.g., Monroe, Rohde, Seeley, & Lewinsohn, 1999). Other researchers have shown that family characteristics contribute risk for emotional and behavioral disorders in childhood, including the effects of the stress of divorce (e.g., Emery, 1999).
- Researchers in clinical psychology have used experimental methods to examine the characteristics of psychopathology under controlled conditions in order to elucidate possible causes. Colin MacLeod in Australia and Andrew Mathews in England, for instance, have elegantly demonstrated that people who are experiencing anxiety disorders show heightened attentional processing of threat-related environmental stimuli (e.g., Mathews & MacLeod, 1985, 1986; Mogg, Mathews, & Eysenck, 1992). Similar results have been found with respect to the attentional processing of depressed patients and, further, have documented that these effects seem to dissipate following the patients' recovery (e.g., Gotlib & Cane, 1997; McCabe & Gotlib, 1993). Such findings are critical in stimulating theory refinement, clinical research, and enhancements in psychotherapy.

Assessment

Psychological assessment and testing represent arenas in which clinical psychology has made perhaps the greatest contributions, and testing and measurement remain a uniquely psychological endeavor. In the late 1800s psychological assessment was limited to the very earliest stages of intelligence testing as represented in the work of Alfred Binet in France. Other methods to measure characteristics of personality or psychopathology that were available at that time were extremely subjective, and there were no standardized tests for the measurement of behavior, personality, or neuropsychological function.

The ensuing century has witnessed major advances in psychological measurement:

- Currently psychologists have at their disposal highly reliable tests for the assessment of intelligence (see chapter 8). Although intelligence tests are not without problems, the Wechsler scales are now the standards for assessment of cognitive or intellectual functioning in preschool children (WPPSI-R), school-age children and adolescents (WISC-III), and adults (WAIS-III). Performance on these tests has been shown to be very stable over short periods of time (reliability) and predictive of some aspects of academic and work performance (validity). These tests have given psychologists valuable tools for measuring cognitive competence to identify children who may have difficulty learning at the expected grade level or who have strengths and weaknesses in different areas of cognitive functioning that may interfere with learning.

- Similar advances have been made in the measurement of personality (see chapter 9). The revision of the MMPI, the MMPI-2, has been used extensively to assess psychopathology (e.g., Stein, Graham, Ben-Porath, & McNulty, 1999) and for understanding the ways that differences in personality may relate to responses to psychological treatment (Butcher, 1997). More recently, measures have been developed to reflect specific theoretical models of the structure of personality. For example, the NEO-PI has been developed based on the five-factor model of personality, and this test has been used successfully in studies of both normal and clinical populations (Ball, Tennen, Poling, Kranzler, & Rounsaville, 1997; McRae & Costa, 1997; McRae, Costa, Del Pilar, Rolland, & Parker, 1998).

- The assessment of psychopathology has seen advances with the development and refinement of structured diagnostic interviews to reliably determine *DSM-IV* diagnoses of different disorders (see chapter 7). Diagnostic interviews have played an important role in increasing precise identification of specific psychological disorders, both for research and for selection of appropriate methods of treatment. Psychologists have been actively involved in the application and testing of the reliability and validity of these interview methods (e.g., Foa, Cashman, Jaycox, & Perry, 1997; Segal, Hersen, & Van Hasselt, 1994).

- Major achievements have been made in methods of behavioral assessment that involve the direct observation of behavior (by a clinician or other trained observer) and in systematic methods for clients to track and record their own behavior (self-monitoring). These methods have proven essential in providing data for behavioral and cognitive-behavioral methods of treatment, because they are important in identifying specific behaviors and thoughts that are changed in treatment (see chapter 10).

- Clinical neuropsychological assessment represents another area of significant accomplishment in psychological assessment and measurement (see chapter 8). Neuropsychological function is assessed indirectly through performance on tasks that are related to specific aspects of brain and central nervous system functioning. With increased understanding of brain function and its role in personality, psychopathology, and virtually all aspects of behavior, methods to assess neuropsychological functioning have become increasingly important.

Intervention

A little more than a century ago, Lightner Witmer developed a treatment with the goal of improving a 14-year-old boy's difficulties with spelling and recognizing written words. At the time that Witmer's work marked the founding of the field of clinical psychology, the only recognized form of psychotherapy was Freud's "talk therapy," which in 1896 was only beginning to attract attention in the United States. Even when psychoanalytic treatment began to gain acceptance and popularity in the early 1900s, psychologists were content, by and large, to leave the practice of psychotherapy to the emerging profession of psychiatry. Significant advances have been achieved by clinical psychologists in interventions in the lives of individuals suffering from emotional and behavioral problems:

- Psychotherapy is now very much an integral part, if not the major focus, of clinical psychology. Indeed, over the last 50 years psychologists have been at the forefront of developing and evaluating innovative and effective forms of psychological treatment. Clinical psychologists, for example, were instrumental figures in the origins and development of behavior therapy (e.g., John Watson), cognitive therapy (e.g., Albert Ellis), cognitive-behavior therapy (e.g., Donald Meichenbaum), and humanistic therapies (e.g., Carl Rogers). Equally important, clinical psychologists have made major contributions in refining these approaches to treatment based on research examining both empirical evaluations of treatments' effectiveness and the mechanisms through which the treatments achieve and maintain their results (Nathan, Stuart, & Dolan, 2000).
- Given the early focus of the field on psychological treatments for children, it is fitting that clinical psychologists have also been responsible for developing therapies for use with younger populations. Psychologists Ivar Lovaas, Philip Kendall, Russell Barkley, and Rex Forehand, for example, all have described innovative and effective extensions of behavioral, cognitive, or cognitive-behavioral therapies to the treatment of children who are experiencing various psychological difficulties, including fears and phobias, depression, and externalizing behavioral and emotional problems (Kazdin & Weisz, 1998).
- Another area in which clinical psychologists have taken a leadership position is in the evaluation of the effectiveness of psychological

therapies for both children and adults. There are several issues and questions that clinical psychologists have begun to address, including the assessment of empirical support for different psychotherapies. Clinical psychology is taking the lead in establishing criteria for empirically supported treatments for psychological difficulties and in identifying specific therapies that meet these criteria (e.g., Chambless & Hollon, 1998). These efforts, which we described in detail in chapter 15, reflect the scientific values that form the foundation of clinical psychology.

CHALLENGES FOR CLINICAL PSYCHOLOGY IN THE TWENTY-FIRST CENTURY

The important accomplishments during the first century of clinical psychology notwithstanding, the field faces significant challenges at the outset of its second century. These challenges include issues related to clinical psychological research, the practice of clinical psychology, and the interface between research and practice. We highlight a few salient issues here, continuing with our focus on psychopathology, assessment, and intervention. The way in which these issues are resolved will profoundly shape the future of the field.

Psychopathology

As the *DSM-IV* has become the standard in research and practice, it is important to recognize that we are still faced with significant gaps in our knowledge of psychopathology. As Widiger and Clark (2000) state in a recent review of the status of psychopathology classification, "There might not in fact be one sentence within *DSM-IV* for which well meaning clinicians, theorists, and researchers could not find some basis for fault" (p. 946). Several issues are important to consider as psychologists continue to apply the *DSM-IV* in research and practice and as the field anticipates the next edition of the classification manual (*DSM-V*) that is likely to appear within the next 5 years (Widiger & Clark).

Challenge 1: The Classification of Psychopathology   Several fundamental issues in the classification of psychopathology remain unresolved. First, the boundary between psychopathology and normality continues to be blurry at best. These boundary problems include difficulties in clearly defining when a given behavior is evidence of psychopathology versus variation in normal functioning, and in identifying the threshold for what constitutes a psychological disorder (Widiger & Clark, 2000). It is not clear if there are qualitative differences associated with the criteria established in the *DSM-IV* to distinguish between the presence or absence of a disorder (e.g., Judd, Paulus, Wells, & Rapaport, 1996). The difference between psychopathology and problems in living that do not reflect underlying pathology in the individual (as specified by *DSM-IV* for the diagnosis of disorder) has not been clearly defined. For example, in reference to Maria, one of the cases we have followed throughout this book, the distinction between normal grief following the death of her husband and a diagnosis of depression is based on somewhat arbitrary criteria involving the duration of the symptoms (2 months or more distinguishes between grief and depression) and impairment in functioning (Wakefield, 1997).

A closely related issue involves reconciling categorical and dimensional approaches to psychopathology. It is widely recognized that many symptoms, and even some disorders, represent extreme deviations of behaviors that also occur to lesser degrees along a continuum. Recent research has begun to address possible relationships between categorical and dimensional approaches to the classification of psychopathology (e.g., Achenbach & McConaughy, 1996; Kreuger, 1999; see chapter 5). However, it remains to be determined if most disorders represent variation along a continuum as opposed to qualitative differences.

Finally, although the *DSM-IV* is a categorical system comprised of discrete disorders, the rates of comorbidity or co-occurrence of disorders are very high. For example, in a major epidemiological study, the National Comorbidity Survey, 56 percent of people who qualified for at least one *DSM* diagnosis at some point during their lifetime met criteria for two or more disorders (Kessler et al., 1994). This comorbidity raises serious questions about the degree to which many of the disorders in the *DSM-IV* are in fact discrete entities. Resolution of these issues will be critical in advancing our understanding of the basic nature of psychopathology (Widiger & Clark, 2000).

Challenge 2: The Role of Culture and Context in Psychopathology   Much or most research on psychopathology has been carried out with samples drawn from the majority cultural group within the United States—middle and upper-middle socioeconomic status individuals of European descent. The changing demographics of the U.S. population (see chapter 2) raises important questions for the future of clinical psychology. For example, do various ethnic, cultural, and age groups differ in clinically meaningful ways in the manifestation of psychopathology and in differential response to various treatments? If there are important cultural differences in psychopathology and response to treatment, how should clinical psychology prepare itself to meet the needs of a diverse, pluralistic society?

To address these issues, we need a better knowledge base of the types of mental health problems and concerns that are faced by individuals in different ethnic and cultural groups. We have precious little knowledge concerning whether the prevalence and manifestation of various forms of psychopathology is similar or different across groups. This information is critical if we are to provide valid and effective means of assessment and treatment to different populations. For example, John Weisz and colleagues have studied differences between Thailand and the United States in the way that emotional and behavioral problems in children and adolescents are viewed (McCarty et al., 1999; Weisz, Suwanlert, Chaiyasit, & Walter, 1987; Weisz et al., 1988). Thai culture is based in Buddhist principles and other aspects of eastern philosophy and values, whereas the U.S. culture, although increasingly pluralistic, is rooted in western European beliefs associated with Protestant Christian values. In Thai culture, children's aggression and disruptive behavior problems are strongly disapproved and discouraged, whereas inhibition and overcontrol of behavior is condoned or even encouraged. Consistent with these differences, internalizing problems (fear, nervousness, somatic problems) were reported much more often by parents for Thai children than for U.S. children, and externalizing problems (e.g., fighting, disobedience, lying) were reported more often for U.S. children than for Thais (Weisz et al., 1987).

Researchers have also begun to examine prevalence rates of disorders among specific ethnic groups within the United States. For example, Takeuchi et al. (1998) reported that the lifetime rates of Major Depressive Disorder and Dysthymia were 6.9 percent and 5.3 percent in a large community sample of Chinese Americans. These types of epidemiological data have been relatively rare, however. A priority for future research is to document both similarities and differences across cultures (Sue, Sue, Sue, & Takeuchi, 1995). As our society continues to become increasingly more diverse, an understanding of cultural differences in psychopathology will become more important.

Challenge 3: Genes and Psychopathology
Biological scientists have now completed the initial mapping of the human genome, opening the door for increasingly more sophisticated research on the role of genes in all aspects of human functioning. Particularly important for clinical psychology is the role of genetics in psychopathology and other psychological characteristics, work that is encompassed in the field of **behavioral genetics.** Dr. Francis Collins, director of the National Human Genome Research Institute, points out that 99.9 percent of the genome is shared by all humans, a percentage that is much higher than is found in other primate species (Collins, 1999). Therefore, groups of people who are often assumed to differ genetically are actually remarkably similar in their genetic makeup. Observed differences between people are therefore likely to be strongly influenced by social, cultural, and environmental factors (Carpenter, 2000). Behavioral genetic research has helped clarify the ways in which the environment influences behavior; specifically, environmental factors and experiences not shared by individuals raised in the same family exert strong influences on psychological functioning (McGue & Bouchard, 1998; O'Connor & Plomin, 2000). Moreover, the fact that some behavioral characteristics are heritable does not mean that they are completely determined by genes. Rather, genes influence behavior through complex interactions with environmental factors. Clinical psychologists must have a better understanding of the role of genetic factors in both their research and in their clinical practice. For example, Plomin and Crabbe (2000) anticipate that clinical psychology will be fundamentally changed by advances in our knowledge of genetics, especially in the form of gene-based diagnoses and treatment programs.

Assessment

In spite of the major improvements that have been made in the quality of psychological tests and other assessment methods, several challenges remain to be addressed. Testing and other forms of assessment are likely to remain a unique skill of clinical psychologists, and continued improvement in these methods is a high priority.

Challenge 1: Broadening Our Models of Intelligence   Although significant advances have been made in the methods used to assess intelligence, critics observe that current standardized intelligence tests measure only a limited range of intellectual functioning while overlooking other forms of intelligence (Sternberg, 2000). For example, psychologist Robert Sternberg has proposed that features of intelligence that are important for success in work and academics involve analytical abilities, creative abilities, and practical abilities that are not tapped by traditional measures of IQ (Sternberg & Kaufman, 1998). Psychologist Peter Salovey and others have observed that there are important differences between individuals in what is referred to as **emotional intelligence.** Emotional intelligence includes self-awareness, impulse control, persistence, self-motivation, and empathy for others (e.g., Goleman, 1995; Salovey, Hsee, & Mayer, 1993; Salovey & Sluyter, 1997). Although it is important to set some limits on what is included within the domain of what we call intelligence, it is clear that there are other important aspects of cognitive functioning that are not measured by current IQ tests. Clinical psychology faces a challenge to develop tests of other aspects of intelligence that can expand the assessment of important human competencies.

Challenge 2: Engaging in Culturally Sensitive Assessment   As the diversity of our culture continues to grow, there is increased need and demand for methods of assessment that are culturally sensitive and fair. Differences in language, fundamental beliefs and values, and differences in perspectives on psychopathology and normality are all evident across different cultural groups. One important step in achieving culturally fair assessment procedures involves generating normative data on psychological tests from samples that include adequate representation of minority groups. Furthermore, provision of culturally sensitive services to a diverse population may be impaired by possible biases and stereotypes on the part of psychologists and other mental health professionals. Although research suggests that biases in clinical judgment may be less pervasive than was previously thought, researchers have identified biases in assessment practices and in clinical judgments on the basis of race, social class, and gender (Garb, 1997). It is important for psychologists to continue to attend to these factors to both prevent bias and to ensure that assessment and treatment are conducted in culturally sensitive ways. As a step in this direction, training programs in clinical psychology are placing more emphasis on cultural factors in mental health, as reflected in the increasing number of programs that require students to complete courses in cultural diversity (e.g., Bernal & Castro, 1994; Hall, 1997). The APA now requires accredited doctoral programs in clinical psychology to include course work and training in cultural diversity as part of their curriculum. This training includes consideration of the role of cultural context for all clients, not simply for ethnic minorities.

Challenge 3: Applying Research Methods to Clinical Practice   Exciting findings are emerging from research using laboratory experimental methods to study cognitive factors in different forms of psychopathology, most notably depression and anxiety disorders. For example, computer-based tasks are used to measure aspects of attention and information processing (e.g., MacLeod, 1999; McCabe, Gotlib, & Martin, 2000; Mogg et al., 2000). Computer-based tasks that involve the presentation of emotional stimuli (e.g., words that are related to sources of anxiety) as contrasted with neutral stimuli (non-anxiety-provoking words) are used to assess biases in attention toward negative information. The extent to which individuals attend to emotionally negative words as contrasted with neutral words reflects a bias to selectively attend to threatening information in the environment. Evidence of selective attention on these types of experimental tasks has been shown to be a predictor of the course of anxiety disorders and differences in response to treatment (MacLeod & Gotlib, 1997). A strength of experimental tasks is that they are not subject to sources of bias or error that affect self-report measures and tests that require subjective interpretation by the examiner. However, experimental methods of assessment that are used in research have not been adapted for use in clinical practice. The significance of these findings will be of limited clinical application if comparable methods cannot be used in practice.

Intervention

Interventions have grown to represent an increasingly larger portion of the research and practice of clinical psychologists. Not surprisingly then, a proportionately larger number of issues and challenges in the future of the field pertain to interventions. The stakes are the highest with regard to interventions, because some of the issues facing the field could fundamentally redefine what it means to be a clinical psychologist.

Challenge 1: Obtaining Prescription Privileges for Psychologists   No issue looms larger in the future of clinical psychology than whether psychologists should obtain **prescription privileges,** that is, limited privileges for the prescription of psychotropic medication (see chapter 2). Two questions are at the center of this controversy: Can clinical psychologists be trained to safely and effectively prescribe medication for psychological problems? And should psychologists be trained to prescribe psychotropic medication?

The answer to the first question appears to be yes, psychologists can be trained to safely and effectively prescribe psychotropic medication. The basis for this conclusion comes primarily from the results of the **Psychopharmacology Demonstration Project** funded and implemented by the Department of Defense (DoD; see

Newman, Phelps, Sammons, Dunivin, & Cullen, 2000). The Psychopharmacology Demonstration Project was initiated by the DoD to train licensed military psychologists to prescribe medication for psychological disorders. Ten psychologists received training between 1988 and 1997, and their work was closely and extensively evaluated. The consensus of the evaluation was that training psychologists in psychopharmacology was feasible and cost effective, and the performance of the trained psychologists was rated as good to excellent (Vector Research, 1996). Many questions remain open about the length and scope of the training that is required to provide adequate knowledge and skill in order to effectively prescribe medication, but the results of the DoD study suggest that it is feasible to train psychologists for this role.

The second question, *should* psychologists be trained to prescribe medication, is much more complex. Recent surveys indicate that the majority of practicing clinical psychologists favor limited prescription rights for psychologists, provided that they have received adequate training in psychopharmacology (Sammons, Gorny, Zinner, & Allen, 2000). Based in part on the results of the DoD project as well as on a growing body of research documenting the effectiveness of psychotropic medication in the treatment of emotional disorders such as depression and anxiety, in 1996 the APA officially endorsed the pursuit of prescription privileges for suitably trained psychologists. Toward this end, the APA has helped develop state legislation to obtain prescription privileges for psychologists and has helped design a model curriculum for both pre- and postdoctoral training in this area. By 1998 legislation for psychology prescription privileges had been introduced, but has not yet passed, in six states, including California, Florida, and Hawaii (Cullen & Newman, 1997; Foxhall, 2000). And in January of 1999, psychologists in the U.S. territory of Guam obtained the right to prescribe psychotropic medication under the supervision of a physician (Sammons et al.). Thus, efforts toward this goal are moving forward. Supporters have argued that the needs of those suffering from psychological problems cannot be adequately met if physicians alone are allowed to prescribe medication for the treatment of such problems as schizophrenia, depression, anxiety disorders, and eating disorders. Finally, one of the arguments offered by advocates of obtaining privileges for psychologists is that other non-physicians, such as nurse practitioners, physician assistants, and dentists, already have limited prescription privileges in many states.

In contrast to the position taken by the APA, there is opposition to prescription privileges for psychologists from both within and outside the field of psychology. The prescription of medication for any disorder, whether the problem is physical or psychological in nature, has been the exclusive purview of physicians. The medical profession has argued that physicians are uniquely trained in the basic biological sciences and in the knowledge base of medical practice to utilize medications as a tool to treat disease, including psychopathology. Psychiatrists have been strongly opposed to granting prescription privileges to psychologists (Klusman, 1998), although other physicians (e.g., family practitioners) have been more mixed in their response (Bell, Digman, & McKenna, 1995).

Despite the APA's endorsement of the movement for prescription privileges, not all psychologists support this objective. Unlike the results of the Sammons et al. (2000) survey, the results of several surveys of psychologists (including nonclinical psychologists) regarding prescription privileges reflect mixed support (e.g., DeNelsky, 1996; Hayes & Heiby, 1996). There are several reasons offered in opposition. First, prescription privileges would profoundly change the training received by clinical psychologists, because it would require extensive additional training in psychopharmacology. Some professionals have proposed training programs targeted at the post-doctoral level, that is, to be taken after the individual has already obtained a PhD in psychology

(Sammons & Brown, 1997). However, others have advocated adding psychopharmacology-related courses, such as biochemistry and physiology, to the PhD graduate curriculum in clinical psychology. In either case, the additional training requirements would be substantial.

Perhaps more important than the amount of additional training that would be required for psychologists to obtain prescription privileges is the unavoidable change in the focus of the graduate and postgraduate training in clinical psychology (see box 16.1). The current curricula of APA accredited training programs in clinical psychology are already extensive and intensive, especially in programs that strive to train students in both science and practice. The addition of such courses as biology, chemistry, and pharmacology would mean the elimination or reduction of courses in psychological assessment, psychotherapy, and statistics and research methods as well as breadth courses in other areas of psychology (learning, developmental, social psychology). These changes would move clinical psychology toward a medical model of psychopathology and its treatment, and away from a psychological perspective. Indeed, it is instructive to note that, before the advent and widespread use of psychotropic medications, psychiatry, too, emphasized the practice of psychotherapy rather than its current strong practice of pharmacotherapy.

Regardless of whether psychologists gain prescription privileges, the role of medication in the treatment of psychopathology is well established. There is a large literature comparing the effectiveness of psychotropic medication and psychotherapy for the treatment of various psychological or emotional disorders. Numerous studies have now compared the efficacy of psychological treatments versus medication and the combination of the two treatments. Although the findings differ depending on the disorder, age of the subjects, and the type of medication used, research suggests that both psychological and pharmacological treatment methods are effective

BOX 16.1

PRESCRIPTION PRIVILEGES FOR CLINICAL PSYCHOLOGISTS: THE IMPACT ON TRAINING

Few issues in clinical psychology have produced more heated debate than the arguments surrounding prescription privileges. Physicians have argued that psychologists lack adequate training necessary to prescribe medications in a careful, ethical, and effective manner. Both the American Medical Association and the American Psychiatric Association have voiced strong opposition to allowing psychologists to obtain prescription privileges (e.g., Leard-Hansson, 2001). Proponents of psychologists acquiring prescription rights, including the APA, argue that such training for psychologists is fully possible to achieve. Further, proponents have argued that it is in the best interest of underserved populations who are in need of psychoactive medication and other psychological services to increase the numbers and types of professionals who are trained to prescribe medication. The level of conflict is especially high within the field of clinical psychology. Indeed, psychologists on both sides of the question have argued that their position is in the best interest of the profession and that those who disagree do not understand the direction in which psychology should be moving (e.g., Barkley, 1991; DeLeon, Fox, & Graham, 1991; Hayes & Heiby, 1996).

In considering the impact of extending prescription rights to psychologists, it is important to understand the effects that this change would have on the nature of the field of clinical psychology and on the ways in which psychologists are trained to think about people and their problems. Doctoral-level training of clinical psychologists is already pressed to the limit in trying to provide the knowledge and necessary skills to graduate scientist-practitioners for the field. The addition of course work and practical training necessary to build the competencies to prescribe psychoactive medication would mean either extending the length of time required for training or replacing aspects of training that are already in place (Adams & Bielianskas, 1994a, 1994b). A concern raised by many professionals is that research training would be decreased in order to accommodate the time and effort needed for training in psychopharmacology, thus further eroding the scientific training of clinical psychologists. Similarly, clinical psychologists may devote less time to keeping up with new developments in psychotherapy and more time to acquiring new information about psychopharmacology (DeNelsky, 1991). Finally, prescription privileges for clinical psychology may have a pervasive effect on the ways that psychologists think about human problems and solutions to those problems. That is, access to prescription rights may lead psychologists away from the continued development of nonmedical explanations and treatments of psychopathology. As psychologist Abraham Maslow (1966) noted, "It is tempting, if the only tool you have is a hammer, to treat everything as if it were a nail" (pp. 15–16).

in treating many forms of psychopathology (e.g., Antonuccio, Danton, & DeNelsky, 1995; Antonuccio, Thomas, & Danton, 1997; Gould, Otto, Pollack, & Yap, 1997; see chapter 15). For example, Barlow, Gorman, Shear, and Woods (2000), in a paper published in the prestigious *Journal of the American Medical Association*, compared cognitive-behavioral therapy, imipramine, and the combination of the two treatments in a ran-

domized, place-controlled trial. Both treatments were superior to a placebo treatment, and the findings suggest that cognitive-behavioral therapy was more durable and was better tolerated by the patients. The ability to understand the complementary roles of psychotherapy and pharmacotherapy is likely to become increasingly important for clinical psychologists in the future. It may be important for clinical psychologists to have expertise in psychopharmacology in order to be informed participants in the treatment of patients when it includes medication (Barnett & Neel, 2000).

In summary, the role of clinical psychology in the prescription of psychotropic medication is far from resolved. The APA is leading the effort to obtain prescription privileges for psychologists, and the psychiatric community is mounting strong opposition. Regardless of the outcome of this issue, it is changing the focus and the character of clinical psychology.

Challenge 2: Linking Research and Practice in Interventions As we discussed in chapter 15, clinical psychologists have made significant advances in the development of treatments for a variety of psychological disorders. However, there remains a large gap between the standardized methods of treatment that have been evaluated in research and psychological interventions as they are practiced in the real world. Despite the goal of training psychologists who are well versed in both research and practice, the communication between researchers and practitioners is poor (e.g., Barlow, 1981; Beutler, Williams, Wakefield, & Entwistle, 1995; Cohen, Sargent, & Sechrest, 1986; Edelson, 1994; Havens, 1994). Researchers are dismayed by reports that most practicing psychologists do not read or stay informed of the latest developments in psychological research. Practitioners bemoan the nature of psychological research, arguing that it often has little relevance for the day-to-day activities that they carry out in the real world. The result has been a breakdown in the link between clinical research and clinical practice (Kanfer, 1991).

One way in which this issue has been framed is in terms of the contrast between research on **treatment efficacy** as opposed to **treatment effectiveness** (e.g., Barlow, 1996; Nathan et al., 2000). Efficacy research is focused on determining if a treatment can work under optimal conditions (i.e., specially trained therapists, clearly

defined treatment manuals, carefully selected samples of clients). In efficacy research, a premium is placed on internal validity, or the degree to which variables in the study have been carefully controlled and the effects of a treatment can be inferred to be causally related to the treatment itself. Effectiveness research, in contrast, is concerned with the degree to which treatment does work in the real world (i.e., practicing psychologists who may not be specially trained in a specific treatment modality, absence of clear treatment guidelines, heterogeneous client samples). An emphasis is placed on external validity in effectiveness research, that is, the degree to which the findings can be generalized to therapists and clients (Nathan et al.). Most psychotherapy research to date has been concerned with efficacy, including the work on empirically supported treatments. There is some evidence, however, that the effects of treatments that have been shown to be efficacious in carefully controlled treatment outcome studies may not be as effective under real-world conditions (Weisz, Donenberg, Han, & Weiss, 1995).

Not surprisingly, psychotherapy researchers have placed greater value on efficacy studies, because they strive to determine if a specific type of therapy can produce reliable changes in the treatment of a specific disorder or problem. In contrast, practitioners question the value of efficacy research, because they recognize that clients do not present with only one disorder and that flexibility is often required in adapting a treatment to the needs of a particular client. Therefore, practicing psychologists often place more value on findings from effectiveness studies. A continuing challenge for clinical psychology is to provide a stronger link between the well-controlled studies that characterize efficacy research and the more externally valid research on treatment effectiveness (see box 16.2).

Challenge 3: Understanding Cultural Factors in Interventions We need a better understanding of how different cultural and ethnic groups

BOX 16.2

THE RELATIONSHIP BETWEEN SCIENCE AND PRACTICE

The need to maintain a strong link between science and practice is a major challenge for clinical psychology. This issue is not unique to our field, however; it is a pervasive concern for all health professions. The problem is personified in two reports issued by the Institute of Medicine, a branch of the National Academy of Sciences. The first report, *To Err Is Human: Building a Safer Medical System* (Kohn, Corrigan, & Donaldson, 2000) provided data on the effects of errors made in medical treatment in the United States. The researchers conducted an intensive study of the medical records of several hospitals in order to evaluate the consequences of mistakes and limitations in medical treatment (e.g., failing to provide the correct medication, inadequate access to proper care, delays in obtaining treatment). Based on their most conservative and cautious estimates, the researchers concluded that medical errors are responsible for at least 44,000 deaths each year in the United States, a rate that exceeds the death rates attributable to motor vehicle accidents (43,000 deaths), breast cancer (42,000 deaths), and AIDS (16,000 deaths).

In a follow-up report, *Crossing the Chasm: A New Health Care System for the Twenty-first Century* (Committee on Quality Health Care in America,

2001), recommendations were proposed to rectify this serious problem in our health care system. One of the major causes of medical errors was attributed to the use of outdated treatments when newer, more effective techniques were available. One of the most startling findings was that it can take more than 17 years for some important medical discoveries to become accepted practice by the average physician. For example, at the time of the study, the use of beta blockers had been established as a highly effective treatment for the prevention of second heart attacks in cardiac patients for over 10 years; however, nearly half the patients in the study did not receive this important medication.

The parallel for clinical psychology is clear. Major advances have been made in the development of efficacious psychological treatments for a wide range of disorders. However, these advances will be of little benefit to patients if practicing psychologists are not informed of the latest treatment developments, are skeptical about the generalizability of the findings, or are not trained in the use of new techniques. The stakes are extraordinarily high for clinical psychology in terms of needless suffering by patients who have failed to receive treatments that could effectively alleviate their problems.

conceptualize solutions to and help for their problems (e.g., Kulka, Veroff, & Douvan, 1979; Tsai & Carstensen, 1996). For example, it is not at all clear that psychotherapy as it is currently practiced is applicable to problems faced by inner-city African American youth or to families that have recently immigrated from different regions (e.g., Southeast Asia). Research by psychologist Stanley Sue and his colleagues has shown that there are differences among ethnic groups in their participation in and response to psychotherapy. For example, Sue et al. (1991) found that the match (or correspondence) between the ethnicity of the therapist and the eth-

nicity of the client was related to the length of treatment for Asian American, African American, and Hispanic American clients and was associated with treatment outcomes among Hispanic American clients. Yeh, Takeuchi, and Sue (1994) found that children who received mental health services at ethnic-specific mental health centers were less likely to drop out of services after the first session (a frequent problem in the treatment of children), utilized more services, and received higher ratings of their functioning at the end of treatment than did those who attended mainstream or non-ethnic-specific mental health centers. Broadening our understanding of the similarities and the differences among various cultural groups is a pressing need for the future development of clinical psychology (Sue, 1998). Increased knowledge and sensitivity to the impact of cultural differences on treatment is a high priority for clinical research and for the practice of clinical psychology with diverse populations (Tsai & Carstensen, 1996).

Challenge 4: Understanding Why Treatments Work   In spite of the strong knowledge base that has developed on the effectiveness and efficacy of psychological treatments, we are still in the early stages of understanding why certain treatments are effective. Some treatments may work for reasons that are quite different than proponents of the approach may think. Research is required to dismantle the different elements through **component analysis.** Component analysis is best accomplished by comparing interventions that include and exclude carefully selected elements of an overall treatment approach. We provided two examples of component analysis of treatments in chapter 15—a study of the effects of different elements of cognitive-behavior therapy for bulimia (Agras et al., 1989) and a study of the eye movement component of EMDR (Feske & Goldstein, 1997). Both these studies were useful in identifying elements of interventions that were not necessary to produce significant positive effects. Component analysis research will be important in determining more efficient and cost effective forms of treatment, a goal that is increasing in importance for clinical psychology.

Challenge 5: Providing Services in the Context of Managed Health Care   The character of health care in America changed dramatically during the 1980s and 1990s, with **managed health care** playing an increasingly greater role in the provision of health care to individuals and families. Under managed health care systems, decisions about an individual's health care are regulated either by companies that provide health care services or by insurance companies that underwrite the cost of services. Managed health care is likely to continue to grow as the United States government remains undecided about the possibility of a broad national program to provide health care to all Americans.

Managed health care has not emerged specifically in regard to mental health care but rather as an effort to deal with the ever-rising costs of health care in general. However, the growth of managed care has had a major impact on the way that psychological services are provided to individuals (Chambliss, 2000). Prior to the development of managed care systems, most health insurance policies included mental health services that covered psychological testing and psychotherapy provided by a clinical psychologist. Individuals who wanted to receive mental health services, most often psychotherapy, were free to choose a psychologist, and the cost of the psychologist's services would be reimbursed by the insurance company. For the most part, there were no stipulations about the types of problems for which an individual could seek help, nor were there limits placed on the number of sessions or type of treatment that would be reimbursed. This situation has changed dramatically under managed care. Most current systems require that approval be obtained from a primary care physician (a general practitioner or family practitioner) or from a managed care worker before services from a psychologist can be sought. The psychologist is typically required to specify a *DSM-IV* diagnosis that is being treated, and a limited number of sessions are approved for reimbursement. Additional sessions are added only after review by a managed care worker.

There have been both problems and benefits for psychologists as a result of managed health care. The most significant problem has been the limits on the degree of independence that clinical psychologists have in working with patients. Patients are no longer free to choose to see a psychologist on their own; they must have received prior approval from their managed care company that their insurance will pay for the services they will receive. The level of independence of practicing psychologists is further limited by constraints on the type of treatment and the number of sessions that can be offered. These problems have led to concerns that managed care is limiting the ability of psychologists to practice as independent health professionals and that some of the limits on practice are not in the best interest of the patients (e.g., Hayes, Barlow, & Nelson-Gray, 1999; Sloan & Mizes, 1999).

On the other hand, there have been positive effects of the increasing role of managed care. Most importantly, monitoring of psychological services by managed care organizations has led to much greater accountability by psychologists (Chambliss, 2000). That is, psychologists are now held accountable to external review in terms of applying a specific diagnosis for each patient, justification of the patient's need for care, the use of treatments with documented efficacy, and measurement and documentation of outcomes to demonstrate effectiveness with individual patients. If cases are reviewed by managed care agents who are knowledgeable of the literature on empirically supported treatments, this accountability could lead to better application of the most effective treatments for specific cases. For example, if a psychologist determines that a patient is suffering from Panic Disorder, in the absence of any form of external monitoring the psychologist could use any form of treatment that he or she chooses, including traditional long-term psychoanalysis, client-centered therapy, or Gestalt therapy. However, none of these therapies have been shown to be effective in the treatment of Panic Disorder. There are, however, cognitive-behavioral methods for treating Panic Disorder that have been shown to be highly effective (e.g., Barlow & Cerney, 1988; Barlow et al., 1989; Clark, 1986; Clark et al., 1999). If managed care agents are aware of these research findings, they could require that in order for the psychologist to be reimbursed for treatment, he or she must use one of the methods that has been shown to be effective for treating Panic Disorder. Although this type of regulation clearly limits the autonomy of psychologists, it just as clearly provides some protection to the public that the treatment they receive has been shown to be effective.

As the role of managed health care increases, it will be essential for clinical psychology to ensure that decisions about diagnosis and treatment of psychological disorders are based on the best available research evidence. In this way, managed care can provide an impetus for a closer link between research and practice and can provide greater assurance to patients that they will receive high quality mental health care.

OPPORTUNITIES IN CLINICAL PSYCHOLOGY

The field of clinical psychology has begun its second century as a vital combination of research and application of scientific knowledge. We anticipate that the field will continue with its existing strengths—assessment and psychotherapy. We now present our best guesses on exciting directions for the future. In some instances these represent increased emphasis in areas in which clinical psychology is already active. In other cases, these reflect new areas for our field. As we pointed out in chapter 2, the history of clinical psychology has been influenced by advances within psychology and by factors and forces outside the field. Drawing on the past, we expect that some of the opportunities for the future will come from accomplishments in psychological research, whereas others will be driven by changes in our world. These opportunities may be helpful to you as you consider the possibility of pursuing a degree and a career in clinical psychology (see box 16.3).

Emerging Themes in Psychological Research

We believe that two current areas of research will have far-reaching consequences for research and

BOX 16.3

GRADUATE STUDY IN CLINICAL PSYCHOLOGY

In this book we have described the field of clinical psychology and the tremendous opportunities that we believe are available to students entering the field. As you know, the first major step to becoming a clinical psychologist (besides taking this course!) is applying to, and entering, a graduate program in clinical psychology. In teaching this course at our own universities over the past few years, we have found that undergraduate students raise some important questions regarding graduate study in clinical psychology. In this box, therefore, we answer these questions and describe the process of applying to graduate school in clinical psychology.

WHY SHOULD I GO TO GRADUATE SCHOOL IN CLINICAL PSYCHOLOGY?

There are several reasons to pursue graduate work in clinical psychology. Some people want to become practicing psychologists, to engage in psychotherapy and psychological testing. Others are interested in studying psychopathology or how psychotherapy works. Some people are interested in both research and clinical practice. Most careers in clinical psychology currently require a doctoral degree (either a PhD or a PsyD), so we suggest that you apply to doctoral programs in clinical psychology rather than to programs that offer only a master's degree.

WHAT ARE THE REQUIREMENTS FOR ADMISSION TO GRADUATE SCHOOL IN CLINICAL PSYCHOLOGY?

Admission to PhD programs in clinical psychology is very competitive. Ratios of 200 to 300 applicants to 8 positions are common (although as many as 10 to 15 students would actually be accepted to fill the 8 slots, because some students who are accepted to a particular program decide to go elsewhere, vacating that slot for another applicant). Different programs emphasize different factors for admission, but it is reasonably safe to say that in all programs Graduate Record Examinations (GREs) and grade point averages (GPAs) are examined closely. In the most com-petitive graduate programs in clinical psychology, students who gain admission to the program have average scores of more than 2,000 on the GRE (Verbal plus Quantitative plus Analytical) and have an average GPA of more than 3.5. GPAs are most important for the last two years of undergraduate schooling, so students with uneven early records still have a good chance of being admitted to graduate school if they've improved over their undergraduate years. There are certainly respectable graduate programs in clinical psychology whose students have lower scores on these measures, but in general, students who score below 1,800 on the GRE or have a GPA of less than 3.3 should expect some difficulty getting into a top graduate program in clinical psychology unless they have some other special qualifications.

Other criteria are also important in gaining admission to a top graduate program in clinical psychology, but these criteria are less standardized than GPA and GRE scores. For example, most (but not all) graduate programs expect applicants to have obtained some research experience as undergraduates. The primary concern is that students should have conducted some psychological research in order to know whether they find it interesting. From an admissions perspective, it is less important that you have had research experience in clinical areas than it is that you have had meaningful research experience at all, that is, that you have not just helped to enter data in someone's lab. It is also important that you be able to solicit a letter of recommendation from at least one research supervisor.

Many graduate schools give a great deal of consideration to the potential match between applicants' and faculty's interests. Your strong interests in a professor's research will make you a much more desirable applicant to that person. But you must be able to convey that your interests are serious, for example, by discussing a specific study. Most faculty will not be impressed if it seems that you merely scanned the departmental brochure searching for topics that sound interesting.

BOX 16.3 (continued)

Finally, you may also want to consider trying some hands-on counseling work. Many agencies accept and train volunteers. This experience is probably more helpful in exploring your own interests than in gaining admission to graduate school, but it certainly won't hurt your chances of being admitted.

WHAT IF I DON'T GET ADMITTED TO GRADUATE SCHOOL?

For a number of reasons, many students do not get admitted to any of the programs to which they have applied. This situation can happen because a student applied to only a few programs, and the faculty with whom they wanted to work were not accepting students that year. It could also reflect the fact that a student is not among the most competitive applicants. To avoid the former possibility, most students should apply to 10 or more programs. Many faculty are receptive to e-mails from potential applicants inquiring about whether they are accepting graduate students for the coming year. If a student is rejected because of shortcomings in her or his academic record, there is still hope for being accepted in the future, but it will take work and commitment. For example, to compensate for an uneven undergraduate record, a student may take additional classes and perform well in them. GREs lower than 1,800 may require that the student attempt to raise them by taking a GRE preparation course. (These courses can often be helpful, but you shouldn't expect them to raise your score more than 200 points or so.) Another possibility is to take a year or two off to work on research. It is often possible to get a paid position in a research laboratory at a university or at an agency such as NIMH. Full-time research experience in a certain area will make you more attractive to other professionals in that area (e.g., schizophrenia research). It will also give you a clearer indication of whether research is for you. Obviously, this employment is a large commitment, one that you should approach carefully.

HOW DO I DECIDE WHERE TO APPLY?

The most important consideration in deciding where to apply to graduate school in clinical psychology concerns your ultimate career goals. Some programs are oriented primarily toward training academic clinical psychologists, that is, future university professors; others focus more strongly on training practitioners, clinical psychologists who might practice full-time. It is important that you are aware that even the most academically oriented graduate programs will prepare you both for practice and for research. Therefore, unless you are absolutely confident right now that you will never want to conduct research once you have your doctoral degree, we strongly encourage you to keep your options open by applying to accredited PhD programs in clinical psychology. In these programs, the faculty are conducting cutting-edge research, and the quality of the clinical training is typically excellent.

The best way to decide which graduate programs to apply to is to figure out what, specifically, you are interested in and then find out which programs are best in training in that area. In your classes, you should pay close attention to the topics that most excite you. What studies do you wish you'd done? In your research experiences, what has excited you most? If you are fortunate enough to get a strong idea about your research interests and if you find people at clinical programs with whom you'd really like to work, let them know, preferably by writing to them. If you are primarily interested in clinical practice, you might seek out and talk to clinical psychologists at sites that seem most interesting to you (for example, hospitals, clinics, or even in private practice). Many practicing clinical psychologists would be flattered and happy to talk about their jobs.

WHAT INFORMATION RESOURCES ARE AVAILABLE?

There are several resources that you can (and should) consult when deciding where to apply for graduate school in clinical psychology. Probably the most informative single source is a book entitled *Insider's Guide to Graduate Programs in Clinical Psychology*, written by Michael A. Sayette, Tracy J. Mayne, and John C. Norcross, and published by Guilford Press. This book's introductory chapter describes the field of clinical psychology and is followed by a number of chapters outlining in considerable detail how you should go about preparing for

BOX 16.3 (concluded)

graduate school, selecting and applying to appropriate graduate programs in clinical psychology, and making a final decision about which program to attend. The book also contains sample letters requesting program information and a sample format for your curriculum vitae, or résumé. And perhaps most importantly, this book contains information on almost 200 graduate programs in clinical psychology across North America. Now, you should bear in mind that these presentations are not objective: Each program provides its own (unedited) information for the book. Nevertheless, these descriptions should give you a fair idea about each program's clinical versus research focus, GRE and GPA cutoffs, and available research areas. This book is updated regularly, although in general the information and program descriptions will change little from one year to the next.

Another useful book is *Graduate Studies in Psychology*, published by the APA. This book lists all doctoral and master's level psychology graduate programs in the United States and Canada, organized by state. To get more information about each

program, send a postcard (really, that's all that's necessary) to the person listed as the director of admissions asking for their graduate brochure and application materials. These postcards should be sent by no later than November 1. Once you begin to receive brochures, you should have a better idea of which programs are best suited to your interests.

Finally, you should feel free to talk with your academic advisor about graduate programs in clinical psychology. If your university or college has a graduate program in clinical psychology, you should talk with the graduate students. They will all have gone through the application process themselves, and most will also have interviewed at a number of different programs. They will be able to give you some firsthand information about the application and interviewing procedure and probably about some specific programs as well.

The information in this box is based on a longer document written by Michael Bailey and Ian Gotlib. The document is on the website of the Psychology Department at Northwestern University.

---

practice in clinical psychology. The first is focused on the role of emotions in normal functioning, psychopathology, health, and illness. The second is the rapidly developing technology for the assessment and measurement of brain function.

Emotion and Emotion Regulation There is an ebb and flow of topics and perspectives that dominate research in psychology. During the early history of the field, a strong emphasis was placed on the importance of emotions, primarily because of the pioneering work of Sigmund Freud and William James. This period was followed by the rise of behaviorism in the 1930s and 1940s, when observable behavior became the focus for much of psychology. Behaviorism held sway until the 1970s when psychology underwent the cognitive revolution and the study of cognitive processes came to dominate. During

the 1990s, with advances in technology and knowledge of underlying biological processes, biology came to predominate. And now at the beginning of the new century, we have come full circle and emotions are once again at center stage (e.g., Lewis & Haviland-Jones, 2000).

The study of emotions holds two major implications for the future of clinical psychology. First, clinical research is needed on all aspects of emotion, including the role of emotions in psychopathology, health, and illness; the measurement of emotion processes; and the role of emotion in psychological interventions. Emotions are central to most or all of human experience. The experience of emotion signals the importance of an event, facilitates or impedes decision making, influences learning and memory, and provides motivation for behavior.

Second, another broad area of opportunity for clinical psychology involves the integration of cutting-edge research on emotion into clinical practice. Central to both research and practice is the process of **emotion regulation.** Emotion regulation refers to the capacity to initiate, modulate, modify, redirect, or optimize emotional arousal, particularly in response to threat or stress. Some aspects of emotion regulation are biologically wired into human beings and are present from birth (e.g., Barr, Young, Wright, Gravel, & Alkawaf, 1999). Most aspects of emotion regulation, however, are learned over the course of development, and many emotion regulation strategies involve complex sets of thoughts and behaviors. For example, extensive research indicates that efforts to suppress emotions are associated with adverse psychological and physical outcomes. Jane Richards and James Gross have shown that efforts to suppress the expression of negative emotion impairs memory and that this effect is due in part to the types of self-talk that individuals use to try to monitor and suppress the expression of their emotions (Richards & Gross, 1999, 2000). In contrast, the modulated expression of emotions appears to be beneficial. For example, writing about one's emotions has been found to have beneficial effects in terms of decreased levels of negative emotion and enhanced health (Pennebaker, 1997). Research on emotion regulation has powerful implications for psychological interventions, because the failure to manage negative emotions is at the core of many forms of psychopathology. Therefore, increased knowledge about adaptive and maladaptive processes of emotion regulation (and dysregulation) will provide a stronger foundation for interventions to enhance processes of managing negative emotions.

Neuroscience There is a long history of the involvement of clinical psychologists in **neuroscience,** or the study of the relationship between brain functioning and human behavior. As we saw in chapter 8, clinical psychologists working in the field of neuropsychology are particularly interested in how performance on tasks assessing cognitive or motor abilities might reflect difficulties or abnormalities in brain function. Most recently, there has been enormous interest in procedures that permit a more direct assessment of brain functioning than is available through the administration of traditional neuropsychological tests. Procedures utilizing electroencephalography (EEG), positron emission tomography (PET), and functional magnetic resonance imaging (fMRI) yield information about brain activity virtually at the moment of assessment and typically in response to different types of stimuli. Whereas EEG records electrical activity at different sites in the brain through electrodes placed on the scalp, PET involves injecting a radioactive chemical into the patient and tracking the rate at which it is metabolized at various sites of the brain. Finally, fMRI uses powerful magnets to determine which specific areas or structures of the brain are activated while the patient is engaging in cognitive or emotional tasks.

The first studies using these procedures focused largely on identifying which areas of the brain are activated when individuals participate in different types of cognitive encoding and memory tasks (e.g., Demb et al., 1995; Gabrieli, Brewer, Desmond, & Glover, 1997). More recently, however, investigators have become interested in studying the relationship between brain activation and emotional functioning. Indeed, our ability now to depict noninvasively the neurometabolic underpinnings of various emotions has advanced our understanding of a number of different mental disorders (e.g., Barlow & Durand, 1995; Institute of Medicine, 1991). For example, a considerable body of research has recently described what appears to be localized brain activation in Panic Disorder (e.g., George, 1992). Other research has elegantly demonstrated that neurobiological dysfunction in obsessive-compulsive patients normalizes following successful treatment with either medication or behavior therapy (e.g., Baxter, 1994; Baxter et al., 1992; Schwartz et al., 1996).

BOX 16.4

EMOTIONS AND EMOTION REGULATION
ACROSS CULTURES AND ACROSS THE LIFE SPAN

Psychological research is rapidly advancing our understanding of the nature, significance, and function of emotion. Although emotion took a back seat during the era of behaviorism and during psychology's cognitive revolution, it has gained a place of prominence in current psychological research and theory. A full appreciation of the role of emotion depends in part on our understanding of how different emotions vary as a function of two fundamental factors—age and culture. Stanford psychologists **Laura Carstensen** and Jeanne Tsai have led the way in research on emotion across the life span and in different cultural groups.

Several observations from their work have particular significance for clinical psychology. There are significant changes in the way people experience and manage emotions across the life span, with important changes occurring in late adulthood (Carstensen & Turk, 1998). In her theory of socioemotional selectivity, Carstensen has shown that as people age they become aware of having less time left in their lives, and this awareness leads to changes in their motivation to direct more attention to emotional rather than knowledge-related goals (Carstensen, 1999). One pronounced change is a shift to increase interactions with others with whom they share close, emotionally meaningful relationships and to expend less time and effort in relationships that are less intimate. Thus, although the

number of social contacts declines with age, this decline is the result of investing time in fewer, closer relationships (Carstensen, 1998). Moreover, older people are better able to regulate their emotions than are their younger counterparts, including the regulation of physiological responses to emotionally arousing stimuli (Tsai, Levenson, & Carstensen, 2000).

There are also important cultural differences in the experience, expression, and regulation of emotions. For example, Tsai and colleagues have examined differences between Asian Americans and Euro-Americans in self-report, behavioral, and physiological indicators of emotion (e.g., Tsai et al., 2000; Tsai, Levenson & McCoy, 1999). There are greater cultural differences in positive than in negative emotions, and in self-report and behavioral measures of emotion than in physiological markers. This finding suggests that those aspects of emotion that are most strongly influenced by social consequences show the greatest cultural differences.

These studies indicate that clinical psychologists need to give greater attention to the role of development and culture in both research and practice. Differences in emotional expression and regulation will be important to consider in understanding individuals' emotional responses in treatment and in the types of regulatory skills that may be appropriate to teach in the context of psychotherapy and other psychological interventions.

These new directions in neuroscience are clearly relevant to the functioning of clinical psychologists. Findings concerning the association between localized brain activation and emotion, for example, are providing the empirical foundation for theoretical integrations of biological and psychological factors in different forms of psychopathology (e.g., Baxter, 1994; Goodman & Gotlib, 1999). Clinical psychologists will play a major role in refining and extending these formulations and in designing and conducting

research to test these models. As a model of this role, we can look to the work of **Richard J. Davidson,** a psychologist at the University of Wisconsin. Drawing on the work of Jeffrey Gray, Davidson has formulated a theory in which he posits that depression is characterized by relatively greater activation of the frontal region of the right rather than the left hemisphere. The right frontal area of the brain is associated with withdrawal tendencies, whereas the left frontal area is related to approach behavior. In a series of

Jeanne L. Tsai, Ph.D., and Laura L. Carstensen, Ph.D., professors at Stanford University, are clinical psychologists who are recognized for their work on cultural aspects of emotion regulation over the life course. Dr. Carstensen has conducted innovative research examining changes in emotional functioning with age. Dr. Tsai has examined differences in the physiology and expressive behaviors of individuals of different cultures as they experience various emotional states. (Photo courtesy of Jeanne Tsai and Laura Carstensen.)

studies using EEG procedures, Davidson and his colleagues (e.g., Davidson, 1994; Davidson, Jackson, & Kalin, 2000; Henriques & Davidson, 1991; Sutton & Davidson, 1997) have demonstrated that depressed persons are typified by greater activation in the right frontal than in the left frontal area of the brain, reflecting the stronger withdrawal rather than approach behavioral tendencies that are characteristic of depression.

As you might imagine, clinical psychologists have drawn on these and similar findings both in attempting to understand possible mechanisms of treatment for psychopathology and in developing

new approaches to therapy. For example, EEG findings concerning the decreased activation of the area of the brain involved in approach behavior in depressed patients might help explain why treatment programs designed to increase the activities of depressed persons have been successful (e.g., Hammen & Glass, 1975; Lewinsohn, Sullivan, & Grosscup, 1980); these findings might also be of use in refining similar treatments. Neuroscience findings can also be used in developing novel approaches to the treatment of emotional disorders. For example, Peter Rosenfeld and his colleagues at Northwestern University (Rosenfeld et al., 1995, 1996) drew on Davidson's findings of hemispheric asymmetry in depression when they tested the effects of biofeedback in the treatment of this disorder. In this treatment, patients learned to increase the relative activation of their left frontal hemisphere, with a resultant elevation of their mood.

Certainly more work needs to be done in this area, but there are already strong indications of the benefits of close collaborations between clinical psychologists and neuroscientists, each bringing their own skills to bear to the assessment and treatment of psychopathology. Clinical psychologists have unique expertise in developing tests and tasks to assess cognitive and emotional functioning and in developing and evaluating approaches to therapy that build on the most current research findings in neuroscience. With the rapid increase of research in the neuroscience of psychopathology, there are exciting opportunities for clinical psychologists to contribute to virtually every aspect of this growth in the coming decades.

Emerging Arenas for Practice

Prevention As we discussed in chapter 11, a much more recent role for clinical psychologists (and psychologists in the related field of community psychology) has been in the prevention of psychopathology and in the promotion of mental and physical health. The notion of prevention of psychopathology and promotion of mental health were remote concepts 100 years ago, because the etiology of most forms of mental disorder was unknown. However, as the sources of risk for various types of psychopathology, and in some instances the causes of certain disorders, have been identified, prevention programs have been developed to reduce these risks and reduce the onset or progression of some forms of psychopathology.

Although advances in the treatment of mental disorders have come from the work of many different disciplines, psychologists have played a leading role in the prevention of psychopathology and mental health promotion and in the development and evaluation of interventions to reduce the onset of psychological disorders. For example, there is new promising evidence that interventions that include multiple components aimed at children, families, and their social environments may help reduce aggressive and violent behavior that is associated with conduct disorder in later childhood and adolescence. One exemplary intervention, the FAST Track program, begins with the identification of children who are at risk for aggression and conduct disorder based on characteristics that are identified before children enter school (e.g., Conduct Problems Prevention Research Group, 1999a, 1999b). Services are then delivered to change the behavior of high-risk children, improve the skills of parents in managing oppositional and aggressive behavior in these children, build structured interventions in the school, and change communities to reduce the risk for violent and aggressive behavior.

There is also some initial evidence that interventions with children at risk for depression can reduce their development of depressive symptoms and depressive disorder. In one approach, children are first identified as being at risk for depression, based on evidence that they are experiencing either high levels of depressive symptoms or a pessimistic or hopeless cognitive style (Gillham, Reivich, Jaycox, & Seligman, 1995; Jaycox, Reivich, Gillham, & Seligman, 1994; Seligman, 1995). Children at high risk are then offered the opportunity to participate in a program to learn more optimistic ways of thinking and skills to manage sources of stress in their lives that can contribute to feelings of hopelessness and depression.

One of the challenges for clinical psychologists in the future is the integration of prevention programs into the mainstream of mental health care. Prevention does not involve the treatment of an individual (or individuals) with an identified or diagnosed problem. Therefore, methods used to treat psychological problems cannot be applied. Furthermore, it has been difficult (or impossible) for psychologists to be paid for delivering preventive services, because insurance companies and other third-party payers have been unwilling to reimburse psychologists unless a diagnosis of a psychological disorder has been made. The increasing role of managed care in mental health care may offer an exciting opportunity for clinical psychologists to become involved in prevention in the future. Managed care companies are invested in providing health care to large numbers of people at the lowest possible cost. The argument can be made that prevention offers an excellent method to contain costs by preventing problems before they occur or at least before they become severe.

One important avenue for developing and implementing prevention programs within managed care organizations involves the identification of children who are at risk for psychopathology because one or both of their parents suffer from psychopathology. Research has clearly shown that children of parents with schizophrenia, depression, alcoholism, and other forms of psychopathology are themselves at dramatically increased risk for psychopathology (e.g., Gotlib & Goodman, 1999; Morey, 1999; Watt, Anthony, Wynne, & Rolf, 1984). If parents are receiving treatment for a mental health problem through a managed care organization, the managed care company is responsible for the health coverage for the children in this family as well. It is financially in the best interest of the company to prevent psychological problems in children in such families before they need to provide coverage for much costlier treatment for psychological disorders. In addition to the economic incentive for managed care companies to invest in prevention, it is also consistent with the basic principles espoused by health maintenance organizations. That is, many managed care companies are committed to providing comprehensive services that are aimed at building and maintaining health and not just treating diseases or disorders once they develop.

One example of preventive interventions for children of parents with psychopathology involves the development of interventions for children of depressed parents. There are multiple mechanisms through which parental depression affects children, including both biological and interpersonal processes. Programs have been developed to address the interpersonal processes within families that place children at risk. Psychiatrist William Beardslee (1998) has created a program for families with a depressed parent that helps these families better understand the nature of depression and that develops ways of protecting children in these families from some of the family interactions that can contribute to children's emotional and behavioral problems.

We have presented here only a few examples of the strides that have been made in identifying factors that place individuals at risk for psychopathology and in translating those risks into programs to prevent the onset of disorder. Much of the important work in prevention has fallen outside the traditional framework of clinical psychology and has been conducted by psychologists who identify themselves as community psychologists. However, there is a clear and important role for clinical psychologists to play in the prevention of psychopathology.

Health   A relatively recent development in the field has been clinical psychologists' increased role in the prevention and treatment of physical disease and illness and concomitantly in the promotion of health. Exciting advances include research that has established a strong relationship between stressful experiences and health. Both the occurrence of stressful life events and chronic stressful conditions are related to higher rates of illness. This research has opened the way for further study into more and less adaptive ways that people can try to manage stress and ultimately to interventions that improve coping and stress responses in order to reduce the risk of illness. Extensive research has shown that emotional symptoms and disorders are related to health and illness. The role of negative emotions in patients' recovery from illness and injury has identified opportunities for psychological interventions that may decrease morbidity and mortality among patients recovering from illness and from the side effects of treatments. Some of the most powerful research in clinical health psychology has come in studies of interventions to enhance patients' health and their ability to cope with and prevent disease. Psychological interventions can promote a better emotional response to serious illness and may facilitate better physical outcomes as well. Preventive interventions have also proved to be promising in reducing the incidence of a number of diseases by changing behaviors that are related to increased risk.

Similar to the state of knowledge with regard to prevention of mental disorders, recognition and knowledge of the role of behavioral factors in health and physical disease was limited or nonexistent a century ago. Since then, behavior has come to be recognized as a major source of risk for a wide range of physical illnesses and diseases, including the two most significant causes of death in the United States—heart disease and cancer. In addition, behavior plays a substantial role in risk for contracting HIV and AIDS and other sexually transmitted diseases. The important issue is to identify the unique contributions that clinical psychologists can make in regard to health and illness.

Cigarette smoking is one of the major sources of morbidity and mortality in the United States through its contribution to both lung cancer and heart disease. However, there are now promising data to suggest that behavioral interventions can reduce the onset of smoking in young people, and some forms of cognitive-behavioral therapy are effective in smoking cessation and preventing relapse (Compas, Haaga, Keefe, Leitenberg, & Williams, 1998). By preventing the onset of smoking and helping smokers to quit, psychologists can play a major role in reducing this enormous cause of cancer and heart disease. AIDS is another major health threat that is the direct consequence of behavior through either unprotected sexual activity or through use of contaminated needles. Psychological and behavioral interventions have been found to be effective in increas-

ing safe sexual behavior and thereby reducing the risk of exposure to the AIDS virus (e.g., Holtgrave & Kelly, 1996; Jemmott, Jemmott, Fong, & McCaffree, 1999; Kelly, 1997; Pinkerton, Holtgrave, DiFranceisco, Stevenson, & Kelly, 1998). Interventions to change unprotected sexual activity represent a second area in which psychologists can help people change behavior and, through changes in behavior, reduce mortality attributable to AIDS.

In addition to these important contributions to the prevention of disease, psychological interventions have also been developed to enhance the quality of life of patients with acute and chronic disease and to aid patients in coping with a major symptom of many diseases—chronic pain (e.g., Gatchel & Turk, 1996, 1999; Keefe, Beaupré, & Gil, 1996). Clinical psychologists work in collaboration with physicians, nurses, and other health care professionals in helping patients and their families cope with illness, increase compliance with important treatments, and manage the emotional effects of illness. Psychological interventions have been shown to be effective in reducing problems such as anxiety and depression that frequently accompany a serious illness (Compas et al., 1998). There is also evidence that psychological interventions may reduce the risk of recurrence of illness and may prolong survival (Spiegel et al., 1989).

With these important findings as a base, clinical psychologists in the future have enormous opportunities to contribute to physical health and emotional well-being. Psychologists can work as members of multidisciplinary teams of health care providers, offering specific expertise in human behavior and behavior change (broadly defined). It is somewhat ironic that while some psychologists are seeking prescription privileges that would duplicate those of physicians, other psychologists are creating a role that is based on the unique skills of psychologists—the scientific study of human behavior and the application of scientific knowledge to behavior change. It will be important for clinical psychologists to identify a role and niche within the health care system that is based on the unique knowledge base and skills that clinical psychologists have to offer.

Changes in Society: The Role of Technology

In chapter 2 we noted the profound impact of the First and Second World Wars on the evolution of clinical psychology. We hope that the future does not hold similar catastrophic events that will influence our field. However, we anticipate that changes outside psychology will continue to shape the science and practice of clinical psychology, most notably the rapid changes that are occurring in technology in our everyday lives.

Telemedicine and Telehealth   Technology now allows health professionals to interact with each other and with patients from remote locations through television. Referred to as **telemedicine** and **telehealth,** this process has allowed health care providers to share information with one another and provide case consultation on a remote basis when practical factors prohibit face-to-face contact. Telecommunications technology can also be used for assessment, diagnosis, and intervention in various aspects of health care, including mental health services (Nickelson, 1998). This technology is now finding its way into psychology and could change the nature of practice (Jerome & Zaylor, 2000). Psychological consultation may be facilitated through two-way televised interactions, particularly for psychologists practicing in rural locations that are typically isolated from contact with other professionals. At present, televised conferences and therapist-client interactions are in their earliest stages of development and warrant attention in future research.

The Internet   The Internet represents one of the greatest technological developments of the last 100 years. It is estimated that the Internet will have as much or more influence on communication as the telephone, and its effect on our access to information is immeasurable. Two questions face psychologists regarding the Internet: Is use of the Internet related to psychological problems? And should therapy be conducted online? Research addressing the first question is still in its early stages; however, there are some studies suggesting that high levels of use of the Internet are associated with psychological and interpersonal difficulties (e.g., Kraut et al., 1998; Sanders, Field, Diego, & Kaplan, 2000). Both Kraut et al. and Sanders et al. found that high Internet use was associated with decreased social interactions with others, decreased communication with family members, and declines in social network size. Kraut et al. but not Sanders et al. found that Internet use was associated with increased depressive symptoms and loneliness. It is unlikely that there will be simple associations between the use of the Internet and psychological problems; however, these early studies suggest that there may be social costs associated with extreme involvement in the Net.

The role of the Internet in the delivery of psychological services is less clear. The use of the telephone in crisis counseling and other types of mental health services has a long history. Jerome and Zaylor (2000) note that newer communication technologies hold significant promise for the provision of psychological services to individuals who are geographically isolated, lacking in personal and financial resources, or confined in such a way that prevents access to face-to-face services. One of the challenges in understanding the place for newer communication technologies is the different level of information that is available compared with face-to-face or even telephone communication (Maheu & Gordon, 2000). In particular, a great deal of the characteristics of emotions are conveyed through facial expression, gestures, and tone of voice. These sources of emotional information are lost in Internet communication (Jerome & Zaylor). The promise of technology for the improvement of mental health services is great but as yet relatively untapped and not well understood. As such, it represents an interesting opportunity for the future of clinical psychology.

SUMMARY AND CONCLUSIONS

We have now completed our introduction to the field of clinical psychology. In this chapter we have summarized some of the many accomplishments and advances that have been achieved by clinical psychologists since the founding of the field a little over 100 years ago. Significant progress is noted in all areas, including our understanding of psychopathology, the development of reliable and valid tools for psychological assessment, and the development and implementation of efficacious psychological interventions. In spite of the tendency toward self-criticism in clinical psychology, the field has made enormous strides in its first century.

Without overlooking the progress that has been achieved, clinical psychology is faced with a number of challenges in our understanding of psychopathology, in the development of methods of assessment, and in the treatment of psychological problems. These challenges include devoting greater attention to social and cultural factors in psychopathology, assessment, and intervention; expanding the scope of our assessment methods, especially in the measurement of intelligence; and increasing the linkages between the science and practice of psychotherapy. Paramount are the issues involved in the pursuit of prescription privileges for psychologists, a step that could change the face of the discipline more than any other development.

For those of you contemplating a career in clinical psychology, the future is filled with exciting possibilities. We have outlined only a few of those possibilities here, including new areas of psychological research on emotions and in neuroscience; new opportunities for practice in prevention and health; and the implications of new technologies for the practice of clinical psychology. We hope we have provided an introduction to the field that has captured some of the challenges, opportunities, and rewards that can be found in research and practice in clinical psychology.

KEY TERMS AND NAMES

Behavioral genetics
Laura Carstensen
Component analysis of treatment
Richard Davidson
Emotion regulation
Emotional intelligence
Managed care

Neuroscience
Prescription privileges
Psychopharmacology Demonstration Project
Telehealth
Telemedicine
Treatment effectiveness
Treatment efficacy

RESOURCES

Books
American Psychological Association. (2001). *Graduate study in psychology.* Washington, DC: American Psychological Association.
Hayes, S. C., & Heiby, E. M. (1998). *Prescription privileges for psychologists: A critical appraisal.* Reno, NV: Context Press.

Sayette, M. A., Mayne, T. J., & Norcross, J. C. (1998). *Insider's guide to graduate programs in clinical and counseling psychology.* New York: Guilford.
Journals
American Psychologist
Professional Psychology: Research and Practice
Monitor on Psychology

GLOSSARY

A-B-A-B design A single-case experimental design in which the target behavior is assessed continuously during a baseline condition (the A phase) in which no treatment is in effect, followed by a condition in which treatment is implemented (the B phase). The A and B phases are then repeated to complete the design. Changes in the target behavior from A to B phases are interpreted as evidence of the effectiveness of the treatment.

Accountability In psychotherapy, the position taken increasingly by managed care organizations that psychotherapists should be able to document the effects of the procedures that they use in treatment. Accountability is an important reason to evaluate empirically the effectiveness of different psychotherapies.

Analog observation In behavioral assessment, observations in which the clinician controls the context and situation and systematically examines their effects on the target behavior.

Army Alpha and Army Beta tests Tests of verbal skills (Army Alpha) and nonverbal skills (Army Beta) developed by a group of psychologists in 1917 to measure the mental abilities of American military recruits in World War I.

Assessment The administration and interpretation of standardized psychological tests, structured clinical interviews, systematic observation of an individual's behavior, and examination of the settings or environments in which the individual functions in order to develop an understanding of the person and her or his current problems.

Attending skills Verbal and nonverbal methods of communication that are used to ensure the accurate monitoring of the client and to communicate sincere interest and concern on behalf of the interviewer.

Aversive conditioning A behavioral technique in which an undesired behavior is followed by a negative consequence, thereby decreasing the strength of the behavior.

Behavior therapy An approach to the treatment of problem behaviors that is based on principles of conditioning or learning. Behavior therapy focuses on the treatment of overt behaviors, and its practice is based on the results of empirical research.

Behavioral genetics A field concerned with understanding the degree to which genetic information can contribute to individual differences in behavior and development. In clinical psychology, behavioral geneticists try to determine the extent to which specific psychological disorders or symptoms are inherited.

Behavioral interviewing Interviewing in which the focus is on describing and understanding the relationships among behaviors and their antecedents and consequences and on obtaining detailed descriptions of the problem behaviors and the individual's current environment.

Behavioral neuroscience A discipline that focuses on understanding neural bases of learning, development, and psychopathology, with an emphasis on the role of the brain and the central nervous system in affecting people's behavior.

Behavioral observation   The most fundamental method of behavioral assessment. Direct observation allows the psychologist to document the frequency and intensity of specific behaviors as well as contextual variables that may be eliciting and maintaining the behaviors.

Between-subjects designs   In psychotherapy research, studies examining the effectiveness of a particular treatment by comparing the outcomes of two or more groups of individuals, some of whom receive the treatment and some do not.

Biological preparedness   A concept rooted in evolutionary theory that suggests that we learn to fear some stimuli (e.g., snakes, heights) more easily and readily than we do other stimuli (e.g., flowers, tables).

Boulder Conference   Conference on Graduate Education in Psychology held in Boulder, Colorado, in 1949. The scientist-practitioner model of training was endorsed at this conference as the accepted model of doctoral training in clinical psychology.

Boulder Model   The model of training in clinical psychology—first defined at a conference held in Boulder, Colorado, in 1949—that emphasizes training in both science and practice (also referred to as the scientist-practitioner model).

Catharsis   In psychoanalytic therapy, the release of strong emotions that have been repressed or blocked from direct expression.

Classical, or Pavlovian, conditioning   A form of learning in which a neutral stimulus is paired, or associated, with a different positive or negative stimulus. As a result of this pairing, the original stimulus elicits the same response that was emitted to the stimulus with which it was paired. Ivan Pavlov and John Watson are researchers associated most strongly with classical conditioning.

Classification   In science, grouping elements according to their similarities and differences. In psychopathology more specifically, classification refers to the process of placing people in various diagnostic categories.

Clinical attitude   Attending to the concerns of individual clients through the application of general knowledge from the field of psychology to understand the unique features of the specific case.

Clinical psychology   The branch of psychology devoted to the generation of psychological knowledge and the application of knowledge from the science of psychology for the purpose of understanding and improving the mental and physical well-being and functioning of an individual or group of individuals.

Clinical significance   The degree to which the effect that is observed in a study is meaningful in relation to a clinical criterion or standard. For example, clinical significance can be measured by the proportion of participants who no longer meet diagnostic criteria for a disorder after receiving a specific treatment.

Clinical social work   A branch of the field of social work that involves work with psychological problems through community agencies or mental health settings. Clinical social workers typically conduct psychotherapy on an individual or group basis and are involved in the coordination of a wide range of social and psychological services for the people they serve.

Clinical versus statistical prediction   A distinction originally described by psychologist Paul Meehl. Clinical prediction involves judgments about an individual made on the basis of a clinician's personal experience and subjective criteria; statistical prediction involves judgments about an individual using quantitative methods based on data from large representative samples of people.

Cognitive theories   Theories of personality and psychopathology that ascribe primary importance to thoughts, or cognitions, to the way we perceive and interpret events around us, in affecting our behaviors and emotions.

Cognitive therapy   An approach to therapy developed by Aaron Beck that emphasizes the importance of thoughts and cognitive processes in the etiology and maintenance of various forms of psychopathology. Cognitive therapy is an active treatment that focuses on changing the individual's dysfunctional thoughts in order to reduce symptoms of psychopathology.

Cognitive-behavioral assessment   The application of behavioral principles and procedures to the measurement of thoughts and cognitive processes.

Collective unconscious   A construct, formulated by Carl Jung, composed of latent memory traces and ancestral memories that are inherited and shared by all human beings. Jung believed that the collective unconscious explains the universality of symbols and mythologies.

Component analysis of psychotherapy The understanding that many cognitive and behavioral treatments are composed of several components. The goal of component analysis is to identify those components that are necessary for the effectiveness of the treatment so that it can be offered and conducted more efficiently.

Concurrent validity The association between a measure of specific construct and a measure of a related construct taken at the same point in time. Concurrent validity is a form of criterion validity in which the construct and the criterion are measured at the same point in time.

Confidentiality Maintaining the privacy of information obtained from and about an individual in the context of a clinical relationship. Confidentiality includes the privacy of information obtained through psychological tests and during psychotherapy sessions.

Construct validity Degree to which the structure of a hypothetical construct is reflected in the structure of a test or procedure that is designed to measure the construct. Construct validity of psychological tests is often tested using the statistical procedure of confirmatory factor analysis.

Consultation The process of advising and providing information, typically to organizations, to help address psychological problems in a group of individuals (e.g., advising a company to help reduce substance abuse among its employees).

Consumer Reports psychotherapy survey A large-scale survey conducted by *Consumer Reports* magazine; subscribers who responded to the survey reported that psychotherapy was effective in helping them deal more effectively with their problems.

Content validity Extent to which items on a measure or test reflect the fundamental nature of the construct of interest and capture the full range and scope of the construct.

Contextual determinants of behavior In behavioral assessment, the situational or environmental variables that are controlling the problem behaviors.

Contingency contracting A contingency management technique in which the therapist and client (or clients) construct and sign a formal agreement describing exactly the behaviors that are expected of the client and the precise consequences of engaging or failing to engage in the behaviors.

Continuous performance tests A group of measures developed to assess the inattention component of specific forms of psychopathology, such as Schizophrenia and Attention Deficit/Hyperactivity Disorder. These measures typically involve the computerized presentation of a series of letters or numbers and require the individual to respond selectively to certain stimuli and not to others.

Correlation Statistic that represents the magnitude and direction of association between two variables. Correlation coefficients can range from -1.00 to $+1.00$; the most common form is the Pearson correlation.

Counseling psychology The branch of psychology concerned primarily with problems of everyday living and with enhancing the adjustment of well-functioning individuals through counseling and psychotherapy. Counseling psychology typically has addressed less severe forms of psychological problems than those that are the focus of clinical psychology.

Crystallized intelligence The aspect of intelligence that includes skills and knowledge that are acquired through interactions specific to one's culture. Crystallized intelligence involves cognitive skills that are acquired through repeated exposure and practice and is reflected in the products and achievements of intellectual activity.

Dead man's test In behavioral assessment, a tongue-in-cheek test to ensure that the clinician selects an active, rather than a passive, behavior for observation. If a dead man can perform the selected behavior, it is a poor choice for assessment.

Dementia praecox An early term used in the nineteenth century by psychiatrist Emil Kraepelin to describe what is currently referred to as schizophrenia.

Department of Defense Psychopharmacology Demonstration Project An experimental training program funded by the U.S. Department of Defense to determine the feasibility of training psychologists to become competent in prescribing medication for psychological disorders.

Description, explanation, prediction, change A series of four steps that characterize the thinking and work of clinical psychologists in research and in clinical practice.

Developmental psychopathology A field of study that focuses on the early origins, often in childhood, of various forms of abnormal behavior. Developmental psychopathologists also often study the changes and continuities of abnormal behavior over the life course.

Deviation IQ Defines the IQ as the ratio between a particular score that an individual attains on a given intelligence test and the score that an average individual of his or her chronological age would be assumed to attain on the same test. Using the deviation method, IQ is one's actual score divided by the expected mean score for one's age. Deviation IQ is a measure of relative intelligence, because it evaluates one's performance relative to others of the same age.

Diagnosis The classification of a disorder based on an accepted and validated classification system. In clinical psychology diagnoses are typically made on the basis of the *Diagnostic and Statistical Manual of Mental Disorders–Fourth Edition (DSM-IV)* of the American Psychiatric Association.

Diagnostic and Statistical Manual of Mental Disorders Fourth Edition (DSM-IV) The manual published by the American Psychiatric Association that is widely used in North America to diagnose individuals with various mental disorders.

Diagnostic axes Dimensions along which individuals who receive psychiatric diagnoses are classified. The five diagnostic axes include clinical disorders, personality disorders, medical conditions, environmental difficulties, and overall level of functioning.

Diagnostic comorbidity The simultaneous co-occurrence of two or more diagnosable disorders in the same individual.

Diagnostic Interview Schedule for Children– Version IV (DISC-IV) A highly structured interview designed to be used by trained lay interviewers for the assessment of *DSM-IV* disorders in children and adolescents. Children and their parents can be interviewed separately to obtain information for deriving diagnoses for children.

Dodo bird verdict A reference to *Alice's Adventures in Wonderland* invoked to illustrate the conclusion of some researchers that there are few differences among various types of therapies with respect to their effectiveness. Current research suggests that this verdict, or conclusion, is wrong.

Dose response In treatment, the question of whether the patient's response (i.e., amount of improvement) is proportional to the dose (i.e., the length) of treatment. Studies examining the dose-response relationship in psychotherapy have found that if therapy is going to be effective at all, it will usually be effective relatively quickly.

Dream analysis A psychoanalytic technique designed to probe the unconscious. Freud believed that dream analysis represented a powerful tool to uncover unconscious material.

Dream work The process of transforming the latent content of dreams into manifest content.

Dysthymia A diagnosable disorder similar to major depression. A diagnosis of Dysthymia requires fewer symptoms than is the case for major depression, but symptoms must have been present for a minimum period of two years rather than two weeks.

Effect size The magnitude or strength of the relationship found in a research study. Examples include the magnitude of the difference between two groups on a measure, or the strength of the correlation between two variables.

Ego psychology A movement led, in part, by Anna Freud and Erik Erikson that focuses on the ego as the critical component of personality and a major determinant of behavior.

Emotion regulation The capacity to initiate, modulate, modify, redirect, or optimize emotional arousal, particularly in response to threat or stress. Emotion regulation is a central focus in many areas of current psychological research.

Emotion schemes A concept in process-experiential psychotherapy that refers to the basic units of emotional experience. Emotional schemes are comprised of emotional memories, hopes, expectations, and fears.

Emotional intelligence Aspects of intelligence that relate to emotional functioning, including self-awareness, impulse control, persistence, self-motivation, and empathy for others. Emotional intelligence is a relatively new concept within psychology and is not measured by standard IQ tests.

Empathy A central skill in humanistic psychotherapy involving the capacity to view and understand the world from the perspective of the client and to convey that understanding to the client in the context of the therapeutic relationship.

Empirical keying An approach to test construction in which items are assigned to particular scales not because of their content or any theoretical rationale, but because they discriminate empirically between normal individuals and members of different diagnostic groups.

Empirically supported treatments Psychological treatments for various disorders that have been demonstrated empirically to meet certain criteria so as to be labeled "well established" or "probably efficacious" in their effectiveness. Updated lists of empirically supported treatments are published periodically by the Society of Clinical Psychology of APA.

Ethical principles A code of conduct for psychologists published by the APA. With respect to testing, these principles require that clinical psychologists be formally trained in the use of assessment instruments and that they should use only those techniques or procedures that are within their competence.

Ethnic diversity In psychopathology, a term used to describe the ethnic composition of different forms of abnormal behavior. As our society becomes more diverse in its ethnic composition, our classification systems for psychopathology will need to be increasingly sensitive to cultural differences in the types of problems that people experience.

Event recording In behavioral observation, the recording by the clinician of each discrete occurrence of the target behavior during the observation period. Event recording is most appropriate for behaviors that have a distinct beginning and end.

Existential psychotherapy The set of approaches to psychotherapy that emphasize the human potential for free will as well as human limitations and the troubling and tragic dimensions of existence. Existential therapy addresses two contrasting sides of free will—the positive sense of *self-determination* and the *existential anxiety* that is inevitable in making important choices.

Experiential processing A method in process-experiential psychotherapy that involves facilitating the client's awareness of her or his experience. Experiential processing includes helping the client become aware of internal physical sensations and external stimuli, both of which are essential components of making clear contact with reality. The therapist further encourages the client to actively and spontaneously express her or his own emotional reactions.

Experimental research design The features of a research study that include the approach that is used to test the primary hypotheses of the study. Common research designs include between-group designs that involve comparison of two or more groups of participants, and within-group designs in which the hypotheses are concerned with relationships among variables within a group of participants.

Exposure with response prevention A behavioral technique used to treat anxiety disorders, most commonly obsessive-compulsive disorder. The client is exposed to the anxiety-inducing stimulus (e.g., dirt) and is prevented from performing the behavior that usually relieves the anxiety (e.g., hand washing).

Externalizing problems An empirically derived dimension of problem behaviors in children that includes conduct difficulties and delinquent and aggressive behaviors.

Five axes of *DSM-IV* Dimensions along which individuals who receive psychiatric diagnoses are classified. The five axes include clinical disorders, personality disorders, medical conditions, environmental difficulties, and overall level of functioning.

Five-Factor Model of Personality An empirically derived, atheoretical model of personality composed of the following five dimensions: Neuroticism, Extraversion, Openness, Conscientiousness, and Agreeableness.

Flexner Report An influential report written by Abraham Flexner in 1910 that called for the introduction of training in basic science as a component in all medical training and education and thus changed the nature of the field of medicine.

Fluid intelligence   The aspect of intelligence that includes nonverbal, relatively culture-free mental skills. Fluid intelligence involves the capacity to adapt to new situations and is represented in basic mental operations and processes.

Free association   A procedure used in Freudian psychoanalysis in which the patient lies on a couch and says everything that comes into her or his mind during the course of a therapeutic session.

Functional analysis of behavior   The evaluation of the function of behaviors and situational variables. The clinician identifies antecedents and consequences of specific problem behaviors in order to understand factors that cause and maintain the behaviors.

Gender differences in psychopathology   The understanding that prevalence rates of certain disorders are different for men and women. Understanding the reasons for these differences is an important task for clinical psychology.

Genotypic IQ   The presumed innate intellectual capacity of an individual.

Halstead-Reitan Neuropsychological Test Battery   A series of tests designed to assess various aspects of neuropsychological functioning, including attention, memory, language skills, and fine motor coordination.

Health-compromising behaviors   Patterns of behavior that are associated with higher morbidity and disease and lower levels of fitness and competence. Certain health-compromising or health-risk behaviors tend to occur together, including substance abuse, unsafe sexual activity, and drunk driving.

Health-enhancing behaviors   Patterns of behavior that are associated with lower morbidity and disease and higher levels of fitness and competence. Research has shown that certain health-promoting behaviors tend to be correlated with one another, including exercise, sleep, healthy diet, dental care, safe driving, and positive social activities.

Heritability index   Statistic that reflects the degree to which scores on intelligence tests (or any measure of a human trait or characteristic) are associated with a genotype. The heritability index can be derived in several different ways; for

example, the correlation of scores obtained by monozygotic twins reared apart is a direct measure of heritability.

Humanistic psychotherapy   A general set of approaches to psychotherapy that emphasize the positive aspects of human nature, the innate human tendency for positive growth, and the role of the therapist in facilitating these positive features of people to emerge in the context of therapy.

Humanistic theories   Theories of personality and psychopathology that are based on the assumption that people have an innate capacity for and a tendency toward positive growth and experience. Humanistic theories of personality generally maintain that people are motivated by a drive for self-actualization.

Hypnosis   A procedure used initially by Freud to probe the unconscious. Freud later rejected the use of hypnosis therapeutically because it bypasses the ego, thereby making psychoanalysis less effective.

Hypothesis   A proposition that is used to guide research. A hypothesis is stated in a way that can be tested using empirical and statistical methods and is based on theory, previous research, or careful clinical observations.

Illusory correlation   In projective testing, a term that describes the tendency of clinicians to make intuitive (but incorrect) interpretations about the associations of individuals to projective stimuli.

Implosive therapy   A behavioral technique that attempts to extinguish a fear response by exposing anxious individuals to fear-eliciting situations and forcing them to remain in those situations until their arousal is reduced or eliminated.

Incidence of problems   The rate of occurrence of new cases of a problem or disorder in a specified period of time; for example, the rate of new cases of depression can be examined over a period of one year.

Indicated preventive interventions   Interventions delivered to high-risk individuals identified as having minimal but detectable signs of or symptoms foreshadowing psychological disorder.

Inferiority complex   In part, the personality characteristics that develop from the different ways in which people deal with feelings of inferiority. Alfred Adler placed considerable importance on feelings of inferiority.

Influencing skills   Responses by the therapist that attempt to guide or shape the verbal and nonverbal behaviors of the client during an interview.

Information gathering   One goal of clinical interviews is to obtain data and knowledge about a client; for example, obtaining data needed to arrive at a diagnosis or make other important decisions.

Informed consent   Principle that participants in any psychological intervention have a right to be fully aware of the nature of the intervention prior to participating; for example, the decision to enter into and to continue psychotherapy must be made knowingly, intelligently, and voluntarily.

Intake interview   Initial interaction between the therapist and client that is intended to establish rapport, gather basic information about the client, and establish the initial concerns or problems that have motivated the client to seek help.

Intelligence quotient (IQ)   Score derived from an intelligence test. Originally the IQ was derived from the relationship between people's chronological age and their mental age (based on their performance on a test). Current approaches to deriving IQ no longer involve the use of the concept of mental age.

Internal consistency   In science, a principle that states that elements of a theory do not contradict each other. In psychometrics, a measure of how strongly items on a scale are intercorrelated.

Internal consistency reliability   The degree to which responses to items on a measure of single constructs are correlated with one another, typically expressed by the statistic coefficient alpha.

Internalizing problems   An empirically derived dimension of problem behaviors in children that includes withdrawn, anxious, and depressed behaviors.

International Classification of Diseases (ICD)   The diagnostic classification system used throughout Europe. Its categories are roughly equivalent to those included in the *DSM,* which is used in North America.

Interpersonal psychotherapy (IPT)   A brief form of psychotherapy developed for the treatment of depression. The rationale for IPT is that by solving interpersonal problems in therapy, patients will improve their life situations and simultaneously relieve the symptoms of the depressive episode.

Interpretation   In psychoanalysis, what the analyst tells patients about the meaning of their unconscious conflicts in order to help the patients gain insight into their behavior. The most important interpretations are usually those that focus on the transference relationship between the therapist and the patient.

Inter-rater reliability   The level of agreement between two observers on a specific task; for example, inter-rater reliability is frequently calculated for methods that involve the direct observation of behavior.

Interval recording   In behavioral observation, recording by the clinician as to whether the target behavior occurred within each of a number of specific time intervals. Interval recording is most appropriate when there are no clear beginning and end points for the behavior.

***Kappa* coefficient**   Statistic, developed by psychologist Jacob Cohen, that reflects the degree of association or agreement between two sets of responses (e.g., ratings of the same client made by two psychologists) after controlling for the degree of association expected to occur by chance.

Latent content   The symbolic meaning of a dream or a free association.

Major depression   One of the most prevalent of the emotional disorders, characterized by at least two weeks of sad mood and/or loss of interest in daily activities, plus a number of associated symptoms such as concentration difficulties and sleep disturbance.

Managed health care   A system of health care that is designed to contain costs by controlling access to and the scope of services (including psychological care); emphasis is placed on accountability of health care professionals to provide efficient and effective services.

Manifest content   The actual content of a dream or a free association.

"Manifesto for a Science of Clinical Psychology"   An influential paper by Richard McFall published in 1991 that articulated the basic principles and importance of the scientific basis of clinical psychology.

Mental age   Concept developed by Binet based on those test items that were passed by a majority of children at a given age level. Certain tasks were selected as representative of each age level, based on the average number of children who solved them correctly at each chronological age.

Mental status exam   One of the oldest forms of clinical interviews, dating back to the work of psychiatrist Adolf Meyer in the early 1900s. The mental status exam typically includes an assessment of the client's general appearance and behavior, speech and thought processes, consciousness, mood and affect, perception, orientation, memory, attention and concentration, general information, intelligence, insight, and judgment.

Meta-analysis   A procedure that statistically pools or combines the results of existing studies on a particular topic—essentially, a study of studies.

MMPI   The Minnesota Multiphasic Personality Inventory, a measure of personality that compares the pattern of an individual's responses to a set of true-false questions to the patterns of answers from a large sample of individuals to statistically determine the personality characteristics of the individual.

MMPI-2   A measure of psychopathology that is the most recent version of the original MMPI. The MMPI-2 is an objective test that consists of 567 true-false items and that was developed using empirical keying. It provides scores on several clinical scales and is one of the most widely used measures of personality and psychopathology.

MMPI-2 clinical scales   The 10 clinical scales of the MMPI-2 that were developed to evaluate the respondent's psychiatric status and personality characteristics.

MMPI-2 validity scales   Scores on the MMPI-2 that are used to evaluate whether the examinee's responses to the test are valid. The validity scales were developed to evaluate the examinee's test-taking attitudes, openness, honesty, cooperativeness, and willingness to share personal information.

Modeling   In behavior therapy, a technique in which the client learns to engage in a behavior by observing the successful performance of the behavior by a live or symbolic model.

Multiple baseline design   A single-case experimental design in which two or more treatment components targeting different outcomes

or behaviors in the same individual are begun at different times, and data are collected continuously on all behaviors throughout treatment. When an intervention is begun, it is applied to only one of the behaviors and not to the others. If the intervention is specific, only the behaviors to which it is applied should change when that treatment is begun.

Multiple regression   Statistical method that tests the magnitude and direction of association between two or more predictor (or independent) variables and an outcome (or dependent) variable.

National Institute of Mental Health Collaborative Depression Research Project   The first and largest major study comparing the relative effectiveness of cognitive therapy, interpersonal therapy, and medication in the treatment of depression.

Naturalistic observation   In behavioral assessment, observations of behaviors as they occur in a natural setting, such as school classroom or playground.

Need for achievement   Also characterized as power motivation, a need to have a strong impact on others. Need for achievement is often assessed using the Thematic Apperception Test.

NEO-PI-R   A self-report measure of the Five-Factor Model of Personality that yields scores on the subscales of Neuroticism, Openness, Extraversion, Conscientiousness, and Agreeableness.

Nonrandomized control group studies   In psychotherapy research, studies in which the participants have not been randomly assigned to different treatment conditions, but rather are self-selected into different groups (e.g., patients who choose to see a psychotherapist versus patients who choose to receive medication from a family physician). The major problem with this design is that it is impossible to know whether the groups differed in any important ways prior to receiving treatment.

Normative standards   Criteria used in comparing an individual to a sample that is representative of the population at large. A normative standard is representative of the population on a number of characteristics, including age, gender, ethnicity, education, and income.

Null hypothesis   The proposition in an experiment that the experimental groups are not different. Statistical tests are designed to reject the null hypothesis at a specified level of certainty; in psychological research a probability that the null hypothesis is rejected at a 95 percent level of confidence is an accepted standard.

Object relations   A theory and school of therapy based on the formulation that early social interactions and interpersonal attachments are critical in affecting an individual's subsequent level of emotional functioning. Melanie Klein and John Bowlby are two of the major theorists in object relations.

Objective personality tests   Measures of personality in which the individual responds to a standard series of questions or statements and in which there is a constrained set of possible responses.

Operant, or instrumental, conditioning   A form of learning in which a behavior or response is followed by a positive or negative consequence, which increases or decreases the probability of the behavior being emitted in the future. B. F. Skinner is the figure most strongly associated with operant conditioning.

Operational definitions of behavior   In behavioral assessment, precisely identifying and quantifying the individual's problem behaviors along any of a number of dimensions. These dimensions often include ratings of intensity, frequency, and duration.

Parsimony   A law of science that states that the simplest explanation of any phenomenon is always preferable.

Performance IQ   Score derived from an IQ test that reflects intellectual abilities that primarily involve visual and spatial skills and are relatively independent of language; examples include solving puzzles of geometric shapes, identifying missing parts of common objects, and repeating sequences of numbers.

Personal unconscious   A construct, formulated by Carl Jung, that is hypothesized to hold repressed memories, wishes, and feelings from infancy and early childhood. The contents of the personal unconscious are unique to each individual.

Personality   The distinctive stable patterns of behavior, thoughts, and emotions that characterize each individual.

PhD in clinical psychology   A doctor of philosophy degree (PhD) in clinical psychology; such graduate programs are typically based in psychology departments in universities and offer balanced training in research and practice.

Phenomenological   The belief that an individual can be understood only from the vantage point of her or his own unique perceptions and feelings. The phenomenological world of the individual includes all that is within her or his sensory awareness at a given moment in time.

Phenotypic IQ   The expression of a person's intelligence as observed on an IQ test.

Placebo   An inert substance or procedure that has no direct or active effect on the outcome in question.

Play therapy   A humanistic approach to psychotherapy with children, originated in the work of psychologist Virginia Axline. The basic principles of Rogerian therapy are followed; however, instead of a reliance on verbal interactions between the therapist and client, as in adult psychotherapy, play is used as the primary vehicle for communication and interaction between the therapist and client.

Positive mental health   The ability and resources to protect oneself from stress and adversity and the skills and resources to involve oneself in personally meaningful activities and generate a sense of personal mastery and competence. Positive mental health is characterized by a set of beliefs or a cognitive style that includes an optimistic outlook on the future, a sense of personal control over one's life, and a sense of self-efficacy.

Prediction   Process of estimating the likelihood of a future behavior or psychological outcome for an individual or group of individuals. Psychologists may be called on to make predictions about the likelihood that an individual will develop a disorder at some point in the future or whether an individual is likely to respond to a specific treatment.

Predictive validity   The association between a measure of specific construct and a measure of a related construct taken at a later point in time. Predictive validity is a form of criterion validity in which the construct and the criterion are measured at two different times.

Prescription privileges for psychologists
An effort, supported by the APA, to allow psychologists who receive specialized training in psychopharmacology to be able to prescribe psychoactive medication for psychological disorders. As of 2001, efforts to obtain prescription privileges for psychologists were underway in several state legislatures in the United States.

Prevention   Interventions aimed at deterring psychological problems before they occur. Prevention can be accomplished by changing factors in the environment that lead to psychological problems and by teaching skills to individuals that can help them reduce the chances that they will develop a problem.

Process-experiential psychotherapy
A contemporary approach to humanistic psychotherapy, represented in the work of psychologist Leslie Greenberg. This approach reflects an integration of Rogers's client-centered therapy, Gestalt therapy, and existential therapy along with current research and theory on the nature of emotions. This integration includes a greater commitment to link the process-experiential approach with psychological research than was evident in earlier existential and humanistic approaches.

Professional competence   Areas in which a psychologist has sufficient expertise and training to provide the basis for practice; psychologists are not allowed to practice in areas outside their professional competence and expertise.

Profile analysis   Interpretation of a number of psychological tests based on analysis of the profile of subscales rather than on the basis of individual scores. Most notably, interpretation of scores on the Wechsler intelligence scales and on the MMPI-2 is based more on the obtained profile than on individual items or scales.

Projective drawing tests   Procedures in which respondents are asked to draw pictures of people and/or objects. The drawings are then interpreted by clinicians with respect to the person's unconscious personality characteristics and conflicts.

Projective personality tests   Measures of personality that typically ask individuals to respond to ambiguous stimuli such as inkblots and pictures. Individuals are hypothesized to "project" unconscious aspects of their personality onto the stimuli, thereby revealing these aspects of themselves to the clinician.

Promotion   Interventions that help clients develop healthy behavior, attitudes, and lifestyles. The emphasis in promotion programs is on the development of positive behaviors rather than the treatment of prevention of problems.

Protective factors   Characteristics of the person or the environment that increase an individual's resistance to risk and, therefore, strengthen the individual against the development of psychological disorder.

PsyD in clinical psychology   A doctor of psychology degree (PsyD) in clinical psychology; such graduate programs are most often based in freestanding professional schools of psychology and offer training that emphasizes clinical practice more than research.

Psychiatry   The subdiscipline of the field of medicine devoted to the study and treatment of mental disorders. Specialization in psychiatry occurs after completion of medical school; psychiatrists are trained to treat mental disorders through the prescription of psychoactive medication.

Psychoanalysis   The form of psychotherapy, developed by Sigmund Freud, that attempts to help patients become aware of information stored in their unconscious.

Psychology licensing laws   State laws that provide guidelines for the accreditation of individuals in the practice of psychology. Licensing laws are designed to protect the public by specifying the level and type of education required to practice psychology and through the administration of a competency exam.

Psychophysiological assessment   In behavioral assessment, the measurement of reactions by the body to environmental demands. Typically the focus is on response reactions that are governed by the sympathetic and parasympathetic portions of the autonomic nervous system, including heart rate, blood pressure, respiration, skin conductance, muscle tension, and electrocortical activity.

Psychotherapy   A broad term used to refer to psychological methods used in the treatment of mental and emotional problems or disorders.

Psychotherapy is characterized by a unique human interaction in which a trained, certified professional attempts to help a client think, feel, or behave differently. The relationship between therapist and client is characterized by confidentiality, trust, and respect. Within the context of this relationship, the therapist typically follows a set of procedures that are, to a greater or lesser extent, prescribed by a certain theory or school of thought.

Quantitative taxonomic systems   Systems developed for the classification of psychopathological behaviors that are based entirely on the results of empirical studies.

Randomized clinical trials   Studies in which participants are randomly assigned to different conditions or treatment groups. This randomization maximizes the likelihood that the groups will not differ systematically at the beginning of the study.

Rating scales   In behavioral assessment, measures intended to provide information on a wider range of an individual's behavior over a longer period of time than is possible with direct observation.

Rational-emotive therapy   An approach to therapy developed by Albert Ellis that teaches individuals to identify and change their illogical thoughts and beliefs. Ellis postulates that illogical beliefs lie at the root of different forms of psychopathology and that changing these beliefs will reduce problematic behaviors.

Real and ideal self   Two aspects of the self concept described by psychologist Carl Rogers. The real self refers to perceptions of the self as the individual is currently functioning—aspects of the self that are currently included in awareness. The ideal self, in contrast, refers to perceptions of the self to which the individual aspires. Our ideal self is often based on the internalized values and goals of others—what others expect and want from us rather than what we want for ourselves.

Reciprocal inhibition   A principle, formulated by Joseph Wolpe, that states that if a response antagonistic to anxiety (such as relaxation) can be made to occur in the presence of anxiety-evoking stimuli, the bond between these stimuli and the anxiety responses will be weakened.

Remoralization, remediation, rehabilitation   The three phases of psychotherapy that represent three steps in the psychotherapeutic process as defined by psychologist Ken Howard and his colleagues. These phases of psychotherapy involve progressive improvement of the client's subjective sense of well-being, reduction in psychological symptoms, and enhancement of overall life functioning.

Representative sample   Group of individuals selected in such a way as to reflect the central characteristics of a population. Important characteristics include the age, gender, ethnicity, education level, and economic status of a population.

Research Diagnostic Criteria   One of the first attempts to establish more precise standards and guidelines for deriving psychiatric diagnoses; the criteria were developed by psychiatrist Robert Spitzer and colleagues as part of the development of standardized diagnostic interviews.

Resistance   In psychoanalysis, a term describing attempts by patients to prevent the therapeutic uncovering of unacceptable unconscious material. Resistance itself usually occurs at an unconscious level.

Risk factors   Characteristics of the person or the environment that, if present for a given individual, make it more likely that this individual, as compared with others in the general population, will develop a disorder.

Rorschach Inkblot Test   A projective technique in which the clinician interprets individuals' responses to a series of 10 inkblots.

Sample versus sign   Behavioral assessment that focuses on obtaining samples of behavior in contrast to more traditional psychodynamic approaches to assessment, which conceptualize test responses as signs of underlying personality characteristics.

Schedule for Affective Disorders and Schizophrenia (SADS)   A semi-structured psychiatric interview designed by psychiatrists Endicott and Spitzer to elicit information necessary for making diagnoses based on the Research Diagnostic Criteria.

Screening   Process of administering a measure or set of measures to determine which individuals in a population have an identifiable disorder or have an increased probability of developing a disorder.

Selective preventive interventions   Interventions targeted to subgroups of the population whose risk is greater than for the population as a whole but who have not yet manifested a problem or disorder.

Self-and-world construct system   A concept from humanistic psychotherapy that is based on the work of psychologist George Kelly. Individuals define themselves and the world in such a way that they are protected from the anxiety that would come from recognizing all of life's possibilities. This system is thought to be only partly conscious and mostly implicit.

Self-determination   A concept from humanistic and existential psychotherapy that reflects the belief that people are capable of controlling and directing their own lives and destinies.

Self-discrepancy theory   Theory of the self developed by social psychologist E. Tory Higgins that states there are three main domains of the self that influence a person's emotional experience: the actual self, the ideal self, and the ought self. Discrepancies between the actual self and the self-guides (ideal and ought selves) are hypothesized to contribute to a person's vulnerability to experience negative emotions.

Self-monitoring   An observational procedure in which clients are instructed to observe and record their own behaviors, thoughts, or feelings as they occur.

Self-referent standards   Comparison of an individual to his or her own previous behavior or performance on a test or measure. Self-referent standards are used to determine if an individual has changed over time, for example in response to an intervention.

Shaping   A technique in which a final desired behavior is established by reinforcing successive approximations to (i.e., increasingly closer versions of) the final behavior.

Single-case experimental designs   Research designs that involves only a single participant. Data are typically obtained during a baseline period, during exposure to a specified experimental condition, and following withdrawal of the experimental condition (return to baseline). Changes in the individual's functioning are assessed as these conditions are changed.

Social competence   Skills and capacities for forming and maintaining social relationships and in solving problems in daily living. Many health promotion and prevention programs are designed to enhance social competence in children and adolescents.

Social skills training   A behavioral technique in which clients are taught specific verbal and nonverbal behaviors to increase their comfort, skill, and effectiveness in social situations.

Society of Clinical Psychology of the American Psychological Association   The division of the APA that is devoted to supporting and encouraging the evolution and development of clinical psychology as both a science and a profession; this division has over 7,000 members.

Statistical significance   The probability that the observed relationship between variables in a research study is not attributable to chance. Statistical significance is typically expressed as the likelihood (out of 100) that a relationship of the same size or greater would be obtained if the study were conducted again. Psychology's accepted standard of statistical significance is that a finding could be expected by chance less than 5 times out of 100 (95 percent confidence).

Statistically versus clinically significant change   The issue of whether the statistically significant improvement in a group of patients from pretreatment to posttreatment is sufficient to place them in the normal range of functioning, or whether, even though they improved significantly, they are still more dysfunctional than normal controls are.

Structured Clinical Interview for *DSM-IV* Disorders (SCID-IV)   A structured psychiatric diagnostic interview developed to provide direct assessment of *DSM-IV* diagnoses. The SCID was developed for use by trained interviewers who are able to use considerable diagnostic judgment over the course of the interview.

Syndrome   A set of symptoms that tend to occur or cluster together.

Systematic desensitization   A behavioral technique, based on the principle of reciprocal inhibition, used to reduce anxiety. Clients practice relaxation while imagining each of a hierarchy of anxiety-inducing scenes. The relaxation breaks the association between the stimuli and the anxiety response.

Tarasoff case   Landmark legal case that established that the duty to protect another person from potential harm takes precedence over the right of the client to privacy within a relationship with a psychologist. In this specific case, Tatiana Tarasoff was stabbed to death by a man who had disclosed to his psychologist that he intended to kill Ms. Tarasoff. The court ruled that the psychologist had a duty to warn Ms. Tarasoff of the threat against her life.

Taxonomy   A system of classification. In clinical psychology, the major taxonomy of psychopathology is that described in the *Diagnostic and Statistical Manual of Mental Disorders (DSM).*

Telemedicine/telehealth   The use of telecommunications technology to allow health professionals, including psychologists, to communicate with one another and with patients from remote locations.

Test bias   A situation in which members of different cultural or ethnic groups obtain different scores on a test for reasons that are unrelated to what the test is measuring.

Test standardization   The practice of presenting psychological tests in the same way to all respondents, using the same instructions and scoring procedures for everyone.

Test-retest reliability   The degree of consistency in scores or responses on a measure over one or more repeated administrations; typically expressed as a correlation coefficient.

Thematic Apperception Test   A projective technique in which the individual is asked to generate a story to each of a series of ambiguous pictures that usually involve people.

Time-Limited Dynamic Psychotherapy (TLDP)   A brief form of psychotherapy developed by Hans Strupp. TLDP attempts to modify the way people relate to others and to themselves by analyzing the relationship between the patient and the therapist.

Token economy   A contingency management technique in which behaviors are reinforced by the administration of tokens or symbolic reinforcers, which can be exchanged for goods, services, or privileges. Token economies are usually used on psychiatric units or in classrooms.

Traits   Stable and enduring characteristics or dimensions of individual differences.

Transference   In psychoanalytic therapy, when the patient responds at an unconscious level to the therapist as if the therapist were an important figure from the patient's past.

Treatment   The process of alleviating or correcting a psychological problem through systematically changing a client's thoughts, emotions, or behaviors. Psychological treatment is most often carried out through psychotherapy with individuals, groups, or families.

Treatment effectiveness   The degree to which a treatment does work in the real world (i.e., under such circumstances as practicing psychologists who may not be specially trained in a specific treatment modality, absence of clear treatment guidelines, heterogeneous client samples). In research on treatment effectiveness the emphasis is placed on external validity, or the extent to which the findings can be generalized to all therapists and clients.

Treatment efficacy   The extent to which a treatment can work under optimal conditions (i.e., specially trained therapists, clearly defined treatment manuals, carefully selected samples of clients). In research on treatment efficacy the emphasis is on internal validity, or the degree to which variables in the study have been carefully controlled and the effects of a treatment can be inferred to be causally related to the treatment itself.

Treatment outcome research   Empirical investigations of the effectiveness or efficacy of different treatments for specific disorders. Treatment outcome research is concerned primarily with the impact of therapy on a client's functioning.

Treatment process research   A focus on those characteristics of therapists, patients, and therapeutic techniques that may account for positive changes in patient functioning.

Type I error   A mistake made in the interpretation of data that occurs when a researcher assumes that the null hypothesis has been rejected when in fact there is not sufficient evidence to do so.

Unconditional positive regard   A central concept in Rogerian psychotherapy that entails warm acceptance of the client's experience, no matter what it is. There are no conditions or qualifications on the therapist's acceptance of the client. A therapist engaging in unconditional positive regard accepts both the good and the bad characteristics of the client.

Universal preventive interventions   Interventions directed to the general population to address factors that contribute to increased risk in the population as a whole.

Vail Conference   Conference on Graduate Education in Psychology held in Vail, Colorado, in 1973. An alternative model of training in clinical psychology was supported at this conference, a model that placed greater emphasis on training in clinical practice and commensurately less emphasis on research training.

Verbal IQ   Score derived from an IQ test that reflects intellectual skills that primarily involve the use of language; examples include tests of vocabulary, analogies, and general fund of information.

WAIS-III   Wechsler Adult Intelligence Scale–Third Edition; the most widely used intelligence test for adults, originally developed by psychologist David Wechsler. The test generates scores for verbal, performance, and full scale IQ.

WISC-III   Wechsler Intelligence Scale for Children–Third Edition; the most widely used intelligence test for children (ages 6 to 16 years old), originally developed by psychologist David Wechsler. The test generates scores for verbal, performance, and full scale IQ.

Within-subject designs   In psychotherapy research, studies examining the effectiveness of a particular treatment by measuring change over time in one treated individual.

REFERENCES

Abikoff, H. (1991). Cognitive training in ADHD children: Less to it than meets the eye. *Journal of Learning Disabilities, 24,* 205–209.

Abikoff, H., Gittelman-Klein, R., & Klein, D. F. (1977). Validation of a classroom observation code for hyperactive children. *Journal of Consulting and Clinical Psychology, 45,* 772–783.

Ablow, J. C., Measelle, J. R., Kraemer, H. C., Harrington, R., Luby, J., Smider, N., Dierker, L., Clark, V., Dubicka, B., Heffelfinger, A., Essex, M., & Kupfer, D. J. (1999). The MacArthur Three-City Outcome Study: Evaluating multi-informant measures of young children's symptomatology. *Journal of the American Academy of Child & Adolescent Psychiatry, 38,* 1580–1590.

Abramowitz, J. S. (1996). Variants of exposure and response prevention in the treatment of obsessive-compulsive disorder: A meta-analysis. *Behavior Therapy, 27,* 583–600.

Abramowitz, J. S. (1997). Effectiveness of psychological and pharmacological treatments for obsessive-compulsive disorder: A quantitative review. *Journal of Consulting Clinical Psychology, 65,* 44–52.

Abramson, L. Y., Alloy, L. B., Hankin, B. L., Haeffel, G. J., MacCoon, D. G., & Gibb, B. E. (in press). Two cognitive theories of depression: Hopelessness theory and Beck's theory. In I.H. Gotlib & C. L. Hammen (Eds.), *Handbook of depression and its treatment.* New York: Guilford Press.

Abramson, L. Y., Metalsky, G. I., & Alloy, L. B. (1989). Hopelessness depression: A theory-based subtype of depression. *Psychological Review, 96,* 358–372.

Abramson, L. Y., Seligman, M. E. P., & Teasdale, J. (1978). Learned helplessness in humans: Critique and reformulation. *Journal of Abnormal Psychology, 87,* 49–74.

Achenbach, T. M. (1985). *Assessment and taxonomy of child and adolescent psychopathology.* Thousand Oaks, CA: Sage.

Achenbach, T. M. (1991). *Integrative guide for the 1991 CBCL/4-18, YSR, and TRF Profiles.* Burlington: University of Vermont, Department of Psychiatry.

Achenbach, T. M. (1991). The derivation of taxonomic constructs: A necessary stage in the development of developmental psychopathology. In D. Cicchetti & S. L. Sheree (Eds.), *Rochester symposium on developmental psychopathology: Vol. 3. Models and integrations* (pp. 43–74). Rochester, NY: University of Rochester Press.

Achenbach, T. M. (1993). Taxonomy and comorbidity of conduct problems: Evidence from empirically based approaches. *Development and Psychopathology, 5,* 51–64.

Achenbach, T. M. (1995). Empirically based assessment and taxonomy: Applications to clinical research. *Psychological Assessment, 7,* 261–274.

Achenbach, T. M. (2000). Assessment of psychopathology. In A. Sameroff & M. Lewis

(Eds.), *Handbook of developmental psychopathology* (2nd ed.; pp. 41–56). New York: Kluwer Academic/Plenum Publishers.

Achenbach, T. M., & McConaughy, S. H. (1996). Relations between DSM-IV and empirically based assessment. *School Psychology Review, 25,* 329–341.

Achenbach, T. M., & McConaughy, S. H. (1997). *Empirically based assessment of child and adolescent psychopathology: Practical applications* (2nd ed.). Thousand Oaks, CA: Sage.

Achenbach, T. M., Bird, H. R., Canino, G., Phares, V., Gould, M. S., & Rubio-Stipec, M. (1990). Epidemiological comparisons of Puerto Rican and U.S. mainland children: Parent, teacher, and self-reports. *Journal of the American Academy of Child and Adolescent Psychiatry, 29,* 84–93.

Achenbach, T. M., Hensely, V. R., Phares, V., & Grayson, D. (1990). Problems and competencies reported by parents of Australian and American children. *Journal of Child Psychology & Psychiatry & Allied Disciplines, 31,* 265–286.

Achenbach, T., & Howell, C. T. (1993). Are American children's problems getting worse? A 13-year comparison. *Journal of the American Academy of Child & Adolescent Psychiatry, 32,* 1145–1154.

Achenbach, T. M., Howell, C. T., McConaughy, S. H., & Stanger, C. (1998). Six-year predictors of problems in a national sample: IV. Young adult signs of disturbance. *Journal of the American Academy of Child and Adolescent Psychiatry, 37,* 718–727.

Achenbach, T. M., Howell, C. T., Quay, H. C., & Conners, C. K. (1991). National survey of problems and competencies among four-to-sixteen-year-olds: Parents' reports for normative and clinical samples. *Monographs of the Society for Research in Child Development, 56,* v–120.

Achenbach, T. M., McConaughy, S. H., & Howell, C. T. (1987). Child/adolescent behavioral and emotional problems: Implications of cross-informant correlations for situational specificity. *Psychological Bulletin, 101,* 213–232.

Acierno, R., Resnick, H. S., & Kilpatrick, D. G. (1997). Health impact of interpersonal violence: I. Prevalence rates, case identification, and risk factors for sexual assault, physical assault, and domestic violence in men and women. *Behavioral Medicine, 23,* 53–64.

Ackerman, S. J., Clemence, A. J., Weatherill, R., & Hilsenroth, M. J. (1999). Use of the TAT in the assessment of *DSM-IV* Cluster B personality disorders. *Journal of Personality Assessment, 73,* 422–448.

Adams, G. (1934). The rise and fall of psychology. *Atlantic Monthly, 153,* 82–92.

Adams, K. M., & Bieliauskas, L. A. (1994a). Could versus should: A reply to Sammons. *Journal of Clinical Psychology in Medical Settings, 1,* 209–215.

Adams, K. M., & Bieliauskas, L. A. (1994b). On perhaps becoming what you had previously despised: Psychologists as prescribers of medication. *Journal of Clinical Psychology in Medical Settings, 1,* 189–197.

Adelman, H. S. (1995). Clinical psychology: Beyond psychopathology and clinical interventions. *Clinical Psychology: Science & Practice, 2,* 28–44.

Adler, A. (1959). *Understanding human nature.* New York: Premier Books.

Adler, N. E., Marmot, M., McEwen, B. S., & Stewart, J. (1999). *Socioeconomic status and health in industrial nations: Social, psychological, and biological pathways.* New York: New York Academy of Sciences.

Agosti, V. (1995). The efficacy of treatments in reducing alcohol consumption: A meta-analysis. *International Journal of the Addictions, 30,* 1067–1077.

Agras, W. S., Schneider, J. A., Arnow, B., Raeburn, S. D., & Telch C. F. (1989). Cognitive-behavioral and response-prevention treatments for bulimia nervosa. *Journal of Consulting and Clinical Psychology, 57,* 215–221.

Agras, W. S., Walsh, B. T., Fairburn, C. G., Wilson, G. T., & Kraemer, H. C. (2000). A multicenter comparison of cognitive-behavioral therapy and interpersonal psychotherapy for bulimia nervosa. *Archives of General Psychiatry, 57,* 459–466.

Aiken, L. R. (1999). *Personality assessment methods and practice* (3rd ed.). Seattle, WA: Hogrefe & Huber.

Akiskal, H., & McKinney, W. T. (1975). Overview of recent research in depression: Integration of ten conceptual models into a comprehensive clinical frame. *Archives of General Psychiatry, 32,* 285–305.

Albee, G. W. (2000). The Boulder model's fatal flaw. *American Psychologist, 55,* 247–248.

Albee, G. W., & Gullotta, T. P. (1997). Primary prevention's evolution. In G. W. Albee & T. P. Gullotta (Eds.), *Primary prevention that works: Issues in children's and families' lives.* Thousand Oaks, CA: Sage Publications.

Albee, G. W., & Loeffler, E. (1971) Role conflicts in psychology and their implications for a reevaluation of training models. *Canadian Psychologist, 12,* 465–481.

Alexander, F., & French, T. M. (1946). *Psychoanalytic therapy: principles and application.* New York: Ronald Press.

Allen, S., Serufilira, A., Gruber, V., & Kegeles, S. (1993). Pregnancy and contraception use among urban Rwandan women after HIV testing and counseling. *American Journal of Public Health, 83,* 705–710.

Alloy, L. B., & Abramson, L. Y. (1979). Judgment of contingency in depressed and nondepressed students: Sadder but wiser? *Journal of Experimental Psychology: General, 108,* 441–485.

Alloy, L. B., Abramson, L. Y., & Francis E. L. (1999). Do negative cognitive styles confer vulnerability to depression? *Current Directions in Psychological Science, 8,* 128–132.

Alloy, L. B., Jacobson, N. S., & Acocella, J. (1999). *Abnormal psychology: Current perspectives* (8th ed.). New York: McGraw-Hill.

Alpert-Gillis, L. J., Pedro-Carroll, J. L., & Cowen, E. L. (1989). The children of divorce intervention program: Development, implementation, and evaluation of a program for young urban children. *Journal of Consulting and Clinical Psychology, 57,* 583–589.

Altemeyer, B. (1996). *The authoritarian specter.* Cambridge, MA: Harvard University Press.

American Cancer Society. (2000). *Cancer facts and figures.* Atlanta: Author.

American Psychiatric Association Commission on Psychotherapies. (1982). *Psychotherapy research: Methodological and efficacy issues.* Washington, DC: American Psychiatric Association.

American Psychiatric Association. (1994). *Diagnostic and statistical manual of mental disorders* (4th ed.). Washington, DC: Author.

American Psychiatric Association. (2000). Practice guidelines for the treatment of patients with major depressive disorder (revision). *American Journal of Psychiatry, 157* (suppl. 4), 1–45.

American Psychological Association. (1967). *Casebook on ethical standards of psychologists.* Washington, DC: Author.

American Psychological Association (1981). *Specialty guidelines for delivery of services by clinical psychologists.* Washington, DC: Author.

American Psychological Association (2001). *Graduate Study in Psychology: 2000 Edition With 2001 Addendum.* Washington, DC: Author.

American Psychological Association. (1992). Ethical principles of psychologists and code of conduct. *American Psychologist, 47,* 1597–1611.

Anastasi, A. (1988). *Psychological testing* (6th ed.). New York: Macmillan.

Anastasi, A. (1997). *Psychological testing* (7th ed.). Upper Saddle River, NJ: Prentice-Hall.

Anastopolous, A. D., Spisto, M. A., & Maher, M. C. (1994). The WISC-III Freedom from Distractibility factor: Its utility in identifying children with attention deficit hyperactivity disorder. *Psychological Assessment. 6,* 368–371.

Andersen, B. L., Farrar, W. B., Golden-Kreutz, D., Kutz, L. A., MacCallum, R., Courtney, M. E., & Glaser R. (1998). Stress and immune responses after surgical treatment for regional breast cancer. *Journal of the National Cancer Institute, 90,* 30–36.

Anderson, B. L., Kiecolt-Glaser, J. K., & Glaser, R. (1994). A biobehavioral model of cancer stress and disease course. *American Psychologist, 49,* 389–404.

Anderson, J. W. (1999). Henry A. Murray and the creation of the Thematic Apperception Test. In L. Geiser & M. I. Stein (Eds.), *Evocative images: The Thematic Apperception Test and the art of projection* (pp. 23–38). Washington, DC: American Psychological Association.

Andrews, G., & Harvey, R. (1981). Does psychotherapy benefit neurotic patients? A reanalysis of the Smith, Glass, and Miller data. *Archives of General Psychiatry, 38,* 1203–1208.

Aneshensel, C. S., Estrada, A. L., Hansell, M. J., & Clark, V. A. (1987). Social psychological aspects of reporting behavior: Lifetime depressive episode reports. *Journal of Health and Social Behavior, 28,* 232–246.

Angold, A. (1988). Childhood and adolescent depression: I. Epidemiological and aetiological aspects. *British Journal of Psychiatry, 152,* 601–617.

Antonuccio, D., Danton, W. G., & DeNelsky, G. Y. (1995). Psychotherapy versus medication for depression: Challenging the conventional wisdom with data. *Professional Psychology: Research and Practice, 26,* 574–585.

Antonuccio, D., Thomas, M. & Danton, W. G. (1997). A cost-effectiveness analysis of cognitive behavior therapy and fluoxetine (prozac) in the treatment of depression. *Behavior Therapy, 28,* 187–210.

Arkes, H. R. (1981). Impediments to accurate clinical judgment and possible ways to minimize their impact. *Journal of Consulting and Clinical Psychology, 49,* 323–330.

Arkes, H. R., & Harkness, A. R. (1983). Estimates of contingency between two dichotomous variables. *Journal of Experimental Psychology: General, 112,* 117–135.

Arlow, J. A. (1984). The psychoanalytic process in regard to the development of transference and interpretation. *Emotions and Behavior Monographs, 3,* 21–44.

Arnold, L. E., Abikoff, H. B., Cantwell, D. P., Conners, C. K., Elliott, G. R., Greenhill, L. L., Hechtman, L., Hinshaw, S. P., Hoza, B., Jensen, P. S., Kraemer, H. C., March, J. S., Newcorn, J. H., Pelham, W. E., Richters, J. E., Schiller, E., Severe, J. B., Swanson, J. M., Vereen, D., & Wells, K. C. (1997). NIMH collaborative multimodal treatment study of children with ADHD (MTA): Design, methodology, and protocol evolution. *Journal of Attention Disorders, 2,* 141–158.

Ax, A. F. (1953). The physiological differentiation between fear and anger in humans. *Psychosomatic Medicine, 15,* 433–442.

Axline, V. M. (1955). Play therapy procedures and results. *American Journal of Orthopsychiatry, 25,* 618–626.

Ayllon, T., & Azrin, N. H. (1965). The measurement and reinforcement of behavior of psychotics. *Journal of the Experimental Analysis of Behavior, 8,* 357–383.

Baker, D. B., & Benjamin, L. T. (2000). The affirmation of the scientist-practitioner. *American Psychologist, 55,* 241–247.

Ball, S. A., Kranzler, H. R., Tennen, H., Poling, J. C., & Rounsaville, B. J. (1998). Personality disorder and dimension differences between Type A and Type B substance abusers. *Journal of Personality Disorders, 12,* 1–12.

Ball, S. A., Tennen, H., Poling, J. C., Kranzler, H. R., & Rounsaville, B. J. (1997). Personality, temperament, and character dimensions and the DSM-IV personality disorders in substance abusers. *Journal of Abnormal Psychology, 106,* 545–553.

Bandura, A. (1969). *Principles of behavior modification.* New York: Holt, Rinehart, & Winston.

Bandura, A. (1986). *Social foundations of thought and action: A social cognitive theory.* Englewood Cliffs, NJ: Prentice-Hall.

Bandura, A. (1989). Human agency in social cognitive theory. *American Psychologist, 44,* 1175–1184.

Bandura, A. (1997). *Self-efficacy: The exercise of control.* New York: W. H. Freeman.

Bandura, A. (2000). Self-efficacy: The foundation of agency. In W. J. Perrig & A. Grob (Eds.), *Control of human behavior, mental processes, and consciousness: Essays in honor of the 60th birthday of August Flammer* (pp. 17–33). Mahwah, NJ: Lawrence Erlbaum.

Bandura, A., Blanchard, E. B., & Ritter, B. (1969). Relative efficacy of desensitization and modeling approaches for inducing behavioral, affective, and attitudinal changes. *Journal of Personality and Social Psychology, 13,* 173–199.

Bandura, A., Grusec, J. E., & Menlove, F. L. (1967). Vicarious extinction of avoidance behavior. *Journal of Personality and Social Psychology, 5,* 16–23.

Barber, J. P., & Muenz, L. R. (1996). The role of avoidance and obsessiveness in matching patients to cognitive and interpersonal psychotherapy: Empirical findings from the Treatment for Depression Collaborative Research Program. *Journal of Consulting and Clinical Psychology, 64,* 951–958.

Barefoot, J. C., Brummett, B. H., Helms, M. J., Mark, D. B., Siegler, I. C., & Williams, R. B. (2000). Depressive symptoms and survival of patients with coronary artery disease. *Psychosomatic Medicine, 62,* 790–795.

Barends, A., Westen, D., Byers, S., Leigh, J., & Silbert, D. (1990). Assessing affect-tone of relationship paradigms from TAT and interview data. *Psychological Assessment, 2,* 329–332.

Barkham, M., Rees, A., Shapiro, D. A., Stiles, W. B., Agnew, R. M., Halstead, J., Culverwell, A., & Harrington, V. M. G. (1996). Outcomes of time-limited psychotherapy in applied settings: Replicating the Second Sheffield Psychotherapy Project. *Journal of Consulting and Clinical Psychology, 64,* 1079–1085.

Barkley, R. A. (1991). Introduction to the special issue: Child psychopharmacology. *Journal of Clinical Child Psychology, 20,* 226–231.

Barkley, R. A. (1997a). *ADHD and the nature of self-control.* New York: Guilford Press.

Barkley, R. A. (1997b). *Defiant children: A clinician's manual for assessment and parent training* (2nd ed.). New York: Guilford Press.

Barkley, R. A. (1998). *Attention-deficit hyperactivity disorder: A handbook for diagnosis and treatment* (2nd ed.). New York: Guilford Press.

Barkley, R. A. (2000). *Taking charge of ADHD: The complete, authoritative guide for parents* (rev. ed.). New York: Guilford Press.

Barkley, R. A., Fischer, M., Newby, R. F., & Breen, M. J. (1988). Development of a multimethod clinical protocol for assessing stimulant drug response in children with attention deficit disorder. *Journal of Clinical Child Psychology, 17,* 14–24.

Barkley, R. A., & Murphy, K. R. (1998). *Attention-deficit hyperactivity disorder: A clinical workbook* (2nd ed.). New York: Guilford Press.

Barlow, D. H. (1981). On the relation of clinical research to clinical practice: Current issues, new directions. *Journal of Consulting and Clinical Psychology, 49,* 147–155.

Barlow, D. H. (1991). Introduction to the Special Issue on Diagnoses, Dimensions, and DSM-IV: The Science of Classification. *Journal of Abnormal Psychology, 100,* 243–244.

Barlow, D. H. (1996). Health care policy, psychotherapy research, and the future of psychotherapy. *American Psychologist, 51,* 1050–1058.

Barlow, D., & Cerney, J. A. (1988). *Psychological treatment of panic.* New York: Guilford Press.

Barlow, D., & Durand (1995). *Abnormal psychology: An integrative approach.* Pacific Grove, CA: Brooks/Cole.

Barlow, D. H., Esler, J. L., & Vitali, A. E. (1998). Psychosocial treatments for panic disorders, phobias, and generalized anxiety disorder. In P. E. Nathan, & J. M. Gorman (Eds.), *A guide to treatments that work* (pp. 288–318). New York: Oxford University Press.

Barlow, D. H., Gorman, J. M., Shear, M. K., & Woods, S. W. (2000). Cognitive-behavioral therapy, imipramine, or their combination for panic disorder: A randomized controlled trial. *Journal of the American Medical Association, 283,* 2529–2536.

Barlow, D. H., & Hersen, M. (1973). Single-case experimental designs: Uses in applied clinical research. *Archives of General Psychiatry, 29,* 319–325.

Barlow, D. H., & Hersen, M. (1984). *Single-case experimental designs: Strategies for studying behavior change* (2nd ed.). Elmsford, NY: Pergamon.

Barnett, J. E., & Neel, M. L. (2000). Must all psychologists study psychopharmacology? *Professional Psychology: Research and Practice, 31,* 619–627.

Barnett, P., & Gotlib, I. (1988). Psychosocial functioning and depression: Distinguishing among antecedents, concomitants, and consequences. *Psychological Bulletin, 104,* 97–126.

Barr, R. G., Young, S. N., Wright, J. H., Gravel, R., & Alkawaf, R. (1999). Differential calming responses to sucrose taste in crying infants with and without colic. *Pediatrics, 103.*

Barrera, S. E., Osinski, W. A., & Davidoff, E. (1994). The use of Antabuse (tetraethylthiuramdisulphide) in chronic alcoholics. *American Journal of Psychiatry,151,* 263–267.

Barrett, P. M., Dadds, M. R., & Rapee, R. M. (1996). Family treatment of childhood anxiety: A controlled trial. *Journal of Consulting and Clinical Psychology, 64,* 333–342.

Barthlow, D. L., Graham, J. R., Ben-Porath, Y. S., & McNulty, J. L. (1999). Incremental validity of the MMPI-2 content scales in an outpatient mental health setting. *Psychological Assessment, 11,* 39–47.

Baucom, D. H., Shoham, V., Mueser, K. T., Daiuto, A. D., & Stickle, T. R. (1998). Empirically supported couple and family interventions for marital distress and adult mental health problems. *Journal of Consulting and Clinical Psychology, 66,* 53–88.

Baumeister, R. (1996). *Evil: Inside human cruelty and violence.* New York: W. H. Freeman.

Baxter, L. R. (1992). Neuroimaging studies of obsessive-compulsive disorder. *Psychiatric Clinics of North America, 15,* 871–884.

Baxter, L. R., Ackermann, R. F., Swerdlow, N. R., Brody, A., Saxena, S., Schwartz, J. M., Gregortich, J. M., Stoessel, P., & Phelps, M. E. (2000). Specific brain system mediation of obsessive-compulsive disorder responsive to either medication or behavior therapy. In W. K. Goodman, & M. V. Rudorfer (Eds.). (2000). *Obsessive-compulsive disorder: Contemporary issues in treatment. Personality and clinical psychology series.* (pp. 573–609). Mahwah, NJ:. Lawrence Erlbaum Associates, Inc.

Beardslee, W. R. (1998). Prevention and the clinical encounter. *American Journal of Orthopsychiatry, 68,* 521–533.

Bechtoldt, H., Norcross, J. C., Wyckoff, L. A., Pokrywa, M. L., & Campbell, L. F. (2001). Theoretical orientations and employment settings of clinical and counseling psychologists: A comparative study. *The Clinical Psychologist, 54,* 3–6.

Beck, A. T. (1967). *Depression: Clinical, experimental, and theoretical aspects.* New York: Harper & Row.

Beck, A. T. (1976). *Cognitive therapy and the emotional disorders.* New York: International Universities Press.

Beck, A. T., Rush, A. J., Shaw, B. F., & Emery, G. (1979). *Cognitive therapy of depression: A treatment manual.* New York: Guilford Press.

Beck, A. T., Steer, R. A., & Garbin, M. G. (1988). Psychometric properties of the Beck Depression Inventory: Twenty-five years of evaluation. *Clinical Psychology Review, 8,* 77–100.

Beck, J. G., Ohtake, P. J., & Shipherd, J. C. (1999). Exaggerated anxiety is not unique to CO-sub-2 in panic disorder: A comparison of hypercapnic and hypoxic challenges. *Journal of Abnormal Psychology, 108,* 473–482.

Beck, S. J. (2000). Behavioral assessment. In M. Hersen, R. T. Ammerman, (Eds.), *Advanced abnormal child psychology* (2nd ed., pp. 177–195). Mahwah, NJ: Lawrence Erlbaum.

Beidel, D. C., Turner, S. M., & Morris, T. L. (2000). Behavioral treatment of childhood social phobia. *Journal of Consulting and Clinical Psychology, 68,* 1072–1080.

Belar, C. D. (1997). Clinical health psychology: A specialty for the 21st century. *Health Psychology, 16,* 411–416.

Belar, C. D. (2000). Scientist-practioner = Science + Practice. *American Psychologist, 55,* 249–250.

Belar, C. D. (Ed.) (1998). *Comprehensive clinical psychology, Vol. 10: Sociocultural and individual differences.* Oxford, England: American Book Co.

Belar, C. D., & Perry, N. W. (1992). The National Conference on Scientist-Practitioner Education and Training for the Professional Practice of Psychology. *American Psychologist, 47,* 71–75.

Bell, P. F., Digman, R. H., & McKenna, J. P. (1995). Should psychologists obtain prescribing privileges? A survey of family physicians. *Professional Psychology: Research and Practice, 26,* 371–376.

Bellack, A. S., & Hersen, M. (Eds.). (1998). *Behavioral assessment: A practical handbook* (4th ed.). Boston: Allyn & Bacon.

Bellack, A. S., & Mueser, K. T. (1994). Schizophrenia. In L. W. Craighead, W. E. Craighead, A. E. Kazdin, & M. J. Mahoney (Eds.), *Cognitive and behavioral interventions: An empirical approach to mental health problems* (pp. 105–122). Boston: Allyn & Bacon.

Bellak, L. (1993). *The TAT, CAT, and SAT in clinical use* (5th ed.). New York: Grune & Stratton.

Benjamin, L. T. (1986). Why don't they understand us? A history of psychology's public image. *American Psychologist, 41,* 941–946.

Benjamin, L. T., & Baker, D. B. (2000). Boulder at 50: Introduction to the section. *American Psychologist, 55,* 233–235.

Bennun, I. (1987). Behavioural marital therapy: A critique and appraisal of integrated models. *Behavioural Psychotherapy, 15,* 1–15.

Ben-Porath, Y. S., Butcher, J. N., & Graham, J. R. (1991). Contribution of the MMPI-2 content scales to the differential diagnosis of schizophrenia and major depression. *Psychological Assessment, 3,* 634–640.

Ben-Porath Y. S., & Waller N. G. (1992). Five big issues in clinical personality assessment: A rejoinder to Costa and McCrae. *Psychological Assessment, 4,* 23–25.

Benton, A. L. (1994). Neuropsychological assessment. *Annual Review of Psychology, 45,* 1–23.

Bergin, A. E. (1971). The deterioration effect: A reply to Braucht. *Journal of Abnormal Psychology, 75,* 300–302.

Bergin, A. E., & Garfield, S. L. (1971). *Handbook of psychotherapy and behavior change: An empirical analysis.* New York: John Wiley.

Berman, J. S., Miller, R. C., & Massman, P. J. (1985). Cognitive therapy versus systematic desensitization: Is one treatment superior? *Psychological Bulletin, 97,* 451–461.

Bernal, M. E., & Castro, F. G. (1994). Are clinical psychologists prepared for service and research with ethnic minorities? Report of a decade of progress. *American Psychologist, 49,* 797–805.

Berney, T. P. (1998). "Born to . . ."—Genetics and behavior. *British Journal of Learning Disabilities, 26,* 4–8.

Berscheid, E. (1994). Interpersonal relationships. *Annual Review of Psychology, 45,* 79–129.

Beutler, L. E. (1996). The clinical interview. In L. E. Beutler, & M. R. Berren, (Eds.), *Integrative assessment of adult personality* (pp. 94–120). New York: Guilford Press.

Beutler, L. E., Crago, M., & Arezmendi, T. G. (1986). Therapist variables in psychotherapy process and outcome. In S. L. Garfield & A. E. Bergin (Eds.), *Handbook of psychotherapy and behavior change* (3rd ed.; pp. 257–310). New York: John Wiley.

Beutler, L. E., Williams, R. E., Wakefield, P. J., & Entwistle, S. R. (1995). Bridging scientist and practitioner in clinical psychology. *American Psychologist, 50,* 984–994.

Bickman, L. (1994). Social influence and diffusion of responsibility in an emergency. In B. Puka (Ed.), *Moral development: A compendium: Vol. 7. Reaching out: Caring, altruism, and prosocial behavior.* (pp. 42–49). New York: Garland.

Biederman, J., Lapey, K. A., Milberger, S., Faraone, S. V., Reed, E. D., & Seidman, L. J. (1994). Motor preference, major depression and psychosocial dysfunction among children with attention deficit hyperactivity disorder. *Journal of Psychiatric Research, 28,* 171–184.

Bijou, S. W., Peterson, R. F., Harris, F. R., Allen, K. E., & Johnston, M. S. (1969). Methodology for experimental studies of young children in natural settings. *Psychological Record, 19,* 177–210.

Binder, J. L., Strupp, H. H., & Henry, W. P. (1995). Psychodynamic therapies in practice: Time-limited dynamic psychotherapy. In B. M. Bongar, & L. E. Beutler, (Eds.), *Comprehensive textbook of psychotherapy: Theory and practice* (pp. 48–63) New York: Oxford University Press.

Blanchard, E. B. (2001). *Irritable bowel syndrome: Psychosocial assessment and treatment.* Washington, DC: American Psychological Association.

Blanchard, E. B., Peters, M. L., & Hermann, C. (1997). Direction of temperature control in the thermal biofeedback treatment of vascular headache. *Applied Psychophysiology and Biofeedback, 22,* 227–245.

Blatt, S. J., & Lerner, H. D. (1983). The psychological assessment of object representation. *Journal of Personality Assessment, 47,* 7–28.

Blatt, S. J., Brenneis, C. B., Schimek, J. G., Glick, M. (1976). Normal development and psychopathological impairment of the concept of the object on the Rorschach. *Journal of Abnormal Psychology, 85,* 364–373.

Blechman, E. A. (1980). Family problem-solving training. *American Journal of Family Therapy, 8,* 3–21.

Block, J. (1995). A contrarian view of the five-factor approach to personality description. *Psychological Bulletin, 117,* 187–215.

Boden, M. (1977). Cognitive science: An integrative approach to the mind. *Communication and Cognition, 10,* 63–66.

Bohart, A. C., & Greenberg, L. S. (Eds.). (1997). *Empathy reconsidered: New Directions in psychotherapy.* Washington, DC: American Psychological Association.

Bohart, A. C., & Tallman, K. (1998). The person as active agent in experiential therapy. In L. S. Greenberg & J. C. Watson (Eds.), *Handbook of experiential psychotherapy* (pp. 178–200). New York: Guilford Press.

Borkovec, T. D. (1997). On the need for a basic science approach to psychotherapy research. *Psychological Science, 8,* 145–147.

Botvin, G. J. (1999). Adolescent drug abuse prevention: Current findings and future directions. In M. D. Glantz, D. Meyer, & C. R. Hartel (Eds.), *Drug abuse: Origins and interventions* (pp. 285–308). Washington, DC: American Psychological Association.

Bouton, M. (1993). Context, time, and memory retrieval in the interference paradigms of Pavlovian learing. *Psychological Bulletin, 114,* 80–99.

Bouton, M. E. (1994). Context, ambiguity, and classical conditioning. *Current Directions in Psychological Science, 3,* 49–53.

Bouton, M. E. (1998). The role of context in classical conditioning: Some implications for cognitive behavior therapy. In W. O'Donohue (Ed.), *Learning and behavior therapy* (pp. 59–84). Boston: Allyn & Bacon.

Bouton, M. E. (2000). A learning theory perspective on lapse, relapse, and the maintenance of behavior change. *Health Psychology, 19,* 57–63.

Bouton, M. E., Mineka, S., & Barlow, D. H. (2001). A modern learning theory perspective on the etiology of panic disorder. *Psychological Review, 108,* 4–32.

Bouton, M. E., & Swartzentruber, D. (1991). Sources of relapse after extinction in Pavlovian and instrumental learning. *Clinical Psychology Review, 11,* 123–140.

Bouvard, M., Mollard, E., Guerin, J., & Cottraux, J. (1997). Study and course of the psychological profile in 77 patients experiencing panic disorder with agoraphobia after cognitive behaviour therapy with or without buspirone. *Psychotherapy and Psychosomatics, 66,* 27–32.

Bowlby, J. (1969–1980). *Attachment and loss.* (Vols. 1–3). New York: Basic Books.

Boyce, P., Gilchrist, J., Talley, N. J., & Rose, D. (2000). Cognitive-behaviour therapy as a treatment for irritable bowel syndrome: A pilot study. *Australian and New Zealand Journal of Psychiatry, 34,* 300–309.

Bradley, J. D. D., Teichner, G., Crum, T. A., & Golden, C. J. (2000). Concurrent validity and analysis of learning curves on the memory scales of the Luria-Nebraska Neuropsychological Battery-third edition. *International Journal of Neuroscience, 103,* 115–126.

Brandwin, M., Trask, P. C., Schwartz, S. M., & Clifford, M. (2000). Personality predictors of mortality in cardiac transplant candidates and recipients. *Journal of Psychosomatic Research, 49,* 141–147.

Braun, A. R., Balkin, T. J., Wesensten, N. J., Gwadry, F., Carson, R. E., Varga, M., Baldwin, P., Belenky, G., & Herscovitch, P. (1998). Dissociated pattern of activity in visual cortices and their projections during human rapid eye movement sleep. *Science, 279,* 91–95.

Brenner, C. (1995). Some remarks on psychoanalytic technique. *Journal of Clinical Psychoanalysis, 4,* 413–428.

Breslau, N., & Klein, D. F. (1999). Smoking and panic attacks: An epidemiologic investigation. *Archives of General Psychiatry, 56,* 1141–1147.

Breuer, J., & Freud, S. (1895). Studies on hysteria. In J. Strachey (Ed. And Trans.), *The standard edition of the complete psychological works of Sigmund Freud* (Vol. 2, pp. 1–335). London: Hogarth Press.

Brody, A. L., Saxena, S., Schwartz, J. M., Stoessel, P. W., Maidment, K., Phelps, M. E., & Baxter, L. R. (1998). FDG-PET predictors of response to behavioral therapy and pharmacotherapy in obsessive compulsive disorder. *Psychiatry Research: Neuroimaging, 84,* 1–6.

Bronfenbrenner, U. (1999). Environments in developmental perspective: Theoretical and operational models. In S. L. Friedman, T. D. Wachs, (Eds.), *Measuring environment across the life span: Emerging methods and concepts* (pp. 3–28). Washington, DC: American Psychological Association.

Brooks-Gunn, J., Klebanov, P. K., & Duncan, G. J. (1996). Ethnic differences in children's intelligence test scores: Role of economic deprivation, home environment, and maternal characteristics. *Child Development, 67,* 396–408.

Brown, A. W. (1935). Report of the committee of clinical section of American Psychological Association. I. The definition of clinical psychology and standards for training clinical psychologists. II. Guide to psychological clinics in the United States. *Psychological Clinic, 23,* 1–140.

Brown, R. J., & Donderi, D. C. (1986). Dream content and self-reported well-being among recurrent dreamers, past-recurrent dreamers, and nonrecurrent dreamers. *Journal of Personality and Social Psychology, 50,* 612–623.

Brown, T. A., DiNardo, P. A., & Barlow, D. H. (1994). *Anxiety disorders interview schedule for DSM-IV (ADIS-IV).* Albany, NY: Graywind Publications.

Brownell, K. D., & Rodin, J. (1994). The dieting maelstrom: Is it possible and advisable to lose weight? *American Psychologist, 49,* 781–792.

Brunello, N., den Boer, J. A., Judd, L. L., Kasper, S., Kelsey, J. E., Lader, M., Lecrubier, Y., Lepine, J. P., Lydiard, R. B., Mendlewicz, J., Montgomery, S. A., Racagni, G., Stein, M. B., & Wittchen, H.-U. (2000). Social phobia: Diagnosis and epidemiology, neurobiology and pharmacology, comorbidity and treatment. *Journal of Affective Disorders, 60,* 61–74.

Bryntwick, S., & Solyom, L. (1973). A brief treatment of elevator phobia. *Journal of Behavior Therapy and Experimental Psychiatry, 4,* 355–356.

Buchanan, G. M., & Seligman, M. E. P. (1995). *Explanatory style.* Hillsdale, NJ: Lawrence Erlbaum.

Buck, J. N. (1948). The H-T-P technique, a qualitative and quantitative scoring manual. *Journal of Clinical Psychology, 4,* 317–396.

Bugental, J. F. T. (1981). *Psychotherapy and process: The fundamentals of an existential-humanistic approach.* New York: McGraw-Hill.

Bugental, J. F. T. (1987). *The art of the psychotherapist.* New York: Norton.

Bugental, J. F. T. (1999). *Psychotherapy isn't what you think: Bringing the psychotherapeutic engagement into the living moment.* Phoenix, AZ: Zeig, Tucker & Co.

Bugental, J. F. T., & Bugental, E. K. (1989). Resistance to fear and change. In F. Flach (Ed.),

Stress and its management (pp. 58–67). New York: Norton.

Bugental, J. F. T, & McBeath, B. (1995). Depth existential therapy: Evolution since World War II. In B. M. Bongar & L. E. Beutler (Eds.), *Comprehensive textbook of psychotherapy: Theory and practice.* (pp. 111–122). New York: Oxford University Press.

Burns, R. C. (1987). *Kinetic House-Tree-Person (KHTP).* New York: Brunner/Mazel.

Burstein, B., & Goodman, G. (1988). Analyzing communication acts in small groups with the response mode model: A training guide. *Small Group Behavior, 19,* 495–515.

Butcher, J. N. (1997). *Personality assessment in managed health care: Using the MMPI-2 in treatment planning.* New York: Oxford University Press.

Butcher, J. N., Dahlstrom, W. G., Graham, J. R., Tellegen, A., & Kaemmer, B. (1989). *Manual for administration and scoring: MMPI-2.* Minneapolis: University of Minnesota Press.

Butcher, J. N., & Rouse, S. V. (1996). Personality: Individual differences and clinical assessment. *Annual Review of Psychology, 47,* 87–111.

Butcher, J. N., Williams, C. L. (1992). *Essentials of MMPI-2 and MMPI-A interpretation.* Minneapolis: University of Minnesota Press.

Butow, P. N., Hiller, J. E., Price, M. A., Thackway, S. V., Kricker, A., & Tennant, C. C. (2000). Epidemiological evidence for a relationship between life events, coping style, and personality factors in the development of breast cancer. *Journal of Psychosomatic Research, 49,* 169–181.

Cacioppo, J. T., Berntson, G. G., & Anderson, B. L. (1991). Psychophysiological approaches to the evaluation of psychotherapeutic process and outcome: Contribution from social psychophysiology. *Psychological Assessment, 3,* 321–336.

Cacioppo, J. T., Berntson, G. G., & Crites, S. L. (1996). Social neuroscience: Principles of psychophysiological arousal and response. In E. T. Higgins & A. W. Kruglanski (Eds.), *Social psychology: Handbook of basic principles* (pp. 72–101). New York: Guilford Press.

Cacioppo, J. T., Gardner, W. L. (1999). Emotions. *Annual Review of Psychology, 50,* 191–214.

Campbell, D. T., & Fiske, D. W. (1959). Convergent and discriminant validation by the multitrait-multimethod matrix. *Psychological Bulletin, 56,* 81–105.

Caplan, M., Weissberg, R. P., Grober, J. S., & Sivo, P. J. (1992). Social competence promotion with inner-city and suburban young adolescents: Effects on social adjustment and alcohol use. *Journal of Consulting and Clinical Psychology, 60,* 56–63.

Caplan, R. D., Vinokur, A. D., Price, R. H., & Van Ryn, M. (1989). Job seeking, reemployment, and mental health: A randomized field experiment in coping with job loss. *Journal of Applied Psychology, 74,* 759–769.

Carey, M. P. (2000). Preventing HIV infection through sexual-behavior change. In F. Cournos & M. Forstein (Eds.). *New directions for mental health services: What mental health practitioners need to know about HIV and AIDS* (pp. 77–84). San Francisco: Jossey-Bass.

Carpenter, S. (2000). Human Genome project director says psychologists will play a critical role in the initiative's success. *Monitor on Psychology, 31,* 14–15.

Carroll, J. (1995). Non-directive play therapy with bereaved children. In S. C. Smith, & M. Pennells (Eds.). *Interventions with bereaved children* (pp. 68–83). London, England: Jessica Kingsley Publishers.

Carstensen, L. L. (1998). A lifespan approach to social motivation. In J. Heckhausen & C. S. Dweck (Eds.). *Motivation and self-regulation across the lifespan* (pp. 341–364). New York, NY: Cambridge University Press.

Carstensen, L. L. (1999). Taking time seriously: A theory of socioemotional selectivity. *American Psychologist, 54,* 165–181.

Carstensen, L. L., & Charles, S. T. (1998). Emotion in the second half of life. *Current Directions in Psychological Science, 7,* 144–149.

Carver, C. S., & Scheier, M. F. (1998). *On the self-regulation of behavior.* New York, NY: Cambridge University Press.

Carver, C. S., & Scheier, M. F. (2000). Autonomy and self regulation. *Psychological Inquiry, 11,* 284–291.

Carver, C. S., & Scheier, M. F. (2001). Optimism, pessimism, and self-regulation. In E. C. Chang (Ed.), *Optimism and pessimism: Implications for theory, research, and practice* (pp. 31–51). Washington, DC: American Psychological Association.

Carver, C. S., Harris, S. D., Lehman, J. M., Durel, L. A., Antoni, M. H., Spencer, S. M., & Pozo-Kaderman, C. (2000). How important is the perception of personal control? Studies of early stage breast cancer patients. *Personality and Social Psychology Bulletin, 26,* 139–149.

Carver, C. S., Pozo, C., Harris, S. D., & Noriega, V. (1993). How coping mediates the effect of optimism on distress: A study of women with early stage breast cancer. *Journal of Personality and Social Psychology, 65,* 375–390.

Casas, J. M. (1995). Counseling and psychotherapy with racial/ethnic minority groups in theory and practice. In Bongar, B. M. & Beutler, L. E. (Eds.), *Comprehensive textbook of Psychotherapy: Theory and practice* (311–335). New York: Oxford.

Cattell, R. B. (1963). Theory of fluid and crystallized intelligence: A critical experiment. *Journal of Educational Psychology, 54,* 1–22.

Cavalli-Sforza, L. L., Menozzi, P., & Piazza, A. (1994). *The History and geography of human genes.* Princeton, NJ: Princeton.

Centers for Disease Control and Prevention (2001). Statistics from the World Health Organization and the Centers for Disease Control. *AIDS, 6,* 1229–1233.

Chambers, W. J., Puig-Antich, J., Hirsch, M., Paez, P., Ambrosia, P. J., & Davies, M. (1985). The assessment of affective disorders in children and adolescents by semistructured interview: Test-retest reliability of the Schedule for Affective Disorders and Schizophrenia for school-age children, present episode version. *Archives of General Psychiatry, 42,* 696–702.

Chambless, D. L. (1996). In defense of dissemination of empirically supported psychological interventions. *Clinical Psychology: Science and Practice, 3,* 230–235.

Chambless, D. (1999). Empirically validated treatments—What now? *Applied and Preventive Psychology, 8,* 281–284.

Chambless, D. L., Baker, M. J., Baucom, D. H., Beutler, L. E., Calhoun, K. S., Crits-Christoph, P., Daiuto, A., DeRubeis, R., Detweiler, J., Haaga, D. A. F., Johnson S. B., McCurry, S., Mueser, K. T., Pope, K. S., Sanderson, W. C., Shoham, V.,

Stickle, T., Williams, D. A., & Woody, S. (1998). Update on empirically validated therapies, II. *The Clinical Psychologist, 51,* 3–16.

Chambless, D. L., Caputo, G. C., Bright, P., & Gallagher, R. (1984). Assessment of fear in agoraphobics: The body sensations questionnaire and the agoraphobic cognitions questionnaire. *Journal of Consulting and Clinical Psychology, 52,* 1090–1097.

Chambless, D. L., & Gillis, M. M. (1996). Cognitive therapy of anxiety disorders. In K. S. Dobson & K. D. Craig, (Eds.), *Advances in cognitive-behavioral therapy, 2* (pp. 116–144). Thousand Oaks, CA: Sage.

Chambless, D. L., & Hollon, S. (1998). Defining empirically supported therapies. *Journal of Consulting and Clinical Psychology, 66,* 7–18.

Chambless, D. L., & Hope, D. A. (1996). Cognitive approaches to the psychopathology and treatment of social phobia. In P. M. Salkovskis (Ed.), *Frontiers of cognitive therapy* (pp. 345–382). New York: Guilford Press.

Chambliss, C. H. (2000). *Psychology and managed care: Reconciling research and policy.* Boston: Allyn & Bacon.

Chapman, L. J., & Chapman J. P. (1967). Genesis of popular but erroneous psychodiagnostic observations. *Journal of Abnormal Psychology, 77,* 193–204.

Chapman, L. J., & Chapman, J. P. (1969). Illusory correlation as an obstacle to the use of valid psychodiagnostic signs. *Journal of Abnormal Psychology, 74,* 271–280.

Chapman, L. J., & Chapman, J. (1971). Test results are what you think they are. *Psychology Today, 5,* 18–22, 106.

Chappell, D., & DiMartino, V. (2000). *Violence at work* (2nd ed.). Geneva: International Labour Office.

Chassin, L., Pitts, S. C., DeLucia, C., & Todd, M. (1999). A longitudinal study of children of alcoholics: Predicting young adult substance use disorders, anxiety, and depression. *Journal of Abnormal Psychology, 108,* 106–119.

Chen, W. J., Faraone, S. V., Biederman, J., & Tsuang, M. T. (1994). Diagnostic accuracy of the Child Behavior Checklist scales for attention-deficit hyperactivity disorder: A receiver-operating

characteristic analysis. *Journal of Consulting and Clinical Psychology, 62,* 1017–1025.

Chorpita, B. F., Brown, T. A., & Barlow, D. H. (1998). Diagnostic reliability of the *DSM-III-R* anxiety disorders: Mediating effects of patient and diagnostician characteristics. *Behavior Modification, 22,* 307–320.

Chorpita, B. F., Vitali, A. E., & Barlow, D. H. (1997). Behavioral treatment of choking phobia in an adolescent: An experimental analysis. *Journal of Behavior Therapy and Experimental Psychiatry, 28,* 307–315.

Christensen, A., & Hazzard, A. (1983). Reactive effects during naturalistic observation of families. *Behavioral Assessment, 5,* 349–362.

Clark, D. M. (1986). A cognitive approach to panic. *Behaviour Research and Therapy, 24,* 461–470.

Clark, D. M., Salkovskis, P. M., Hackmann, A., Wells, A., Ludgate, J., & Gelder, M. (1999). Brief cognitive therapy for panic disorder: A randomized controlled trial. *Journal of Consulting and Clinical Psychology, 67,* 583–589.

Clark, D., Beck, A. T., & Alford, B. A. (1999). *Scientific foundations of cognitive theory and therapy of depression.* New York: John Wiley.

Clark, L. A., Watson, D., & Reynolds, S. (1995). Diagnosis and classification of psychopathology: Challenges to the current system and future directions. *Annual Review of Psychology, 46,* 121–153.

Clarke, G. N. (1999). Prevention of depression in at-risk samples of adolescents. In C. A. Essau, & F. Petermann, (Eds.), *Depressive disorders in children and adolescents: Epidemiology, risk factors, and treatment* (pp. 341–360). Northvale, NJ: Jason Aronson.

Clarke, G. N., Hawkins, W., Murphy, M., Sheeber, L. B., Lewinsohn, P. M., & Seeley, J. R. (1995). Targeted prevention of unipolar depressive disorder in an at-risk sample of high school adolescents: A randomized trial of group cognitive intervention. *Journal of the American Academy of Child and Adolescent Psychiatry, 34,* 312–321.

Clarke, G. N., Rohde, P., Lewinsohn, P. M., Hops, H., & Seeley, J. R. (1999). Cognitive-behavioral treatment of adolescent depression: Efficacy of acute group treatment and booster sessions. *Journal of the American Academy of Child and Adolescent Psychiatry, 38,* 272–279.

Clum, G. A., Clum, G. A., & Surls, R. (1993). A meta-analysis of treatments for panic disorder. *Journal of Consulting and Clinical Psychology, 61,* 317–326.

Coates, T. J., & Collins, C. (1999). HIV prevention: We don't need to wait for a vaccine. In M. D. Glantz & C. R. Hartel, (Eds.), (1999). *Drug abuse: Origins and interventions* (pp. 309–329). Washington, DC: American Psychological Association.

Cogan, J. C., & Ernsberger, P. (1999). Dieting, weight, and health: Reconceptualizing research and policy. *Journal of Social Issues, 55,* 187–205.

Cohen, J. (1988). *Statistical power analysis for the behavioral sciences* (rev. ed.). Hillsdale, NJ: Lawrence Erlbaum.

Cohen, J. (1992). A power primer. *Psychological Bulletin, 112,* 155–159.

Cohen, J. (1994). The earth is round (p < .05). *American Psychologist, 49,* 997–1003.

Cohen, L. H., Sargent, M. M., & Sechrest, L. B. (1986). Use of psychotherapy research by professional psychologists. *American Psychologist, 41,* 198–206.

Cohen, P., Johnson, J. G., Pine, D. S., Klein, D. F., Kasen, S., & Brook, J. S. (2000). Association between cigarette smoking and anxiety disorders during adolescence and early adulthood. *Journal of the American Medical Association, 284,* 2348–2351.

Cohen, S., Doyle, W. J., & Skoner, D. P. (1999). Psychological stress, cytokine production, and severity of upper respiratory illness. *Psychosomatic Medicine, 61,* 175–180.

Cohen, S., Frank, E., Doyle, W. J., Skoner, D. P., Rabin, B. S., & Gwaltney, J. M. Jr. (1998). Types of stressors that increase susceptibility to the common cold in healthy adults. *Health Psychology, 17,* 214–223.

Coie, J. D., Cillessen, A. H. N., Dodge, K. A., Hubbard, J. A., Schwartz, D., Lemerise, E. A., & Bateman, H. (1999). It takes two to fight: A test of relational factors and a method for assessing aggressive dyads. *Developmental Psychology, 35,* 1179–1188.

Coie, J. D., Miller-Johnson, S., & Bagwell, C. (2000). Prevention science. In A. J. Sameroff, M. Lewis, & S. M. Miller (Eds.), *Handbook of developmental psychopathology* (2nd ed.;

pp. 93–112). New York: Kluwer Academic/Plenum Publishers.

Coie, J. D., Watt, N. F., West, S. G., & Hawkins, J. D. (1993). The science of prevention: A conceptual framework and some directions for a national research program. *American Psychologist, 48,* 1013–1022.

Cole, D. A., Hoffman, K., Tram, J. M., & Maxwell, S. E. (2000). Structural differences in parent and child reports of children's symptoms of depression and anxiety. *Psychological Assessment, 12,* 174–185.

Collins, F. S. (1999). Shattuck lecture—Medical and societal consequences of the human genome project. *New England Journal of Medicine, 341,* 28–37.

Committee on Quality Health Care in America. (2001). *Crossing the chasm: A new health care system for the twenty-first century.* Washington, DC: National Academy Press.

Compas, B. E. (1993). Promoting positive mental health during adolescence. In S. G. Millstein, A. C. Petersen, E. Nightengale, & R. Takanishi (Eds.), *Promoting the health of adolescents: New directions for the twenty-first century* (pp. 159–179). New York: Oxford University Press.

Compas, B. E., & Hammen, C. L. (1996). Child and adolescent depression: Covariation and comorbidity in development. In R. J. Haggerty & L. R. Sherrod (Eds.), *Stress, risk, and resilience in children and adolescents: Processes, mechanisms, and interventions* (p. 225–267). New York: Cambridge University Press.

Compas, B. E., Connor, J., & Wadsworth, M. (1997). Prevention of depression. In R. P. Weissberg, T. P. Gullotta, R. L. Hampton, B. A. Ryan, & G. R. Adams (Eds.), *Healthy children 2010: Enhancing children's wellness* (pp. 129–174). Thousand Oaks, CA: Sage.

Compas, B. E., Connor-Smith, J. K., Saltzman, H., Thomsen, A. H., & Wadsworth, M. E. (2001). Coping with stress during childhood and adolescence: Problems, progress, and potential in theory and research. *Psychological Bulletin, 127,* 87–127.

Compas, B. E., Ey, S., & Grant, K. (1993). Taxonomy, assessment, and diagnosis of depression during adolescence. *Psychological Bulletin, 114,* 323–344.

Compas, B. E., Haaga, D. A. F., Keefe, F. J., Leitenberg, H. L., & Williams, D. A. (1998). Sampling of empirically supported psychological treatments from health psychology: Smoking, chronic pain, cancer, and bulimia nervosa. *Journal of Consulting and Clinical Psychology, 66,* 89–112.

Compas, B. E., & Oppedisano, G. (2000). Mixed anxiety/depression in childhood and adolescence. In A. J. Sameroff, M. Lewis, & S. M. Miller (Eds.), *Handbook of developmental psychopathology* (2nd ed., pp. 531–548). New York: Kluwer Academic/Plenum.

Compas, B. E., Oppedisano, G., Connor, J. K., Gerhardt, C. A., Hinden, B., Achenbach, T. M., & Hammen, C. (1997). Gender differences in depressive symptoms in adolescence: Comparison of national samples of clinically referred and nonreferred youths. *Journal of Consulting and Clinical Psychology, 65,* 617–626.

Compas, B. E., Worsham, N. L., Epping-Jordan, J. E., Grant, K. E. (1994).When Mom or Dad has cancer: Markers of psychological distress in cancer patients, spouses, and children. *Health Psychology, 13,* 507–515.

Conduct Problems Prevention Research Group (1992). A developmental and clinical model for the prevention of conduct disorder: The FAST Track Program. *Development & Psychopathology, 4,* 509–527.

Conduct Problems Prevention Research Group. (1999a). Initial impact of the fast track prevention trial for conduct problems: I. The high-risk sample. *Journal of Consulting and Clinical Psychology, 67,* 631–647.

Conduct Problems Prevention Research Group. (1999b). Initial impact of the fast track prevention trial for conduct problems: II. Classroom effects. *Journal of Consulting and Clinical Psychology, 67,* 648–657.

Conners, C. K., Sitarenios, G., Parker, J. D. A., & Epstein, J. N. (1998). The revised Conners' Parent Rating Scale (CPRS-R): Factor structure, reliability, and criterion validity. *Journal of Abnormal Child Psychology, 26,* 257–268.

Conners, C. K., Wells, K. C., Parker, J. D. A., Sitarenios, G., Diamond, J. M., & Powell, J. W. (1997). A new self-report scale for assessment of adolescent psychopathology: Factor structure, reliability, validity, and diagnostic sensitivity. *Journal of Abnormal Child Psychology, 25,* 487–497.

Consumer Reports. (1995, November). Mental health: Does therapy help? pp. 734–739.

Cook, M., & Mineka, S. (1990). Observational conditioning of fear to fear-relevant versus fear-irrelevant stimuli in rhesus monkeys. *Journal of Abnormal Psychology, 98,* 448–459.

Cooper, J. (1998). Unlearning cognitive dissonance: Toward an understanding of the development of dissonance. *Journal of Experimental Social Psychology, 34,* 562–575.

Cooper, P. J. & Steere, J. (1995). A comparison of two psychological treatments for bulimia nervosa: Implications for models of maintenance. *Behaviour Research and Therapy, 33,* 875–886.

Cornes, C. & Frank, E. (1996). Interpersonal psychotherapy. *American Psychiatric Press Review of Psychiatry, 15,* 91–107.

Costa, F. M., Jessor, R., & Turbin, M. S. (1999). Transition into adolescent problem drinking: The role of psychosocial risk and protective factors. *Journal of Studies on Alcohol, 60,* 480–490.

Costa, P. T., Jr. & McCrae, R. R. (1992). *Manual for the Revised NEO Personality Inventory (NEO-PI-R) and NEO Five-Factor Inventory (NEO-FFI).* Odessa, FL: Psychological Assessment Resources.

Costello, E. J., & Edelbrock, C. S. (1985). Detection of psychiatric disorders in pediatric primary care: A preliminary report. *Journal of the American Academy of Child Psychiatry, 24,* 771–774.

Costello, E. J., Edelbrock, C. S., & Costello, A. J. (1985). Validity of the NIMH Diagnostic Interview Schedule for Children: A comparison between psychiatric and pediatric referrals. *Journal of Abnormal Child Psychology, 13,* 570–595.

Cowen, E. L. (1991). In pursuit of wellness. *American Psychologist, 46,* 404–408.

Cowen, E. L. (1994). The enhancement of psychological wellness: Challenges and opportunities. *American Journal of Community Psychology, 22,* 149–179.

Craighead, L. W., Craighead, W. E., Kazdin, A. E., & Mahoney, M. J. (Eds.). (1994). *Cognitive and behavioral interventions: An empirical approach to mental health problems.* Boston: Allyn & Bacon.

Cranston-Cuebas, M. A., & Barlow, D. H. (1990). Cognitive and affective contributions to sexual functioning. *Annual Review of Sex Research, 1,* 119–161.

Crary, M. A., Fucci, D. J., & Bond, Z. S. (1981). Interaction of sensory feedback: A child/adult comparison of oral sensory and temporal articulatory feedback. *Perceptual & Motor Skills, 53,* 979–988.

Crary, W. G., & Johnson, C. W. (1970). Attitude therapy in a crisis-intervention program. *Hospital & Community Psychiatry, 21,* 165–168.

Crijnen, A. A. M., Achenbach, T. M., & Verhulst, F. C. (1999). Problems reported by parents of children in multiple cultures: The Child Behavior Checklist syndrome constructs. *American Journal of Psychiatry, 156,* 569–574.

Crits-Christoph, P. (1992). The efficacy of brief dynamic psychotherapy: A meta-analysis. *American Journal of Psychiatry, 149,* 151–158.

Cronbach, L. J. (1951). Coefficient alpha and the internal structure of tests. *Psychometrika, 16,* 297–334.

Cross National Collaborative Group (1992). The changing rate of major depression: Cross-national comparisons. *JAMA: Journal of the American Medical Association, 268,* 3098–3105.

Cullen, E. A., & Newman, R. (1997). In pursuit of prescription privileges. *Professional Psychology: Research & Practice, 28,* 101–106.

Cumella, E. J., Wall, A. D., & Kerr-Almeida, N. (2000). MMPI-2 in the inpatient assessment of women with eating disorders. *Journal of Personality Assessment, 75,* 387–403.

Cummings, E. M. (1998). Children exposed to marital conflict and violence: Conceptual and theoretical directions. In G. W. Holden, R. Geffner, (Eds.), *Children exposed to marital violence: Theory, research, and applied issues* (pp. 55–93). Washington, DC: American Psychological Association.

Cummings, E. M., & Davis, P. (1992). Parental depression, family functioning, and child adjustment: Risk factors, processes, and pathways. *Rochester symposium on developmental psychology: Developmental perspectives of depression, 4,* 283–322.

Cummings, E. M., & Davis, P. (1994). *Children and marital conflict: The impact of family dispute and resolution.* New York: Guilford Press.

Curtis, G. C., Magee, W. J., Eaton, W. W., Wittchen, H.-U., & Kessler, R. C. (1998). Specific fears and phobias: Epidemiology and classification. *British Journal of Psychiatry, 173,* 212–217.

Da Costa, D., Larouche, J., Dritsa, M., & Brender, W. (1999). Variations in stress levels over the course of pregnancy: Factors associated with elevated hassles, state anxiety, and pregnancy-specific stress. *Journal of Psychosomatic Research, 47,* 609–621.

Dana, R. H. (Ed.). (2000). *Handbook of cross-cultural and multicultural personality assessment.* Mahwah, NJ: Erlbaum.

Daniels, T. G., Rigazio-DiGilio, S. A., & Ivey, A. E. (1997). Microcounseling: A training and supervision paradigm for the helping professions. In C. E. Watkins, Jr., (Ed.), *Handbook of psychotherapy supervision* (pp. 277–295). New York: John Wiley.

Davanloo, H. (Ed.). (1978). *Basic principles and techniques in short-term dynamic psychotherapy.* New York: Spectrum.

Davanloo, H. (Ed.). (1980). *Short-term dynamic psychotherapy.* New York: Jason Aronson.

Davenport, S., Hobson, R., & Margison, F. (2000). Treatment development in psychodynamic-interpersonal psychotherapy (Hobson's 'Conversational Model') for chronic treatment resistant schizophrenia: Two single case studies. *British Journal of Psychotherapy, 16,* 287–302.

Davidson, J. R. T., & Foa, E. B. (1991). Diagnostic issues in posttraumatic stress disorder: Considerations for the DSM-IV. *Journal of Abnormal Psychology, 100,* 346–355.

Davidson, P. R., & Parker, K. C. H. (2001). Eye movement desensitization and reprocessing (EMDR): A meta-analysis. *Journal of Consulting and Clinical Psychology, 69,* 305–316.

Davidson, R. J. (1994). Asymmetric brain function, affective style, and psychopathology: The role of early experience and plasticity. *Development & Psychopathology, 6,* 741–758.

Davidson, R. J. (2000a). Award for distinguished scientific contributions. *American Psychologist, 55,* 1193–1196.

Davidson, R. J. (2000b). Affective style, psychopathology, and resilience: Brain mechanisms and plasticity. *American Psychologist, 55,* 1196–1214.

Davidson, R. J., Jackson, D. C., & Kalin, N. H. (2000). Emotion, plasticity, context, and regulation: Perspectives from affective neuroscience. *Psychological Bulletin, 126,* 890–909.

Davidson, R. J., Marshall, J. R., Tomarken, A. J., & Henriques, J. B. (2000). While a phobic waits: Regional brain electrical and autonomic activity in social phobics during anticipation of public speaking. *Biological Psychiatry, 47,* 85–95.

Davison, G. C., Navarre, S., & Vogel, R. (1995). The articulated thoughts in simulated situations paradigm: A think-aloud approach to cognitive assessment. *Current Directions in Psychological Science, 4,* 29–33.

Davison, G. C. (1997). The mutual enrichment of basic and applied research in psychological science and practice. *Psychological Science, 8,* 194–197.

Davison, G. C., & Lazarus, A. A. (1994). Clinical innovation and evaluation: Integrating practice with inquiry. *Clinical Psychology: Science and Practice, 1,* 157–168.

Davison, G. C., & Neale, J. M. (1998). *Abnormal psychology* (7th ed.). New York, NY: John Wiley & Sons, Inc.

Dawes, R. M. (1994). *House of cards: Psychology and psychotherapy built on myth.* New York: Free Press.

Dawes, R. M. (1995). Standards of practice. In S. C. Hayes & V. M. Follette, (Eds.), *Scientific standards of psychological practice: Issues and recommendations* (pp. 31–43). Reno, NV: Context Press.

Dawes, R. M., Faust, D., & Meehl, P. E. (1989). Clinical versus actuarial judgment. *Science, 243,* 1668–1674.

De Renzi, A., & Vignolo, L. A. (1962). Token test: A sensitive test to detect receptive disturbances in aphasics. *Brain, 85,* 665–678.

De Renzi, E., & Faglioni, P. (1978). Normative data and screening power of a shortened version of the Token Test. *Cortex 14,* 41–49.

DeLeon, P. H., & Wiggins, J. G. (1996). Prescription privileges for psychologists. *American Psychologist, 51,* 225–229.

DeLeon, P. H., Fox, R. E., & Graham, S. R. (1991). Prescription privileges: Psychology's next frontier? *American Psychologist, 46,* 384–393.

Demb, J. B., Desmond, J. E., Wagner, A. D., & Vaidya, C. J. (1995). Semantic encoding and retrieval in the left inferior prefrontal cortex: A functional MRI study of task difficulty and process specificity. *Journal of Neuroscience, 15,* 5870–5878.

Dember, W. N. (1974). Motivation and the cognitive revolution. *American Psychologist, 29,* 161–168.

den Boer, J. A. (2000). Social anxiety disorder/social phobia: Epidemiology, diagnosis, neurobiology, and treatment. *Comprehensive Psychiatry, 41,* 405–415.

DeNelsky, G. Y. (1991). Prescription privileges for psychologists: The case against. *Professional Psychology: Research and Practice, 22,* 188–193.

DeNelsky, G. Y. (1996). The case against prescription privileges for psychologists. *American Psychologist, 51,* 207–211.

DeRubeis, R. J., & Crits-Christoph, P. (1998). Empirically supported individual and group psychological treatments for adult mental disorders. *Journal of Consulting and Clinical Psychology, 66,* 37–52.

DeRubeis, R. J., Evans, M. D., Hollon, S. D., Garvey, M. J., Grove, W. M., & Tuason, V. B. (1990). How does cognitive therapy work? Cognitive change and symptom change in cognitive therapy and pharmacotherapy for depression. *Journal of Consulting and Clinical Psychology, 58,* 862–869.

DeRubeis, R. J., Gelfand, L. A., Tang, T. Z., & Simons, A. D. (1999). Medication versus cognitive behavior therapy for severely depressed outpatients: Mega-analysis of four randomized comparisons. *American Journal of Psychiatry, 156,* 1007–1013.

DiBartolo, P. M., Albano, A. M., Barlow, D. H., & Heimberg, R. G. (1998). Cross-informant agreement in the assessment of social phobia in youth. *Journal of Abnormal Child Psychology, 26,* 213–220.

DiNardo, P. A., Moras, K., Barlow, D. H., & Rapee, R. M., (1993). Reliability of *DSM-III-R* anxiety disorder categories: Using the Anxiety Disorders Interview Schedule–Revised (ADIS-R). *Archives of General Psychiatry, 50,* 251–256.

Dickens, W. T., & Flynn, J. R. (2001). Heritability estimates versus large environmental effects: The IQ paradox resolved. *Psychological Review, 108,* 346–369.

Diener, E., & Suh, E. M. (Eds.). (2000). *Culture and subjective well-being.* Cambridge, MA: MIT Press.

DiLalla, L. F., & Gottesman, I. (1991). Biological and genetic contributors to violence: Widom's untold tale. *Psychological Bulletin, 109,* 125–129.

DiNardo, P. A., & Barlow, D. H. (1988). *Anxiety Disorders Interview Schedule-Revised (ADIS-R).* Albany: Phobia and Anxiety Disorder Clinic, State University of New York at Albany.

DiNardo, P. A., O'Brien, G. T., Barlow, D. H., Waddell, M. T., & Blanchard, E. B. (1983). Reliability of DSM-III anxiety disorder categories using a new structured interview. *Archives of General Psychiatry, 40,* 1070–1074.

Dobson, K. S. (1989). A meta-analysis of the efficacy of cognitive therapy for depression. *Journal of Consulting and Clinical Psychology, 57,* 414–419.

Dodge, K. A. (2000). Conduct disorder. In A. J. Sameroff, M. Lewis, & S. M. Miller (Eds.), *Handbook of developmental psychopathology* (2nd ed.) (pp. 447–463). New York, NY: Plenum Publishers.

Dohrenwend, B. P. (2000). The role of adversity and stress in psychopathology: Some evidence and its implications for theory and research. *Journal of Health and Social Behavior, 41,* 1–19.

Donohue, B., Van Hasselt, V. B., Hersen, M., & Perrin, S. (1998). Role-play assessment of social skills in conduct disordered and substance abusing adolescents: An empirical review. *Journal of Child and Adolescent Substance Abuse, 8,* 1–28.

Donovan, J. E., Jessor, R., & Costa, F. M. (1993). Structure of health-enhancing behavior in adolescence: A latent-variable approach. *Journal of Health and Social Behavior, 34,* 346–362.

Dornbusch, S. M., Mont-Reynaud, R., Ritter, P. L., Chen, Z. Y., & Steinberg, L. (1991). Stressful events and their correlates among adolescents of diverse backgrounds. In M. E. Colten & S. Gore

(Eds.), *Adolescent stress: Causes and consequences* (pp. 111–130). New York: Aldine De Gruyter.

Doyle, A. E., Biederman, J., Seidman, L. J., Weber, W., & Faraone, S. V. (2000). Diagnostic efficiency of neuropsychological test scores for discriminating boys with and without attention deficit-hyperactivity disorder. *Journal of Consulting and Clinical Psychology, 68,* 477–488.

Driskell, J. E., & Olmstead, B. (1989). Psychology and the military: Research applications and trends. *American Psychologist, 44,* 43–54.

Drum, D. J., & Hall, J. E. (1993). Psychology's self-regulation and the setting of professional standards. *Applied and Preventive Psychology, 2,* 151–161.

Druss, B. G., Rosenheck, R. A., & Sledge, W. H. (2000). Health and disability costs of depressive illness in a major U. S. corporation. *American Journal of Psychiatry, 157,* 1274–1278.

DuPaul, G. J., Guevremont, D. C., & Barkley, R. A. (1994). Attention deficit hyperactivity disorder. In L. W. Craighead, W. E. Craighead, A. E. Kazdin, & M. J. Mahoney (Eds.), *Cognitive and behavioral interventions: An empirical approach to mental health problems* (pp. 235–250). Boston: Allyn & Bacon.

Durlak, J. A., Fuhrman, T., & Lampman, C. (1991). Effectiveness of cognitive-behavior therapy for maladapting children: A meta-analysis. *Psychological Bulletin, 110,* 204–214.

Dusenbury, L., & Falco, M. (1977). School-based drug abuse prevention strategies: From research to policy and practice. In R. P. Weissberg & T. P. Gullotta, (Eds.), *Healthy children 2010: Enhancing children's wellness* (pp. 47–75). Thousand Oaks, CA: Sage.

Eaton, W. W. (2001). *The sociology of mental disorders* (3rd ed.). Westport, CT: Praeger Publishers/Greenwood Publishing Group.

Edelbrock, C. & Costello, A. J. (1988). Convergence between statistically derived behavior problem syndromes and child psychiatric diagnoses. *Journal of Abnormal Child Psychology, 16,* 219–231.

Edelbrock, C., Costello, A. J., Dulcan, M. K., Conover, N. C., & Kala, R. (1986). Parent-child agreement on child psychiatric symptoms assessed via structured interview. *Journal of*

Child Psychology & Psychiatry & Allied Disciplines, 27, 181–190.

Edelbrock, C., Costello, A .J., Dulcan, M. K., Kalas, R., & Conover, N. C. (1985). Age differences in the reliability and validity of the psychiatric interview of the child. *Child Development, 56,* 265–275.

Edelbrock, C., Costello, A. J., & Kessler, M. D. (1984). Empirical corroboration of attention deficit disorder. *Journal of the American Academy of Child Psychiatry, 22,* 285–290.

Edelbrock, C., Crnic, K., & Bohnert, A. (1999). Interviewing as communication: An alternative way of administering the Diagnostic Interview Schedule for Children. *Journal of Abnormal Child Psychology, 27,* 447–453.

Edelson, M. (1994). Can psychotherapy research answer this psychotherapist's questions? In P. F. Talley, H. H. Strupp, & S. F. Butler (Eds.), *Psychotherapy research and practice: Bridging the gap* (pp. 60–87). New York: Basic Books.

Eisenbruch, M. (1992). Toward a culturally sensitive DSM: Cultural bereavement in Cambodian refugees and the traditional healer as taxonomist. *Journal of Nervous and Mental Disease, 180,* 8–10.

Ekman, P. (1999). Facial expressions. In T. Dalgleish & M. J. Power (Eds.), *Handbook of cognition and emotion* (pp. 301–320). Chichester, England: John Wiley.

Elkin, I. (1994). The NIMH treatment of depression collaborative research program: Where we began and where we are. In A. E. Bergin and S. L. Garfield (Eds.), *Handbook of psychotherapy and behavior change* (4th ed.; pp. 114–139). New York: John Wiley.

Elkin, I., Gibbons, R. D., Shea, M. T., Sotsky, S. M., Watkins, J. T., Pilkonis, P. A., & Hedecker, D. (1995). Initial severity and differential treatment outcome in the National Institute of Mental Health Treatment of Depression Collaborative Research Program. *Journal of Consulting and Clinical Psychology, 63,* 841–847.

Elkin, I., Parloff, M. B., Hadley, S. W., & Autry, J. H. (1985). NIMH treatment of Depression Collaborative Research Program: Background and research plan. *Archives of General Psychiatry, 42,* 305–316.

Elkin, I., Shea, M. T., Watkins, J. T., Imber, S. D., Sotsky, S. M., Collins, J. F., Glass, D. R., Pilkonis, P. A., Leber, W. R., Docherty, J. P., Fiester, S. J., & Parloff, M. B. (1989). National Institute of Mental Health Treatment of Depression Collaborative Research Program: General effectiveness of treatments. *Archives of General Psychiatry, 46,* 971–983.

Elliott, R. (1999). Editor's introduction to special issue on qualitative psychotherapy research: Definitions, themes and discoveries. *Psychotherapy Research. 9,* 251–257.

Elliott, R., Davis, K. L., & Slatick, E. (1998). Process-experiential therapy for posttraumatic stress difficulties. In L. S. Greenberg & J. C. Watson (Eds.), *Handbook of experiential psychotherapy* (pp. 249–271). New York: The Guilford Press.

Elliott, R., Fischer, C. T., & Rennie, D. L. (1999). Evolving guidelines for publication of qualitative research studies in psychology and related fields. *British Journal of Clinical Psychology, 38,* 215–229.

Elliott, R., & Greenberg, L. S. (1995). Experiential therapy in practice: The process-experiential approach. In B. M. Bongar & L. E. Beutler (Eds.), *Comprehensive textbook of psychotherapy: Theory and practice.* (pp. 123–139). New York: Oxford University Press.

Ellis, A. (1962). *Reason and emotion in psychotherapy.* New York: Lyle Stuart.

Ellis, A. (1994). *Reason and emotion in psychotherapy, revised and updated.* New York: Carol Publishing.

Ellis, A. (2000). Rational-emotive behavior therapy as an internal control psychology. *Journal of Rational-Emotive and Cognitive Behavior Therapy, 18,* 19–38.

Ellis, A., & Grieger, R. (Eds.). (1977). *Handbook of rational-emotive therapy.* New York: Springer.

Emanuels-Zuurveen, L., & Emmelkamp, P. M. G. (1996). Individual behavioural-cognitive therapy v. marital therapy for depression in maritally distressed couples. *British Journal of Psychiatry, 169,* 181–188.

Emery, R. E. (1999). Postdivorce family life for children: An overview of research and some implications for policy. In R. A. Thompson & P. R. Amato (Eds.), *The postdivorce family: Children, parenting, and society* (pp. 3–27). Thousand Oaks, CA: Sage.

Emery, R. E, & Forehand, R. (1996). Parental divorce and children's well-being: A focus on resilience. In R. J. Haggerty, L. R. Sherrod, M. Rutter, & N. Garmezy (Eds.), *Stress, risk and resilience in children and adolescents: Processes, mechanisms, and interventions* (pp. 64–99). New York: Cambridge University Press.

Emmelkamp, P. M. G. (1994). Behavior therapy with adults. In A. E. Bergin & S. L. Garfield (Eds.), *Handbook of psychotherapy and behavior change* (4th ed.; pp. 379–427). New York: John Wiley.

Endicott, J., & Spitzer, R. L. (1978). A diagnostic interview: The Schedule for Affective Disorders and Schizophrenia. *Archives of General Psychiatry, 35,* 837–844.

Endicott, J., Spitzer, R. L., Fleiss, J. L., & Cohen, J. (1976). The Global Assessment Scale: A procedure for measuring overall severity of psychiatric disturbance. *Archives of General Psychiatry, 33,* 766–771.

Entwisle, D. R. (1972). To dispel fantasies about fantasy-based measures of achievement motivation. *Psychological Bulletin, 77,* 377–391.

Epstein, N. B., Baucom, D. H., & Daiuto, A. (1997). Cognitive-behavioral couples therapy. In W. K. Halford & H. J. Markman (Eds.), *Clinical handbook of marriage and couples interventions* (pp. 415–449). Chichester: John Wiley.

Erdberg, P. (1990). Rorschach assessment. In G. Goldstein & M. Hersen (Eds.), *Handbook of psychological assessment* (2nd ed., pp. 387–399). New York: Pergamon Press.

Erikson, E. (1950). *Childhood and society.* New York: Norton.

Erikson, E. (1956). The problem of ego identity. *Journal of the American Psychoanalytic Association, 4,* 56–121.

Erikson, E. (1959). *Identity and the life cycle: Vol 1. Selected papers, psychological issues.* New York: International Universities Press.

Evans, D. R., Hearn, M. T., Uhlemann, M. R., & Ivey, A. E. (1998). *Essential interviewing: A programmed approach to effective communication* (5th ed.). Pacific Grove, CA: Brooks/Cole.

Exner, J. E., Jr. (1978). *The Rorschach: A comprehensive system: Vol. 2. Current research and advanced interpretation.* New York: John Wiley.

Exner, J. E., Jr. (1986). Some Rorschach data comparing schizophrenics with borderline and schizotypal personality disorders. *Journal of Personality Assessment, 50,* 455–471.

Exner, J. E., Jr. (1993). *The Rorschach: A comprehensive system: Vol. 1. Basic foundations* (3rd ed.). New York: John Wiley.

Exner, J. E., Jr. (1997). The future of Rorschach in personality assessment. *Journal of Personality Assessment, 68,* 37–46.

Exner, J. E., Jr., & Exner, D. E. (1972). How clinicians use the Rorschach. *Journal of Personality Assessment, 36,* 403–408.

Eysenck, H. J. (1952). The effects of psychotherapy: An evaluation. *Journal of Consulting Psychology, 16,* 319–324.

Eysenck, H. J. (Ed.). (1960). *Behaviour therapy and the neuroses: Readings in modern methods of treatment derived from learning theory.* Oxford, England: Pergamon Press.

Eysenck, H. J. (1981). *The intelligence controversy: H. J. Eysenck versus Leon Kamin.* New York: Wiley.

Fabrega, H. (1992). Diagnosis interminable: Toward a culturally sensitive DSM-IV. *Journal of Nervous and Mental Disease, 180,* 5–7.

Fairburn, C. G. (1998). Interpersonal psychotherapy for bulimia nervosa. In J. C. Markowitz (Ed.), *Interpersonal psychotherapy* (pp. 99–128). Washington, DC: American Psychiatric Press.

Fairburn, C. G., Jones, R., Peveler, R. C., Carr, S. J., Solomon, R. A., & O'Connor, M. E. (1991). Three psychological treatments for bulimia nervosa: A comparative trial. *Archives of General Psychiatry, 48,* 463–469.

Fairburn, C. G., Jones, R., Peveler, R. C., Hope, R. A., & O'Connor, M. E. (1993). Predictors of 12-month outcome in bulimia nervosa and the influence of attitudes to shape and weight. *Journal of Consulting and Clinical Psychology, 61,* 696–698.

Fairburn, C. G., Marcus, M. D., & Wilson, G. T. (1993). Cognitive-behavioral therapy for binge eating and bulimia nervosa: A comprehensive treatment manual. In C. G. Fairburn, & G. T. Wilson, (Eds.), *Binge eating: Nature, assessment, and treatment* (pp. 361–404). New York: Guilford Press.

Fairburn, C. G., Norman, P. A.,Welch, S. L., O'Connor, M. E., Doll, H. A., & Peveler, R. C. (1995). A prospective study of outcome in bulimia nervosa and the long-term effects of three psychological treatments. *Archives of General Psychiatry, 52,* 304–312.

Fairburn, W. R. D. (1952). *Pyschoanalytical studies of the personality.* London: Routledge & Kegan Paul.

Falls, W. A. (1998). Extinction: A review of evidence suggesting that memories are not erased with nonreinforcement. In W. T. O'Donahue (Ed.), *Learning and behavior therapy* (pp. 205–229). Boston, MA: Allyn & Bacon.

Faraone, S. V., Biederman, J., Feighner, J. A., & Monuteaux, M. C. (2000). Assessing symptoms of attention deficit hyperactivity disorder in children and adults: Which is more valid? *Journal of Consulting and Clinical Psychology, 68,* 830–842.

Farrell, A. D., Danish, S. J., & Howard, C. W. (1992). Risk factors for drug use in urban adolescents: Identification and cross-validation. *American Journal of Community Psychology, 20,* 263–286.

Farrington, D. P. (2000). Adolescent violence: Findings and implications from the Cambridge Study. In G. Boswell, (Ed.), *Violent children and adolescents: Asking the question why* (pp. 19–35). London, England: Whurr Publishers.

Farrington, D. P., & Loeber, R. (2000). Epidemiology of juvenile violence. *Child and Adolescent Psychiatric Clinics of North America, 9,* 733–748.

Farris, M. A. (1988). Differential diagnosis of borderline and narcissistic personality disorders. In H. D. Lerner & P. M. Lerner (Eds.), *Primitive mental states and the Rorschach* (pp. 299–337). Madison, CT: International Universities Press.

Fawzy, F. I., Fawzy, N. W., Arndt, L. A., & Pasnau, R. O. (1995). Critical review of psychosocial interventions in cancer care. *Archives of General Psychiatry, 52,* 100–113.

Fawzy, F. I., Fawzy, N. W., Hyun, C. S., & Elashoff, R. (1993). Malignant melanoma: Effects of an early structured psychiatric intervention, coping, and affective state on recurrence and survival 6 years later. *Archives of General Psychiatry, 50,* 681–689.

Feighner, J. P., Robins, E., Guze, S. B., Woodruff, R. A., Winokur, G., & Muñoz, R. (1972).

Diagnostic criteria for use in psychiatric research. *Archives of General Psychiatry, 26,* 57–63.

Ferenczi, S., & Rank, O. (1925). *The development of psycho-analysis.* New York and Washington, DC: Nervous and Mental Diseases Publishing Co.

Feske, U., & Chambless, D. L. (1995). Cognitive behavioral versus exposure only treatment for social phobia: A meta-analysis. *Behavior Therapy, 26,* 695–720.

Feske, U., & Goldstein, A. J. (1997). Eye movement desensitization and reprocessing treatment for panic disorder: A controlled outcome and partial dismantling study. *Journal of Consulting and Clinical Psychology, 65,* 1026–1035.

Festinger, L. (1957). *A theory of cognitive dissonance.* Evanston, IL: Row, Peterson.

Fink, P. J., & Tasman, A. (1992). *Stigma and mental illness.* Washington, DC: American Psychiatric Press.

Finn, S. E. (1996). *Manual for using the MMPI-2 as a therapeutic intervention.* Minneapolis: University of Minnesota Press.

First, M. B., Spitzer, R. L., Gibbon, M., & Williams, J. B. W. (1995a). The Structured Clinical Interview for *DSM-III-R* Personality Disorders (SCID-II): I. Description. *Journal of Personality Disorders, 9,* 83–91.

First, M. B., Spitzer, R. L., Gibbon, M., & Williams, J. B. W., (1995b). The Structured Clinical Interview for *DSM-III-R* Personality Disorders (SCID-II): II. Multi-site test-retest reliability study. *Journal of Personality Disorders, 9,* 92–104.

Fiske, S. T. (1993). Social cognition and social perception. *Annual Review of Psychology, 44,* 155–194.

Fleiss, J. L., & Cohen, J. (1973). The equivalence of weighted kappa and the intraclass correlation coefficient as measures of reliability. *Educational and Psychological Measurement, 33,* 613–619.

Flynn, J. R. (1999). Searching for justice: The discovery of IQ gains over time. *American Psychologist, 54,* 5–20.

Foa, E. B., & Goldstein, A. J. (1978). Continuous exposure and complete response prevention in the treatment of obsessive-compulsive neurosis. *Behavior Therapy, 9,* 821–829.

Foa, E. B., Cashman, L., Jaycox, L., & Perry, K. (1997). The validation of a self-report measure of posttraumatic stress disorder: The Posttraumatic

Diagnostic Scale. *Psychological Assessment, 9,* 445–451.

Foa, E. B., Hearst-Ikeda, D., & Perry, K. J. (1995). Evaluation of a brief cognitive-behavioral program for the prevention of chronic PTSD in recent assault victims. *Journal of Consulting and Clinical Psychology, 63,* 948–955.

Foa, E. B., Keane, T. M., & Friedman, M. J. (2000). *Effective treatments for PTSD: Practice guidelines for the International Society for Traumatic Stress Studies.* New York: Guilford Press.

Foa, E. B., Kozak, M. J., Steketee, G. J., & McCarthy, P. R. (1992). Treatment of depressive and obsessive-compulsive symptoms in OCD by imipramine and behaviour therapy. *British Journal of Clinical Psychology, 31,* 279–292.

Fordyce, W. E. (1988). Pain and suffering: A reappraisal. *American Psychologist, 43,* 276–283.

Fordyce, W. E. (1993). Effects of marital interaction on chronic pain and disability: Examining the down side of social support [Comment] *Rehabilitation Psychology, 38,* 211–212.

Forgatch, M. S., & Patterson, G. R. (1998). Behavioral family therapy. In F. Dattilio (Ed.), *Case studies in couple and family therapy: Systemic and cognitive perspectives* (pp. 85–107). New York: Guilford Press.

Foundas, A. L., Eure, K. F., Luevano, L. F., & Weinberger, D. R. (1998). fMRI asymmetries of Broca's area: The pars triangularis and pars opercularis. *Brain & Language, 64,* 282–296.

Foxhall, K. (2000). Psychology as a leader in Internet culture. *Monitor on Psychology, 31,* 26–28.

Foxx, R. M. (1998). A comprehensive treatment program for inpatient adolescents. *Behavioral Interventions, 13,* 67–77.

Frank, E., Frank, N., Cornes, C., Imber, S. D., Miller, M. D., Morris, S. M., & Reynolds, C. F., III. (1993). Interpersonal psychotherapy in the treatment of late-life depression. In G. L. Klerman & M. M.Weissman (Eds.), *New applications of interpersonal psychotherapy* (pp. 167–198). Washington, DC: American Psychiatric Press.

Frank, E., Kupfer, D. J., Perel, J. M., Cornes, C., Jarrett, D. B., Mallinger, A. G., Thase, M. E., McEachran, A. B., & Grochocinski, V. J. (1990). Three-year outcomes for maintenance therapies in recurrent depression. *Archives of General Psychiatry, 47,* 1093–1099.

Frank, J. D. (1982). Therapeutic components shared by all psychotherapies. In J. H. J. Harvey, & M. M. Parks (Eds.), *Psychotherapy research and behavior change.* Washington, D.C.: American Psychological Association.

Frank, J. D., & Frank, J. B. (1991). *Persuasion and healing: A comparative study of psychotherapy* (3rd ed.). Baltimore: Johns Hopkins University Press.

Frank, L. K. (1948). *Projective methods.* Springfield, IL: Thomas.

Frankl, V. E. (1963). *Man's search for meaning* (rev. ed.). New York: Washington Square Press.

Frankl, V. E. (1965). The concept of man in logotherapy. *Journal of Existentialism, 6,* 53–58.

Frankl, V. E. (1967). *Psychotherapy and existentialism: Selected papers on logotherapy.* New York: Washington Square Press.

Frankl, V. E. (1969). *The will to meaning,: foundations and applications of logotherapy.* New York: World Pub. Co.

Frankl, V. E. (1992). The first published cases of paradoxical intention. *International Forum for Logotherapy, 15,* 2–6.

Franklin, M. E., Abramowitz, J. S., Kozak, M. J., Levitt, J. T., & Foa, E. B. (2000). Effectiveness of exposure and ritual prevention for obsessive-compulsive disorder: Randomized compared with nonrandomized samples. *Journal of Consulting and Clinical Psychology, 68,* 594–602.

Franz, D., & Gross, A. M. (1998). Assessment of child behavior problems: Externalizing disorders. In A. S. Bellack & M. Hersen (Eds.), *Behavioral assessment: A practical handbook* (pp. 361–377). Elmsford, NY: Pergamon Press.

Frasure-Smith, N., Lesperance, F., Juneau, M., Talajic, M., & Bourassa, M. G. (1999). Gender, depression, and one-year prognosis after myocardial infarction. *Psychosomatic Medicine, 61,* 26–37.

Frasure-Smith, N., Lesperance, F., & Talajic, M. (1995). The impact of negative emotions on prognosis following myocardial infarction: Is it more than depression? *Health Psychology, 14,* 388–398.

Fredrickson, B. L. (2000). Cultivating positive emotions to optimize health and well-being. *Prevention and Treatment, 3,* n.p.

Freud, A. (1928). *Introduction to the technique of child analysis.* New York: International Universities Press.

Freud, A. (1946). *The ego and the mechanisms of defense.* New York: International Universities Press.

Freud, S. (1893). *Some points for a comparative study of organic and hysterical motor paralyses.* Standard Edition (Vol. 1), 160–172.

Freud, S. (1896). *The etiology of hysteria.* Standard Edition (Vol. 3), 189–224.

Freud, S. (1900). *The interpretation of dreams.* Translated by J. Strachey (1998 edition). New York: Avon Books.

Freud, S. (1911). On the mechanism of paranoia. In S. Freud, *General psychological theory: Papers on metapsychology.* New York: Collier Books.

Freud, S. (1912). The dynamics of transference. In J. Strachey (Ed. And Trans.), *The standard edition of the complete psychological works of Sigmund Freud* (Vol. 12, pp. 99–108). London: Hogarth Press.

Freud, S. (1913). On beginning the treatment (Further recommendations on the technique of psychoanalysis). In J. Strachey (Ed. And Trans.), *The standard edition of the complete psychological works of Sigmund Freud* (Vol. 12, pp. 121–144). London: Hogarth Press.

Freud, S. (1917). *Introductory lectures on psychoanalysis.* In J. Strachey (Ed. and Trans.), *The standard edition of the complete psychological works of Sigmund Freud* (Vol. 15, pp. 1–239; Vol. 16, pp. 241–496). London: Hogarth Press.

Freud, S. (1923). *The ego and the id* (Vol. 19; J. Strachey, Ed.). London: Hogarth Press.

Freund, K., & Watson, R. J. (1991). Assessment of the sensitivity and specificity of a phallometric test: An update of phallometric diagnosis of pedophilia. *Psychological Assessment, 3,* 254–260.

Friedlander, M. L., & Phillips, S. D. (1984). Preventing anchoring errors in clinical judgment. *Journal of Consulting and Clinical Psychology, 52,* 366–371.

Friedman, M., Fleischmann, N., & Price, V. A. (1996). Diagnosis of Type A behavior pattern. In R. Allan, & S. S. Scheidt, (Eds.), *Heart and mind: The practice of cardiac psychology* (pp. 179–195). Washington, DC: American Psychological Association.

Friedman, S. L., & Wachs, T. D. (Eds.). (1999). *Measuring environment across the life span: Emerging methods and concepts.* Washington, DC: American Psychological Association.

Friman, P. C., & Vollmer, D. (1995). Successful use of the nocturnal urine alarm for diurnal enuresis. *Journal of Applied Behavior Analysis, 28,* 89–90.

Gabrieli, J. D. E., Brewer, J. B., Desmond, J. E., & Glover, G. H. (1997). Separate neural bases of two fundamental memory processes in the human medial temporal lobe. *Science, 276,* 264–266.

Garb, H. (1997). Race bias, social class bias, and gender bias in clinical judgment. *Clinical Psychology: Science and Practice, 4,* 99–120.

Garber, J. (2000). Development and depression. In A. J. Sameroff, M. Lewis, & S. M. Miller (Eds.), *Handbook of developmental psychopathology* (2nd ed., pp. 467–490). New York: Kluwer Academic/Plenum.

Garcia, J., & Koelling, R. A. (1966). Relation of cue to consequence in avoidance learning. *Psychonomic Science, 4,* 123–124.

Gardner, H. (1993). *Multiple intelligences: The theory and practice.* NY: Basic Books.

Gardner, H. (1999). Intelligence reframed: *Multiple intelligences for the 21st century.* NY: Basic Books.

Garfield, S. L. (1996). Some problems associated with "validated" forms of psychotherapy. *Clinical Psychology: Science and Practice, 3,* 218–229.

Garfield, S. L., & Kurtz, R. M. (1978). Illusory correlation: A further exploration of Chapman's paradigm. *Journal of Consulting and Clinical Psychology, 46,* 1009–1015.

Garner, D. M. (1991). *Eating Disorders Inventory-2.* Odessa, FL: Psychological Assessment Resources.

Gatchel, R. J., & Turk, D. C. (1996). *Psychological approaches to pain management: A practitioner's handbook.* New York: Guilford Press.

Gatchel, R., J., & Turk, D. C. (1999). *Psychosocial factors in pain: Critical perspectives.* New York: The Guilford Press.

Genero, N., & Cantor, N. (1987). Exemplar prototypes and clinical diagnosis: Toward a cognitive economy. *Journal of Social and Clinical Psychology, 5,* 59–78.

Gerhardt, C. A., Compas, B. E., Connor, J. K., & Achenbach, T. M. (1999). Association of a mixed anxiety-depression syndrome and symptoms of major depressive disorder during adolescence. *Journal of Youth & Adolescence, 28,* 305–323.

Ghaderi, A., & Andersson, G. (1999). Meta-analysis of CBT for bulimia nervosa: Investigating the effects using *DSM-III-R* and *DSM-IV* criteria. *Scandinavian Journal of Behaviour Therapy, 28,* 79–87.

Gil, K. M., Carson, J. W., Sedway, J. A., Porter, L. S., Schaeffer, J. J. W., & Orringer, E. (2000). Follow-up of coping skills training in adults with sickle cell disease: Analysis of daily pain and coping practice diaries. *Health Psychology, 19,* 85–90.

Gillham, J. E., & Reivich, K. J. (1999). Prevention of depressive symptoms in school children: A research update. *Psychological Science, 10,* 461–462.

Gillham, J. E., Reivich, K. J., Jaycox, L. H., & Seligman, M. E. P. (1995). Prevention of depressive symptoms in school children: Two-year follow-up. *Psychological Science, 6,* 343–351.

Gillham, J. E., Shatte, A. J., & Freres, D. R. (2000). Preventing depression: A review of cognitive-behavioral and family interventions. *Applied and Preventive Psychology, 9,* 63–88.

Glinder, J. G., & Compas, B. E. (1999). Self-blame attributions in women with newly diagnosed breast cancer: A prospective analysis. *Health Psychology, 18,* 475–481.

Glinder, J. G., Compas, B. E., & Kaiser, C. (2001). *Cognitive bias in women with newly diagnosed breast cancer.* Unpublished raw data. University of Vermont.

Gloaguen, V., Cottraux, J., Cucherat, M., & Blackburn, I. (1998). A meta-analysis of the effects of cognitive therapy in depressed patients. *Journal of Affective Disorders, 49,* 59–72.

Gnys, J. A., Willis, W. G., Faust, D. (1995). School psychologists' diagnoses of learning disabilities: A study of illusory correlation. *Journal of School Psychology, 33,* 59–73.

Goetze, H. (1994). Processes in person-centered play therapy. In J. Hellendoorn & R. van der Kooij (Eds.), *Play and intervention.* (pp. 63–76). Albany: State University of New York Press.

Golden, C. J., Moses, J. A., Graber, B., & Berg, R. A. (1981). Objective clinical rules for interpreting the Luria-Nebraska Neuropsychological Battery: Derivation, effectiveness, and validation. *Journal of Consulting and Clinical Psychology, 49,* 616–618.

Goldenberg, I., & Goldenberg, H. (2000). *Family therapy: An overview* (5th ed.). Pacific Grove, CA: Brooks/Cole.

Goldman, H., Pincus, H., Taube, C., & Regier, D. (1984). Prospective payment for psychiatric hospitalization: Questions and issues. *Hospital and Community Psychiatry, 35,* 460–464.

Goldstein, R. B., Weissman, M. M., Adams, P. B., Horwath, E., Lish, J. D., Chamey, D., Woods, S. W., Sobin, C., & Wickramaratne, P. J. (1994). Psychiatric disorders in relatives of probands with panic disorder and/or major depression. *Archives of General Psychiatry, 51,* 383–394.

Goldstein, R. B., Wickramaratne, P. J., Horwath, E., & Weissman, M. M. (1997). Familial aggregation and phenomenology of "early"-onset (at or before age 20 years) panic disorder. *Archives of General Psychiatry, 54,* 271–278.

Goleman, D. (1994, April 19). Revamping psychiatrists' bible. *The New York Times,* pp. C1, C11.

Goleman, D. (1995). *Emotional intelligence.* New York: Bantam Books.

Goodenough, F. (1926). *Measurement of intelligence by drawings.* New York: World Book.

Goodglass, H., Kaplan, E., Weintraub, S., & Ackermann, N. (1976). The "tip of the tongue" phenomenon in aphasia. *Cortex, 12,* 145–153.

Goodman, G. & Dooley, D. (1976). A framework for help-intended communication. *Psychotherapy: Theory, Research & Practice, 13,* 106–117.

Goodman, L. A., Koss, M. P., Fitzgerald, L. F., & Russo, N. F., (1993). Male violence against women: Current research and future directions. *American Psychologist, 48,* 1054–1058.

Goodman, S. H., & Gotlib, I. H. (1999). Risk for psychopathology in the children of depressed mothers: A developmental model for understanding mechanisms of transmission. *Psychological Review, 106,* 458–490.

Goodman, W. K., Price, L. H., Rasmussen, S. A., Mazure, C., Fleischmann, R. L., Hill, C.L., Heninger, G. R., & Charney, D. S. (1989). The

Yale-Brown Obsessive Compulsive Scale: I. Development, use, and reliability. *Archives of General Psychiatry, 46,* 1006–1011.

Gormally, J., Black, S., Daston, S., & Rardin, D. (1982). The assessment of binge eating severity among obese persons. *Addictive Behaviors, 7,* 47–55.

Gortner, E. T., Gollan, J. K., Dobson, K. S., & Jacobson, N. S. (1998). Cognitive-behavioral treatment for depression: Relapse prevention. *Journal of Consulting and Clinical Psychology, 66,* 377–384.

Gotlib, I. H., & Abramson, L. Y. (1999). Attributional theories of emotion. In T. Dalgleish & M. Power (Eds.), *The handbook of cognition and emotion* (pp. 613–636). Chichester, England: John Wiley.

Gotlib, I. H., & Beach, S. (1995). A marital/family discord model of depression: Implications for therapeutic intervention. In N. S. Jacobson & A. S. Gurman (Eds.), *Clinical handbook of couple therapy* (pp. 411–436). New York: Guilford Press.

Gotlib, I. H., & Cane, D. B. (1987). Construct accessibility and clinical depression: A longitudinal approach. *Journal of Abnormal Psychology, 96,* 199–204.

Gotlib, I. H., & Goodman, S. H. (1999). Children of parents with depression. In W. K. Silverman & T. H. Ollendick (Eds.), *Developmental issues in the clinical treatment of children* (pp. 415–432). Boston: Allyn & Bacon.

Gotlib, I. H., & Hammen, C. L. (1992). *Psychosocial aspects of depression: Toward a cognitive-interpersonal integration.* Chichester, England: Wiley.

Gotlib, I. H., & Hammen, C. L. (Eds.). (in press). *Handbook of depression and its treatment.* New York: Guilford Press.

Gotlib, I. H., Kurtzman, H. S., & Blehar, M. C. (1997). The cognitive psychology of depression: Introduction to the special issue. *Cognition and Emotion, 11,* 497–500.

Gotlib, I. H., Lewinsohn, P. M., & Seeley, J. R. (1995). Symptoms versus a diagnosis of depression: Differences in psychosocial functioning. *Journal of Abnormal Psychology, 63,* 90–100.

Gotlib, I. H., Lewinsohn, P. M., & Seeley, J. R. (1998). Consequences of depression during adolescence: Marital status and marital functioning in early adulthood. *Journal of Abnormal Psychology, 107,* 686–690.

Gotlib, I. H., & MacLeod, C. (1997). Information processing in anxiety and depression: A cognitive-developmental perspective. In J. A. Burack, & J. T. Enns (Eds.). *Attention, development, and psychopathology* (pp. 350–378). New York, NY: The Guilford Press.

Gotlib, I. H., & Neubauer, D. L. (2000). Information-processing approaches to the study of cognitive biases in depression. In S. L. Johnson, A. M. Hayes, T. M. Field, N. Schneiderman, & P. M. McCabe (Eds.), *Stress, coping, and depression* (pp. 117–143). Mahwah, NJ: Lawrence Erlbaum.

Gotlib, I. H., Whiffen, V. E., Wallace, P. M., & Mount, J. H. (1991). A prospective investigation of postpartum depression: Factors involved in onset and recovery. *Journal of Abnormal Psychology, 100,* 122–132.

Gottman, J. M, & Levenson, R. W. (1992). Marital processes predictive of later dissolution: Behavior, physiology, and health. *Journal of Personality and Social Psychology, 63,* 221–233.

Gough, H. G. (1990). The California Psychological Inventory. In C. E. Watkins & V. L. Campbell (Eds.), *Testing in counseling practice* (pp. 37–62). Hillsdale, NJ: Lawrence Erlbaum.

Gould, R. A., Buckminster, S., Pollack, M. H., Otto, M. W., & Yap, L. (1997). Cognitive-behavioral and pharmacological treatment for social phobia: A meta-analysis. *Clinical Psychology: Science and Practice, 4,* 291–306.

Gould, R. A., Otto, M. W., & Pollack, M. H. (1995). A meta-analysis of treatment outcome for panic disorder. *Clinical Psychology Review, 15,* 819–844.

Gould, R. A., Otto, M. W., Pollack, M. H., & Yap, L. (1997). Cognitive behavioral and pharmacological treatment of generalized anxiety disorder: A preliminary meta-analyis. *Behavior Therapy, 28,* 285–305.

Gould, R. A., Otto, M. W., Pollack, M. H., & Yap, L. (1997). Cognitive-behavioral and pharmacological treatment for social phobia: A meta-analysis.

Clinical Psychology: Science and Practice, 4, 291–306.

Graham, J. R. (2000). *MMPI-2: Assessing personality and psychopathology* (3rd ed.). New York: Oxford University Press.

Graham, P., & Rutter, M. (1968). The reliability and validity of psychiatric assessment of the child: II. Interviews with the parent. *British Journal of Psychiatry, 114,* 563–579.

Grant, B. (1994). Epidemiologic Bulletin: Prevalence of *DSM-IV* alcohol abuse and dependence, United States 1992. *Alcohol Health and Research World, 18,* 243–248.

Greenberg, L. S. (1996). The power of empathic exploration: A process-experiential/Gestalt perspective on the case of Jim Brown. In B. A. Farber & D. C. Brink (Eds.), *The psychotherapy of Carl Rogers: Cases and commentary* (pp. 251–260). New York: Guilford Press.

Greenberg, L. S., & Elliott, R. (1997). Varieties of empathic responding. In A. C. Bohart & L. S. Greenberg (Eds.), *Empathy reconsidered: New directions in psychotherapy* (pp. 167–186). Washington, DC: American Psychological Association.

Greenberg, L. S., Elliott, R., & Lietaer, G. (1994). Research on humanistic and experiential psychotherapies. In A. E. Bergin & S. L. Garfield (Eds.), *Handbook of psychotherapy and behavior change* (4th ed.; pp. 509–539). New York: John Wiley.

Greenberg, L. S., & Goldman, R. L. (1988). Training in experiential therapy. *Journal of Consulting and Clinical Psychology, 56,* 696–702.

Greenberg, L. S., & Paivio, S. C. (1997). *Working with emotions in psychotherapy.* New York: Guilford.

Greenberg, L. S., & Van Balen, R. (1998). The theory of experience-centered therapies. In L. S. Greenberg & J. C. Watson (Eds.), *Handbook of experiential psychotherapy* (pp. 28–57). New York: Guilford Press.

Greenberg, L. S., Rice, L. N., & Elliott, R. (1993). *Facilitating emotional change: The moment-by-moment process.* New York: Guilford Press.

Greenberg, L. S., & Watson, J. (1998). Experiential therapy of depression: Differential effects of client-centered relationship conditions and process experiential interventions. *Psychotherapy Research, 8,* 210–224.

Greenberg, L. S., Watson, J. C., & Goldman, R. (1998). Process-experiential therapy of depression. In L. S. Greenberg & J. C. Watson (Eds.), *Handbook of experiential psychotherapy* (pp. 227–248). New York: Guilford.

Greenberg, M. T., Lengua, L. J., Coie, J. D., Pinderhughes, E. E., Bierman, K. D., Lochman, K. A., McMahon, J. E., & Robert, J. (1999). Predicting developmental outcomes at school entry using a multiple-risk model: Four American communities. *Developmental Psychology, 35,* 403–417.

Greenberger, D., & Padesky, C. A. (1995). *Mind over mood: A cognitive therapy treatment manual for clients.* New York: Guilford Press.

Greenfield, S. F., Reizes, J. M., Magruder, K. M., Muenz, L. R., Kopans, B., & Jacobs, D. G. (1997). Effectiveness of community-based screening for depression. *American Journal of Psychiatry, 154,* 1391–1397.

Greenfield, S. F., Reizes, J. M., Muenz, L., Kopans, B., Kozloff, R. C., & Jacobs, D. G. (2000). Treatment for depression following the 1996 National Depression Screening Day. *American Journal of Psychiatry, 157,* 1867–1869.

Greenson, R. (1967). *The technique and practice of psycho-analysis.* New York: International Universities Press.

Greenwald, M. K., Cook, E. W., & Lang, P. J. (1989). Affective judgment and psychophysiological response: Dimensional covariation in the evaluation of pictorial stimuli. *Journal of Psychophysiology, 3,* 51–64.

Gresham, F. M. (1993). "What's wrong with this picture?": Response to Motta et al.'s review of human figure drawings. *School Psychology Quarterly, 8,* 182–186.

Groth-Marnat, G. (1997). *Handbook of psychological assessment* (3rd ed.). New York: John Wiley.

Grove, W. M., Zald, D. H., Lebow, B. S., Snitz, B. E., & Nelson, C. (2000). Clinical versus mechanical prediction: A meta-analysis. *Psychological Assessment, 12,* 19–30.

Grundy, C. T., Lunnen, K. M., Lambert, M. J., & Ashton, J. E. (1994). The Hamilton Rating Scale for Depression: One scale or many? *Clinical Psychology: Science & Practice, 1,* 197–205.

Guntrip, H. (1973). Science, psychodynamic reality and autistic thinking. *Journal of the American Academy of Psychoanalysis, 1,* 3–23.

Guthrie, R. (1998). *Even the rat was white: A historical view of psychology* (2nd ed.). Needham Heights, MA: Allyn & Bacon.

Haaga, D. A., DeRubeis, R. J., Stewart, B. L., & Beck, A. T. (1991). Relationship of intelligence with cognitive therapy outcome. *Behaviour Research and Therapy, 29,* 277–281.

Haaga, D. A., Dyck, M. J., & Ernst, D. (1991). Empirical status of cognitive theory of depression. *Psychological Bulletin, 110,* 215–236.

Haaga, D. A. F., & Stiles, W. B. (2000). Randomized clinical trials in psychotherapy research: Methodology, design, and evaluation. In C. R. Snyder & R. E. Ingram (Eds.), *Handbook of psychological change* (pp. 14–39). New York: John Wiley.

Hall, C. C. I. (1997). Cultural malpractice: The growing obsolescence of psychology with the changing U.S. population. *American Psychologist, 52,* 642–651.

Hall, J. A., Carter, J. D., & Horgan, T. G. (2000). Gender differences in nonverbal communication of emotion. In A. H. Fischer (Ed.), *Gender and emotion: Social psychological perspectives. Studies in emotion and social interaction. Second series* (pp. 97–117). New York: Cambridge University Press.

Halmi, K. A., Sunday, S. R., Strober, M., Kaplan, A., Woodside, D. B., Fichter, M., Treasure, J., Berrettini, W. H., & Kaye, W. H. (2000). Perfectionism in anorexia nervosa: Variation by clinical subtype, obsessionality, and pathological eating behavior. *American Journal of Psychiatry, 157,* 1799–1805.

Hamilton, M. (1960). A rating scale for depression. *Journal of Neurology, Neurosurgery & Psychiatry, 23,* 56–61.

Hamilton, M. (1967). Development of a rating scale for primary depressive illness. *British Journal of Social and Clinical Psychology, 6,* 278–296.

Hamm, A. O., Greenwald, M. K., Bradley, M. M., & Lang, P. J. (1993). Emotional learning, hedonic change, and the startle probe. *Journal of Abnormal Psychology, 102,* 453–465.

Hammen, C. L., & Glass, D. R. (1975). Expression, activity, and evaluation of reinforcement. *Journal of Abnormal Psychology, 84,* 718–721.

Hankin, B. L., Abramson, L. Y., Moffitt, T. E., Silva, P. A., McGee, R., & Angell, K. E. (1998). Development of depression from preadolescence to young adulthood: Emerging gender differences in a 10-year longitudinal study. *Journal of Abnormal Psychology, 107,* 128–140.

Hankin, B. L., Roberts, J., & Gotlib, I. H. (1997). Elevated self-standards and emotional distress during adolescence: Emotional specificity and gender differences. *Cognitive Therapy and Research, 21,* 663–679.

Hankin, J. R., & Locke, B. Z. (1983). Extent of depressive symptomatology among patients seeking care in a prepaid group practice. *Psychological Medicine, 13,* 121–129.

Hardy, G. E., Shapiro, D. A., Stiles, W. B., & Barkham, M. (1998). When and why does cognitive-behavioural treatment appear more effective than psychodynamic-interpersonal treatment? Discussion of the findings from the Second Sheffield Psychotherapy Project. *Journal of Mental Health, 7,* 179–190.

Harris, D. B. (1963). *Children's drawings as measures of intellectual maturity.* New York: Harcourt, Brace, & World.

Hartlage, S., Alloy, L. B., Vasquez, C., & Dykman, B. (1993). Automatic and effortful processing in depression. *Psychology Bulletin, 113,* 247–278.

Hartman, H. (1939). *Ego psychology and the problem of adaptation.* New York: International Universities Press.

Hartmann, D. P. (1984). Assessment strategies. In D. H. Barlow & M. Hersen (Eds.), *Single case experimental designs: Strategies for studying behavior change* (pp. 107–139). New York: Pergamon Press.

Hathaway, S. R. (1943). *The Minnesota Multiphasic Personality Inventory.* Minneapolis: University of Minnesota Press.

Hathaway, S. R., & McKinley, J. C. (1942). *The Minnesota Multiphasic Personality Schedule.* Minneapolis: University of Minnesota Press.

Havens, L. (1994). Some suggestions for making research more applicable to clinical practice. In P. F. Talley, H. H. Strupp, & S. F. Butler (Eds.), *Psychotherapy research and practice: Bridging the gap* (pp. 88–98). New York: Basic Books.

Hayes, S. C., Barlow, D. H., & Nelson-Gray, R. O. (1999). *The scientist practitioner: Research and accountability in the age of managed care* (2nd ed.). Boston, MA: Allyn & Bacon.

Hayes, S. C., & Heiby, E. (1996). Psychology's drug problem: Do we need a fix or should we just say no? *American Psychologist, 51*, 198–206.

Haynes, S. N. (1991). Clinical applications of psychophysiological assessment: An introduction and overview. *Psychological Assessment, 3*, 356–365.

Haynes, S. N., & O'Brien, W. H. (2000). *Principles and practice of behavioral assessment*. New York: Kluwer Academic/Plenum Press.

Hayward, C., Gotlib, I. H., Schraedley, P. K., & Litt, I. F. (1999). Ethnic differences in the association between pubertal status and symptoms of depression in adolescent girls. *Journal of Adolescent Health, 25*, 143–149.

Hayward, C., Killen, J. D., Kraemer, H. C., & Taylor, C. B. (2000). Predictors of panic attacks in adolescents. *Journal of the American Academy of Child and Adolescent Psychiatry, 39*, 207–214.

Hedlund, J. (1977). Automated psychiatric information systems: A critical review of Missouri's Standard System of Psychiatry (SSOP). *Journal of Operational Psychiatry, 8*, 5–26.

Heine, R. W. (1953). A comparison of patients' reports on psychotherapeutic experience with psychoapsychoanalytic, nondirective, and Adlerian therapists. *American Journal of Psychotherapy, 7*, 16–23.

Helmes, E., & Reddon, J. R. (1993). A perspective on developments in assessing psychopathology: A critical review of the MMPI and MMPI-2. *Psychological Bulletin, 113*, 453–471.

Helzer, J. E. (1983). Standardized interviews in psychiatry. *Psychiatric Developments, 1*, 161–178.

Helzer, J. E. (1984). "Inferring causes—some constraints in the social psychiatry of depressive disorders": Commentary. *Integrative Psychiatry, 2*, 79–80.

Helzer, J. E., Brockington, I. F., & Kendell, R. E. (1981). Predictive validity of DSM-III and Feighner definitions of schizophrenia: A comparison with research diagnostic criteria and CATEGO. *Archives of General Psychiatry, 38*, 791–797.

Helzer, J. E., Robins, L. N., Croughan, J. L., & Welner, A. (1981). Renard Diagnostic Interview: Its reliability and procedural validity with physicians and lay interviewers. *Archives of General Psychiatry, 38*, 393–398.

Helzer, J. E., Spitznagel, E. L., & McEvoy, L. (1987). The predictive validity of lay Diagnostic Interview Schedule diagnoses in the general population: A comparison with physician examiners. *Archives of General Psychiatry, 44*, 1069–1077.

Henrich, C. C., Blatt, S. J., Kuperminc, G. P., Zohar, A., & Leadbeater, B. J. (2001). Levels of interpersonal concerns and social functioning in early adolescent boys and girls. *Journal of Personality Assessment, 76*, 48–67.

Henriques, J., & Davidson, R. (1991). Left frontal hypoactivation in depression. *Journal of Abnormal Psychology, 100*, 535–545.

Herjanic, B., & Campbell, W. (1977). Differentiating psychiatrically disturbed children on the basis of a structured interview. *Journal of Abnormal Child Psychology, 5*, 127–134.

Herjanic, B., Herjanic, M., Brown, F., & Wheatt, T. (1975). Are children reliable reporters? *Journal of Abnormal Child Psychology, 3*, 41–48.

Herrnstein, R. J., & Murray, C. (1994). *The bell curve: Intelligence and class structure in American life*. New York: Simon and Schuster.

Hibbard, S., Tang, P., Latko, R., Park., J. H., Munn, S., Bolz, S., & Somerville, A. (2000). Differential validity of the defense mechanism manual for the TAT between Asian Americans and whites. *Journal of Personality Assessment, 75*, 351–372.

Higgins, E. T. (1987). Self-discrepancy: A theory relating self and affect. *Psychological Review, 94*, 319–340.

Higgins, E. T., Bond, R. N., Klein, R., & Strauman, T. (1986). Self-discrepancies and emotional vulnerability: How magnitude, accessibility, and type of discrepancy influence affect. *Journal of Personality and Social Psychology, 51*, 5–15.

Higgins, E. T., Klein, R., & Strauman, T. (1985). Self-concept discrepancy theory: A psychological model for distinguishing among different aspects of depression and anxiety. *Social Cognition, 3*, 51–76.

Higgins, E. T., Roney, C. J. R., Crowe, E., & Hymes, C. (1994). Ideal versus ought predilections for approach and avoidance distinct self-regulatory systems. *Journal of Personality and Social Psychology, 66*, 276–286.

Hiller, J. B., Rosenthal, R., Bornstein, R. F., Berry, D. T. R., & Brunell-Neuleib, S. (1999).

A comparative meta-analysis of Rorschach and MMPI validity. *Psychological Assessment, 11,* 278–296.

Hinshaw, S. P. (1992). Academic underachievement, attention deficits, and aggression: Comorbidity and implications for intervention. *Journal of Consulting and Clinical Psychology, 60,* 893–903.

Hinshaw, S. P., & Nigg, J. T. (1999). Behavior rating scales in the assessment of disruptive behavior problems in childhood. In D. Shaffer & C. P. Lucas (Eds.), *Diagnostic assessment in child and adolescent psychopathology* (pp. 91–126). New York: Guilford Press.

Hinshaw, S. P., Owens, E. B., Wells, K. C., Kraemer, H. C., Abikoff, H. B., Arnold, L. E., Conners, C. K., Elliott, G., Greenhill, L. L., Hechtman, L., Hoza, B., Jensen, P. S., March, J. S., Newcorn, J. H., Pelham, W. E., Swanson, J. M., Vitiello, B., & Wigal, T. (2000). Family processes and treatment outcome in the MTA: Negative/ineffective parenting practices in relation to multimodal treatment. *Journal of Abnormal Child Psychology, 28,* 555–568.

Hobson, R. P. (1985). Self-representing dreams. *Psychoanalytic Psychotherapy, 1,* 43–53.

Hoch, E. L., Ross, A. E., & Winder, C. L. (Eds.). (1966). *Professional education of clinical psychologists.* Washington, DC: American Psychological Association.

Holaday, M., Smith, D. A., & Sherry, A. (2000). Sentence completion tests: A review of the literature and results of a survey of members of the Society for Personality Assessment. *Journal of Personality Assessment, 74,* 371–383.

Hollon, S. D. (1996). The efficacy and effectiveness of psychotherapy relative to medications. *American Psychologist, 51,* 1025–1030.

Hollon, S. D., & Beck, A. T. (1994). Cognitive and cognitive-behavioral therapies. In A. E. Bergin & S. L. Garfield (Eds.), *Handbook of psychotherapy and behavior change* (4th ed.; pp. 428–466). New York: John Wiley.

Hollon, S. D., DeRubeis, R. J., & Evans, M. D. (1996). Cognitive therapy in the treatment and prevention of depression. In P. M. Salkovskis (Ed.), *Frontiers of cognitive therapy* (pp. 293–317). New York: Guilford Press.

Hollon, S. D., Haman, K. L., & Brown, L. L. (in press). Cognitive behavioral treatment of depression. In I. H. Gotlib and C. L. Hammen (Eds.), *Handbook of depression: Research and treatment.* New York: Guilford Press.

Hollon, S. D., & Kendall, P. C. (1980). Cognitive self-statements in depression: Development of an automatic thoughts questionnaire. *Cognitive Therapy and Research, 4,* 383–395.

Hollon, S. D., Shelton, R. C., & Davis, D. D. (1993). Cognitive therapy for depression: Conceptual issues and clinical efficacy. *Journal of Consulting and Clinical Psychology, 61,* 270–275.

Holmbeck, G. N., Kendall, P. C., & Butcher, J. N. (Eds.). (1999). *Handbook of research methods in clinical psychology* (2nd ed.). New York: John Wiley.

Holtgrave, D. R., & Kelly, J. A. (1996). Preventing HIV/AIDS among high-risk urban women: The cost-effectiveness of a behavioral group intervention. *American Journal of Public Health, 86,* 1442–1445.

Hooley, J. M., & Gotlib, I. H. (2000). A diathesis-stress conceptualization of expressed emotion and clinical outcome. *Applied and Preventive Psychology, 9,* 135–151.

Horn, J. (1985). Bias? Indeed. *Child Development, 56,* 779–780.

Horn, J., & Cattell, R. (1967). Age differences in fluid and crystallized intelligence. *Acta Psychologica, 26,* 107–129.

Horton, A. M. (1997). The Halstead-Reitan Neuropsychological Test Battery: Problems and prospects. In A. M. Horton & D. Wedding (Eds.), *The neuropsychology handbook, Vol. 1: Foundations and assessment* (2nd ed., pp. 221–254). New York, NY, USA: Springer.

Horvath, A. O., & Luborsky, L. (1993). The role of the therapeutic alliance in psychotherapy. *Journal of Consulting and Clinical Psychology, 61,* 561–573.

Horvath, A. O., & Symonds, B. D. (1991). Relation between working alliance and outcome in psychotherapy: A meta-analysis. *Journal of Counseling Psychology, 38,* 139–149.

Howard, K. I., Kopta, M. S., Krause, S. M., & Orlinsky, D. E. (1986). The dose effect relationship in psychotherapy. *American Psychologist, 41,* 159–164.

Howard, K. I., Lueger, R. J., Maling, M. S., & Martinovich, Z. (1993). A phase model of psychotherapy outcome: Causal mediation of change. *Journal of Consulting and Clinical Psychology, 61,* 678–685.

Howard, K. I., Moras, K., Brill, P. L., & Martinovich, Z. (1996). Evaluation of psychotherapy: Efficacy, effectiveness, and patient progress. *American Psychologist, 51,* 1059–1064.

Howland, R. H., & Thase, M. E. (1999). Affective disorders: Biological aspects. In T. Millon, P. H. Blaney, & R. D. Davis (Eds.), *Oxford textbook of psychopathology* (pp. 166–202). New York: Oxford University Press.

Hudziak, J. J., Wadsworth, M. E., Heath, A. C., & Achenbach, T. M. (1999). Latent class analysis of Child Behavior Checklist attention problems. *Journal of the American Academy of Child and Adolescent Psychiatry, 38,* 985–991.

Hulse, W. C. (1951). The emotionally disturbed child draws his family. *Quarterly Journal of Child Behavior, 3,* 152–174.

Hunsley, J., & Bailey, M. J. (1999). The clinical utility of the Rorschach: Unfulfilled promises and an uncertain future. *Psychological Assessment, 11,* 266–277.

Institute of Medicine. (1991). *Mapping the brain and its functions: Integrating enabling technologies into neuroscience research.* National Academy Press: Washington D.C.

Iribarren, C., Sidney, S., Bild, D. E., Liu, K., Markovitz, J. H., Roseman, J. M., & Matthews, K. (2000). Association of hostility with coronary artery calcification in young adults: The CARDIA study. *Journal of the American Medical Association, 283,* 2810–2815.

Ito, T. A., & Cacioppo, J. T. (2001). Affect and attitudes: A social neuroscience approach. In J. P. Forgas (Ed.), *Handbook of affect and social cognition* (pp. 50–74). Mahwah, NJ: Lawrence Erlbaum.

Ivey, A. E. (1994). *Intentional interviewing and counseling: Facilitating client development in a multicultural society* (3rd ed.). Pacific Grove, CA: Brooks/Cole.

Ivey, A. E. (1995). Psychotherapy as liberation: Toward specific skills and strategies in multicultural counseling and therapy. In J. G. Ponterotto & J. M. Casas (Eds.), *Handbook of multicultural counseling* (pp. 53–72). Thousand Oaks, CA: Sage.

Ivey, A. E., Ivey, M. B., & Simek-Downing, L. (1987). *Counseling and psychotherapy: Integrating skills. theory. and practice.* Englewood Cliffs, NJ: Prentice-Hall.

Jackson, D. (1989). *Basic personality inventory manual.* Port Huron, MI: Sigma Assessment Systems.

Jacobson, E. (1938). *Progressive relaxation* (2nd ed.). Chicago: Chicago Press.

Jacobson, N. S., Dobson, K. S., Truax, P. A., Addis, M. E., Koerner, K., Gollan, J. K., Gortner, E., & Prince, S. E. (1996). A component analysis of cognitive-behavior therapy for depression. *Journal of Consulting and Clinical Psychology, 64,* 295–304.

Jacobson, N. S., Gottman, J. M., Gortner, E., Berns, S., & Shortt, J. W. (1996). Psychological factors in the longitudinal course of battering: When do the couples split up? When does the abuse decrease? *Violence and Victims, 11,* 371–392.

Jacobson, N. S., & Truax, P. (1991). Clinical significance: A statistical approach to defining meaningful change in psychotherapy research. *Journal of Consulting and Clinical Psychology, 59,* 12–19.

Jarrett, R. B., Eavers, G. G., Grannemann, B. D., & Rush, A. J. (1991). Clinical, cognitive, and demographic predictors of response to cognitive therapy for depression: A preliminary report. *Psychiatry Research, 37,* 245–260.

Jaycox, L. H., Reivich, K. J., Gillham, J. E., & Seligman, M. E. P. (1994). Prevention of depressive symptoms in school children. *Behaviour Research and Therapy, 32,* 801–816.

Jemmott, J. B., Hellman, C., McClelland, D. C., Locke, S. E., Kraus, L., & Williams, R. M. (1990). Motivational syndromes associated with natural killer cell activity. *Journal of Behavioral Medicine, 13,* 53–73.

Jemmott, J. B., Jemmott, L. S., Fong, G. T., & McCaffree, K. (1999) Reducing HIV risk-associated sexual behavior among African American adolescents: Testing the generality of intervention effects. *American Journal of Community Psychology, 27,* 161–187.

Jensen, A. R. (1969). How much can we boost IQ and scholastic achievement? *Harvard Educational Review, 39,* 1–123.

Jensen, A. R. (1998). *The g factor: The science of mental ability.* Westport, CT: Praeger.

Jensen, J. A., McNamara, J. R., & Gustafson, K. E. (1999). Parents' and clinicians' attitudes toward the risks and benefits of child psychotherapy: A study of informed-consent content. *Professional Psychology: Research & Practice, 22,* 161–170.

Jerome, L. W., & Zaylor, C. (2000). Cyberspace: Creating a therapeutic environment for telehealth applications. *Professional Psychology: Research and Practice, 31,* 478–483.

Jessor, R. (Ed). *New perspectives on adolescent risk behavior.* New York: Cambridge University Press.

John, O., & Srivastava, S. (1999). The Big Five Trait taxonomy: History, measurement, and theoretical perspectives. In L. A. Pervin & O. John (Eds.), *Handbook of personality: Theory and research* (2nd ed.; pp. 102–138). New York: Guilford Press.

Johnson, D. L. (1997). Weight loss for women: Studies of smokers and nonsmokers using hypnosis and multicomponent treatments with and without overt aversion. *Psychological Reports, 80,* 931–933.

Johnson, S. M., & Greenberg, L. S. (1985). Differential effects of experiential and problem-solving interventions in resolving marital conflict. *Journal of Consulting and Clinical Psychology, 53,* 175–184.

Johnson, S. M., Hunsley, J., Greenberg, L., & Schindler, D. (1999). Emotionally focused couples therapy: Status and challenges. *Clinical Psychology: Science and Practice, 6,* 67–79.

Johnson, S. M., & Talitman, E. (1997). Predictors of success in emotionally focused marital therapy. *Journal of Marital and Family Therapy, 23,* 135–152.

Jonas, B. S., & Mussolino, M. E. (2000). Symptoms of depression as a prospective risk factor for stroke. *Psychosomatic Medicine, 62,* 463–471.

Jones, E. E., Ghannam, J., Nigg, J. T., & Dyer, J. F. (1993). A paradigm for single-case research: The time series study of a long-term psychotherapy for depression. *Journal of Consulting and Clinical Psychology, 61,* 381–394.

Jones, E. E., & Windholz, M. (1990). The psychoanalytic case study: Toward a method for systematic inquiry. *Journal of the American Psychoanalytic Association, 38,* 985–1015.

Jones, M. C. (1924a). The elimination of children's fears. *Journal of Experimental Psychology, 7,* 383–390.

Jones, M. C. (1924b). A laboratory study of fear: The case of Peter. *Journal of Genetic Psychology, 31,* 308–315.

Jones, M. C. (1974). Albert, Peter, and John B. Watson. *American Psychologist, 29,* 581–583.

Judd, L., Paulus, M. P., Wells, K. B., & Rapaport, M. H. (1996). Socioeconomic burden of subsyndromal depressive symptoms and major depression in a sample of the general population. *American Journal of Psychiatry, 153,* 1411–1417.

Judson, H. F. (1980). *The search for solutions.* New York: Holt, Rinehart, & Winston.

Jung, C. G. (1933). *Modern man in search of a soul.* New York: Harcourt, Brace.

Jung, C. G. (1935/1956). *Collected works: Two essays on analytical psychology.* (Vol. 17). Princeton, NJ: Princeton University Press.

Jung, C. G. (1956). Psychotherapists or the clergy. *Pastoral Psychology, 7,* 27–44.

Kabat-Zinn, J., Lipworth, L., & Burney, R. (1985). The clinical use of mindfulness meditation for the self-regulation of chronic pain. *Journal of Behavioral Medicine, 8,* 163–190.

Kabat-Zinn, J., Massion, A. O., Kristeller, J., Petersen, L. G., Fletcher, K. E., Pbert, L., Lenderking, W. R., & Santorelli, S. F. (1992). Effectiveness of a meditation-based stress reduction program in the treatment of anxiety disorders. *American Journal of Psychiatry, 149,* 936–943.

Kabat-Zinn, J., Wheeler, E., Light, T., Skillings, A., Scharf, M. J., Cropley, T. G., Hosmer, D., & Bernhard, J. D. (1998). Influence of a mindfulness meditation-based stress reduction intervention on rates of skin clearing in patients with moderate to severe psoriasis undergoing phototherapy (UVB) and photochemotherapy (PUVA). *Psychosomatic Medicine, 60,* 625–632.

Kalish, H. (1981). *From behavioral science to behavior modification.* New York: McGraw-Hill.

Kamin, L. J. (1978). A positive interpretation of apparent "cumulative deficit." *Developmental Psychology, 14,* 195–196.

Kanfer, F. H. (1989). The scientist-practitioner connection: Myth or reality? A response to Perrez. *New Ideas in Psychology, 7,* 147–154.

Kanfer, F. H., & Goldstein, A. P. (Eds.). (1991). *Helping people change: A textbook of methods* (4th ed.). New York: Pergamon Press.

Kaplan, R. M. (2000). Two pathways to prevention. *American Psychologist, 55,* 382–396.

Karon, B. P., & Widener, A. J. (1995). Psychodynamic therapies in historical perspective: "Nothing human do I consider alien to me." In B. M. Bongar & L. E. Beutler, (Eds.), *Comprehensive textbook of psychotherapy: Theory and practice* (pp. 24–47). New York: Oxford University Press.

Kaufman, A. (1983). Some questions and answers about the Kaufman Assessment Battery for Children (K-ABC). *Journal of Psychoeducational Assessment , 1,* 205–218.

Kaufman, A. S., & Kamphaus, R. W. (1984). Factor analysis of the Kaufman Assessment Battery for Children (K-ABC) for ages 2 through 12 years. *Journal of Educational Psychology, 76,* 623–637.

Kaufman, A. S., & Kaufman, N. D. (1983). *Kaufman Assessment Battery for Children (K-ABC).* Circle Pines, MN: American Guidance Service.

Kaufman, A., & Kaufman, N. (2000). Nature, applications, and limitations of neuropsychological assessment following traumatic brain injury. In A. Christensen, & B. Uzzel (Eds.), *International handbook of neuropsychological rehabilitation* (pp. 67–79). New York: Kluwer Academic/Plenum Publishers.

Kaufman, A. S., Kaufman, J. C., Lincoln, A. J., & Kaufman, J. L. (2000). Intellectual and cognitive assessment. In M. Hersen & R. T. Ammerman, (Eds.), *Advanced abnormal child psychology* (2nd ed., pp. 153–175). Mahwah, NJ: Lawrence Erlbaum.

Kazdin, A. E. (1994). *Behavior modification in applied settings.* Pacific Grove, CA: Brooks/Cole.

Kazdin, A. E. (1994). Methodology, design, and evaluation in psychotherapy research. In A. E. Bergin & S. L. Garfield (Eds.), *Handbook of psychotherapy and behavior change* (4th ed.) (pp. 19–71). New York: John Wiley.

Kazdin, A. E. (1998). *Research design in clinical psychology* (3rd ed.). Boston: Allyn & Bacon.

Kazdin, A. E., & Weisz, J. R. (1998). Identifying and developing empirically supported child and adolescent treatments. *Journal of Consulting and Clinical Psychology, 66,* 19–36.

Kazdin, A. E., & Wilcoxon, L. A. (1976). Systematic desensitization and nonspecific treatment effects: A methodological evaluation. *Psychological Bulletin, 83,* 729–758.

Kazdin, A. E., & Wilson, G. T. (1978). *Evaluation of behavior therapy: Issues, evidence, and research strategies.* Cambridge, MA : Ballinger.

Keefe, F. J., & France, C. R. (1999). Pain: Biopsychosocial mechanisms and management. *Current Directions in Psychological Science, 8,* 137–141.

Keefe, F. J., Beaupre, P. M., & Gil, K. M. (1996). Group therapy for patients with chronic pain. In R. J. Gatchel & D. C. Turk (Eds.), *Psychological approaches to pain management: A practitioner's handbook* (pp. 259–282). New York: Guilford Press.

Keiser, R. E., & Prather, E. N. (1990). What is the TAT? A review of ten years of research. *Journal of Personality Research, 55,* 800–803.

Keith, S. J., Regier, D. A., Rae, D. S., & Matthews, S. (1991). Schizophrenic disorder. In L. N. Robins & D. A. Regier (Eds.), *Psychiatric disorders in America* (pp. 33–52). New York: Free Press.

Keith-Speigel, P. (1994). The 1992 Ethics Code: Boon or bane. *Professional Psychology: Research and Practice, 25,* 315–316.

Kelley, H. H. (1967). Attribution theory in social psychology. *Nebraska Symposium on Motivation, 15,* 192–238.

Kelley, H. H. (1973). The processes of causal attribution. *American Psychologist, 28,* 107–128.

Kelly, A. B., Halford, W. K., & Young, R. M. (2000). Maritally distressed women with alcohol problems: The impact of a short-term alcohol-focused intervention on drinking behaviour and marital satisfaction. *Addiction, 95,* 1537–1549.

Kelly, G. A. (1955). *The psychology of personal constructs* (Vols. 1, 2). New York: Norton.

Kelly, J. A. (1997). HIV risk reduction interventions for persons with severe mental illness. *Clinical Psychology Review, 17,* 293–309.

Kelly, J. A., Murphy, D. A., Bahr, G. R., & Kalichman, S. C. (1993). Outcome of cognitive-behavioral and support group brief therapies for depressed, HIV-infected persons. *American Journal of Psychiatry, 150,* 1679–1686.

Kendall, P. C. (1998). Empirically supported psychological therapies. *Journal of Consulting and Clinical Psychology, 66,* 3–6.

Kendall, P. C., Flannery-Schroeder, E., Panichelli-Mindel, S. M., & Southam-Gerow, M. (1997). Therapy for youths with anxiety disorders: A second randomized clinical trial. *Journal of Consulting and Clinical Psychology, 65,* 366–380.

Kendall, P. C., & Hammen, C. (1998). *Abnormal psychology: Understanding human problems.* Boston: Houghton Mifflin.

Kendler, K. S., Kessler, R. C., Walters, E. E., MacLean, C., Neale, M. C., Heath, A. C., & Eaves, L. J. (1995). Stressful life events, genetic liability, and onset of an episode of major depression in women. *American Journal of Psychiatry, 152,* 833–842.

Kendler, K. S., Neale, M. C., Kessler, R. C., Heath, A. C., & Eaves, L. J. (1992). A population-based twin study of major depression in women: The impact of varying definitions of illness. *Archives of General Psychiatry, 49,* 257–266.

Kernberg, O. F. (1976). Technical considerations in the treatment of borderline personality organization. *Journal of the American Psychoanalytic Association, 24,* 795–829.

Kernberg, O. F. (1980). Symposium on object relations theory and love—Love, the couple, and the group: A psychoanalytic frame. *Psychoanalytic Quarterly, 49,* 78–108.

Kernberg, O. F., Burstein, E. D., Coyne, L., Appelbaum, A., Horwitz, L., & Voth, H. (1972). Psychotherapy and psychoanalysis: Final report of the Menninger Foundation's psychotherapy research project. *Bulletin of the Menninger Clinic, 36,* 275.

Kerr, M. E., & Bowen, M. (1988). *Family evaluation: An approach based on Bowen theory.* New York: Norton.

Kerwin, M. E., Ahearn, W. H., Eicher, P. S., & Burd, D. (1995). The costs of eating: A behavioral economic analysis of food refusal. *Journal of Applied Behavior Analysis, 28,* 245–260.

Kessler, R. C. (1994). The National Comorbidity Survey of the United States. *International Review of Psychiatry, 6,* 365–376.

Kessler, R. C., DuPont, R. L., Berglund, P., & Wittchen, H. U. (1999). Impairment in pure and comorbid generalized anxiety disorder and major depression in two national surveys. *American Journal of Psychiatry, 156,* 1915–1923.

Kessler, R. C., McGonagle, K. A., Zhao, S., Nelson, C. B., Hughs, M., Eshleman, S., Wittchen, H.-U., & Kendler, K. S. (1994). Lifetime and 12-month prevalence of DSM-III-R psychiatric disorders in the United States: Results from the National Comorbidity Survey. *Archives of General Psychiatry, 51,* 8–19.

Kessler, R. C., Stang, P. E., Wittchen, H., Ustun, T. B., Roy-Burne, P. P., & Walters, E. E. (1998). Lifetime panic-depression comorbidity in the National Comorbidity Survey. *Archives of General Psychiatry, 55,* 801–808.

Kessler, R. C., Walters, E. E., & Forthofer, M. S. (1998). The social consequences of psychiatric disorders, III: Probability of marital stability. *American Journal of Psychiatry, 155,* 1092–1096.

Kessler, R. C., Zhao, S., Blazer, D. G., Swartz, M. (1997). Prevalence, correlates, and course of minor depression and major depression in the National Comorbidity Survey. *Journal of Affective Disorders, 45,* 19–30.

Kiecolt-Glaser, J. K., Page, G. G., Marucha, P. T., MacCallum, R. C., & Glaser, R. (1998). Psychological influences on surgical recovery: Perspectives from psychoneuroimmunology. *American Psychologist, 53,* 1209–1218.

Kihlstrom, J. F. (1995). Psychology, the basic science for mental health. *Psychological Science, 6,* 189–191.

Kilpatrick, D. G., Resnick, H. S., & Acierno, R. (1997). Health impact of interpersonal violence: III. Implications for clinical practice and public policy. *Behavioral Medicine, 23,* 79–85.

King, C. A., Hovey, J. D., Brand, E., & Wilson, R. (1997). Suicidal adolescents after hospitalization: Parent and family impacts on treatment follow-through. *Journal of the American Academy of Child and Adolescent Psychiatry, 36,* 85–93.

Kinoy, B. P. (Ed.). (2001). *Eating disorders: New directions in treatment and recovery* (2nd ed.). New York: Columbia University Press.

Kirk, S. A., & Kutchins, H. (1994). The myth of the reliability of DSM. *Journal of Mind and Behavior, 15,* 71–86.

Klein, D. F. (1993). False suffocation alarms, spontaneous panics, and related conditions: An integrative hypothesis. *Archives of General Psychiatry, 50,* 306–317.

Klein, D. F. (1998). Control groups in pharmacotherapy and psychotherapy evaluations. *Prevention and Treatment, 1,* n.p.

Klein, M. (1932). *The psycho-analysis of children.* New York: Norton.

Klein, M. (1948). *Contributions to psychoanalysis, 1921–1945.* London: Hogarth Press.

Klein, M. (1955). The psychoanalytic play technique. *American Journal of Orthopsychiatry, 25,* 223–237.

Klerman, G. (1986). Adaptation, depression, and transitional life events. *Adolescent Psychiatry, 8,* 301–308.

Klerman, G. L., & Weissman, M. M. (Eds.) (1993). *New applications of interpersonal psychotherapy.* Washington, DC: American Psychiatric Press.

Klerman, G. L., Weissman, M. M., Rounsaville, B. J., & Chevron, E. S. (1984). *Interpersonal psychotherapy of depression.* New York: Basic Books.

Klerman, G., & Weissman, M. (1989). Continuities and discontinuities in anxiety disorders. In P. Williams & G. Wilkinson, (Eds.), *The scope of epidemiological psychiatry: Essays in honour of Michael Shepard* (pp. 1725–2003). Florence, KY: Taylor & Francis/Routledge.

Klusman, L. E. (1998). Military health care providers' views on prescribing privileges for psychologists. *Professional Psychology: Research and Practice, 29,* 223–229.

Knox, M., Funk, J., Elliott, R., & Bush, E. G. (1998). Adolescents' possible selves and their relationship to global self-esteem. *Sex Roles, 39,* 61–80.

Koestenbaum, P. (1978). *The new image of the person: The theory and practice of clinical philosophy.* Westport, CT: Greenwood Press.

Kohn, L. T., Corrigan, J. M., & Donaldson, M. S. (2000). *To err is human: building a safer medical system.* Washington, DC: National Academy Press.

Kohut, H. (1971). *The analysis of the self.* New York: International Universities Press.

Kohut, H. (1977). *The restoration of the self.* New York: International Universities Press.

Korchin, S. (1976). *Modern clinical psychology: Principles of intervention in the clinic and community.* New York: Basic Books.

Korman, M. (1974). National conference on levels and patterns of professional training in psychology: The major themes. *American Psychologist, 29,* 441–449.

Koss, M. P. (1993). Rape: Scope, impact, interventions, and public policy responses. *American Psychologist, 48,* 1062–1069.

Koss, M. P. (2000). Blame, shame, and community: Justice responses to violence against women. *American Psychologist, 55,* 1332–1343.

Kratochwill, T. R. (1985). Selection of target behaviors in behavioral consultation. *Behavioral Assessment, 7,* 49–61.

Kraut, R., Patterson, M., Lundmark, V., Kiesler, S., Mukophadhyay, T., & Scherlis, W. (1998). Internet paradox: A social technology that reduces social involvement and psychological well-being? *American Psychologist, 53,* 1017–1031.

Kropp, P., Gerber, W.-D., Keinath-Specht, A., Kopal, T., & Niederberger, U. (1997). Behavioral treatment in migraine. Cognitive-behavioral therapy and blood-volume-pulse biofeedback: A cross-over study with a two-year followup. *Functional Neurology: New Trends in Adaptive and Behavioral Disorders, 12,* 17–24.

Krueger, R. F. (1999). The structure of common mental disorders. *Archives of General Psychiatry, 56,* 921–926.

Kubie, L. S. (1950). *Practical and theoretical aspects of psychoanalysis.* New York: International Universities Press.

Kubzansky, L. D., & Kawachi, I. (2000). Going to the heart of the matter: Do negative emotions cause coronary heart disease? *Journal of Psychosomatic Research, 48,* 323–337.

Kulka, R. A., Veroff, J., & Douvan, E. (1979). Social class and the use of professional help for personal problems: 1957 and 1976. *Journal of Health and Social Behavior, 20,* 2–17.

Kung, W. W. (2000). The intertwined relationship between depression and marital distress: Elements of marital therapy conducive to effective treatment outcome. *Journal of Marriage and Family Counseling, 26,* 51–63.

Kutchins, H., & Kirk, S. A. (1997). *Making us crazy—DSM: The psychiatric bible and the creation of mental disorders.* New York: Free Press.

Ladouceur, R., Freeston, M. H., Gagnon, F., Thibodeau, N., & Dumont, J. (1993). Idiographic considerations in the behavioral treatment of intrusive thoughts. *Journal of Behavior Therapy and Experimental Psychiatry, 24,* 301–310.

Laessle, R. G., & Zoettl, C. and Pirke, K. M. (1987). Meta-analysis of treatment studies for bulimia. *International Journal of Eating Disorders, 6,* 647–653.

Lah, M. I., & Rotter, J. B. (1981). Changing college student norms on the Rotter Incomplete Sentences Blank. *Journal of Consulting and Clinical Psychology, 49,* 985.

Lambert, M. C., Lyubansky, M., & Achenbach, T. M. (1998). Behavioral and emotional problems among adolescents of Jamaica and the United States: Parent, teacher, and self-reports for ages 12 to 18. *Journal of Emotional and Behavioral Disorders, 6,* 180–187.

Lambert, M. J., & Bergin, A. E. (1994). The effectiveness of psychotherapy. In A. E. Bergin & S. L. Garfield (Eds.), *Handbook of psychotherapy and behavior change* (4th ed.; pp. 143–189). New York: John Wiley.

Lambert, M. J., & Hill, C. E. (1994). Assessing psychotherapy outcomes and processes. In A. E. Bergin & S. L. Garfield (Eds.), *Handbook of psychotherapy and behavior change* (4th ed.; pp. 72–113). New York: John Wiley.

Lamm, D. H., Jones, S. H., Hayward, P., & Bright, J. A. (1999). *Cognitive therapy for bipolar disorder: A therapist's guide to concepts, methods, and practice.* Chichester: John Wiley.

Landreth, G. L., & Sweeney, D. S. (2001). Child-centered group play therapy. In G. L. Landreth (Ed.). *Innovations in play therapy: Issues, process, and special populations* (pp. 181–202). Philadelphia, PA: Brunner-Routledge.

Lang, P. J. (1995). The emotion probe: Studies of motivation and attention. *American Psychologist, 50,* 372–385.

Lang, P. J., Levin, D. N., Miller, G. A. & Kozak, M. J. (1983). Fear behavior, fear imagery, and the psychophysiology of emotion: The problem of affective response integration. *Journal of Abnormal Psychology, 92,* 276–306.

Lapouse, R. & Monk, R. (1964). Behavior deviations in a representative sample of children: Variation by sex, age, race, social class, and family size. *American Journal of Orthopsychiatry, 34,* 436–446.

Lapouse, R., & Monk, M. A. (1959). Fears and worries in a representative sample of children. *American Journal of Orthopsychiatry, 29,* 803–818.

Larson, C. L., Sutton, S. K., & Davidson, R. J. (1998). Affective style, frontal EEG asymmetry, and the time course of the emotion-modulated startle. *Psychophysiology, 35,* 552.

Latane, B., & Darley, J. M. (1968). Group inhibition of bystander intervention in emergencies. *Journal of Personality and Social Psychology, 10,* 215–221.

Lazarus, A. A. (1973). Multimodal behavior therapy: Treating the "BASIC ID." *Journal of Nervous and Mental Disease, 156,* 404–411.

Lazarus, A. A. (1989). Multimodal therapy. In R. Corsini & D. Wedding (Eds.), *Current psychotherapies* (4th ed., pp. 503–544). Itasca, IL: F. E. Peacock.

Lazarus, R. S. (1991). *Emotion and adaptation.* New York, NY: Oxford University Press.

Lazarus, R. S. (1991). Progress on a cognitive-motivational-relational theory of emotion. *American Psychologist, 46,* 819–834.

Lazarus, R. S. (1995). Emotions express a social relationship, but it is an individual mind that creates them. *Psychological Inquiry, 6,* 253–265.

Lazarus, R. S. (1999). *Stress and emotion: A new synthesis.* New York: Springer.

Leard-Hansson, J. B. E. (2001). Psychologist-prescribing efforts: A brief history. *Psychiatric News, 36,* 31.

Leijssen, M. (1998). Focusing microprocesses. In L. S. Greenberg & J. C. Watson (Eds.), *Handbook of experiential psychotherapy* (pp.121–154). New York: Guilford Press.

Leitenberg, H. (1973). The use of single-case methodology in psychotherapy research. *Journal of Abnormal Psychology, 82,* 87–101.

Leitenberg, H., Rosen, J. C., Gross, J., Nudelman, S., & Vara, J. R. (1988). Exposure plus response-prevention treatment of bulimia nervosa. *Journal of Consulting and Clinical Psychology, 56,* 535–541.

Levenson, H. (1995). *Time-limited dynamic psychotherapy: A guide to clinical practice.* New York: Basic Books.

Levenson, R. W., Carstensen, L. L., & Gottman, J. M. (1994). Influence of age and gender on affect, physiology, and their interrelations: A study of long-term marriages. *Journal of Personality and Social Psychology, 67,* 56–68.

Leventhal, H., & Keeshan P. (1993). Promoting healthy alternatives to substance abuse. In S. G. Millstein, A. C. Petersen, E. Nightengale, & R. Takanishi (Eds.), *Promoting the health of adolescents: New directions for the twenty-first century* (pp. 260–284). New York: Oxford University Press.

Lewandowski, L. M., Gebing, T. A., Anthony, J. L., & O'Brien, W. H. (1997). Meta-analysis of cognitive-behavioral treatment studies for bulimia. *Clinical Psychology Review, 17,* 703–718.

Lewinsohn, P. M. (1974). A behavioral approach to depression. In R. J. Friedman & M. M. Katz (Eds.), *The psychology of depression: Contemporary theory and research* (pp. 157–185). New York: John Wiley.

Lewinsohn, P. M., Allen, N. B., Seeley, J. R., & Gotlib, I. H. (1999). First onset versus recurrence of depression: Differential processes of psychosocial risk. *Journal of Abnormal Psychology, 108,* 483–489.

Lewinsohn, P. M., & Clarke, G. N. (1999). Psychosocial treatments for adolescent depression. *Clinical Psychology Review, 19,* 329–342.

Lewinsohn, P. M., Clarke, G. N., Rohde, P., Hops, H., & Seeley, J. R. (1996). A course in coping: A cognitive-behavioral approach to the treatment of adolescent depression. In E. D. Hibbs & P. S. Jensen, (Eds.), *Psychosocial treatments for child and adolescent disorders: Empirically based strategies for clinical practice* (pp. 109–135). Washington, DC: American Psychological Association.

Lewinsohn, P. M., & Gotlib, I. H. (1995). Behavioral theory and treatment of depression. In E. E. Beckham & W. R. Leber (Eds.), *Handbook of depression* (2nd ed., pp. 352–375). New York: Guilford Press.

Lewinsohn, P. M., Hoberman, H., Teri, L., & Hautzinger, M. (1985). An integrative theory of depression. In S. Reiss & R. Bootzin (Eds.), *Theoretical issues in behavior therapy* (pp. 331–359). New York: Academic Press.

Lewinsohn, P. M., Hops, H., Roberts, R. E., Seeley, J. R., & Andrews, J. A. (1993). Adolescent psychopathology: I. Prevalence and incidence of depression and other DSM-III-R disorders in high school students. *Journal of Abnormal Psychology, 102,* 133–144.

Lewinsohn, P. M., Rohde, P., & Seeley, J. R. (1996). Adolescent suicidal ideation and attempts: Prevalence, risk factors, and clinical implications. *Clinical Psychology: Science and Practice, 3,* 25–46.

Lewinsohn, P., Sullivan, J. M., & Grosscup, S. J. (1980). Changing reinforcing events: An approach to the treatment of depression. *Psychotherapy: Theory, research and practice, 17,* 322–334.

Lewis, M., & Haviland-Jones, J. M. (Eds.). (2000). *Handbook of emotions* (2nd ed.). New York: Guilford Press.

Lewontin, R. C., Rose, S., & Kamin, L. J. (1984). *Not in our genes: Biology, ideology, and human nature.* New York: Pantheon Books.

Lezak, M. D. (1995). *Neuropsychological assessment* (3rd ed.). New York: Oxford University Press.

Lichtenstein, E. (1982). The smoking problem: A behavioral perspective. *Journal of Consulting and Clinical Psychology, 50,* 804–819.

Liebowitz, M. R., Salman, E., Jusino, C. M., Garfinkel, R., Street, L., Cardenas, D. L., Silvestre, J., Fyer, A. J., Carrasco, J. L., & Davies, S. (1994). *Atacqaue de nervios* and panic disorder. *American Journal of Psychiatry, 151,* 871–875.

Lilienfeld, S. O., Wood, J. M., & Garb, H. N. (2000). The scientific status of projective techniques. *Psychological Science in the Public Interest, 1,* 27–66.

Lindsley, O. R. (1968, March). *Training parents and teachers to precisely manage children's behavior.* Address presented at the C. S. Mott Foundation Children's Health Center.

Lindzey, G. (1959). On the classification of projective techniques. *Psychological Bulletin, 56,* 158–168.

Linscott, J., & DiGiuseppe, R. (1998). Cognitive assessment. In A. S. Bellack & M. Hersen (Eds.), *Behavioral assessment: A practical handbook* (pp. 104–125). Elmsford, NY: Pergamon Press.

Lipson, K. J., Stevens, M. J., Graybill, D., & Mark, K. I. (1995). MMPI-2 and family environment differences between bulimic and nonbulimic women and their families. *Assessment, 2,* 203-218.

Lobitz, W. C., & LoPiccolo, J. (1972). New methods in the behavioral treatment of sexual dysfunction.

Journal of Behavior Therapy and Experimental Psychiatry, 3, 265–271.

Loevinger, J. (1998). *Technical foundations for measuring ego development: The Washington University Sentence Completion Test.* Mahwah, NJ: Lawrence Erlbaum.

London, P. (1986). *The modes and morals of psychotherapy* (2nd ed.). New York, NY: Hemisphere Publishing Corp./Harper & Row Publishers, Inc.

Long, P., Forehand, R., Wierson, M., & Morgan, A. (1994). Does parent training with young noncompliant children have long-term effects? *Behaviour Research and Therapy, 32,* 101–110.

Lorenz, K. (1966). *On aggression.* New York: Harcourt, Brace & World.

Lovaas, O. I. & Buch, G. (1997). Intensive behavioral intervention with young children with autism. In N. N. Singh (Ed.), *Prevention and treatment of severe behavior problems: Models and methods in developmental disabilities* (pp. 61–86). Pacific Grove, CA: Brooks/Cole.

Luborsky, L., Singer, B., & Luborsky, L. (1975). Comparative studies of psychotherapies: Is it true that "everyone has won and all must have prizes"? *Archives of General Psychiatry, 32,* 995–1008.

Lucas, C. P., Fisher, P., Piacentini, J., Zhaug, H., Jenson, P. S., Shaffer, D., Dulcan, M., Schwab-Stone, M., Regier, D., & Camino, G. (1999). Features of interview questions associated with attenuation of symptom reports. *Journal of Abnormal Child Psychology, 27,* 429–437.

Lucyshyn, J. M., Albin, R. W., & Nixon, C. D. (1997). Embedding comprehensive behavioral support in family ecology: An experimental, single case analysis. *Journal of Consulting and Clinical Psychology, 65,* 241–251.

Lueger, R. L. & Petzel, T. P. (1979). Illusory correlation in clinical judgment: Effects of amount of information to be processed. *Journal of Consulting and Clinical Psychology, 47,* 1120–1121.

Lukas, E. (1984). *Meaningful living: Logotherapeutic guide to health.* New York: Grove Press.

Lynam, D., Moffitt, T., & Stouthamer-Loeber, M. (1993). Explaining the relation between IQ and delinquency. Class, race, test motivation, school failure, or self-control? *Journal of Abnormal Psychology, 102,* 187–196.

Lytle, L. A., Stone, E. J., Nichaman, M. Z., & Perry, C. L. (1996). Changes in nutrient intakes of elementary school children following a school-based intervention: Results from the CATCH study. *Preventive Medicine, 25,* 465–477.

Machado, P. P., Beutler, L. E., & Greenberg, L. S. (1999). Emotion recognition in psychotherapy: Impact of therapist level of experience and emotional awareness. *Journal of Clinical Psychology, 55,* 39–57.

Machover, K. (1949). *Personality projection in the drawing of the human figure.* Springfield, Ill.: Charles C. Thomas.

MacLeod, C., & Rutherford, E. M. (1998). Automatic and strategic cognitive biases in anxiety and depression. In K. Kirsner & C. Spellman (Eds.). *Implicit and explicit mental processes* (pp. 223–254). Mahwah, NJ: Erlbaum.

MacLeod, C. (1999). Anxiety and anxiety disorders. In T. Dalgleish & M. J. Power (Eds.), *Handbook of cognition and emotion* (pp. 447–477). New York: John Wiley.

Maheu, M. M., & Gordon, B. L. (2000). The internet versus the telephone: What is telehealth anyway? *Professional Psychology: Research and Practice, 31,* 484–489.

Mahler, M., Pine, F., & Bergman, A. (1975). *The psychological birth of the human infant.* New York: Basic Books.

Mahoney, M. (1998). Essential themes in the training of psychotherapists. *Psychotherapy in Private Practice, 17,* 43–59.

Mahoney, M. J. (1974). *Cognition and behavior modification.* Cambridge, MA: Ballinger.

Mahoney, M. J. (1976). *Scientist as subject: The psychological imperative.* Cambridge: Ballinger.

Mahoney, M. J. (1984). Behaviorism, cognitivism, and human change processes. In M. A. Reda & M. J. Mahoney (Eds.), *Cognitive psychotherapies: Recent developments in theory, research, and practice* (pp. 3–30). Cambridge, MA: Ballinger Publishing Company.

Mahoney, M. J. (1989). Scientific psychology and radical behaviorism: Important distinctions based in scientism and objectivism. *American Psychologist, 44,* 1372–1377.

Malan, D. H. (1976). *The frontier of brief psychotherapy: An example of the convergence of research and clinical practice.* New York: Plenum Medical Book Co.

Malan, D. H. (1979). *Individual psychotherapy and the science of psychodynamics.* London: Butterworth.

Maloney, M. P., & Ward, M. P. (1976). *Psychological assessment: A conceptual approach.* New York: Oxford.

Mann, J. (1973). *Time-limited psychotherapy.* Cambridge, MA: Harvard University Press.

Margolin, G., & Gordis, E. B. (2000). The effects of family and community violence on children. *Annual Review of Psychology, 51,* 445–479.

Marks, I. (1987). Agoraphobia, panic disorder, and related conditions in the *DSM-III-R* and *ICD-10. Journal of Psychopharmacology, 1,* 6–12.

Marks, I. M., & Mathews, A. M. (1979). Brief standard self-rating for phobic patients. *Behavior Research & Therapy, 17,* 263–267.

Marlatt, G. A., & George, W. H. (1998). Relapse prevention and the maintenance of optimal health. In S. A. Shumaker, & E. B. Schron, (Eds.), *The handbook of health behavior change* (2nd ed., pp. 33–58). New York: Springer.

Marshall, P. J., & Fox, N. A. (2000). Emotion regulation, depression, and hemispheric asymmetry. In S. L. Johnson, A. M. Hayes, T. M. Field, N. Schneiderman, & P. M. McCabe (Eds.), *Stress, coping, and depression* (pp. 35–50). Mahwah, NJ: Lawrence Erlbaum.

Martin, E. D., & Sher, K. J. (1994). Family history of alcoholism, alcohol use disorder, and the five-factor model of personality. *Journal of Studies on Alcohol, 55,* 81–90.

Maser, J. D., & Cloninger, C. R. (1990). *Comorbidity of mood and anxiety disorders.* Washington, DC: American Psychiatric Press.

Maser, J. D., Klaeber, C., & Weise, R. (1991). International use and attitudes toward DSM-III and DSM-III-R: Growing consensus in psychiatric classification. *Journal of Abnormal Psychology, 100,* 271–279.

Mash, E. J., & Barkley R. A. (1986). Assessment of family interaction with the response-class matrix. *Advances in Behavioral Assessment of Children and Families, 2,* 29–67.

Maslow, A. (1966). *The psychology of science: A reconnaissance.* New York: Harper & Row.

Maslow, A. H. (1971). *The farther reaches of human nature.* New York: Viking.

Maslow, A. H. (1987). *Motivation and personality* (3rd ed.). New York: Harper & Row.

Mason, B. J., Markowitz, J. C., & Klerman, G. L. (1993). Interpersonal psychotherapy for dysthymic disorders. In G. L. Klerman & M. M. Weissman, (Eds.), *New applications of interpersonal psychotherapy* (pp. 225–264). Washington, DC: American Psychiatric Press, Inc.

Masters, J. C., & Burish, T. G. (1987). *Behavior therapy: Techniques and empirical findings* (3rd ed.). San Diego, CA: Harcourt Brace Jovanovich.

Mathews, A., & MacLeod, C. (1985). Selective processing of threat cues in anxiety states. *Behaviour Research and Therapy, 23,* 563–569.

Mathews, A., & MacLeod, C. (1986). Discrimination of threat cues without awareness in anxiety states. *Journal of Abnormal Psychology, 95,* 131–138.

Mathews, A., & MacLeod, C. (1994). Cognitive approaches to emotions and emotional disorders. *Annual Review of Psychology, 45,* 25–50.

May, R. (1981). *Freedom and destiny.* New York: Norton.

May, R. (1990). Will, decision and responsibility. In K. Hoeller (Ed.), *Readings in existential psychology and psychiatry* (pp. 269–278). Seattle, WA: Review of Existential Psychology and Psychiatry.

May, R., & Yalom, I. D. (1989). Existential psychotherapy. In R. J. Corsini & D. Wedding (Eds.), *Current psychotherapies* (4th ed., pp. 363–402). Itasca, IL: F. E. Peacock.

Mayes, S. D., Calhoun, S. L., & Crowell, E. W. (1998). WISC-III Freedom from Distractibility as a measure of attention in children with and without attention deficit hyperactivity disorder. *Journal of Attention Disorders, 2,* 217–227.

McAdams, D. P. (1992). The five-factor model in personality: A critical appraisal. *Journal of Personality, 60,* 329–361.

McAuley, C. (2000). Children's adjustment over time in foster care: Cross-informant agreement, stability, and placement disruption. *British Journal of Social Work, 30,* 91–107.

McCabe, S. B. & Gotlib, I. (1993). Attentional processing in clinically depressed subjects: A longitudinal investigation. *Cognitive Therapy and Research, 17*, 359–377.

McCabe, S. B., Gotlib, I. H., & Martin, R. A. (2000). Cognitive vulnerability for depression: Development of attention as a function of history of depression and current mood state. *Cognitive Therapy and Research, 24*, 427–444.

McCall, R. B. (1979). The development of intellectual functioning in infancy and prediction of later IQ. In J. D. Osofsky (Ed.), *Handbook of infant development* (pp. 707–741). New York: Wiley.

McCarty, C. A., Wesiz, J. R., Wanitromanee, K., Eastman, K. L., Suwanlert, S., Chaiyasit, W., & Band, E. B. (1999). Culture, coping, and context: Primary and secondary control among Thai and American youth. *Journal of Child Psychology and Psychiatry and Allied Disciplines, 40*, 809–818.

McClelland, D. C. (1961). *The achieving society.* Princeton, NJ: Van Nostrand.

McClelland, D. C. (1985). How motives, skills, and values determine what people do. *American Psychologist, 40*, 812–825.

McClelland, D. C., Alexander, C., & Marks, E. (1982). The need for power, stress, immune function, and illness among male prisoners. *Journal of Abnormal Psychology, 91*, 61–70.

McClelland, D. C., Atkinson, J. W., Clark, R. A., & Lowell, E. L. (1976). *The achievement motive.* New York, NY: Irvington.

McClelland, D. C., & Jemmott, J. B. (1980). Power motivation, stress, and physical illness. *Journal of Human Stress, 6*, 6–15.

McConaughy, S. H. (2000). Self-report: Child clinical interviews. In E. S. Shapiro & T. R. Kratochwill (Eds.), *Conducting school-based assessments of child and adolescent behavior. The Guilford school practitioner series* (pp. 170–202). New York: Guilford Press.

McCrady, B. S., & Epstein, E. E. (Eds.), (1999). *Addictions: A comprehensive guidebook.* New York, NY: Oxford University Press.

McEwen, B. S. (1998). Stress, adaptation, and disease: Allostasis and allostatic load. In S. M. McCann, & J. M. Lipton, (Eds.), *Annals of the New York Academy of Sciences: Vol. 840. Neuroimmunomodulation: Molecular aspects, integrative systems, and clinical advances*

(pp. 33–44). New York: New York Academy of Sciences.

McFall, R. M. (1991). Manifesto for a science of clinical psychology. *The Clinical Psychologist, 44*, 75–88.

McGee, L., & Newcomb, M. (1992). General deviance syndrome: Expanded hierarchical evaluations at four ages from early adolescence to adulthood. *Journal of Consulting and Clinical Psychology, 60*, 766–776.

McGlynn, F. D., & Rose, M. P. (1998). Assessment of anxiety and fear. In A. S. Bellack & M. Hersen (Eds.), *Behavioral assessment: A practical handbook* (pp. 179–209). Elmsford, NY: Pergamon Press.

McGue, M., & Bouchard, T. J. (1998). Genetic and environmental influences on human behavioral differences. *Annual Review of Neuroscience, 21*, 1–24.

McKay, J. R. (1991). Assessing aspects of object relations associated with immune function: Development of the Affiliative Trust-Mistrust coding system. *Psychological Assessment, 3*, 641–647.

McKeown, R. E., Garrison, C. Z., Cuffe, S. P., Waller, J. L., Jackson, K. L., & Addy, C. L. (1998). Incidence and predictors of suicidal behaviors in a longitudinal sample of young adolescents. *Journal of the American Academy of Child and Adolescent Psychiatry, 37*, 612–619.

McLoyd, V. C., (1998). Socioeconomic disadvantage and child development. *American Psychologist, 53*, 185–204.

McRae, R. R., & Costa, P. T. (1997). Conceptions and correlates of openness to experience. In R. Hogan & J. A. Johnson (Eds.), *Handbook of personality psychology* (pp. 825–847). San Diego, CA: Academic Press.

McRae, R. R., & Costa, P. T. (1997). Personality trait structure as a human universal. *American Psychologist, 52*, 509–516.

McRae, R. R., Costa, P. T., Del Pilar, G. H., Rolland, J., & Parker, W. D. (1998). Cross-cultural assessment of the five-factor model: The Revised NEO Personality Inventory. *Journal of Cross-Cultural Psychology, 29*, 171–188.

McReynolds, P. (1987). Lightner Witmer: Little-known founder of clinical psychology. *American Psychologist, 42*, 849–858.

McReynolds, P. (1997). *Lightner Witmer: His life and times.* Washington, DC: American Psychological Association.

Medin, D. L., & Heit, E. (1999). Categorization. In B. M. Bly & D. E. Rumelhart (Eds.), *Cognitive science* (pp. 99–143). San Diego: Academic Press.

Meehl, P. (1986). Diagnostic taxa as open concepts: Metatheoretical and statistical questions about reliability and construct validity in the grand strategy of nosological revision. In T. Millon & G. Klerman (Eds.), *Contemporary directions in psychopathology: Toward the DSM-IV* (pp. 215–231). New York: Guilford Press.

Meehl, P. E. (1945). An investigation of a general normality or control factor in personality testing. *Psychological Monographs, 59*(4, Whole No. 274).

Meehl, P. E. (1954). *Clinical versus statistical prediction: A theoretical analysis and a review of the evidence.* Minneapolis: University of Minnesota Press.

Meehl, P. E. (1986). General remarks on quantification of clinical material. In H. R. Arkes & K. R. Hammond (Eds.), *Judgment and decision making: An interdisciplinary reader* (pp. 549–550). Cambridge, England: Cambridge University Press.

Meehl, P. E. (1996). *Clinical versus statistical prediction: A theoretical analysis and a review of the evidence.* Northvale, NJ: Aronson. (Original work published 1954)

Meehl, P. E. (1997). Credentialed persons, credentialed knowledge. *Clinical Psychology: Science and Practice, 4,* 91–98.

Meichenbaum, D. (1977). *Cognitive-behavior modification: An integrative approach.* New York: Plenum.

Meichenbaum, D. H. (1995). Cognitive-behavioral therapy in historical perspective. In B. Bongar & L. E. Beutler (Eds.), *Comprehensive textbook of psychotherapy: Theory and practice* (pp. 140–158). New York: Oxford University Press.

Meltzoff, J., & Kornriech, M. (1970). *Research in psychotherapy.* New York: Atherton.

Menninger, K. (1958). *Theory of psychoanalytic technique.* New York: Basic Books.

Mercer, J. R. (1989). Why haven't schools changed the focus from pathology to prevention? Conceptual and legal obstacles. In L. A. Bond & B. E. Compas (Eds.), *Primary prevention and promotion in the schools. Primary prevention of psychopathology, Vol. 12* (pp. 345–360). Newbury Park, CA: Sage Publications.

Merikangas, K. R., & Swendsen, J. D. (1997). Genetic epidemiology of psychiatric disorders. *Epidemiological Reviews, 19,* 144–155.

Merrell, K. W. (1999). *Behavioral, social, and emotional assessment of children and adolescents.* NJ: Lawrence Erlbaum.

Messer, D. J. (1994). *The development of communication: From social interaction to language.* Chichester, England: John Wiley.

Metalsky, G., & Joiner, T. E. (1992). Vulnerability to depressive symptomatology: A prospective test of the diathesis-stress and causal mediation components of the hopelessness theory of depression. *Journal of Personality and Social Psychology, 63,* 667–675.

Meyer, A. (1957). *Psychobiology: A science of man.* Springfield, IL: Charles C. Thomas.

Milich, R., Loney, J., & Landau, S. (1982). Independent dimensions of hyperactivity and aggression: A validation with playroom observation data. *Journal of Abnormal Psychology, 91,* 183–198.

Miller, G. A., & Kozak, M. J. (1993). Three-systems assessment and the construct of emotion. In N. Birbaumer & A. Ohman (Eds.), *The structure of emotion: Psychophysiological, cognitive, and clinical aspects* (pp. 31–47). Seattle, WA: Hogrefe & Huber.

Miller, J. J., Fletcher, K., & Kabat-Zinn, J. (1995). Three-year follow-up and clinical implications of a mindfulness meditation-based stress reduction intervention in the treatment of anxiety disorders. *General Hospital Psychiatry, 17,* 192–200.

Millon, T. (1992). Millon Clinical Multiaxial Inventory: I and II. *Journal of Counseling and Development, 70,* 422–426.

Millon, T. (1996). *The Millon Inventories.* New York: Guilford Press.

Mineka, S. (1992). Evolutionary memories, emotional processing, and the emotional disorders. In D. Medin (Ed.), *The psychology of learning and motivation* (Vol. 28; pp. 161–206). New York: Academic Press.

Mineka, S., & Cook, M. (1986). Immunization against the observational conditioning of fear in rhesus monkeys. *Journal of Abnormal Psychology, 95,* 307–318.

Mineka, S., & Cook, M. (1993). Mechanisms involved in the observational conditioning of fear. *Journal of Experimental Psychology: General, 122,* 23–38.

Mineka, S., Davidson, M., Cook, M., & Keir, R. (1984). Observational conditioning of snake fear in rhesus monkeys. *Journal of Abnormal Psychology, 93,* 355–372.

Mineka, S., & Zinbarg, R. (1996). Conditioning and ethological models of anxiety disorders: Stress-in-Dynamic-Context Anxiety Models. In D. Hope (Ed.), *Perspectives on anxiety, panic, and fear: Nebraska symposium on motivation* (pp. 135–210). Lincoln: University of Nebraska Press.

Minuchin, S. (1974). *Families and family therapy.* Cambridge, MA: Harvard University Press.

Mischel, W. (1968). *Personality and assessment.* New York: John Wiley.

Mischel, W. (1998). *Introduction to personality* (6th ed.). Fort Worth, TX: Harcourt Brace College Publishers.

Mischel, W., & Shoda, Y. (1995). A cognitive-affective system theory of personality: Reconceptualizing situations, dispositions, dynamics, and invariance in personality structure. *Psychological Review, 102,* 246–268.

Mitchell, S. A., & Black, M. J. (1995). *Freud and beyond: A history of modern psychoanalytic thought.* New York: Basic Books.

Mitsis, E. M., McKay, K. E., Schulz, K. P., Newcorn, J. H., & Halperin, J. M. (2000). Parent-teacher concordance for *DSM-IV* attention-deficit/hyperactivity disorder in a clinic-referred sample. *Journal of the American Academy of Child and Adolescent Psychiatry, 39,* 308–313.

Modestin, J., & Puhan, A. (2000). Comparison of assessment of personality disorder by patients and informants. *Psychopathology, 33,* 265–270.

Moffitt, T. (1993). Adolescence-limited and life-course-persistent antisocial behavior: A developmental taxonomy. *Psychological Review, 100,* 674–701.

Mogg, K., Bradley, B. P., Dixon, C., Fisher, S., Twelftree, A., & McWilliams, A. (2000). Trait anxiety, defensiveness, and selective processing of threat: An investigation using two measures of attentional bias. *Personality and Individual Differences, 28,* 1063–1077.

Mogg, K., Mathews, A., & Eysenck, H. (1992). Attentional bias to threat in clinical anxiety states. *Cognition & Emotion, 6,* 149–159.

Mohanty, S., Pati, N. C., & Kumar, R. (1998). Effects of token economy on the rate of envelope making in the persons with mental retardation. *Social Science International, 14,* 84–97.

Monroe, S. M., & Hadjyannakis, K. (in press). The social environment and depression. In I. H. Gotlib & C. L. Hammen (Eds.), *Handbook of depression: Research and treatment.* New York: Guilford Press.

Monroe, S. M., Rohde, P., Seeley, J. R., & Lewinsohn, P. M. (1999). Life events and depression in adolescence: Relationship loss as a prospective risk factor for first onset of major depressive disorder. *Journal of Abnormal Psychology, 108,* 606–614.

Moore, J. E., Von Korff, M., Cherkin, D., Saunders, K., & Lorig, K. (2000). A randomized trial of a cognitive-behavioral program for enhancing back pain self care in a primary care setting. *Pain, 88,* 145–153.

Moretti, M. M., & Higgins, E. T. (1999a). Internal representations of others in self-regulation: A new look at a classic issue. *Social Cognition, 17,* 186–208.

Moretti, M. M., & Higgins, E. T. (1999b). Own versus other standpoints in self-regulation: Developmental antecedents and functional consequences. *Review of General Psychology, 3,* 188–223.

Morey, L. C. (1999) Personality Assessment Inventory. In M. E. Maruish (Ed.), *The use of psychological testing for treatment planning and outcomes assessment* (2nd ed., pp. 1083–1121). Mahwah, NJ: Lawrence Erlbaum.

Morley, S., Eccleston, C., & Williams, A. (1999). Systematic review and meta-analysis of randomized controlled trials of cognitive behaviour therapy and behaviour therapy for chronic pain in adults, excluding headache. *Pain, 80,* 1–13.

Morrison, D. L. (1988). Predicting diagnosis performance with measures of cognitive style. *Current Psychology: Research & Reviews, 7,* 136–156.

Mowrer, O. H., & Mowrer, W. M. (1938). Enuresis—a method for its study and treatment. *American Journal of Orthopsychiatry, 8,* 436–459.

Mowrer, R. R., & Klein, S. B. (1989). A contrast between traditional and contemporary learning theory. In S. B. Klein, & R. R. Mowrer (Eds.), *Contemporary learning theories: Instrumental conditioning theory and the impact of biological constraints on learning* (p. 1–10). Hillsdale, NJ: Lawrence Erlbaum Associates.

Mowrer, R. R., & Klein, S. B. (2001). *Handbook of contemporary learning theories.* Mahwah, NJ: Lawrence Erlbaum Associates.

Mrazek, P. J., & Haggerty, R. J. (Eds.). (1994). *Reducing risks for mental disorders: Frontiers for preventive intervention research.* Washington, DC: National Academy Press.

Mueser, K. T., & Liberman, R. P. (1995). Behavior therapy in practice. In B. Bongar & L. E. Beutler (Eds.), *Comprehensive textbook of psychotherapy: Theory and practice* (pp. 84–110). New York: Oxford University Press.

Mufson, L., Moreau, D., Weissman, M. M., & Klerman, G. L. (1993). *Interpersonal psychotherapy for depressed adolescents.* New York: Guilford Press.

Mufson, L., Weissman, M. M., Moreau, D., & Garfinkel, R. (1999). Efficacy of interpersonal psychotherapy for depressed adolescents: *Archives of General Psychiatry, 56,* 573–579.

Muñoz, R. F, Le, H-N., & Ghosh Ippen, C. (2000). We should screen for major depression. *Applied and Preventive Psychology, 9,* 123–133.

Muñoz, R. F., Le, H-N., Clarke, G., & Jaycox, L. (in press). Preventing the onset of major depression. In I. H. Gotlib & C. L. Hammen (Eds.), *Handbook of depression: Research and treatment.* New York: Guilford Press.

Muñoz, R. F., Mrazek, P. J., & Haggerty, R. J. (1996). Institute of Medicine report on prevention of mental disorders: Summary and commentary. *American Psychologist, 51,* 1116–1122

Muñoz, R. F., Ying, Y, Perez-Stable, E. J., & Miranda, J. (1993). *The prevention of depression: Research and practice.* Baltimore, MD: The Johns Hopkins University Press.

Muñoz, R. F., Ying, Y., Bernal, G., & Perez-Stable, E. J. (1995). Prevention of depression with primary care patients: A randomized controlled trial. *American Journal of Community Psychology, 23,* 199–222.

Munsinger, H. (1975). *Fundamentals of child development* (2nd ed.). New York: Holt, Rinehart & Winston.

Murphy, E., & Carr, A. (2000). Enuresis and encopresis. In A. Carr (Ed.), *What works with children and adolescents? A critical review of psychological interventions with children, adolescents, and their families* (pp. 49–64). New York: Routledge.

Murray, C. J. L., & Lopez, A. D. (Eds.). (1996). *The global burden of disease: A comprehensive assessment of mortality and disability from diseases, injuries, and risk factors in 1990 and projected to 2020.* Cambridge, MA: Harvard University Press.

Murray, H. A. (1938). *Explorations in personality: A clinical and experimental study of fifty men of college age.* New York: Oxford University Press.

Murray, H. A. (1943). *Thematic Apperception Test manual.* Cambridge, MA: Harvard University Press.

Naglieri, J. A. (1988). *Draw A Person: A quantitative scoring system.* San Antonio, TX: Psychological Corporation.

Nathan, P. E., & Gorman, J. M. (Eds.). (1998). *A guide to treatments that work.* New York: Oxford University Press.

Nathan, P. E., Stuart, S. P., & Dolan, S. L. (2000). Research on psychotherapy efficacy and effectiveness: Between Scylla and Charybdis? *Psychological Bulletin, 126,* 964–981.

National Advisory Mental Health Council Behavioral Science Task Force. (1995). Basic behavioral science research for mental health: A national investment. *Psychological Science, 6,* 192–202.

National Institutes of Health Consensus Development Conference statement: Diagnosis and treatment of attention-deficit/hyperactivity disorder (ADHD). (2000). *Journal of the American Academy of Child and Adolescent Psychiatry, 39,* 182–193.

Nelson, T. O., Graf, A., Dunlosky, J., Marlatt, G. A., Walker, D., & Luce, K. (1998). Effect of acute alcohol intoxication on recall and on judgments of learning during the acquisition of new information. In G. Mazzoni, E. Giuliana, & T. O. Nelson (Eds.), *Metacognition and cognitive neuropsychology:*

Monitoring and control processes (pp. 161–180). Mahwah, NJ: Lawrence Erlbaum.

Nelson, T. O., McSpadden, M., Fromme, K., & Marlatt, G. A. (1986). Effects of alcohol intoxication on metamemory and on retrieval from long-term memory. *Journal of Experimental Psychology: General, 115,* 247–254.

Newman, R., Phelps, R., Sammons, M. T., Dunivin, D. L., & Cullen, E. A. (2000). Evaluation of the psychopharmacology demonstration project: A retrospective analysis. *Professional Psychology: Research and Practice, 31,* 598–603.

Nezu. A., & Nezu, C. M. (1993). Identifying and selecting target problems for clinical interventions: A problem-solving model. *Psychological Assessment, 5,* 254–263.

Nezu, A. M., Ronan, G. F., Meadows, E. A., & McClure, K. S. (Eds.). (2000). *Practitioner's guide to empirically based measures of depression.* New York: Kluwer Academic/Plenum Press.

Nezworski, M. T., & Wood, J. M. (1995). Narcissism in the Comprehensive System for the Rorschach. *Clinical Psychology: Science and Practice, 2,* 179–199.

Nicholas, M. K., Wilson, P. H., & Goyen, J. (1991). Operant-behavioural and cognitive-behavioural treatment for chronic low back pain. *Behaviour Research and Therapy, 29,* 225–238.

Nickelson, D. (1998). Telehealth and the evolving health care system: Strategic opportunities for professional psychology. *Professional Psychology: Research and Practice, 29,* 527–535.

Nietzel, M. T., Bernstein, D. A., & Russell, R. L. (1988). Assessment of anxiety and fear. In A. S. Bellack & M. Hersen (Eds.), *Behavioral assessment: A practical handbook* (pp. 280–312). Elmsford, NY: Pergamon Press.

Nietzel, M. T., Russell, R. L., Hemmings, K. A., & Gretter, M. L. (1987). Clinical significance of psychotherapy for unipolar depression: A meta-analytic approach to social comparison. *Journal of Consulting and Clinical Psychology, 55,* 156–161.

Nietzel, M. T., & Trull, T. J. (1988). Meta-analytic approaches to social comparisons: A method for measuring clinical significance. *Behavioral Assessment, 10,* 159–169.

Nigg, J. T., Hinshaw, S. P., & Halperin, J. M. (1996). Continuous performance test in boys with attention deficit hyperactivity disorder: Methylphenidate dose response and relations with observed behaviors. *Journal of Clinical Child Psychology, 25,* 330–340.

Nigg, J. T., Quamma, J. P., Greenberg, M. T., & Kusche, C. A. (1999). A two-year longitudinal study of neuropsychological and cognitive performance in relation to behavioral problems and competencies in elementary school children. *Journal of Abnormal Child Psychology, 27,* 51–63.

Nisbett, R. E. (1998). Race, genetics, and IQ. In C. Jencks, & M. Phillips (Eds.), *The Black-White test score gap.* (pp. 86–102). Washington, DC, USA: Brookings Institution.

Nisbett, R. E., & Wilson, T. D. (1977). Telling more than we can know: Verbal reports on mental processes. *Psychological Review, 84,* 231–259.

Nobre, P., & Gouveia, J. P. (2000). Erectile dysfunction: An empirical approach based on Beck's cognitive theory. *Sexual and Relationship Therapy, 15,* 351–366.

Nolen-Hoeksema, S. (1998). *Abnormal psychology.* Boston: McGraw-Hill.

Nolen-Hoeksema, S. (2000). Further evidence for the role of psychosocial factors in depression chronicity. *Clinical Psychology: Science and Practice, 7,* 224–227.

Nolen-Hoeksema, S. (in press). Gender differences in depression. In I. H. Gotlib & C. L. Hammen (Eds.), *Handbook of depression: Research and treatment.* New York: Guilford Press.

Nolen-Hoeksema, S., Larson, J., & Grayson, C. (1999). Explaining the gender difference in depressive symptoms. *Journal of Personality and Social Psychology, 77,* 1061–1072.

Norcross, J. C., Krag, R., & Prochaska, J. O. (1997). Clinical psychologists in the 1990's: I. *The Clinical Psychologist, 50,* 4–9.

O'Connor, T. G., & Plomin, R. (2000). Developmental behavioral genetics. In A. J. Sameroff, M. Lewis, & S. Miller (Eds.), *Handbook of developmental psychopathology* (2nd ed., pp. 217–235). New York: Kluwer Academic/ Plenum Publishers.

O'Donohue, W. T. (Ed.) (1998). *Learning and behavior therapy.* Boston: Allyn & Bacon.

O'Leary, D., & Wilson, G. T. (1987). *Behavior therapy: Application and outcome* (2nd ed.). Englewood Cliffs, NJ: Prentice-Hall.

O'Reilly, M. F., Lancioni, G. E., & O'Kane, N. (2000). Using a problem-solving approach to teach social skills to workers with brain injuries in supported employment settings. *Journal of Vocational Rehabilitation, 14,* 187–194.

Ogles, B. M., Lambert, M. J., & Sawyer, J. D. (1995). Clinical significance of the National Institute of Mental Health Treatment of Depression Collaborative Research Program data. *Journal of Consulting and Clinical Psychology, 63,* 321–326.

Ohman, A. (1996). Preferential preattentive processing of threat in anxiety: Preparedness and attentional biases. In R. M. Rapee (Ed.), *Current controversies in the anxiety disorders* (pp. 253–290). New York: Guilford Press.

Olds, D. L. (1986). Case studies of factors interfering with nurse home visitors' promotion of positive care-giving methods in high risk families. In A. S. Honig (Ed.), *Risk factors in infancy* (pp. 149–165). Amsterdam, Netherlands: Gordon and Breach Publishers.

Olds, D. L. (1988). The prenatal/early infancy project. In R. H. Price, E. L. Cowen, R. P. Lorian, & J. Ramos-McKay (Eds.), *Fourteen ounces of prevention: A casebook for practitioners* (pp. 9–23). Washington, DC: American Psychological Association.

Olds, D. L. (1989). The prenatal/early infancy project: A strategy for responding to the needs of high-risk mothers and their children. *Prevention in Human Services, 7,* 59–87.

Olds, D. L., Henderson, C. R., & Tatelbaum, R. (1994). Intellectual impairment in children of women who smoke cigarettes during pregnancy. *Pediatrics, 93,* 221–227.

Olds, D. L., Henderson, C. R., Kitzman H., & Cole R. (1995). Effects of prenatal and infancy nurse home visitation on surveillance of child maltreatment. *Pediatrics, 95,* 365–372.

Olds, D. L., Henderson, C. R., Phelps, C., Kitzman, H., & Hanks C. (1993). Effect of prenatal and infancy nurse home visitation on government spending. *Medical Care, 31,* 155–174.

Olin, J. T. & Zelinski, E. M. (1991). The 12-month reliability of the Mini-Mental State Examination. *Psychological Assessment, 3,* 427–432.

O'Neill, P. (1998). *Negotiating consent in psychotherapy.* New York: New York University Press.

Onken, L. S., & Blaine, J. D. (1997). Behavioral therapy development and psychological science: Reinforcing the bond. *Psychological Science, 8,* 143–144.

Orlinsky, D. E., Geller, J. D., Tarragona, M., & Farber, B. (1993). Patients' representations of psychotherapy: A new focus for psychodynamic research. *Journal of Consulting and Clinical Psychology, 61,* 596–610.

Ornish, D., Scherwitz, L. W., Billings, J. H., Gould, K. L., Merritt, T. A., Sparler, S., Armstrong, W. T., Ports, T. A., Kirkeeide, R. L., Hogeboom, C., & Brand, R. J. (1998). Intensive lifestyle changes for reversal of coronary heart disease. *Journal of the American Medical Association, 280,* 2001–2007.

Ouellet, J. V. (1976). On Locke's counter-cartesianism. *American Psychologist, 31,* 93.

Overall, J. E., & Gorham, D. R. (1962). The Brief Psychiatric Rating Scale. *Psychological Reports, 10,* 799–812.

Overholser, J. C., & Fine, M. A. (1990). Defining the boundaries of professional competence: Managing subtle cases of clinical incompetence. *Professional Psychology: Research & Practice, 21,* 462–469.

Overmier, J. B. & Seligman, M. E. (1967). Effects of inescapable shock upon subsequent escape and avoidance responding. *Journal of Comparative and Physiological Psychology, 63,* 28–33.

Ozer, D. J., & Reise, S. P. (1994). Personality assessment. *Annual Review of Psychology, 45,* 357–388.

Paivio, S. C., & Greenberg, L. S. (1995). Resolving "unfinished business": Efficacy of experiential therapy using empty-chair dialogue. *Journal of Consulting and Clinical Psychology, 63,* 419–425.

Paivio, S. C., & Greenberg, L. S. (1998). Experiential theory of emotion applied to anxiety and depression. In W. F. Flack, & J. D. Laird (Eds.), *Emotions in psychopathology: Theory and research. Series in affective science.* (pp. 229–242). New York: Oxford University Press.

Parker, K. C., Hanson, R. K., & Hunsley, J. (1988). MMPI, Rorschach, and WAIS: A meta-analytic comparison of reliability, stability, and validity. *Psychological Bulletin, 103,* 367–373.

Patterson, C. H. (2000). *Understanding psychotherapy: Fifty years of client-centered theory and practice.* Ross-on-Wye, England: PCCS Books.

Patterson, G. R. (1997). Performance models for parenting: A social interactional perspective. In J. E. Grusec, & L. Kuczynski (Eds.), *Parenting and children's internalization of values: A handbook of contemporary theory* (pp. 193–226). New York: John Wiley.

Patterson, G. R., & Chamberlain, P. (1994). A functional analysis of resistance during parent training therapy. *Clinical Psychology: Science and Practice, 1,* 53–70.

Paul, G. (1967). Strategy of outcome research in psychotherapy. *Journal of Consulting and Clinical Psychology, 31,* 109–118.

Paul, G. L., Redfield, J. P., & Lentz, R. J. (1976). The Inpatient Scale of Minimal Functioning: A revision of the Social Breakdown Syndrome Gradient Index. *Journal of Consulting and Clinical Psychology, 44,* 1021–1022.

Pedersen, P. B., & Ivey, A. E. (1993). *Culture-centered counseling and interviewing skills: A practical guide.* Westport, CT: Praeger Publishers/Greenwood Publishing.

Pedro-Carroll, J. L., & Cowen, E. L. (1985). The children of divorce intervention program: An investigation of the efficacy of a school-based prevention program. *Journal of Consulting and Clinical Psychology, 53,* 603–611.

Pennebaker, J. W. (1997). *Opening up: The healing power of expressing emotions* (rev. ed.). New York: The Guilford Press.

Pennebaker, J. W. (1997). Writing about emotional experiences as a therapeutic process. *Psychological Science, 8,* 152–166.

Perlin, M. L. (1994). Law and the delivery of mental health services in the community. *American Journal of Orthopsychiatry, 64,* 194–208.

Perls , F. S. (1947). *Ego, hunger, and aggression.* London: Allen and Unwin.

Perls, F. (1969*). Gestalt therapy verbatim.* Lafayette, CA: Real People Press.

Perls, F. S. (1973). *The Gestalt approach and eyewitness to therapy.* Palo Alto, CA: Science and Behavior Books.

Perry, C. L., Story, M., & Lytle, L. A. (1997). Promoting healthy dietary behaviors. In R. P. Weissberg, T. P. Gullotta, R. L. Hampton, B. A. Ryan, & G. R. Adams (Eds.), *Healthy children 2010: Enhancing children's wellness* (pp. 214–249). Thousand Oaks, CA: Sage.

Persons, J. B., & Fresco, D. M. (1998). Assessment of depression. In A. S. Bellack & M. Hersen (Eds.), *Behavioral assessment: A practical handbook* (4th ed., pp. 210–231). Boston: Allyn & Bacon.

Petersen, A. C., Compas, B. E., Brooks-Gunn, J., Stemmler, M., Ey, S., & Grant, K. E. (1993). Depression in adolescence. *American Psychologist, 48,* 155–168.

Peterson, D. R. (1968). The doctor of psychology program at the University of Illinois. *American Psychologist, 23,* 511–516.

Peterson, D. R. (1995). The reflective educator. *American Psychologist, 50,* 975–983.

Peterson, L., & Sobell, L. C. (1994). Introduction to the state-of-the-art review series: Research contributions to clinical assessment. *Behavior Therapy, 25,* 523–531.

Piacentini, J., Roper, M., Jensen, P., Lucas, C., Fisher, P., Bird, H., Bourdon, K., Schwab-Stone, M., Rubio-Stipec, M., Davies, M., & Dulcan, M. (1999). Informant-based determinants of symptom attenuation in structured child psychiatric interviews. *Journal of Abnormal Child Psychology, 27,* 417–428.

Piaget, J. (1954). *The construction of reality in the child.* NY: Basic Books.

Pinkerman, J. E., Haynes, J. P., & Keiser, T. (1993). Characteristics of psychological practice in juvenile court clinics. *American Journal of Forensic Psychology, 11,* 3–12.

Piotrowski, C., & Belter, R. W. (1999). Internship training in psychological assessment: Has managed care had an impact? *Assessment, 6,* 381–385.

Piotrowski, C., & Zalewski, C. (1993). Training in psychodiagnostic testing in APA-approved PsyD and PhD clinical training programs. *Journal of Personality Assessment, 61,* 394–405.

Piper, W. E., Joyce, A. S., McCallum, M., & Azim, H. F. (1993). Concentration and correspondence of transference interpretations in short-term psychotherapy. *Journal of Consulting and Clinical Psychology, 61,* 586–595.

Plomin, R. (1990). *Nature and nurture: An introduction to human behavioral genetics.* Pacific Groove, CA: Brooks/Cole.

Plomin, R. (1991). Genetic risk and psychosocial disorders: Links between the normal and abnormal. In M. Rutter & P. Casaer (Eds.),

Biological risk factors for psychosocial disorders (pp. 101–138). New York: Cambridge University Press.

Plomin, R. (1997). Genetics and intelligence: What's new? *Intelligence, 24,* 53–77.

Plomin, R., & Crabbe, J. (2000). DNA. *Psychological Bulletin, 126,* 806–828.

Plomin, R., DeFries, J. C., McClearn, G. E., & Rutter, M. (1997). *Behavioral genetics* (3rd ed.). New York: W. H. Freeman.

Plomin, R., & Rutter, M. (1998). Child development, molecular genetics, and what to do with genes once they are found. *Child Development, 69,* 1223–1242.

Pope, K. S., Borys, D. S., Gutheil, T. G., Gabbard, G. O., Bersoff, D. N., Strasburger, L. H., Jorgenson, L., Randles, R., & Blevins-Knabe, B. (1995). Multiple relationships. In D. N. Bersoff, (Ed.), *Ethical conflicts in psychology* (pp. 207–248). Washington, DC: American Psychological Association.

Pope, K. S., Sonne, J. L., & Holroyd, J. (1993). *Sexual feelings in psychotherapy: Explorations for therapists and therapists-in-training.* Washington, DC: American Psychological Association.

Pope, K. S., & Vasquez, M. J. T. (1998). *Ethics in psychotherapy and counseling: A practical guide* (2nd ed.). San Francisco: Jossey-Bass.

Porter, S. C., Fein, J. A., & Ginsburg, K. R. (1997). Depression screening in adolescents with somatic complaints presenting to the emergency department. *Annals of Emergency Medicine, 29,* 141–145.

Power, K. G., Simpson, R. J., Swanson, V., & Wallace, L. A. (1990). A controlled comparison of cognitive-behaviour therapy, diazepam, and placebo, alone and in combination, for the treatment of generalised anxiety disorder. *Journal of Anxiety Disorders, 4,* 267–292.

Price, R. H., Cowen, E. L., Lorion, R. P., & Ramos-McKay, J. (1988). *Fourteen ounces of prevention: A casebook for practitioners.* Washington, DC: American Psychological Association.

Price, R. H., Johnson, S. B. (1999). Cognitive behavioral approaches to the prevention of depression, anxiety and health problems: New results and future prospects. *Prevention & Treatment, 2,* n.p.

Prochaska, J. O. (1994). Strong and weak principles for progressing from precontemplation to action

on the basis of twelve problem behaviors. *Health Psychology, 13,* 47–51.

Prout, S. M., & Prout, H. T. (1998). A meta-analysis of school-based studies of counseling and psychotherapy: An update. *Journal of School Psychology, 36,* 121–123.

Puig-Antich, J., Perel, J. M., Laputkin, W., Chambers, W. J., Shea, C., Tabrizi, M. A., & Stiller, R. L. (1979). Plasma levels of imipramine (IMI) and desmethylimipramine (DSI) and clinical response in major depressive disorders: A preliminary report. *Journal of the American Academy of Child and Adolescent Psychiatry, 18,* 616–627.

Puig-Antich, J., Perel, J. M., Lupatkin, W., & Chambers, W. J. (1987). Imipramine in prepubertal major depressive disorders. *Archives of General Psychiatry, 44,* 81–89.

Quay, H. C. (1983). A dimensional approach to behavior disorder: The Revised Behavior Problem Checklist. *School Psychology Review, 12,* 244–249.

Rachman, S. (1990). The determinants and treatment of simple phobias. *Advances in Behaviour Research and Therapy, 12,* 1–30.

Rachman, S., & Hodgson, R. (1997). The treatment of chronic obsessive-compulsive neurosis. In D. J. Stein & M. H. Stone (Eds.), *Essential papers on obsessive-compulsive disorder* (pp. 203–217). New York: New York University Press.

Raichle, M. (1994a). Images of the human mind. *Neuropsychopharmacology, 10*(3, Suppl. Pt. 1), 28S–33S.

Raichle, M. (1994b). Images of the mind: Studies with modern imaging techniques. *Annual Review of Psychology, 45,* 333–356.

Raichle, M. E. (1997). Functional brain imaging and verbal behavior. J. W. Donahoe & V. P. Dorsel (Eds.). *Neural-network models of cognition: Biobehavioral foundations. Advances in psychology, Vol. 121.* (pp. 438–454). Amsterdam, Netherlands: North-Holland/Elsevier Science Publishers.

Raimy, V. C. (Ed.). (1950). *Training in clinical psychology.* New York: Prentice-Hall.

Rajigah, L. S. (1996). Treatment of choice for nocturnal enuresis: Review and recommendations. *Journal of Psychological Practice, 2,* 33–42.

Rank, O. (1936). *Truth and reality. A life history of the human will.* NY: Knopf.

Rank, O. (1936). *Will therapy; and, Truth and reality.* NY: Knopf.

Rappaport, J., & Seidman, E. (Eds.). (2000). *Handbook of community psychology,* New York, NY: Kluwer Academic/Plenum Publishers.

Rayfield, A., Eyberg, S. M., & Foote, R. (1998). Revision of the Sutter-Eyberg Student Behavior Inventory: Teacher ratings of conduct problem behavior. *Educational and Psychological Measurement, 58,* 88–98.

Regan-Smith, M. G. (1998). Teachers' experiential learning about learning. *International Journal of Psychiatry in Medicine, 28,* 11–20.

Reiman, E. M., Lane, R. D., Van Patten, C., & Bandettini, P. A. (2000). Positron emission tomography and functional magnetic resonance imaging. In J. T. Cacioppo & L. G. Tassinary (Eds.), *Handbook of psychophysiology* (2nd ed.) (pp. 85–118). NY: Cambridge University Press.

Reinecke, M. A., Ryan, N. E., & DuBois, D. L. (1998). Cognitive-behavioral therapy of depression and depressive symptoms during adolescence: A review and meta-analysis. *Journal of the American Academy of Child and Adolescent Psychiatry, 37,* 26–34.

Reisman, J. R. (1976). *A history of clinical psychology.* New York: Irvington.

Reiss, S., Peterson, R. A., Gursky, D. M., & McNally, R. J. (1986). Anxiety sensitivity, anxiety frequency and the predictions of fearfulness. *Behaviour Research and Therapy, 24,* 1–8.

Reitan, R. M., & Wolfson, D. (1992). Conventional intelligence measurements and neuropsychological concepts of adaptive abilities. *Journal of Clinical Psychology, 48,* 521–529.

Reitan, R. M., & Wolfson, D. (1996). Theoretical, methodological, and validational bases of the Halstead-Reitan Neuropsychological Test Battery. In I. Grant & K. M. Adams (Eds.), *Neuropsychological assessment of neuropsychiatric disorders* (2nd ed., pp. 3–42). New York, NY: Oxford University Press.

Reithmiller, R. J., & Handler, L. (1997). Problematic methods and unwarranted conclusions in DAP research: Suggestions for improved research procedures. *Journal of Personality Assessment, 69,* 459–475.

Rescorla, R. A. (1988). Pavlovian conditioning: It's not what you think it is. *American Psychologist, 43,* 151–160.

Rescorla, R. A. (2001). Experimental extinction. In R. R. Mowrer & S. B. Klein (Eds.), *Handbook of contemporary learning theories* (pp. 119–154). Mahwah, NJ: Lawrence Erlbaum.

Resnick, H., Acierno, R., Holmes, M., Kilpatrick, D. G., & Jager, N. (1999). Prevention of post-rape psychopathology: Preliminary findings of a controlled acute rape treatment study. *Journal of Anxiety Disorders, 13,* 359–370.

Resnick, H. S., Kilpatrick, D. G., Dansky, B. S., & Saunders, B. E. (1993). Prevalence of civilian trauma and posttraumatic stress disorder in a representative national sample of women. *Journal of Consulting and Clinical Psychology, 61,* 984–991.

Rey, J., & Morris-Yates, A. (1991). Adolescent depression and the Child Behavior Checklist. *Journal of the American Academy of Child and Adolescent Psychiatry, 30,* 423.

Reynolds, C. F., III., Frank, E., Perel, J. M., Imber, S. D., Cornes, C., Miller, M. D., Mazumdar, P. R., Houck, P. R., Dew, M. A., Stack, J. A., Pollock, B. G., & Kupfer, D. J. (1999). Nortriptyline and interpersonal psychotherapy as maintenance therapies for recurrent major depression: A randomized controlled trial in patients older than fifty-nine years. *Journal of the American Medical Association, 281,* 39–45.

Ricca, V., Mannucci, E., Zucchi, T., Rotella, C. M., & Faravelli, C. (2000). Cognitive-behavioural therapy for bulimia nervosa and binge eating disorder: A review. *Psychotherapy and Psychosomatics, 69,* 287–295.

Richards, J. M., & Gross, J. J. (1999). Composure at any cost? The cognitive consequences of emotion suppression. *Personality and Social Psychology Bulletin, 25,* 1033–1044.

Richards, J. M., & Gross, J. J. (2000). Emotion regulation and memory: The cognitive costs of keeping one's cool. *Journal of Personality and Social Psychology, 79,* 410–424.

Rielly, N. E., Cunningham, C. E., Richards, J. E., Elbard, H., & Mahoney, W. J. (1999). Detecting attention deficit hyperactivity disorder in a communications clinic: Diagnostic utility of the Gordon Diagnostic System. *Journal of Clinical and Experimental Neuropsychology, 21,* 685–700.

Roberts, J., Gotlib, I. H., & Kassel, J. (1996). Adult attachment security and symptoms of depression: The mediating roles of dysfunctional attitudes and low self-esteem. *Journal of Personality and Social Psychology, 70,* 310–320.

Robins, L. N., Helzer, J. E., Croughan, J. L., & Ratcliff, K. S. (1981). National Institute of Mental Health Diagnostic Interview Schedule: Its history, characteristics, and validity. *Archives of General Psychiatry, 38,* 381–389.

Robinson, L. A., Berman, J. S., & Niemeyer, R. A. (1990). Psychotherapy for the treatment of depression: A comprehensive review of controlled outcome research. *Psychological Bulletin, 108,* 30–49.

Rogers, C. R. (1940). The processes of therapy. *Journal of Consulting Psychology, 4,* 161–164.

Rogers, C. R. (1942). *Counseling and psychotherapy.* Boston: Houghton Mifflin.

Rogers, C. R. (1949a). The attitude and orientation of the counselor in client-centered therapy. *Journal of Consulting Psychology, 13,* 82–94.

Rogers, C. R. (1949b). A coordinated research in psychotherapy; a nonobjective introduction. *Journal of Consulting Psychology, 13,* 149–153.

Rogers, C. R. (1951). *Client-centered therapy: Its current practice, implications, and theory.* Boston: Houghton Mifflin.

Rogers, C. R. (1952). "Client-centered" psychotherapy. *Scientific American, 187,* 66–74.

Rogers, C. R. (1954). *Psychotherapy and personality change.* Chicago: University of Chicago Press.

Rogers, C. R. (1957). The necessary and sufficient conditions of therapeutic personality change. *Journal of Consulting Psychology, 21,* 95–103.

Rogers, C. R. (1961). The place of the person in the new world of the behavioral sciences. *Personnel and Guidance Journal, 39,* 442–451.

Rogers, C. R. (1961). The process equation of psychotherapy. *American Journal of Psychotherapy, 15,* 27–45.

Rorschach, H. (1921). *Psychodiagnostik.* Bern, Switzerland: Huber.

Rorty, M., Yager, J., Buckwalter, J. G., & Rossotto, E. (1999). Social support, social adjustment, and recovery status in bulimia nervosa. *International Journal of Eating Disorders, 26,* 1–12.

Rosen, J. C., & Reiter, J. (1996). Development of the Body Dysmorphic Disorder Examination. *Behaviour Research and Therapy, 34,* 755–766.

Rosen, J. C., Orosan, P., & Reiter, J. (1995). Cognitive behavior therapy for negative body image in obese women. *Behavior Therapy, 26,* 25–42.

Rosenfeld, J. P., Baehr, R., Gotlib, I. H., & Rangauath, C. (1996). Preliminary evidence that daily changes in frontal asymmetry correlate with changes in affect in therapy sessions. *International Journal of Psychophysiology, 23,* 137–141.

Rosenfeld, J. P., Cha, G., Blair, T., & Gotlib, I. H. (1995). Operant (biofeedback) control of left-right frontal alpha power differences: Potential neurotherapy for affective disorders. *Biofeedback and Self Regulation, 20,* 241–258.

Rosenthal, R. (1991). *Meta-analytic procedures for social research, revised edition.* Newbury Park, CA: Sage.

Rosenthal, T. L., & Steffek, B. D. (1991). Modeling methods. In F. H. Kanfer & A. P. Goldstein, (Eds.), *Helping people change: A textbook of methods* (4th ed., pp. 70–121). New York: Pergamon Press.

Ross, M. W., & Kelly, J. A. (2000). Interventions to reduce HIV transmission in homosexual men. In J. L. Peterson, & R. J. DiClemente, (Eds.), *Handbook of HIV prevention, AIDS prevention, and mental health* (pp. 201–216). New York: Kluwer Academic/Plenum Publishers.

Rothbaum, B. O., Foa, E. B., Riggs, D. S., & Murdock, T., (1992). A prospective examination of posttraumatic stress disorder in rape victims. *Journal of Traumatic Stress, 5,* 455–475.

Rottenberg, J., Gross, J. J., Wilhelm, F. H., Najmi, S., & Gotlib, I. H. (2001). *The crying response in depression.* Unpublished manuscript, Stanford University.

Rotter, J. B. (1954). *Social learning and clinical psychology.* New York, NY: Prentice-Hall.

Routh, D. K. (1994). *Clinical psychology since 1917: Science, practice, and organization.* New York: Plenum.

Rubio-Stipec, M., Shrout, P. E., Bird, H., & Canino, G. (1989). Symptom scales of the Diagnostic Interview Schedule: Factor results in Hispanic and Anglo samples. *Psychological Assessment, 1,* 30–34.

Rueter, M. A., & Conger, R. D. (1998). Reciprocal influences between parenting and adolescent problem-solving behavior. *Developmental Psychology, 34,* 1470–1482.

Rush, A. J., Beck, A. T., Kovacs, M., & Hollon, S. (1977). Comparative efficacy of cognitive therapy and pharmacotherapy in the treatment of depressed outpatients. *Cognitive Therapy and Research, 1,* 17–37.

Russell, M. A., Armstrong, E., & Patel, U. A. (1976). Temporal contiguity in electric aversion therapy for cigarette smoking. *Behaviour Research and Therapy, 14,* 103–123.

Rutter, M., Silberg, J., O'Connor, T., & Siminoff, E. (1999). Genetics and child psychiatry: II. Empirical research findings. *Journal of Child Psychology & Psychiatry & Allied Disciplines, 40,* 19–55.

Ryan, R. M. (1985). Thematic Apperception Test. In D. J. Keyser & R. C. Swetland (Eds.), *Test critiques* (Vol. 2, pp. 799–814). Kansas City, MO: Test Corporation of America.

Ryan, R. M., Avery, R. R., & Grolnick, W. S. (1985). A Rorschach assessment of children's mutuality of autonomy. *Journal of Personality Assessment, 49,* 6–12.

Ryan, R. M., & Deci, E. L. (2000). Self-determination theory and the facilitation of intrinsic motivation, social development, and well-being. *American Psychologist, 55,* 68–78.

Safran, J. D., & Greenberg, L. S. (1987). Affect and the unconscious: A cognitive perspective. In R. Stern (Ed.), *Theories of the unconscious and theories of the self* (pp. 191–212). Hillsdale, NJ: Analytic Press.

Salkovskis, P. M., & Kirk, J. (1989). Obsessional disorders. In K. Hawton, P. M. Salkovskis, J. Kirk, & D. M. Clark, (Eds.), *Cognitive behaviour therapy for psychiatric problems: A practical guide* (pp. 129–168). Oxford, England: Oxford University Press.

Sallis, J. F., Patrick, K., Frank, E., Pratt, M., Wechsler, H., & Galuska, D. A. (2000). Interventions in health care settings to promote healthful eating and physical activity in children and adolescents. *Preventive Medicine: An International Journal Devoted to Practice & Theory, 31,* 112–120.

Salmon, P. G., Santorelli, S. F., & Kabat-Zinn, J. (1998). Intervention elements promoting adherence to mindfulness-based stress reduction programs in the clinical behavioral medicine setting. In S. A. Shumaker & E. B. Schron (Eds.), *The handbook of health behavior change* (2nd ed., pp. 239–266). New York: Springer Publishing.

Salovey, P., Hsee, C. K., & Mayer, J. D. (1993). Emotional intelligence and the self-regulation of affect. In D. M. Wegner & J. W. Pennebaker (Eds.), *Handbook of mental control* (pp. 258–277). Englewood Cliffs, NJ: Prentice-Hall.

Salovey, P., & Sluyter, D. J. (1997). *Emotional development and emotional intelligence: Educational implications.* New York: Basic Books.

Salter, A. (1949). *Conditioned reflex therapy: The direct approach to the reconstruction of personality.* New York: Creative Age Press.

Sammons, M. T., & Brown, A. B. (1997). The Department of Defense Psychopharmacology Demonstration Project: An evolving program for postdoctoral education in psychology. *Professional Psychology: Research and Practice, 28,* 107–112.

Sammons, M. T., Gorny, S. W., Zinner, E. S., & Allen, R. P. (2000). Prescriptive authority for psychologists: A consensus of support. *Professional Psychology: Research and Practice, 31,* 604–609.

Sanders, C. E., Field, T. M., Diego, M., & Kaplan, M. (2000). The relationship of Internet use to depression and social isolation among adolescents. *Adolescence, 35,* 237–242.

Sanderson, W. C., & Rego, S. A. (2000). Empirically supported treatment for panic disorder: Research, theory, and application of cognitive behavioral therapy. *Journal of Cognitive Psychotherapy, 14,* 219–244.

Sandler, I. N. (1999). Progress in developing strategies and theory for the prevention of depression and anxiety. *Prevention and Treatment, 2,* n.p.

Sandler, I. N., Tein, J., Mehta, P., Wolchik, S. A., & Ayers, T. (2000). Coping efficacy and psychological problems of children of divorce. *Child Development, 71,* 1099–1118.

Sapolosky, R. M. (1998). *Why zebras don't get ulcers: An updated guide to stress, stress-related diseases, and coping.* New York: W. H. Freeman.

Sarafino, E. P., & Goehring, P. (2000). Age comparisons in acquiring biofeedback control and success in reducing headache pain. *Annals of Behavioral Medicine, 22,* 10–16.

Sarwer, D. B., & Sayers, S. L. (1998). Behavioral interviewing. In A. S. Bellack & M. Hersen (Eds.), *Behavioral assessment: A practical handbook* (4th ed., pp. 63–78). Boston: Allyn & Bacon.

Sattler, J. (1988). *Assessment of children* (3rd ed.). San Diego, CA: Author.

Sattler, J. (1992a). *Assessment of children: WISC-III and WPPSI-R supplement.* San Diego, CA: Jerome M. Sattler.

Sattler, J. (1992b). Assessment of children's intelligence. In C. Walker, & M. Roberts, (Eds.), *Handbook of clinical child psychology* (2nd ed., pp. 85–100). New York: John Wiley.

Saxon, A. J., Calsyn, D. A., Kivlahan, D. R., & Roszzell, D. K. (1993). Using drugs to facilitate sexual behavior is associated with sexual variety among injection drug users. *Journal of Nervous and Mental Disease, 181,* 626–631.

Sayette, M. A., Mayne, T. J., & Norcross, J. C. (1998). *Insider's guide to graduate programs in clinical and counseling psychology. 1998/99 edition.* New York: Guilford.

Scheier, M. F., & Carver, C. S. (1985). Optimism, coping, and health: Assessment and implications of generalized outcome expectancies. *Health Psychology, 4,* 219–247.

Scheier, M. F., Carver, C. S., & Bridges, M. W. (1994). Distinguishing optimism from neuroticism (and trait anxiety, self-mastery, and self-esteem): A reevaluation of the Life Orientation Test. *Journal of Personality and Social Psychology, 67,* 1063–1078.

Scheier, M. F., Matthews, K. A., Owens, J. F., Magovern, G. J., Lefebvre, R. C., Abbott, R. A., & Carver, C. S. (1989). Dispositional optimism and recovery from coronary artery bypass surgery: The beneficial effects on physical and psychological well-being. *Journal of Personality and Social Psychology, 57,* 1024–1040.

Schmidt, N. B., & Woolaway-Bickel, K. (2000). The effects of treatment compliance on outcome in cognitive-behavioral therapy for panic disorder: Quality versus quantity. *Journal of Consulting and Clinical Psychology, 68,* 13–18.

Schmidt, N. B., Lerew, D. R., & Jackson, R. J. (1999). Prospective evaluation of anxiety sensitivity in the pathogenesis of panic: Replication and extension. *Journal of Abnormal Psychology, 108,* 532–537.

Schmidt, N. B., Woolaway-Bickel, K., Trakowski, J., Santiago, H., Storey, J., Koselka, M., & Cook, J. (2000). Dismantling cognitive-behavioral treatment for panic disorder: Questioning the

utility of breathing retraining. *Journal of Consulting and Clinical Psychology, 68,* 417–424.

Schneider, K. J., & May, R. (1995). *The psychology of existence: An integrative, clinical perspective.* New York: McGraw-Hill.

Schraedley, P. K., Gotlib, I. H., & Hayward, C. (1999). Gender differences in correlates of depressive symptoms in adolescents. *Journal of Adolescent Health, 25,* 98–108.

Schuckit, M. C. (2000). Genetics of the risk for alcoholism. *American Journal on Addictions, 9,* 103–112.

Schultz, D. P., & Schultz, S. E. (1987). *A history of modern psychology* (4th ed.). San Diego, CA: Harcourt, Brace, Jovanovich.

Schwab-Stone, M., Fallon, T., Briggs, M., & Crowther, B. (1994). Reliability of diagnostic reporting for children aged 6–11 years: A test-retest study of the Diagnostic Interview Schedule for Children–Revised. *American Journal of Psychiatry, 151,* 1048–1054.

Schwab-Stone, M., Shaffer, D., Dulcan, M., Jensen, P., Fisher, P., Bird, H., Goodman, S., Lahey, B., Lichtman, J., Canino, G., Rubio-Stipec, M., & Rae, D. S. (1996). Criterion validity of the NIMH Diagnostic Interview Schedule for Children Version 2.3 (DISC 2.3). *Journal of the American Academy of Child and Adolescent Psychiatry, 35,* 878–888.

Schwartz, J. M., Stoessel, P. W., Baxter, L. R., Martin, K. M., & Phelps, M. E. (1996). Systematic changes in cerebral glucose metabolic rate after successful behavior modification treatment of obsessive-compulsive disorder. *Archives of General Psychiatry, 53,* 109–113.

Scott, L., & O'Hara, M. W. (1993). Self-discrepancies in clinically anxious and depressed university students. *Journal of Abnormal Psychology, 102,* 282–287.

Sechrest, L., McKnight, P., & McKnight, K. (1996). Calibration of measures for psychotherapy outcome studies. *American Psychologist, 51,* 1065–1071.

Segal, Z., Hersen, M., & Van Hasselt, V. B. (1994). Reliability of the Structured Clinical Interview for *DSM-III-R:* An evaluative review. *Comprehensive Psychiatry, 35,* 316–327.

Segrin, C., & Flora, J. (2000). Poor social skills are a vulnerability factor in the development of psychosocial problems. *Human Communication Research, 26,* 489–514.

Seligman, M. E. P. (1971). Phobias and preparedness. *Behavior Therapy, 2,* 307–320.

Seligman, M. E. P. (1975). *Helplessness: On depression, development, and death.* San Francisco: W. H. Freeman.

Seligman, M. E. P. (1994). *What you can change and what you can't: The complete guide to successful self-improvement.* New York: Knopf.

Seligman, M. E. P. (1995). The effectiveness of psychotherapy: The Consumer Reports study. *American Psychologist, 50,* 965–974.

Seligman, M. E. P. (1996). Science as an ally of practice. *American Psychologist, 51,* 1072–1079.

Seligman, M. E. P., & Csikszentmihalyi, M. (2000). Positive psychology: An introduction. *American Psychologist, 55,* 5–14.

Seligman, M. E. P., & Maier, S. F. (1967). Failure to escape traumatic shock. *Journal of Experimental Psychology, 74,* 1–9.

Seligman, M. E. P., Maier, S. F., & Greer, J. H. (1968). Alleviation of learned helplessness in the dog. *Journal of Abnormal Psychology, 73,* 256–262.

Seligman, M. E. P., Schulman, P., DeRubeis, R. J., & Hollon, S. D. (1999). The prevention of depression and anxiety. *Prevention and Treatment, 2,* n.p.

Shadish, W. R., Navarro, A. M., Matt, G. E., & Phillips, G. (2000). The effects of psychological therapies under clinically representative conditions: A meta-analysis. *Psychological Bulletin, 126,* 512–529.

Shaffer, D., Fisher, P., Dulcan, M., Davies, M., Piacentini, J., Schwab-Stone, M., Lahey, B., Bourdon, K., Jensen, P., Bird, H., Canino, G., & Regier, D. (1996). The NIMH Diagnostic Interview Schedule for Children (DISC-2): Description, acceptability, prevalences, and performance in the MECA study. *Journal of the American Academy of Child and Adolescent Psychiatry, 35,* 865–877.

Shaffer, D., Fisher, P., Lucas, C. P., Dulcan, M. K., & Schwab-Stone, M. E. (2000). NIMH Diagnostic Interview Schedule for Children Version IV (NIMH DISC-IV): Description, differences from previous versions, and reliability of some common diagnoses. *Journal of the American Academy of Child and Adolescent Psychiatry, 39,* 28–38.

Shakow, D. (1948). Clinical training facilities, 1948: Report of the Committee on Training in Clinical Psychology. *American Psychologist, 3,* 317–318.

Shapiro, A. K., & Morris, L. A. (1978). The placebo effect in medical and psychological therapies. In S. L. Garfield & A. E. Bergin (Eds.), *Handbook of psychotherapy and behavior change: An empirical analysis* (pp. 369–410). New York: Wiley.

Shapiro, D. A., Barkham, M., Rees, A., & Hardy, G. E. (1994). Effects of treatment duration and severity of depression on the effectiveness of cognitive-behavioral and psychodynamic-interpersonal psychotherapy. *Journal of Consulting and Clinical Psychology, 62,* 522–534.

Shapiro, D. A., Rees, A., Barkham, M., Hardy, G., Reynolds, S., Startup, M. (1995). Effects of treatment duration and severity of depression on the maintenance of gains after cognitive-behavioral and psychodynamic-interpersonal psychotherapy. *Journal of Consulting and Clinical Psychology, 63,* 378–387.

Shapiro, D. A., & Shapiro, D. (1982). Meta-analysis of comparative therapy outcome research: A critical appraisal. *Behavioural Psychotherapy, 10,* 4–25.

Shapiro, F. (1995). *Eye movement desensitization and reprocessing.* New York: Guilford Press.

Shapiro, J. P., Leifer, M., Martone, M. W., & Kassem, L. (1990). Multimethod assessment of depression in sexually abused girls. *Journal of Personality Assessment, 55,* 234–248.

Shea, M. T., Elkin, I., & Sotsky, S. M. (1999). Patient characteristics associated with successful treatment: Outcome findings from the NIMH Treatment of Depression Collaborative Research Program. In D. S. Janowsky (Ed.), *Psychotherapy indications and outcomes* (pp. 71–90). Washington, DC: American Psychiatric Press.

Shea, M. T., Widiger, T. A., & Klein, M. H. (1992). Comorbidity of personality disorders and depression: Implications for treatment. *Journal of Consulting and Clinical Psychology, 60,* 857–868.

Shelton, R. C., Hollon, S. D., Purdon, S. E., & Loosen, P. T. (1991). Biological and psychological aspects of depression. *Behavior Therapy, 22,* 201–228.

Short, J. L., Roosa, M. W., Sandler, I. N., & Ayers, T. S. (1995). Evaluation of a preventive intervention for a self-selected subpopulation of children. *American Journal of Community Psychology, 23,* 223–247.

Siever, L. J., & Davis, K. L. (1985). Overview: Toward a dysregulation hypothesis of depression. *American Journal of Psychiatry, 142,* 1017–1031.

Sifneos, P. E. (1972). *Short-term psychotherapy and emotional crisis.* Cambridge, MA: Harvard University Press.

Sifneos, P. E. (1987). *Short-term dynamic psychotherapy: Evaluation and technique.* New York: Plenum Press.

Silverman, D. K. (1996). Arithmetic of a one- and two-person psychology: Merton M. Gill, an essay. *Psychoanalytic Psychology, 13,* 267–274.

Silverman, W. K., & Serafini, L. T. (1998). Assessment of child behavior problems: Internalizing disorders. In A. S. Bellack & M. Hersen (Eds.), *Behavioral assessment: A practical handbook* (pp. 342–360). Elmsford, NY: Pergamon Press.

Sivers, H., Canli, T., Thomason, M. E., Benson, E., Gabrieli, J. D. E., Bower, G. H., & Gotlib, I. H. (March, 2001). *Neural response to performance feedback in depressed and psychologically healthy adults.* Paper presented at the Conference of the Cognitive Neuroscience Society, New York.

Skinner, B. F. (1953). *Science and human behavior.* New York: Macmillan.

Skodol, A. E., Rosnick, L., Kellman, D., Oldham, J. M., & et al. (1988). Validating structured DSM-III-R personality disorder assessments with longitudinal data. *American Journal of Psychiatry, 145,* 1297–1299.

Sloan, D. M., & Mizes, J. S. (1999). Foundations of behavior therapy in the contemporary healthcare context. *Clinical Psychology Review, 19,* 255–274.

Sloan, R. B., Staples, F. R., Cristol, A. H., Yorkston, N., J., & Whipple, K. (1975). *Psychotherapy versus behavior therapy.* Cambridge, MA: Harvard University Press.

Sloane, R. B., Staples, F. R., & Schneider, L. S. (1985). Interpersonal therapy versus nortriptyline for depression in the elderly. In G. D. Burrows, T. R. Norman, & L. Dennerstein (Eds.), *Clinical and pharmacological studies in psychiatric disorders* (pp. 344–346). London: John Libbey.

Smith, M. L., & Glass, G. V. (1977). Meta-analysis of psychotherapy outcome studies. *American Psychologist, 32,* 752–760.

Smith, M. L., Glass, G. V., & Miller, T. I. (1980). *The benefits of psychotherapy.* Baltimore: Johns Hopkins University Press.

Smith-Bell, M., & Winslade, W. J. (1994). Privacy, confidentiality, and privilege in psychotherapeutic relationships. *American Journal of Orthopsychiatry, 64,* 180–193.

Snyder, C. R., McDermott, D. S., Leibowitz, R. Q., & Cheavens, J. (2000). The roles of female clinical psychologists in changing the field of psychotherapy. In C. R. Snyder & R. E. Ingram (Eds.), *Handbook of psychological change: Psychotherapy processes and practices for the twenty-first century* (pp. 640–659). New York: John Wiley.

Snyder, D. K., & Wills, R. M. (1989). Behavioral versus insight-oriented marital therapy: Effects on individual and interspousal functioning. *Journal of Consulting and Clinical Psychology, 57,* 39–46.

Snyderman, M., & Rothman, S. (1987). Survey of expert opinion on intelligence and aptitude testing. *American Psychologist, 42,* 137–144.

Sotsky, S. M., Glass, D. R., Shea, M. T., & Pilkonis, P. A. (1991). Patient predictors of response to psychotherapy and pharmacotherapy: Findings in the NIMH Treatment of Depression Collaborative Research Program. *American Journal of Psychiatry, 48,* 997–1008.

Spearman, C. (1927a). *The abilities of man.* New York: Macmillan.

Spearman, C. (1927b). Material versus abstract factors in correlation. *British Journal of Psychology, 17,* 322–326.

Spence, S. H., & Donovan, C. (1998). Interpersonal problems. In P. J. Graham (Ed.), *Cognitive-behaviour therapy for children and families* (pp. 217–245). New York: Cambridge University Press.

Sperry, R. (1961). Cerebral organization and behavior. *Science, 133,* 1749–1757.

Spiegel, D. (1991). Effects of group support for metastatic breast cancer patients on coping, mood, pain, and survival. In J. ten Have-de Labije & H. Balner (Eds.), *Coping with cancer and beyond: Cancer treatment & mental health* (pp. 11–29). Amsterdam, Netherlands: Swets & Zeitlinger.

Spiegel, D., Bloom, J. R., Kraemer, H. C., & Gottheil E. (1989). Effect of psychosocial treatment on survival of patients with metastatic breast cancer. *Lancet, 2(8668),* 888–891.

Spiegel, D., & Classen, C. (2000). *Group therapy for cancer patients: A research-based handbook of psychosocial care.* New York: Basic Books.

Spiegel, D., Morrow, G. R., Classen, C., Raubertas, R., Stott, P., Mudaliar, M., Pierce, H. I., Flynn, P. J., Heard, L., & Riggs, G. (1999). Group psychotherapy for recently diagnosed breast cancer patients: A multicenter feasibility study. *Psycho-Oncology, 8,* 482–493.

Spiegler, M. D. (1998). *Contemporary behavior therapy* (3rd ed.). Pacific Grove, CA: Brooks/Cole.

Spitzer, R. L., Endicott, J., Robins, E. (1978). Research Diagnostic Criteria: Rationale and Reliability. *Archives of General Psychiatry, 35,* 773–782.

Spitzer, R. L, & Fleiss, J. L. (1974). A re-analysis of the reliability of psychiatric diagnosis. *British Journal of Psychiatry, 125,* 341–347.

Spitzer, R. L., Gibbon, M., Skodol, A. E., Williams, J. B. W., & First, M. B. (1994). *DSM-IV casebook: A learning companion to the Diagnostic and Statistical Manual of Mental Disorders—4th ed.* Washington, DC: American Psychiatric.

Spitzer, R. L., Williams, J. B., Gibbon, M., & First, M. B. (1992). The Structured Clinical Interview for DSM-III-R (SCID): I. History, rationale, and description. *Archives of General Psychiatry, 49,* 624–629.

St. Lawrence, J. S., Brasfield, T. L., Jefferson, K. W., Alleyne, E., & et al. (1995). Cognitive behavioral intervention to reduce African American adolescents' risk for HIV infection. *Journal of Consulting and Clinical Psychology, 63,* 221–237.

Stampfl, T. G., & Levis, D. J. (1967). Essentials of implosive therapy: A learning-theory-based psychodynamic behavioral therapy. *Journal of Abnormal Psychology, 72,* 496–503.

Stanger, C., Achenbach, T., & McConaughy, S. (1993). Three-year course of behavior/emotional problems in a national sample of 4- to 16-year-olds: III. Predictors of signs of disturbance. *Journal of Consulting and Clinical Psychology, 61,* 839–848.

Stark, K. D., Swearer, S., Kurowski, C. A., Sommer, D. H., & Bowen, B. (1996). Targeting the child and the family: A holistic approach to treating

child and adolescent depressive disorders. In E. D. Hibbs & P. S. Jensen (Eds.), *Psychosocial treatments for child and adolescent disorders: Empirically based strategies for clinical practice* (pp. 207–238). Washington, DC: American Psychological Association.

Startup, M., & Shapiro, D. A. (1993). Therapist treatment fidelity in prescriptive vs. exploratory psychotherapy. *British Journal of Clinical Psychology, 32,* 443–456.

Stasiewicz, P. R., Carey, K. B., Bradizza, C. M., & Maisto, S. A. (1996). Behavioral assessment of substance abuse with co-occurring psychiatric disorder. *Cognitive and Behavioral Practice, 3,* 91–105.

Steer, R. A., Clark, D. A., Beck, A. T., & Ranieri, W. F. (1999). Common and specific dimensions of self-reported anxiety and depression: The BDI-II versus the BDI-IA. *Behaviour Research and Therapy, 37,* 183–190.

Steering Committee of the Physicians' Health Study Research Group. (1989). Final report on the aspirin component of the ongoing Physicians' Health Study. *New England Journal of Medicine, 321,* 129–135.

Stein, L. A. R., Graham, J. R., Ben-Porath, Y. S., & McNulty, J. L. (1999). Using the MMPI-2 to detect substance abuse in an outpatient mental health setting. *Psychological Assessment, 11,* 94–100.

Sternberg, R. J. (1984). Toward a triarchic theory of human intelligence. *Behavioral and Brain Sciences, 7,* 269–315.

Sternberg, R. J. (1985). *Beyond IQ: A triarchic theory of human intelligence.* New York: Cambridge University Press.

Sternberg, R. J. (1990). *Metaphors of mind: Conceptions of the nature of intelligence.* New York: Cambridge University Press.

Sternberg, R. J. (1992). Metaphors of mind underlying the testing of intelligence. In J. C. Rosen & P. McReynolds (Eds.), *Advances in psychological assessment* (Vol. 8, pp. 1–39). New York: Plenum Press.

Sternberg, R. J. (1997). The concept of intelligence and its role in lifelong learning and success. *American Psychologist, 52,* 1030–1037.

Sternberg, R. J. (1999). Looking back and looking forward on intelligence: Toward a theory of successful intelligence. In M. Bennett,

Developmental psychology: Achievements and prospects (pp. 289–308). Philadelphia: Psychology Press/Taylor & Francis.

Sternberg, R. J. (2000). Successful intelligence: A unifying view of giftedness. In C. F. M. van Lieshout & P. G. Heymans (Eds.), *Developing talent across the lifespa*n (pp. 43–65). Philadelphia: Psychology Press/Taylor Francis.

Sternberg, R. J., & Kaufman, J. C. (1998). Human abilities. *Annual Review of Psychology, 49*, 479–502.

Stillings, N., Feinstein, M., Garfield, J., Rissland, E., Rosenbaum, D., Weisler, S., & Baker-Wars, L. (1987). *Cognitive science: An introduction.* Cambridge, MA: MIT Press.

Stolberg, A. L., & Mahler, J. (1994). Enhancing treatment gains in a school-based intervention for children of divorce through skill training, parental involvement, and transfer procedures. *Journal of Consulting and Clinical Psychology, 62,* 147–156.

Stone, A. A., Turkkan, J. S., Bachrach, C. A., Jobe, J. B., Kurtzman, H.S., & Cain, V. S. (Eds.). (2000). *The science of self-report: Implications for research and practice.* Mahwah, NJ: Lawrence Erlbaum.

Stoolmiller, M., Eddy, J. M., & Reid, J. B. (2000). Detecting and describing preventive intervention effects in a universal school-based randomized trial targeting delinquent and violent behavior. *Journal of Consulting and Clinical Psychology, 68,* 296–306.

Stoolmiller, M., & Patterson, G. R. (1997). Parental discipline and child antisocial behavior: A contingency-based theory and some methodological refinements. *Psychological Inquiry, 8,* 223–229.

Strauman, T. J. (1989). Self-discrepancies in clinical depression and social phobia: Cognitive structures that underlie emotional disorders? *Journal of Abnormal Psychology, 98,* 14–22.

Strauman, T. J. (1992). Self-guides, autobiographical memory, and anxiety and dysphoria: Toward a cognitive model of vulnerability to emotional distress. *Journal of Abnormal Psychology, 101*, 87–95.

Strauman, T. J., & Higgins, E. T. (1987). Automatic activation of self-discrepancies and emotional syndromes: When cognitive structures influence affect. *Journal of Personality and Social Psychology, 53*, 1004–1014.

Strauss, J., & Ryan, R. M. (1987). Autonomy disturbances in subtypes of anorexia nervosa. *Journal of Abnormal Psychology, 96,* 254–258.

Street, L. L., & Barlow, D. H. (1994). Anxiety disorders. In L. W. Craighead, W. E. Craighead, A. E. Kazdin, & M. J. Mahoney (Eds.), *Cognitive and behavioral interventions: An empirical approach to mental health problems* (pp. 71–87). Boston: Allyn & Bacon.

Stricker, G., & Healey, B. J. (1990). Projective assessment of object relations: A review of the empirical literature. *Psychological Assessment, 2,* 219–230.

Strickland, B. R. (1986). Over the Boulder(s) and through the Vail. *Clinical Psychologist, 38,* 52–56.

Strickland B. R. (1988). Clinical psychology comes of age. *American Psychologist, 43,* 104–107.

Strupp, H. H. (1996). The tripartite model and the Consumer Reports study. *American Psychologist, 51, 1017–1024.*

Strupp, H. H., & Binder, J. (1984). *Psychotherapy in a new key: A guide to Time-Limited Dynamic Psychotherapy.* New York: Basic Books.

Strupp, H. H., & Hadley, S. W. (1977). A tripartite model of mental health and therapeutic outcomes: With special reference to negative effects in psychotherapy. *American Psychologists, 32,* 187–196.

Stuart, G. L., Treat, T. A., & Wade, W. A. (2000). Effectiveness of an empirically based treatment for panic disorder delivered in a service clinic setting: 1-year follow-up. *Journal of Consulting and Clinical Psychology, 68,* 506–512.

Stumpf, H. (1993a). The factor structure of the Personality Research Form: A cross-national evaluation. *Journal of Personality, 61,* 27–48.

Stumpf, H. (1993b). Performance factors and gender-related differences in spatial ability: Another assessment. *Memory and Cognition, 21,* 828–836.

Stunkard, A. J. (1991). Genetic contributions to human obesity. In P. R. McHugh & V. A. McKusick, (Eds.), *Genes, brain, and behavior. Research Publications: Association for Research in Nervous and Mental Disease,* Vol. 69 (pp. 205–218). NY: Raven Press.

Sturgis, E. T., & Gramling, S. E. (1998). Psychophysiological assessment. In A. S. Bellack

& M. Hersen (Eds.), *Behavioral assessment: A practical handbook* (4th ed., pp. 126–157). Boston: Allyn & Bacon.

Sue, D. W., Ivey, A. E., & Pedersen, P. B. (Eds.). (1996). *A theory of multicultural counseling and therapy.* Pacific Grove, CA: Brooks/Cole.

Sue, S. (1991). Ethnicity and culture in psychological research and practice. In J. D. Goodchilds (Ed.). *Psychological perspectives on human diversity in America. The Master lectures.* (pp. 51–85). Washington, DC: American Psychological Association.

Sue, S. (1998). In search of cultural competence in psychotherapy and counseling. *American Psychologist, 53,* 440–448.

Sue, S., Fujino, D. C., Hu, L., & Takeuchi, D. T. (1991). Community mental health services for ethnic minority groups: A test of the cultural responsiveness hypothesis. *Journal of Consulting and Clinical Psychology, 59,* 533–540.

Sue, S., Kuraski, K. S., & Srinivasan, S. (1999). Ethnicity, gender, and cross-cultural issues in clinical research. In P. C. Kendall, J. N. Butcher, & G. Holmbeck (Eds.), *Handbook of research methods in clinical psychology* (2nd ed., pp. 54–71). New York, NY: John Wiley & Sons, Inc.

Sue, S., Sue, D. W., Sue, L., & Takeuchi, D. T. (1995). Psychopathology among Asian Americans: A model minority? *Cultural Diversity and Mental Health, 1,* 39–51.

Sullivan, H. S. (1940). Conceptions of modern psychiatry: The first William Alanson White memorial lectures. *Psychiatry, 3,* 1–117.

Sullivan, H. S. (1953). *The interpersonal theory of psychiatry.* New York: Norton.

Sullivan, H. S. (1956). *Clinical studies in psychiatry.* New York: Norton.

Sundberg, N. D. (1961). The practice of psychological testing in clinical services in the United States. *American Psychologist, 16,* 79–83.

Suomi, S. J. (1998). Compelling retrospective results call for creative prospective investigations. *Psychosomatic Medicine, 60,* 245–246.

Sutton, S., & Davidson, R. (1997). Prefrontal brain asymmetry: A biological substrate of the behavioral approach and inhibition systems. *Psychological Science, 8,* 204–210.

Svartberg, M., & Stiles, T. S. (1991). Comparative effects of short-term psychodynamic psychotherapy: A meta-analysis. *Journal of Consulting and Clinical Psychology, 59,* 704–714.

Swain, J. C., & McLaughlin, T. F. (1998). The effects of bonus contingencies in a classwide token program on math accuracy with middle-school students with behavioral disorders. *Behavioral Interventions, 13,* 11–19.

Takeuchi, D. T., Chung, R. C.-Y., Lin, K.-M., Shen, H., Kurasaki, K., Chun, C.-A., & Sue, S. (1998). Lifetime and twelve-month prevalence rates of major depressive episodes and dysthymia among Chinese Americans in Los Angeles. *American Journal of Psychiatry, 155,* 1407–1414.

Talbert, F. S., Braswell, L. C., Albrecht, J. W., & Hyer, L. A. (1993). NEO-PI profiles in PTSD as a function of trauma level. *Journal of Clinical Psychology, 49,* 663–669.

Tarrier, N., & Humphreys, L. (2000). Subjective improvement in PTSD patients with treatment by imaginal exposure or cognitive therapy: Session by session changes. *British Journal of Clinical Psychology, 39,* 27–34.

Tarrier, N., Pilgrim, H., Sommerfield, C., Faragher, B., Reynolds, M., Graham, E., & Barrowclough, C. (1999). A randomized trial of cognitive therapy and imaginal exposure in the treatment of chronic posttraumatic stress disorder. *Journal of Consulting and Clinical Psychology, 67,* 13–18.

Task Force on Promotion and Dissemination of Psychological Procedures. (1995). Training in and dissemination of empirically validated psychological treatments. *Clinical Psychologist, 48,* 3–23.

Tavris, C. (1992). *The mismeasure of woman.* New York: Simon & Schuster.

Taylor, L. & Adelman, H. S. (1998). Confidentiality: Competing principles, inevitable dilemmas. *Journal of Educational and Psychological Consultation, 9,* 267–275.

Taylor, S. (1996). Meta-analysis of cognitive-behavioral treatment for social phobia. *Journal of Behavior Therapy and Experimental Psychiatry, 27,* 1–9.

Taylor, S. E., Repetti, R. L., & Seeman, T. (1997). Health psychology: What is an unhealthy environment and how does it get under the skin? *Annual Review of Psychology, 48,* 411–447.

Tellegen, A. (1991). Personality traits: Issues of definition, evidence, and assessment. In D. Cicchetti & W. M. Grove, (Eds.), *Thinking clearly about psychology: Essays in honor of Paul E. Meehl, Vol. 2: Personality and psychopathology* (pp. 10–35); Minneapolis: University of Minnesota Press.

Tellegen, A., & Waller, N. G. (in press). Exploring personality through test construction: Development of the Multidimensional Personality Questionnaire. In S. R. Briggs & J. M. Cheek (Eds.), *Personality Measures: Development and evaluation* (Vol. 1). Greenwich, CT: JAI Press.

Terman, L. M., Lyman, G., Ordahl, G., Ordahl, L., Galbreath, N., & Talbert, W. (1916). The Stanford revision of the Binet-Simon scale and some results from its application to 1000 non-selected children. *Journal of Educational Psychology, 6,* 551–562.

Teusch, L., & Boehme, H. (1952). Is the exposure principle really crucial in agoraphobia? The influence of client-centered "nonprescriptive" treatment on exposure. *Psychotherapy Research, 9,* 115–123.

Tharp, R. G. (1989). Psychocultural variables and constants: Effects on teaching and learning in schools. *American Psychologist, 44,* 349–359.

Tharp, R. G. (1991). Cultural diversity and treatment of children. *Journal of Consulting and Clinical Psychology, 59,* 799–812.

Thase, M. E., Greenhouse, J. B., Frank, E., Reynolds, C. F., Pilkonis, P. A., Hurley, K., Grochocinski, V., & Kupfer, D. J. (1997). Treatment of major depression with psychotherapy or psychotherapy-pharmacotherapy combinations. *Archives of General Psychiatry, 54,* 1009–1015.

Thorndike, E. L. (1927). The law of effect. *American Journal of Psychology, 39,* 212–222.

Tillich, P. (1952). *The courage to be.* New Haven, CT: Yale University Press.

Timbrook, R. E., & Graham, J. R. (1994). Ethnic differences on the MMPI-2? *Psychological Assessment, 6,* 212–217.

Tjaden, P., & Thoennes, N. (2000). Prevalence and consequences of male-to-female and female-to-male intimate partner violence as measured by the National Violence Against Women Survey. *Violence & Victims, 15,* 427–441.

Tolman, E. C. (1932). *Purposive behavior in animals and men.* London: Century/Random House.

Tolman, E. C. (1952). A cognition motivation model. *Psychological Review, 59,* 389–400.

Truax, C. B. (1966). Influence of patient statements on judgments of therapist statements during psychotherapy. *Journal of Clinical Psychology, 22,* 335–337.

Truax, C. B. (1968). Therapist interpersonal reinforcement of client self-exploration and therapeutic outcome in group psychotherapy. *Journal of Counseling Psychology, 15,* 225–235.

Truax, C. B., & Carkhuff, R. R. (1967). *Toward effective counseling and psychotherapy.* Chicago: Aldine-Atherton.

Truax, C. B., & Mitchell, K. M. (1971). Research on certain therapist interpersonal skills in relation to process and outcome. In A. E. Bergin & S. L. Garfield (Eds.), *Handbook of psychotherapy and behavior change.* New York: John Wiley.

Trull, T. J., Useda, J. D., Costa, P. T., & McCrae, R. R. (1995). Comparison of the MMPI-2 Personality Psychopathology Five (PSY-5), the NEO-PI, and NEO-PI-R. *Psychological Assessment, 7,* 508–516.

Tsai, J. L., & Carstensen, L. L. (1996). Clinical intervention with ethnic minorities. In L. L. Carsetensen, B. A. Edelstein, & L. Dornbrand (Eds.), *The practical handbook of gerontology* (pp. 76–106). Thousand Oaks, CA: Sage.

Tsai, J. L., Levenson, R. W., & Carstensen, L. L. (2000). Autonomic, subjective, and expressive responses to emotional films in older and younger Chinese Americans and European Americans. *Psychology and Aging, 15,* 684–693.

Tsai, J. L., Levenson, R. W., & McCoy, K. (1999). *Cultural similarities and differences in emotional responding: Chinese American and European American dating couples during conflict.* Unpublished manuscript. Stanford University.

Tucker, G. J. (1998). Putting DSM-IV in perspective. *American Journal of Psychiatry, 155,* 159–161.

Turner, J. A., Clancy, S., McQuade, K. J, & Cardenas, D. D. (1990). Effectiveness of behavioral therapy for chronic low back pain: A component analysis. *Journal of Consulting and Clinical Psychology, 58,* 573–579.

Tversky, A., & Kahneman, D. (1974). Judgment under uncertainty: Heuristics and biases. *Science, 185,* 1124–1131.

Urist, J. (1977). The Rorschach Test and the assessment of object relations. *Journal of Personality Assessment, 41,* 3–9.

Valla, J., Bergeron, L., & Smolla, N. (2000). The Dominic-R: A pictorial interview for 6 to 11-year-old children. *Journal of the American Academy of Child & Adolescent Psychiatry, 39,* 85–93.

Van Beek, N., & Griez, E. (2000). Reactivity to a 35% CO-sub-2 challenge in healthy first-degree relative of patients with panic disorder. *Biological Psychiatry, 47,* 830–835.

Vandiver, T. & Sher, K. J. (1991). Temporal stability of the Diagnostic Interview Schedule. *Psychological Assessment, 3,* 277–281.

Vector Research. (1996). *Cost-effectiveness and feasibility of the DoD Psychopharmacology Demonstration Project: Final report.* Arlington, VA: Author.

Verhulst, F. C., Achenbach, T. M., Ferdinand, R. F., & Kasius, M. C. (1993). Epidemiological comparisons of American and Dutch adolescents' self-reports. *Journal of the American Academy of Child and Adolescent Psychiatry, 32,* 1135–1144.

Verlinden, S., Hersen, M., & Thomas, J. (2000). Risk factors in school shootings. *Clinical Psychology Review, 20,* 3–56.

Vinokur, A. D., Price, R. H., & Schul, Y. (1995). Impact of the JOBS intervention on unemployed workers varying in risk for depression. *American Journal of Community Psychology, 23,* 39–74.

von Bertalanffy, L. (1973). *General systems theory* (Revised Edition). New York: George Braziller.

Wadsworth, M. E., Hudziak, J. J., Heath, A. C., & Achenbach, T. M. (2001). Latent class analysis of Child Behavior Checklist anxiety/depression in children and adolescents. *Journal of the American Academy of Child and Adolescent Psychiatry, 40,* 106–114.

Wagner, B. M. (1997). Family risk factors for child and adolescent suicidal behavior. *Psychological Bulletin, 121,* 246–298.

Wakefield, J. C. (1997). Diagnosing *DSM-IV*: Part I. *DSM-IV* and the concept of disorder. *Behavior Research and Therapy, 35,* 633–649.

Wallace, J., Schneider, T., & McGuffin P. (in press). The genetics of depression. In I. H. Gotlib & C. L. Hammen (Eds.), *Handbook of depression: Research and treatment.* New York: Guilford Press.

Waller, R. W., & Keeley, S. M. (1978). Effects of explanation and information feedback on the illusory correlation phenomenon. *Journal of Consulting and Clinical Psychology, 46,* 342–343.

Walters, G. D. (2000). Behavioral self-control training for problem drinkers: A meta-analysis of randomized control studies. *Behavior Therapy, 31,* 135–149.

Wampold, B. E., Mondin, G. W., Moody, M., Stich, F., Benson, K., & Ahn, H. (1997). A meta-analysis of outcome studies comparing bona fide psychotherapies: Empirically, "all must have prizes." *Psychological Bulletin, 122,* 203–215.

Wanderer, Z., & Ingram, B. L. (1990). Physiologically monitored implosion therapy of phobias. *Phobia Practice and Research Journal, 3,* 61–77.

Warner, D. L. & Bradley, J. R. (1991). Undergraduate psychology students' views of counselors, psychiatrists, and psychologists: A challenge to academic psychologists. *Professional Psychology: Research and Practice, 22,* 138–140.

Warrington, E. K., & Leff, A. P. (2000). Jargon dyslexia: A single case study of intact reading comprehension in a jargon dysphasic. *Neurocase, 6,* 499–507.

Waters, A. M., Lipp, O. V., & Cobham, V. E. (2000). Investigation of threat-related attentional bias in anxious children using the startle eyeblink modification paradigm. *Journal of Psychophysiology, 14,* 142–150.

Watkins, C. E., Campbell, V. L., Nieberding, R., & Hallmark, R. (1995). Contemporary practice of psychological assessment by clinical psychologists. *Professional Psychology: Research and Practice, 26,* 54–60.

Watson, D., & Pennebaker, J. W. (1989). Health complaints, stress, and distress: Exploring the central role of negative affectivity. *Psychological Review, 96,* 234–254.

Watson, J. B. (1924). *Behaviorism.* New York: People's Institute.

Watson, J. B., & Rayner, R. (1920). Conditioned emotional reactions. *Journal of Experimental Psychology, 3,* 1–14.

Watt, N. F., Anthony, E. J., Wynne, L. C., & Rolf, J. E. (1984). *Children at risk for schizophrenia: A longitudinal perspective.* Cambridge, England: Cambridge University Press.

Wechsler, D. (1939). *The measurement of adult intelligence.* Baltimore, MD: Williams & Wilkins.

Wechsler, D. (1981). The psychometric tradition: Developing the Wechsler Adult Intelligence Scale. *Contemporary Educational Psychology, 6,* 82–85.

Wechsler, D. (1989). *The Wechsler Preschool and Primary Scale of Intelligence-Revised (WPPSI-R).* San Antonio, TX: The Psychological Corporation.

Wechsler, D. (1991). *The Wechsler Intelligence Scale for Children—Third Edition (WISC-III).* San Antonio, TX: The Psychological Corporation.

Wechsler, D. (1997). *Wechsler Adult Intelligence Scale—Third Edition (WAIS-III).* San Antonio, TX: The Psychological Corporation.

Wegner, J. T., & Wegner, A. Z. (2001). Cognitive-behavioral therapy and other short-term approaches in the treatment of eating disorders. In B. P. Kinoy (Ed.), *Eating disorders: New directions in treatment and recovery* (2nd ed., pp. 112–126). New York: Columbia University Press.

Weiner, I. B. (1999). What the Rorschach can do for you: Incremental validity in clinical applications. *Assessment, 6,* 327–338.

Weiss, B., & Weisz, J. R. (1995). Effectiveness of psychotherapy. *Journal of the American Academy of Child and Adolescent Psychiatry, 34,* 971–972.

Weiss, B., & Weisz, J. R. (1995). Relative effectiveness of behavioral versus nonbehavioral child psychotherapy. *Journal of Consulting and Clinical Psychology, 63,* 317–320.

Weissberg, R. P. (2000). Improving the lives of millions of school children. *American Psychologist, 55,* 1360–1372.

Weissman, A., & Beck, A. T. (1978, November). *Development and validation of the dysfunctional attitudes scale.* Paper presented at the annual meeting of the Association for the Advancement of Behavior Therapy, Chicago.

Weissman, M. M., & Klerman, G. L. (1993). Conjoint interpersonal psychotherapy for depressed patients with marital disputes. In G. L. Klerman & M. M. Weissman (Eds.), *New applications of interpersonal psychotherapy,* (p. 103–127). Washington, DC: American Psychiatric Press.

Weissman, M. M., & Markowitz, J. C. (in press). Interpersonal psychotherapy for depression. In I. H. Gotlib & C. L. Hammen (Eds.), *Handbook of depression: Research and treatment.* New York: Guilford Press.

Weissman, M. M., Markowitz, J. C., & Klerman, G. L. (2000). *Comprehensive guide to interpersonal psychotherapy.* New York: Basic Books.

Weisz, J. R., Donenberg, G. R., Han, S. S., & Weiss, B. (1995). Bridging the gap between laboratory and clinic in child and adolescent psychotherapy. *Journal of Consulting and Clinical Psychology, 63,* 688–701.

Weisz, J. R., Hawley, K. M., Pilkonis, P. A., Woody, S. R., & Follette, W. C. (2000). Stressing the (other) three r's in the search for empirically supported treatments: Review procedures, research quality, relevance to practice and the public interest. *Clinical Psychology: Science and Practice, 7,* 243–258.

Weisz, J. R., Rudolph, K. D., Granger, D. A., & Sweeney, L. (1992). Cognition, competence, and coping in child and adolescent depression: Research findings, developmental concerns, therapeutic implications. *Development and Psychopathology, 4,* 627–653.

Weisz, J. R., Suwanlert, S., Chaiyasit, W., Weiss, B., Walter, B. R., & Anderson, W. W. (1988). Thai and American perspectives on over- and undercontrolled child behavior problems: Exploring the threshold model among parents, teachers, and psychologists. *Journal of Consulting and Clinical Psychology, 56,* 601–609.

Weisz, J. R., Suwanlert, S., Chaiyasit, W., & Walter, B. R. (1987). Over- and undercontrolled referral problems among children and adolescents from Thailand and the United States: The wat and wai of cultural differences. *Journal of Consulting and Clinical Psychology, 55,* 719–726.

Weisz, J. R., Suwanlert, S., Chaiyasit, W., Weiss, B., Achenbach, T. M., & Walter, B. R. (1987). Epidemiology of behavioral and emotional problems among Thai and American children: Parent reports for ages 6 to 11. *Journal of the American Academy of Child and Adolescent Psychiatry, 26,* 890–897.

Weisz, J. R., Weiss, B., & Donenberg, G. R. (1992). The lab versus the clinic: Effects of child and adolescent psychotherapy. *American Psychologist, 47,* 1578–1585.

Weisz, J. R., Weiss, B., Han, S. S., & Granger, D. A. (1995). Effects of psychotherapy with children and adolescents revisited: A meta-analysis of treatment outcome studies. *Psychological Bulletin, 117,* 450–468.

Wells, A. (1997). *Cognitive therapy of anxiety disorders: A practice manual and conceptual guide.* Chichester: John Wiley & Sons.

Wells, K. B., Golding, J. M., & Burnam, M. A. (1989). Chronic medical conditions in a sample of the general population with anxiety, affective, and substance use disorders. *American Journal of Psychiatry, 146,* 1440–1446.

Wells, K. B., Manning, W. G., Duan, N., & Newhouse, J. P. (1986). Use of outpatient mental health services by a general population with health insurance coverage. *Hospital and Community Psychiatry, 37,* 1119–1125.

Westen, D. (1991). Clinical assessment of object relations using the TAT. *Journal of Personality Assessment, 56,* 56–74.

Westen, D., Lohr, N., Silk, K. R., Gold, L., & Kerber, K. (1990). Object relations and social cognition in borderlines, major depressives, and normals: A Thematic Apperception Test analysis. *Psychological Assessment, 2,* 355–364.

Westermeyer, J., & Specker, S. (1999). Social resources and social function in comorbid eating and substance disorder: A matched-pairs study. *American Journal on Addictions, 8,* 332–336.

Whisman, M. (1993). Mediators and moderators of change in cognitive therapy of depression. *Psychological Bulletin, 114,* 248–265.

Whitbread, J., & McGown, A. (1994). The treatment of bulimia nervosa: What is effective? A meta-analysis. *Indian Journal of Clinical Psychology, 21,* n.p.

Whittal, M. L., Agras, W. S., & Gould, R. A. (1999). Bulimia nervosa: A meta-analysis of psychosocial and pharmacological treatments. *Behavior Therapy, 30,* 117–135.

Widiger, T. A., & Clark, L. A. (2000). Toward *DMS-V* and the classification of psychopathology. *Psychological Bulletin, 126,* 946–964.

Widiger, T. A., & Costa, P. T. (1994). Personality and personality disorders. *Journal of Abnormal Psychology, 103,* 78–91.

Widiger, T. A., Frances, A. J., Pincus, H. A., Davis, W. W., & First, M. B. (1991). Toward an empirical classification for the DSM-IV. *Journal of Abnormal Psychology, 100,* 280–288.

Widiger, T. A., & Shea, M. T. (1991). Differentiation of Axis I and Axis II disorders. *Journal of Abnormal Psychology. Special Issue: Diagnoses, dimensions, and DSM-IV—The science of classification, 100,* 399–406.

Widom, C. S. (2000). Motivation and mechanism in the "cycle of violence." In D. J. Hansen (Ed.), *Nebraska Symposium on Motivation: Vol. 46. Motivation and child maltreatment* (pp. 1–37). Lincoln: University of Nebraska Press.

Wiener-Levy, D., & Exner, J. E. (1981). The Rorschach EA-ep variable as related to persistence in a task frustration situation under feedback conditions. *Journal of Personality Assessment, 45,* 118–124.

Wiens, A. N. (1991). Diagnostic interviewing. In M. Hersen, & A. E. Kazdin, (Eds,), *The clinical psychology handbook* (2nd ed., pp. 345–361). New York: Pergamon Press.

Wierson, M. & Forehand, R. (1994). Parent behavioral training for child noncompliance: Rationale, concepts, and effectiveness. *Current Directions in Psychological Science, 3,* 146–150.

Wiggins, J. S., & Pincus, A. L. (1992). Personality: Structure and assessment. *Annual Review of Psychology, 43,* 473–504.

Wilfley, D. E., Schwartz, M. B., Spurrell, E. B., & Fairburn, C. G. (1997). Assessing the specific psychopathology of binge eating disorder patients: Interview or self-report? *Behaviour Research and Therapy, 35,* 1151–1159.

Wilken, J. A., Smith, B. D., Tola, K., & Mann, M. (2000). Trait anxiety and prior exposure to non-stressful stimuli: Effects on psychophysiological arousal and anxiety. *International Journal of Psychophysiology, 37,* 233–242.

Willcutt, E. G., Hartung, C. M., Lahey, B. B., Loney, J., & Pelham, W. E. (1999). Utility of behavior ratings by examiners during assessments of preschool children with attention-deficit/hyperactivity disorder. *Journal of Abnormal Child Psychology, 27,* 463–472.

Williams, J. B., Gibbon, M., First, M. B., Spitzer, R. L., et al. (1992). The Structured Clinical

Interview for *DSM-III-R* (SCID): II. Multisite test-retest reliability. *Archives of General Psychiatry, 49,* 630–636.

Wilson, E. O. (1978). *On human nature.* Cambridge, MA: Harvard University Press.

Wilson, F. E., & Evans, I. M. (1983). The reliability of target-behavior selection in behavioral assessment. *Behavioral Assessment, 5,* 15–32.

Wilson, G. T. (1999). Cognitive behavior therapy for eating disorders: Progress and problems. *Behaviour Research and Therapy, 37* (Suppl. 1), S79–S95.

Wilson, G. T., Eldredge, K. L., Smith, D., & Niles, B. (1997). Cognitive-behavioural treatment with and without response prevention for bulimia. In S. Rachman (Ed.), *Best of behavior research and therapy* (pp. 131–139). New York: Pergamon/Elsevier Science.

Wilson, G. T., & Fairburn, C. G. (1998). Eating disorders. In P. E. Nathan & J. M. Gorman (Eds.), *A guide to treatments that work* (2nd ed.). New York: Oxford University Press.

Wilson, G. T., Rossiter, E., Kleifield, E. I., & Lindholm, L. (1986). Cognitive-behavioral treatment of bulimia nervosa: A controlled evaluation. *Behaviour Research and Therapy, 24,* 277–288.

Wilson, G. T., & Vitousek, K. M. (1999). Self-monitoring in the assessment of eating disorders. *Psychological Assessment, 11,* 480–489.

Winson, J. (1990). The meaning of dreams. *Scientific American, 263,* 86–88, 90–92, 94–96.

Wiseman, H., & Rice, L. N. (1989). Sequential analyses of therapist-client interaction during change events: A task-focused approach. *Journal of Consulting and Clinical Psychology, 57,* 281–286.

Witmer, L. (1907). Clinical psychology. *The Psychological Clinic, 1,* 1–9.

Witmer, L. (1909). The study and treatment of retardation: A field of applied psychology. *Psychological Bulletin, 6,* 121–126.

Witmer, L. (1996). Clinical psychology: Reprint of Witmer's 1907 article. *American Psychologist, 51,* 248–251.

Wiznitzer, M., Verhulst, F., Van den Brink, W., Koeter, M., Van der Ende, J., Giel, R., & Koot, H. M. (1992). Detecting psychopathology in young adults: The Young Adult Self Report, the General Health Questionnaire, and the Symptom Checklist as screening instruments. *Acta Psychiatrica Scandinavica, 86,* 32–37.

Wolchik, S. A., West, S. G., Sandler, I. N., Tein, J.-Y., Coatsworth, D., Lengua, L., Weiss, L., Anderson, E. R., Greene, S. M., & Griffin, W. A. (2000). An experimental evaluation of theory-based mother and mother-child programs for children of divorce. *Journal of Consulting and Clinical Psychology, 68,* 843–856.

Wolfe, B. E., & Sigl, P. (1998). Experiential psychotherapy of the anxiety disorders. In L. S. Greenberg & J. C. Watson (Eds.), *Handbook of experiential psychotherapy* (pp. 272–294). New York: Guilford Press.

Wolfner, G., Faust, D., & Dawes, R. M. (1993). The use of anatomically detailed dolls in sexual abuse evaluations: The state of the science. *Applied and Preventive Psychology, 2,* 1–11.

Wolpe, J. M. (1958). *Psychotherapy by reciprocal inhibition.* Stanford, CA: Stanford University Press.

Wood, J. M., Lilienfeld, S. O., Garb, H. N., & Nezworski, M. T. (2000). The Rorschach test in clinical diagnosis: A critical review, with a backward look at Garfield (1947). *Journal of Clinical Psychology, 56,* 395–430.

Wood, J. M., Nezworski, M. T., Garb, H. N., & Lilienfeld, S. O. (in press). The misperception of psychopathology: Problems with the norms of the Comprehensive System for the Rorschach. *Clinical Psychology: Science and Practice.*

Wood, J. M., Nezworski, M. T., & Stejskal, W. J. (1996). The comprehensive system for the Rorschach: A critical examination. *Psychological Science, 7,* 3–10.

Woodruff, R. A., Goodwin, D. W., & Guze, S. B. (1974). *Psychiatric diagnosis.* New York: Oxford.

Woody, S. R., & Sanderson, W. C. (1998). Manuals for empirically supported treatments: 1998 update. *The Clinical Psychologist, 51,* 17–21.

World Health Organization. (1990). *International Classification of Diseases* (10th ed.). Geneva: World Health Organization.

Yalom, Y. D. (1980). *The theory and practice of group psychotherapy* (4th ed.). New York: Basic Books.

Yeh, M., Takeuchi, D. T., & Sue, S. (1994). Asian-American children treated in the mental health system: A comparison of parallel and mainstream outpatient service centers. *Journal of Clinical Child Psychology, 23,* 5–12.

Yeung, P. P., & Greenwald, S. (1992). Jewish Americans and mental health: Results of the NIMH Epidemiologic Catchment Area Study. *Social Psychiatry and Psychiatric Epidemiology, 27,* 292–297.

Young, A. S., Klap, R., Sherbourne, C. D., & Wells, K. B. (2001). The quality of care for depressive and anxiety disorders in the United States. *Archives of General Psychiatry, 58,* 55–61.

Zajonc, R. B. (2000). Feeling and thinking: Closing the debate over the independence of affect. In J. P. Forgas, et al. (Eds.), *Feeling and thinking: The role of affect in social cognition. Studies in emotion and social interaction, second series* (pp. 31–58). New York: Cambridge University Press.

Zvolensky, M. J., Eifert, G. H., Lejuez, C. W., & McNeil, D. W. (1999). The effect of offset control over 20% carbon-dioxide-enriched air on anxious responding. *Journal of Abnormal Psychology, 108,* 624–632.

CREDITS

Chapter 11

Chapter 12

Chapter 15

AUTHOR INDEX

SUBJECT INDEX